Communication
Yearbook

MICHAEL E. ROLOFF, Editor
GAYLEN D. PAULSON, Editorial Assistant

Communication Yearbook

Published Annually for the
International Communication Association

SAGE Publications
International Educational and Professional Publisher
Thousand Oaks   London   New Delhi

For information:

Sage Publications, Inc.
2455 Teller Road
Thousand Oaks, California 91320
E-mail: order@sagepub.com

SAGE Publications Ltd.
6 Bonhill Street
London EC2A 4PU
United Kingdom

SAGE Publications India Pvt. Ltd.
M-32 Market
Greater Kailash I
New Delhi 110 048 India

Printed in the United States of America

Library of Congress: 76-45943

ISBN: 0-7619-1935-X

ISSN: 0147-4642

99 00 01 02 03 04 10 9 8 7 6 5 4 3 2 1

Acquisition Editor:	Margaret H. Seawell
Editorial Assistant:	Renée Piernot
Production Editor:	Denise Santoyo
Editorial Assistant:	Nevair Kabakian
Designer/Typesetter:	Danielle Dillahunt
Indexer:	Will Ragsdale

CONTENTS

THE INTERNATIONAL COMMUNICATION ASSOCIATION

The International Communication Association (ICA) was formed in 1950, bringing together academicians and other professionals whose interests focus on human communication. The Association maintains an active membership of more than 2,900 individuals, of whom some two-thirds are teaching and conducting research in colleges, universities, and schools around the world. Other members are in government, the media, communication technology, business, law, medicine, and other professions. The wide professional and geographic distribution of the membership provides the basic strength of the ICA. The Association is a meeting ground for sharing research and useful dialogue about communication interests.

Through its Divisions and Interest Groups, publications, annual conferences, and relations with other associations around the world, the ICA promotes the systematic study of communication theories, processes, and skills.

In addition to *Communication Yearbook,* the Association publishes the *Journal of Communication, Human Communication Research, Communication Theory, A Guide to Publishing in Scholarly Communication Journals, ICA Newsletter,* and the *ICA Membership Directory.*

For additional information about the ICA and its activities, contact Robert L. Cox, Executive Director, International Communication Association, P.O. Box 9589, Austin, TX 78766; phone (512) 454-8299; fax (512) 454-4221; e-mail icahdq@uts.cc.utexas.edu

Editors of the *Communication Yearbook* series:

Volumes 1 and 2, Brent D. Ruben
Volumes 3 and 4, Dan Nimmo
Volumes 5 and 6, Michael Burgoon
Volumes 7 and 8, Robert N. Bostrom
Volumes 9 and 10, Margaret L. McLaughlin
Volumes 11, 12, 13, and 14, James A. Anderson
Volumes 15, 16, and 17, Stanley A. Deetz
Volumes 18, 19, and 20, Brant R. Burleson
Volumes 21, 22, and 23, Michael E. Roloff

INTERNATIONAL COMMUNICATION ASSOCIATION
EXECUTIVE COMMITTEE

President and Chair
Peter Monge, *University of Southern California*

President-Elect
Howard Giles, *University of California, Santa Barbara*

Immediate Past-President
Stanley A. Deetz, *University of Colorado, Boulder*

Finance Chair
Bradley Greenberg, *Michigan State University*

Executive Director
Robert L. Cox (ex-officio), *ICA Headquarters*

BOARD OF DIRECTORS

Members-at-Large

Christine Ogan, *Indiana University*
Esther Thorson, *University of Missouri*
Youichi Ito, *Higashikaigan Minami*

Student Members

Adrianne W. Kunkel, *Purdue University*
Kory Floyd, *University of Arizona*

Division Chairs and Vice Presidents

Information Systems
Annie Lang, *Indiana University*

Interpersonal Communication
Steven Wilson, *Northern Illinois University*

Mass Communication
James Ettema, *Northwestern University*

Organizational Communication
Katherine Miller, *University of Kansas*

Intercultural/Development Communication
Fred Casmir, *Pepperdine University*

Political Communication
Wolfgang Donsbach, *University of Dresden*

Instructional/Developmental Communication
Cynthia Hoffner, *Illinois State University*

Health Communication
Peter G. Northouse, *Western Michigan University*

Philosophy of Communication
Briankle Chang, *University of Massachusetts*

Communication and Technology
Leah A. Lievrouw, *University of California, Los Angeles*

Popular Communication
Barbie Zelizer, *University of Pennsylvania*

Public Relations
Shirley Ramsey, *Oklahoma University*

Feminist Scholarship
Rashmi Luthra, *University of Michigan*

Language and Social Interaction
Anita Pomerantz, *Temple University*

Special Interest Group Chairs

Communication Law and Policy
John Soloski, *University of Iowa*

Visual Communication
Robert L. Craig, *University of St. Thomas*

Gay, Lesbian, Bisexual, and Transgender Studies
Lisa Henderson, *University of Massachusetts*
John Nguyet Erni, *University of New Hampshire*

CONSULTING EDITORS

The following individuals helped make possible this volume of the *Communication Yearbook*. The editor gratefully acknowledges these scholars for the gifts of their time and wisdom.

EDITOR'S INTRODUCTION

WELCOME to Volume 22 of the *Communication Yearbook*. This collection continues the format, begun with Volume 19, of publishing state-of-the-art reviews of communication research. Under the able editorship of Brant Burleson, *Communication Yearbook* established itself as an essential source for in-depth analyses of communication scholarship representing the broad array of research areas evident within the field. The chapters contained in this volume are of high quality and should add to the reputation of *Communication Yearbook*.

To help the reader understand this volume, I will describe the process by which the chapters were selected, the content of each chapter, and the individuals who played essential roles in putting the volume together.

CHAPTER CREATION

Approximately 18 months prior to the publication of this volume, a call for submissions was circulated. Drafts of chapters and proposals for chapters were solicited that would review important, specific areas of scholarship. An attempt was made to solicit reviews from across research specializations. To that end, copies of the call were sent to the leadership of all divisions and interest groups of the International Communication Association with a request that they identify potential contributors and circulate the call to the membership. I am grateful to those who assisted with these tasks. In addition, the call was sent to the editors of 20 newsletters published by organizations both within (e.g., the National Communication Association) and outside the field of communication (e.g., the Society for the Study of Personality and Social Psychology), most of whom published it. Finally, given that dissertations are often a rich source for literature reviews, more than 100 letters were sent to professors at Ph.D.-granting institutions asking them to identify recently completed dissertations that contained quality literature reviews.

We received 33 new submissions and also considered 5 papers that were submitted to *Communication Yearbook 21* but were not completed by the deadline for publication. The proposed reviews reflected the diversity of our field and addressed issues in health communication, intercultural communication, interpersonal communication, legal communication, mass communication, organizational communication, political communication, public relations, and rhetoric. All 38 prospective chapters were subjected to blind review by at least two referees. Each referee was asked to make the following assessments: (a) Is the submission a literature review? (b) Is the literature worthy of review? (c) Is the review comprehensive and current? (d) Is there a coherent organizational pattern and procedure for conducting the review?

(e) Are the conclusions clear and valid? (f) Is the review sufficiently critical? and (g) Does the review set forth future issues and directions for research? The authors of those proposals and papers that were judged to conform to each standard were encouraged to submit chapters, which were subjected to further evaluation. In most cases, the manuscripts went through several revisions.

The 11 chapters contained in this volume are those that survived this rigorous review process. They are truly a select group. Of the total, 7 were drawn from the 33 new submissions and 4 emerged from the 5 projects originally proposed for *CY21*.

CHAPTER CONTENT

Although proposals were sought from all interest areas in communication, the selection of chapters was based entirely upon their judged quality. Had the proposals from a single interest area all been judged to be the best, *CY22* would have a singular focus. However, as testimony to the vibrancy of all of our research specializations, the final chapters reflect the diverse interests that constitute our field. Therefore, readers will find some chapters that fit into our formal divisional structures and some that blend two or more. Hence readers will likely find in-depth reviews focused on important topics in their own specializations and well-written syntheses that inform as to scholarship in other domains.

In a way, each of the chapters addresses one of the most pressing issues currently facing individuals: how to communicate with others who are different from them. Increasingly, individuals have the opportunity to communicate with others who come from cultures and backgrounds different from their own. Consequently, individuals may be uncertain about how they should act toward others and what types of behaviors to expect in return. To reduce this uncertainty, they turn to researchers for advice. As a result, scholars have become interested in whether or not individuals differ in their communication behaviors, and if they do differ, what impacts such differences might have. The chapters contained in this volume explore the variations in how individuals communicate and how these differences are related to problematic communication, influence attempts, and support processes.

The first two chapters review literature that informs as to how groups of individuals might differ in their communication behaviors. Sex differences in communication have been of critical interest not only to scholars but also to the general public. Hence a variety of books have been published by popular presses that describe basic differences between males and females. One of the most widely read and influential of these is Tannen's *You Just Don't Understand*. In Chapter 1, Goldsmith and Fulfs provide a detailed, critical analysis of the claims contained in Tannen's book. By comparing each conclusion with published research, and by applying rigorous scholarly standards to an analysis of the support for Tannen's claims, they uncover a number of apparent shortcomings. Although their own review identifies some sex differences in communication, they also note substantial similarities between males and females. They conclude that Tannen's analysis overstates the degree to which males and females differ, and that readers should be cautious when deciding whether or not to accept her claims.

As technological advances continue to make international communication more frequent, it is not surprising that individuals are as interested in cross-cultural differences in communication as they are in sex differences. One of the most studied areas focuses on how individuals from different cultures vary in the degree to which they are verbally assertive. In Chapter 2, Kim provides a thorough review of research focused on cross-cultural differences in the motivation to approach or avoid communication. Beyond presenting and critiquing prior research, the chapter culminates in a theoretical perspective that might guide future inquiry.

When individuals with differing characteristics come into contact, many positive things may happen. For example, diverse viewpoints might be brought to bear on common problems and creative solutions might be uncovered. However, such encounters might also lead to actions that have negative consequences for the communicators. The next three chapters focus on such problematic situations. In Chapter 3, Leets and Giles focus on forms of harmful speech. They offer an integrative framework that for the first time brings together scholarship on problematic forms of communication arising from racism, sexism, ageism, and discrimination against the disabled. Working within the assumptions of a social identity framework, they examine research that informs as to the types of messages that are harmful, how such messages are interpreted, the kinds of harms that result, and the reactions that result from receiving such messages.

One of the most difficult issues facing society has been that of pornography. Although many individuals find pornographic images to be offensive, standards of freedom of speech render government restrictions problematic. Unless a clear danger can be established, individuals retain the right to consume such material regardless of the objections of others. In Chapter 4, Allen, D'Alessio, and Emmers-Sommer report on a meta-analysis of research that examines the possible impact of exposure to pornography on criminal sexual offenders. They conclude that sexual criminal offenders and nonoffenders do not differ in their exposure to pornography, but that the former appear to be more aroused by it and especially so when the pornographic images depict acts similar to their own crimes.

Some individuals have a tendency to interpret any criticism or negative statements as being a direct, intentional attack on their self-concept. In Chapter 5, Hample reviews research that informs as to tendency of some individuals to take conflict personally. He focuses on underlying psychological processes that make individuals prone to feel personally affronted by others as well how they behave in conflict situations.

When individuals encounter disagreement, they often try to convince one another to change. The next three chapters are all focused on influence processes. In Chapter 6, O'Keefe reports a meta-analysis of research focused on the effects of one-sided versus two-sided persuasive messages. Researchers have long been interested in whether it is more persuasive only to include arguments in favor of one's own position in a message or whether it might be better also to include the opposing side's arguments along with a refutation. O'Keefe finds that the relative advantage of two-sided over one-sided messages depends upon whether or not the two-sided messages refute the opposing side's arguments and whether or not the messages appear in an advertising context. He then analyzes how well existing persuasion theory can account for these various findings and suggests new research directions.

Whenever individuals have interdependent outcomes, they may feel compelled to convince each other to behave in ways that will facilitate reward attainment, or at least minimize potential hindrances to doing so. Such is the case in organizational life. Traditionally, researchers have focused on how superiors in organizations can motivate subordinates to work harder, obey organizational rules, and be loyal to the organization. As organizations have become more decentralized and employees have become more vocal, increased research attention has focused on how subordinates attempt to exert upward influence on their superiors. In Chapter 7, Waldron reviews this growing body of research. He examines how subordinates seek feedback, express disagreement with organizational decisions, and acquire power. He also describes the relationship between the use of influence strategies and relational, individual, and contextual characteristics.

Influence is also a central part of societal governance. Citizen knowledge and participation are critical for democratic representatives to formulate wise and fair policies and laws. However, when the electorate becomes alienated and cynical about the government, it exerts little influence and the system fails. Some have argued that the news media have contributed toward such a crisis in citizenship. In Chapter 8, Bucy and D'Angelo review normative theories that examine and critique how the press and democratic governments should interact. These theories and resulting research provide insights into how the news media might contribute to a lack of citizen involvement in government. Interestingly, Bucy and D'Angelo have argued that such theories have also been a source of friction among scholars interested in political communication, and they examine current perspectives that might unify scholars with different theoretical and methodological approaches.

It is axiomatic that individuals often require the assistance of others and that communication is a means by which we negotiate and receive needed resources. However, acquiring needed resources can be made problematic by a variety of factors. The last three chapters highlight research focused on acquiring resources.

Organizations inherently survive based upon their ability to provide needed services to clients. In Chapter 9, Ford summarizes research that informs as to the interchange between organizational service provider and customer. She presents research related to the enactment of courteous, personalized, and manipulative service. The factors that lead to the enactment of a given style, and the outcomes associated with each, are discussed.

Not all resources are provided by formal organizations. Personal relationships such as families are essential sources of rewards that maintain a person's sense of well-being. As an individual grows older, his or her needs may change and so might the family roles that he or she plays. In Chapter 10, Fox reviews the burgeoning research investigating how family communication changes over the life span, and especially how adult children communicate with an aging parent. She reviews traditional theories of aging and posits a new perspective based on social identity theory and communication accommodation theory.

Not only do individuals acquire needed support from their families, they also turn to friends in time of need. Hence the ability to form quality friendships is essential to a person's well-being. However, that ability may be impeded when the individual is living outside of the culture in which he or she was raised. In Chapter 11, Gareis reviews the research and theory related to the ability of foreign sojourners to form friendships with U.S. citizens during their stay in this country. Her review of research conducted among foreign exchange students identifies a variety of challenges to the formation of intercultural friendships.

Although broadly cast, all of the chapters included here address issues that are important for communication researchers as well as for society as a whole. The reader will find that each chapter provides an excellent summary and critique of the literature. The authors have done a fine job.

ACKNOWLEDGMENTS

Putting together a volume such as the *Communication Yearbook* is labor-intensive, and an editor relies upon the cooperation and goodwill of many people. I would be quite remiss if I did not acknowledge the critical contributions of my support system.

My able editorial assistant, Gaylen Paulson, worked countless hours on this project. He computerized the review process, and his finally honed copyediting skills were invaluable. He kept me on track and was an effective problem solver. He deserves a great deal of credit for the completion of this huge project.

My colleagues from Northwestern and around the country also contributed to this endeavor. Dean David Zarefsky provided financial support from the School of Speech at Northwestern, as did the Department of Communication Studies. Two Northwestern staff members, Rita Lutz and Martha Kayler, helped me process the internal paperwork necessary to keep the review processing functioning. Professors Peter Miller, Linda Putnam, and Brant Burleson were extremely helpful in directing me to referees. Two doctoral students at Northwestern, Joy Shih and Lefki Anastasiou, assisted with copyediting tasks. I must also extend my appreciation to the many students who tolerated my delayed response to their assignments and inquiries when my editorial duties beckoned.

Clearly, a volume such of this could not exist without submitters and reviewers. I am very appreciative of the interest expressed by those who sent in proposals, and I applaud the time and effort they expended on proposals that in some cases did not come to fruition. The referees provided thorough, insightful responses to the proposals, and most were completed in a timely fashion.

I want to acknowledge the assistance and support of the communication editor at Sage Publications, Margaret Seawell, and her assistant, Renée Piernot. They efficiently moved the volume through the production phase.

Finally, I need to express my gratitude to my wife, Karen, and my daughters, Erika, Katrina, and Carlissa, for tolerating my periodic inattention to the travails of family life.

Michael E. Roloff

CHAPTER CONTENTS

1   "You Just Don't Have the Evidence": An Analysis of Claims and Evidence in Deborah Tannen's *You Just Don't Understand*

DAENA J. GOLDSMITH
University of Illinois, Urbana-Champaign

PATRICIA A. FULFS
University of Texas, Austin

This chapter separates fact from fiction in Tannen's *You Just Don't Understand* (1990b), a book widely cited by scholars as an authoritative source for claims about the communicative differences between men and women. The authors determined that Tannen's claims are treated as factual generalizations based on their outline of claims and evidence in the text, their analysis of citations to the book, and other information within the text. When they tested the evidence for these factual generalizations, they discovered problems with the adequacy, sufficiency, relevance, and consistency of Tannen's evidence and with her use of empirical studies. Consequently, scholars and policy makers should be cautious about relying on Tannen's book as a source of empirical generalizations about men's and women's communicative behavior.

I N the past 20 years we have seen an explosion of interest in gender and communication. Several early works drew attention to the relationships among gender, language, and communication (e.g., Key, 1975; Lakoff, 1975; Thorne & Henley, 1975), and a steady stream of scholarly interest in these issues has followed. Popular writings on gender and communication abound (e.g., Gray, 1993; Reardon, 1995; Schloff & Yudkin, 1993). Perhaps the best-known work on the subject is linguist Deborah Tannen's *You Just*

Correspondence and requests for reprints: Daena J. Goldsmith, Department of Speech Communication, 244 Lincoln Hall, University of Illinois, 702 S. Wright Street, Urbana, IL 61801-3631; e-mail goldsmit@uiuc.edu

Don't Understand: Women and Men in Conversation (1990b; hereafter referred to as *YJDU*).

Tannen's book is distinctive in that it has successfully influenced both scholarly and popular audiences. Tannen draws on scholarly research as a basis for her claims, and her book is frequently treated as a source of generalizations about gender differences in communication in its own right. Our purpose in this chapter is to evaluate the adequacy of the evidence for the claims about gender differences in communication within *YJDU*.

TANNEN'S INFLUENCE WITH
LAY AND SCHOLARLY AUDIENCES

To say that *YJDU* has been a popular book is an understatement. The cover of the 1990 paperback edition proudly proclaims that the book has appeared on the *New York Times* best-seller list for more than 4 years, generated more than 1.5 million printed copies, and received favorable reviews from the *New York Times Book Review, Washington Post, Los Angeles Times*, and *San Francisco Chronicle*. The book has been excerpted and cited for millions of readers in such popular magazines as *Newsweek, Time, Redbook, Reader's Digest, Working Woman, Ladies' Home Journal*, and *People* and in newspapers such as the *Christian Science Monitor* and *USA Today*.[1]

Following the success of the book, Tannen has made numerous television appearances and has written articles and book reviews in a wide variety of publications with large circulation, including *Reader's Digest*, the *Washington Post, McCall's, USA Today*, and *New York Times Magazine*, to name only a few. Tannen's influence is evident in works of fiction, such as in David Carkeet's *The Full Catastrophe* (1990). The producers of *Home Improvement*, one of the most successful television situation comedies of the 1990s, urged star Tim Allen to read Tannen's book ("The Men's Movement," 1998), and one of the series creators has stated that Tannen's book "should be every sitcom writer's guide to humor" (*"Home Improvement*," 1998).

Clearly, Tannen has succeeded in reaching a large mainstream audience. What may be less well-known is her impact upon academic audiences and scholarly research. In the period from *YJDU*'s release in 1990 to August 1995, we found it cited in 247 scholarly articles in 41 different disciplines. Tannen's claims have been used by scholars to explain everything from Aristotle's conception of human nature (Arnhart, 1994) to our choices of entertainment media (Bhatia & Desmond, 1993), and from the ability to negotiate salaries (Stevens, Bavetta, & Gist, 1993) to erectile dysfunctions (Leiblum & Rosen, 1991).

Tannen's dual popularity with lay and scholarly audiences is likely due to the dual messages in her book about the basis of her claims. The book is written in an accessible self-help style and is chock-full of examples from

Tannen's own experience, from popular culture, and from stories relayed by Tannen's friends and fans. However, the book repeatedly reminds readers that Tannen's claims about the communication behaviors of men and women are based not only on her own insight and experience but also on scholarly research. Both popular and scholarly audiences treat her as one who makes scholarly findings and theories accessible to a nonexpert audience (e.g., Rose, 1990; Safier, 1992; Trnka, 1991). For example, *Washington Post* staff writer Henry Allen (1992) declares in an article about the value of *YJDU:* "Unlike the purveyors of self-help weepology, Tannen actually knows what she is talking about. She's done the research" (p. D6). Such adulation is not, however, limited to the popular press. In a *Journal of Pragmatics* review of the book, sociologist Stephen Murray (1992) concludes: "I think that Tannen writes better than Goffman or Hall, and I also think that she has a more coherent theory of culture and its reproduction than either of them. Her data add up" (p. 513). Even neutral characterizations of Tannen's work nonetheless treat it as grounded in research findings. For example, in citing *YJDU* in the *Philosophical Forum,* Piper (1993) says that the book is "a popularization of her research in linguistics on gender differences in language use" (p. 231).

In this review, we examine the appropriateness of treating *YJDU* as a source of empirical generalizations about the communication behavior of adult men and women in the United States. We recognize the value of making theory and scholarly research accessible to a mainstream audience. We acknowledge that some readers say they have been helped by this book and that there may be utility in this work that is independent of its factual accuracy and scholarly credentials. Similarly, we will not address the political implications of Tannen's work. For example, others have agreed with Tannen that there are gender differences in communication but have then gone on to criticize her for ignoring the degree to which these differences come about because of gender differences in power, male dominance, and social inequality (Cameron, 1992; DeFrancisco, 1992; Henley & Kramarae, 1991; Kramarae, 1992; Perry, 1991; Uchida, 1992). Our concern is with the factual accuracy of Tannen's claims about gender differences in communication. Questions that motivate this project include the following: Are readers of *YJDU* led to believe these are factual generalizations about male and female communication styles? Are such generalizations supported by the appropriate use of evidence? Is it appropriate for scholars to cite Tannen's work as empirically based evidence of gender differences in communication?

Whether Tannen is writing to a popular or an academic audience, there are similar standards for the evidence needed to support a factual generalization. We are particularly concerned about scholars who cite *YJDU* as a source of empirically based generalizations about gender differences, because it is reasonable to expect that scholars who cite Tannen would share our concern with factual accuracy rather than purely personal interest or heuristic use. Our analysis proceeded in three stages: (a) identification of claims and evidence,

(b) determination of what types of claims are made, and (c) evaluation of the support for Tannen's claims.

IDENTIFYING CLAIMS AND EVIDENCE

Tannen's claims about communication behavior and the evidence used to support them are dispersed and repeated throughout *YJDU*. For example, one of Tannen's central ideas—that boys and girls learn different patterns of communication in their same-sex play—is repeated and developed in several passages throughout the book. Consequently, we began our analysis by identifying each of the claims made about gender and communication and then creating topical groupings of claims with their corresponding evidence.

One of the authors recorded each claim as it appeared in the text and then grouped together identical claims that appeared at various places in the text, noting the page numbers where the claims were asserted. This author also recorded the evidence Tannen provides with each claim, indicating page number and type of evidence (e.g., citation to a study or scholarly paper, example from a novel). After she had recorded every claim with its corresponding evidence, this author generated a topical outline in which she placed subclaims under the larger claims they support. The length of the resulting detailed outline precludes its inclusion here,[2] but Table 1.1 summarizes the seven main claims identified. The appendix to this chapter shows the full outline for the fourth main claim, that adult men and women represent cross-cultural communication.

IDENTIFYING TYPES OF CLAIMS

Before we could evaluate the adequacy of Tannen's evidence, we needed to determine what kinds of claims she makes (and thus the appropriate standards for evaluation). We examined how Tannen presents her claims as well as how scholars who cite Tannen have interpreted her claims.

How Tannen Presents Her Claims

To determine how Tannen intends for her claims to be taken, we examined three aspects of the text itself. First, one author classified each of the claims in the topical outline as a claim of fact (an assessment of whether something is true or false, exists or does not exist, has or has not happened, and so on), value (an assessment of the whether something is positive or negative, or an evaluation of the worth or merit of an object, idea, behavior, and so on), or policy (advocacy of a particular action that should or should not be performed).[3]

TABLE 1.1
Main Claims and Illustrative Subclaims in *YJDU*

I. All conversations serve universal human needs for involvement and independence.
(For example: There is asymmetry and symmetry in each conversation. Men and women both want independence and intimacy but pursue them under the guise of their respective goals.)

II. Boys and girls grow up in different cultures.
(For example: Boys seek to preserve status and independence. Girls seek to create connections.)

III. Boys and girls create different worlds, which men and women go on inhabiting.
(For example: Women gossiping is a grown-up version of girls telling secrets.)

IV. Adult men and women represent cross-cultural communication.
(For example: Men try to preserve independence and see the world as hierarchical. Women try to preserve intimacy and see the world as a network of connections.)

V. Men and women are judged differently for the same behaviors.
(For example: Women's silence is construed as weakness; men's silence is seen as powerful.)

VI. Conversational style differences lead to misunderstandings.
(For example: Interruption is not always the result of intention to dominate; rather, it comes about because of different styles.)

VII. Recognizing and understanding differences enables us to adjust to and learn from one another.
(For example: Both men and women need to develop flexibility and could benefit from learning each other's styles.)

Claims of fact include both claims about what happened in a particular instance to a particular man or woman and claims about what is true of men and women generally. Consequently, we examined a second aspect of the text: How frequently does Tannen make qualified and unqualified generalizations about the behavior of men and women as classes? One author classified every sentence in the book as an unqualified generalization, a qualified generalization, or not a generalization about men's and/or women's communication (kappa = .96 for the other author's independent coding of 5% of the pages of the book).

Finally, one author counted every sentence in which Tannen referred to her status as an academic authority or to how her work has helped others. These kinds of statements suggest that Tannen's claims are not based simply on her own experience or opinion but are validated by others' experiences and/or are grounded in scientific research. Both kinds of statements implicitly encourage the reader to treat claims as factual generalizations (kappa = .99 for the other author's independent coding of 5% of the pages of the book).

The overwhelming majority of Tannen's claims (213 of 223) were classified as claims of fact. This is not surprising, given that Tannen explicitly states that she wants to avoid evaluating men's or women's style as good or bad. Instead, she prefers to document that their styles are different and to press the argument that each is equally valid. True to her word, Tannen rarely advances claims of value (7 of 223) or policy (3 of 223). The few that do occur are related to her sixth and seventh main claims about the consequences and conclusions of her larger argument.

Tannen's claims of fact are not limited to assertions about what occurred in particular episodes. We located 479 generalizations about men's and/or women's communication in the 298-page book. Of these, 193 are unqualified and 286 are qualified by words and phrases such as *many, most,* and *typically.* These kinds of qualifiers are less precise than specific information about percentages of men or women or likelihood of occurrence, and they also portray exceptions to the generalization as less common than cases consistent with the generalization.

Finally, we located 40 instances in which Tannen refers to her scholarly status and 16 instances in which she asserts that others have found her work useful, sensible, and/or valuable. For example, in a passage claiming that men and women take different roles as audiences, Tannen chooses to describe a personal example in the following way: "I recall a speaking engagement before which I was taken to lunch by a group of women. *They were so attentive to my expertise* that they plied me with questions" (p. 146, emphasis added). Another more general reference to Tannen's expertise and popularity appears early in *YJDU*: "Most people exclaim that what I say is true, that it explains their own experience" (p. 14). In the text that follows, individuals who don't "exclaim that what I say is true" are portrayed not as providing counterexamples or as exclaiming that Tannen's claims are not true, but rather as objecting to her claims on political grounds.

Based on an analysis of the text itself, it appears that Tannen intends for her work to be taken as a source of factual generalizations about men and women—if not all men and women, then at least "most" or "many" of them. As we examine how readers have taken Tannen's claims, we find these features of the text are not lost on those who cite *YJDU* as a source of factual generalizations.

How Scholarly Readers
Interpret Tannen's Claims

To gauge how Tannen's claims are treated by scholars who cite *YJDU*, we searched for Tannen's name and the book's title in *Social Sciences Citation Index & Source Index* (1990-August 1995), *Arts & Humanities Citation Index & Source Index* (1990-August 1995), the ERIC database of education journals and related fields (1990-1996), and the PsycINFO database (1990-1995). We used subject category listings within the *Social Sciences* and *Arts & Humanities* citation indexes to classify journals according to discipline. In all, 247 scholarly articles cited *YJDU*;[4] the 180 journals in which these citations appeared came from 41 different academic disciplines. In order to understand how Tannen's claims are treated by scholars who cite her, we developed coding systems to characterize the type of article in which Tannen is cited and the way in which the citation to the book is used.

We first classified the *type of article* in which the book is cited, including book reviews of *YJDU* or of other books, letters, editorials, articles reporting empirical studies, and essays or literature reviews (one author coded every work; kappa = 1.00 for a randomly selected 5% of works). Second, we identified *how the book is used* by the scholars who cite it. In a *mention* of the book, an author refers to Tannen in relation to general content or methodology but does not identify any specific claims, does not assume Tannen's claims are true in explaining his or her own claims, and does not test or evaluate the veracity of any of Tannen's claims. In a *reference* to the book, the author identifies, utilizes, and extends one or more of Tannen's specific claims in support of the author's own position. A *discussion* of Tannen's book involves extensive analysis or evaluation of multiple claims advanced in *YJDU* but does not collect empirical data to test Tannen's claims. A *test* does collect empirical data directed toward one or more of Tannen's claims. We coded as *other* three articles that did not fit the mention, reference, discussion, or test categories (one author coded every work; kappa = .73 for a random sample of 10% of the works). Within the reference, discussion, and test categories, we further differentiated citations that assume Tannen's claims to be true or provide reasoning or evidence consistent with Tannen's claims (positive citations) from citations that question some or all of Tannen's claims (mixed/negative citations) (one author coded every work; kappa for valence = .71 for a random sample of 10% of the works).

Table 1.2 shows the results of our analysis of scholarly citations. Tannen is cited in a variety of genres of academic writing. Only 31.2% of the citations appear in articles reporting empirical studies, and nearly half of these empirical studies did not test Tannen's claims; rather, the authors simply mention, refer to, or discuss *YJDU*. Thus only 16.2% of all the scholarly citations to *YJDU* involve empirical tests of Tannen's claims. The most common type of citation, making up slightly more than 50% of all citations, is a positive reference (i.e., accepting Tannen's claims without evaluation to forward the author's own claim[s]). In fact, citations to Tannen are overwhelmingly positive: Across the reference, discussion, and testing categories, more than 78% of the authors treat Tannen's work positively and accept her claims as true.

Because so many authors have used Tannen's work uncritically as a positive reference to advance their own claims, we examined which claims from the topical outline are the main focus of positive references. A given article could refer to more than one of Tannen's claims, resulting in 212 positive references. Of these, 136 (64%) cite Tannen's claims regarding communication differences between adult men and women (main point IV). The second most cited claims involve recommendations about what people should do as a result of these differences (main claim VII, 16 positive references, 7.5%) and the

TABLE 1.2
Frequency of Citation to *YJDU* by Academic Genre and Type of Citation

Genre	Mention	Reference		Discussion		Test		Other
		+	–/mixed	+	–/mixed	+	–/mixed	
Reviews of YJDU (19)	0	0	0	10	9	0	0	0
Other book reviews (9)	1	6	2	0	0	0	0	0
Letters (3)	2	1	0	0	0	0	0	0
Editorials (4)	1	2	1	0	0	0	0	0
Empirical studies (77)	3	29	0	3	0	23	17	2
Essays, literature reviews, reports (135)	19	87	17	6	5	0	0	1
Total (247)	26	125	20	19	14	23	17	3

assertion that men and women are judged differently for the same behaviors (main claim V, 15 positive references, 7.1%).

EVALUATING THE ADEQUACY OF EVIDENCE
FOR GENDER DIFFERENCES IN COMMUNICATION

We limited our evaluation of the adequacy of Tannen's evidence to those sources used in support of the claims regarding communication differences between adult men and women (main point IV; see the appendix to this chapter). As communication scholars, we find these claims to be of greatest interest; these are also the claims most frequently cited in other scholars' positive references to *YJDU*. In addition, the topical outline revealed that the greatest number of Tannen's claims are devoted to enumerating these differences. Finally, claims about communication differences between adult men and women are central to other main claims. For instance, if there are no differences in the behaviors of adult men and women, then the significance of claims about boys and girls becomes unclear (main claims II and III) and the defense of a conversational style-based explanation (main claim VI) and recommendations for greater understanding (main claim VII) are unnecessary.

We attempted to locate all the published scholarly evidence Tannen cites in support of her claims under main claim IV, a total of 43 sources. Of these, 3 are cited for the use of a term or concept only and not for evidence of gender differences in communication.[5] Of the 40 remaining sources, we were able to locate 37.[6] To evaluate the adequacy of Tannen's evidence, we used several traditional tests of evidence from argumentation theory (as set out in Vancil, 1993, pp. 178-201). Tests of the *evidence-claim* relationship focus on how well evidence supports a claim. These include assertion, sufficiency, relevance, and recency. Tests of *evidence substance* are concerned with the trustworthiness of the evidence. Of the four substance tests Vancil (1993) describes, we focus on "consistency" and "statistics," and we expand our evaluation of statistics to consider the appropriate use of empirical data of all types. Although they are relevant to Tannen's anecdotal evidence, we have no basis for applying the "integrity" and "context" tests of substance. Similarly, we did not apply Vancil's tests of *evidence source* (including identification, expertise, and bias). It was impossible to examine the accessibility or authenticity of Tannen's references to personal experiences, and we took for granted that Tannen's scholarly citations refer to studies whose researchers possess appropriate credentials and engaged in unbiased analysis.

Assertion and Sufficiency

The criterion of assertion applies simply to whether or not there is any evidence that supports the claim; sufficiency involves a judgment of whether enough evidence is provided. Perusal of the outline for main claim IV (see the appendix) reveals how many of Tannen's main claims have no supporting evidence and stand primarily on Tannen's authority and/or the reader's own judgment of plausibility. The first five lettered subclaims (A-E) point to various kinds of differences that suggest men and women constitute different cultures (e.g., differences in what is natural, differences in reasons for action, differences in what is considered important). These claims rest on 28 citations to evidence, only 6 of which are scholarly studies. Of these 6, 1 is an error: Sternberg and Grajek's (1984) study does not provide any evidence that men and women differ in who they name as best friends. Another is a citation to a highly controversial set of studies carried out in the late 1960s (Horner, 1972; see Paludi, 1984, for a review of the "fear of success" construct). The rest of the evidence consists of 16 anecdotes, an excerpt from a short story, an analogy to a book about an American tourist imprisoned in Turkey, a poem, an opinion piece from *Newsweek* magazine, and scenes from two films. The final three lettered subclaims include all of Tannen's specific claims about how men communicate (F), how women communicate (G), and how they misinterpret one another's communication (H). Of the 34 claims about men's communication, more than one-third (13) have no scholarly citation to support the claim. Even those claims that are accompanied by scholarly citation rest on thin documentation: 13 of the 21 claims with scholarly support rely on the results of a single study. In her claims about the communication behavior of men, Tannen cites more than twice as many nonscholarly sources (62) as scholarly sources (26). A similar pattern emerges for her claims about the behavior of women (in part because Tannen frequently makes claims about the behavior of men and women in the same passage and with the same evidence to support both claims). Of the 27 statements describing women's communication, 9 have no scholarly reference for support. Of the 16 claims that do cite a scholarly source, 6 rest on a single study.

Claims with no evidence are insufficiently supported, and even claims evidenced by citation of a single empirical study are problematic: If that study is flawed, irrelevant to Tannen's claim, or inconsistent with her conclusions, the claim has no additional support. Even if a single study is valid, generalizations from its findings are limited by the particulars of the study (e.g., the type of situation observed or type of task used, the age and background of participants, the type of measures used). We also question the many claims that rest only on examples from works of fiction, from Tannen's own experience, and/or from experiences reported to Tannen by others. How many personal or fictional examples are sufficient to support a generalization that "women do this" or "men do that," and how do we reconcile Tannen's examples with disconfirming instances in our own experience? Rather than using examples as *illustrations* of points documented by empirical research, Tannen often presents examples as the sole support for her claims. It is unclear whether this pattern of citation may have been dictated by the demands of publishing in a popular genre. Nonetheless, scholarly and popular audiences alike should be cautious about accepting factual generalizations that rest on anecdotal support or on no support at all.

Relevance

The relevance criterion applies to the degree to which evidence directly supports the claim made and, if the evidence does not provide direct support, if there is an explanation of how the evidence is relevant. Two problems with the relevance of Tannen's scholarly evidence stem from her reliance on studies conducted in other cultures (7 of the 43 studies cited under main claim IV) and on studies of children's behavior (another 6 of the 43 studies cited under main claim IV).

A key claim in Tannen's work is that differences in the communication patterns of adult men and women come about because of their socialization as children. This would seem to suggest that the communicative behavior of men and women is a result of particular practices to which children are socialized in a particular cultural group and not of any innate, universal, biological factors.[7] Indeed, the cross-cultural communication analogy on which Tannen relies for her analysis presumes that different cultures have distinctive ways of communicating, and we cannot assume similarity from one group to another. Given this stance, it is puzzling to see Tannen use studies conducted in Iran (Beeman, 1986), Mexico (Brown, 1990), Greece (Caraveli, 1986; Dubisch, 1986), Indonesia (Kuipers, 1986), and Panama (Sherzer, 1987), as well as in an ethnic subcultural group of Jewish Americans

(Schiffrin, 1984), as evidence for the behavior of men and women in the "mainstream American" society that appears to be the focus of her analysis. At best, similar communication patterns in these other cultural groups are irrelevant to Tannen's claims; given Tannen's belief that communicative practices are culture specific, evidence that men and women in other cultures behave in particular ways cannot count as evidence that men and women in the United States will do the same. At worst, the findings of these studies ought to raise questions about the adequacy of socialization alone as an account for differences in male-female communication. If men and women in diverse cultures display similar communicative patterns, we ought to wonder at the coincidence that cultures around the world socialize men and women in such similar ways.

However, there is reason to doubt that the patterns in other cultures are in fact all that similar to the communication of Tannen's mainstream American culture. For example, Beeman (1986) emphasizes the fundamental differences between Iranian and North American social ethics of symmetry and asymmetry. He claims it is difficult for Americans truly to understand the quality of intimate life in Iran and, therefore, suggests that parallels between interpersonal lives cannot be drawn accurately. Similarly, Sherzer (1987) says that cross-cultural universals in male and female speech may be possible, but insists "that any such universals be sought out and analyzed in relation to significant cross-cultural and individual differences as well. . . . generalizations and universals must come to terms with this complexity and try not to simplify it" (pp. 119-120).

Another problem with the relevance of Tannen's evidence is her use of studies of children as support for claims about the behavior of adults. Studies of children are obviously relevant to claims about the behavior of children (main claim II), but Tannen also cites six studies of children as support for claims about the behaviors of *adults* (Corsaro & Rizzo, 1990; Goodwin, 1990; Greenwood, 1989; Hughes, 1988; Newman, 1971; Tannen, 1990a). In order to clarify the relevance of these studies, Tannen would need to provide evidence that childhood behavior in same-sex play groups persists unchanged into same- and opposite-sex behavior by adults in adult contexts. We grouped all claims relevant to this issue under main claim III and found that this argument rests solely on Tannen's (1990a) assertion that it is so (based on her observation that behavior in six children's friendship pairs bore similarity to the behavior of two pairs of 25-year-old friends) and on Fox's (1990) report of two college students in his writing class. In contrast to Tannen's willingness to assume that childhood behavior persists unchanged into adulthood, several of her sources on children's behavior warn against generalizing from their results. Eckert (1990), Goodwin (1990), and Hughes (1988) all caution against generalizing about boys' and girls' behavior across activities and social class. Lever (1978) states explicitly, "That those social skills might carry over and influence their adult behavior is pure speculation" (p. 481).

Recency

The recency criterion addresses whether the time referent of the evidence is consistent with the time referent of the claim. Although we will not attempt to present evidence of our own that the communication of men and women has changed over the past four decades,[8] we do note that 12 of the 43 studies Tannen cites were based on data collected in the 1950s, 1960s, or 1970s. Strodtbeck and Mann's study was published in 1956. Horner's article, though published in 1972, reports on research conducted in 1964 and 1971. Seven studies were published in the 1970s (Aries, 1976; Eakins & Eakins, 1976; Fishman, 1978; Hirschman, 1973; Kalčik, 1975; Newman, 1971; Swacker, 1976), one study published in 1990 is based on a conversation recorded in 1974 (Erickson, 1990), and Mitchell's 1985 chapter is based on a 1976 dissertation. Although the publication date of Maltz and Borker's article is 1982, theirs is a literature review of research conducted in the 1950s, 1960s, and 1970s. If men's and women's behaviors are culturally based, we might expect change over time in the nature and magnitude of gender differences, particularly given dramatic social change during this particular time period.

Appropriate Use of Empirical Findings

In examining the appropriateness of Tannen's use of empirical findings, we focus on her citation of 19 empirical studies and 3 reviews of empirical research on communication by adult men and women in the United States.[9] We are not evaluating the studies per se but rather Tannen's use of these studies to support generalizations about male and female communication patterns.

If we wish to generalize about how men and women communicate based on the results of a study, the findings of that study ought to be based on a reasonably large and representative sample of individuals. Of the 19 studies Tannen cites, 14 provide small and unrepresentative samples for the purposes of generalization. Eakins and Eakins (1976) base their conclusions on recordings of seven meetings of a faculty. Edelsky (1981) bases her findings on observations of a single 11-member faculty committee of which she was a member. Erickson (1990) reports on a dinnertime conversation in one Italian American family with five children. Fishman (1978) examines recordings of three couples. Fox (1990) provides an analysis of writing samples by two students in one of his courses. Frank (1988) analyzes a tape of a 30-minute argument she had with her husband. Hirschman's (1973) findings are based on four people. Kalčik (1975) reports on the meetings of two women's consciousness-raising groups and an unspecified number of additional "one-shot women's functions such as workshops, NOW conventions, and women's career days" (p. 4). Johnstone (1989) draws conclusions based on 25 stories told by men and 33 stories told by women. Smith's (1990) conclusions are based on analysis of sermons by 4 women and 11 men enrolled in a Baptist seminary in Texas. Swacker (1976) observed meetings of the Linguistic Society of America plus two colloquia. Other studies involve a reasonably large numbers of participants, but analysis is complicated by nonindependent data because the individuals interacted together in groups: Aries examined 6 groups of college students (1976) and 21 groups of students (1982); Strodtbeck and Mann (1956) observed the deliberations of 12 mock juries.

Tannen's claims that a particular kind of behavior or interpretation is more frequent for one gender than the other require a clear and consistent way of identifying and counting all occurrences of the behavior or interpretation in question. Intercoder reliability is one widely accepted way of demonstrating that a phenomenon can be consistently identified by multiple independent observers. Of the studies we examined, 14 rely on some sort of classification or coding of observed or recorded interaction and subsequent comparison of the frequencies with which different categories are performed by men or women (Aries, 1976, 1982; Eakins & Eakins, 1976; Edelsky, 1981; Fishman, 1978; Hirschman, 1994; Johnstone, 1989; Leet-Pellegrini, 1980; Mitchell, 1985; Riessman, 1990; Smith, 1990; Strodtbeck & Mann, 1956; Swacker, 1976; Tannen, 1990a). Yet only 3 of these provide any evidence of intercoder reliability, and 2 of these 3 studies obtained intercoder reliability for only some categories.[10] In fairness to the authors, some of the discourse features that were coded in these studies were relatively straightforward (e.g., number of words, length of turn as timed by a stopwatch, use of the phrase "D'ya know what?"). However, many of the features classified by a single coder are open to interpretation, such as type of response to another's comment (Hirschman, 1973), topical content of a story or presence of extrathematic detail (Johnstone, 1989), emphasis on freedom versus obligation in stories about one's divorce (Riessman, 1990), asking tangential questions (Swacker, 1976), and features of physical alignment and gaze (Tannen, 1990a). Finally, none of the studies indicates that coders were blind to speaker gender, leaving open the possibility that observers were influenced by expectations or stereotypes of how men and women speak.

Claims that a particular behavior or interpretation is more frequent for one gender than the other also require some means of determining whether the difference is likely to have occurred by chance alone. Tests of statistical significance provide this information. In assessing how different men and women really are, it is also useful to know how large the difference is (i.e., an estimate of effect size). Of the studies we examined, 15 make claims about the differential frequency with which men and women behave (Aries, 1976, 1982; Blumstein & Schwartz, 1984; Eakins & Eakins, 1976; Edelsky, 1981; Fishman, 1978; Hirschman, 1994; Johnstone, 1989; Leet-Pellegrini, 1980; Mitchell, 1985; Riessman, 1990; Smith, 1990; Strodtbeck & Mann, 1956; Swacker, 1976; Tannen, 1990a); only 6 of these provide tests of statistical significance to support their conclusions of gender difference. Nonindependence of data and extremely small samples may account for some authors' reliance on narrative summary, raw frequency counts, percentages, or simple display of means. Although some studies provide tabled comparisons of frequencies or percentages (and some of the differences do appear to be large), this does not provide information that a test of statistical significance is designed to provide: We cannot be confident that within-gender variability does not exceed between-gender variability, and we cannot know the likelihood that observed differences were a matter of chance. Similarly, none of the studies discusses effect size for gender differences. In one study, the authors note that gender differences occurred in the context of a high degree of similarity in behaviors; they conclude: "By and large the jurors' interaction profiles are quite similar. In the face of this similarity, the direction of attention of the differences associated with gender roles should not be permitted to obscure the determinative influences of the problem situation" (Strodtbeck & Mann, 1956, p. 10).

In addition to the studies Tannen cites as evidence for her generalizations, she also refers to three literature reviews. Maltz and Borker (1982) make essentially the same argument Tannen later popularized, and their review is based on many of the studies already discussed (Fishman, 1978; Hirschman, 1973; Kalčik, 1975; Strodtbeck & Mann, 1956). In addition, they cite a descriptive study of the interactions of two married couples on a weekend vacation (Soskin & John, 1963) and studies of interruption by West and Zimmerman. One of these studies examined parent-child conversation (West & Zimmerman, 1977), another examined five pairs of college students in a laboratory setting (West, 1979; the conversations appear to have been coded by the author alone and no tests of significance are reported), and another reported on 31 naturally occurring conversations in dyads of differing gender composition (Zimmerman & West, 1975; the authors independently coded for interruption and overlap but no tests of significance were conducted). As we shall see below, Zimmerman and West's conclusions about the relative frequency of male and female interruptions are not entirely consistent with the findings of other subsequent studies. Maltz and Borker also rely on several ethnographic studies concerned with describing and interpreting a form of talk that happens to occur in male or female groups. None of these ethnographic studies attempted to document the relative frequency or distribution across gender of the type of talk described. Furthermore, these studies took place in other cultural or ethnic groups than the (presumably) white, middle-class, American demographic to whom Tannen's book is addressed. For example, Abrahams (1975, 1976) and Hannerz (1969) studied in urban black communities, Bauman (1972) and Faris (1966) studied in a small Newfoundland town, and Philipsen (1975) and LeMasters (1975) studied in working-class neighborhoods (and took great pains to describe how these communities' ways of speech were distinctive from those of the broader American culture). Tannen's references to Maltz and Borker do little to shore up the empirical basis for her generalizations, because most of the studies they review are subject to the same problems of relevance and representativeness that pertain to Tannen's other empirical sources.

Tannen also refers to literature reviews by James and colleagues, one a review of research on gender differences in amount of talk (James & Drakich, 1993) and the other a review of gender differences in interruptions (James & Clarke, 1993).[11] Because both reviews draw conclusions that are inconsistent with some of Tannen's claims, we discuss these reviews below as part of our consideration of the internal and external consistency of Tannen's evidence.

To summarize our review of the appropriateness of Tannen's use of empirical studies, we note that of the empirical studies available to us and relevant to Tannen's claims, only two (Blumstein & Schwartz, 1984; Horner, 1972) are not limited by small or unrepresentative samples, coding systems of unknown reliability, and/or unsystematic comparisons of frequencies. These are not necessarily flaws in the studies themselves but rather problems in Tannen's using these studies as evidence for her generalizations. Many of these studies were designed to support claims of a different sort from the claims for which Tannen uses them as evidence, and many of the authors of these studies caution against the very kinds of conclusions Tannen draws from their findings—an issue of consistency, to which we now turn.

Internal Consistency

The internal consistency criterion applies to whether evidence for various claims agrees with other information provided by the sources of that evidence. The most noticeable problem with the internal consistency of Tannen's evidence is her citation of studies to support generalizations when the authors of the studies give explicit warnings against doing so. We noted above that several authors of cross-cultural studies and studies of children caution against such generalization and so do the authors of several of the studies of adult men and women. Fox's (1990) analysis of two students is one of the studies Tannen cites most frequently, yet he explicitly states:

> There is nothing either predictable or predictive about these case studies. . . . If I wished to propose a generalization in these cases, this generalization would apply only to these students in my course; it would not apply to other students in different courses, nor to the same students next month or next year, nor to other students in my class with the same social background. . . .
>
> . . . Stereotypical predictions of language use ignore the important shaping power of context and, worse, underestimate people's ability to vary their language creatively according to their perception of context. Conclusions about the relationship between gender, reading, and writing need to be situationally specific, for neither men's language nor women's language is stable across contexts. (pp. 49-51)

Hirschman (1994) is equally explicit:

Because of the sample size (four people), clearly it is impossible to make any kinds of generalizations about female and male patterns of conversational inter-action. However, this research does enable us to construct detailed, empirically testable hypotheses about sex-related differences. The next step, of course, is to collect data in large quantities, in order to test these hypotheses. (p. 430)

Likewise, Kalčik (1975) cautions, "No definitive statement about women's storytelling, interaction, or use of language is attempted except in terms of the rap group situation and narratives analyzed here" (p. 3).

Another inconsistency involves Tannen's use of studies whose findings or conclusions are inconsistent with her own position. For example, Tannen cites Aries (1982) in support of the claim that women adopt a "ladylike" posture and talk about different topics in mixed-sex groups; however, when advancing her claim that men talk more than women, Tannen neglects to note Aries's finding that women initiate *more* turns at talk than men in the mixed-group setting. Similarly, Tannen refers to literature reviews by James and colleagues whose conclusions differ from her own. For example, in their reviews of the literature on gender differences in amount of talk (James & Drakich, 1993) and interruptions (James & Clarke, 1993), James and her coauthors conclude that Tannen's explanation for gender differences is insufficient to account for the empirical findings. We acknowledge that the versions of these papers available to Tannen at the writing of *YJDU* might have differed from the published versions of these reviews to which we now have access. However, the empirical literature that James and colleagues reviewed was available to Tannen and is inconsistent with her claims—an issue of external consistency.

External Consistency

The external consistency criterion focuses on the extent to which Tannen's evidence agrees with other sources of information. As the outline in the appendix to this chapter makes clear, Tannen's claims about gender differences in communication are far-reaching. The scholarly literature on gender differences in communication is even more extensive. It is beyond the scope of this chapter for us to provide a review of all of the scholarly literature relevant to all of Tannen's claims about communication behavior. However, it is instructive to contrast Tannen's claims about gender differences in communication with the conclusions reached by other authors who have conducted more extensive and systematic reviews of the empirical literature on various topics.[12] If it is appropriate to treat *YJDU* as a synthesis of findings on gender and communication (as many scholars do), then we ought to find that the conclusions Tannen reaches and the generalizations she draws are consistent with conclusions reached in other literature reviews and syntheses of research. We found reviews of literature or meta-analyses for the following topics about which Tannen makes claims: compliance gaining, conflict, verbal presumptuousness versus attentiveness, conversational maintenance, amount of talk, topics of talk, seeking and giving help, nonverbal communication, and the role of talk in intimate relationships.

Compliance Gaining

Tannen claims that men give orders (F1) whereas women make requests (G1) and that men are not comfortable consulting their partners (F2) whereas women prefer to consult and discuss (G2). Canary and Emmers-Sommers (1997) have reviewed studies on how men and women exercise power and control in personal relationships. Contrary to Tannen's claims, they conclude that, "although women appear to use a wider variety of indirect and negative influence behaviors, the effect sizes due to gender differences are small. Some research has shown that men and women largely prefer the same strategies. Other research shows that women appear to use more unilateral and controlling behaviors in romantic relationships" (p. 80).

Tannen's contrast between giving orders and making requests could also be interpreted as a difference in politeness. A review of studies of men and women from Western industrialized nations found mixed evidence of differences in politeness (Goldsmith & MacGeorge, 1997). However, some of the studies finding no difference between men and women employed small samples with low statistical power. Of the studies that did find differences, women were found to be more polite than men or to use different forms of politeness than men. Similarly, Aries (1996) concludes her review of differences in language use by noting that there is research to suggest that women use more politeness strategies than men. However, she cautions:

> When we take another perspective on these data and pay more careful attention to the methodological problems that plague many of the studies—the power, status, and roles of the participants and the contextual variability in the use of language forms—another understanding of the literature emerges. We see that gender differences in language are few in number. They do not appear consistently but are situationally variable depending on the setting, topic, role, status, and gender of the participants. Many studies report no gender differences. The magnitude of these gender differences has not been assessed. Researchers in the area of language have paid attention to statistical significance but not to effect sizes. (p. 139)

There does not appear to be a clear empirical basis for concluding that men give orders and decline to consult with their partners whereas women make requests and engage in consensus building. Findings on control and politeness strategies are mixed, perhaps due to methodological limitations or to variability in the tasks and situations studied. When differences do occur, studies of politeness suggest women are more polite than men, but the effect sizes are small. Studies of close romantic relationships (the context from which many of Tannen's examples are drawn) suggest that women may actually engage in more unilateral control strategies than do men.

Conflict

The common thread in Tannen's claims about gender differences in conflict (F5-F9, G4-G6) is that men engage in conflict more directly than women do, because men view conflict as a natural expression of the contest for status whereas women view conflict as a threat to solidarity and harmony. There is limited support for these claims in the empirical literature.

Gayle, Preiss, and Allen (1994) report a meta-analysis of 31 studies that examined gender differences in the use of conflict strategies (avoidance, accommodation, competition, compromise, and collaboration) across a wide variety of situations. The findings indicate that women engaged in avoidance, accommodation, compromise, and collaboration more frequently than men, and men behaved competitively more frequently than women. However, the effect sizes were small, accounting for less than 1% of the variability in individual behavior. A somewhat different picture emerges from two litera-ture reviews focused on conflict in personal relationships. Canary and Emmers-Sommers (1997) note that in personal relationships, women tend to use more competitive, negative conflict behavior than men do; however, gender is a less powerful predictor of these behavior patterns than are other factors, including the partner's antecedent behavior, overall relational satisfaction, occupation, and whether an individual is trying to change the status quo or defend it. Similarly, Cupach and Canary (1995) conclude: "Although men and women may exhibit *some* differences in conflict management behavior, these differences are found inconsistently. . . . Sex differences in conflict tend to be small in magnitude and are often greatly overshadowed by other contex-tual, personal, and relational factors" (p. 237).

The empirical literature surveyed in these reviews focuses on self-reported and observed conflict behaviors and thus does not speak to Tannen's claims about the intentions and interpretations men and women may have for con-flict. However, the empirical literature is quite clear in showing that men and women do not display consistent, dichotomous differences in their conflict behavior. There are small tendencies for women to use conflict behaviors that might be seen as more cooperative and accommodating and for men to engage in competitive conflict behaviors, but the small effect sizes suggest that men and women are much more similar than different. In addition, in the context of close personal relationships it appears that women can be just as competi-tive as men, if not more so.

Verbal Presumptuousness
Versus Attentiveness

Tannen claims that in informal conversation, men offer information and engage in lecturing (F10). They do so both as a means of asserting their status and as a way of charming the hearer (F10-F11), and they assume their conversational partners will do likewise if they have something to contribute (F12). In contrast, Tannen says that women are more inclined to give praise, ask questions, and offer agreement or disagreement with the speaker; they do this both to charm the hearer and to attempt to minimize status differences by sharing information (G7, G8). These constellations of communicative behavior resemble a distinction drawn by Stiles and colleagues (1997) between verbal presumptuousness and attentiveness.[13] In five studies of various populations engaged in various kinds of tasks, they found no evidence that men were more presumptuous than women. Instead, the degree of presumptuousness was linked to the type of task in which the dyad engaged, the relationship between partners (e.g., spouses were more presumptuous with one another than were strangers), and partner's level of presumptuousness. In four of the five studies, women were more attentive than men; however, these effects were quite small and in two of the studies gender of speaker interacted with other factors (relationship to partner, which member of a dyad received instructions first) in predicting attentiveness.

Conversational Maintenance

Tannen claims that men remain silent when they listen (F13) whereas women ask questions and provide back-channel responses (G9). She asserts that both men and women engage in interruption, but they do so for different reasons. Men interrupt to assume control of the conversation (F14) whereas women interrupt to show rapport (G10).

Canary and Emmers-Sommers (1997) suggest that the question of whether men or women do more to maintain a conversation remains unresolved, due to variability in the tasks and methods employed in various studies and to small sample sizes that limit statistical power to detect differences. Some studies have found that women produce more back channels than do men, some have found that men produce more back channels than do women, and some have found no significant differences. Aries (1996) concludes that women are more likely than men to use back-channel behaviors; however, gender interacts with other variables, including whether the task is cooperative or competitive and whether the researcher focuses on interactive or narrative segments of discourse. Similarly, Wannaruk (1997) identifies several factors that influence back-channel behavior, including status, social role, occupational and educational experience, intimacy between participants, and setting. She also notes the difficulty in generalizing across studies using different methodologies and small subject samples.

Although there is a large and varied literature on the question of interruptions, most of the research has examined whether men or women interrupt more frequently. James and Clarke (1993) report that "most research has found no significant difference between the genders in the number of interruptions initiated, in either cross-sex or same-sex interaction" (p. 231), and Aries (1996) concurs. In contrast, Tannen's claims concern gender differences in how interruptions are intended and interpreted. Although they acknowledge that few studies have differentiated among various types of interruptions, James and Clarke (1993) conclude that "the research to date provides no firm evidence" (p. 231) that men are more likely to use interruptions to dominate. They present some evidence that women use interruptions to show involvement and rapport; however, this conclusion is based in part on research conducted solely in women's groups rather than on research that compares women's behavior to men's behavior in comparable situations.

Research on conversational maintenance provides a tenuous basis for any sort of claim. Studies of back-channel responses are few in number, highly variable in method, and limited by small sample sizes, so perhaps it is not surprising that findings are inconsistent. A number of studies examine interruption, but most focus on sheer frequency rather than meaning. The literature does not provide conclusive evidence that Tannen is wrong, but it is inaccurate to say that the literature shows men and women have distinctly different styles of conversational maintenance.

Amount of Talk

Tannen claims that men talk more than women in mixed-sex public settings whereas women talk more than men in private settings (F15-F17, G11-G12). Smythe and Schlueter (1989) reviewed 65 studies and found no consistent gender-associated effect on amount of talk produced; however, they did not differentiate between different settings of talk. Eagly (1987) examines three different meta-analyses of gender differences in speech production in discussion groups. None found any overall gender difference in amount of talk. In a review of 56 studies of mixed-sex interactions, James and Drakich (1993) found that men talked more than women in 42.9% of the studies and that women talked more than men in only 3.6% of the studies. They further differentiated studies according to whether the interaction occurred in formal task settings, formally structured but not formal task settings (e.g., classrooms, TV panel discussions), and informal nontask settings. They conclude that men talk more than women in formal task settings whereas findings of no difference were more frequent in informal nontask settings. However, they also found that methodological differences accounted for variability in findings. With respect to Tannen's claims, it is noteworthy that these authors did not find that women talked more than men in the informal nontask settings—a third of these studies still found that men talked more than women. James and

Drakich explicitly evaluate and reject Tannen's account of gender differences as an explanation for these findings and argue instead that results "cannot be adequately understood either from a power perspective or from the perspective of differential gender-based interactional styles" (p. 302). Unfortunately, their tallying of statistically significant differences ignores variability in sample size and overlooks effect size.

Topics of Talk

Tannen claims that men prefer to talk about politics, news, and sports; to gossip about themselves and about political figures; and to tell stories about individual contests in which they prevailed (F18-F20). In contrast, women are more interested in talking about details of personal relationships, and their narratives emphasize themes of community (G13-G14). Bischoping (1993), who reviewed 10 studies on topics of talk, concludes that "a clear pattern of gender differences in topic choice emerges" (p. 7); however, because she was interested in changes over time, she included in her summary 6 studies conducted prior to 1950. She found that later studies show smaller gender differences than do earlier studies, though it is not clear whether this reflects change over time or differences in samples (i.e., college students were sampled more often in later studies). Unfortunately, Bischoping relies on chi-square analyses of the gender-by-topic relationship for the findings of each individual study; consequently, her conclusions about differences for specific topics are suspect and her generalizations across studies are impressionistic. For example, in her own results from observation of college students in 1990, a chi-square analysis indicates topic of conversation is not independent of the gender of speakers, but there are no tests for differences on particular topics. Nonetheless, Bischoping reports that men talk about work, money, and leisure more than women do and women talk about the opposite sex and appearances more than men do; however, for both men and women, work, money, and leisure are the most frequent topics. Fehr's (1996) review of differences in the conversational topics of friends concludes that gender differences in topics of talk are "rather striking": women talk more about relationships, personal problems, and secrets from the past than men do, and men talk more about sports, hobbies, and activities than women do. Like Bischoping, Fehr reviews studies that focus on who talks more about various topics and neglects to ask whether the most- and least-frequent topics are similar or different for men and women.

Significance of Talk to Relational Intimacy

Tannen characterizes men's friendship as activity based (F21-F22) and women's friendships as sustained by small talk, gossip, and the sharing of secrets (G15-G16). These differences are also related to her broader claims that men and women have different understandings of intimacy (claim D). In her book reviewing the empirical research on friendship, Fehr (1996, p. 117) observes that although these characterizations of men's and women's friendships are quite common, they have recently come under critical scrutiny.

Research on self-disclosure is one body of work relevant to these claims. If Tannen is correct, we ought to find that women disclose more than men, particularly in same-sex relationships. There is some support for this in the research literature; however, differences tend to be small and highly variable. Dindia and Allen's (1992) meta-analysis of 205 studies produced a small average effect size of gender on self-disclosure, indicating that women disclose slightly more than men. Effect sizes varied significantly from one study to another, depending on the gender of the target person to whom a disclosure was made and the way in which self-disclosure was measured. Gender differences in disclosure are greater in same-sex interactions than in opposite-sex interactions; however, female-to-male self-disclosure was not greater than male-to-male self disclosure. In a meta-analysis of 71 studies of self-disclosure, Belk (1991) similarly concludes that women tend to disclose more than men; however, a variety of moderating variables also had a significant impact on gender differences, including age and social class of subjects, region in the United States, self-report versus observation measures, and survey versus experimental methods. Two narrative literature reviews have also emphasized the situational variability in gender differences in self-disclosure (Aries, 1996; Hill & Stull, 1987). That women friends disclose more than men friends is consistent with Tannen's claims. However, if this difference were due to men's and women's pursuing different goals and styles across various situations and relationships, we might not expect to see such small differences and so much variability in the size of these differences.

Several recent studies have examined the larger issue of whether men and women differ in their perceptions of the role of talk in close relationships. Duck and Wright (1993) note that in everyday conversations, college men and women both report "mere talk" as the primary purpose for getting together with friends. Burleson, Kunkel, Samter, and Werking (1996) asked college men and women to rate the importance of various types of communication skills for same-sex friendships and for opposite-sex romantic relationships. Although women placed slightly greater value on affective communication skills than did men, and men placed slightly greater value on instrumental communication skills than did women, both men and women saw affective communication skills as more important in close relationships than instrumental communication skills. Burleson (1997) summarizes the results of several studies comparing the meanings of intimacy and closeness for men and women and concludes that "although some small gender differences are regularly found, the meanings that men and women have for these concepts are much more similar than different" (p. 236). Lundquist (1993) reports a meta-analysis of 146 studies comparing men's and women's expressions and understandings of intimacy in romantic relationships (including 257 effect sizes and 40,600 participants). She reports that women outscored men by a statistically insignificant amount and that the way in which intimacy was measured produced significant variability in effect size: "When intimacy was defined and measured according to feelings rather than actions, the differences favored females, while the opposite was true for more behavior-oriented measures of intimacy" (p. 186). Even so, the effect sizes were small, indicating that men and women are much more similar than different in the ways they express and understand intimacy. In addition, Lundquist found that studies published later and studies employing larger samples tended to find smaller gender differences than did earlier studies and studies based on small samples.

Taken together, these results suggest that men may place slightly greater value on activities in their close relationships whereas women may place slightly greater value on intimate and expressive talk. However, to thematize and polarize this small difference is to ignore much greater similarities between men and women. For both men and women, ordinary small talk is a more common purpose of getting together with friends than is intimate talk, and for both men and women, intimate and expressive forms of talk are valued as ways of being close. In addition, a focus on gender differences should not divert attention from a variety of other situational and methodological factors that influence whether or not men and women differ.

Giving and Seeking Help

A number of Tannen's claims focus on how men and women talk about their problems, stresses, and negative emotions. Tannen claims that men do not express their doubts and fears, speak abstractly and indirectly about personal feelings, withhold their problems to protect women, and don't like to ask for help (F25-F27). In contrast, women express their fears and doubts and feel comfortable asking for help (F17-F18). Tannen also suggests that men and women differ in how they respond to other persons' disclosure of troubles: Men try to fix problems whereas women sympathize and talk about their own similar troubles (F27-F28, G19-G20).

There is evidence that women display a more diverse range of negative emotion than men do. LaFrance and Banaji (1992) report that men and women differ in the public expression of emotion despite similarity in subjective experience of emotion. However, Canary and Emmers-Sommers (1997) note that much of the existing research has not examined emotional expression in the context of close relationships. They also show how the degree to which men and women differ in their willingness to express emotion varies for different types of emotion. Men may be less likely than women to express fear, but men and women both become angry and express anger in a similar manner. Both men and women may express sadness in indirect ways; however, men may be more likely to divert attention to activities whereas women may be more likely to dwell on and internalize sadness. Canary and Emmers-Sommers conclude by noting that "the research on men, women, and emotion suggests that, although gender similarities far outweigh differences in the experience of emotions, women appear to have a wider latitude of emotional expression than do men" (p. 46).

Goldsmith and Dun (1997) reviewed research on what kinds of social support men and women provide to others who are distressed. They found some evidence that women are more likely than men to offer emotional support; however, there was little evidence that men were more likely than women to offer advice and problem-focused support. In contrast to Tannen's claims that men are problem solvers whereas women offer sympathy, Goldsmith and Dun found more consistent support for the notion that men deny and trivialize other persons' problems more often than women do. Finally, when gender differences occurred, they were typically small and inconsistent across studies. This may be due to variability across and within studies in the type of situation, type of relationship, age of provider and receiver, and sex of receiver.

Partial and indirect support for Tannen's claims may be found in Eagly and Crowley's (1986) meta-analysis of 172 studies of helping behavior. In contrast to the social support literature, which usually reports studies examining assistance received in close relationships, most of the helping studies involved brief encounters with strangers and forms of help that might be characterized as chivalrous or heroic (e.g., responding to an emergency, assisting a stranger with a package). In these circumstances, men were more likely than women to engage in helping behavior (various estimates of effect size are provided, ranging from .34 to .07). Eagly (1987) concludes, "Because the effect sizes in the present meta-analysis were extremely heterogeneous, mean effect sizes implying an overall gender difference are much less important than successful prediction of variability in the magnitude of effect sizes" (p. 66). The tendency for men to help more than women was most pronounced in off-campus settings, with an audience and other potential helpers present, and with an appeal for help presented as a need rather than a direct request. In addition, men were more likely to help a woman than to help another man, whereas women were equally likely to help a man or a woman. Similarly, men were equally likely to receive help from a man or a woman but women were more likely to receive help from a man. Eagly's findings are similar in some respects to Tannen's claims that men prefer to help in settings in which this reflects their status and ability and that men are sensitive to the status implications of giving or receiving help from other men. However, it is important to note that this generalization is based on studies of strangers providing a particular kind of help to other strangers.

Finally, there is the issue of whether men and women differ in their preferences for different types of responses to their problems. Kunkel and

Burleson (1998) propose that Tannen's analysis implies four specific areas in which men and women would differ with respect to comforting and emotional support: (a) Men and women will have different criteria for evaluating better and worse emotional support responses, (b) men and women will prefer a same-sex support provider to an opposite-sex support provider, (c) women will place greater value on emotional support skills in close relationships than will men, and (d) men and women will express greater liking for those who behave in gender-typical ways than for those who provide counternormative supportive responses. Kunkel and Burleson's review of the research uncovers "virtually no support" for any of these predictions. Instead, they found that men and women are highly similar in their criteria, preferences, values, and interpersonal evaluations of emotional support. However, they note that men and women do differ in their skill at providing emotional support: Men are more likely than women to provide responses that deny or trivialize the other person's emotions.

In sum, there is evidence for some small differences in the ways in which men and women express negative emotions and respond to the problems and negative emotions of others. However, these differences are not entirely consistent with Tannen's claims. Differences in emotional expression are more pronounced for some emotions than for others, and differences in supportive responses are observed for some types of responses but not for others. Tannen's portrayal of women's helping responses may be most accurate in close relationships, whereas her portrayal of men's responses may be more appropriate to chivalrous forms of help offered to strangers. Despite these differences in behaviors, men and women do not appear to have different understandings of or preferences for emotional support.

Nonverbal Communication

Tannen claims that men and women differ in their physical positioning and patterns of gaze during informal conversation (F29, G21). Hall's (1984) extensive meta-analyses of nonverbal communication research provide some support for these claims. Hall reports that women do engage in more gaze at their conversational partners than do men (mean effect size between .16 and .32). These differences are largest in same-sex pairs and in cooperative rather than competitive situations. There is a small tendency for women to orient more directly to conversational partners (mean effect size between .02 and .15), however, this conclusion is based on a limited literature. Similarly, Hall found few studies of gender differences in body movement and positioning. Women's body movements and positions appear to be less restless, less expansive, more involved, more expressive, and more self-conscious than men's (mean effect sizes range from .06 to .46). These gender differences in nonverbal behavior tend to be larger than those for verbal behaviors. However, Hall (1984) cautions that observer bias may inflate differences in nonverbal communication because it is difficult to obscure the gender of the person observed. In addition, Hall notes her fear that at the time she conducted her analysis, publication biases may have favored studies that found differences, resulting in an inflated estimate of effect sizes. Finally, Hall (1987) observes that a relatively narrow range of situations have been studied, making it difficult to determine how effects may vary in different settings. In this later essay, Hall (1987) points out that no one theoretical explanation (e.g., Tannen's emphasis on childhood socialization) provides a satisfactory account for the range of nonverbal behaviors she examined; instead, her findings suggest that multiple factors (both distal and proximate) work in concert and that different factors may be important for different behaviors.

Summary

In the extensive literature external to Tannen's evidence, it is possible to extract partial and qualified support for some of her specific claims. However, the bigger picture suggests small differences between men and women and differences that are contingent on other factors. Thus, even if there is some support for Tannen's subclaims about specific behaviors, the empirical literature is inconsistent with her broader characterizations of men and women as having different styles and of men and women as clustering at opposite ends of a status-connection continuum. The notion that men and women represent cross-cultural communication is also inconsistent with several widely held propositions about gender and communication.

First, there is widespread agreement that gender differences in communication are typically small. This pattern is evident in the foregoing review of research in various areas and has also been noted by other authors who have conducted similar reviews. For example, Canary and Hause (1993) reviewed 15 meta-analyses on various communication topics, summarizing more than 1,200 studies of gender differences in communication. The average effect size is small (average weighted $d = .24$) and accounts for about 1% of the variance.[14] Some of the largest gender differences in communication are in the area of nonverbal communication, and even these differences are small to moderate (Hall, 1984; Hyde, 1990). Although small differences can be meaningful and merit theoretical explanation (Eagly, 1995), Tannen's claim that communication between men and women is cross-cultural communication would seem to suggest much greater differences between the two groups than empirical research has revealed.

Second, men and women are typically more similar than different in their communication behavior. For small effect sizes (such as those typical in research on gender and communication), the distributions of scores are 15% nonoverlapping and 85% overlapping (Cohen, 1977). The focus on gender differences and on tests of statistical significance has frequently obscured the degree to which men and women are similar (Favreau, 1997; Unger, 1990; Wright, 1988). Several recent studies have paid explicit attention to the degree of similarity in men's and women's communication and have found it to be substantial (Burleson et al., 1996; Duck & Wright, 1993; Goldsmith & Dun, 1997; Jones, 1991; Vangelisti & Daly, 1997).

Third, there is ample evidence that the presence and magnitude of gender differences in communication vary depending on a host of situational factors. On the basis of her meta-analyses of gender differences in many areas of human ability and behavior, Eagly (1994) concludes that "the inconsistencies in the magnitude of gender-difference findings (and sometimes in their direction) are their most challenging features" (p. 516). Canary and Hause (1993) note that in each of the meta-analyses they reviewed, "there were significant moderating or interacting variables that suggest when sex affects social behavior it does so under particular conditions" (p. 134). Linn (1986) concludes an edited book of meta-analyses on gender differences for a wide range of abilities and behaviors by stating:

> Results reported in this volume from over a thousand studies of close to half a million individuals show that gender differences can be moderated or potentiated by the context in which they are measured. These results warn us against unwarranted generalizations. They illustrate how widely held stereotypes can interact with small differences to make them appear larger. (p. 229)

Perhaps one of the most compelling features of Tannen's analysis is the way in which she attempts to show that overarching differences in communicative style can account for gender differences in a wide variety of situations and for a wide variety of communicative behaviors. In contrast, the empirical research literature makes it clear that how men and women communicate and whether there are differences in communication are contingent on many situational variables. Rather than viewing gender differences in communication as matters of individual style, many theorists are calling for a view of gendered communication as a matter of situated, social interaction (e.g., Canary & Emmers-Sommers, 1997; Crawford, 1995; Deaux & Major, 1990; Eagly, 1987; Ragan, 1989; Risman & Schwartz, 1989).

In short, we found that Tannen's claims are based on a narrow, selective review of the research literature. Our summary of the conclusions drawn in other literature reviews and meta-analyses suggests that although some specific findings are consistent with Tannen's claims, other findings are not. Even more important, Tannen's portrayal of men and women as representing different cultures is inconsistent with a widespread consensus that gender differences in communication tend to be small and situationally variable whereas gender similarities are large.

CONCLUSIONS

The text of *YJDU* leads readers to believe that Tannen has distilled from scholarly research a set of factual generalizations about the communication of men and women. She goes on to propose an explanation for these differences and a prescription for dealing with them productively. This textual self-presentation may account for the widespread acceptance of *YJDU* by the scholarly community, as evidenced by the number and range of citations to this work in scholarly journals. More than half of these citations refer to Tannen's work positively and uncritically, taking for granted the truth of her claims and using them to advance the authors' own claims. Unfortunately, our analysis of Tannen's evidence indicates that this confidence is unfounded. Our organization of Tannen's claims with their evidence reveals that many of the claims are not supported by scholarly research at all, and others rest on the findings of single studies. Of the studies Tannen cites to support claims about differences in men's and women's communication, all but one are unavailable, controversial, irrelevant, or outdated; used methods or analyses inappropriate to the kinds of claims Tannen makes; or are otherwise inconsistent with Tannen's claims. In addition, a large body of research on gender differences is not included in Tannen's citations. Comprehensive reviews and meta-analyses of this empirical research provide a much more complicated and much less dramatic picture of gender similarity as well as difference and of situational variables that affect the size and nature of gender differences in communication.

One direct implication of our findings is that scholars should not treat *YJDU* as a scholarly source of factual generalizations about the communicative behavior of men and women. We note a disturbing tendency for scholars to treat Tannen's work as if it were a review of literature and to cite Tannen rather than empirical research or scholarly literature reviews. We are equally bothered by Tannen's admission (in the 1994 preface to the publication of Hirschman's 1973 conference paper) that she had cited the findings of Hirschman's study for years without ever having read the actual paper.[15] There is a similar pattern of secondary citation throughout Tannen's book. For example, when she refers to Horner's studies of women's motivation to avoid success (p. 217), Tannen does not cite the studies that are the basis for this claim; instead, she cites Carol Gilligan's citation of a review article by Horner in which Horner summarizes the results of the original studies. This practice of secondhand (and even thirdhand) citation obscures potential problems with using a study based on a particular methodology to advance claims for which that methodology is inappropriate. It also overlooks authors' explicit warnings against generalizing from their findings.

We would also caution teachers and policy makers against accepting Tannen's book uncritically as a basis for pedagogy or behavioral prescriptions. For example, Tannen has been recommended for reading in psychology courses (Dunn, 1993), interpersonal sensitivity programs (Capuzza, 1993), and multicultural classrooms (Jacob, 1995); for women trying to establishing themselves in leadership positions in mental health administration (Scheidt, 1994); for couples trying to understand one another (Hawkins, Roberts, Christiansen, & Marshall, 1994); for libraries of all kinds (McMaster, 1992); and as a way to enhance arbitration (Fraser, 1992) and business interactions (Emerson, 1992). Without appropriate evidence that men and women differ in the ways Tannen proposes, we should be wary of using the text in undergraduate courses or accepting prescriptions for action derived from Tannen's analysis.

Our analysis also suggests implications beyond this particular book regarding potential difficulties in synthesizing findings from studies produced in different research paradigms. We have shown that Tannen advances a particular kind of claim: factual generalization about the relative frequencies of certain communicative behaviors, intentions, and interpretations by certain classes of individuals. This is a common type of claim within a particular research paradigm, and scholars who advance these types of claims have developed procedures and standards that are useful in defending their claims against possible rival claims (e.g., observations should be based on a reasonably large and representative sample; the method for identifying the behaviors, intentions, or interpretations should be explicit and replicable; observed differences should be tested for statistical significance). When we criticize Tannen for reliance on anecdotal evidence or on studies that do not meet these standards, it is not because we believe all research must adhere to the standards of this particular paradigm but because this is a reasonable "burden of proof" for claims about how men and women, as classes of individuals, communicate (see Jackson, 1986).

We believe that Tannen's failure to meet this burden of proof can be traced to her attempt to use research designed for one kind of claim to try to support a different kind of claim. Tannen's own published research (e.g., Tannen, 1984, 1990a, 1994) and many of the studies she cites come out of ethnographic and discourse-analytic traditions with methods designed to provide evidence for different kinds of claims. Case studies, intensive analysis of examples of discourse, and extensive observation of a few individuals are methods particularly well suited for claims about the meaning and structure of discourse (e.g., What are some of the meaningful patterns of behavior that occur? When those patterns occur, what do they mean to participants? What principles can account for the order and coherence of these patterns?). Such claims are not concerned with the frequency or distribution of these patterns but rather with their internal structure and meaning *when* they do occur (see Jacobs, 1986, 1990). In an essay characterizing the work of conversation analysts, for example, Pomerantz (1990) explains, "While we make insightful proposals about the ways in which 'at least some' participants accomplish actions, we have not made rigorous claims about the extent to which particular methods are used, who the users are, or the circumstances of their use" (p. 234). Although it appeared before *YJDU,* Jackson's (1986) discussion of the appropriate use of methods of discourse analysis provides an apt characterization of the problems with Tannen's use of evidence:

> Certain kinds of claims just have to have a different sort of evidence. Quantitative claims, even vague and casual ones, require quantitative evidence. These include claims about what usually happens, what frequently happens, or what typically happens. Claims about individual or situational variations in discourse likewise require evidence other than examples. A claim that men and women use different speech styles cannot be supported by showing examples of male and female speech. Instead, evidence must be gathered which reflects the variability among individual women and men, and that permits comparison of the frequency of certain features in women's speech with the frequency of those features in men's speech. (pp. 138-139)

Tannen's insights, and those of most of the authors she cites, suggest possible variations in the functions and meanings of various communicative behaviors. However, the documentation that these patterns of behavior and their interpretation are more or less frequent depending on an individual's gender is an entirely different order of claim requiring different kinds of evidence.

Tannen's failure to distinguish between these different types of claims is evident not only from our analysis of *YJDU,* but also from a published statement Tannen makes in a preface to the 1994 publication of the 1973 Hirschman paper. Tannen notes that Hirschman's original conference paper (based on 60 minutes of conversation by four individuals)

> is perennially cited for the finding that females are inclined to offer more "back-channel responses" in conversation. . . . Like everyone else, I regularly cited Hirschman's findings but assumed I would never read the study itself. . . . [This publication] allows us to see, and (perhaps?) to be surprised at, the small scale of the study that carries on its shoulders the weight of so many citations. It is not a criticism, but a testament to Hirschman's perceptiveness and the pervasiveness of the phenomena, that the patterns she found in a study of four speakers have since been replicated by other researchers. It is not unusual for studies of conversational interaction to be relatively small-scale, and to use anthropological case-study methods or the close textual reading of literary analysis rather than the survey methods of sociology. If one wants to examine conversation closely, it is not possible to record a thousand conversations and hire a battery of undergraduates to serve as coders. The insight must be in the texture of the particular discourse. (in Hirschman, 1994, pp. 428-429)

The claim for which Tannen cites Hirschman's study as support—"females are inclined to offer more 'back-channel responses' in conversation"—is a claim about the relative frequency of a particular behavior by a class of individuals. Tannen says this finding has been replicated (but offers no citations to studies that do so)[16] and then speciously dismisses the possibility of obtaining adequate samples of behavior and coding them systematically. She justifies this dismissal with the cryptic statement that "the insight must be in the texture of the particular discourse." This ignores the distinction between claims about frequency (and their evidentiary burdens) and claims about "texture." In contrast, Hirschman (1994) notes: "This paper was not published originally, because it was very exploratory research. . . . To verify the hypotheses formulated in the paper, I would have needed substantial funding in order to collect, transcribe, and analyze enough data to obtain statistically significant findings" (pp. 439-440).

Our analysis has shown that many scholars uncritically accept Tannen's word as truth. Even many of Tannen's critics take for granted her analysis of gender differences, disagreeing only about the implications of and explanations for these differences. In contrast, our analysis indicates that the evidence presented in *YJDU* is an unsuitable basis upon which to accept Tannen's claims about gender differences. It is inappropriate for scholars to cite this work as an authoritative synthesis of the research literature. Research on gender differences in communication does point to differences in how men and women communicate, but it is equally clear that simplistic representations of dichotomous differences are unfounded. In contrast, the literature we have reviewed reveals substantial similarity in the communication of men and women punctuated by situations in which modest differences may appear. Accounting for this kind of variability requires a different sort of model than the one Tannen proposes.

Appendix: Subclaims and Evidence for Main Claim IV

Claim	Pages	Research	Other Evidence
IV. Men and women represent cross-cultural communication.	18, 42, 47, 268, 281		story, 280
A. Men and women approach the world differently; their senses of what is natural and important are different.	72, 79, 80, 176, 257, 279, 282, 287, 288	Tannen (1990a), 277	short story 72; examples, 80, 288, 289; film, 80
B. Men and women view the same situation differently; they do the same things for different reasons; they approach the same task with different goals.	13, 26, 38, 62, 70, 79, 133, 139, 261, 290	Fox (1990), 132	Gurney (1989), 138; examples, 26, 39, 70, 71, 289-290; film, 79

(continued)

Appendix *(Continued)*

Claim	Pages	Research	Other Evidence
C. Women and men do not have the same options for communicating some things.	238		example, 238
1. Can't show mutual affection in the same way; physical alignments are expected to be different.	283-284		example, 283-284
2. Sleep in different positions.	284-286		poem, 284-285; film, 286
D. Men and women have different understandings of intimacy and independence.	290-291		
1. Being protective is central to men's ideas of intimacy, whereas being helpful is central to women's ideas of intimacy.	288-290		examples, 288, 289
2. Men prefer asymmetrical independence, whereas women prefer symmetrical independence.	292	Blumstein & Schwartz (1984), 292	
3. Men name wives as best friends; women name other women with whom they are in constant contact. Women want time away from partners to preserve intimacy with friends.	80, 101, 294	Sternberg & Grajek (1984), n80; Blumstein & Schwartz (1984), 294	example, 101
4. The essence of male friendship is activity, whereas the essence of female friendship is talk.	80, 85, 104		
E. Men and women cluster at opposite ends of the status-connection continuum.	290		

Appendix *(Continued)*

Claim	Pages	Research	Other Evidence
1. Crucial to women to be liked by their peers; crucial to men to be respected.	108, 129	Goodwin (1990), 108	
2. Women seem to fear success.	217	Horner (1972), 217	
3. Women measure and adapt behavior based on potential for gossip.	107		
F. Men try to preserve independence and see the world as a hierarchical social order where they attempt to stay "one-up" and avoid being "one-down."	24, 25, 36, 38, 40, 42, 67, 77, 85, 128, 130, 277, 279	Riessman (1990), 40; Leet-Pellegrini (1980), 128-129; Aries (1976), 130; Tannen (1990a), 277	"The Pros and Cons" (1989), 41; personal examples, 23-25; examples, 26, 29, 40
1. Men give orders.	154	Smith (1990), 154	
2. Men are not comfortable consulting their partners.	26-27		examples, 26, 27
3. Men don't want it to look like anyone is telling them what to do.	151	Blumstein & Schwartz (1984), 151	2 examples, 151
4. Men resent evidence of women's authority, respond with verbal challenge.	128	Leet-Pellegrini (1980), 128	
5. Men see conflict as means of status negotiation.	150	Ong (1981), 150	
6. Men may use aggression, conflict, or disagreement to initiate friendship and intimacy.	159, 163-165, 167, 168, 170, 277	Corsaro & Rizzo (1990), 160, 163-165; Tannen (1990a), 277; Schiffrin (1984), 160; Frank (1988), 160	examples, 159, 163, 167, 168, 170
7. Men may issue verbal challenges out of respect, rather than as attempts to undercut other.	168-170		personal examples, 168-170

(continued)

Appendix *(Continued)*

Claim	Pages	Research	Other Evidence
8. Men may ritualize conflict.	150-151	Ong (1981), 150	
9. Men (particularly American men) make conversation into a contest.	293		example, 293
10. Men lecture, set agendas, offer opinions, and give lengthy, factual explanations in order to be superior; will listen to lectures from higher-status men.	125, 126, 130, 131, 133, 138	Aries (1976), 130; Fox (1990), 131; Leet-Pellegrini (1980), 131	Gurney (1989), 138; personal examples, 123-126
11. Men try to charm or ingratiate by offering information.	143, 145		personal example, 145
12. Men expect that women will volunteer information.	143-145	Aries (1976), 145	personal example, 143
13. Men remain silent when listening.	142-143	Maltz & Borker (1982), n142; Fishman (1978), n142; Hirschman (1973), n142; Strodtbeck & Mann (1956), n142	
14. Men interrupt because they view conversation as conflict, interpret overlaps as attempts at control.	210		examples, 210-211
15. Men talk longer and more than women, will talk first in mixed-sex, public settings.	75, 76, 88	Eakins & Eakins (1976), 75; Swacker (1976), 76; James & Drakich (1993), 75	personal example, 76; *Diane Rehm Show*, 88
16. Men will control beginnings and ends of conversations with women, but only ends with other men.	128	Leet-Pellegrini (1980), 128	

Appendix *(Continued)*

Claim	Pages	Research	Other Evidence
17. Men are more comfortable with public speaking: do not speak their thoughts in private, think home means freedom to be silent; tell jokes in public to take center stage and gain status.	77, 81, 83, 86-88, 140	Greenwood (1989), 86; Aries (1976), 139; Newman (1971), 139; Chafe (1987), 140	cartoon, 81; examples, 83, 87; *Diane Rehm Show,* 88; examples, 140
18. Men like to talk about details of politics, news, and sports; need to know what's going on in the world.	110, 275	Tannen (1990a), 275	Stephens (1988), 111; example, 110
19. Men gossip about themselves and political rather than personal relationships.	101	Tannen (unpub. ms.), 101	
20. Men tell stories about contests in order to make themselves look good. Their stories tell how power comes from individuals.	176-178	Johnstone (1989), 177, 178	informal student comparison, 176
21. Men "do" things and are interested in action.	27, 291		personal example, 291
22. Men find it difficult to find serious topics to discuss with male friends and appear uncomfortable sitting and talking.	275-276	Tannen (1990a), 275-276	
23. Men don't express doubts and fears.	84		example, 83
24. Men speak abstractly and indirectly about personal feelings and topics.	275-276	Tannen (1990a), 275-276	

(continued)

Appendix *(Continued)*

Claim	Pages	Research	Other Evidence
25. Men don't like to ask for help because it makes them appear subordinate; don't like to disclose problems, would rather lie than say, "I don't know"; expected to be experts.	62, 63, 69, 71, 109	Riessman (1990), 109	
26. Men withhold information about their troubles to protect women.	288		examples, 288, 289
27. Men provide information, fix things, and talk about solutions to problems in order to display their status and help others.	52, 61, 64-69, 71, 102		examples, 52; personal examples, 64-66; examples, 67, 68-69; short story, 71, 72
28. Men think matching troubles is belittling.	49-51		examples, 49-51
29. Men sit stretched out and at angles to others, don't make eye contact with one another.	130, 275	Aries (1976), 130; Tannen (1990a), 275	
30. Men focus on the message and report aspects of talk and interpret metamessages in terms of status differences.	33-35, 53, 62, 63, 67, 174	concept from Goffman (1974), 33; Frank (1988), 176	examples, 34, 35; hypothetical example, 62-63; examples, 67, 174; novel, 175
31. Men make categorical statements of right and wrong and use formal logic.	92, 150	Roberts & Jupp (1985), 91; Ong (1981), 150	example, 115
32. Men don't want to mix business with unrelated things.	118		
33. Men feel boasting is suitable in public.	223, 224		example, 223-224
34. Men see apologies as one-down.	232, 234		example, 233-234

Appendix *(Continued)*

Claim	Pages	Research	Other Evidence
G. Women try to preserve intimacy and negotiate for consensus and support. They see the world as a network of connections and community.	25, 36, 28, 40, 42, 67, 77, 81, 130, 277, 279	Riessman (1990), 40; Aries (1976), 130; Tannen (1990a), 277	"The Pros and Cons" (1989), 41; personal examples, 23-25; examples, 26, 29, 40
1. Women make requests.	154	Smith (1990), 154	
2. Women are comfortable consulting their partners. They like discussion and consensus.	27		examples, 26, 27
3. Women will try to play a one-down role to create symmetry and rapport.	274	Tannen (1990a), 274; Beeman (1986), 274	
4. Women eschew conflict in order to espouse connection and harmony; they play peacemaker and seek agreement.	150, 154, 167, 168, 271, 272	Ong (1981), 150; Tannen (1990a), 271, 272	examples, 167, 168
5. Women may use cooperation, praise, gossip, and helpful suggestions to be competitive or critical.	171-174	Goodwin (1990), 171; Hughes (1988), 171; Brown (1990), 172	examples, 173
6. Women may ritualize community.	150, 151		
7. Women are expected to give praise rather than information. They lack experience in defending themselves against challenges to their authority and instead try to minimize appearance of superiority and share knowledge.	69, 125, 128-129, 131	Leet-Pellegrini (1980), 127, 128; Aries (1976), n129; Aries (1982), n130; Fox (1990), 130	

(continued)

Appendix *(Continued)*

Claim	Pages	Research	Other Evidence
8. Women support a speaker rather than volunteering information and gaining attention. They may try to charm others by listening.	125, 126, 130, 131, 135-138, 143-145	Aries (1976), 130; Fox (1990), 131; Erickson (1990), 136, 137; Aries (1976), 145	personal examples, 123-126; Feiffer (1982), 133, 134; personal examples, 143, 145
9. When listening, women will ask questions and respond positively, give listening responses, offer agreement or disagreement with speaker.	142, 143	Maltz & Borker (1982), 142; Fishman (1978), n142; Hirschman (1973), n142; Strodtbeck & Mann (1956), n142	
10. Women interrupt to show support and agreement. They prefer overlapping speech as sign of rapport and make false interruptions to eliminate silences.	203, 205, 211	Kalčik (1975), 203; James & Drakich (1993), 203; Edelsky (1981), 203; Hornyak (n.d.), 203, 204	personal example, 205; example, 211
11. Women talk less than men in mixed-sex public settings.	75, 77, 188	James & Drakich (1993), n75; Edelsky (1981), n75; Sadker & Sadker (1985), n77	joke, 188
12. Women are more comfortable with private speaking: speak their thoughts in private, think home means freedom to talk; feel they must be on good behavior in public or with men. They do not tell jokes in public or around men but prefer smaller, private groups; in public, they laugh at others' jokes.	77, 81, 83, 86, 87, 89, 90, 93, 94, 140, 236	term from Goffman (1959), n89; Aries (1982), 236; Mitchell (1985), 89; Greenwood (1989), 86	cartoon, 81; examples, 83, 87; *Diane Rehm Show,*, 88

Appendix *(Continued)*

Claim	Pages	Research	Other Evidence
13. Women like to talk about details of personal relationships; withhold details from those with whom they don't want to be intimate.	110, 113, 117, 148		example, 110; Stephens (1988), 111; example, 117; Aron (1988), 117
14. Women tell stories about other people. Their stories show how power comes from community and suffering comes from acting alone.	176-178	Johnstone (1989), 177, 178	informal student comparison, 176
15. Women appear comfortable sitting and talking with friends.	271	Tannen (1990a), 271	
16. Women use gossip to keep intimate conversations and relationships going; having and telling secrets can establish openness and create friendships so may feel obligated to tell secrets, may find themselves in trouble if they have to none to tell; need small talk to maintain connections so they don't feel alone.	98, 102, 104, 109, 113		examples, 98; novel, 98; story, 99; short story, 102; student recordings, 103; examples, 113; novel, 114
17. Women express fears and doubts.	84		example, 83
18. Women feel comfortable asking for help, obligated to seek and accept it, and display gratitude for it because it supports bonds.	63, 65-69, 71		personal examples, 64-66; examples, 67-68, 69

(continued)

Appendix *(Continued)*

Claim	Pages	Research	Other Evidence
19. Women bond with one another through lamenting and troubles talk.	100, 277	Caraveli (1986), 100; Kuipers (1986), 100; Sherzer (1987), 100; Tannen (1990a), 277; term from Jefferson (1988), n53	
20. Women want to match troubles, receive sympathy, confirm feelings. They like to have technical things fixed, but don't like advice, information, or fixing of emotions.	49-51, 58, 59, 61, 277, 291	Tannen (1990a), 277	examples, 49-51; short story, 58; personal example, 291
21. Women sit closed in; they sit closer to and look at others directly.	130, 248, 271	Aries (1976), 130; Tannen (1990a), 248, 271	
22. Women focus on metamessage and what it says about rapport and connection.	53, 142, 176	Frank (1988), 176	example, 174; novel, 175
23. Women want to hear explanations and reasons for things.	159		example, 158-159
24. Women use personal experiences rather than abstract argumentation because they prefer private speaking.	91	Roberts & Jupp (1985), 91	example, 91, 92-93
25. Women will mix business with unrelated things, will choose friendships over business if they conflict morally.	117, 118		Loftus (1987), 118; examples, 118
26. Women feel boasting is only suitable in private.	223, 224		examples, 223, 224

Appendix *(Continued)*

Claim	Pages	Research	Other Evidence
27. Women apologize frequently to show support and sympathy; they believe apologies should be matched or deflected to reduce asymmetry.	231-234		examples, 232-234
H. Men and women honestly don't understand each other.	81		
1. Women feel men don't talk to them, whereas men feel wrongly accused when women claim they don't talk enough.	78-79, 81-83		Hacker (1979), n78; Ann Landers, 78; film, 79; cartoon, 81; example, 83
2. Men find it intrusive when women ask for explanations, whereas women think men don't give enough details and see this as a sign of not caring.	159		example, 158-159
3. Men think women shift and change topic frequently, whereas women are annoyed by men changing topics.	92-93, 212-214		examples, 92, 93; short story, 212-214
4. Men think women talking about their relationships is disloyal.	110	Dubisch (1986), 110	example, 110
5. Men feel hurt when women don't appreciate advice; women feel attacked when they don't receive sympathy and affirmation of their feelings.	52, 61		examples, 52; Carlson (1989), n53

NOTES

1. Citations to these newspaper and magazine articles appear in Fulfs and Goldsmith (1997).

2. This detailed outline of claims, subclaims, their location in the text, and the evidence for each claim appears in Fulfs and Goldsmith (1997).

3. We provide these classifications in Fulfs and Goldsmith (1997).

4. Two additional articles listed in the *Social Sciences* and *Arts & Humanities Citation Indexes* did not cite Tannen, and we found three articles in languages other than English (two in French, one in Spanish).

5. Chafe (1987) discusses the disabling function of humor but makes no claims about gender differences in the use of this function. Similarly, Tannen credits Goffman (1974, 1981) with the term *alignment* prior to her discussion of gender differences in alignment, and she credits Jefferson (1988) with the term *troubles talk* prior to her discussion of this activity.

6. Tannen cites an unpublished paper by Hornyak and provides no bibliographic information. Our attempts to contact Dr. Hornyak were unsuccessful. Tannen refers to interviews she has conducted but provides no citations (we cite these as "unpublished manuscripts"). No bibliographic information is provided for a conference presentation by Roberts and Jupp; we have been unable to locate either the paper or the authors. A published book chapter by Johnstone (1993) bears the same title as the 1989 conference paper Tannen cites, so we have used the published chapter.

7. Tannen clarifies her position on this matter in a later book, *Gender and Discourse* (1994), saying: "To describe differences is not to ascribe them to either biological or cultural sources. . . . Although the question of the origins of the patterns I describe has not been a focus of my concern, probably because of my anthropological orientation I have been inclined to regard socialization (that is, cultural experience) as the main influence shaping patterns of behavior. Thus, in *You Just Don't Understand,* as in the present volume, I cite research on the role of childhood peer groups as the source of gendered patterns in ways of speaking." In a footnote, she goes on to say, "I realize, however, that biological factors may be at work as well" (pp. 12-13).

8. For example, Hyde (1990) summarizes several meta-analytic studies in which the magnitude of gender differences in aggression and cognitive ability vary as a function of publication date. This may be due to an increase in the publication of studies finding no gender difference rather than any changes in the phenomena under study. Whatever the reason for changes in findings over time, such trends indicate it is reasonable to be concerned with the recency of evidence.

9. The reader may be surprised to learn that the weight of Tannen's claims in main point IV rest on 19 empirical studies. Of the 37 sources Tannen cites that are available to us and used for more than just a conceptual label, 13 are irrelevant to claims about the communication behavior of adult men and women in the United States because they involve children or members of other cultures. Of the remaining 24 sources, we have excluded 3 more from our evaluation. Tannen's citation to Sadker and Sadker (1985) is a *Psychology Today* report of their research. That article does not provide sufficient information to evaluate the study on which the report is based, nor does the article provide a citation to a publication containing this information. Similarly, we have not included Sternberg and Grajek (1984). Tannen refers to this study as support for the claim that men name their wives as best friends whereas women name other women as best friends, but the study has no bearing on this claim and appears to be an error of citation. We have excluded Ong's (1981) book because it uses humanistic rather than empirical methods to make claims about male aggression. This leaves 19 empirical studies (Aries, 1976, 1982; Blumstein & Schwartz, 1984; Eakins & Eakins, 1976; Edelsky, 1981; Erickson, 1990; Fishman, 1978; Fox, 1990; Frank, 1988; Hirschman, 1994; Horner, 1972; Johnstone, 1993; Kalcik, 1975; Leet-Pellegrini, 1980; Mitchell, 1985; Riessman, 1990; Smith, 1990; Strodtbeck & Mann, 1956; Swacker, 1976) and 3 reviews of empirical research (James & Clarke, 1993; James & Drakich, 1993; Maltz & Borker, 1982).

10. It is unclear whether a study by Strodtbeck and Mann (1956) used multiple coders with acceptable levels of agreement. They appear to have used Bales's interaction process categories,

but they do not provide details regarding how they implemented this system. Aries (1976) provides definitions and intercoder reliability estimates for assessments of who initiated and received interaction. She relied on a computer content analysis program to code topical contents. However, she goes on to attribute intentions and functions to behaviors, with no indication of how these classifications were made and no evidence that an independent rater would reach similar conclusions (e.g., we are told that male groups engaged in more "brain-picking" and "sizing up the competition"). Similarly, Leet-Pellegrini (1980) obtained ratings from (and reports high levels of agreement among) several observers and the participants for variables such as perceived control of the conversation; however, she gives no intercoder reliability estimates for measures of discourse features (e.g., interruptions, active listenership).

11. Tannen refers to an unpublished paper by James and Drakich on gender differences in amount of talk; she also attributes to James and Drakich a review paper on gender differences in interruptions but provides no bibliographic information. In response to our request for these papers, Deborah James referred us to two 1993 chapters in a volume edited by Tannen (James & Clarke, 1993; James & Drakich, 1993). We used these published sources as the basis for our review.

12. Having seen how other authors have uncritically cited Tannen's conclusions about gender differences, apparently without consulting or evaluating the original evidence, we are wary of engaging in a similar pattern of secondary citation. We offer this discussion of conclusions reached by other reviewers so that the reader might have a sense of the larger body of opinion and research within which Tannen's claims are situated. We encourage readers with interest in a particular topic to consult both the reviews to which we refer *and* the original research.

13. Stiles et al. (1997) define verbal presumptuousness as having to do with "being one-up, with knowing the other, with assuming one is important to the other" (p. 761). In contrast, verbal attentiveness "has to do with manifest interest in the other and attempts to ensure that the other's thoughts are expressed and considered in the conversation" (p. 761).

14. Eagly (1995) claims that effect sizes for gender differences are not necessarily any smaller than effect sizes for other independent variables in psychological research. However, this claim is based on a more encompassing review of gender differences that includes some rather large differences in noncommunication variables. In addition, Hyde and Plant (1995) point out that most of the effect sizes for gender are zero or small.

15. To Tannen's credit, she has been instrumental in bringing a number of previously unpublished papers into the published literature (e.g., Hirschman, 1994; James & Clark, 1993; James & Drakich, 1993; Johnstone, 1993).

16. Several studies suggest that women do not provide more back-channel responses (Kollock, Blumstein, & Schwartz, 1985; McMullen, Vernon, & Murton, 1995; Robey, Canary, & Burggraf, 1998). Only one of these studies had been published at the time Tannen claimed that this was a well-proven finding. At the same time, we are uncertain to which studies Tannen is referring when she asserts that Hirschman's claims have been replicated.

REFERENCES

Abrahams, R. D. (1975). Negotiating respect: Patterns of presentation among black women. *Journal of American Folklore, 88,* 58-30.

Abrahams, R. D. (1976). *Talking black.* Rowley, MA: Newbury House.

Allen, H. (1992, March 14). Keep talking. She's still listening. *Washington Post,* p. D1.

Aries, E. (1976). Interaction patterns and themes of male, female, and mixed groups. *Small Group Behavior, 7,* 7-18.

Aries, E. (1982). Verbal and nonverbal behavior in single-sex and mixed-sex groups: Are traditional sex roles changing? *Psychological Reports, 51,* 127-134.

Aries, E. (1996). *Men and women in interaction: Reconsidering differences.* New York: Oxford University Press.

Arnhart, L. (1994). A sociobiological defense of Aristotle's sexual politics. *International Political Science Review, 15,* 289-415.

Aron, E. (1988, May). [Letter to the editor]. *Psychology Today,* p. 5.

Bauman, R. (1972). The La Have Island General Store: Sociability and verbal art in a Nova Scotia community. *Journal of American Folklore, 85,* 330-343.

Beeman, W. O. (1986). *Language, status, and power in Iran.* Bloomington: Indiana University Press.

Belk, S. S. (1991). A meta-analysis of gender differences in self-disclosure (Doctoral dissertation, University of Texas, Austin, 1991). *Dissertation Abstracts International, 52,* 2349.

Bhatia, A. S., & Desmond, R. J. (1993). Emotion, romantic involvement, and loneliness: Gender differences among inner states and choice of entertainment. *Sex Roles, 28,* 655-665.

Bischoping, K. (1993). Gender differences in conversation topics, 1922-1990. *Sex Roles, 28,* 1-18.

Blumstein, P., & Schwartz, P. (1984). *American couples: Money, work, sex.* New York: William Morrow.

Brown, P. (1990). Gender, politeness, and confrontation in Tenejapa. *Discourse Processes, 13,* 123-141.

Burleson, B. R. (1997). A different voice on different cultures: Illusion and reality in the study of sex differences in personal relationships. *Personal Relationships, 4,* 229-241.

Burleson, B. R., Kunkel, A. W., Samter, W., & Werking, K. J. (1996). Men's and women's evaluation of communication skills in personal relationships: When sex differences make a difference—and when they don't. *Journal of Social and Personal Relationships, 13,* 201-224.

Cameron, D. (1992). [Review of the book *You just don't understand: Women and men in conversation,* by D. Tannen]. *Feminism & Psychology, 2,* 465-468.

Canary, D. J., & Emmers-Sommers, T. M. (1997). *Sex and gender differences in personal relationships.* New York: Guilford.

Canary, D. J., & Hause, K. S. (1993). Is there any reason to research sex differences in communication? *Communication Quarterly, 41,* 129-144.

Capuzza, J. C. (1993). Curriculum inclusion and small group communication courses. *Communication Education, 42,* 172-178.

Caraveli, A. (1986). The bitter wounding: The lament as social protest in rural Greece. In J. Dubisch (Ed.), *Gender and power in rural Greece* (pp. 169-194). Princeton, NJ: Princeton University Press.

Carkeet, D. (1990). *The full catastrophe.* New York: Simon & Schuster.

Carlson, R. (1989, October 8). Clobbering her ex [Review of the book *After you've gone,* by A. Adams]. *New York Times Book Review,* p. 27.

Chafe, W. (1987). Humor as a disabling mechanism. *American Behavioral Scientist, 30*(3), 16-25.

Cohen, J. (1977). *Statistical power analysis for the behavioral sciences* (Rev. ed.). New York: Academic Press.

Corsaro, W., & Rizzo, T. (1990). Disputes in the peer culture of American and Italian nursery school children. In A. Grimshaw (Ed.), *Conflict talk* (pp. 21-66). Cambridge: Cambridge University Press.

Crawford, M. (1995). *Talking difference: On gender and language.* London: Sage.

Cupach, W. R., & Canary, D. J. (1995). Managing conflict and anger: Investigating the sex stereotype hypothesis. In P. J. Kalbfleisch & M. J. Cody (Eds.), *Gender, power, and communication in human relationships* (pp. 233-252). Hillsdale, NJ: Lawrence Erlbaum.

Deaux, K., & Major, B. (1990). A social-psychological model of gender. In D. L. Rhode (Ed.), *Theoretical perspectives on sexual difference* (pp. 89-279). New Haven, CT: Yale University Press.

DeFrancisco, V. L. (1992). [Review of the book *You just don't understand: Women and men in conversation,* by D. Tannen]. *Language in Society, 21,* 319-324.

Dindia, K., & Allen, M. (1992). Sex differences in self-disclosure: A meta-analysis. *Psychological Bulletin, 112,* 106-124.

Dubisch, J. (1986). Culture enters through the kitchen: Women, food, and social boundaries in rural Greece. In J. Dubisch (Ed.), *Gender and power in rural Greece* (pp. 195-241). Princeton, NJ: Princeton University Press.

Duck, S., & Wright, P. H. (1993). Re-examining gender differences in same-gender friendships: A close look at two kinds of data. *Sex Roles, 28,* 709-727.

Dunn, D. S. (1993). Integrating psychology into the interdisciplinary core curriculum. *Teaching of Psychology, 20,* 213-218.

Eagly, A. H. (1987). *Sex differences in social behavior: A social-role interpretation.* Hillsdale, NJ: Lawrence Erlbaum.

Eagly, A. H. (1994). On comparing men and women. *Feminism & Psychology, 4,* 513-522.

Eagly, A. H. (1995). The science and politics of comparing women and men. *American Psychologist, 50,* 145-158.

Eagly, A. H., & Crowley, M. (1986). Gender and helping behavior: A meta-analytic review of the social psychological literature. *Psychological Bulletin, 100,* 283-308.

Eakins, B. W., & Eakins, R. G. (1976). Verbal turn-taking and exchanges in faculty dialogue. In B. L. Dubois & I. Crouch (Eds.), *Papers in Southwest English IV: Proceedings of the Conference on the Sociology of the Languages of American Women* (pp. 53-62). San Antonio, TX: Trinity University Press.

Eckert, P. (1990). Cooperative competition in adolescent "Girl Talk." *Discourse Processes, 13,* 91-122.

Edelsky, C. (1981). Who's got the floor? *Language in Society, 10,* 383-421.

Emerson, A. F. (1992). Women as competitive advantage. *Harvard Business Review, 70*(3), 158.

Erickson, F. (1990). Social construction of discourse coherence in a family dinner table conversation. In B. Dorval (Ed.), *Conversational organization and its development* (pp. 207-228). Norwood, NJ: Ablex.

Faris, J. C. (1966). The dynamics of verbal exchange: A Newfoundland example. *Anthropologica, 8,* 235-248.

Favreau, O. E. (1997). Sex and gender comparisons: Does null hypothesis testing create a false dichotomy? *Feminism & Psychology, 7,* 63-81.

Fehr, B. (1996). *Friendship processes.* Thousand Oaks, CA: Sage.

Feitter, J. (1982). *Grown ups.* New York: Samuel French

Fishman, P. M. (1978). Interaction: The work women do. *Social Problems, 25,* 397-406.

Fox, T. (1990). Gender interests in reading and writing. In G. W. Noblit, W. Pink, & T. Fox (Eds.), *The social uses of writing: Politics and pedagogy* (pp. 51-70). Norwood, NJ: Ablex.

Frank, J. (1988). A comparison of intimate conversations: Pragmatic theory applied to examples of invented and actual dialog. *SECOL Review, 12*(3), 186-208.

Fraser, B. (1992). New diversity in the American workplace: A challenge to arbitration. *Arbitration Journal, 47*(1), 5-15.

Fulfs, P. A., & Goldsmith, D. J. (1997, November). *"You just don't have the evidence": An analysis of claims and evidence in Deborah Tannen's* You just don't understand. Paper presented at the annual meeting of the National Communication Association, Chicago.

Gayle, B. M., Preiss, R. W., & Allen, M. (1994). Gender differences and the use of conflict strategies. In L. H. Turner & H. M. Sterk (Eds.), *Differences that make a difference: Examining the assumptions in gender research* (pp. 13-26). Westport, CT: Bergin & Garvey.

Goffman, E. (1959). *The presentation of self in everyday life.* Garden City, NY: Doubleday.

Goffman, E. (1974). *Frame analysis.* New York: Harper & Row.

Goffman, E. (1981). *Forms of talk.* Philadelphia: University of Pennsylvania Press.

Goldsmith, D. J., & Dun, S. A. (1997). Sex differences and similarities in the communication of social support. *Journal of Social and Personal Relationships, 14,* 317-337.

Goldsmith, D. J., & MacGeorge, E. L. (1997, May). *Sex differences and similarities in politeness of advice.* Paper presented at the annual meeting of the International Communication Association, Montreal.

Goodwin, M. H. (1990). *He-said-she-said: Talk as social organization among black children.* Bloomington: Indiana University Press.

Gray, J. (1993). *Men are from Mars, women are from Venus: A practical guide for improving communication and getting what you want in your relationships.* New York: HarperCollins.

Greenwood, A. (1989). Discourse variation and social comfort: A study of topic initiation and interruption patterns in the dinner conversation of pre-adolescent children (Doctoral dissertation, City University of New York, 1989). *Dissertation Abstracts International, 50,* 2472.

Gurney, A. R. (1989, June 26). Conversation piece. *Newsweek,* pp. 10-11.

Hacker, A. (1979, May 3). Divorce à la mode [Review of the book *Husbands and wives: A nationwide survey of marriage,* by A. Pietropinto & J. Simenauer]. *New York Review of Books,* p. 24.

Hall, J. A. (1984). *Nonverbal sex differences: Accuracy of communication and expressive style.* Baltimore: Johns Hopkins University Press.

Hall, J. A. (1987). On explaining gender differences: The case of nonverbal communication. In P. Shaver & C. Hendrick (Eds.), *Sex and gender* (pp. 177-200). Newbury Park, CA: Sage.

Hannerz, U. (1969). *Soulside.* New York: Columbia University Press.

Hawkins, A. J., Roberts, T. A., Christiansen, S. L., & Marshall, C. M. (1994). An evaluation of a program to help dual-earner couples share the second shift. *Family Relations, 43,* 213-220.

Henley, N. M., & Kramarae, C. (1991). Gender, power, and miscommunication. In N. Coupland, H. Giles, & J. M. Wiemann (Eds.), *"Miscommunication" and problematic talk* (pp. 18-43). Newbury Park, CA: Sage.

Hill, C. T., & Stull, D. E. (1987). Gender and self-disclosure: Strategies for exploring the issues. In V. J. Derlega & J. H. Berg (Eds.), *Self-disclosure: Theory, research, and therapy* (pp. 81-100). New York: Plenum.

Hirschman, L. (1973). *Female-male differences in conversational interaction.* Paper presented at the annual meeting of the Linguistics Society of America, San Diego, CA.

Hirschman, L. (1994). Female-male differences in conversational interaction. *Language in Society, 23,* 427-442.

Home improvement—production notes. (1998, April 24). [On-line]. Available: http://src.doc.ic.ac.uk/public/media/tv/collections/tardis/us/comedy/HomeImprovement/html/prodnotes.html

Horner, M. S. (1972). Toward an understanding of achievement-related conflicts in women. *Journal of Social Issues, 28,* 157-175.

Hughes, L. A. (1988). "But that's not *really* mean": Competing in a cooperative mode. *Sex Roles, 19,* 669-687.

Hyde, J. S. (1990). Meta-analysis and the psychology of gender differences. *Signs, 16,* 55-73.

Hyde, J. S., & Plant, E. A. (1995). Magnitude of psychological gender differences: Another side to the story. *American Psychologist, 50,* 159-161.

Jackson, S. (1986). Building a case for claims about discourse structure. In D. G. Ellis & W. A. Donohue (Eds.), *Contemporary issues in language and discourse processes* (pp. 129-147). Hillsdale, NJ: Lawrence Erlbaum.

Jacob, E. (1995). Reflective practice and anthropology in culturally diverse classrooms. *Elementary School Journal, 95,* 451-463.

Jacobs, S. (1986). How to make an argument from example in discourse analysis. In D. G. Ellis & W. A. Donohue (Eds.), *Contemporary issues in language and discourse processes* (pp. 149-167). Hillsdale, NJ: Lawrence Erlbaum.

Jacobs, S. (1990). On the especially nice fit between qualitative analysis and the known properties of conversation. *Communication Monographs, 57,* 243-249.

James, D., & Clarke, S. (1993). Women, men, and interruptions: A critical review. In D. Tannen (Ed.), *Gender and conversational interaction* (pp. 231-280). New York: Oxford University Press.

James, D., & Drakich, J. (1993). Understanding gender differences in amount of talk: A critical review of research. In D. Tannen (Ed.), *Gender and conversational interaction* (pp. 281-312). New York: Oxford University Press.

Jefferson, G. (1988). On the sequential organization of troubles-talk in ordinary conversation. *Social Problems, 35,* 418-441.

Johnstone, B. (1989). *Community and contest: How women and men construct their worlds in conversational narrative.* Paper presented at the conference Women in America: Legacies of Race and Ethnicity, Georgetown University, Washington, DC.

Johnstone, B. (1993). Community and contest: Midwestern men and women creating their worlds in conversational storytelling. In D. Tannen (Ed.), *Gender and conversational interaction* (pp. 62-80). New York: Oxford University Press.

Jones, D. C. (1991). Friendship satisfaction and gender: An examination of sex differences in contributors to friendship satisfaction. *Journal of Social and Personal Relationships, 8,* 167-185.

Kalčik, S. J. (1975). " . . . Like Ann's gynecologist or the time I was almost raped": Personal narratives in women's rap groups. *Journal of American Folklore, 88,* 3-11.

Key, M. R. (1975). *Male/female language.* Metuchen, NJ: Scarecrow.

Kollock, P., Blumstein, P., & Schwartz, P. (1985). Sex and power in interaction: Conversational privileges and duties. *American Sociological Review, 50,* 34-46.

Kramarae, C. (1992). [Review of the book *You just don't understand: Women and men in conversation,* by D. Tannen]. *Signs, 17,* 666-671.

Kuipers, J. C. (1986). Talking about troubles: Gender differences in Weyewa speech use. *American Ethnologist, 13,* 448-462.

Kunkel, A. W., & Burleson, B. R. (1998). Social support and the emotional lives of men and women: An assessment of the different cultures perspective. In D. J. Canary & K. Dindia (Eds.), *Sex differences and similarities in communication: Critical essays and empirical investigations of sex and gender in interaction* (pp. 101-125). Mahwah, NJ: Lawrence Erlbaum.

LaFrance, M., & Banaji, M. (1992). Toward a re-consideration of the gender-emotion relationship. In M. S. Clark (Ed.), *Emotion and social behavior* (pp. 178-201). Newbury Park, CA: Sage.

Lakoff, R. (1975). *Language and women's place.* New York: Harper & Row.

Leet-Pellegrini, H. M. (1980). Conversational dominance as a function of gender and expertise. In H. Giles, W. P. Robinson, & P. M. Smith (Eds.), *Language: Social psychological perspectives* (pp. 97-104). Oxford: Pergamon.

Leiblum, S. R., & Rosen, R. C. (1991). Couples therapy for erectile disorders: Conceptual and clinical considerations. *Journal of Sex & Marital Therapy, 17,* 147-159.

LeMasters, E. E. (1975). *Blue collar aristocrats: Life styles at a working class tavern.* Madison: University of Wisconsin Press.

Lever, J. (1978). Sex differences in the complexity of children's play and games. *American Sociological Review, 43,* 471-483.

Linn, M. C. (1986). Meta-analysis of studies of gender differences: Implications and future directions. In J. S. Hyde & M. C. Linn (Eds.), *The psychology of gender: Advances through meta-analysis* (pp. 210-231). Baltimore: Johns Hopkins University Press.

Loftus, E. (1987, June 29). Trials of an expert witness. *Newsweek,* p. 10.

Lundquist, A. R. (1993). Gender differences in the intimacy of romantic relationships: A meta-analysis (Doctoral dissertation, University of Wisconsin, Madison, 1993). *Dissertation Abstracts International, 54,* 5927.

Maltz, D. N., & Borker, R. A. (1982). A cultural approach to male-female miscommunication. In J. J. Gumperz (Ed.), *Language and social identity* (pp. 196-216). Cambridge: Cambridge University Press.

McMaster, T. (1992). [Review of the book *You just don't understand: Women and men in conversation,* by D. Tannen]. *Library Journal, 117,* 134-135.

McMullen, L. M., Vernon, A. E., & Murton, T. (1995). Division of labor in conversations: Are Fishman's results replicable and generalizable? *Journal of Psycholinguistic Research, 24,* 255-268.

The men's movement and *Home improvement.* (1998, April 24). [On-line]. Available: http://src.doc.ic.ac.uk/public/media/tv/collections/tardis/us/comedy/HomeImprovement/html/mensmovement.html

Mitchell, C. (1985). Some differences in male and female joke-telling. In R. A. Jordan & S. J. Kal̃cik (Eds.), *Women's folklore, women's culture* (pp. 163-186). Philadelphia: University of Pennsylvania Press.

Murray, S. O. (1992). [Review of the book *You just don't understand: Women and men in conversation,* by D. Tannen]. *Journal of Pragmatics, 18,* 507-514.

Newman, B. M. (1971). Interpersonal behavior and preferences for exploration in adolescent boys: A small group study (Doctoral dissertation, University of Michigan, 1971). *Dissertation Abstracts International, 32,* 6625.

Ong, W. J. (1981). *Fighting for life: Contest, sexuality, and consciousness.* Ithaca, NY: Cornell University Press.

Paludi, M. A. (1984). Psychometric properties and underlying assumptions of four objective measures of fear of success. *Sex Roles, 10,* 765-781.

Perry, L. (1991). [Review of the book *You just don't understand: Women and men in conversation,* by D. Tannen]. *Communication Quarterly, 39,* 376-377.

Philipsen, G. (1975). Speaking "like a man" in Teamsterville: Culture patterns of role enactment in an urban neighborhood. *Quarterly Journal of Speech, 61,* 13-22.

Piper, A. M. S. (1993). Xenophobia and Kantian rationalism. *Philosophical Forum, 24,* 188-232.

Pomerantz, A. (1990). Conversation analytic claims. *Communication Monographs, 57,* 231-235.

The pros and cons of an academic career: Six views from Binghamton. (1989, January 25). *Chronicle of Higher Education,* p. A15.

Ragan, S. L. (1989). Communication between the sexes: A consideration of sex differences in adult communication. In J. F. Nussbaum (Ed.), *Life-span communication* (pp. 179-193). Hillsdale, NJ: Lawrence Erlbaum.

Reardon, K. (1995). *They don't get it, do they? Communication in the workplace: Closing the gap between women and men.* Boston: Little, Brown.

Riessman, C. K. (1990). *Divorce talk: Women and men make sense of personal relationships.* New Brunswick, NJ: Rutgers University Press.

Risman, B. J., & Schwartz, P. (1989). *Gender in intimate relationships: A micro-structural approach.* Belmont, CA: Wadsworth.

Roberts, C., & Jupp, T. (1985). [Study findings presented at the Linguistic Institute, Georgetown University].

Robey, E. B., Canary, D. J., & Burggraf, C. S. (1998). Conversational maintenance behaviors of husbands and wives: An observational analysis. In D. J. Canary & K. Dindia (Eds.), *Sex differences and similarities in communication: Critical essays and empirical investigations of sex and gender in interaction* (pp. 373-392). Mahwah, NJ: Lawrence Erlbaum.

Rose, R. (1990, August 5). I hear you, I hear you [Review of the book *You just don't understand: Women and men in conversation,* by D. Tannen]. *New York Times Book Review,* pp. 8-9.

Sadker, M., & Sadker, D. (1985, March). Sexism in the schoolroom of the '80s. *Psychology Today,* pp. 54-57.

Safier, E. J. (1992). New directions in family therapy. *Bulletin of the Menninger Clinic, 56*(1), 33-47.

Scheidt, S. D. (1994). Great expectations: Challenges for women as mental health administrators. *Journal of Mental Health Administration, 21,* 419-429.

Schiffrin, D. (1984). Jewish argument as sociability. *Language in Society, 13,* 311-335.

Schloff, L., & Yudkin, M. (1993). *He and she talk: How to communicate with the opposite sex.* New York: Plume.

Sherzer, J. (1987). A diversity of voices: Men's and women's speech in ethnographic perspective. In S. Philips, S. Steele, & C. Tanz (Eds.), *Language, gender, and sex in comparative perspective* (pp. 95-120). Cambridge: Cambridge University Press.

Smith, F. (1990). Gender and the framing of exegetical authority in sermon performances (Doctoral dissertation, Georgetown University, 1990). *Dissertation Abstracts International, 51,* 3728.

Smythe, M. J., & Schlueter, D. W. (1989). Can we talk? A meta-analytic review of the sex differences in language literature. In C. M. Lont & S. A. Friedley (Eds.), *Beyond boundaries: Sex and gender diversity in communication* (pp. 31-48). Fairfax, VA: George Mason University Press.

Soskin, W. F., & John, V. P. (1963). The study of spontaneous talk. In R. G. Barker (Ed.), *The stream of behavior* (pp. 228-281). New York: Appleton-Century-Crofts.

Stephens, M. (1988). *A history of news: From the drum to the satellite.* New York: Viking.

Sternberg, R. J., & Grajek, S. (1984). The nature of love. *Journal of Personality and Social Psychology, 47,* 312-329.

Stevens, C. K., Bavetta, A. G., & Gist, M. E. (1993). Gender differences in the acquisition of salary negotiation skills: The role of goals, self-efficacy and perceived control. *Journal of Applied Psychology, 78,* 723-735.

Stiles, W. B., Lyall, L. M., Knight, D. P., Ickes, W., Waung, M., Hall, L. C., & Primeau, R. E. (1997). Gender differences in verbal presumptuousness and attentiveness. *Personality and Social Psychology Bulletin, 23,* 759-772.

Strodtbeck, F. L., & Mann, R. D. (1956). Sex role differentiation in jury deliberations. *Sociometry, 19,* 3-11.

Swacker, M. (1976). Women's verbal behavior at learned and professional conferences. In B. L. Dubois & I. Crouch (Eds.), *The sociology of the languages of American women* (pp. 155-160). San Antonio, TX: Trinity University Press.

Tannen, D. (1984). *Conversational style: Analyzing talk among friends.* Norwood, NJ: Ablex.

Tannen, D. (1990a). Gender differences in conversational coherence: Physical alignment and topical cohesion. In B. Dorval (Ed.), *Conversational organization and its development* (pp. 167-206). Norwood, NJ: Ablex.

Tannen, D. (1990b). *You just don't understand: Women and men in conversation.* New York: Ballantine.

Tannen, D. (1994). *Gender and discourse.* New York: Oxford University Press.

Thorne, B., & Henley, N. M. (1975). *Language and sex: Difference and dominance.* Rowley, MA: Newbury House.

Trnka, S. (1991). [Review of the book *You just don't understand: Women and men in conversation,* by D. Tannen]. *Socialist Review, 21,* 201-205.

Uchida, A. (1992). When "difference" is "dominance": A critique of the "anti-power-based" cultural approach to sex differences. *Language in Society, 21,* 547-568.

Unger, R. K. (1990). Imperfect reflections of reality: Psychology constructs gender. In R. T. Hare-Mustin & J. Marecek (Eds.), *Making a difference: Psychology and the construction of gender* (pp. 102-149). New Haven, CT: Yale University Press.

Vancil, D. L. (1993). *Rhetoric and argumentation.* Boston: Allyn & Bacon.

Vangelisti, A. L., & Daly, J. A. (1997). Gender differences in standards for romantic relationships. *Personal Relationships, 4,* 203-219.

Wannaruk, A. (1997). Back-channel behavior in Thai and American casual telephone conversations (Doctoral dissertation, University of Illinois, Urbana-Champaign, 1997). *Dissertation Abstracts International, 58,* 3866.

West, C. (1979). Against our will: Male interruptions of females in cross-sex conversation. *Annals of the New York Academy of Sciences, 327,* 81-97.

West, C., & Zimmerman, D. H. (1977). Women's place in everyday talk: Reflections on parent-child interaction. *Social Problems, 24,* 521-529.

Wright, P. H. (1988). Interpreting research on gender differences in friendship: A case for moderation and a plea for caution. *Journal of Social and Personal Relationships, 5,* 367-373.

Zimmerman, D. H., & West, C. (1975). Sex roles, interruptions and silences in conversation. In B. Thorne & N. M. Henley (Eds.), *Language and sex: Difference and dominance* (pp. 105-129). Rowley, MA: Newbury House.

CHAPTER CONTENTS

2 Cross-Cultural Perspectives on Motivations of Verbal Communication: Review, Critique, and a Theoretical Framework

MIN-SUN KIM
University of Hawaii at Manoa

There has been an immense amount and variety of scholarship on the topic of motivation to communicate verbally (e.g., communication apprehension, assertiveness). The work in the area of communication motivation has been biased by the individualist assumption, explicit or implicit, that communication approach is more desirable than communication "avoidance." The author agrees that extreme forms of communication "avoidance" and lack of verbal assertiveness can be a handicap in any culture. However, she is critical of the ethnocentric preoccupation with the Western view of the self, which sees communication "avoidance" solely as a "deficiency." The purposes of this review are (a) to synthesize and evaluate critically prior cross-cultural research on verbal communication motivation, (b) to examine the philosophical/cultural basis of that research, and (c) to propose a theoretical framework for studying communication motivation from a derived etic perspective. Throughout, limitations in current knowledge are noted and avenues for future research are proposed. This review also provides practical suggestions for coping with the different degrees of communication motivation within various interaction contexts (classrooms, organizations, and counseling).

> An empty cart makes more noise.
>
> *Korean proverb*

> In the beginning was the Word.
>
> *John 1:1*

AUTHOR'S NOTE: I would like to thank the editor, Michael Roloff, and anonymous reviewers for their useful suggestions that improved this chapter. Also, I gratefully acknowledge Krystyna Aune, Don Klopf, and Hyun-Joo Kim for their constructive comments on an earlier draft.

Correspondence and requests for reprints: Min-Sun Kim, Department of Speech, George Hall 331, University of Hawaii at Manoa, Honolulu, HI 96822; e-mail kmin@hawaii.edu

Communication Yearbook 22, pp. 51-89

IT is no secret that theories of human communication, as studied in Western academia, have been based in large part on individualist assumptions and empirical research involving subjects from the mainstream U.S. culture. With the advent of the "cybercultural revolution" (Harris & Moran, 1979), the "global village" is now a reality rather than a forecast. The assumption that appropriate and effective styles of communication in U.S. culture may apply to people in other parts of the world is no longer valid. As people are increasingly involved in situations where intercultural communication is required, its difficulties are painfully recognized. Two serious sources of miscommunication and misunderstanding in intercultural contexts seem to be (a) the "how" of communication (e.g., degrees of directness) and (b) the amount of communication (e.g., the general tendency to approach or "avoid" communication).[1] In the area of intercultural communication, less attention has been given to the latter than to the former. On the other hand, numerous "nonintercultural" studies have investigated issues related to the amount of verbal communication (i.e., variability in the motivation to communicate verbally).

There have been several attempts to summarize the empirical findings and major trends on the topic of communication approach or "avoidance" (Allen & Bourhis, 1996; Allen, Hunter, & Donohue, 1989; Daly & Stafford, 1984; Infante & Rancer, 1996; Lustig & Andersen, 1991; McCroskey, 1977; Patterson & Ritts, 1997). The general conclusions drawn from studies using U.S. American subjects have been well established. However, cross-cultural research on the topic has yet to be synthesized and critically evaluated. A substantial body of research already exists involving other cultures, as well as subgroups in the United States, that warrants a critical synthesis. Research on predispositional communication motivation is available regarding Hawaii, Micronesia, Japan, Korea, Australia, Germany, England, the People's Republic of China, Puerto Rico, South Africa, the Philippines, Finland, Russia, Sweden, Taiwan, various subcultures in the United States, and others.

Notably, most cross-cultural research on communication disposition has explored how it applies/operates in U.S. culture in comparison with other cultures. Because culture shapes human communication behavior, the amount of talking in which a person engages is dependent, at least in part, on that person's cultural orientation (Barraclough, Christophel, & McCroskey, 1988). For instance, it is likely that different cultures perceive, manifest, and respond (reward/sanction) to communication approach and "avoidance" differently (Olaniran & Roach, 1994). For this reason, it is important to review the cross-cultural applicability of various constructs related to verbal communication motivation (e.g., communication apprehension and assertiveness).

Communication approach (e.g., assertiveness) is generally linked to healthy personality adjustment in the mainstream U.S. context (Cook & St. Lawrence, 1990; Henderson & Furnham, 1982; Zakahi, 1985). However, there is a danger in assuming communication "avoidance" (e.g., nonassertiveness, communication apprehension) merely as maladaptive. I agree that extreme forms of communication "avoidance" and lack of verbal assertiveness can be a handicap in any culture. However, I am critical of the ethnocentric preoccupation with the Western view of the self, which sees communication "avoidance" solely as a "deficiency." Clearly, viewed from an individualist standpoint, "avoidance" of communication or a lack of verbal assertiveness becomes anything but a deficiency. In this review, I discuss the necessity of reformulating theories in this and related areas, arguing that the conceptualizations and interpretations of results have been flawed or incomplete because of the individualist bias of work in this area.

Culture is one of the major influences that may contribute to preferences for communication approach and "avoidance" as well as related constructs of predispositions toward communication (e.g., unwillingness to communicate). The contrast between independence on the one hand and interdependence on the other seems to be the most useful theoretical framework for integrating findings on cross-cultural research into communication motivation (Gudykunst et al., 1996; Kim et al., 1996; Markus & Kitayama, 1991; Singelis & Brown, 1995). These two images of self are conceptualized as reflecting the emphasis on connectedness and relations often found in non-Western cultures (interdependent) and the separatedness and uniqueness of the individual (independent) stressed in the West (Markus & Kitayama, 1991, 1994a, 1994b).

The social and cultural backgrounds of most theoreticians in this area would probably lead them to assume that the desire to be an autonomous and effectual individual is a human universal. They might, therefore, take the desirability of high verbal communication (which serves the needs of individualists) as self-evident. The evidence, however, suggests that this is far from the case. Being an independent and efficacious individual has been the goal of only a small portion of humankind (Inkeles & Smith, 1974; Schooler, 1990). In fact, societies with such individualist values are so relatively rare that Meyer (1988) has formulated a theoretical approach aimed at specifying the nature of the institutional supports that Western societies provide for such an individualist view of the self. Furthermore, such differences in emphasis may exist not only between cultures, but also within societies, particularly those that are not socially or culturally homogeneous (Schooler, 1990). Although the development of communication theory that would generalize only to the mainstream U.S. culture would still be of value, the tendency to assume that what is true of the mainstream United States is true of other parts of the world is representative of general Western ethnocentrism (McCroskey, Burroughs, Daun, & Richmond, 1990).

In this chapter, I review and critically synthesize, from a cultural standpoint, research on people's willingness to approach or avoid social interaction. My review is limited to cross-cultural research on communication predisposition—that is, the motivation for verbal communication—rather than the actual verbal communication behavior. Thus I do not include research that deals with communication *styles* or language per se (for example, research on self-disclosure [e.g., Gudykunst & Nishida, 1984], direct and indirect forms of verbal behavior [e.g., Okabe, 1987], persuasive strategies [Hirokawa & Miyahara, 1986], to name only a few of the possibilities). I also omit such constructs as "social anxiety" and "shyness" (Buss, 1980; Leary, 1983), which typically been studied in the field of social psychology as personality characteristics, not directly linked to communication.

For the purposes of this review, I focus on two main areas of verbal communication motivations: (a) communication apprehension, and (b) assertiveness and its subset, argumentativeness. Within each of these two areas, I present a critique of current research from a cultural perspective along with agendas for future investigations. I then move beyond synthesis and propose a theoretical framework to incorporate findings on cultural variations in people's willingness to approach or "avoid" social interaction. I conclude the chapter with a discussion of cross-cultural misunderstandings in the interpretation and evaluation of the amount of verbal communication in various interaction settings.

VERBAL COMMUNICATION: MOTIVATIONS FOR APPROACH AND "AVOIDANCE"

Predispositions toward communication have been a central focus of theory-building efforts in communication for almost three decades. The importance of studying communication from this perspective is understandable, given that communication traits and predispositions have been found to account for significant variance in both observed communication behavior and communication-based perceptions (Infante & Rancer, 1996; McCroskey, 1977).

The disposition toward verbal communication has a number of different labels, such as *communication apprehension* (McCroskey, 1984), *unwillingness to communicate* (Burgoon, 1976), *predisposition toward verbal behavior* (Mortensen, Arnston, & Lustig, 1977), *social-communicative anxiety* (Daly & Stafford, 1984; Patterson & Ritts, 1997), *argumentativeness,* and *assertiveness* (Infante & Rancer, 1996). The constructs associated with each of these labels differ in emphasis, but the general thrust of all of them is the differing proclivity of people to participate in and enjoy, or "avoid" and fear, social interaction (Daly & Stafford, 1984; Kelly, 1982). In their review of the major trends of social-communicative anxiety and related constructs, Daly and Stafford (1984) found considerable evidence suggesting that, by and large, the many different constructs within this area tap a single, broad disposition. In their recent meta-analysis, Patterson and Ritts (1997) echo the same observation.

The focus of this review is on a presumed traitlike predisposition toward communication. In this section, I review cross-cultural research on two of the most popularly researched areas of verbal communication motivation: (a) communication apprehension (representing "avoidant" communication motivation) and (b) assertiveness and its subset, argumentativeness (representing "approach" motivation).

Cross-Cultural Research on Motivation to "Avoid" Verbal Communication

Communication Apprehension

Lustig and Andersen (1991) argue that "no communication variable has been examined more during the past two decades than has communication apprehension" (p. 299). Communication apprehension (CA) has been defined as "an individual's level of fear or anxiety associated with either real or anticipated communication with another person or persons" (McCroskey, 1977, p. 78). CA is typically divided into "state" and "trait" aspects. State CA is specific to the immediate communication episode that the person is facing—for example, an interview. Trait CA has been defined as a relatively enduring, personality-type orientation toward a given mode of communication across a wide variety of encounters (McCroskey, 1984).

Perhaps the most striking feature of communication apprehension is that the outcomes of apprehension and "avoidance" are solely negative. Researchers have found that individuals who are low on emotional maturity, adventurousness, self-control, self-esteem, and tolerance for ambiguity are more inclined to exhibit communication apprehension (McCroskey, Richmond, Daly, & Falcione, 1977). These findings, however, may not apply among people of different cultural orientations. In our predominantly individualist culture (i.e., the mainstream United States), talk is viewed positively and is generally rewarded. Many other cultures may not place as high a premium on the amount/frequency of talk as does the mainstream U.S. culture.

Previous cross-cultural studies on communication apprehension have focused on comparisons of other cultures as either higher or lower in communication motivation (e.g., CA and willingness to communicate) than the U.S. culture. It has been shown that culture or national origin influences the level of communication apprehension. Klopf, Cambra, and Ishii (1981) found that the Japanese are more apprehensive in communication situations than are Americans, and research by McCroskey, Gudykunst, and Nishida (1985) confirms this finding. Similarly, Klopf (1984) found that the Japanese were significantly more apprehensive than all the other groups studied: Americans, Australians, Koreans, Micronesians, People's Republic Chinese, and Filipinos. With the impact of culture influencing the development of all aspects of the individual's life, Klopf, Ishii, and Cambra (1995) conclude that culture seems to be an important determinant of communication apprehension.

Several studies have compared European cultures with U.S. culture. McCroskey et al. (1990) found that adult Swedes and Americans hold substantially different orientations toward verbal communication. Although Swedes see themselves as more competent as communicators than do Americans, they are less prone to initiate communication than are Americans. It is important to consider the fact that verbal communication skills seem to be valued much more highly in mainstream American culture than in the Swedish culture. According to McCroskey et al., this is reflected in the stress that is placed on verbal performance in American schools and colleges, and in the fact that verbal ability, in most colleges, even influences the formal grading of students. Such emphasis is unheard of in Sweden. Another indication is the large quantity of research that has been conducted on speech anxiety and related constructs in the United States, whereas very little interest in this area has been expressed in Sweden, where quietness and reticence are generally looked upon as individual differences rather than problems.

Moving beyond the two-culture comparison, McCroskey and Richmond (1990) summarize data from five cultures that they have studied. Among the participants from the five countries studied (the United States, Sweden, Australia, Micronesia, and Puerto Rico), they found that there were large differences in mean scores. With regard to the Willingness to Communicate Scale, the U.S. subjects reported the highest willingness and the Micronesians reported the lowest. For most of the countries, public speaking drew the least willingness and talking in a dyad drew the most. McCroskey and Richmond conclude that any generalizations concerning the association of self-perceived competence with willingness to communicate must be qualified with reference to culture.

Studies involving various other cultures also confirm the finding that general levels of communication apprehension vary from one culture to another. Chesebro et al. (1992) found that the Hispanic group in their sample included a substantially greater proportion of highly apprehensive students than did either their white group or their black group. Thus ethnicity was highly predictive of the proportion of students classified as highly communication apprehensive. In a study by Hackman and Barthel-Hackman (1993), the New Zealand students sampled were significantly less willing to communicate than were U.S. students in all four contexts (public speaking, meeting, group, and dyad) and with all three types of receivers (stranger, acquaintance, and friend). The authors attribute these results to the collectivist Maori society in New Zealand. Maoris utilize silence rather than verbal expression when they are uncomfortable or are attempting to gather their thoughts. Also, Olaniran and Roach (1994) found that the average CA scores for the Nigerian high school students in their sample seemed to be lower than the average CA scores for American high school students.

More recent research also indicates that culture influences "avoidant" communication motivations. Hutchinson, Neuliep, and More (1995) compared U.S. and Australian samples on the Personal Report of Communication Apprehension (PRCA-24) and its subscales. The Australian sample scored significantly lower on the overall PRCA-24 and on three of the four subscales (group, meeting, and interpersonal). Christophel's (1996) recent study has added data from Russia to the set of cultures available for comparative studies on verbal communication orientation. Christophel examined the communication orientations of Russian students and compared the results with those of previous studies conducted in the United States, Sweden, Finland, Australia, Micronesia, and Puerto Rico. The Russians indicated a lower willingness to engage in communication (as measured by the Willingness to Communicate Scale) than did subjects in the comparative countries, with the exception of Micronesians. The mean PRCA-24 score for the Russian sample was identical to that of Finland's and comparable with the scores for the United States, Sweden, and Australia. The highest score was reported by Micronesians and the lowest by Puerto Ricans.

There is further support for the cultural differences outlined above. Zhang, Butler, and Pryor (1996) found that a Chinese sample yielded a significantly higher mean score on apprehension about communication than did an American sample. These authors claim that if they had used the mean (65.6) and standard deviation (15.3) of CA from McCroskey's (1982) original sample (of 25,000 Americans) for comparison instead of the American sample collected for their study, the mean of the Chinese sample would have been close to that of "highly apprehensive" individuals. They argue that high scores for communication apprehensiveness among Chinese may not carry the same negative implications as high scores in the United States. According to Zhang et al., individual assertiveness is valued less highly in Chinese society than it is in U.S. society. As an example, they note that the Chinese society de-emphasizes self-expression and oral participation in public schools.

Differing levels of communication apprehension have been observed among children as well. Watson, Monroe, and Atterstrom (1989) examined the levels of CA among American and Swedish elementary school children in their native languages. They found both cultural and developmental differences, with Swedish subjects reporting more CA than American subjects and combined Swedish and American older subjects (ages 9 through 11) reporting more CA than younger subjects (ages 5 through 8). These authors had found similar differences in a previous study involving American and Swedish subjects (Watson, Monroe, & Atterstrom, 1984).

Some cross-cultural studies on communication "avoidance" have also addressed the role of second language in levels of CA. McCroskey, Fayer, and Richmond (1985) found that the Puerto Ricans in their sample were much less apprehensive about communication in their native language (Spanish) than were U.S. students but much more apprehensive about communication in their second language (English) than were the U.S. students. These findings have been further endorsed in a study by Burroughs and Marie (1990), who found that, when using a second language, not only do Micronesian students report feeling more apprehensive and less competent, they also are less willing to communicate than when using their first language.

Critique and Summary

I have examined above some cross-cultural variations in general levels of communication apprehension. The cross-cultural research reviewed clearly demonstrates that the norms for verbal behavior, as well as the consequent perceptions associated with these norms, may vary to an extraordinary degree from one culture to the next. The overall results of the past research indicate that samples from collectivist cultures such as China, Japan, and Micronesia display higher levels of verbal communication apprehension than do comparable samples in individualist cultures such as Australia and the mainland United States. Gudykunst and Ting-Toomey (1988) contend that the finding that members of collectivist cultures have higher levels of communication apprehension than do members of individualist cultures should not be taken to imply that communication apprehension is a "problem" in collectivist cultures. In fact, probably the opposite is true. Hence, without information about a culture's general predisposition toward verbal communication, research on communication apprehension in a given culture may not be very useful. The amount of talk and the degree of quietness endorsed by a culture may have an overwhelming impact on the communication motivation of most people in that culture.

A few of the cross-cultural studies reviewed made use of cultural variability dimensions (i.e., individualism and collectivism) to explain the differences in their findings (post hoc cultural explanations). However, the use of broad cultural variability dimensions has been criticized by many authors for its lack of explanatory power (Gaines et al., 1997; Gudykunst et al., 1996; Kâgitçibasi, 1987; Kim et al., 1996; Kitayama, Markus, Matsumoto, & Norasakkunkit, 1997; Schwartz, 1990; Singelis & Brown, 1995). Given the complexities of the influence of culture on communication behavior, it is necessary to find relevant intervening variables in order to understand "what in culture" accounts for cultural differences. According to Hofstede (1980), his four cultural dimensions (individualism, masculinity, tolerance for ambiguity, and power distance) together explain only 49% of the variance in the data. The other 51% remain specific to individual countries. Surely, the division of the world into individualist and collectivist cultures is a broad simplification that deserves a more systematic and detailed examination (Schwartz, 1990). Clarifying the "social-cultural processes" resulting in motivation to "avoid" or approach verbal communication is an integral step toward culture-sensitive theorizing. Given this overview of "avoidant" motivations in different cultures, we now turn to a discussion of the approach motivations for verbal communication: assertiveness and its subset, argumentativeness.

Cross-Cultural Research on Motivation to Communicate Verbally

Assertiveness

Assertiveness is defined as behaviors that enable an individual to act in his or her best interest, or to stand up for him- or herself without undue anxiety; to express his or her rights without denying the rights of others (Alberti & Emmons, 1970). At least within the U.S. context, assertiveness has been viewed as a measure of social competence or as an indicator of interpersonal communication competence. Assertive behaviors are perceived as more competent and attractive than unassertive behaviors in the United States (Cook & St. Lawrence, 1990: Henderson & Furnham, 1982; Zakahi, 1985). People who are perceived as high in assertiveness are considered to be competitive, risk takers, fast to take action, take-charge individuals, and directive. People perceived as low in assertiveness are characterized as cooperative, risk avoiders, slow to take action, "go-along" persons, and nondirective.

Previous research on cross-cultural differences in assertiveness has focused on comparisons of other cultures with the U.S. culture, ranking those other cultures as either higher or lower on assertiveness than U.S. culture. Several studies have reported that Asians are less assertive than Caucasians (Fukuyama & Greenfield, 1983; Johnson & Marsella, 1978). Fukuyama and Greenfield (1983) compared the responses of Asian American and Caucasian American students on the College Self-Expression Scale and found that the former had significantly lower assertion scores on the following items: expressing feelings or making difficult requests in public, disagreeing with parents, and expressing annoyance to the opposite sex. Nagao (1991) found a significant difference in assertive behaviors between Americans and Japanese. Specifically, she found that Japanese students, more so than American students, perceived it to be inappropriate for a student to question a professor if the student disagrees with the professor's statement. These results are consistent with Thompson and Ishii's (1990) findings. Thompson and Ishii also found that, based on assertiveness scores, the Japanese are similar to the Finns, with both holding a moderate level of assertiveness. In addition, they found that the American students in their sample were more assertive than were the Japanese in their behaviors. The Koreans and Americans showed a high degree of assertiveness, with mean scores above 34. The Koreans, however, were significantly different from the Americans, with the Americans being more assertive.

Focusing on subcultures in the United States, Sue, Ino, and Sue (1983) found that Chinese American men reported more anxiety and apprehension in social situations than did their Caucasian counterparts, but claimed to behave equally assertively. Similarly, Sue, Sue, and Ino (1990) found that the self-reported assertiveness scores of Chinese American and Caucasian American women were not significantly different. They speculate as to whether, in real life, Chinese Americans would exhibit assertive responses, even though they were able to demonstrate the same level of assertiveness as Caucasians in laboratory settings. It should also be noted that the participants in this study were Chinese American college students who had spent the majority of their lives in the midwestern United States. Chinese Americans who have had more contact with Chinese culture might respond very differently.

Assertiveness has typically been treated as a unidimensional construct, but different types of assertiveness may play varied roles in different situational contexts. Recent evidence from Goldberg and Botvin (1993) supports the concept of assertiveness as a multidimensional construct and also provides evidence for situation-specific, assertive skills. Carmona and Lorr (1992) found a strong similarity in the dimensions of the assertiveness trait in Chilean and U.S. participants: defense of rights, social assertiveness, directiveness, and independence. Wheeless (1975) views assertiveness as the task-oriented dimension of interpersonal communication. By being assertive, communicators can get things done. Nonassertive persons are characterized, on the other hand, as inhibited, submissive, self-deprecating, self-denying, and conforming. However, it would be imprudent to generalize the "negative" description of low argumentative individuals (based on studies using subjects from the United States) to people belonging to other cultures.

Argumentativeness

Argumentativeness is another predisposition toward verbal communication that has been studied extensively (Dowling & Flint, 1990; Infante & Rancer, 1996). Argumentativeness is considered a subset of assertiveness (Infante & Rancer, 1996). Not all assertive behavior, therefore, entails argument. Specifically, argumentativeness is defined as a generally stable trait that predisposes individuals in communication situations to advocate positions on controversial issues and to challenge verbally the positions others hold on those issues (Infante & Rancer, 1982). Argumentativeness and verbal aggressiveness are similar in that both are aggressive, attacking forms of communication. However, they can be distinguished from each other according to the locus of attack: Argumentativeness attacks the *positions* taken by others on the issues, whereas verbal aggressiveness attacks the *self-concepts* of others instead of, or in addition to, their positions on issues (Infante, Trebing, Shepherd, & Seeds, 1984). In individualist cultures (e.g., the mainland United States), argumentativeness has been found to be a constructive form and verbal aggressiveness a counterproductive form of aggressive communication.

Argumentativeness within the mainstream U.S. context is supposedly related positively to learning, intellectual development, and problem-solving abilities for the individual (Infante, 1982). Research in the organizational context has shown that argumentativeness is positively related to job satisfaction (Infante & Gordon, 1985, 1987). Research in the marital context has shown that argumentativeness is negatively related to individuals' involvement in interspousal violence (Infante, Chandler, & Rudd, 1989). Infante (1985) also found that speaker credibility is enhanced by arguing.

According to Prunty, Klopf, and Ishii (1990), it would be imprudent to generalize this description of argumentativeness traits across different cultures as well as to the many subcultures within the United States. Prunty et al. found that the Japanese in their sample were significantly less inclined to approach argument situations and had a significantly weaker argumentativeness trait than did the Americans. Compared with Americans, researchers report, typical Japanese are more apprehensive (Klopf et al., 1981), speak less frequently (Klopf & Ishii, 1976), are less predisposed to talk, are less fluent (Klopf, Ishii, & Cambra, 1976), and are more prone to attain unanimous agreement on any matter (Doi, 1973)—all qualities that are antithetical to argumentative (highly verbal) behavior.

Further confirming the above observations, Jenkins, Klopf, and Park (1991) have found that Japanese and Koreans are not significantly different from each other in argumentativeness, but Americans are significantly more argumentative than either of these groups. These authors found no significant differences among the three groups on "avoidance" tendencies. According to Becker (1986), the Japanese are more intuitive and nonargumentative than Americans, valuing group harmony and shunning controversy. Confronting differences in Japan, Barnlund (1989) avers, would be a serious blunder. Prunty et al. (1990) concur with the findings of other researchers regarding the nonargumentativeness of Japanese. They contend that argumentativeness is a Western practice that is both impractical and inconceivable to the Japanese. Americans do not perceive arguments as necessarily negative, and relationships between Americans might not be severely disrupted by an argument. Even if some tension is caused, the parties involved may be likely to repair their relationship. In contrast, because the Japanese view argument negatively, friendships between Japanese that are disrupted by argument are rarely repaired (Barnlund, 1989).

Critique and Summary

Although research on verbal communication approach has been conducted primarily in the United States, cross-cultural studies on the topic are still numerous. Past research has reported that Asians are less assertive than

Caucasians. The general conclusion that can be drawn from these results is that people from individualist cultures are generally more assertive than are people from collectivist cultures. The general outcomes and perceptions of argumentativeness, however, are mostly based on research involving predominantly Anglo-Saxon subjects in the United States whose self-identity is autonomous and bounded. A consistent personality profile of assertive and nonassertive individuals has emerged in the literature within the U.S. context. Assertive behavior is said to be characterized by individuals standing up for their rights and being able to express their thoughts, feelings, and beliefs directly and honestly. Assertiveness is often regarded as an individualist interpersonal-oriented behavior in contrast to a collectivist interpersonal-oriented behavior. Assertive behaviors are demonstrated by those who value individual events, beliefs, and feelings above the events, beliefs, and feelings of the group (Shoemaker & Satterfield, 1977).

The previous conceptualization of communication approach tendencies (argumentativeness and assertiveness) is too narrow. A person who is more susceptible to low levels of assertiveness or argumentativeness may not have an idealized role identity that is characterized as neurotic and/or introverted, as some researchers have asserted. For instance, Hamid (1994), focusing on a measure of what has come to be known as the "Big Five" personality factors, found that assertive students are more emotionally expressive, outgoing, and expansive in their self-expression. On the other hand, they are less agreeable and conscientious than are nonassertive students among Hong Kong Chinese. Thus the cultural meanings of personality styles may be associated with the different values placed on different personality displays. Similarly, in individualist cultures, assertiveness is generally seen as a characteristic of a well-adjusted person. In collectivist cultures, however, nonassertiveness and nonargumentativeness are probably more socially desirable, as shown by findings that "agreeableness" is closely associated with "nonassertiveness" in such cultures. Typically, for example, the Chinese tend to equate assertiveness with aggressiveness and arrogance (Yeo, 1990). In the collectivist context, a conscientious person may be seen as unobtrusively getting on with the job. These results highlight the importance of cultural differences in perceptions of assertive and argumentative behaviors.

General Conclusion and
Limitations of Past Research

Based on the results of the various cross-cultural studies reviewed above, it is clear that there are substantial differences in the approach and "avoidant" tendencies of verbal communication among the countries of the world. In addition, and possibly even more important, the relationships among these orientations also differ. Talk probably is a vital component in interpersonal communication and the development of interpersonal relationships in all cultures. However, people differ dramatically in the degree to which they actually value talking behavior. Clearly, any generalization concerning the differences in verbal communication motivations or the associations among variables must be qualified with reference to culture.

In addition, much of the accumulated research on cross-cultural communication motivation is descriptive in nature. Typically, investigations have attempted merely to describe different mean levels of various communication orientations. Although this line of research provides an important descriptive base, a fundamental problem stands out: It does not enhance our *understanding* of the different levels of verbal communication motivation across cultures. Why does a given cultural group prefer certain levels of verbal communication? Typically, studies do not deal with the theoretical reasons *why* particular groups prefer particular levels of verbal communication motivation.

A major purpose of cross-cultural communication orientation research is to improve communication and understanding between members of different cultural groups. Thus understanding and predicting others' verbal orientations is an important component in developing cross-cultural communication competence. In order to understand we must predict, and in order to predict we must have background knowledge as to why different levels of verbal communication motivations are found across cultures and how general impressions of competence are formed, based on the levels of verbal communicativeness. We now turn our attention to the cultural ideologies that influence verbal communication motivation.

CULTURAL PERSPECTIVES ON MOTIVATION TO APPROACH OR "AVOID" VERBAL COMMUNICATION

According to Gudykunst, Guzley, and Ota (1993), when one studies concepts that have culture-specific meanings (e.g., communication apprehension, assertiveness), it is necessary to begin by looking at emic conceptualizations of the concepts. Then, as a next step, it is critical to generate etic conceptualizations of concepts that are compatible with culturally specific emic conceptualizations (i.e., derived etic conceptualizations). (For example, see Gudykunst et al., 1993, for discussion of derived etic conceptualizations of "face.") In this section, I will isolate the emic conceptualizations of verbal communication motivations and then arrive at a derived etic conceptualization.

The research on communication motivation, like many other branches of communication research, was born and nourished by the philosophical foundations of individualism. We now discover that individualism is not a universal, but a culture-specific belief system (Greenfield, 1994). The view of communication motivation from interdependence-oriented societies can help to balance the ethnocentric picture of individualist value toward communication approach. To what extent does a culture idealize personhood in terms of individual achievement and autonomy? To what extent does a culture idealize personhood in terms of interdependence with others? This emphasis, with its implications for verbal communication motivation, may provide a unifying conceptual framework for researching the relationship between cultural values and the motivation to communicate verbally.

Numerous scholars have noted the propensity for the Western cultural value of individualism to shape theorists' views of psychological functioning (Gilligan, 1982; Markus & Kitayama, 1994a; Sampson, 1988; Sharkey & Singelis, 1995). From an individualist point of view, the individual, in contrast to some larger social grouping, is the unit of central importance, both in the selection of means and in the evaluation of ends. The individual is conceived of as "essentially" existing independent of society. The individualist view coincides with Sampson's (1977) notion of a centralized, equilibrium concept of personhood (i.e., individualism). A centralized, equilibrium concept of personhood holds that only through mastery and personal control can one prevent chaos while maintaining order and coherence (Sampson, 1988). This notion of personhood is typically a part of Western cultures. Given the general assumption of the desirability of direct confrontation stemming from independent view of the self, it is not surprising that researchers have conceptualized the "avoidance" style as a deficiency. This assumption is taken so much for granted in individualist cultures that it has rarely been stated explicitly. As emic conceptualizations, I propose that differing degrees of verbal communication motivations may stem from (a) the strength of the individual's idealized role identity (as bounded and separate) in interaction, and (b) the individual's sensitivity to others' evaluations as the interaction unfolds, depending on the degree to which the individual's identity is entwined with and dependent on others.

The Individualist View:
Communication "Avoidance" as a Deficit

Traditionally, communication anxiety or reticence has been attributed to a weak sense of the independent self. Thus from an individualist point of view, an individual who has low communication motivation is thought to have an unstable or uncertain sense of his or her own role identity as bounded and separate from others. It is claimed that this fragile sense of role identity is inherently vulnerable to threats during interaction, which causes communication anxiety. The hypersensitivity to evaluation is related to an uncertain sense of self and the accompanying fear of negative evaluation. This represents the deficit view of verbal communication "avoidance."

It is unlikely that either tendency (i.e., individualist or group-based evaluation of outcomes) ever becomes the sole determinant of behavior. In most circumstances, people's choices of actions probably represent some balance of the two. All in all, the definition of individualism implies that persons in individualist societies would be likely to wish themselves to be self-directed and to value highly the phenomenological experience of freedom of choice. Personal efficacy would be valued not only because individuals value their independence, but also because they see themselves as primarily responsible for what happens to them. If one assumes that the individual should be a bounded, autonomous, self-sufficient social unit, then nonassertiveness becomes a deficiency. That is, being silent or "avoiding" argument becomes an indicator of anxiety or lack of social confidence.

In individualist societies, the development of strong interpersonal relationships is heavily dependent on the amount of communication in which interactants are willing to engage. Hence, other things being equal, the more a person is willing to talk and to be nonverbally expressive, the more likely that person is to develop positive interpersonal relationships. Although research in the mainstream American culture strongly supports this conclusion, the generalizability of these research findings to other cultures is questionable. Rather than viewing communication "avoidance" as a personal deficiency, it is possible to view it as a sensitivity to the social context.

The Collectivist View:
Communication "Avoidance"
Stemming From a Sensitivity to Social Context

The deficit view is ethnocentric in its conceptualization of the self as a bounded, independent, and autonomous entity. A second way in which the individual's social role is threatened involves others' evaluations. In this case, rather than viewing communication "avoidance" as arising from the individual's insecurity about his or her independent role identity, it can be viewed as arising from his or her sensitivity to social context and a heightened awareness of others' evaluations (Sharkey & Singelis, 1995). All else being equal, people who are highly conscious of their social identities might experience more anxiety because others' perceptions of what takes place in the social context are particularly important to them. A generalized sensitivity to others' evaluations and "fitting in" is one of the central characteristics of the collectivist self.

Further confirming the heightened social sensitivity of interdependents, Sharkey and Singelis (1995) found that interdependence was positively correlated with embarrassability. They propose that sensitivity to the social context and embarrassability may be viewed as positive characteristics that contribute to the individual's ability to adapt to and fit into a social system, especially one that emphasizes groups and cooperative effort (i.e., collectivist cultures). In individualist cultures, a sensitivity to the social context can be useful, even though it is not emphasized. The disruption of an interaction would certainly have stronger effects on a presentation of self that emphasizes fitting in and being sensitive to social contexts (Sharkey & Singelis, 1995).

"Avoidance" of verbal expression can help the individual to control emotion and may at times also allow the passive expression of discontent without the dangers of a direct challenge. Just as messages of silence (extreme forms of indirectness) might be evaluated differently within different relationship contexts (Tannen, 1985), "avoidant" styles can be seen as positive or negative by people with different cultural orientations. In individualist contexts, there often appears to be a "demand to interact" that characterizes much of dyadic communication—a built-in assumption that when people are engaged in focused conversation it is their responsibility to keep verbal communication active. Silence or "avoidant" communication styles might, at times, represent a threat to this responsibility. Hence low motivation for verbal output among independents may be seen as the failure of positive politeness—the need to be involved with others. The benefit of low verbal output among interdependents comes from being understood without putting one's meaning on record, so that understanding is seen not as the result of putting meaning into words, but rather as the greater understanding of shared perspective, expectations, and intimacy.

Given the above emic conceptualizations of verbal communication motivation, I propose the following derived etic conceptualization of the construct: *Verbal communication motivation is a person's predisposition toward verbally expressing his or her beliefs, attitudes, and feelings to others in various social contexts.* In the current review I seek to examine the role of cultural values in determining levels of verbal communication motivation. The next section is devoted to outlining the theoretical framework from a derived etic perspective.

INTEGRATIVE FRAMEWORK: TOWARD A CULTURAL MODEL OF VERBAL COMMUNICATION MOTIVATION

There have been numerous empirical studies of cross-cultural verbal communication motivation, but few theoretical analyses. As a step toward conceptual integration, in this section I bring together extant empirical findings within a cultural framework. The major premise underlying the framework described below is that culture influences mediating processes (self-construals and beliefs about arguing) that affect the motivations for verbal communication. Stated differently: Cultural variability does not directly affect verbal communication motivations per se; rather, its influence is indirect. Similar mediation models have been adopted to explain communication processes across cultures, including low- and high-context communication styles (Gudykunst et al., 1996; Singelis & Brown, 1995) and the perceived importance of

conversational constraints (Kim et al., 1996). To understand individual behavior, we must take into consideration both culture-level individualism and
collectivism as well as individual-level factors that mediate the influence of
culture (see Gudykunst et al., 1996). To do so, we need to isolate the
individual-level factors that mediate the influence of culture-level individualism and collectivism on communication motivation.

One way to understand the mediating influence of culture-level individualism and collectivism on individuals' communication motivation is to determine the way individuals conceive of themselves (e.g., self-concept) and the
belief structures that people have about verbal communicativeness. Below, I
present culture-level as well as individual-level factors that may be related to
aspects of verbal communication motivation: (a) the cultural variability
dimensions of individualism and collectivism, (b) individual-level correlates
of individualism and collectivism (i.e., independent self-construals, interdependent self-construals), and (c) beliefs about verbal communicativeness.

Culture-Level Individualism and Collectivism

The concept of individualism and collectivism has been described by
Triandis (1988) as perhaps the most important dimension of cultural differences in social behavior across the diverse cultures of the world. Numerous
cross-cultural studies have provided empirical evidence supporting the usefulness of the individualism and collectivism dimension as a way of categorizing cultures (see, e.g., Bond & Forgas, 1984; Hofstede, 1980; Hui &
Triandis, 1986). In dealing with the constructs of individualism and collectivism, Triandis, Bontempo, Villareal, Asai, and Lucca (1988) posit that the
emphasis is usually on the goals of the collective more than personal goals in
collectivist cultures, and the reverse in individualist cultures. Specifically,
these authors have defined collectivism as having (a) great emphasis on the
views, needs, and goals of the in-group rather than of oneself; (b) great
readiness to cooperate with in-group members; and (c) intense emotional
attachment to the in-group. Individualism is reflected in (a) self-reliance, (b)
low concern for in-groups, and (c) distance from in-groups. In other words,
individualism is defined as the tendency to be more concerned about one's
behavior for one's own needs, interests, and goals, whereas collectivism
refers to the tendency to be more concerned about the consequences of one's
behavior for in-group members and to be more willing to sacrifice personal
interests for the attainment of collective interests and harmony.

Individualism and collectivism (sometimes under different names) have
often been identified as "relational" attributes of a *culture as a whole*. Within
a given culture, however, individuals vary in the extent to which they are
"typical" and construe the self in the "typical" way. Thus not all people who are
part of an individualist culture possess primarily independent self-construals,

nor do all those who are part of a collectivist culture possess primarily interdependent self-construals.

Furthermore, culture is not uniform within what we nominally designate as one "culture." This is obvious in the case of a country like India, where many cultural details differ between linguistic groups and religions, and even within religions across castes. It is less obvious in other countries, but analysis of all the countries examined by researchers in recent years suggests that heterogeneity of culture is true for most countries in the world today. Therefore, broad culture-level tendencies in individualism and collectivism alone cannot be used to explain individuals' motivations for verbal communication. The individual-level factors that mediate the influence of culture-level individualism and collectivism also must be taken into consideration. Whereas individualism and collectivism define broad differences between cultures, self-construals, discussed below, focus upon the ways individuals conceive of themselves.

Independent and Interdependent Self-Construals

A growing body of cross-cultural studies of the self-concept (Gudykunst et al., 1996; Kashima et al., 1995; Kim et al., 1996; Kim, Sharkey, & Singelis, 1994; Markus & Kitayama, 1991, 1994a, 1994b; Singelis & Brown, 1995) reveals that an exclusive focus on culture-level generalizations is no longer appropriate for studying intercultural communication styles. It is necessary to identify the theoretical elements or processes that explain these cultural differences. The findings from Gudykunst et al.'s (1996) study also suggest that individual-level factors (i.e., self-construals) are better predictors of low- and high-context communication styles across cultures than is cultural individualism/collectivism.

In the pages that follow, I propose a pancultural model of the self in terms of the relative salience of its components. This model states that, irrespective of their cultural backgrounds, people have complex selves that contain qualitatively different cognitions, and one way to divide up these cognitions is to separate them into independent and interdependent self-construals (Markus & Kitayama, 1991). The current literature proposes that people construe the self in two divergent ways. One type of construal may be described using such concepts as *independent, autonomous, agentic,* and *separate,* whereas the other type may be described using the antonyms to these terms: *interdependent, communal,* and *relational* (Gaines et al., 1997; Kitayama et al., 1997; Markus & Kitayama, 1991, 1994a, 1994b).

Markus and Kitayama (1991) suggest two types of self-construal (independent and interdependent) and argue for the systematic influence of these differing self-concepts on cognition, emotion, and motivation. These two images of self were originally conceptualized as reflecting the emphasis on connectedness and relations often found in "non-Western" cultures (interdependent) and the separateness and uniqueness of the individual (independent) stressed in "the West." The *independent* construal views self as an entity that (a) comprises a unique, bounded configuration of internal attributes (e.g., preferences, traits, abilities, motives, values, and rights) and (b) behaves primarily as a consequence of these internal attributes (see Markus & Kitayama, 1994a). This view of the self derives from a belief in the wholeness and uniqueness of each person's configuration of internal attributes (Johnson, 1985). According to Lebra (1991), European-American culture naturally embraces the individual level of reality—the person's seemingly separate and private store of thoughts and feelings—because it is rooted in an ontological tradition that favors the "theistic/Cartesian split self" (i.e., the self/other split).

By contrast, in the *interdependent* construal, the self is viewed not as an independent entity, separate from the collective, but instead as fundamentally interdependent with others (Markus & Kitayama, 1991). This is not to say that the person with an interdependent view of the self has no conception of internal traits, characteristics, or preferences that are unique to him or her; rather, these internal, private aspects of the self are not primary in directing or guiding the individual's behavior. This view of the self and of the collective requires adjusting to and fitting into important relationships, occupying one's proper place in the group, engaging in collectively appropriate actions, and promoting the goals of others. Lebra (1991) contends that East Asian cultural groups are more attuned to a social or relational level of reality because they are tied to an ontological tradition that favors a notion of the submerged self, in which the goal is the connection with others and the surrounding context. Within such a construal, the self becomes most meaningful and complete when it is cast in the appropriate social relationship. Thus the variability of independent and interdependent construals of self seems to frame our existential experience and serves as an anchoring point in terms of how we view verbal communication.

Cultural differences in self-construal have been well established by recent studies (Bochner, 1994; Bond & Cheung, 1983; Cousins, 1989; Gudykunst et al., 1996; Kashima et al., 1995; Kim et al., 1996). Singelis (1994; Singelis & Brown, 1995) has developed a measure that taps the independent and interdependent dimensions of the self and has found that in Hawaii participants from an Asian background were both more interdependent and less independent relative to those with a European background. Bochner (1994) found that Malaysian self-construals were more interdependent and less independent than Australian and British self-construals. Recent studies (Kim et al., 1994, 1996; Kim & Sharkey, 1995) also show that the degree of independent and interdependent construal of self systematically affects the perceived importance of "conversational constraints" (Kim, 1994, 1995; Kim & Wilson, 1994) within a culture as well as across different cultural groups. In their study of four different cultural groups (in Japan, Korea, Australia, and the

United States), Gudykunst et al. (1996) also found that the degree of independent and interdependent construal of self systematically varies across cultures. I propose that self-concept alone, however, does not explain the approach and "avoidance" tendencies of verbal communication among individuals. An individual's general beliefs about verbal communicativeness may also affect his or her motivations toward verbal communication.

Beliefs About Verbal Communicativeness

Desire to communicate verbally may be conceived as a continuum that goes from high willingness to low willingness. In order to understand the argumentativeness trait more fully, Rancer, Baukus, and Infante (1985) utilized Fishbein and Ajzen's (1975) theory of reasoned action, which proposes that human behavior is directly linked to attitudes and beliefs. Further, a predisposition (an inclination to behave in a particular way) is controlled by the set of beliefs that the individual learns to associate with the object of the predisposition (Kim & Hunter, 1993a, 1993b; Rancer, Kosberg, & Baukus, 1992). For example, one way to understand verbal approach versus "avoidance" tendencies is to determine the belief structures people have about arguing: If beliefs control predispositions, a person's level of argumentativeness may be related to his or her beliefs about arguing.

In measuring beliefs about arguing, Rancer et al. (1985) found that more argumentative individuals had predominantly positive beliefs about arguing, whereas less argumentative individuals had predominantly negative beliefs about arguing. Early research in communication apprehension suggested that individuals with high public speaking apprehension would experience high levels of negative thinking, both in anticipation of presenting a speech and in the delivery of the speech (Meichenbaum, 1977). More recent studies support these ideas with respect to both positive and negative thinking (Buhr, Pryor, & Sullivan, 1991; Daly, Vangelisti, Neel, & Cavanaugh, 1989). Based on these findings, it appears worthwhile to examine how beliefs about arguing are related to verbal communication motivations among individuals of different cultural orientations. Within a given speech community, social values and norms strongly influence the amount of talk and the amount of argument that is considered normal or appropriate. It is possible that among people of high interdependence, arguing is perceived as an unpleasant activity of dubious value that leads to anger and unreasonable behavior. Interdependents may foster negative beliefs about arguing, which may significantly dampen motivation to argue and heighten verbal communication "avoidance."

East Asian tradition appears to value the preservation of the harmony of the social group above the expression of individuals' inner thoughts and negative feelings (Barnlund, 1989). Because of the belief that meaning can be sensed but not phrased, a talkative person is often considered a "show-off" or insincere. The Korean term *noon-chi* ("reading the other person's mind," grasping a situation) and the Japanese term *haragei* (wordless communication) capture the essence of East Asians' positive feelings toward communication without words. For example, a person who "has *noon-chi*" should not ask a favor if he or she knows it cannot be granted, or that granting it would inconvenience the other person.

Several writers have argued that Japanese do not value verbal communication and "avoid" it whenever possible (Gudykunst & Nishida, 1993; Ishii, 1982; Nakane, 1970). For instance, Gudykunst and Nishida (1993) assert that the Japanese concept of *enryo* (a ritualized verbal self-deprecation process used for the purpose of maintaining group harmony) explains these patterns. Similarly, Ishii (1982) claims that it is traditional in the Japanese culture for people to go out of their way to conceal their sentiments, so that they may not disturb the general atmosphere of harmony. Hiroshi Ota argues that *enryo* is an "active" process in Japan, not a "passive" process like reticence (the nearest equivalent concept) in the United States (personal communication cited in Gudykunst & Nishida, 1993). Compatible with this argument, Giles, Coupland, and Wiemann (1992) compared the beliefs of Chinese and Americans about talking. The Americans described talking as pleasant and important, and as a way of controlling what goes on. The Chinese were more "tolerant" of silence and saw quietness as a way of controlling what goes on.

In a more philosophical and complex account of Chinese relationships, Chang and Holt (1991) argue that Chinese feel no need to develop verbal communicative strategies to maintain their relationships. They note that Chinese cherish the chance of association and allow relationships to develop according to their own course. Chang and Holt further claim that Chinese do not perceive verbal communication as the chief factor in determining relationships. Thus communication "avoidance" should not be interpreted as merely a "passive" form of communication. As Katriel and Philipsen (1981) point out, many North Americans feel that they need "communication" to make a relationship "work." On the other hand, interdependents may hold a considerably less instrumental view of the role of verbal communication in relationships. These inherent differences lead to fundamentally different views of verbal communication.

Takai and Ota's (1994) work also supports the observations of Japanese interpersonal behavior reported above. These researchers describe five factors as essential to Japanese communication competence. Among these factors, at least three (perceptive ability, self-restraint, and interpersonal sensitivity) seem to be closely related to the "low motivation for verbal communication" among Japanese. Takai and Ota describe their first factor, perceptive ability, as sensing the cues in the interaction context and empathizing with the other person, without having the other directly transmit a message using the verbal code. They identify their second factor, self-restraint, as the key value in Japanese communication, in which the "avoidance" of confrontation is often preferred over direct communication of negative feelings or conflict-raising issues. The third factor, interpersonal sensitivity, involves the encoding and decoding of sensitive messages. According to Takai and Ota, being direct and frank toward another person can sometimes be embarrassing to the hearer. Hence, among Japanese, a speaker must be sensitive enough to get his or her message across using hints.

In the West, the Chomskyan notion of communicative competence consists mainly of the grammatical knowledge that is displayed in most communicative processes, whereas for Japanese, communicative competence means "the ability to send and receive subtle, unstated messages" (Lebra, 1991, p. 14). Assuming that these culture-level generalizations are generally consistent with the individual's self-concept, views of verbal communicativeness among people of high interdependent self-construals may possibly be different from those of people high in independent self-construals. Recently, Kim et al. (1996) found that culture-level individualism influences independent self-construals, which in turn correlate positively with two outcome-oriented conversational constraints ("clarity" and "effectiveness"). They also found that culture-level collectivism affects interdependent self-construals, which correlate positively with three relational constraints ("concern for not imposing," "avoiding hurting the hearer's feelings," and "avoiding negative evaluation"). In their study of four different cultural groups (in Japan, Korea, Australia, and the United States), Gudykunst et al. (1996) found that independent self-construals negatively predicted use of indirect messages and interdependent self-construals positively predicted sensitivity. However, the findings regarding interdependent self-construals and negative attitudes toward silence did not fit the expected pattern. Gudykunst et al. believe that the reason for this is that the factor focuses on positive attitude toward silence, not on how much silence is used. Overall, prior research seems to confirm that those who emphasize interdependent self-construals desire to be accepted by group members and to avoid losing face. Consequently, the social interaction among those who emphasize interdependent self-construal requires individuals to read others' minds, which contributes to the tendency for low verbal output.

Among individuals with high independent self-construals, "elaborated talk" (Hall, 1976) is necessary to establish identity—to make oneself "stand out in the crowd." Thus it should be expected that the highly verbal person will be perceived in a positive light because he or she is more successful at establishing "identity" (Elliot, Scott, Jensen, & McDonough, 1982). Independents should be motivated to seek out, exert greater effort in, and derive greater satisfaction from situations allowing personal control. Thus oral communication skills are highly valued, and people are far more likely to be attracted to individuals blessed with the "gift of gab" than to those who are less inclined to speak their minds (Elliot et al., 1982). In contrast, in Eastern cultures the low verbal person should be perceived more positively because he or she is successful at maintaining the social order without saying more than needs to be said.

In a similar vein, Tannen (1985) discusses cultural variability in evaluating talkativeness and silence. Silence (an outcome of low verbal communication motivation) is the extreme manifestation of indirectness (Tannen, 1985). Silence helps the individual to control his or her emotions, and may at times also allow the passive expression of discontent without the dangers of a direct challenge (Saunders, 1985). Specifically, silence among interdependents can be seen as negative politeness—that is, not imposing on others. One may speculate that silence among interdependents often comes from being understood without putting one's meaning on record. Thus understanding may result from empathy, rather than from putting meaning into words. Independents, in contrast, may perceive silence as the failure of positive politeness (i.e., the need to be involved with others). Recently, Kim, Shin, and Cai (1998), in a study using participants from Korea, Hawaii, and the mainland United States, found that the higher a person's independent cultural orientations, the less likely he or she is to remain silent in both first- and second-attempt requests. Thus I predict that individuals with highly independent self-construals will value talk more than will those with highly interdependent self-construals.

To summarize, it is likely that high interdependents tend to discourage aggressive communication, regardless of its locus of attack ("position" or "self-concept" of the other person), because it is regarded as negative and disruptive behavior. Accordingly, people of high interdependent self-construals may want to "avoid" "aggressive" forms of communication and may feel anxious if they have to be "aggressive" in communication situations. Among people of high interdependent self-construals, taking the opposite side of an argument (argumentativeness) necessarily means becoming a personal rival and antagonist of the one who holds the other side (Becker, 1986). Thus argumentativeness may be seen negatively among high interdependents. Concern regarding others' feelings and regarding negative evaluation by others seems to be at the heart of such interdependent (collectivist) characteristics as need for approval. As concern for the reactions of others increases, so may the importance of "avoidance" motivation, especially in problem situations such as conflicts.

This discussion of culture-level individualism and collectivism, self-construals, and beliefs about verbal communicativeness suggests the existence of processes underlying predispositions to verbal communication. These processes are summarized in Figure 2.1, which illustrates the interrelationships among the constructs. Specifically, I propose an integrated cultural model of verbal communication motivation that includes the influence of culture-level individualism and collectivism, self-construals, and beliefs about verbal communicativeness on verbal communication motivation. According to this model, individualism and collectivism have an indirect effect on verbal communication motivation that is mediated through self-construals and beliefs about arguing. That is, culture-level individualism and collectivism affect self-construals, which in turn become causal antecedents to beliefs about verbal communicativeness. Specifically, I expect that independent self-construals tend to predominate in individualist cultures and interdependent self-construals tend to predominate in collectivist cultures. Then, regarding the mediation process, I expect that the greater the individual's construal of self as independent, the more positive his or her beliefs regarding verbal communicativeness, which in turn leads to the higher degree of motivation to communicate verbally. The model also suggests that the greater the individual's construal of self as interdependent, the more negative his or her beliefs regarding verbal communicativeness, which in turn leads to the higher degree of communication "avoidance." As I have noted throughout this chapter, an "avoidance" motivation toward verbal communication should not be interpreted solely from an individualist perspective. The use of *enryo* (as a form of "avoidant" communication motivation) in Japan, for example, is not viewed merely as unwillingness to communication or "avoiding" communication. Enryo may be perceived as an "active" process in Japan, although it is viewed as "avoidance" from a Western perspective (Gudykunst & Nishida, 1993).

In developing this model, I have relied in part on Rancer et al.'s (1992) conceptualization of beliefs about arguing. However, this model departs from the previous conceptualization in an important way. For instance, Rancer et al. (1992) claim that individuals with high motivation to argue appear to "feel better" about themselves; they have high communicative competence, high credibility, high perceived leadership, and the ability to see things from the other person's perspective. My model, on the other hand, recognizes that culture and self-construals may significantly influence whether or not arguing is considered desirable.

In-Group Versus Out-Group Interactant Distinction

According to conventional findings concerning individualism and collectivism, one might assume that independent selves would always be "assertive" and interdependent selves would always be "avoidant" in communication behavior. This, however, is an overly simplistic conclusion. Although it may be true that independent selves prefer "approaching" styles, interdependent selves can also be "assertive" and even controlling under certain circumstances. The situational variable that I examine below for its impact on communication motivation is the in-group versus out-group distinction.

Triandis (1988) argues that members of collectivist cultures draw a sharper distinction between in-group and out-group than do members of individualist cultures. Gudykunst and his colleagues have conducted a systematic line of research on in-group and out-group communication. Gudykunst, Yoon, and Nishida's (1987) findings indicate that the greater the degree of collectivism present in a culture, the greater the differences in in-group (i.e., classmate)

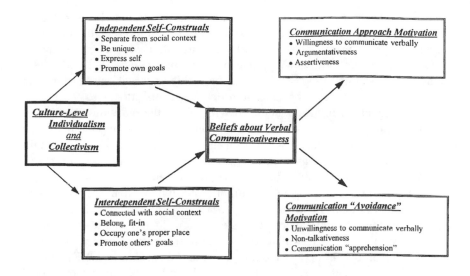

Figure 2.1. Cultural Framework of Approach Versus "Avoidance" of Verbal Communication

and out-group (i.e., stranger) communication in terms of amount of personalization (e.g., intimacy of communication), synchronization (e.g., coordination of communication), and difficulty in communication. Focusing on uncertainty reduction, Gudykunst, Nishida, and Schmidt (1989) found that there are differences in uncertainty-reduction processes between members of ingroups and members of out-groups in collectivist cultures, but not in individualist cultures.

The findings outlined above are consistent with the general descriptions regarding self-construals. Markus and Kitayama (1991) propose that independent and interdependent selves differ in their cognitions, emotions, and motivations as a consequence of their differing beliefs regarding the self in relation to others. One such difference is the degree to which the two distinguish between in-group and out-group members. Interdependent self-construal is based on specific, significant interpersonal relationships. This view of self is able to modulate according to changes in the social context, which in turn may lead to differences in behavior when dealing with people who are part of the individual's network of relationships and with those who are not. On the other hand, the independent self emphasizes remaining "true to oneself" (i.e., maintaining constant attitude and behavior) regardless of changes in the social context. Therefore, it is expected that verbal communication motivation according to the group membership of the conflict interactant will vary more with interdependent self-construals than with independent self-construals.

Furthermore, many individualism/collectivism researchers hold that allo-
centrics (i.e., individuals of collectivist cultures) seem to be highly cooperative with in-group members but generally distrustful, uncooperative, manipulative, and even exploitative with out-group members (Leung & Bond, 1984;
Triandis & Vassiliou, 1972). Consistent with this observation, Markus and
Kitayama (1991) contend that the interdependent self attends to the needs,
desires, and goals of in-group members with whom the individual has reciprocal and equitable relationships. On the other hand, out-group members are
not treated with any special regard; Markus and Kitayama (1991) maintain
that out-group members "are treated quite differently [from in-group mem-
bers] and are unlikely to experience either the advantages or disadvantages
of interdependence" (p. 229). On the other hand, independent selves' behavior is much less contingent on that of others. Although independents are
selective in their associations with others, they do not make as severe a
distinction in the degree to which they attend to the needs, goals, and desires
of in-group members as opposed to out-group members (Markus & Kitayama,
1991). Thus, whereas interdependents would tend to be more "assertive"
toward out-group members as opposed to in-group members (due to in-group
bias), independents would probably behave more uniformly, irrespective of
in-group or out-group.

PRACTICAL IMPLICATIONS

Many intercultural misunderstandings seem to stem from differing perceptions regarding verbal communication motivation. As this review indicates,
people from different cultural backgrounds may react in totally different ways
to varying degrees of verbal behavior. Thus intercultural communication is
fraught with the potential for misattribution and miscommunication. This is
especially so when those involved are unaware of differences about preferred
levels of verbal loquacity. Numerous studies have linked high communication
apprehension and a low level of argumentativeness/assertiveness to a wide
variety of social, organizational, academic, and communicative problems.
People with "avoidant" communication tendencies have been known to be
less likely to desire advancement in organizations (McCroskey & Richmond,
1979), to score lower than average on academic tests (McCroskey, Andersen,
Richmond, & Wheeless, 1981), to avoid or fail to participate meaningfully in
classroom communication with teachers and peers, and to need clinical
attention (Comadena & Prusank, 1988). The association of these constructs
with communication "avoidance" misrepresents the sources of communication "avoidance" solely as deficiencies or inadequacies.
    Different degrees of communication approach and "avoidance" may be
generated by differing concepts of self, which in part stem from individuals'
different cultural backgrounds. Increased knowledge about the preferred

levels of verbal communication can help individuals to avoid misinterpreting the communication behaviors of people from other cultures. The idea that verbal communication motivation may function differently across cultures suggests a useful framework for explaining intercultural misunderstanding. The prevailing culture determines what level of verbal communication will be seen as normal, who will be required to adapt to whose level of verbal communicativeness, and whose verbal style will be seen as deviant, irrational, or inferior. The implications of these relationships for cross-cultural communication are far-reaching. The interdependent individual, who is less verbal, interacting within the independent social group is potentially at a disadvantage socially, perceived as less attractive than other potential communication partners. Independent individuals operating within interdependent social groups may encounter a similar reversal regarding the perception of their verbal behavior. In the remainder of this section, I discuss some practical implications of the findings reported above for three important types of interaction: counseling, education, and organizational behavior.

Implications for Counseling

Assertive interpersonal skills are a basic necessity for effective functioning in many aspects of life in the United States. The "nonassertive" pattern common among ethnic minorities has been judged by some to be psychologically dysfunctional and has become a target for intervention. Because the lack of these skills can be a source of much unhappiness, it is not surprising that assertiveness training is one of the most frequently prescribed therapeutic interventions (Masters, Burish, Hollon, & Rimm, 1987). Members of many ethnic minority groups have values about assertive responding that differ markedly from those of the dominant culture.

Systematic desensitization is the primary technique that has been used to help people cope with the unpleasant feelings associated with public speaking anxiety (McCroskey, 1972). Cognitive-based interventions are designed to change the way the individual thinks about giving a speech (Ayres & Hopf, 1993). A considerable amount of time has been spent trying to prove that one intervention is superior to another in reducing communication apprehension (Allen et al., 1989). Only rarely have researchers pointed out that the therapist must be sensitive to cultural differences in values regarding assertiveness and must try to understand the client's frame of reference. Cultural sensitivity is crucial not only to the success of the intervention but also to the development of rapport between client and counselor. For example, misunderstandings arising from cultural variations in values or communication patterns may lead to a client's having difficulty in developing trust and rapport with a therapist (Sue, 1981). In fact, the very idea of teaching assertiveness skills is based on an individualist value orientation; it is a value-laden process. The dominant culture and the culture of psychology have deemed certain assertive behaviors to be appropriate. This valuing of assertive behaviors may lead therapists to adopt a "let's fix the minority" approach that blinds them to other possible alternatives—including the alternative in which the client rejects the values of the dominant culture (Wood & Mallinckrodt, 1990).

Sue et al. (1983) propose the concept of "situational assertiveness" to explain the assertive behavior of Asian Americans. They point out that "Asian Americans may be assertive in some situations (with friends, in informal settings, or with members of their own race) and deferential in others (with authority figures, in classroom settings, or in counseling situations)" (pp. 581-582). They suggest that assessment should involve helping the client to determine which situations require culturally appropriate deference and which require assertiveness. For instance, Sue et al. found that Chinese American men were as behaviorally assertive as white American men in many situations. However, Chinese American men experienced more difficulty in a situation that involved an authority figure (a professor) than did white men, which suggests a situation-specific response pattern. It is clear that counselors should avoid attributing interdependent individuals' lack of assertiveness to a stable trait such as shyness.

In helping people to make choices in their communication styles, therapists must avoid implying that there is one best way to behave. Rather, there are more or less effective ways of behaving in different situations. It must be clear to clients that the goal of training is not to persuade them to reject their cultural values; rather, it is to help them to develop an understanding of assertive behavior in various cultural contexts, to recognize cues that discriminate these different situations, and to build an increased repertoire for responding effectively in each of these contexts (Ponterotto, Casas, Suzuki, & Alexander, 1995). The therapist's task is to help clients acquire a repertoire of culturally appropriate skills in order to give them the power of choice. The therapist's openness to the clients' experience and genuine respect for the choices that they make is the most fundamental element of cultural sensitivity (Wood & Mallinckrodt, 1990).

Implications for Education

Training students to argue effectively and constructively has been a central part of the Western communication discipline for more than 2,000 years (Infante & Rancer, 1996). The rather massive and unequivocal finding that argumentativeness is constructive upholds this tradition. Verbal communication has been considered extremely important in the achievement of educational goals. The school in the individualist society is an oral environment in which the principal means of transmitting knowledge is speech. The more a person talks, unless the talk is overly negative or morally reprehensible, the more positively the person is perceived. In U.S. classrooms, the individual is expected to be an active participant in class discussion, and speech is essential

(Klopf et al., 1995). Infante (1982) found that students with high argumentativeness trait reported higher grade point averages.

Instructional approaches offer short-term relief from the "debilitating" effects of communication apprehension and "avoidance," whereas therapeutic approaches offer long-term "cures" for the problem. As the review presented in this chapter shows, one of the most significant influences on the development of communication motivation seems to be cultural orientation. Many researchers who have studied verbal communication motivation end their reports of their work with the following pedagogical recommendations: Students should be encouraged to recognize the favorable, demonstrable pragmatic outcomes associated with motivation to argue and argumentative ability. One specific goal would be to stimulate individuals low in argumentativeness to enhance their motivation to argue and to develop their argumentative skills. A more culturally sensitive approach may include sensitizing educators to the problems associated with grading on participation, providing alternatives to some oral assignments, and removing the stereotype that quietness signifies ignorance or disinterest (McCroskey & Richmond, 1987). Continued research in this area will enhance our understanding of the classroom consequences of low levels of verbal communicativeness among students and will help to develop specific instructional practices that teachers may use to create learning environments that are sensitive to cultural influences.

Implications for Organizational Behavior

In any kind of employment in the U.S. context, an employee's speaking capability is the key to success, promotion, and higher pay (Klopf et al., 1995). Many jobs rely on the individual's ability to speak well—sales and managerial positions, teaching, and service occupations, among others (Pitt & Ramaseshan, 1990). For the highly apprehensive businessperson, negative economic and social consequences can be expected. According to Richmond and McCroskey (1992), high apprehensives, compared with low apprehensives, are perceived by employers as less task attractive and less socially adept. They are thought to be less satisfied in their jobs and have poorer relationships with their fellow employees and supervisors. They are less likely to advance to higher-paying positions. Socially, the highly apprehensive interact less with peers and strangers. They often are considered maladaptive even though they may be psychologically normal in other aspects of their behavior. Richmond and Roach (1992), for example, found that employers who read written descriptions of two prospective employees that differed only in the amount the person talked preferred the description of the talkative individual to the description of the reticent individual. This supports the contention that verbal ability is much valued in mainstream U.S. society.

Worldwide, business organizations have discovered that intercultural communication is a subject of importance, not just because they have to deal increasingly with foreigners, but because the workforce of the future within their own national borders is growing more and more diverse, ethnically and culturally (Limaye & Victor, 1991). Traditionally, American writers have defined miscommunication in organizations as failure to be understood, authentic, honest, and disclosive and failure to establish an open and clear dialogue. Recently, however, some writers have pointed out that the "ideology of openness" might be a cultural assumption, possibly a Western ideology (Eisenberg, 1984; Eisenberg & Phillips, 1991; Pascale & Athos, 1981).

Eisenberg (1984; Eisenberg & Witten, 1987) claims that one of the major reasons organizational participants and theorists uncritically endorse open communication is an implicit belief in the sharing metaphor. "The sharing metaphor implies that effective communication requires the cultivation of shared cognitions and emotions between interactants" (Eisenberg & Phillips, 1991, p. 252). The tendency toward "openness" models of communication is uniquely associated with the mainland United States and reflects a desire to resolve differences rather than learn to live with them (Eisenberg & Phillips, 1991). Many managers place excessive trust in increasing the amount of "open" communication between people (Pascale & Athos, 1981). This philosophy, however, may not lead to productive communication among the predominantly interdependent workforce. On the other hand, within independent cultural organizations, ambiguous or implicit ("unspoken") business messages may not be rewarded. In the end, any acceptable definition of effective communication must take into account the social context, the worldviews and values of the participants, and the point in time (Eisenberg & Phillips, 1991; Kim & Sharkey, 1995).

The "theory of independent-mindedness" (Infante & Gordon, 1987, 1991) recognizes the importance of culture in organizational communication (albeit, in this case, American culture). The theory suggests that independent-mindedness is a norm valued in the mainstream U.S. society, and that micro-structures (i.e., organizations) of this culture should encourage rather than frustrate its expression. Gordon and Infante (1987) claim that organizations in the United States have missed the opportunity to function as a major source of value satisfaction for employees. Independent-mindedness is nurtured in organizations that allow for healthy debate and discourage verbal aggression, especially in superior-subordinate communication (Infante & Gordon, 1987, 1991). It is important, therefore, to determine the type of organizational communication climate that permits value satisfaction for employees.

The consequences of failing to understand each other's sociolinguistic systems may well result in communication breakdown, failure to achieve organizational goals, social isolation, negative sanctions, loss of self-esteem, negative effects on work performance, and/or loss of jobs (Fine, 1991). Understanding people's attitudes toward verbal communication will help individuals to appreciate the complexity of communication in multicultural business organizations. The pace and intensity of change in today's business organizations are unprecedented, making tremendous demands on the individual's ability to adjust. To enhance productivity, employers must incorporate new strategies to work with employees from different cultures and backgrounds who emphasize varying levels of verbal communication motivation. People from different cultural backgrounds bring different meanings, value assumptions, and discourse styles into the workplace conversation.

CONCLUSIONS

Few things are more basic to an individual's communication style than how much he or she talks. A simple description of an unknown person as "quiet" or "talkative" will evoke many different images in different people's minds. Research that has employed such descriptions has found dramatically different perceptions of the persons described. A substantial body of cross-cultural research exists in the area of verbal communication predisposition. Studies indicate that significant differences exist both cross-culturally and intraculturally in regard to communication approach and "avoidance." However, the role communication motivation plays in intercultural communication is virtually unknown. The challenge of understanding communicative behaviors across cultures should include questions concerning individuals' predispositions toward talking and the reactions of others to the manifestations of such predispositions. Because predispositional communication motivation is a relational phenomenon, and those susceptible to anxiety may be more relationally aware and connected, further studies should focus on relational orientations and their effects on communication anxiety and "avoidance." Further, I believe that those with a predominantly interdependent self will be particularly susceptible to what may be termed "other-face communication anxiety." An identity that encompasses the other will be more likely to share in the feelings of others' face concern.

The field of communication is still dominated by a Euro-American perspective and somewhat oblivious to its ethnocentrism. It has consistently been presumed that high communication "avoidance" is a pathology that visits disagreeable consequences on people unfortunate enough to be so afflicted. Recently, the construct of compulsive communication and a measure of this orientation, the Talkaholic Scale, were introduced into the literature (McCroskey & Richmond, 1995). In a recent article, McCroskey and Richmond (1995) refer to extremely low CAs as "talkaholics" and indicate that this propensity for communication may cause problems for these individuals. Just as a certain degree of communication approach tendency is essential for competent interpersonal communication in some situations, too much approach tendency or an aggressive styles could be a problem. Future research should focus more on the potential negative consequences of "talkaholism." A major thrust of research in the future should be in the areas of the causes of excessive communication approach and "avoidance" and the development of treatments from a cultural perspective.

The development of human communication theory in the United States has been based, in large part, on individualist orientations and empirical research involving subjects representing the mainstream U.S. culture. The low external validity of such research and theory has been recognized by many researchers, but the proposed solution to the problem frequently has consisted only of recommendations to examine other samples of the population to test generalizability. This area of research needs to move toward the construction of a truly universal theory of communication motivation through the empirical and theoretical understanding of cultural diversity. We need to recognize that the central components of communication motivation are cultural value orientations. I have criticized this line of research on conceptual grounds for its ethnocentric biases, noting that in some situations and cultural contexts an "avoidant" style can have adaptive consequences.

With new communication technologies, personal intercultural contact is now a daily fact of life for literally millions of people. The forecast of the "global village" is contemporary reality. We are rapidly learning that not all "villagers" are alike, however. Understanding the cultural underpinnings of communication motivation will foster maximum effectiveness in pluralist societies. With the increasing commonness of intercultural encounters, the likelihood of negative impacts from ethnocentric tendencies in research/ theorizing has also grown tremendously. This review provides a theoretical basis for replacing a single, monocultural view of communication motivation with a multiperspective, multicultural view. Communication scholars need to be aware of different cultural perspectives so that they do not attempt to generalize too broadly from their own cultural orientations.

NOTE

1. People in the United States usually interpret "avoiding communication" as something negative. In an attempt to indicate that the term *communication avoidance* should not simply be taken at face value and interpreted negatively, I put it within quotes whenever appropriate.

REFERENCES

Alberti, R. E., & Emmons, M. L. (1970). *Your perfect right: A guide to assertive behavior.* San Luis Obispo, CA: Impact.

Allen, M., & Bourhis, J. (1996). The relationship of communication apprehension to communication behavior: A meta-analysis. *Communication Quarterly, 44,* 214-226.

Allen, M., Hunter, J. E., & Donohue, W. (1989). Meta-analysis of self-report data on the effectiveness of public speaking anxiety treatment techniques. *Communication Education, 38,* 54-76.

Ayres, J., & Hopf, T. (1993). *Coping with speech anxiety.* Norwood, NJ: Ablex.

Barnlund, D. (1989). *Communication styles of Japanese and Americans.* Belmont, CA: Wadsworth.

Barraclough, R. A., Christophel, D. M., & McCroskey, J. C. (1988). Willingness to communicate: A cross-cultural investigation. *Communication Research Reports, 5,* 187-192.

Becker, C. (1986). Reasons for the lack of argumentation and goodness-of-fit in the analysis of covariance structures. *Psychological Bulletin, 10,* 93-98.

Bochner, S. (1994). Cross-cultural differences in the self concept: A test of Hofstede's individualism/collectivism distinction. *Journal of Cross-Cultural Psychology, 25,* 273-283.

Bond, M. H., & Cheung, T. S. (1983). College students' spontaneous self-concept: The effect of culture among respondents in Hong Kong, Japan, and the United States. *Journal of Cross-Cultural Psychology, 14,* 153-171.

Bond, M. H., & Forgas, J. P. (1984). Linking person perception to behavior intention across cultures: The role of cultural collectivism. *Journal of Cross-Cultural Psychology, 15,* 337-352.

Buhr, T. A., Pryor, B., & Sullivan, M. (1991). A further examination of communication apprehension and information processing. *Cognitive Therapy and Research, 15,* 303-317.

Burgoon, J. K. (1976). The unwillingness-to-communicate scale: Development and validation. *Communication Monographs, 43,* 60-69.

Burroughs, N. F., & Marie, V. (1990). Communication orientations of Micronesian and American students. *Communication Research Reports, 7,* 139-146.

Buss, A. H. (1980). *Self-consciousness and social anxiety.* San Francisco: Freeman.

Carmona, A. E., & Lorr, M. (1992). Dimensions of assertiveness: A cross-cultural comparison of Chilean and U.S. subjects. *Personality and Individual Differences, 13,* 45-48.

Chang, H. C., & Holt, G. R. (1991). The concept of *yuan* and Chinese interpersonal relationships. In S. Ting-Toomey & F. Korzenny (Eds.), *Cross-cultural interpersonal communication* (pp. 28-57). Newbury Park, CA: Sage.

Chesebro, J. W., McCroskey, J. C., Atwater, D. F., Bahrenfuss, R. M., Cawelti, G., Gaudino, J. L., & Hodges, H. (1992). Communication apprehension and self-perceived communication competence of at-risk students. *Communication Education, 41,* 345-360.

Christophel, D. M. (1996). Russian communication orientations: A cross-cultural examination. *Communication Research Reports, 13,* 43-51.

Comadena, M. E., & Prusank, D. T. (1988). Communication apprehension and academic achievement among elementary and middle school students. *Communication Education, 37,* 270-277.

Cook, D. J., & St. Lawrence, J. S. (1990). Variations in presentation format: Effect on interpersonal evaluations of assertive and unassertive behavior. *Behavior Modification, 14,* 21-36.

Cousins, S. D. (1989). Culture and self-perception in Japan and the United States. *Journal of Personality and Social Psychology, 56,* 124-131.

Daly, J. A., & Stafford, L. (1984). Correlates and consequences of social-communicative anxiety. In J. A. Daly & J. C. McCroskey (Eds.), *Avoiding communication: Shyness, reticence, and communication apprehension* (pp. 125-143). Beverly Hills, CA: Sage.

Daly, J. A., Vangelisti, A. L., Neel, H. L., & Cavanaugh, P. D. (1989). Pre-performance concerns associated with public speaking anxiety. *Communication Quarterly, 37,* 39-53.

Doi, L. T. (1973). The Japanese pattern of communication and the concept of *amae. Journal of Speech, 53,* 180-185.

Dowling, R. E., & Flint, L. J. (1990). The argumentativeness scale: Problems and promise. *Communication Studies, 41,* 183-198.

Eisenberg, E. M. (1984). Ambiguity as strategy in organizational communication. *Communication Monographs, 51,* 1713-1722.

Eisenberg, E. M., & Phillips, S. R. (1991). Miscommunication in organizations. In N. Coupland, H. Giles, & J. M. Wiemann (Eds.), *"Miscommunication" and problematic talk* (pp. 244-258). Newbury Park, CA: Sage.

Eisenberg, E. M., & Witten, M. G. (1987). Reconsidering openness in organizational communication. *Academy of Management Review, 12,* 418-426.

Elliot, S., Scott, M. D., Jensen, A. D., & McDonough, M. (1982). Perceptions of reticence: A cross-cultural investigation. In M. Burgoon (Ed.), *Communication yearbook 5* (pp. 591-602). New Brunswick, NJ: Transaction.

Fine, M. G. (1991). New voices in the workplace: Research directions in multicultural communication. *Journal of Business Communication, 28,* 259-275.

Fishbein, M., & Ajzen, I. (1975). *Belief, attitude, intention, and behavior: An introduction to theory and research.* Reading, MA: Addison-Wesley.

Fukuyama, M. A., & Greenfield, T. K. (1983). Dimensions of assertiveness in an Asian-American student population. *Journal of Counseling Psychology, 30,* 429-432.

Gaines, S. O., Jr., Marelich, W. D., Bledsoe, K. L., Steers, W. N., Henderson, M. C., Granrose, C. S., Barajas, L., Hicks, D., Lyde, M., Takahashi, Y., Yum, N., Rios, D. I., Garcia, B. F., Farris, K. R., & Page, M. S. (1997). Links between race/ethnicity and cultural values as mediated by racial/ethnic identity and moderated by gender. *Journal of Personality and Social Psychology, 72,* 1460-1476.

Giles, H., Coupland, N., & Wiemann, J. M. (1992). "Talk is cheap" . . . but "my word is my bond": Beliefs about talk. In K. Bolton & H. Kwok (Eds.), *Sociolinguistics today: Eastern and Western perspectives* (pp. 218-243). London: Routledge.

Gilligan, C. (1982). *In a different voice: Psychological theory and women's development.* Cambridge, MA: Harvard University Press.

Goldberg, C. J., & Botvin, G. J. (1993). Assertiveness in Hispanic adolescents: Relationship to alcohol use and abuse. *Psychological Reports, 73,* 227-238.

Gordon, W. I., & Infante, D. A. (1987). Employee rights: Content, argumentativeness, verbal aggressiveness and career satisfaction. In C. A. B. Osigweh (Ed.), *Communicating employee responsibilities and rights: A modern management mandate* (pp. 149-163). New York: Quorum.

Greenfield, P. M. (1994). Independence and interdependence as developmental scripts: Implications for theory, research, and practice. In P. M. Greenfield & R. R. Cocking (Eds.), *Cross-cultural roots of minority child development* (pp. 1-37). Hillsdale, NJ: Lawrence Erlbaum.

Gudykunst, W. B., Guzley, R. M., & Ota, H. (1993). Issues for future research on communication in Japan and the United States. In W. B. Gudykunst (Ed.), *Communication in Japan and the United States* (pp. 291-322). Albany: State University of New York Press.

Gudykunst, W. B., Matsumoto, Y., Ting-Toomey, S., Nishida, T., Kim, K., & Heyman, S. (1996). The influence of cultural individualism-collectivism, self-construals, and individual values on communication styles across cultures. *Human Communication Research, 22,* 510-543.

Gudykunst, W. B., & Nishida, T. (1984). Individual and cultural influences on uncertainty reduction. *Communication Monographs, 51,* 23-36.

Gudykunst, W. B., & Nishida, T. (1993). Interpersonal and intergroup communication in Japan and the United States. In W. B. Gudykunst (Ed.), *Communication in Japan and the United States* (pp. 149-214). Albany: State University of New York Press.

Gudykunst, W. B., Nishida, T., & Schmidt, K. L. (1989). Cultural, relational, and personal influences on uncertainty reduction processes. *Western Speech Communication Journal, 53,* 13-29.

Gudykunst, W. B., & Ting-Toomey, S. (1988). *Culture and interpersonal communication.* Newbury Park, CA: Sage.

Gudykunst, W. B., Yoon, Y. C., & Nishida, T. (1987). The influence of individualism-collectivism on perceptions of communication in ingroup and outgroup relationships. *Communication Monographs, 54,* 295-306.

Hackman, M. Z., & Barthel-Hackman, T. A. (1993). Communication apprehension, willingness to communicate, and sense of humor: United States and New Zealand perspectives. *Communication Quarterly, 41,* 282-291.

Hall, E. T. (1976). *Beyond culture.* Garden City, NY: Doubleday.

Hamid, P. N. (1994). Assertiveness and personality dimensions in Chinese students. *Psychological Reports, 75,* 127-130.

Harris, P. R., & Moran, R. T. (1979). *Managing cultural differences.* Houston, TX: Gulf.

Henderson, M., & Furnham, A. (1982). Self-reported and self-attributed scores on personality, social skills, and attitudinal measures as compared between high nominated friends and acquaintances. *Psychological Reports, 50,* 88-90.

Hirokawa, R., & Miyahara, A. (1986). A comparison of influence strategies utilized by managers in American and Japanese organizations. *Communication Quarterly, 34,* 250-265.

Hofstede, G. (1980). *Culture's consequences: International differences in work-related values.* Beverly Hills, CA: Sage.

Hui, C. H., & Triandis, H. C. (1986). Individualism-collectivism: A study of cross-cultural researchers. *Journal of Cross-Cultural Psychology, 17,* 225-248.

Hutchinson, K. L., Neuliep, J. W., & More, E. (1995). Communication apprehension across cultures: A test of the PRCA-24 and comparisons between Australia and the United States. *Australian Journal of Communication, 22,* 59-69.

Infante, D. A. (1982). The argumentative student in the speech communication classroom: An investigation and implications. *Communication Education, 31,* 141-148.

Infante, D. A. (1985). Response to high argumentativeness: Message and sex differences. *Southern Communication Journal, 54,* 159-170.

Infante, D. A., Chandler, T. A., & Rudd, J. E. (1989). Test of an argumentative skill deficiency model of interspousal violence. *Communication Monographs, 56,* 163-177.

Infante, D. A., & Gordon, W. I. (1985). Superiors' argumentativeness and verbal aggressiveness as predictors of subordinates' satisfaction. *Human Communication Research, 12,* 117-125.

Infante, D. A., & Gordon, W. I. (1987). Superior and subordinate communication profiles: Implications for independent-mindedness and upward effectiveness. *Central State Speech Journal, 38,* 73-80.

Infante, D. A., & Gordon, W. I. (1991). How employees see the boss: Test of an argumentativeness and affirming model of supervisors' communication behavior. *Western Journal of Speech Communication, 55,* 294-304.

Infante, D. A., & Rancer, A. S. (1982). A conceptualization and measure of argumentativeness. *Journal of Personality Assessment, 46,* 72-80.

Infante, D. A., & Rancer, A. S. (1996). Argumentativeness and verbal aggressiveness: A review of recent theory and research. In B. R. Burleson (Ed.), *Communication yearbook 19* (pp. 318-351). Thousand Oaks, CA: Sage.

Infante, D. A., Trebing, J. D., Shepherd, P. E., & Seeds, D. E. (1984). The relationship of argumentativeness to verbal aggression. *Southern Speech Communication Journal, 50,* 67-77.

Inkeles, A., & Smith, D. H. (1974). *Becoming modern: Individual change in six developing countries.* Cambridge, MA: Harvard University Press.

Ishii, S. (1982). Thought patterns as modes of rhetoric: The United States and Japan. *Communication, 11,* 81-86.

Jenkins, G., Klopf, D., & Park, M. S. (1991, July). *Argumentativeness in Korean and American college students: A comparison.* Paper presented at the annual meeting of the World Communication Association, Jyvaskyla, Finland.

Johnson, F. (1985). The Western concept of self. In A. Marsella, G. De Vos, & F. L. K. Hsu (Eds.), *Culture and self* (pp. 91-138). London: Tavistock.

Johnson, F. A., & Marsella, A. J. (1978). Differential attitudes toward verbal behavior in students of Japanese and European ancestry. *Genetic Psychology Monographs, 97,* 43-76.

Kâgitçibasi, Ç. (1987). Individual and group loyalties: Are they possible? In Ç. Kâgitçibasi (Ed.), *Growth and progress in cross-cultural psychology* (pp. 94-103). Lisse, Netherlands: Swets & Zeitlinger.

Kashima, Y., Yamaguchi, S., Kim, U., Choi, S. C., Gelfand, M. J., & Yuki, M. (1995). Culture, gender, and self: A perspective from individualism-collectivism research. *Journal of Personality and Social Psychology, 69,* 925-937.

Katriel, T., & Philipsen, G. (1981). "What we need is communication": "Communication" as a cultural category in some American speech. *Communication Monographs, 48,* 301-317.

Kelly, L. (1982). A rose by any other name is still a rose: A comparative analysis of reticence, communication apprehension, unwillingness to communicate, and shyness. *Human Communication Research, 8,* 99-113.

Kim, M.-S. (1994). Cross-cultural comparisons of the perceived importance of conversational constraints. *Human Communication Research, 21,* 128-151.

Kim, M.-S. (1995). Toward a theory of conversational constraints: Focusing on individual-level dimensions of culture. In R. L. Wiseman (Ed.), *Intercultural communication theory* (pp. 148-169). Thousand Oaks, CA: Sage.

Kim, M.-S., & Hunter, J. E. (1993a). Attitude-behavior relations: A meta-analysis of past research—focusing on attitudinal relevance and topic. *Journal of Communication, 43*(1), 101-142.

Kim, M.-S., & Hunter, J. E. (1993b). Relationships among attitudes, behavioral intentions, and behavior: A meta-analysis of past research, part 2. *Communication Research, 20,* 331-364.

Kim, M.-S., Hunter, J. E., Miyahara, A., Horvath, A., Bresnahan, M., & Yoon, H. J. (1996). Individual- vs. culture-level dimensions of individualism and collectivism: Effects on preferred conversational styles. *Communication Monographs, 63,* 29-49.

Kim, M.-S., & Sharkey, W. F. (1995). Independent and interdependent construals of self: Explaining cultural patterns of interpersonal communication in multi-cultural organizational settings. *Communication Quarterly, 43,* 20-38.

Kim, M.-S., Sharkey, W. F., & Singelis, T. M. (1994). The relationship between individual's self-construals and perceived importance of interactive constraints. *International Journal of Intercultural Relations, 18,* 117-140.

Kim, M.-S., Shin, H.-C., & Cai, D. (1998). The influence of cultural orientations on the preferred forms of requesting and rerequesting. *Communication Monographs, 65,* 47-66.

Kim, M.-S., & Wilson, S. R. (1994). A cross-cultural comparison of implicit theories of requesting. *Communication Monographs, 61,* 210-235.

Kitayama, S., Markus, H. R., Matsumoto, H., & Norasakkunkit, V. (1997). Individual and collective processes in the construction of the self: Self-enhancement in the United States and self-criticism in Japan. *Journal of Personality and Social Psychology, 72,* 1245-1267.

Klopf, D. W. (1984). Cross-cultural apprehension research: A summary of Pacific Basin studies. In J. A. Daly & J. C. McCroskey (Eds.), *Avoiding communication: Shyness, reticence, and communication apprehension* (pp. 157-169). Beverly Hills, CA: Sage.

Klopf, D. W., Cambra, R. E., & Ishii, S. (1981). A comparison of the communication styles of Japanese and American college students. *Current English Studies, 20,* 66-71.

Klopf, D. W., & Ishii, S. (1976). A comparison of the communication activities of Japanese and American adults. *ELEC Bulletin, 53,* 22-26.

Klopf, D. W., Ishii, S., & Cambra, R. E. (1976). Patterns of oral communication among the Japanese. *Cross-Currents, 5,* 37-49.

Klopf, D. W., Ishii, S., & Cambra, R. E. (1995). *Japanese communication behavior: Recent research findings.* Tokyo: Pacific and Asian Press.

Leary, M. R. (1983). Social anxiousness: The construct and its measurement. *Journal of Personality Assessment, 47,* 66-75.

Lebra, T. S. (1991, March). *Cultural factors that influence communication in Japan and the United States.* Paper presented as a plenary address at a conference on communication in Japan and the United States, California State University, Fullerton.

Leung, K., & Bond, M. (1984). The impact of cultural collectivism on reward allocation. *Journal of Personality and Social Psychology, 47,* 793-804.

Limaye, M. R., & Victor, D. A. (1991). Cross-cultural business communication research: State of the art and hypotheses for the 1990s. *Journal of Business Communication, 28,* 277-299.

Lustig, M. W., & Andersen, P. A. (1991). Generalizing about communication apprehension and avoidance: Multiple replications and meta-analyses. In J. W. Neuliep (Ed.), *Replication research in the social sciences* (pp. 297-328). Newbury Park, CA: Sage.

Markus, H. R., & Kitayama, S. (1991). Culture and the self: Implications for cognition, emotion, and motivation. *Psychological Review, 98,* 224-253.

Markus, H. R., & Kitayama, S. (1994a). A collective fear of the collective: Implications for selves and theories of selves. *Personality and Social Psychology Bulletin, 20,* 568-579.

Markus, H. R., & Kitayama, S. (1994b). The cultural construction of self and emotion. In S. Kitayama & H. R. Markus (Eds.), *Culture, self, and emotion* (pp. 89-130). Washington, DC: American Psychological Association.

Masters, J. C., Burish, T. G., Hollon, S. D., & Rimm, D. C. (1987). *Behavior therapy: Techniques and empirical findings.* New York: Harcourt Brace Jovanovich.

McCroskey, J. C. (1970). Measures of communication-bound anxiety. *Speech Monographs, 37,* 269-277.

McCroskey, J. C. (1972). The implementation of a large-scale program of systematic desensitization for communication apprehension. *Speech Teacher, 21,* 255-264.

McCroskey, J. C. (1977). Oral communication: A summary of recent theory and research. *Human Communication Research, 4,* 78-96.

McCroskey, J. C. (1982). Oral communication apprehension: A reconceptualization. In M. Burgoon (Ed.), *Communication yearbook 6* (pp. 136-170). Beverly Hills, CA: Sage.

McCroskey, J. C. (1984). The communication perspective. In J. A. Daly & J. C. McCroskey (Eds.), *Avoiding communication: Shyness, reticence, and communication anxiety* (pp. 136-170). Beverly Hills, CA: Sage.

McCroskey, J. C., Andersen, J. F., Richmond, V. P., & Wheeless, L. R. (1981). Communication apprehension of elementary and secondary students and teachers. *Communication Education, 30,* 122-132.

McCroskey, J. C., Burroughs, N. F., Daun, A., & Richmond, V. P. (1990). Correlates of quietness: Swedish and American perspectives. *Communication Quarterly, 38,* 127-137.

McCroskey, J. C., Fayer, J., & Richmond, V. P. (1985). Don't speak to me in English: Communication apprehension in Puerto Rico. *Communication Quarterly, 33,* 185-192.

McCroskey, J. C., Gudykunst, W. B., & Nishida, T. (1985). Communication apprehension among Japanese students in native and second language. *Communication Research Reports, 2,* 11-15.

McCroskey, J. C., & Richmond, V. P. (1979). The impact of communication apprehension on individuals in organizations. *Communication Quarterly, 27,* 55 61.

McCroskey, J. C., & Richmond, V. P. (1987). Willingness to communicate. In J. C. McCroskey & J. A. Daly (Eds.), *Personality and interpersonal communication* (pp. 129-156). Newbury Park, CA: Sage.

McCroskey, J. C., & Richmond, V. P. (1990). Willingness to communicate: Differing cultural perspectives. *Southern Communication Journal, 56,* 72-77.

McCroskey, J. C., & Richmond, V. P. (1995). Correlates of compulsive communication: Quantitative and qualitative characteristics. *Communication Quarterly, 43,* 39-52.

McCroskey, J. C., Richmond, V. P., Daly, J. A., & Falcione, R. L. (1977). Studies of the relationship between communication apprehension and self-esteem. *Human Communication Research, 3,* 269-277.

Meichenbaum, D. (1977). *Cognitive behavior modification.* New York: Plenum.

Meyer, J. W. (1988). The social construction of the psychology of childhood: Some contemporary processes. In R. M. Lerner & E. M. Hetherington (Eds.), *Child development in life span perspective* (pp. 47-65). Hillsdale, NJ: Lawrence Erlbaum.

Mortensen, C. D., Arnston, P. H., & Lustig, M. (1977). The measurement of verbal predispositions. *Human Communication Research, 3,* 146-158.

Nagao, M. (1991). *Assertive behaviors and perceptions of assertiveness as communication competence: A comparative study of American and Japanese students.* Unpublished master's thesis, Ohio University, Athens.

Nakane, C. (1970). *Japanese society.* Berkeley: University of California Press.

Okabe, K. (1987). Indirect speech acts of the Japanese. In D. L. Kincaid (Ed.), *Communication theory from Eastern and Western perspectives* (pp. 127-136). New York: Academic Press.

Olaniran, B. A., & Roach, K. D. (1994). Communication apprehension and classroom apprehension in Nigerian classrooms. *Communication Quarterly, 42,* 379-389.

Pascale, R. T., & Athos, A. G. (1981). *The art of Japanese management.* New York: Simon & Schuster.

Patterson, M. L., & Ritts, V. (1997). Social and communicative anxiety: A review and meta-analysis. In B. R. Burleson (Ed.), *Communication yearbook 20* (pp. 263-303). Thousand Oaks, CA: Sage.

Pitt, L. F., & Ramaseshan B. (1990). Apprehension about communication and salespersons' performance. *Psychological Reports, 67,* 1355-1362.

Ponterotto, J. G., Casas, J. M., Suzuki, L. A., & Alexander, C. M. (Eds.). (1995). *Handbook of multicultural counseling.* Thousand Oaks, CA: Sage.

Prunty, A., Klopf, D. W., & Ishii, S. (1990). Argumentativeness: Japanese and American tendencies to approach and avoid conflict. *Communication Research Reports, 7,* 75-79.

Rancer, A. S., Baukus, R. A., & Infante, D. A. (1985). Relations between argumentativeness and belief structures about arguing. *Communication Education, 34,* 37-47.

Rancer, A. S., Kosberg, R. L., & Baukus, R. A. (1992). Beliefs about arguing as predictors of trait argumentativeness: Implications for training in argument and conflict management. *Communication Education, 41,* 375-387.

Richmond, V. P., & McCroskey, J. C. (1992). *Communication apprehension: Avoidance and effectiveness.* Scottsdale, AZ: Gorsuch Scarisbrick.

Richmond, V. P., & Roach, K. D. (1992). Willingness to communicate and employee success in U.S. organizations. *Journal of Applied Communication Research, 20,* 95-115.

Sampson, E. E. (1977). Psychology and the American ideal. *Journal of Personality and Social Psychology, 35,* 767-782.

Sampson, E. E. (1988). The debate on individualism: Indigenous psychologies of the individual and their role in personal and societal functioning. *American Psychologist, 43,* 15-22.

Saunders, G. R. (1985). Silence and noise as emotion management styles: An Italian case. In D. Tannen & M. Saville-Troike (Eds.), *Perspectives on silence* (pp. 165-183). Norwood, NJ: Ablex.

Schooler, C. (1990). Individualism and the historical and social-structural determinants of people's concerns over self-directedness and efficacy. In J. Rodin, C. Schooler, & K. W. Schaie (Eds.), *Self-directedness: Cause and effects through the life course* (pp. 19-49). Hillsdale, NJ: Lawrence Erlbaum.

Schwartz, S. H. (1990). Individualism-collectivism: Critique and proposed refinements. *Journal of Cross-Cultural Psychology, 21,* 139-157.

Sharkey, W. F., & Singelis, T. M. (1995). Embarrassability and self-construal: A theoretical integration. *Personality and Individual Differences, 19,* 919-926.

Shoemaker, M., & Satterfield, D. O. (1977). Assertion training: An identity crisis that's coming on strong. In R. E. Alberti (Ed.), *Assertiveness: Innovations, applications, issues* (pp. 49-58). San Luis Obispo, CA: Impact.

Singelis, T. M. (1994). The measurement of independent and interdependent self-construals. *Personality and Social Psychology Bulletin, 20,* 580-591.

Singelis, T. M., & Brown, W. J. (1995). Culture, self, and collectivist communication: Linking culture to individual behavior. *Human Communication Research, 21,* 354-389.

Sue, D., Ino, S., & Sue, D. M. (1983). Nonassertiveness of Asian Americans: An inaccurate assumption? *Journal of Counseling Psychology, 30,* 581-588.

Sue, D., Sue, D. M., & Ino, S. (1990). Assertiveness and social anxiety in Chinese-American Women. *Journal of Psychology, 124,* 155-163.

Sue, D. W. (1981). *Counseling the culturally different: Theory and practice.* New York: John Wiley.

Takai, J., & Ota, H. (1994). Assessing Japanese interpersonal communication competence. *Japanese Journal of Experimental Social Psychology, 33,* 224-236.

Tannen, D. (1985). Silence: Anything but. In D. Tannen & M. Saville-Troike (Eds.), *Perspectives on silence* (pp. 93-111). Norwood, NJ: Ablex.

Thompson, C. A., & Ishii, S. (1990). Japanese and American compared on assertiveness/responsiveness. *Psychological Reports, 66,* 829-830.

Triandis, H. C. (1988). Collectivism vs. individualism: A reconceptualization of a basic concept in cross-cultural psychology. In C. Bagley & G. K. Verma (Eds.), *Cross-cultural studies of personality, attitudes, and cognition* (pp. 60-95). London: Macmillan.

Triandis, H. C., Bontempo, R., Villareal, M. J., Asai, M., & Lucca, N. (1988). Individualism and collectivism: Cross-cultural perspectives on self-ingroup relationships. *Journal of Personality and Social Psychology, 54,* 323-338.

Triandis, H. C., & Vassiliou, V. (1972). A comparative analysis of subjective culture. In H. C. Triandis (Ed.), *The analysis of subjective culture* (pp. 299-335). New York: John Wiley.

Watson, K. W., Monroe, E. E., & Atterstrom, A. (1984). American and Swedish children's apprehension about communication: A comparative study. *Perceptual and Motor Skills, 59,* 129-133.

Watson, K. W., Monroe, E. E., & Atterstrom, A. (1989). Comparison of communication apprehension across cultures: American and Swedish children. *Communication Quarterly, 37,* 67-76.

Wheeless, L. R. (1975). An investigation of receiver apprehension and social context dimensions of communication apprehension. *Speech Teacher, 24,* 261-268.

Wood, P. S., & Mallinckrodt, B. (1990). Culturally sensitive assertiveness training for ethnic minority clients. *Professional Psychology: Research and Practice, 21,* 5-11.

Yeo, A. (1990). Development and trends of counseling in Singapore: A personal view. *Asian Counselling Bulletin, 1,* 14-17.

Zakahi, W. R. (1985). The relationship of assertiveness to communication competence and communication satisfaction: A dyadic assessment. *Communication Research Reports, 2,* 36-40.

Zhang, Y., Butler, J., & Pryor, B. (1996). Comparison of apprehension about communication in China and the United States. *Perceptual and Motor Skills, 82,* 1168-1170.

CHAPTER CONTENTS

3 Harmful Speech in Intergroup Encounters: An Organizational Framework for Communication Research

LAURA LEETS
Stanford University

HOWARD GILES
University of California, Santa Barbara

Verbally disturbing communication, or what is broadly referred to as harmful speech (e.g., racist, sexist, and ageist speech), is a growing but fragmented area of inquiry in need of integration. In an effort to capitalize on various traditions' insights and make connections across academic boundaries, the authors present a model for summarizing findings and generating and guiding research for several intergroup forms of deprecating speech. To begin, seven of the more established research areas—verbal aggression, gender, age, physical disability, ethnicity, jurisprudence, and rhetoric—are overviewed. These are then integrated into a model that describes the dynamics and processes underlying the type of communication that results in harm. The general utility of the framework lies in (a) its comprehensive elucidation of many types of harmful speech; (b) its specificity, because it allows for the complexity and interaction of a variety of situational, psychological, affective, social, and communicative factors; and (c) its ability to serve as a complex and heuristic model that can frame and guide future research.

S INCE at least the late 1980s, the politics of identity (ethnicity, sexuality, religion, age) or the need for recognition (Taylor, 1995) has had a prominent place in academic (e.g., Arthur & Shapiro, 1995; Choi & Murphy, 1992; Goldberg, 1994; Gordon & Newfield, 1996) and popular (e.g., Bloom, 1987; D'Souza, 1991; Kimball, 1990) discourse. This intellectual movement stems from the long-standing and broader struggle to advance civil

Correspondence and requests for reprints: Laura Leets, Department of Communication, Stanford University, Stanford, CA 94305-2050; e-mail leets@leland.stanford.edu

Communication Yearbook 22, pp. 91-137

rights, a movement largely responsible for opening new vistas of scholarship. In the past 30 years there has been an explosion of literature concentrating on traditionally overlooked topics as well as advancing research and theories designed to end injustices based on ethnicity, sex, class, and other social factors. The literature is now broad, expansive, and interdisciplinary (e.g., involving the social sciences, the humanities, and cultural, ethnic, and gender studies). In a previous volume of the *Communication Yearbook,* this trend is evidenced by three chapters regarding age (Nussbaum, Hummert, Williams, & Harwood, 1996) and sexual harassment (Keyton, 1996; Metts & Spitzberg, 1996).

One way to view this literature's emergence is as an attempt to understand and manage the growing pluralism in our contemporary society. Most countries are striving to create communities that allow diverse populations to reside together in harmony. Living in a post-civil rights era, most people believe themselves to be opposed to prejudice and in favor of diversity. Any act of overt discrimination and prejudice is strongly frowned upon. Although working and living with diverse others often brings understanding, it does not always encourage greater acceptance and tolerance of differences. Inherent tension arising out of diversity can find expression through deprecating speech, a phenomenon that has become increasingly pervasive (e.g., Ehrlich, 1990; U.S. Merit Systems Protection Board, 1981, 1987; Vissing, Straus, Gelles, & Harrop, 1991). For example, derogatory epithets are aimed at individuals' sexuality in the form of sexual harassment or with regard to sexual orientation: In an interview, one female reported that a male colleague at work said to her, "Why don't you wear miniskirts to work? I'll buy you a nice leather one. Best quality. It would look great on you." In San Francisco, a gay and lesbian activist group (GLAAD) was told, "It's time for you and your kind (Devil's spawn) to run back into the closet and slam the door behind you!!! We're waiting . . . start running." Moreover, deprecating speech also is aimed at ethnic or religious identity: A college newspaper reported the distribution of a flier claiming, "Blacks don't belong in classrooms, they belong hanging from trees," and a national newspaper quoted Louis Farrakhan, the leader of the Nation of Islam, as publicly stating, "You wonder why I call it Jew-nited Nations . . . Jew York City . . . Jew-niversity. Because [Jews] control it." Even a person's age can serve as an impetus to denigrate another: In one survey, a 49-year-old man wrote that a 20-year-old had brushed by him in the airport and said, "Hey, watch where you're going, you ol' fart."

To date, the research examining verbally disturbing communication, or what we will term *harmful speech* (e.g., Infante & Rancer, 1996; Lederer & Delgado, 1995; Smolla, 1993; Whillock & Slayden, 1995a), has received attention among critical and postmodern theorists, but has only recently been addressed by social scientists. One of our main reasons for writing this chapter is that the empirical investigations that have been conducted have not been integrated or critically analyzed. Conceivably, the examples given above reflect different domains of a larger underlying process. Uniting these currently fragmented yet related areas into an organizing framework will allow us to capitalize on different fields' insights, make connections among them, and assess our current knowledge base. The research included in our review is diverse, crossing several academic boundaries and approaching the study of harmful speech in several different ways, with a variety of different vocabularies, methods (quantitative and qualitative), and purposes in mind. In particular, the communication discipline is well positioned to synthesize such work, as it is an inclusive field, easily spanning disciplinary divides. Moreover, harmful speech is undeniably a communication phenomenon.

The importance of harmful speech lies in its potentially powerful consequences (Bradac, 1989). Communication can promote or hinder a person's quality of life, which at a fundamental level can be defined as a person's subjective well-being (e.g., Cella, 1994; Green & Henderson, 1993). As Viktor Frankl (1984), a longtime prisoner in a Nazi concentration camp, argues, it was the cumulative impact of negative messages, the undermining of worth, that contributed to the loss of human dignity, the loss of the sense of being an individual with a mind and personal value that in turn robbed Jewish prisoners of their will to live. Although empirical research has not adequately substantiated the harmful effects of messages such as the loss of dignity proposed by Frankl, it has been shown that a variety of stressors, ranging from relatively mild and short-lived (one-time events) to severe and chronic (repetitive events), increase the risk of illness (Maddi, Bartone, & Puccetti, 1987) and decrease immunity (Geiser, 1989). Beyond potential physical and psychological effects, deprecating messages also may harm society. For instance, when speech is divisive and antagonistic, it tears at the very fabric of a community, planting seeds of doubt about the trustworthiness of others, which in turn aggravates efforts at managing diversity (e.g., Leets & Bowers, 1997; Whillock & Slayden, 1995b).

Social identity theory (SIT; Tajfel, 1978, 1982; Tajfel & Turner, 1986) and its extension as self-categorization theory (SCT; Turner, 1987; Turner & Oakes, 1989; Turner, Oakes, Haslam, & McGarty, 1994) provide a theoretical basis for our review. More than 20 years of social psychology research (e.g., Hogg & Abrams, 1988) and 10 years of communication research (e.g., Giles & Coupland, 1992; Gudykunst, 1986) have provided compelling evidence for the distinction between interpersonal and intergroup interactions, which depend on the salience of personal or social identity, respectively. That is, people's language production and reception are markedly affected by whether the interaction is classified according to the participants' perceptions of each other as individuals with unique personality characteristics (interpersonal) or in terms of socially definable groups, with interactants viewing each other as exemplars of particular social categories (intergroup). For instance, different processes underlie an interaction when interpersonal conflict is construed as racial tension between a "typical white" and a "typical black" than when viewed as conflict between "John" and "Jack." Thus qualitatively distinct phenomena with different social processes are represented when derogatory communication takes place on either an interpersonal (e.g., between spouses, siblings, parents and children, dating couples) or an intergroup (e.g., ethnicity, religion, gender) dimension. Evidence for such a distinction also has been documented empirically through the hostile communication typology (Kinney, 1994), which identifies three aspects of a person's identity likely to be attacked: group membership (intergroup) and personal and relational failings (interpersonal). Although both dimensions are worthy of study, we have chosen to narrow our discussion to primarily an intergroup context, with brief reference to the germane aspects of interpersonal research. Expressions of prejudice, such as harmful speech, increase as a result of salient group identities. The more an interaction is seen in intergroup terms, the greater the tendency for discriminatory behavior (Cargile & Giles, 1996).

Specifically, our two objectives in this chapter are (a) to provide an overview of isolated yet overlapping domains of intergroup research on harmful speech and (b) to introduce a model that integrates the literatures as well as casts light on the dynamics of and processes underlying deprecating speech. To this end, the chapter is organized into three major sections. First, we posit a definition of harmful speech. Second, we review research within its purview. Specifically, we ask the reader to bear in mind that at this initial stage we focused our effort on integration and thus identification of trends rather than on providing an exhaustive survey of research results and methodological critique in each intergroup domain. Our aim is to organize the prolific and diverse research conducted on harmful speech into one unifying framework. Third, we present the harmful speech model itself. Finally, we summarize potential lines of future research afforded by this conceptual framework.

DEFINING HARMFUL SPEECH

Several related terms have been used to refer to deprecating speech. These include *verbal aggression* (e.g., Infante & Wigley, 1986), *hate speech* (e.g., Sedler, 1992), *dignity harm* (Harcum & Rosen, 1990a, 1990b), *verbal abuse* (e.g., Ney, 1987), *psychological abuse* (e.g., Langone, 1992) or *maltreatment* (e.g., Hart & Brassard, 1987), *emotional abuse* (e.g., Lucas, 1982) or *maltreatment* (e.g., Garbarino & Garbarino, 1987), and *mental abuse* (e.g., Briere, 1992). The conceptual similarities and differences among these terms have not been explicated. However, there appears to be overlap in that the researchers who use these terms all share an interest in examining communication that tends to generate emotional or psychological pain. One major difference, however, is that some definitions, such as those in communication and social psychology research, limit their focus to speech, whereas others (e.g., in the mental health professions) include both verbal and nonverbal communication (e.g., McGee & Wolfe, 1991). In this chapter, we focus our attention on *speech* and paralinguistics that occur in an intergroup context and result in damage. In particular, we draw on the well-established terms *aggression* and *verbal aggression* defined in the social sciences. Generally, aggression is defined as "any form of behavior that is intended to injure someone physically or psychologically" (Berkowitz, 1993, p. 3). More specifically, in relation to verbal aggression the definition is narrowed; verbal aggression is "an exchange of messages between two people where at least one person in the dyad attacks the self-concept of the other person in order to hurt the person psychologically" (Infante & Wigley, 1986, p. 61). A significant component of these two definitions is the *intention* to hurt a person physically or psychologically.

Although a person's intention is an important element in the definition of aggressive behavior, we question whether a speaker's intention should be the sole criterion for defining utterances that result in damage. For example, from the "fighting words" exception to the First Amendment or the tort of intentional infliction of emotional distress, the law would view intention as critical. However, in sexual harassment cases the law would find the receiver's *perception* to be more important than the sender's actual intention to harm. Thus we extend the above definitions further to define harmful speech as *utterances that are both intended to cause and/or, irrespective of intent, perceived by their receivers to result in damage.* This definition takes into consideration that communication is transactional in nature, open to multiple interpretations and intrinsically flawed (Coupland, Giles, & Wiemann, 1991). We allow for miscommunication, recognizing that interactants may not share a mutual understanding of any given message and that both a speaker's intent and a receiver's perception are important factors for definitional and legal discussions concerning harmful speech.

The issue of intentionality (e.g., Bradac, 1989) is a familiar one to communication scholars, as it is a key construct in the general conceptualization of communication (Littlejohn, 1992). Using the source-message-receiver model of communication, Bowers and Bradac (1982) delineate two metatheoretical interpretations of intentionality. The *traditional approach* views communication as a purposeful activity where the locus of intention is the source of the message. The *nontraditional approach* is favored by stimulus-response theorists and transactional-systems theorists who not only highlight the problematic nature of discerning and measuring intentionality but also prefer to analyze the interdependent (reciprocal) nature of interaction. In an attempt to transcend some of these definitional issues, Bowers and Bradac (1982) modify the word *intention* into the phrase *attribution of intention.* The shift is important because it makes "intention a communicative phenomenon . . . [and turns the spotlight] on the meaning of a message to others" (p. 9).

Finding this shift applicable to the conceptualization of harmful speech, we have incorporated it into the above definition.

Our interaction with others is based largely on what we attribute to be the motives and intentions of their actions (Heider, 1958). A number of theories have been presented that attempt to explain the inference process. Although there are distinctions among these approaches, they can be classified generally as "attribution theories" (see Hewstone, 1990a). Fundamentally, attribution theories attempt to specify the conditions under which a behavior will be attributed to the person, to the environment, or to a combination of both. For example, in an intergroup context, the likelihood of miscommunication increases because differences in meaning are given to the same behavior (Detweiler, 1986). That is, the attributions people make to explain the behaviors of in-group members and out-group members are often different (Hewstone, 1990b; Hewstone, Wagner, & Machleit, 1989). Taylor and Jaggi (1974) found that internal attributions are used when the behavior of an in-group member is positive or when the behavior of an out-group member is negative, whereas external (situational) attributions are given when the behavior of an in-group member is negative or when the behavior of an out-group member is positive. Inferences influence the behavior that we expect from others and how we will subsequently behave toward them (see Felson & Tedeschi, 1993).

In light of the above discussion, scholarly attempts to define and clarify the essence of harmful speech will most likely entail a complicated and difficult journey. Take, for example, the problem with psychological or emotional harm resulting from deprecating speech. It is difficult to measure or prove because it is intangible and highly subjective (Delgado, 1982). Different people react to the same messages in different ways. The event, the personality, and the past of the receiver are a few of the many factors that play roles in a person's response (Ehrlich, 1990). Additionally, meanings change depending upon the speaker, the hearer, the context, and even who is overhearing them (Allen, 1990). As D'Amato (1991) keenly observes, we live in

> an indeterminate culture that is changing so rapidly in the television age that today's startling expression is next year's parody and the following year's playground yell. We can follow a given expression through its initial shock value a year ago to today's rap music lyric and to next year's television commercial. At an accelerating and almost dizzying pace, our culture is legitimizing expression that in the recent past it considered outrageous, if not sinful. (p. 344)

This illustrates why some scholars have considered the concept of intention as a necessary element for establishing responsibility for harm in moral philosophy and jurisprudence (e.g., Shultz & Wright, 1985). Yet moral and legal philosophers also have acknowledged that intention may not always be required for accountability of harm in terms of negligence, which is construed to be simply a lack of caring. Although a person may not have intended to harm, he or she may still be held legally responsible for actions that result in harm. Hence, as our definition suggests, both the speaker's intention to harm and the receiver's perception of harm appear to be key criteria for evaluating potential damage.

We have selected *harmful speech* as the term we use to encompass the distinct yet complementary traditions noted at the beginning of this section because it has not been used previously and because it can be more inclusive than some other terms, especially in the discussion of intergroup rather than interpersonal interaction. Arguably, harmful speech can encompass a large spectrum of interacting factors, such as motivations, consequences, appraisals of threat, coping styles or organization of psychological defenses, and the social milieu, which are all needed for a dynamic perspective on deprecating speech in varied situations.

Because harm and hurt are variegated constructs in everyday usage, it is necessary to distinguish between them. According to the *Oxford Dictionary of the English Language* (1989 edition), hurt is associated with both mental and physical damage to a person. With regard to mental injury, hurt often is viewed as an emotional category: a blend of sadness and anger (Shaver, Schwartz, Dirson, & O'Connor, 1987). For example, a person feels hurt when he or she has been wronged in a way that warrants anger but believes that the offender does not care enough to rectify matters (Alschuler & Alschuler, 1984; Shaver et al., 1987). Hurt constitutes one type of harm, and the word *hurt* is more appropriate for use in describing some interpersonal contexts, such as parents' deprecating speech directed at their children (Bayer & Cegala, 1992) or verbal aggression between spouses (Eggeman & Moxley, 1985). Given our focus on an intergroup perspective, however, we want to cast a wider net, investigating not only personal consequences but also group and societal consequences. For example, racist slurs have incurred legal action for being injurious to the status and prospects of group members (Delgado, 1982), a position that holds stronger international than national support (Henkin, 1995). Moreover, deprecating speech can harm society by impeding a healthy emotional climate (Leets & Bowers, 1997). That is, divisive speech can affect solidarity, fear, hostility, and security among people (de Rivera, 1992). Thus *harm* is a broad referent that can denote both interpersonal and intergroup consequences.

As a point of entry, we associate personal harm with the elicitation of anxiety and distress (Selye, 1993) and give a more detailed discussion of both short- and long-term effects in the model. With regard to group and societal analyses of harm, traditional social science methods need to be cautious of system jumping—that is, mixing sociological and psychological/emotional variables (see McLeod & Blumer, 1987).[1] In particular, reductionism points to the danger of basing data on one unit of analysis (e.g., individuals) and translating it to another unit of analysis (e.g., society). This difficulty, however, is not insurmountable. For example, some scholars (e.g., Buckner, 1988;

Linz et al., 1991) have successfully approached this issue by arguing that the mean score from aggregated individual-level data can quantify some setting-level attributes.

LITERATURE REVIEW
OF HARMFUL SPEECH

Having established and justified our preferred working definition of harmful speech, we turn our attention to pertinent intergroup literature subsumed under the rubric of harmful speech, a scholarly area with growing momentum. For this reason, we begin our review with the research area that has traditionally defined this type of inquiry in the communication discipline—namely, verbal aggression—and then extend what has previously been predominantly an interpersonal level of analysis to an intergroup one through four of the more established research domains in which harmful speech has been documented: gender, age, physical disability, and ethnicity. This is not to say that harmful speech does not permeate other intergroup settings (e.g., between religions, in occupational groups, in homo/heterosexual encounters), as clearly it does. However, we examine areas that have most obviously contained an intergroup component, hoping that our framework will promote work in other areas less developed along these lines. Thus, within each sphere we cover, our review focuses on work that appears to have an intergroup focus. We then conclude with an overview of jurisprudential and rhetorical scholarship on harmful speech in an attempt to broaden the parameters of our intergroup analyses for the reasons stated therein. One final caveat: Any review of such a wide-ranging and far-reaching body of literature could not claim to be exhaustive; rather, this review aims to be representative of the present knowledge base.

Verbal Aggression

Although scholars have not gathered many data on those who receive harm, they have examined the perpetrators of it extensively. We make no attempt to overview an area of research as broad and distinguished as human aggression (see, e.g., Berkowitz, 1993; Blanchard & Blanchard, 1986; Donnerstein, Slaby, & Eron, 1995). Rather, we limit our discussion to verbal aggression, a central line of research within this tradition (Buss, 1961). It is here that utterances degrading some aspect of a person's identity have been examined as one of many types of aggression. Working from a communicative perspective, Infante and Wigley (1986) contend that verbal aggression is worthy of study in its own right; they have derived a line of research focused on verbally aggressive interpersonal messages, their causes, and their consequences (e.g., Infante, 1987; Infante, Chandler, Rudd, & Shannon, 1990; Infante, Rancer,

& Jordan, 1996). Infante's (1981) initial work investigated the relationship between argumentativeness (Infante & Rancer, 1982, 1996) and verbal aggression, demonstrating that a lack of argumentative skill by one or both persons often results in verbal aggression. Infante and his colleagues then explored argumentativeness and verbal aggression in several contexts, such as organizational settings (Infante & Gorden, 1985) and intimate relationships (Infante, Chandler, & Rudd, 1989; Infante et al., 1990; Sabourin, Infante, & Rudd, 1993; Vangelisti, 1994). Within this body of literature, most studies have adopted a pragmatic bent, providing immediate and practical value. For example, one research area guided by argumentation theory (Infante & Rancer, 1996) delineates how people can argue constructively and effectively. Another domain focuses on understanding and controlling verbal aggression, so that Infante (1995) has created a course in which students are taught to recognize and restrain verbal aggression, and Sabourin (1991, 1995; Stamp & Sabourin, 1995) has examined patterns of abusive couples to assist in the development of couple-appropriate treatment programs and interpersonal skills training. These efforts toward ameliorating interpersonal verbal aggression on both micro (e.g., distressed relationships) and macro (e.g., workplace environments) levels are both needed and worthwhile endeavors. As a whole, we use this body of work as a foundation and extend our efforts into an intergroup context.

Intergroup Domains

Gender (Linguistic Sexism)

Research in the area of language, gender, and sexism is voluminous (e.g., Aries, 1996; Beall & Sternberg, 1993; Bem, 1993; Coates, 1992; Wood, 1996). For our purposes, the gender communication literature can be characterized and viewed broadly as forming two classes: difference (e.g., Tannen, 1987, 1990; Wood, 1997) and dominance (e.g., Henley, 1995; Kalbfleisch & Cody, 1995; Kramarae, Schulz, & O'Barr, 1984; Lakoff, 1990; Pearson & Cooks, 1995). The difference approach focuses on the many ways men and women use words, on the differences in words used about men and women, and on the variability in verbal and nonverbal interaction (e.g., Boxer, 1993; DeFrancisco, 1991; Reardon, 1996). This literature has produced findings that both support and challenge the extent of differences, leading some to consider gender differences in communication to be more perceptual than real (e.g., Hopper, 1986). Nonetheless, there is fair agreement now that men and women, in general, do differ in some communicative behaviors (Mulac & Lundell, 1986; Wood, 1997), although these are clearly noncategorical (Swann, 1989), and many mechanisms have been identified (such as sex roles, social networks) to account for them (Coates, 1992).

Along these lines, the dominance perspective (which overlaps implicitly and sometimes explicitly with the difference position) argues that language differences in males' and females' speech are a reflection of men's dominance and women's subordination. Consequently, differences in language (e.g., in patterns of turn taking or interruptions) can be seen as power moves. This approach arose in large part out of the work of Lakoff (1973), who has contended that women's style of speaking reflects and sustains their powerless position vis-à-vis men (see Ng & Bradac, 1993). For example, it is frequently argued that sexual harassment is not about sex, but about power (Tinsley & Stockdale, 1993). Moreover, theorists are now questioning whether gender statically drives communicative differences or whether differences are negotiated and constructed in discourse (e.g., Fenstermaker, West, & Zimmerman, 1991).

West (1995) has argued that notions of communicative competence are inherently sexist and imply different models for men and women. No wonder, therefore, that a growing body of work has considered how women are represented in language, with much of it oriented toward suggesting that linguistically sexist devices such as the use of generic male pronouns need to be revised in all forms of communication (e.g., Khosroshahi, 1989; Prentice, 1994). Henley and Kramarae (1991) have argued that attention to gender differences in language—and especially the view that these are due to cultural differences in conversational rules (e.g., Tannen, 1990)—ought to correspond in importance to the ways in which women are abused and harassed (see Wood, 1992). Hence considerable attention has recently been paid to issues of battering (Bograd, 1990), spouse abuse (Kurz, 1989), sexual assault (Coates, Bavelas, & Gibson, 1994), and so forth. Indeed, Pence and Paymar (1993) discuss the ways in which men talk about women and their relationships that function to conceal and/or justify abuse and to justify males' more powerful positions. Wood and Rennie (1994) also discuss the ways in which some women who have been raped communicate about these events and their consequences in ways that can revictimize them. Interestingly, Henley, Miller, and Beazley (1995) suggest that the language in which the news media report violent acts against women, mainly in the passive voice, can lead (especially among men) to acceptance of such actions.

In tandem, some research has highlighted the ways in which women have been, and still are in the 1990s, stereotypically represented across virtually all genres of the media (e.g., Broverman, Vogel, Broverman, Clarkson, & Rosenkrantz, 1994). Most pernicious has been the representation of women in pornography, which has become increasingly aggressive against women, often perpetuating rape myths that can sustain and even exacerbate traditional sex roles and power differentials between the sexes (e.g., Linz & Malamuth, 1993). For example, one rape myth continues the false belief that a woman who is being forced to have sex initially may react very negatively but at some point will become sexually aroused and come to enjoy the experience (Perse, 1994). Indeed, others across the social sciences have argued that even non-violent media representations of sexual relations between men and women, with their implied notions of dominance differentials, can have such effects (e.g., Allen, Emmers, Gebhardt, & Giery, 1995).

Turning more specifically to verbal aggression, there is an emerging literature focused specifically on sexual harassment (for an overview of sexual harassment, see Keyton, 1996) that, according to Tata (1993), has developed along two main lines, which are worthy of note in terms of our purposes. The first has examined the *structure* of sexual harassment, identifying the conceptual and operational definitions as well as the categories of behavior that constitute sexual harassment, whereas the second has investigated the *nature* of sexual harassment. Tata points out that both areas have progressed largely independent of each other and are in need of integration. Conceptually, the construct of sexual harassment is believed to be multidimensional. Till (1980) divides the construct into five categories of behavior: gender harassment (sexist remarks and behavior), seductive behavior (inappropriate but sanction-free sexual advances), sexual bribery (solicitation of sexual activity with promise of rewards), sexual coercion (coercion of sexual activity), and sexual assault. Consistent with Till's multidimensional definition, the legal definition reduces sexual harassment to two general forms of behavior. The first, quid pro quo harassment, involves the exchange of sexual favors for tangible rewards or the exchange of punishments for refusal to grant sexual favors. The second, hostile work environment harassment, involves behavior of a sexual nature that creates an intimidating or hostile work or learning environment. For our purposes, we are interested in sexual harassment that would be exemplified legally in terms of the hostile environment, and most likely would include repeated sexual comments, requests for dates, sexist jokes, and leering. Moreover, this appears to be the most commonly reported type of harassment (LaFontaine & Tredeau, 1986; Vaux, 1993).

As some scholars point out (e.g., Fitzgerald & Shullman, 1993; Keyton, 1996; Wood, 1993), there are several glaring omissions in this research domain, one being a conceptual framework linking relations between various factors of sexual harassment (see Cleveland & Kerst, 1993). Tangri, Burt, and Johnson (1982) offer three popular explanations for sexual harassment: the natural/biological model, the organization model, and the sociocultural/gender model. The biological model focuses on courtship, the organization model suggests that harassment results from the misuse of organizational authority (by both men and women), and the sociocultural model posits that harassment is a consequence of men's domination in the workplace. Additionally, Gutek and Morasch (1982) argue for a sex role spillover model in which culturally based gender stereotypes result in differential treatment for women and men holding similar organizational roles. More recently, Pryor and his colleagues have offered a person-environment interaction model, arguing that harassment is the result of a stable, individual predisposition to harass in the context of norms that facilitate such behavior (Pryor, Giedd, & Williams, 1995; Pryor, LaVite, & Stroller, 1993). Stockdale (1993), however, argues for a misperception model of sexual harassment, focusing on men's misinterpretation of women's behavior (e.g., refusal, attractive dress) and its role in explaining men's sexual harassment of women. Although these models and others (see Keyton, 1996) offer plausible and useful explanations, none provides a comprehensive framework that integrates the multiple elements surrounding sexual harassment.

Age (Ageism)

Recent interest in the relationship between aging and communication has documented the fact that, at least in Western societies, older people are often communicated to in an ageist fashion (e.g., Hummert, Wiemann, & Nussbaum, 1994; Nussbaum & Coupland, 1995; Nussbaum et al., 1996). Often this stems from negative stereotypes that portray elderly people as unhealthy, weak, verbose, and cognitively deficient (Braithwaite, 1986). For instance, when the same message is presented by an older speaker and a younger speaker, young adults display an in-group bias toward the younger speaker and downgrade the older speaker (Giles, Coupland, Henwood, & Coupland, 1990). Young people also seek information from older people ageistly, in that they orient their initial questioning strategies to explore issues of cognitive incompetence more than they do with younger people in similar situations (Ng, Giles, & Moody, 1991). Moreover, when seeking the compliance of older individuals, young people tend to use more forceful strategies than they employ when seeking compliance from younger people (Dillard, Henwood, Giles, Coupland, & Coupland, 1990).

It is also not uncommon for elderly people to be the recipients of patronizing and overaccommodative communication (Ryan, Hummert, & Boich, 1995) that is ideationally simpler, slower, and childlike in intonation (e.g., Kemper, Vandeputte, Rice, Cheung, & Gabarchuk, 1995). In addition, they are susceptible to inappropriate forms of address (Wood & Ryan, 1991) and overly familiar nonverbals, such as frequent touching (Lancely, 1985). In other words, older people often are not spoken to as though they are individuals with distinctive idiosyncratic qualities; rather, they are addressed in a depersonalized manner that—for the very many elderly people who are socially and cognitively alert—can be received as very demeaning. Ageist communication has been acknowledged in a number of applied settings, including caring (Ashburn & Gordon, 1981) and medical (Adelman, Greene, Charon, & Friedman, 1990) contexts.

Language and communication research in the intergenerational arena has been characterized as "age-decremental" in that the elderly are documented as having certain deficiencies in communicative competence. For example, they have been found to speak more slowly (Stewart & Ryan, 1982), in less sophisticated grammatical ways (Emry, 1986), and are more verbose (Gold, Arbuckle, & Andres, 1994) than younger adults. However, Coupland and Coupland (1990), in their review of the literature, point to many important contextual caveats underlying this kind of work and underscore the fact that the above-mentioned "deficits" (and others) can actually be understood in far more functionally advantageous ways for older people. Indeed, such interpretations have led these authors to promote an "anti-ageist" ideology in their own empirical and theoretical work (e.g., Coupland, Coupland, & Grainger, 1991). Notwithstanding the fact that some frail elderly can collude in promoting their own dependence (see Baltes & Wahl, 1996), the fact remains that many healthy older people are communicated to in stereotypical ways that can be uncomplimentary at best (Ryan et al., 1995).

When they are the topics of conversation, older people often suffer the indignity of having numerous ageist terms applied to them, such as *biddy* and *codger* (Nuessel, 1993). This is a situation that has been criticized in literature (Berman & Sobkowska-Ashcroft, 1986) and social scientific writing (Schaie, 1993) for some years. Furthermore, in the American media, elderly people are relatively invisible. When the elderly are portrayed, the vast majority of the portrayals are stereotypical (approximately 82% of portrayals have been found to be so in some studies; see Gerbner, 1994; Gerbner, Gross, Signorielli, & Morgan, 1980). Specifically, elderly women, apart from soap operas, are particularly negatively portrayed as "past it," and elderly men are either authority figures or rather villainous (Bell, 1992). Harwood and Giles (1992) argue that even the supposedly anti-ageist TV program *The Golden Girls* perpetuates rather than dispels ageist assumptions. Many elderly people are "heavy viewers" of television and so potentially are the most cognizant that their age group is not being represented adequately or appropriately (Gerbner et al., 1980; Passuth & Cook, 1985).

In sum, older people have been documented as talking, talked to, and talked about in an age-discriminatory fashion. This is not to say that older people are not guilty of shaping their communication with younger people any less stereotypically (Giles & Williams, 1994), or that more favorable images of elderly people and their activities are not emerging (although whether this signals a change in the status of older people in our society is perhaps a moot issue). Recent research has focused on potential short-term effects of ageist communication in an empirically controlled manner. Further, alarming data suggest that elder abuse can be far more pernicious and direct than any of that outlined above and sometimes is extremely physical (e.g., Baumhover & Beall, 1996; Pillemer & Finkelhor, 1989). As in the area of language, gender, and feminism (see Laws, 1995), undoubtedly work in communication on aging and ageism soon will endeavor to identify and comment upon manifestations of neglect, abuse, and harassment. In the meantime, however, there is no framework to guide any movement toward integrating the variable manifestations of communicative ageism.

Physical Disability (Ableism)

The elderly are not the only recipients of patronizing speech; such speech is often directed toward people with a range of physical disabilities (Fichten & Bourdon, 1986).[2] Similar to elderly individuals, there are people with disabilities who seem to enjoy, accept, and facilitate patronizing speech and others who find it inappropriate and harmful. Fox (1994) interviewed a sample of people from the latter group and reports that they found three types of talk to be most irritating: (a) baby talk (e.g., "Poor little dear" or "honey," spoken in a condescending tone), (b) depersonalizing language (e.g., "It's nice that you people get out of the house"), and (c) third-party talk, in which a nondisabled person directs communication not to the person with the disability, but to an accompanying nondisabled person (e.g., "Does he take cream in his coffee?"). Consequently, such messages as well as undesirable descriptive labels (Yuker, 1987) most likely harm those with disabilities by reflecting perceptions that they are helpless and inadequate (Fox & Giles, 1996a). However, to date there is only a modest, albeit growing, body of research exploring the impact of speech targeted at those with disabilities as well as communication exchanges between able and disabled people (Fichten, Amsel, Bourdon, & Creti, 1988). Investigations conducted on this topic for the most part have tended to highlight the attitudinal component of how people view those with disabilities (e.g., Yuker, 1988; Yuker & Block, 1986)—quite negatively (Livneh, 1988; Wright, 1988). According to Emry and Wiseman (1987), these attitudes create expectations that disabled people are socially introverted, emotionally unstable, depressed, hypersensitive, and easily offended. Although people with disabilities are seldom studied, they are a relevant population for deprecating speech and reasonably can be included in this genre.

Ethnicism and Language

As with the preceding social categories, definitions of racial and ethnic categories are not unproblematic and have a history of controversy (Leets, Giles, & Clément, 1996). In addition, ethnicism has been examined across several disciplines and thus under many rubrics: racism (e.g., Miles, 1993), ethnocentrism (e.g., Levine & Campbell, 1972), prejudice (e.g., Allport, 1979), discrimination (e.g., Cherry, 1989), and moral exclusion (e.g., Opotow, 1990).

Much intercultural communication work has been devoted to documenting the plethora of communication and sociolinguistic practices that differentiate between ethnic groups in contact (see Giles, 1979; Gudykunst & Asante, 1989; Hecht, Collier, & Ribeau, 1993) and the manner in which they are accommodated (Gallois, Giles, Jones, Cargile, & Ota, 1995) and adjusted (Kim, 1995). Not unexpectedly, and despite the fact that other social, historical, and psychological forces can critically come into play (Cargile & Giles, 1996), such cultural differences in conversational rules and communicative habits can be responsible for intercultural miscommunications that can be interpreted as variably subtle, amusing, refreshing, irritating, or leading to hostilities (Banks, Gao, & Baker, 1991). In tandem, work on interethnic language effects also often demonstrates in- and out-group biases in evaluating speakers from contrasting ethnolinguistic groups (see Giles & Coupland, 1992), sometimes in simulated applied settings such as legal and occupational. Similarly, many ethnic groups have been the subjects of negative stereotypical images in the media, in terms of both labels (e.g., Hartmann & Husband, 1974) and visual depictions (O'Barr, 1994), thereby exacerbating ethnic intolerances (see Baldwin & Hecht, 1995). Inescapably, the history of intercultural relations has been all too tragic and extremely complex.

Researchers have cataloged the many ethnic epithets and slurs that can be used to derogate (Khlief, 1979; Kinney, 1996; Kirkland, Greenberg, & Pyszczynski, 1987; Lukens, 1979)—and the variable and changing forms of language with which groups can self-identify to bolster their sense of worth (e.g., *African American, Chicano*; see Flores & Hopper, 1975; Hecht & Ribeau, 1987; Lampe, 1982), and civil rights laws in many cultures now prohibit certain language that is defined as racially offensive. The less frequent public, verbal invocation of racism, of course, does not mean that racism has dissipated. In fact, some scholars argue that because any expression of racial prejudice is now frowned upon, people favor disguised and indirect ways to express their bigotry (see Sniderman & Piazza, 1993; van Dijk, 1995; Whillock & Slayden, 1995a). Members of ethnic minorities often argue that indirect expressions of racism are more common (e.g., Billig et al., 1988; Essed, 1991; Feagin & Sikes, 1994; van Dijk, 1992, 1993) and more problematic than overt expressions, as objections to them can be dismissed as overreactions by the recipients (e.g., Nairn & McCreanor, 1990, 1991). However, Louw-Potgeiter (1989) found that black South African students weighed social data in a comprehensive manner before labeling an incident as racist and by no means reacted in an "overly sensitive" manner by classifying all discriminatory instances as racist. Additionally, subtle racist messages are difficult to identify and often are perceived by minority recipients as more harmful than overt messages (Leets & Giles, 1997).

Rowe (1990, 1993) describes ethnic slurs as "micro-inequities," unjust acts that are traumatic for the recipients because of the uncertainty they raise as to how to interpret and respond to the messages. Recipients can spend inordinate amounts of time and energy sorting out a source's intentions and/or the meaning of a message, usually in the absence of any avenue of redress. Van Dijk (e.g., 1984, 1987) has been a pioneer in documenting the varying degrees of subtlety and illocutionary force that linguistically deprecating comments have assumed in the United States and the Netherlands, as has Essed (e.g., 1990, 1991). For instance, people may deny their prejudices, justify "nonracist" yet discriminatory practices (Billig, 1988), and account for them by presenting corroborating "facts" to demonstrate they are not racist (Potter & Wetherell, 1987). Importantly, it has been pointed out that racist attitudes and stereotypes are not purely cognitive entities, but are instantiated, modified, and evolved through communication (Condor, 1988; Potter & Wetherell, 1987). This research domain is congruent with the previous four in that it also lacks an organizing framework.

Despite the recent, more theoretically rich work focusing on gender and communication on the one hand and the descriptive work on the effects of verbal aggression, ageism, ethnicism, pornography, and the discourse of violence on the other, we have no general model of harmful communication upon which to draw. Clearly, we believe the development of a framework capable of integrating various forms of harmful speech—that has no intent to subjugate other approaches (e.g., Tedeschi & Felson, 1994)—will be advantageous, if not emancipating, for all. Before we attempt to present such a framework, we survey below two other relevant literatures, jurisprudential and rhetorical, that complement the empirical research discussed above and render a more complete picture of scholarship on harmful speech in an intergroup arena.

Jurisprudence

The jurisprudence literature amply discusses hate (or assaultive) speech and its First Amendment implications (e.g., Lederer & Delgado, 1995; Matsuda, Lawrence, Delgado, & Crenshaw, 1993; Smolla, 1993). The discussions tend to be organized around whether hate speech is legally protected by the First Amendment and thus beyond regulation or whether legislators may carve out exceptions based on fighting words (Saad, 1991), the 14th Amendment (Sedler, 1991, 1992), and tort law objections (Hodulik, 1991). Some legal scholars believe that the effects of hate speech can be addressed within a First Amendment framework (e.g., Becker, 1995; Leidholdt, 1995), whereas other encourage a rethinking of the framework, one that does not privilege free speech in favor of other rights (e.g., equality; see Delgado & Yun, 1995 MacKinnon, 1995). The latter group includes an emerging cadre of critical race scholars who take a subjective and political approach to racist expressions, viewing them not "as isolated instances of conscious bigoted decision making or prejudiced practice, but as larger, systemic, structural and cultural [custom]" (Lawrence, Matsuda, Delgado, & Crenshaw, 1993, p. 5). Hence, in opposition to recent U.S. Supreme Court decisions that have recognized hate speech as protected, these scholars argue for its regulation as a means to advance racial justice. More recently, Heyman (1996) has articulated a middle-ground position, arguing that free speech and other rights can be balanced and do not necessarily result in an irreconcilable conflict. He presents a rights-based model and argues that when hate speech violates rights to personal security, privacy, dignity, emotional well-being, and full and equal citizenship it can be restricted unless the injury to these rights is outweighed by the value of the speech in question.

A particular emphasis in the jurisprudential tradition is the process of how hate speech harms. Lederer and Delgado (1995) argue that at the core of hate speech is a desire to subordinate another group. On these grounds, some contend that hate speech and pornography should not receive First Amendment protection (e.g., Butler, 1995; Lawrence, 1995; Lederer, 1995; Ross, 1995). However, Smolla (1993) points out that the courts will not prohibit or punish speech merely because it is lewd, profane, or otherwise vulgar and offensive. Smolla provides a comprehensive overview of three types of injuries that legally qualify as "harms": (a) physical harms, which have impacts on persons or property; (b) relational harms, which interfere with various kinds of relationships; and (c) reactive harms, which are injuries caused by emotional or intellectual responses to the content of speech (see Table 3.1). Legal and scientific scholarship overlap as to the identification of possible harm resulting from hateful speech, but social science has the potential to define and delineate the *process* of such harms in order to inform the court's assessment of any particular *claim* to harm. Thus an integration of the literatures is a vital step in the tandem efforts of judicial and communication scholarship to understand and subsequently guard against genuinely deleterious effects of harmful speech.

Rhetoric

Rhetorical scholars have forged a different entry point into the domain of harmful communication, examining rhetors' expressions and strategies of hate (Whillock & Slayden, 1995a) as well as the potential outcome of marginalization (Goldberg, 1995; van Dijk, 1995). Thus the focus shifts away from both the social science emphasis on offensiveness and the jurisprudential emphasis on legal protection. According to Whillock and Slayden (1995b), hateful speech is an integral part of daily life and not an exception to the rule that occurs only in moments of cultural tension. Rhetors often use hate actively or symbolically to assert the superiority of their identity while annihilating another's (see Tajfel & Turner, 1986). For example, in Pat Buchanan's 1991 speech announcing his presidential candidacy, he stated:

TABLE 3.1
Harmful Speech Injuries Sufficient to Justify Regulation of Speech

Harms	*Examples*
Physical harms	
Injuries to persons	solicitation of murder
	incitement to riot on behalf of speaker's cause
	reactive violence against the speaker in response to the message
Injuries to property	solicitation of arson
	incitement to destroy property
	reactive violence against the property of the speaker in response to the message
Relational harms	
Injuries to social relationships	libel and slander
	alienation of affections
Injuries to transactions or business relationships	fraud and misrepresentation
	false advertising
	interference with contractual relations
	interference with prospective economic gain
	insider trading
Injuries to information/ownership interests	copyright, trademark, or patent infringement
	appropriation of name or likeness for commercial purposes
Injuries to interests in confidentiality	disclosure of national security secrets
	unauthorized revelation of private personal information
Reactive harms	
Injuries to individual emotional tranquillity	infliction of emotional distress
	invasion of privacy caused by placing the individual in a false light in the public eye
	invasion of privacy involving intrusion upon seclusion
	invasion of privacy involving publication of embarrassing facts
	distress caused by intellectual disagreement with the content of the speech
Injuries to communal sensibilities	insults to human dignity (racist or sexist)
	vulgarity
	obscenity
	interference with political or social cohesiveness or harmony arising from collective disagreement with the content of speech

SOURCE: From *Free Speech in an Open Society* by Rodney A. Smolla. Copyright (c) 1992 by Rodney A. Smolla. Reprinted by permission of Alfred A. Knopf, Inc.

> Every year millions of undocumented aliens break our laws, cross our borders, and demand social benefits paid for with the tax dollars of American citizens. California is being bankrupted . . . yet our leaders, timid and fearful of being called names, do nothing. . . . So, the Custodians of Political Correctness do not frighten me. And I will do what is necessary to defend the borders of my country even if it means putting the National Guard all along our southern frontier. (Buchanan, 1995)

Buchanan identified illegal aliens as a cause of social disorder and violence ("break our laws"), economic misfortune ("California is being bankrupted"), and an intrusive threat to the American way of life ("defend the borders"). As Whillock (1995) points out, such hate appeals encourage a divisive social climate by creating a harm-blame-threat cycle: "They harmed us, we blame them, they continue to threaten us, we must respond" (p. 38). Consequently, rhetorical messages of this genre are harmful, as they "subvert rational argument, denigrate whole groups of people, . . . [and break] down the tentative bonds of trust between differing groups" (p. 48).

In sum, the scholarly traditions discussed above overlap in that each attempts to explore the phenomenon of deprecating speech as well as to identify the types of harms it produces. Broadly, they are distinct in that the social science research has exerted more effort in ameliorating *problems* associated with harmful speech in its various domains, jurisprudential work has focused on the *protection* of such speech, and rhetorical studies have examined its *production.* Indeed, as harmful speech has received increased scholarly attention in recent years, an attempt to unite these efforts under one comprehensive schema would be a logical next step.

We offer a framework as an initial effort toward this end. We recognize that our model will be incomplete, but our goals are to facilitate conceptual integration, inventory, and synthesis of currently held knowledge and to map out possible terrain from which to formulate questions and refine issues. The model is not parsimonious; rather, its complexity is representative of the difficulty involved in trying to provide a comprehensive account of any social interaction. We want to depict the main elements involved in the process of harmful speech and the interrelationships among these elements. The potential utility of this framework lies not only in its inclusiveness of many types of harmful speech, such as racism, sexism, and ageism, but also in its specificity, as it allows for the complexity and interaction of a variety of situational, psychological, affective, social, and communicative factors. The model was developed through an eclectic approach. We drew on several different literatures (e.g., communication, social psychology, intergroup relations, critical race theory), recognizing the tension involved in welding diverse scholarly domains but not viewing this task as overly problematic.

To contextualize the harmful speech model, we begin by making explicit several key assumptions that underlie it. Specifically, we discuss the notion of self-concept and locate it in social psychology, particularly within social identity theory (Tajfel & Turner, 1986). One of our model's central tenets is that people want to maintain a positive self-concept (see Deaux, 1993; Goffman, 1963; Tajfel & Turner, 1986), and when speech undermines a person's identity, it is an unpleasant experience (Berkowitz, 1993).

HARMFUL SPEECH MODEL

Theoretical Basis

Social identity and self-categorization theories, as we have noted, focus largely on the structure and function of the self-concept and provide a foundation from which to understand how the identification process affects interaction. This theoretical basis accounts for the dialectical relationship between society and the individual, incorporating both macro-level (group relations) and micro-level (interpersonal relations) analyses. In its original formulation, social identity theory argued that individuals seek a *positive social identity*; the sought positive self-concept is based partly on the individuals' group memberships, through social *comparisons* between their own and other groups. People try to achieve *positive distinctiveness* for their own group in order to protect and maintain their self-esteem as group members. Essentially, this perspective is based on four fundamental assumptions: (a) social categorization, (b) social identity, (c) social comparison, and (d) psychological group distinctiveness. The categorization process is the first step, as individuals naturally segment the world so as to impose a structure on their environment and establish a sense of self. The part of the self-concept that derives from social group membership is then referred to as one's "social" identity. People not only assess the position and status of their social identity, they also classify others on the basis of their similarities (in-group) and differences (out-group) through a process of social comparison (Festinger, 1954). It is through social comparison that people attempt to establish a positive and distinct social identity. As Taylor and Moghaddam (1987) note, this concept of psychological distinctiveness is influenced by Marx and Freud, who, with a Western bias, characterize individuals as self-centered and irrational beings struggling to improve their position in a conflict-based society. Life is portrayed in a competitive rather than cooperative light, with individuals desiring a positive and distinct identity. This bias to favor the in-group can be extreme, resulting from both the motivation to value oneself positively and the process of simplification and clarification that stems from categorization (Hogg & Abrams, 1988).

Working from this theoretical framework, Hogg and Abrams (1988) define self-concept as "the totality of self-descriptions and self-evaluations [that are] subjectively available to the individual [and] . . . structured into . . . distinct constellations" (p. 24). Moreover, they delineate the self-concept into two relatively separate categories: *social identity,* referring to self-descriptions stemming from group membership (e.g., ethnicity, gender, occupation) and *personal identity,* pertaining to self-descriptions that are unique in nature and based on specific attributes of the individual (e.g., attributes based on close interpersonal relationships). These two different levels of identity are relatively stable and definable and may be contradictory and/or complementary to each other, because an individual's self-concept is never completely experienced as a whole unit but rather is influenced and activated in varying contexts. Thus people can construe communication encounters as either *interpersonal* (i.e., dependent on the individuals' moods, temperaments, and personalities) or *intergroup* (i.e., based entirely on the interactants' dealing with each other as representatives of different social categories). Many researchers in this area find it more productive to consider interpersonal and intergroup constructs as opposites along a single, bipolar continuum instead of as two separate continua where, for instance, one could define an interaction as low or high on both interpersonal and intergroup dimensions (see, e.g., Giles & Hewstone, 1982; Gudykunst & Ting-Toomey, 1990).[3]

In addition, Turner (1987) has noted that in terms of self-categorization theory it is more accurate to speak of multiple social identities, and Deaux (1993) argues this even further, suggesting that the distinction between personal and social identities may be arbitrary and misleading. She proposes instead that the two types of identities are interrelated: "Personal identity is defined, at least in part, by group memberships, and social categories are infused with personal meaning" (p. 5). Consequently, identity can be represented as a hierarchical structure in which sets of identities are related to categories of attributes. The question of individual self-concepts in this view becomes one of position and salience in a given situation. Individuals have multiple identities (social and personal) that are structured hierarchically as a function of context. As a result, the salience and importance of a particular identity can vary according to the context, magnifying or attenuating harmful speech.

Regardless of how we conceptualize identity, an intergroup framework recognizes that social categorization is one of the major cognitive tools individuals use to define themselves vis-à-vis the world. When social identity predominates, intergroup behavior occurs and is separate from interpersonal behavior, as its locus of control is social, not personal, identity (Gallois, Franklyn-Stokes, Giles, & Coupland, 1988; Gudykunst & Lim, 1986). From this standpoint, intergroup relations and behavior are analyzed in terms of the cognitive process of social categorization and the motivational process of self-esteem. As Hogg and Abrams (1993) explain, the categorization process satisfies a fundamental motive to simplify the environment by imposing a structure on it in a meaningful way, and the motivational process of self-esteem encourages individuals and groups to strive for relatively positive social identity. The application of this perspective has been broad, but, for our purposes, it allows a reexamination of research conducted on deprecating speech, not only by distinguishing between intergroup and interpersonal dimensions, but by explaining the causes, consequences, and generative processes underlying intergroup communication. Arguably, the same categorization and motivational processes are operating regardless of the group membership—ethnicity, age, gender, religion, class, and so forth. Thus interrelationships between previously unintegrated areas can be understood within the social identity framework.

Description of the Model

Communicative Contexts

Having noted our theoretical basis, we begin our description of the harmful speech model (see Figure 3.1) in the center, where we present four general communicative contexts that differ in terms of senders' intentions and receivers' attributions. Again, our guiding assumption is that the desire for a positive social identity mediates the kinds of intentions and attributions realized in an intergroup context. Thus the model emphasizes harmful speech directed to a person (interpersonal or mediated) as opposed to speech *about* some other person or group (e.g., Kirkland et al., 1987). However, the model still can adequately address some situations in which harmful speech is not directly expressed to its target but is said more broadly (e.g., public broadcast, overheard conversation). Recognizing that we could not capture all harmful interactions, we began with a set of situations that are generic and could typify many episodes of harmful speech. In Context 1, a speaker utters a comment intended to degrade the receiver's self-concept and successfully accomplishes this task. It is usually in this straightforward case that legal action has been pursued under the tort of intentional infliction of emotional distress or the fighting words exception to the First Amendment. For example, radio disc jockey Howard Stern was accused by a black business association of racist pandering. Stern has broadcast a "black" *Jeopardy!* game show with contestants named "Tyrone Shoelaces," "Buck Wheaties," "Malcolm Excrement," "Highly Salami," and "Marcus Welfare," and has interviewed Daniel Carver, a Ku Klux Klan spokesman, whose comments included: "Niggers have destroyed most of our public schools already. Niggers carry their dope to school. Niggers carry AIDS to school. Niggers stink up the whole classroom." Conversely, Leonard Jeffries, chair of the African American Studies Department at New York's City College, was accused of bigotry by the *Washington Post* with regard to remarks he made during a speech at an Empire State Black

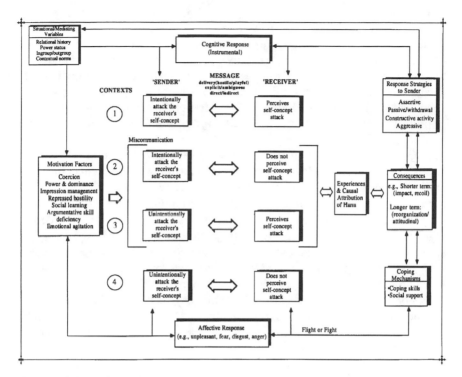

Figure 3.1. Harmful Speech Model

Arts and Cultural Festival. Jeffries claimed that "whites are pathological, dirty, dastardly, devilish folks," and that "Diane Ravitch, Assistant U.S. Secretary of Education, is a sophisticated Texas Jew, a debonair racist."

Turning to Contexts 2 and 3, there is a mismatch between the speaker's and the receiver's mental states. Context 2 represents a hearer-based misunderstanding, whereas Context 3 illustrates a speaker-based misrepresentation. Gender harassment cases often fall within these contexts. Gender harassment is defined by Till (1980) as generalized sexist remarks and behavior that are often claimed to be "misunderstandings." When men in an office or on campus whistle and comment on a woman's appearance (e.g., "Hey, great legs"), the men may intend this to be playful flirting, but the woman recipient may view it as disempowering and/or offensive. Alternatively, men's sexual remarks and joking may be meant to communicate superior power, but some women recipients may interpret them as innocent comments. Although this is a possibility, we also want to note that the most stable finding in the harassment literature is that women are far more likely than men to view gender harassment as offensive (Fitzgerald & Shullman, 1993; Tata, 1993). An incident that took place at Western Kentucky University further illustrates the potential misrepresentations inherent in communication. The university's student newspaper published a feature article with photographs of a 20-year-old unwed black student who was studying for finals with one child and about to give birth to a second. The paper's editors saw the story, which won a Hearst Award, as a sympathetic portrayal of the black woman struggling to keep her family together. However, 175 African American students gathered to protest what they thought was an attempt to stereotype the black community negatively.

In Context 4, the sender does not intend to attack the receiver's identity and is not perceived to do so. For instance, patronizing comments communicating "ageism" from young to elderly (Giles & Williams, 1994) or elderly to young (Giles, Fox, & Smith, 1993; Ryan, Meredith, & Shantz, 1994) may be viewed by the interactants as nurturing. Giles and Williams (1994) identify eight categories that describe elderly-to-young patronization based on college students' self-reports of actual comments, but it is conceivable that the use of such comments may be neither intended nor interpreted negatively. That is, when an elderly person states to a younger person, "You're doing just great, dear," or, "I'll take care of it for you," this may or may not be construed by the recipient as "condescending pet names" or "parental treatment," respectively. In other words, patronizing talk is a social attribution attached to communication rather than a message form per se. However, a third party, perhaps someone eavesdropping, may perceive the message exchange to be harmful. Another scenario further exemplifies this point. A group of Anglos and African Americans were watching a televised football game in a dorm lounge, and one white male yelled in relation to the game, "Go, nigger, go!" The speaker did not intend to denigrate blacks with this statement, and no one watching the sporting event was upset by the comment, but an African American woman who was walking past the lounge at the time was offended and reported the incident to university officials.

Message Characteristics

Characteristics of messages that invalidate an individual's self-concept or group concept (Hogg & Abrams, 1988; Kinney, 1994, 1996; Tedeschi & Felson, 1994) also are addressed in the harmful speech model (see Figure 3.1). Message characteristics are infinite, and some communication scholars have investigated the kinds of messages that result in personal harm (see Harris, 1993; Kinney, 1994; Vangelisti, 1994). Harmful messages may be couched in hostility, whereas others may be delivered playfully. The messages can be direct or indirect (i.e., through a statement directed at another person or an abstract statement). For example, directly telling a Caucasian that he has "white man's disease" (i.e., no rhythm) may have the same effect as casually stating that white people cannot dance. Subsequently, statements that are potentially deprecating may be examined on a continuum of explicitness, including comments such as insults, nasty remarks, hostile jokes, character attacks, competence attacks, profanity, and teasing (Infante & Wigley, 1986). Operationally, this means there are many types of statements that can possibly result in harmful effects. Moreover, Kinney (1994) conducted a multidimensional scaling analysis on a large sample of messages respondents identified as deprecating and found that three message characteristics defined a speaker's strategy: (a) the self-concept under attack, (b) the form, and (c) the force. Kinney then related various combinations of the three message characteristics to different emotional reactions in respondents. Conceptually, these linguistic strategies also may be linked to Brown and Levinson's (1978, 1987) theory of politeness and Searle's (1969, 1975) speech act theory.

Motivations

The framework also attends to potential motives underlying harmful speech, as identified in the aggression literature (e.g., Infante & Wigley, 1986; Taylor, 1986). Beginning with psychological explanations (see Berkowitz, 1993), it is feasible that invalidating communication may be driven by an attempt at *coercion.* That is, a speaker may be attempting to influence a receiver's behavior. Other times, verbally reducing someone else's status is done to elevate one's own group (or personal) position (Cialdini et al., 1976). Gaining the upper hand verbally preserves or enhances the sender's *power and dominance.* This motive would incorporate personal attitudes such as racism and sexism. Alternatively, harmful speech results from *impression management.* The sender is interested in promoting his or her self-image and uses verbal "jesting" to maintain or protect it. Another plausible factor is that harmful speech stems from repressed hostility, which in its extreme form may fall under the classification of psychopathy. The potentially degrading message is transferred to people who represent unresolved conflict. It is important to note that whereas psychopathy is a term often used as a substitute for mental illness or psychiatric disturbance, the notion of transference can occur without a serious disorder (Moberly, 1985).

Turning to developmental matters, Bandura's (1978) *social learning* theory proposes that aggressive behavior (verbal in our case) results from social modeling. Thus the use of deprecating speech may result from a person's learning history. Individual response patterns can stem from both direct experiences with family and friends and vicarious experience through television and film. From a communicative perspective, Infante, Trebing, Shepherd, and Seeds (1984) point out that, at least in argumentative situations, people who lack an ability to refute and defend positions tend to attack the self-concepts of others. Consequently, harmful speech also may result because a person does not have the *argumentative skills* to recognize controversial issues, to advocate positions on them, and to refute other positions (e.g., Infante & Rancer, 1982, 1996).

Lastly, *emotional agitation* refers to impulsive utterances that occur when a person is emotionally aroused. For example, Pankratz, Levendusky, and Glaudin (1976) asked college students to identify situations that elicit in them anger or a loss of temper and constructed seven categories based upon responses. Students apparently become emotionally agitated (a) as a result of totalizing, that is, assessing a person in terms of only one characteristic (e.g., stingy, unfair); (b) in response to aversive traits, behaviors, or characteristics (e.g., a person has a bad attitude or is bothersome); (c) if they perceive a personal affront (e.g., humiliation, rejection, embarrassment); (d) if they perceive their roles and options to be restricted (e.g., control and authority issues); (e) because of a pressure buildup (e.g., frustration, stress, repeated provocation); (f) in response to their own behavior (e.g., failings or inadequacies); and (g) when they perceive themselves as victims of cruelty (e.g., hostility, physical or psychological injury). Any one of these situations could ignite a verbal attack. Taken together, the above motivations may—either individually or in combination—account for many of the occurrences of harmful speech.

Experience and Causal Attribution of Harm

The experience and causal attribution of harm recognizes that harm may be evaluated on several *levels,* such as societal (deontic harm), group, relational, and individual (e.g., Post, 1991), and that not all people will experience any particular message as harmful. For example, Infante (1987) points out that verbal aggression can be constructive. He reminds us that whether an act is considered constructive or destructive can vary with the vantage point of the person making the attribution. Like all communication, responses are mediated by past experiences, psychological and physical strength, status, needs, goals, and so forth (Haiman, 1993). For each person who experiences hurt or lowered self-esteem as a result of degrading utterances, another may let the same words bounce off of him or her, and the experience may even result in a strengthening of that individual's tolerance and restraint (Hyde & Fishman, 1991). Some people are more resilient to the vicissitudes of life than others. On a Southern California university campus, a group of Asian women were walking to class and a Caucasian male walking by shouted, "A.I., A.I.," which stood for "Asian invasion" (Nishita, 1993). Although some of the women interpreted the epithet as a self-concept attack, others in the group did not. They all, however, felt the speech was harmful in that they expressed personal hurt (individual level), disappointment with the intergroup dynamics (group level), and outrage at its occurrence (deontic harm). Moreover, with respect to different levels and kinds of harm, Smolla's (1993) legal categorization of speech injuries further demonstrates the variability conceivable in this dimension (see Table 3.1).

Aside from having varying impacts and occurring on several levels, the harm resulting from verbal aggression may be conceptualized in several ways (Calvert, 1997). The first approach stems from an effects research tradition in communication that focuses on emotional, attitudinal, and behavioral changes (e.g., Giles & Street, 1995; Katz, 1980). Working from this perspective, the harm resulting from speech would be operationalized as negative emotions, hurt feelings, physical changes, mental anguish, and other undesired personal changes. Alternatively, the second approach is endorsed by traditions such as cultural studies (Grossberg, Nelson, & Treichler, 1992), critical race theory (Matsuda et al., 1993), and feminism (MacKinnon, 1993). From this frame of reference, harm is interpreted as the production of a social reality and environment of hate. That is, verbally disturbing communication creates and perpetuates a hostile reality. In this vein, and under Title VII of the U.S. Civil Rights Act of 1964, sexually offensive speech is a legally redressable harm when it results in a hostile working environment. Thus the notion of harm is extended outside the individual and reasonably believed to reside also in the environment's effect on the individual. Both operationalizations of harm can be useful, and the two are not mutually exclusive.

Response Strategies to Sender

Next, we have identified four general responses to communication that may deprecate self-worth and/or group worth, based on our own observations and the very limited literature available. First, a person may be *passive,* choosing to withdraw and remain silent. Although this is often associated with feelings of helplessness and low self-worth, it may sometimes represent strength and self-control. A second response can be one of *assertiveness* (e.g., Harwood & Giles, 1996). The receiver may directly and appropriately express his or her thoughts and feelings in a way that does not invalidate the sender. However, the receiver also may choose to divert attention creatively to other matters, or turn the comment into a joke. This third strategy is referred to as *constructive activity.* A fourth response could be one of *retaliatory aggression,* broadly construed as physical or verbal behavior intended to harm the sender. Certainly more response strategies may be empirically derived from subsequent research aimed at discovering a typology, but in the meantime, the four above can be used as a springboard for exploring how victims of harmful speech manage the speech.

Consequences

The full implications of harmful speech are still unclear (VandenBos & Bryant, 1987), and more research is needed, but the Center for the Applied Study of Prejudice and Ethnoviolence has found some evidence to support claims of both long- and short-term damage in individuals (Ehrlich, Larcom, & Purvis, 1995). There is also growing research on the effect of traumatic events (Frieze, Hymer, & Greenberg, 1987). Quantitative and qualitative studies examining the behavior of victims have found commonality across a range of traumatic situations (e.g., rape, domestic violence, assault, burglary). Although exact components vary, Bard and Sangrey (1986) argue that traumatic events will result in a predictable sequence of three stages: (a) impact-disorganization, (b) recoil, and (c) reorganization. In the impact-disorganization phase immediately following the traumatizing event, recipients display emotional reactions that may include anger, denial, disbelief, and a feeling of violation or vulnerability. This stage can last from hours to days. Giles and Harwood (1997) contend that a person's ability to manage the reception of harmful speech "successfully" (e.g., by rebuttal or defusing) and immediately may be a powerful element in dictating short-term effects. Moreover, regularly experiencing interactive failures to manage harmful speech encounters can accumulate over the life span and result in longer-term effects, such as depression and low life satisfaction. In the next stage, recoil, other short-term emotional reactions emerge. Specifically, the individual experiences emotional swings (e.g., fear to anger) or conflicting reactions (self-blame to other-blame). Loss of identity, self-respect, and trust are also common. The long-term reorganization phase involves attempts at coping and behavioral changes. That is, the individual is able to resolve the trauma of the event in this last stage by establishing more effective defensive-vigilant behaviors and revising values and attitudes to readjust to everyday life. According to Bard and Sangrey's (1986) three-stage framework of traumatic events, the model depicts potential consequences in both the short run (e.g., various psychological burdens) and the long run (e.g., lower self-esteem). The emotional consequences of the first two stages, impact-disorganization and recoil, are short-term effects, whereas the consequences of the third stage, reorganization, defined by attitudinal and behavioral changes, are long-term effects.[4]

Coping Mechanisms

Additionally, the coping mechanisms of the targets of deprecating speech are recognized as an important element and incorporated into the model. It appears that the receiver's interpretation of and reaction to a harmful message is determined in part by his or her coping strategies. For example, Feagin and Sikes (1994) argue that the experience of discrimination is not just a personal matter. It has an impact on the individual, but it also affects that person's family and community: "Victims frequently share their stories with family and friends, often to lighten the burden, and this sharing creates a domino effect of anguish and anger rippling across an extended group" (p. 16). Friedman, Bischoff, Davis, and Person (1982) found that the more supporters the victims of traumatic events have, the sooner they recover from the stress of the experience. Social support appears to protect people in crisis from a variety of pathological states, including physical illness and depression (Dakof

& Taylor, 1990; Kaniasty & Norris, 1992). It seems that the victim's distress and attribution of harm is related to the victim's choice of coping response. Coping mechanisms such as shared accounts of the event move particular incidents from the "I" of personal experience to the "we" of a broad group consciousness (Feagin & Sikes, 1994) and influence the relational history and intergroup dynamics. In the model, individuals' coping skills and social supports, or absence thereof, are depicted as mutually intertwined with all other aspects of the model.

Cognitive and Affective Processes

In light of recent theoretical advances examining the mutual interaction between cognition and affect (e.g., Hamilton & Mackie, 1993), the harmful speech model incorporates both processes as important antecedents of behavior for both the sender and the receiver. For example, consider the sender. Smith (1993) hypothetically illustrates that prejudice can stem from either a cognitive or an emotional base. That is, prejudice may be conceptualized as an attitude, such as when an individual decides that he or she does not *like* members of "group A" because they are dirty and lazy. Thus he or she prefers to avoid members of group A. On the other hand, prejudice also can be conceptualized as an emotion, such as when an individual *feels* anger and resentment toward members of group A because they are receiving benefits that are supported by that person's hard-earned tax dollars. Consequently, she or he may want to hurt group A and end this type of government handout. In addition, Marcus, Sullivan, Theiss-Morse, and Wood (1995) found that asking people to attend to their thoughts or feelings had a highly significant effect on their tolerance judgments of a disliked group. When asked to attend to their feelings, individuals focused on their dislike of the group and therefore reacted with intolerance. When asked to attend to their thoughts, they focused on the benefits of tolerance so as to override their natural instinct to be intolerant. Although it is important to acknowledge emotionally and cognitively triggered behavior, actions are most likely a combination of these two processes and not one or the other. The double arrows in Figure 3.1 are meant to indicate that the two processes are in continuous and mutual interaction. To what degree the affective and cognitive factors exert influence on each other is difficult to delineate. At times, as cognitive-oriented theorists would point out, thoughts may shape both the nature of emotional experience and the behavior that is displayed. For example, a person who views homosexual behavior as perverse may experience feelings of revulsion and disgust when encountering a person identified as gay. In other instances, people can be carried away by their emotions, and their behavior may be spontaneous, as in acts of passion. That is, emotion can potentially elicit behavior with minimal cognitive processing and even be an antecedent of cognition. For instance, intergroup scholars have argued that stereotypes may reflect a justification for emotions felt around an out-group (e.g., Dijker, 1989): An emotion of fear may be translated into a stereotype of group aggressiveness.

With regard to affectively driven behavior, the model appeals to Berkowitz's (1993) theoretical framework of emotional aggression. Berkowitz proposes that it is *unpleasant feelings* rather than stressful events that serve as the basic spur to emotional aggression. As a result of our biological programming, unpleasant feelings give rise to "fight" or "flight" tendencies: "Fight tendencies [constitute] the inclination to attack someone (preferably but not only the perceived source of the felt unpleasantness) while . . . flight reactions [comprise] the inclination to escape or to avoid the aversive situation" (p. 57). Likewise, in terms of the receivers' responses to utterances intended and/or perceived to be insulting, their strategies are very likely also to be governed by flight (passiveness) or fight (aggression) propensities. Even though flight-versus-fight contrasts may seem overly simplistic, the inclusion of this dichotomy is meant to encourage consideration of advances in emotion theory and methodology (e.g., Vanman & Miller, 1993) at this initial stage of theory building on harmful speech.

Situational Dynamics

Conversations occur against a complex backdrop of circumstances. For example, consider the "n-word": Its meaning depends upon who uses it, and in what context. When whites use the word, its meaning is almost always taken by blacks as contemptuous, unmistakably conveying the notion that blacks are second-class citizens or worse. When young male blacks use it, it can be a benign, even positive, word. From a diverse number of disciplines ranging from anthropology to social psychology, it has been observed that situational factors can have important influences on a wide number of aspects of speech (Hewstone & Giles, 1986). Each situation has its own set of norms. As Furnham (1986) notes, it is unquestionably not *whether* situational factors influence communication, but *which* aspects of the situation influence speech, and how. For example, it is a person's background (immediate and past history), the relationship between people (personal, role, group membership), the norms of a given situation, the setting (formal or informal), and the larger structure of society that encloses the interaction that can contribute to the exchange of messages. Berkowitz (1993) reviewed a broad list of experimental studies showing that factors such as irritating cigarette smoke, foul odors, and disgusting scenes increase the punishment given to, or hostility displayed toward, another person. When analyzing communication, it is important to locate individuals in their social and cultural contexts.

All the double arrows throughout the model indicate relationships between variables, which reflects a systems-based view of communication (Ruesch & Bateson, 1951/1968). Each element in the model is dynamically interrelated with every other element, just as these elements are interrelated in reality. For example, the communication between the sender and receiver is viewed as transactional, occurring between and mutually influencing the people as they act together. Additionally, cognitive and affective dimensions work separately and together to influence the sender's motivations and the receiver's response strategies. The double arrows linking the receiver's perception of self-concept attack, attribution of harm, the response strategy, and consequences also point to reciprocal influence. For example, the consequence of the degrading speech will affect the receiver's response strategy as well as the extent to which the receiver interprets the speech as harmful and whether the utterance is viewed as a self-concept attack and vice versa. Finally, double arrows connecting the situational variables, response strategies, and consequences indicate that in the long run these factors may affect the broader group dynamics and change intergroup relations. Moreover, the situational context, such as the intergroup dynamics or the relational history between the interactants, may affect the interpretation of the message and thus the influence, the response to, and the consequences of a particular message.

In sum, the harmful speech model identifies four communicative contexts that provide a base from which we can examine the motivations and consequences underlying, as well as the cognitive and emotional processes operating on, utterances that result in harm. Moreover, the sender's intentions along with the receiver's attributions allow for the processes of miscommunication to be incorporated in the framework. Thus harmful speech is located in a complex system of broader contextual factors that operate in a cyclical fashion, depicting a complex interplay of all elements. As a result, the potential for social and individual change also can be examined within the framework that we have proposed.

EPILOGUE

Future Research Agenda

The study of harmful speech is in its infancy, and thus it is neither theoretically nor methodologically sophisticated. We have presented the harmful speech model in an attempt to fill an immediate need for common-ground exchange among interdisciplinary scholars concerned with this phenomenon. We believe that communication researchers are especially well situated to push this emerging field toward greater coherence and rigor. Whether this conceptual scheme or another is adopted, the area is eminently in need of more specific and detailed pictures of the processes and dynamics underlying harmful speech. As our review suggests, there is much to be done, and we hope that our model can serve as a complex heuristic, a catalyst serving as one of many potential construction blocks that may help us build our way out of a theoretical void. However, our framework does have its problems.

Despite the value of a nonrecursive model, the boundaries are somewhat indeterminate (e.g., cognitive and affective processes). Moreover, it lacks empirical support as well as explication of the various interrelationships not previously addressed. Notwithstanding these inevitable limitations, the model's objective is to make connections among diverse literatures and thus promote descriptive understanding and predictive possibilities. In keeping with this goal, we want to point out several future directions afforded by features of this new model.

To begin, many core questions exist regarding the potential damage of harmful speech. On a micro level, we do not fully understand the physiological effects that may result from harmful speech. Some communication scholars have begun a programmatic effort to link emotional (e.g., distress) and cognitive responses with messages (Dillard & Kinney, 1994; Kinney, 1994; Kinney & Cloven, 1994, 1995). However, we need further investigation of how harmful speech may affect a person's well-being. In addition, what environmental conditions, personal qualities, message characteristics, and perceived motivations facilitate or constrain the experience and causal attribution of harm? Recall that scholars have conducted extensive research across many traumatic events and have documented a similar predictive sequence: impact-disorganization, recoil, and reorganization. When speech is perceived as harmful, do individual responses follow Bard and Sangrey's (1986) three-stage process, undergoing emotional then cognitive and/or behavioral actions? Content analyses of racist exchanges, sexual harassment, and other such accounts may reveal dynamics similar to those found in victims of other traumatic events. Furthermore, do the immediate and/or long-term consequences of harmful speech vary by form (if at all)? Are there differences in the ways harmful speech is experienced (cognitively and affectively) when it is aimed at an individual's personal identity as opposed to social identity? Do attitudes (e.g., Simon & Greenberg, 1996) or emotions regarding the speaker and receiver mitigate the perception of harm? It would also be interesting to investigate how responses to harmful speech vary over the life span (see Nussbaum, 1989). For example, anti-Semitic speech may have a graver impact on a child in his or her developmental years than on an adult. Finally, when we consider macro-level effects, can we find evidence that harmful speech results in group and societal consequences such as the divisive social climate Whillock (1995) and critical race theorists (e.g., Matsuda et al., 1993) suggest? Although there are inherent design difficulties in capturing these societal effects, the full implications of harmful speech will be incomplete without such investigation.

Answers to the above questions as well as others may provide pragmatic contributions to the legal system in terms of First Amendment implications. Research able to identify and document damage resulting from harmful speech may inform the evolving controversy over hate speech. It may help disentangle the times when speech should be endured and dismissed as the rough edges of society from those when speech has superseded tolerable limits and thus warrants liability. In terms of sexual harassment, it may encourage victims to pursue formal action and help courts adjudicate claims. In general, programmatic efforts aimed at addressing legal and policy issues need more attention.

Although we do not expect to eliminate the occurrence of harmful speech, a central goal for future research may include the identification of strategies that could effectively mitigate negative personal and societal effects. For example, what coping skills and social support aid or hinder the recovery process? Are successful restoration strategies consistent across different kinds of damage and manifestations of harmful speech? Can cognitive- and affective-based responses be connected to specific types of response strategies, consequences, and coping mechanisms? In particular, we would encourage more investigation of response strategies and effective coping mechanisms. It is likely that the two factors are closely linked; successful coping strategies may lead to some insight into appropriate response strategies, which subsequently may mediate short- and long-term consequences. In addition, the perceived motivation underlying harmful speech will in some measure contribute to a person's response, the consequences he or she perceives, and the coping strategy he or she selects.

Other important considerations may include the exploration of how situational factors influence the attribution and experience of harmful speech. For example, sociohistorical relations between ethnic groups may magnify the effects of ethnic epithets; the more adverse the intergroup relationship (e.g., the relations between Korean Americans and African Americans in Los Angeles), the greater the perceived harm and potential repercussions for present intergroup relations. Along these lines, studies on harmful speech have been either overly speaker oriented or overly receiver oriented (mainly in studies of sexual harassment); they have not fully integrated both participants into a common interactive framework. We encourage the examination of reciprocal aspects of both interactants. Just as cognitive and affective responses to harmful speech may be linked to different management strategies, future research may also examine the connection between cognitive and affective responses to motivations underlying deprecating speech. Additionally, message characteristics (e.g., force, form) will probably vary in systematic and predictable ways depending upon whether the behavior is emotionally or attitudinally driven. As more work is conducted along these lines and others, the model should contribute to an understanding of the processes underlying and associated with harmful speech.

Summary

In this chapter we have integrated a wide and diverse scholarship under the rubric of harmful speech. We have broadened a predominantly interpersonal focus to include an intergroup one. We have extended Infante and Wigley's (1986) definition of verbal aggression to incorporate analysis of both the speaker's intent to harm and the listener's attribution of harm as well as expanded potential effects beyond a personal analysis to denote possible group and societal consequences. We have briefly contextualized our discussion in the verbal aggression tradition, and we have overviewed four of the more established intergroup areas along with jurisprudential and rhetorical work. We have also presented the harmful speech model in an effort to tie together factors and research that could increase our understanding of the processes underlying harmful speech. Our goal has been to provide a framework that can make useful connections across academic boundaries, summarize findings, and generate and guide future research. We have highlighted its inclusive nature, potentially encompassing intergroup domains such as ageism, racism, ableism, and sexual harassment at the workplace or in the schoolyard (Title IX of the Federal Education Amendments of 1972), while at the same time recognizing that each area comes with its separate scholarly dynamics, culture, and history. Finally, we have offered some leads for future investigations.

Although some may perceive verbally communicated prejudices such as sexism, racism, anti-Semitism, ageism, ableism, and homophobia as independent processes that should be examined in conceptual isolation, we contend that it is more advantageous to organize our efforts under some common framework. Arguably, a harmful speech model and/or theory does not require a context-specific explanation. The communication field often has been criticized for its high level of fragmentation (e.g., Berger, 1991), and we believe integrative efforts have greater potential for generating theoretical activity, which the field lacks (Berger & Chaffee, 1987; Hawkins, Wiemann, & Pingree, 1988). Harmful speech is a vital issue that societies must confront as they deal with demographic changes (e.g., aging population, ethnic diversity, changing workforce) and their resulting implications for notions of community and equal opportunity. As Nardi and Bolton (1991) note, derogatory epithets are the most commonly reported hate crime for all intergroup domains, but this category is often omitted in the statistical reports of such crimes. The field of communication stands in a unique position to contribute to public scholarship with regard to this neglected societal ill. It would behoove us to do so.

NOTES

1. For the sake of clarity, the unit of analysis concern is discussed in relation to measuring one possible dependent variable: harm. This does not translate into a methodological dilemma for interpersonal and intergroup analyses. In light of SIT and SCT, we are defining the group as a psychological entity. That is, we are looking at the identifications of individuals. As Hogg and

Abrams (1988) note, it is a simple transition from regarding the group as external to regarding it as part of the self-concept: "By avoiding the reduction of groups to individuals, it allows us to conceptualize the relationship between individual and society and to place theoretically the group within the individual" (p. 218). Thus measuring social identity is as effective as measuring any other psychological phenomenon.

2. According to Fox and Giles (1996b), *disability* refers to people who experience group differentiation due to physical abnormality (i.e., facial and body) that limits their mobility but who otherwise are not cognitively or linguistically impaired.

3. Arguably, two continua may be conceptually superior to the bipolar option in the sense that an encounter mapped at the center of the latter could actually imply high intergroup plus high interindividual or low for both. The two-dimensional space would clarify such ambiguity as well as add further specificity.

4. The turmoil resulting from traumatic events is usually resolved within 6 months to a year (Salasin, 1981). Some individuals are able to adjust without any distress whereas others experience chronic stress.

REFERENCES

Adelman, R., Greene, M., Charon, R., & Friedman, E. (1990). Issues in physician-geriatric patient relationship. In H. Giles, N. Coupland, & J. M. Wiemann (Eds.), *Communication, health and the elderly: Fulbright International Colloquium 8* (pp. 126-134). Manchester: Manchester University Press.

Allen, I. (1990). *Unkind words: Ethnic labeling from redskin to WASP.* South Hadley, MA: Bergin & Garvey.

Allen, M., Emmers, T. M., Gebhardt, L., & Giery, M. (1995). Pornography and rape myth acceptance. *Journal of Communication, 45*(1), 5-26.

Allport, G. W. (1979). *The nature of prejudice.* Reading, MA: Addison-Wesley.

Alschuler, C., & Alschuler, A. (1984). Developing healthy responses to anger: The counselor's role. *Journal of Counseling and Development, 63,* 26-29.

Aries, E. (1996). *Men and women in interaction.* New York: Oxford University Press.

Arthur, J., & Shapiro, A. (Eds.). (1995). *Campus wars: Multi-culturalism and the politics of difference.* Boulder, CO: Westview.

Ashburn, G., & Gordon, A. (1981). Features of a simplified register in speech to elderly conversationalists. *International Journal of Psycholinguistics, 8,* 7-31.

Baldwin, J. R., & Hecht, M. L. (1995). The layered perspective of cultural (in)tolerance(s): The roots of a multidisciplinary approach. In R. L. Wiseman (Ed.), *Intercultural communication theory* (pp. 59-91). Thousand Oaks, CA: Sage.

Baltes, M., & Wahl, H. (1996). Patterns of communication in old age: The dependency-support and independence-ignorance script. *Health Communication, 8,* 217-231.

Bandura, A. (1978). Social learning theory of aggression. *Journal of Communication, 28*(3), 1-26.

Banks, S. P., Gao G., & Baker, B. (1991). Intercultural encounters and miscommunication. In N. Coupland, H. Giles, & J. M. Wiemann (Eds.), *"Miscommunication" and problematic talk* (pp. 103-120). Newbury Park, CA: Sage.

Bard, M., & Sangrey, D. (1986). *The crime victim's book* (2nd ed.). New York: Brunner/Mazel.

Baumhover, L., & Beall, S. (Eds.). (1996). *Abuse, neglect and exploitation of older persons.* Baltimore: Health Professions.

Bayer, C. L., & Cegala, D. J. (1992). Trait verbal aggressiveness and argumentativeness: Relations with parenting style. *Western Journal of Communication, 56,* 301-310.

Beall, A., & Sternberg, R. (1993). *The psychology of gender.* New York: Guilford.

Becker, M. (1995). The legitimacy of judicial review in speech cases. In L. Lederer & R. Delgado (Eds.), *The price we pay: The case against racist speech, hate propaganda, and pornography* (pp. 208-215). New York: Hill & Wang.

Bell, J. (1992). In search of a discourse of aging: The elderly on television. *Gerontologist, 32,* 305-311.

Bem, S. L. (1993). *The lenses of gender: Transforming the debate on sexual inequality.* New Haven, CT: Yale University Press.

Berger, C. R. (1991). Why are there so few communication theories? Communication theories and other curios [Chautauqua]. *Communication Monographs, 58,* 101-113.

Berger, C. R., & Chaffee, S. H. (1987). The study of communication as a science. In C. R. Berger & S. H. Chaffee (Eds.), *Handbook of communication science* (pp. 15-19). Newbury Park, CA: Sage.

Berkowitz, L. (1993). *Aggression: Its causes, consequences and control.* Philadelphia: Temple University Press.

Berman, L., & Sobkowksa-Ashcroft, I. (1986). The old in language and literature. *Language and Communication, 6,* 139-145.

Billig, M. (1988). The notion of "prejudice": Some rhetorical and ideological aspects. *Text, 8,* 91-110.

Billig, M., Condor, S., Edwards, D., Gane, M., Middleton, D., & Radley, A. (1988). *Ideological dilemmas.* Newbury Park, CA: Sage.

Blanchard, R., & Blanchard, D. (Eds.). (1986). *Advances in the study of aggression* (Vol. 2). Orlando, FL: Academic Press.

Bloom, A. (1987). *The closing of the American mind: Education and the crisis of reason.* New York: Simon & Schuster.

Bograd, M. (1990). Why we need gender to understand human violence. *Journal of Interpersonal Violence, 5,* 132-135.

Bowers, J. W., & Bradac, J. J. (1982). Issues in communication theory: A metatheoretical analysis. In M. Burgoon (Ed.), *Communication yearbook 5* (pp. 1-27). New Brunswick, NJ: Transaction.

Boxer, D. (1993). Complaining and commiserating: Exploring gender issues. *Text, 13,* 371-396.

Bradac, J. J. (Ed.). (1989). *Message effects in communication science.* Newbury Park, CA: Sage.

Braithwaite, V. (1986). Old age stereotypes: Reconciling contradictions. *Journal of Gerontology, 41,* 353-360.

Briere, J. N. (1992). *Child abuse trauma: Theory and treatment of the lasting effects.* Newbury Park, CA: Sage.

Broverman, I. K., Vogel, S. R., Broverman, D. M., Clarkson, F. E., & Rosenkrantz, P. S. (1994). Sex-role stereotypes: A current appraisal. In B. Puka (Ed.), *Caring voices and women's moral frames: Gilligan's view. Moral development: A compendium* (Vol. 6, pp. 191-210). New York: Garland.

Brown, P., & Levinson, S. (1978). Universals in language usage: Politeness phenomena. In E. Goody (Ed.), *Questions and politeness: Strategies in social interaction* (pp. 56-289). Cambridge: Cambridge University Press.

Brown, P., & Levinson, S. (1987). *Politeness: Some universals in language usage.* London: Cambridge University Press.

Buchanan, P. (1995, March 20). *Announcement speech,* Manchester, New Hampshire [On-line]. Available: http://www.buchanan.org/pessay.html

Buckner, J. (1988). The development of an instrument to measure neighborhood cohesion. *American Journal of Community Psychology, 16,* 771-791.

Buss, A. (1961). *The psychology of aggression.* New York: John Wiley.

Butler, T. (1995). Why the First Amendment is being used to protect violence against women. In L. Lederer & R. Delgado (Eds.), *The price we pay: The case against racist speech, hate propaganda, and pornography* (pp. 160-168). New York: Hill & Wang.

Calvert, C. (1997). Hate speech and its harms: A communication theory perspective. *Journal of Communication, 47*(1), 4-19.

Cargile, A. C., & Giles, H. (1996). Intercultural communication training: Review, critique, and a new theoretical framework. In B. R. Burleson (Ed.), *Communication yearbook 19* (pp. 385-423). Thousand Oaks, CA: Sage.

Cella, D. (1994). Quality of life: Concepts and definition. *Journal of Pain and Symptom Management, 9,* 186-192.

Cherry, R. (1989). *Discrimination: Its impact on blacks, women and Jews.* Lexington, MA: Lexington.

Choi, J., & Murphy, J. (1992). *The politics and philosophy of political correctness.* Westport, CT: Praeger.

Cialdini, R., Borden, R., Thorne, A., Walker, M., Freeman, S., & Sloan, L. (1976). Basking in reflected glory: Three (football) field studies. *Journal of Personality and Social Psychology, 34,* 366-374.

Cleveland, J., & Kerst, M. (1993). Sexual harassment and perceptions of power: An under-articulated relationship. *Journal of Vocational Behavior, 42,* 49-67.

Coates, J. (1992). *Women, men and language* (2nd ed.). London: Longman.

Coates, L., Bavelas, J., & Gibson, J. (1994). Anomalous language in sexual assault trail judgments. *Discourse and Society, 5,* 189-206.

Condor, S. (1988). "Race stereotypes" and racist discourse. *Text, 8,* 69-90.

Coupland, J., Coupland, N., & Grainger, K. (1991). Intergenerational discourse: Contextual versions of aging and elderliness. *Ageing and Society, 11,* 189-208.

Coupland, N., & Coupland, J. (1990). Language and later life. In H. Giles & W. Robinson (Eds.), *Handbook of language and social psychology* (pp. 451-468). London: John Wiley.

Coupland, N., Giles, H., & Wiemann, J. M. (Eds.). (1991). *"Miscommunication" and problematic talk.* Newbury Park, CA: Sage.

D'Amato, A. (1991). Harmful speech and the culture of indeterminacy. *William and Mary Law Review, 32,* 329-351.

Dakof, G., & Taylor, S. (1990). Victims' perceptions of social support: What is helpful from whom? *Journal of Personality and Social Psychology, 58,* 80-89.

Deaux, K. (1993). Reconstructing social identity. *Personality and Social Psychology Bulletin, 19,* 4-12.

DeFrancisco, V. (1991). The sounds of silence: How men silence women in marital relations. *Discourse and Society, 2,* 413-424.

Delgado, R. (1982). Words that wound: A tort action for racial insults, epithets, and name-calling. *Harvard Civil Rights-Civil Liberties Law Review, 17,* 133-181.

Delgado, R., & Yun, D. (1995). Pressure valves and bloodied chickens: An assessment of four paternalistic arguments for resisting hate-speech regulation. In L. Lederer & R. Delgado (Eds.), *The price we pay: The case against racist speech, hate propaganda, and pornography* (pp. 290-300). New York: Hill & Wang.

de Rivera, J. (1992). Emotional climate: Social structure and emotional dynamics. In K. Strongman (Ed.), *International review of studies on emotion* (Vol. 2, pp. 197-218). New York: John Wiley.

Detweiler, R. (1986). Categorization, attribution and intergroup communication. In W. B. Gudykunst (Ed.), *Intergroup communication* (pp. 62-73). London: Edward Arnold.

Dijker, A. (1989). Ethnic attitudes and emotions. In J. van Oudenhoven & T. Willemsen (Eds.), *Ethnic minorities: Social psychological perspectives* (pp. 77-93). Amsterdam: Swets & Zeitlinger.

Dillard, J. P., Henwood, K., Giles, H., Coupland, N., & Coupland J. (1990). Compliance-gaining young and old: Beliefs about influence in different age groups. *Communication Reports, 3,* 84-91.

Dillard, J. P., & Kinney, T. (1994). Experiential and physiological responses to interpersonal influence. *Human Communication Research, 20,* 502-528.

Donnerstein, E., Slaby, R., & Eron, L. (1995). The mass media and youth aggression. In L. Eron, J. Gentry, & P. Schlegel (Eds.), *Reason to hope: A psychological perspective on violence and youth* (pp. 219-250). Washington, DC: American Psychological Association.

D'Souza, D. (1991). *Illiberal education*. New York: Free Press.

Eggeman, K., & Moxley, V. (1985). Assessing spouses' perceptions of Gottman's temporal form in marital conflict. *Psychological Reports, 57*, 171-181.

Ehrlich, H. (1990). *Campus ethnoviolence and the policy options* (Institute Report No. 4). Baltimore: National institute Against Prejudice and Violence.

Ehrlich, H., Larcom, B., & Purvis, R. (1995). The traumatic impact of ethnoviolence. In L. Lederer & R. Delgado (Eds.), *The price we pay: The case against racist speech, hate propaganda, and pornography* (pp. 62-79). New York: Hill & Wang.

Emry, O. (1986). Linguistic decrement in normal aging. *Language and Communication, 6*, 47-64.

Emry, R., & Wiseman, R. L. (1987). An intercultural understanding of able-bodied and disabled persons' communication. *International Journal of Intercultural Relations, 11*, 7-27.

Essed, P. (1990). *Everyday racism*. Claremont, CA: Hunter House.

Essed, P. (1991). *Understanding everyday racism: An interdisciplinary theory*. Newbury Park, CA: Sage.

Feagin, J. R., & Sikes, M. (1994). *Living with racism: The black middle-class experience*. Boston: Beacon.

Felson, R., & Tedeschi, J. T. (Eds.). (1993). *Aggression and violence: Social interactionist perspectives*. Washington, DC: American Psychological Association.

Fenstermaker, S., West, C., & Zimmerman, D. H. (1991). Gender inequality: New conceptual terrain. In R. Blumberg (Ed.), *Gender, family, and economy: The triple overlap* (pp. 289-307). Newbury Park, CA: Sage.

Festinger, L. (1954). A theory of social comparison processes. *Human Relations, 7*, 117-140.

Fichten, C., Amsel, R., Bourdon, C., & Creti, L. (1988). Interaction between college students with physical disabilities and their professors. *Journal of Applied Rehabilitation Counseling, 19*, 13-20.

Fichten, C., & Bourdon, C. (1986). Social skill deficit or response inhibition: Interaction between disabled and nondisabled college students. *Journal of College Student Personnel, 27*, 326-333.

Fitzgerald, L., & Shullman, S. (1993). Sexual harassment: A research analysis and agenda for the 1990s. *Journal of Vocational Behavior, 42*, 5-27.

Flores, N., & Hopper, R. (1975). Mexican Americans' evaluations of spoken Spanish and English. *Speech Monographs, 42*, 91-98.

Fox, S. (1994). *Patronizing others in intergroup encounters: The experiences and evaluations of people in interability situations*. Unpublished doctoral dissertation,University of California, Santa Barbara, Department of Communication.

Fox, S., & Giles, H. (1996a). Interability communication: Evaluating patronizing encounter. *Journal of Language and Social Psychology, 15*, 265-290.

Fox, S., & Giles, H. (1996b). "Let the wheelchair through!": An intergroup approach to interability communication. In W. Robinson (Ed.), *Social psychology and social identity: Festschrift in honor of Henri Tajfel* (pp. 215-248). Amsterdam: Elsevier.

Frankl, V. (1984). *Man's search for meaning: An introduction to logotherapy* (3rd ed.). New York: Simon & Schuster.

Friedman, K., Bischoff, H., Davis, R., & Person, A. (1982). *Victims and helpers: Reactions to crime*. New York: Victim Services Agency.

Frieze, I. H., Hymer, S., & Greenberg, M. (1987). Describing the crime victim: Psychological reactions to victimization. *Professional Psychology: Research and Practice, 18*, 299-315.

Furnham, A. (1986). Assertiveness through different media. *Journal of Language and Social Psychology, 5*, 1-11.

Gallois, C., Franklyn-Stokes, A., Giles, H., & Coupland, N. (1988). Communication accommodation in intercultural encounters. In Y. Y. Kim & W. B. Gudykunst (Eds.), *Theories in intercultural communication* (pp. 157-185). Newbury Park, CA: Sage.

Gallois, C., Giles, H., Jones, E., Cargile, A. C., & Ota, H. (1995). Accommodating intercultural encounters: Elaborations and extensions. In R. L. Wiseman (Ed.), *Intercultural communication theory* (pp. 115-147). Thousand Oaks, CA: Sage.

Garbarino, J., & Garbarino, A. (1987). *Emotional maltreatment of children.* Chicago: National Committee for the Prevention of Child Abuse.

Geiser, D. (1989). Psychosocial influences on human immunity. *Clinical Psychology Review, 9,* 689-715.

Gerbner, G. (1994). Learning productive aging as a social role: The lessons of television. In S. Bass, F. Caro, & Y. Chen (Eds.), *Achieving a productive aging society* (pp. 207-219). Westport, CT: Greenwood.

Gerbner, G., Gross, L., Signorielli, N., & Morgan, M. (1980). Aging with television: Images on television drama and conceptions of social reality. *Journal of Communication, 30*(1), 37-47.

Giles, H. (1979). Ethnicity markers in speech. In K. Scherer & H. Giles (Eds.), *Social markers in speech* (pp. 251-290). Cambridge: Cambridge University Press.

Giles, H., & Coupland, N. (1992). *Language: Contexts and consequences.* Pacific Grove, CA: Brooks/Cole.

Giles, H., Coupland, N., Henwood, K., & Coupland J. (1990). The social meaning of RP: An intergenerational perspective. In S. Ramsaran (Ed.), *Studies in the pronunciation of English: A commemorative volume in honor of A. C. Gimson* (pp. 191-210). London: Routledge.

Giles, H., Fox, S., & Smith, E. (1993). Patronizing the elderly: Intergenerational evaluations. *Research on Language and Social Interaction, 26,* 129-149.

Giles, H., & Harwood, J. (1997). Managing intergroup communication: Lifespan issues and consequences. In S. Eliasson & E. Jahr (Eds.), *Language and its ecology: Essays in memory of Einar Haugen* (pp. 105-130). Berlin: de Gruyter.

Giles, H., & Hewstone, M. (1982). Cognitive structures, speech, and social situations. *Language Sciences, 4,* 187-219.

Giles, H., & Street, R. L., Jr. (1995). Communicator characteristics and behavior. In M. L. Knapp & G. R. Miller (Eds.), *Handbook of interpersonal communication* (2nd ed., pp. 103-161). Thousand Oaks, CA: Sage.

Giles, H., & Williams, A. (1994). Patronizing the young: Forms and evaluations. *International Journal of Aging and Human Development, 39,* 33-53.

Goffman, E. (1963). *Behavior in public places: Notes on the social organization of gatherings.* New York: Free Press.

Gold, D. P., Arbuckle, T. Y., & Andres, D. (1994). Verbosity in older adults. In M. L. Hummert, J. M. Wiemann, & J. F. Nussbaum (Eds.), *Interpersonal communication in older adulthood: Interdisciplinary theory and research* (pp. 107-129). Thousand Oaks, CA: Sage.

Goldberg, D. T. (Ed.). (1994). *Multiculturalism: A critical reader.* Oxford: Basil Blackwell.

Goldberg, D. T. (1995). Afterword: Hate, or power? In R. K. Whillock & D. Slayden (Eds.), *Hate speech* (pp. 267-276). Thousand Oaks, CA: Sage.

Gordon, A. F., & Newfield, C. (Eds.). (1996). *Mapping multiculturalism.* Minneapolis: University of Minnesota Press.

Green, J., & Henderson, F. (1993). Quality of life and social function. In P. Tyrer & P. Casey (Eds.), *Social function in psychiatry: The hidden axis of classification exposed* (pp. 140-152). Petersfield, England: Wrightson Biomedical.

Grossberg, L., Nelson, C., & Treichler, P. A. (Eds.). (1992). *Cultural studies.* New York: Routledge.

Gudykunst, W. B. (Ed.). (1986). *Intergroup communication.* London: Edward Arnold.

Gudykunst, W. B., & Asante, M. K. (Eds.). (1989). *Handbook of international and intercultural communication.* Newbury Park, CA: Sage.

Gudykunst, W. B., & Lim, T. S. (1986). A perspective for the study of intergroup communication. In W. B. Gudykunst (Ed.), *Intergroup communication* (pp. 1-9). London: Edward Arnold.

Gudykunst, W. B., & Ting-Toomey, S. (1990). Ethnic identity, language, and communication breakdowns. In H. Giles & W. Robinson (Eds.), *Handbook of language and social psychology* (pp. 309-327). Chichester: John Wiley.

Gutek, B. A., & Morasch, B. (1982). Sex ratios, sex-role spillover, and sexual harassment of women at work. *Journal of Social Issues, 38,* 55-74.

Haiman, F. (1993). *Speech acts and the First Amendment.* Carbondale: Southern Illinois University Press.

Hamilton, D. L., & Mackie, D. M. (1993). Cognitive and affective processes in intergroup perception: The developing interface. In D. M. Mackie & D. L. Hamilton (Eds.), *Affect, cognition, and stereotyping: Interactive processes in group perception* (pp. 1-12). San Diego, CA: Academic Press.

Harcum, E., & Rosen, E. (1990a). Perceived dignity of persons with minimal voluntary control over their own behaviors. *Psychological Reports, 67,* 1275-1282.

Harcum, E., & Rosen, E. (1990b). The two faces of freedom and dignity: Credit or extenuation. *Psychological Reports, 66,* 1295-1298.

Harris, M. (1993). How provoking! What makes men and women angry? *Aggressive Behavior, 19,* 199-211.

Hart, S., & Brassard, M. (1987). A major threat to children's mental health: Psychological maltreatment. *American Psychologist, 42,* 160-165.

Hartmann, P., & Husband, C. (1974). *Racism and the mass media.* London: Davis-Poynter.

Harwood, J., & Giles, H. (1992). "Don't make me laugh": Age representations in a humorous context. *Discourse and Society, 3,* 403-436.

Harwood, J., & Giles, H. (1996). Reactions to older people being patronized: The roles of response strategies and attributed thoughts. *Journal of Language and Social Psychology, 15,* 395-422.

Hawkins, R., Wiemann, J. M., & Pingree, S. (Eds.). (1988). *Advancing communication science: Merging mass and interpersonal processes.* Newbury Park, CA: Sage.

Hecht, M. L., Collier, M. J., & Ribeau, S. A. (1993). *African American communication: Ethnic identity and cultural interpretation.* Newbury Park, CA: Sage.

Hecht, M. L., & Ribeau, S. (1987). Afro-American identity labels and communicative effectiveness. *Journal of Language & Social Psychology, 6,* 319-326.

Heider, F. (1958). *The psychology of interpersonal relations.* New York: John Wiley.

Henkin, L. (1995). Group defamation and international law. In M. Freedman & E. Freedman (Eds.), *Group defamation and freedom of speech: The relationship between language and violence* (pp. 123-134). Westport, CT: Greenwood.

Henley, N. M. (1995). Body politics revisited: What do we know today? In P. J. Kalbfleisch & M. J. Cody (Eds.), *Gender, power, and communication in human relationships* (pp. 27-61). Hillsdale, NJ: Lawrence Erlbaum.

Henley, N. M., & Kramarae, C. (1991). Gender, power, and miscommunication. In N. Coupland, H. Giles, & J. M. Wiemann (Eds.), *"Miscommunication" and problematic talk* (pp. 18-43). Newbury Park, CA: Sage.

Henley, N. M., Miller, M., & Beazley, J. (1995). Syntax, semantics, and sexual violence: Agency and the passive voice. *Journal of Language and Social Psychology, 14,* 60-84.

Hewstone, M. (1990a). *Causal attribution: From cognitive processes to collective beliefs.* Oxford: Basil Blackwell.

Hewstone, M. (1990b). The "ultimate attribution error"? A review of the literature on intergroup causal attribution. *European Journal of Social Psychology, 20,* 311-335.

Hewstone, M., & Giles, H. (1986). Social groups and social stereotypes in intergroup communication. In W. B. Gudykunst (Ed.), *Intergroup communication* (pp. 10-26). London: Edward Arnold.

Hewstone, M., Wagner, U., & Machleit, U. (1989). Self-, ingroup, and outgroup achievement attributions of German and Turkish pupils. *Journal of Social Psychology, 129,* 459-470.

Heyman, S. (1996). *Hate speech and the constitution.* New York: Garland.

Hodulik, P. (1991). Racist speech on campus. *Wayne Law Review, 37,* 1433-1449.

Hogg, M. A., & Abrams, D. (1988). *Social identifications: A social psychology of intergroup relations and group processes.* London: Routledge.

Hogg, M. A., & Abrams, D. (1993). Towards a single-process uncertainty-reduction model of social motivation in groups. In M. A. Hogg & D. Abrams (Eds.), *Group motivation: Social psychological perspectives* (pp. 173-190). New York: Harvester Wheatsheaf.

Hopper, R. (1986). Social evaluation of intergroup dialect differences: The shibboleth schema. In W. B. Gudykunst (Ed.), *Intergroup communication* (pp. 127-136). London: Edward Arnold.

Hummert, M. L., Wiemann, J. M., & Nussbaum, J. F. (Eds.). (1994). *Interpersonal communication in older adulthood: Interdisciplinary theory and research.* Thousand Oaks, CA: Sage.

Hyde, H., & Fishman, G. (1991). The Collegiate Speech Protection Act of 1991: A response to the new intolerance in the academy. *Wayne Law Review, 37,* 1469-1525.

Infante, D. A. (1981). Trait argumentativeness as a predictor of communicative behavior in situations requiring argument. *Central States Speech Journal, 32,* 265-272.

Infante, D. A. (1987). Aggressiveness. In J. C. McCroskey & J. A. Daly (Eds.), *Personality and interpersonal communication* (pp. 157-192). Newbury Park, CA: Sage.

Infante, D. A. (1995). Teaching students to understand and control verbal aggression. *Communication Education, 44,* 51-63.

Infante, D. A., Chandler, T. A., & Rudd, J. E. (1989). Test of an argumentative skill deficiency model of interspousal violence. *Communication Monographs, 56,* 163-177.

Infante, D. A., Chandler, T. A., Rudd, J. E., & Shannon, E. A. (1990). Verbal aggression in violent and nonviolent marital disputes. *Communication Quarterly, 38,* 361-371.

Infante, D. A., & Gorden, W. I. (1985). Superiors' argumentativeness and verbal aggressiveness as predictors of subordinates' satisfaction. *Human Communication Research, 12,* 117-125.

Infante, D. A., & Rancer, A. S. (1982). A conceptualization and measure of argumentativeness. *Journal of Personality Assessment, 46,* 72-80.

Infante, D. A., & Rancer, A. S. (1996). Argumentativeness and verbal aggressiveness: A review of recent theory and research. In B. R. Burleson (Ed.), *Communication yearbook 19* (pp. 319-351). Thousand Oaks, CA: Sage.

Infante, D. A., Rancer, A. S., & Jordan, F. (1996). Affirming and nonaffirming style, dyad sex, and the perception of argumentation and verbal aggression in an interpersonal dispute. *Human Communication Research, 22,* 315-334.

Infante, D. A., Trebing, J. D., Shepherd, P. E., & Seeds, D. E. (1984). The relationship of argumentativeness to verbal aggression. *Southern Speech Communication Journal, 50,* 67-77.

Infante, D. A., & Wigley, C. J. (1986). Verbal aggressiveness: An interpersonal model and measure. *Communication Monographs, 53,* 61-69.

Kalbfleisch, P. J., & Cody, M. J. (Eds.). (1995). *Gender, power, and communication in human relationships.* Hillsdale, NJ: Lawrence Erlbaum.

Kaniasty, K., & Norris, F. (1992). Social support and victims of crime: Matching event, support and outcome. *American Journal of Community Psychology, 20,* 211-241.

Katz, E. (1980). On conceptualizing media effects. *Studies in Communication, 1,* 119-141.

Kemper, S., Vandeputte, D., Rice, K., Cheung, H., & Gubarchuk, J. (1995). Speech adjustments to aging during a referential communication task. *Journal of Language and Social Psychology, 14,* 40-59.

Keyton, J. (1996). Sexual harassment: A multidisciplinary synthesis and critique. In B. R. Burleson (Ed.), *Communication yearbook 19* (pp. 93-155). Thousand Oaks, CA: Sage.

Khlief, B. (1979). Insiders, outsiders and renegades: Towards a classification of ethnolinguistic labels. In H. Giles & B. Saint-Jacques (Eds.), *Language and ethnic relations* (pp. 159-172). Oxford: Pergamon.

Khosroshahi, F. (1989). Penguins don't care, but women do: A social identity analysis of a Whorfian problem. *Language in Society, 18,* 505-527.

Kim, Y. Y. (1995). Cross-cultural adaptation: An integrative theory. In R. L. Wiseman (Ed.), *Intercultural communication theory* (pp. 170-193). Thousand Oaks, CA: Sage.

Kimball, R. (1990). *Tenured radicals: How politics has corrupted higher education.* New York: Harper & Row.

Kinney, T. (1994). An inductively derived typology of verbal aggression and its association to distress. *Human Communication Research, 21,* 183-222.

Kinney, T. (1996, May). *Dimensions and functions of racial, ethnic, and gender slurs.* Paper presented at the annual meeting of the International Communication Association, Chicago.

Kinney, T., & Cloven, D. (1994, May). *A model linking interpersonal stress to well-being.* Paper presented at the annual meeting of the International Communication Association, Sydney.

Kinney, T., & Cloven, D. (1995). The relationship of thoughts to coping with an interpersonal threat [Abstract]. *Psychosomatic Medicine, 57,* 78.

Kirkland, S., Greenberg, J., & Pyszczynski, T. (1987). Further evidence of the deleterious effects of overheard derogatory ethnic labels: Derogation beyond the target. *Personality and Social Psychology Bulletin, 13,* 216-227.

Kramarae, C., Schulz, M., & O'Barr, W. M. (Eds.). (1984). *Language and power.* Beverly Hills, CA: Sage.

Kurz, D. (1989). Social science perspectives on wife abuse: Current debates and future directions. *Gender & Society, 3,* 489-505.

LaFontaine, E., & Tredeau, L. (1986). The frequency, source and correlates of sexual harassment among women in traditional male occupations. *Sex Roles, 15,* 433-442.

Lakoff, R. (1973). Language and women's place. *Language in Society, 2,* 45-79.

Lakoff, R. (1990). *Talking power: The politics of language in our lives.* New York: Basic Books.

Lampe, P. (1982). Ethnic labels: Naming or name calling? *Ethnic and Racial Studies, 5,* 542-548.

Lancely, A. (1985). Use of controlling language in the rehabilitation of the elderly. *Journal of Advanced Nursing, 36,* 12-29.

Langone, M. (1992). Psychological abuse. *Cultic Studies Journal, 9,* 206-218.

Lawrence, C. (1995). Cross-burning and the sound of silence: Anti-subordination theory and the First Amendment. In L. Lederer & R. Delgado (Eds.), *The price we pay: The case against racist speech, hate propaganda, and pornography* (pp. 114-121). New York: Hill & Wang.

Lawrence, C., Matsuda, M., Delgado, R., & Crenshaw, K. (1993). Introduction. In M. Matsuda, C. Lawrence, R. Delgado, & K. Crenshaw (Eds.), *Words that wound: Critical race theory, assaultive speech and the First Amendment* (pp. 1-16). Boulder, CO: Westview.

Laws, G. (1995). Understanding ageism: Lessons from feminism and postmodernism. *Gerontologist, 35,* 112-118.

Lederer, L. (1995). Pornography and racist speech as hate propaganda. In L. Lederer & R. Delgado (Eds.), *The price we pay: The case against racist speech, hate propaganda, and pornography* (pp. 131-140). New York: Hill & Wang.

Lederer, L., & Delgado, R. (Eds.). (1995). *The price we pay: The case against racist speech, hate propaganda, and pornography.* New York: Hill & Wang.

Leets, L., & Bowers, P. (1997, May). *Loud and angry voices: The insidious influence.* Paper presented at the annual meeting of the International Communication Association, Montreal.

Leets, L., & Giles, H. (1997). Words as weapons: When do they wound? Investigations of harmful speech. *Human Communication Research, 24,* 260-301.

Leets, L., Giles, H., & Clément, R. (1996). Explicating ethnicity in theory and communication research. *Multilingua, 15,* 115-147.

Leidholdt, D. (1995). Pornography in the workplace: Sexual harassment litigation under title VII. In L. Lederer & R. Delgado (Eds.), *The price we pay: The case against racist speech, hate propaganda, and pornography* (pp. 216-232). New York: Hill & Wang.

Levine, R., & Campbell, D. (1972). *Ethnocentrism.* New York: John Wiley.

Linz, D., Donnerstein, E., Land, K., McCall, P., Scott, J., Shafer, B., Klein, L., & Lance, L. (1991). Estimating community standards: The use of social science evidence in an obscenity prosecution. *Public Opinion Quarterly, 55,* 80-112.

Linz, D., & Malamuth, N. M. (1993). *Pornography.* Newbury Park, CA: Sage.

Littlejohn, S. W. (1992). *Theories of human communication* (4th ed.). Belmont, CA: Wadsworth.

Livneh, H. (1988). A dimensional perspective on the origin of negative attitudes toward persons with disabilities. In H. Yuker (Ed.), *Attitudes toward persons with disabilities* (pp. 35-46). New York: Springer.

Louw-Potgeiter, J. (1989). Covert racism: An application of Essed's analysis in a South African context. *Journal of Language and Social Psychology, 8,* 307-320.

Lucas, D. (1982). An overview of emotional abuse. In J. Hurd (Ed.), *Proceedings of the Fourth Conference on Emotional Abuse of Children* (pp. 1-3). Winnipeg: University of Manitoba.

Lukens, J. (1979). Interethnic conflict and communicative distance. In H. Giles & B. Saint-Jacques (Eds.), *Language and ethnic relations* (pp. 143-158). Oxford: Pergamon.

MacKinnon, C. A. (1993). *Only words.* Cambridge, MA: Harvard University Press.

MacKinnon, C. A. (1995). Speech, equality, and harm: The case against pornography. In L. Lederer & R. Delgado (Eds.), *The price we pay: The case against racist speech, hate propaganda, and pornography* (pp. 301-314). New York: Hill & Wang.

Maddi, S., Bartone, R., & Puccetti, M. (1987). Stressful events are indeed a factor in physical illness: Reply to Schroeder and Costa (1984). *Journal of Personality and Social Psychology, 52,* 833-843.

Marcus, G., Sullivan, J., Theiss-Morse, E., & Wood, S. (1995). *With malice toward some: How people make civil liberties judgments.* Cambridge: Cambridge University Press

Matsuda, M., Lawrence, C., Delgado, R., & Crenshaw, K. (Eds.). (1993). *Words that wound: Critical race theory, assaultive speech and the First Amendment.* Boulder, CO: Westview.

McGee, R., & Wolfe, D. (Eds.). (1991). Defining psychological maltreatment: Reflections and future directions [Special issue]. *Development and Psychopathology, 3*(1).

McLeod, J. M., & Blumer, J. (1987). The macrosocial level of communication science. In C. R. Berger & S. H. Chaffee (Eds.), *Handbook of communication science* (pp. 271-324). Newbury Park, CA: Sage.

Metts, S., & Spitzberg, B. H. (1996). Sexual communication in interpersonal contexts: A script-based approach. In B. R. Burleson (Ed.), *Communication yearbook 19* (pp. 49-91). Thousand Oaks, CA: Sage.

Miles, R. (1993). *Racism after race relations.* London: Routledge.

Moberly, E. (1985). *The psychology of self and other.* London: Tavistock.

Mulac, A., & Lundell, T. (1986). Linguistic contributions to the gender-linked language effect. *Journal of Language and Social Psychology, 5,* 81-102.

Nairn, R., & McCreanor, T. (1990). Insensitivity and hypersensitivity: An imbalance in Pakeha accounts of racial conflict. *Journal of Language and Social Psychology, 9,* 293-308.

Nairn, R., & McCreanor, T. (1991). Race talk and common sense: Patterns in Pakeha discourse on Maori/Pakeha relations in New Zealand. *Journal of Language and Social Psychology, 10,* 245-262.

Nardi, P., & Bolton, R. (1991). Gay-bashing: Violence and aggression against gay men and lesbians. In R. Baenninger (Ed.), *Targets of violence and aggression* (pp. 349-400). Amsterdam: North Holland.

Ney, P. (1987). Does verbal abuse leave deeper scars? A study of children and parents. *Canadian Journal of Psychiatry, 32,* 371-378.

Ng S. H., & Bradac, J. J. (1993). *Power in language: Verbal communication and social influence.* Thousand Oaks, CA: Sage.

Ng S. H., Giles, H., & Moody, J. (1991). Information-seeking triggered by age. *International Journal of Aging and Human Development, 33,* 269-277.

Nishita, K. (1993, October 19). We're Americans, not invaders. *Daily Nexus,* p. 7.

Nuessel, F. (1993). *The semiotics of aging.* Louisville, KY: University of Louisville Press.

Nussbaum, J. F. (1989). *Lifespan communication: Normative processes.* Hillsdale, NJ: Lawrence Erlbaum.

Nussbaum, J. F., & Coupland, J. (Eds.). (1995). *Handbook of communication and aging research.* Mahwah, NJ: Lawrence Erlbaum.

Nussbaum, J. F., Hummert, M. L., Williams, A., & Harwood, J. (1996). Communication and older adults. In B. R. Burleson (Ed.), *Communication yearbook 19* (pp. 1-47). Thousand Oaks, CA: Sage.

O'Barr, W. M. (1994). *Culture and the ad: Exploring otherness in the world of advertising.* Boulder, CO: Westview.

Opotow, S. (1990). Moral exclusion and injustice: An introduction. *Journal of Social Issues, 46,* 1-20.

Pankratz, L., Levendusky, P., & Glaudin, V. (1976). The antecedents of anger in a sample of college students. *Journal of Psychology, 92,* 173-178.

Passuth, P., & Cook, F. (1985). Effects of television viewing on knowledge and attitudes about older adults: A critical re-examination. *Gerontologist, 25,* 69-77.

Pearson, J., & Cooks, L. (1995). Gender and power. In P. J. Kalbfleisch & M. J. Cody (Eds.), *Gender, power, and communication in human relationships* (pp. 331-349). Hillsdale, NJ: Lawrence Erlbaum.

Pence, E., & Paymar, M. (1993). *Education groups for men who batter: The Duluth model.* New York: Springer.

Perse, E. M. (1994). Uses of erotica and acceptance of rape myths. *Communication Research, 21,* 488-515.

Pillemer, K., & Finkelhor, D. (1989). Causes of elder abuse: Caregiver stress versus problem relatives. *American Journal of Orthopsychiatry, 59,* 179-187.

Post, R. (1991). Racist speech, democracy and the First Amendment. *William and Mary Law Review, 32,* 267-327.

Potter, J., & Wetherell, M. (1987). *Discourse and social psychology.* London: Sage.

Prentice, D. (1994). Do language reforms change our way of thinking? *Journal of Language and Social Psychology, 13,* 3-19.

Pryor, J., Giedd, J., & Williams, K. (1995). A social psychological model for predicting sexual harassment. *Journal of Social Issues, 51,* 69-84.

Pryor, J., LaVite, C., & Stroller, L. (1993). A social psychological analysis of sexual harassment: The person/situation interaction. *Journal of Vocational Behavior, 42,* 68-83.

Reardon, K. K. (1996). *They don't get it, do they? Communication in the workplace—closing the gap between men and women.* Boston: Little, Brown.

Ross, L. (1995). Hate groups, African Americans, and the First Amendment. In L. Lederer & R. Delgado (Eds.), *The price we pay: The case against racist speech, hate propaganda, and pornography* (pp. 151-156). New York: Hill & Wang.

Rowe, M. (1990). Barriers to equality: The power of subtle discrimination to maintain unequal opportunity. *Employee Responsibilities and Rights Journal, 3,* 153-163.

Rowe, M. (1993). Fostering diversity: Some major hurdles remain. *Change, 25,* 35-39.

Ruesch J., & Bateson, G. (1968). *Communication: The social matrix of psychiatry.* New York: W. W. Norton. (Original work published 1951)

Ryan, E. B., Hummert, M. L., & Boich, L. L. (1995). Communication predicaments of aging: Patronizing behavior toward older adults. *Journal of Language and Social Psychology, 14,* 144-166.

Ryan, E. B., Meredith, S. D., & Shantz, G. B. (1994). Evaluative perceptions of patronizing speech addressed to institutionalized elders in varied contexts. *Canadian Journal on Aging, 13,* 236-248.

Saad, H. (1991). The case for prohibitions of racial epithets in the university classroom. *Wayne Law Review, 37,* 1351-1362.

Sabourin, T. C. (1991). Perceptions of verbal aggression in interspousal violence. In D. D. Knudsen & J. A. Miller (Eds.), *Abused and battered: Social and legal responses of family violence* (pp. 135-142). New York: Aldine de Gruyter.

Sabourin, T. C. (1995). The role of negative reciprocity in spouse abuse: A relational control analysis. *Journal of Applied Communication Research, 23,* 271-283.

Sabourin, T. C., Infante, D. A., & Rudd, J. E. (1993). Verbal aggression in marriages: A comparison of violent, distressed but nonviolent, and nondistressed couples. *Human Communication Research, 20,* 245-267.

Salasin, S. (Ed.). (1981). *Evaluating victims' services* (Vol. 7). Beverly Hills, CA: Sage.

Schaie, K. W. (1993). Ageist language in psychological research. *American Psychologist, 48,* 49-51.

Searle, J. (1969). *Speech acts: An essay in the philosophy of language.* Cambridge: Cambridge University Press.

Searle, J. (1975). Indirect speech acts. In P. Cole & J. Morgan (Eds.), *Syntax and semantics 3: Speech acts* (pp. 59-82). New York: Academic Press.

Sedler, R. (1991). *Doe v. University of Michigan* and campus bans on "racist speech": The view from within. *Wayne Law Review, 37,* 1325-1349.

Sedler, R. (1992). The unconstitutionality of campus bans on "racist speech": The view from without and within. *University of Pittsburgh Law Review, 53,* 631-683.

Selye, H. (1993). History of the stress concept. In L. Goldberger & S. Breznitz (Eds.), *Handbook of stress: Theoretical and clinical aspects* (pp. 7-17). New York: Free Press.

Shaver, P., Schwartz, J., Dirson, D., & O'Connor, C. (1987). Emotion knowledge. *Journal of Personality and Social Psychology, 52,* 1061-1086.

Shultz, T., & Wright, K. (1985). Concepts of negligence and intention in the assignment of moral responsibility. *Canadian Journal of Behavioral Science, 17,* 97-108.

Simon, L., & Greenberg, J. (1996). Further progress in understanding the effects of derogatory ethnic labels: The role of preexisting attitudes toward the targeted group. *Personality and Social Psychology Bulletin, 22,* 1195-1204.

Smith, E. (1993). Social identity and social emotions: Toward new conceptualizations of prejudice. In D. M. Mackie & D. L. Hamilton (Eds.), *Affect, cognition, and stereotyping. Interactive processes in group perception* (pp. 297-316). San Diego, CA: Academic Press.

Smolla, R. (1993). *Free speech in an open society.* New York: Vintage.

Sniderman, P. M., & Piazza, T. (1993). *The scar of race.* Cambridge, MA: Belknap.

Stamp, G., & Sabourin, T. C. (1995). Accounting for violence: An analysis of male spousal abuse narratives. *Journal of Applied Communication Research, 23,* 284-307.

Stewart, M., & Ryan, E. B. (1982). Attitudes toward younger and older adult speakers: Effects of varying speech rates. *Journal of Language and Social Psychology, 1,* 91-109.

Stockdale, M. (1993). The role of sexual misperceptions of women's friendliness in an emerging theory of sexual harassment. *Journal of Vocational Behavior, 42,* 84-101.

Swann, J. (1989). Talk control: An illustration from the classroom of problems in analyzing male dominance in education. In J. Coates & D. Cameron (Eds.), *Women in their speech communities* (pp. 122-140). London: Longman.

Tajfel, H. (Ed.). (1978). *Differentiation between social groups: Studies in the social psychology of intergroup relations.* London: Academic Press.

Tajfel, H. (Ed.). (1982). *Social identity and intergroup relations.* Cambridge: Cambridge University Press.

Tajfel, H., & Turner, J. (1986). The social identity theory of intergroup behavior. In S. Worchel & W. G. Austin (Eds.), *Psychology of intergroup relations* (pp. 7-24). Chicago: Nelson-Hall.

Tangri, S., Burt, M., & Johnson, L. (1982). Sexual harassment at work: Three explanatory models. *Journal of Social Issues, 38,* 33-54.

Tannen, D. (1987). *That's not what I meant! How conversational style makes or breaks relationships.* New York: Ballantine.

Tannen, D. (1990). *You just don't understand: Women and men in conversation.* New York: Ballantine.

Tata, J. (1993). The structure and phenomenon of sexual harassment: Impact of category of sexually harassing behavior, gender, and hierarchical level. *Journal of Applied Social Psychology, 23,* 199-211.

Taylor, C. (1995). The politics of recognition. In J. Arthur & A. Shapiro (Eds.), *Campus wars: Multi-culturalism and the politics of difference* (pp. 249-263). Boulder, CO: Westview.

Taylor, D., & Jaggi, V. (1974). Ethnocentrism and causal attribution in a South Indian context. *Journal of Cross-Cultural Psychology, 5,* 162-171.

Taylor, D., & Moghaddam, F. (1987). *Theories of intergroup relations: International social psychological perspectives.* New York: Praeger.

Taylor, S. (1986). The regulation of aggressive behavior. In R. Blanchard & D. Blanchard (Eds.), *Advances in the study of aggression* (pp. 92-120). Orlando, FL: Academic Press.

Tedeschi, J. T., & Felson, R. (1994). *Violence, aggression, and coercive actions.* Washington, DC: American Psychological Association.

Till, F. (1980). *Sexual harassment: A report on the sexual harassment of students.* Washington, DC: National Advisory Council on Women's Educational Programs.

Tinsley, H., & Stockdale, M. (1993). Sexual harassment in the workplace. *Journal of Vocational Behavior, 42,* 1-4.

Turner, J. (1987). *Rediscovering the social group: A self-categorization theory.* Oxford: Basil Blackwell.

Turner, J., & Oakes, P. (1989). Self-categorization theory and social influence. In P. Paulus (Ed.), *The psychology of group influence* (pp. 233-275). Hillsdale, NJ: Lawrence Erlbaum.

Turner, J., Oakes, P., Haslam, S., & McGarty, C. (1994). Self and collective: Cognition and social context. *Personality and Social Psychology Bulletin, 20,* 454-463.

U.S. Merit Systems Protection Board. (1981). *Sexual harassment in the federal workplace: Is it a problem?* Washington, DC: Government Printing Office.

U.S. Merit Systems Protection Board. (1987). *Sexual harassment in the federal workplace: An update.* Washington, DC: Government Printing Office.

VandenBos, G., & Bryant, B. (Eds.). (1987). *Cataclysms, crises, and catastrophes: Psychology in action.* Washington, DC: American Psychological Association.

van Dijk, T. A. (1984). *Prejudice in discourse.* Amsterdam: Benjamins.

van Dijk, T. A. (1987). *Communicating racism: Ethnic prejudice in thought and talk.* Newbury Park, CA: Sage.

van Dijk, T. A. (1992). Discourse and the denial of racism. *Discourse and Society, 3,* 87-118.

van Dijk, T. A. (1993). *Elite discourse and racism.* Newbury Park, CA: Sage.

van Dijk, T. A. (1995). Elite discourse and the reproduction of racism. In R. K. Whillock & D. Slayden (Eds.), *Hate speech* (pp. 1-27). Thousand Oaks, CA: Sage.

Vangelisti, A. (1994). Messages that hurt. In W. R. Cupach & B. H. Spitzberg (Eds.), *The dark side of interpersonal communication* (pp. 53-82). Hillsdale, NJ: Lawrence Erlbaum.

Vanman, E., & Miller, N. (1993). Applications of emotion theory and research to stereotyping and intergroup relations. In D. M. Mackie & D. L. Hamilton (Eds.), *Affect, cognition, and stereotyping: Interactive processes in group perception* (pp. 213-238). San Diego, CA: Academic Press.

Vaux, A. (1993). Paradigmatic assumptions in sexual harassment research: Being guided without being misled. *Journal of Vocational Behavior, 42,* 116-135.

Vissing, Y., Straus, M. A., Gelles, R. J., & Harrop, J. (1991). Verbal aggression by parents and psychosocial problems of children. *Child Abuse & Neglect, 15,* 223-238.

West, C. (1995). Women's competence in conversation. *Discourse and Society, 6,* 107-131.

Whillock, R. K. (1995). The use of hate as a stratagem for achieving political and social goals. In R. K. Whillock & D. Slayden (Eds.), *Hate speech* (pp. 28-54). Thousand Oaks, CA: Sage.

Whillock, R. K., & Slayden, D. (Eds.). (1995a). *Hate speech.* Thousand Oaks, CA: Sage.

Whillock, R. K., & Slayden, D. (1995b). Introduction. In R. K. Whillock & D. Slayden (Eds.), *Hate speech* (pp. ix-xvi). Thousand Oaks, CA: Sage.

Wood, J. T. (Ed.). (1992). "Telling our stories": Sexual harassment in the communication discipline [Symposium]. *Journal of Applied Communication Research, 20,* 349-418.

Wood, J. T. (1993). Naming and interpreting sexual harassment: A conceptual framework for scholarship. In G. L. Kreps (Ed.), *Sexual harassment: Communication implications* (pp. 9-26). Cresskill, NJ: Hampton.

Wood, J. T. (Ed.). (1996). *Gendered relationships.* Mountain View, CA: Mayfield.

Wood, J. T. (1997). *Gendered lives: Communication, gender, and culture* (2nd ed.). Belmont, CA: Wadsworth.

Wood, L., & Rennie, H. (1994). Formulating rape. *Discourse and Society, 5,* 125-148.

Wood, L., & Ryan, E. B. (1991). Talk to elders: Social structure, attitudes, and address. *Ageing and Society, 11,* 167-188.

Wright, B. (1988). Attitudes and the fundamental negative bias: Conditions and corrections. In H. Yuker (Ed.), *Attitudes toward persons with disabilities* (pp. 3-21). New York: Springer.

Yuker, H. (1987). Labels can hurt people with disabilities. *Etc., 44,* 16-22.

Yuker, H. (Ed.). (1988). *Attitudes toward persons with disabilities.* New York: Springer.

Yuker, H., & Block, J. (1986). *Research with the Attitude Toward Disabled Persons Scales (ATDP) 1960-1985.* New York: Hofstra University Press.

CHAPTER CONTENTS

4 Reactions of Criminal Sexual Offenders to Pornography: A Meta-Analytic Summary

MIKE ALLEN
University of Wisconsin–Milwaukee

DAVID D'ALESSIO
University of Conneticut, Storrs

TARA M. EMMERS-SOMMER
University of Oklahoma

This chapter provides a summary of existing data on the impacts of pornography for a specially defined sample. The studies included were studies that used only criminal sexual offenders, either incarcerated or in treatment. The findings indicate no difference in the frequency of consuming sexually explicit materials ($r = -.05$) between criminal sexual offenders and noncriminal controls. However, criminal sexual offenders were more likely to use pornography prior to engaging in sexual behaviors ($r = .23$) than were noncriminal controls. Physiological measures of arousal indicate that although sexual offenders are generally more aroused by such material ($r = .15$), the correlation increases dramatically when the content of the material is matched to the crime committed by the individual ($r = .48$). The findings illustrate that it is the reaction to and function of the mass media material, *not* the frequency of consumption, that differentiates criminal sexual offenders from noncriminal controls.

O NE of the major questions surrounding the effects of pornography considers whether mass communication of sexually explicit material generates any negative consequences for members of society. One particular issue concerns the relationship of sexually explicit materials to sexual crimes and sexual criminals. The common assumption is that sexual criminals use pornography more frequently or respond to the material differ-

Correspondence and requests for reprints: Mike Allen, Department of Communication, University of Wisconsin, Milwaukee, WI 53201; e-mail mikealle@csd.uwm.edu

Communication Yearbook 22, pp. 139-169

ently than do "normals." Conflicting interpretations exist, specifically: (a) that pornography consumption reflects existing predisposition and is not the cause of antisocial behavior and (b) that exposure to sexually explicit materials is one cause of antisocial behavior. This suggestion is only one of many possibilities (not all exclusive), including bidirectional causality (both claims are true) and noncausal relations (typically resulting from a common root factor that creates a "correlation" between the subsequent outcomes). Whatever the relationship, an improved understanding of what the available research indicates would contribute to the eventual testing, confirmation, or elimination of the current explanations.

Whether one believes that pornography serves as a model for the eventual actions of the sexual criminal or represents an ideology that supports the practice of rape, the argument is for a link between mass communication content and individual (as well as social) action. The basis for the belief is found in some form of social learning (Bandura, 1973, 1977; Check & Malamuth, 1986) or excitation transfer theory (Zillmann, Hoyt, & Day, 1974; Zillmann & Sapolsky, 1977). All these theories share the assumption that the experience of the material by the consumer creates a response. As the consumer of the material views the content of the material as desirable (either psychologically or physiologically), a set of responses creates the belief in the consumer that the behavior depicted would create a reward if enacted in real life. The separation of the mediated experience and lived experience becomes confused or fused. As a result, the content of the media material consumed (for whatever reason or based on whatever cues) serves as a basis for behavior. The media experience becomes the model for the actions of the person. That orientation sums up the essential assumptions of those who argue that the media produce antisocial effects. Whether one argues that rape is a crime of aggression and power or is a sexually motivated act (or a combination of both), sex becomes the weapon used to victimize another person. Sexual materials provide "training" or "justification" for the use of that weapon. Surveys of college students provide evidence that pornography serves as a source of information about sexual behavior (Bryant & Brown, 1989; Duncan, 1990; Duncan & Donnelly, 1991; Duncan & Nicholson, 1991). The findings from this set of surveys indicate that explicit sexual materials are in fact a source of information about sexual behavior for some consumers.

In this chapter we use the following definition of pornography, which is consistent with that used in previous meta-analyses: Pornography is material that intends to increase or has the effect of increasing sexual arousal (Allen, D'Alessio, & Brezgel, 1995; Allen, D'Alessio, Emmers, & Gebhardt, 1996; Allen, Emmers, Gebhardt, & Giery, 1995).[1] This is a functional definition of the material as opposed to a structural definition. The definition assumes that how a person uses the material or the effect that the material creates is the relevant factor in determining the suitability of the material. The difficulty of simply using a content definition of the material lies in the wide variety of sexual practices and expectations that individuals possess. However, the lowest common denominator suggests that explicit descriptions or depictions of sexual behavior or reproductive body parts generally are considered to increase sexual arousal for most individuals. This ideal represents an illustrative example rather than the definitive set of boundary conditions that most definitions would provide. For the purposes of understanding, we use terms such as *pornography, sexually explicit material,* and *erotica* interchangeably. The reason for this lack of distinction is the inability to separate, on the basis of content, the functions of the various forms of material. The definition offered above is suitable for scientific purposes because the typical design invariably incorporates some measure of sexual arousal or sexual interest in the material. Measurement, in the form of manipulation checks, confirms that the participants in the investigation interpret the material as sexual, corroborating the assumptions of the particular investigator. In the next section, we consider the effects that consumption of such material has on the message receivers.

UNDERSTANDING THE
EFFECTS OF PORNOGRAPHY

The "smoking gun" evidence necessary to establish a causal connection between exposure to pornography and antisocial outcomes is currently lacking in the scientific literature. There exist three broad classes of designs used to evaluate the connection of sexual materials to social outcomes: (a) relationships among social indicators, (b) experimental and survey designs, and (c) experiential designs using interviews or individual accounts. Researchers using social indicators examine the relationships between records of various indicators (e.g., circulation of pornographic magazines and rape rates) as a means of examining their impacts. Experimental and survey studies examine the impact of material on individual reactions in controlled settings or through the use of self-reports of exposure. Experiential designs use interviews with women, rape survivors, and/or rapists to investigate reactions to and use of sexual materials. Researchers in this last group often employ qualitative analysis of information using various interpretive, critical, or ethnographic techniques.

Social indicator analyses generally have shown little association between the availability or use of pornography and rates of violent sexual crime (Baron & Straus, 1989; Kutchinsky, 1970, 1973a, 1973b, 1985, 1991). Generally, the hypothesis of a connection between the availability of such material and the frequency of sexual crime remains unsupported. Reliance on these data is problematic, however, because many sexual crimes are believed to go unreported, and the use of sexual materials is difficult to assess within the population.

An examination of the experimental and survey designs reveals contradictory outcomes. A recent meta-analysis established that exposure to pornography in laboratories increases antiwoman attitudes (rape myths), whereas surveys relating self-reports of exposure to antiwoman attitudes do not show such a relationship (Allen, Emmers, et al., 1995). A meta-analysis of experimental studies examining the relationship of exposure to pornography to subsequent to behavioral aggression has demonstrated that sexual acts (consensual or nonconsensual) increase behavioral aggression, whereas pictorial nudity diminishes subsequent behavioral aggression (Allen, D'Alessio, & Brezgel, 1995). No theoretical explanation has been offered as to why material with explicit sexual contact would increase behavioral aggression and nude pictures would diminish aggression. This is theoretically troubling, because nude pictures increase sexual arousal. No correlation has been observed between the level of sexual arousal produced by a stimulus and the subsequent behavioral aggression. One explanation for the relationship considers the nature of involvement for the male subject. The nude female image can permit involvement and fantasy about the potential for sexual interaction and relational development. The material featuring explicit sexual contact is less involving and less satisfying given the level of sexual arousal. The analysis did not reject the excitation transfer model, so a psychological framework could provide an interpretation of the images contextualized by the emotional state of the consumer.

Two meta-analyses have examined the issues surrounding sexual aggression and reactions to sexual material. Hall, Shondrick, and Hirschman (1993), who reviewed 9 studies ($N = 434$), conclude that sexually aggressive males demonstrate higher levels of sexual arousal to sexual material ($r = .13$). This is supported by Lalumiere and Quinsey's (1994) meta-analysis of 16 studies ($N = 607$), in which the researchers found that rapists show a higher level of reaction ($d = .82$). These meta-analyses included only a portion of the available literature and the researchers did not consider the nature of the content of the material matched to the particular offenses of the criminal audience.

The problem is that the current state of theoretical development for these issues does not provide an explicit model for the connections among cognitive, emotional, and physiological impacts of pornography on the individual. The explanation for the observed effects awaits the development of a more general model combining the elements of these related but separate outcomes. One potential model is the confluence model of sexual aggression (Malamuth & Billings, 1986). Malamuth and Billings (1986) indicate that rapists may have less exposure to sexual materials than do others, but may be more strongly affected by the exposure they have. Perhaps the response or function of the material rather than the frequency or total amount of exposure may be the important factor in the impact of sexual materials. The confluence model argues that various interacting factors create a synergy between forces that contribute to sexual aggression under certain conditions. In this view, sexually explicit materials provide one potential catalyst for an effect that promotes sexual aggression.

Experiential evidence is often reported in the form of case studies or examples taken from "survivor" testimony (Everywoman, 1983; Palczewski, 1992, 1993). This evidence takes the form of statements by women about their experiences with sexuality and how the existence of pornography creates problems. Rape victims point to the prominence that pornography played in their victimization. Incest victims recount how their victimizers used pornography as part of the process. Women claim that the existence of pornography creates a rape culture. The basis for this claim comes from the experiences of women and their reflections (MacKinnon, 1993). Proponents of the use of experiential evidence argue that "scientific" evidence fails to give a voice to women, in effect "silencing" them. The result is the collection and generation of a body of evidence that provides support for one conclusion.

One issue raised by the use of experiential evidence is the lack of a method to resolve conflicts between divergent sets of experience. Strossen (1995), for instance, provides examples of women who find sexual material liberating and necessary for sexual expression. The problem with using experiential evidence is that it raises the possibility of multiple reactions to the same material. At the current time, no method exists for resolving the inconsistencies between different persons' accounts of their lived experiences. The problem created, then, is that any choice of which set of experiences to use as a basis for belief must "silence" one group of women in preference to another. Without a rational basis for a decision, the effect is to create a paradox in which the failure to choose creates silence and any choice must also create silence.

Another problem with the use of experiential evidence in the study of pornography and its relationship to sexual crime is that it involves an attempt by members of one group (women) to describe the motivations of members of another group (men). The ability of any one group to portray accurately the motivations of members of other groups remains unknown. We have no way to replicate and test such conclusions. Currently, explanations offered for the causality of rape by victims are not always accepted; for example, rape, incest, or pedophile victims who blame themselves for their victimization offer explanations few would accept. The "silencing" of these explanations exists for good reason, but this example illustrates that not all explanations offered by victims should be accepted. Rather, such explanations should serve only as one part of the story; all accounts must be evaluated and compared with other accounts.

The status of the proof provides a necessary condition for the making of a causal claim (for either diminishing or increasing aggression) but fails to meet sufficiency conditions for causality. There are a number of other possible theoretical configurations that would generate the same data but not generate causal claims. The problem is a lack of theoretical explanations for the split in the findings of the available research. One possible area for examination concerns the lifestyles (sexual practices) of individuals and their relative use and reaction to materials that depict sexual behavior.

ISSUES DEALING WITH
SPECIAL POPULATIONS

One set of concerns about the impact of pornography has to do with whether or not pornography contributes to rape, sexual assault, and other actions as well as the attitudes that men have toward women. One means of assessing arguments about causality is to determine whether convicted sexual offenders, compared with nonoffenders, show a higher level of consumption of sexual materials and/or exhibit differences in physiological effects when exposed to such materials. The argument for a relationship between sexual crime and pornography would assume some type of outcome difference: One would expect that convicted sexual offenders should consume more sexual materials and, when exposed, exhibit higher levels of physiological arousal than nonoffenders.

Consider the definition of pornography advanced above. The definition takes a functional approach to defining material in terms of sexual arousal. The logical corollary of this definition is that persons should find material most sexually arousing that matches their own sexual desires and practices. If mass media material reflects desires and fantasy, then sexual material (which should sexually arouse) should reflect the desires and practices of the consumer. This is an important issue in the consideration of trends in the content of sexual materials. Researchers who conduct content analysis consider whether the content of various kinds of materials has changed over time (e.g., the level of violence in sexual depictions). Changes in the content of sexual material may be related to the incidence of sexual crimes, although analyses considering the impact of general availability of sexual materials on rape rates generally provide little evidence of an association (e.g., Kutchinsky, 1991).

Given the above reasoning, rapists should be aroused more by material that depicts rape, whereas nonrapists interested in consensual sexual relations should find depictions of consensual sex more arousing. This finding was supported by the 16 studies included in Lalumiere and Quinsey's (1994) meta-analysis; rapists were found to be more aroused by violent material than were members of nonoffender control groups. This finding also receives support from Hall et al.'s (1993) meta-analysis of 9 studies. These two meta-analyses included only a portion of the available literature, however, and were not exhaustive. More important, there is a logical extension to other sexual offenders and sexually explicit material.

Pedophiles should find depictions of sex with children more arousing than other types of sexual material. The key is that the maintenance of the fantasy and the sexual desire should be consistent with the desires of the consumer. This argument considers a "match" between the crime committed and the preference for sexual material. If sexual crimes are crimes of violence and power, where sex is simply the weapon, then the material demonstrating the weapon should be most satisfying to those using that weapon. The associations among types of sexual material, particular physiological responses, and criminal actions indicate a necessary correspondence for theories arguing causality. Although such evidence is not sufficient to establish causality, it indicates part of the basis for the preference for sexual materials.

Feminist arguments often consider pornography as a form of sexual discrimination in which the material creates a sexually oppressive social system (MacKinnon, 1986, 1993). The testimony of victims of sexual assault is used to argue that sexually explicit material contributed to the actions taken against the victims (Everywoman, 1983). The problem with reliance on such evidence is that it fails to provide material capable of meeting traditional scientific standards. Victim testimony was used extensively in the generation of the issues surrounding the establishment of the Minneapolis and Indianapolis statutes limiting availability of sexual materials (Everywoman, 1983), which were overturned by the courts in the *Hudnut* decision (Downs, 1989). A troubling feature of the use of victim testimony is that it raises new questions. How, for example, does one evaluate the testimony of a victim who says that an acquaintance who raped her was "addicted" to material depicting the behavior eventually enacted?

The Minneapolis and Indianapolis statutes focused on sexual material that portrays women as victims. Social learning theory would argue that material portraying women as willing and sometimes eager victims of sexual assault creates the basis for action. To the extent that the material reflects or justifies a fantasy that discriminates, it is cause for concern. Demonstration of a connection between the physiological responses of convicted sexual offenders and material depicting the criminal acts of which those persons were convicted would add validation to victim testimony. Although the conditions for causality may not be met, the association would provide an indicator of potential behavioral outcomes.

Consider the issues surrounding the identification of sexual criminals. There exists a body of evidence indicating that perpetrators of sexual crimes rate low in social skills (Lipton, McDonel, & McFall, 1987; Segal & Marshall, 1985; Whitman & Quinsey, 1981). Thus sexual offenders are less likely than nonoffenders to initiate and sustain normal heterosexual relationships. An entire body of research considers methods of increasing social skills for this population in an effort to reduce the potential risk these individuals pose to the rest of the population (Allen, Bourhis, Emmers, & Sahlstein, 1998; Christensen, Arkowitz, & Anderson, 1975; Twentyman & McFall, 1975). The social skills hypotheses are arguments for considering the underlying causes of the eventual antisocial acts that become outcomes.

The strong sexual feelings that an adolescent has may be manifested in the use of pornography, which functions as a source of learning about sexual interaction. The maladaptive use of such materials for learning and reinforcing social behavior and values rather than reflecting an expression of sexual fantasy for a vicarious sense of excitation might become a problem. For a person unable to sustain relationships, the ideas contained in the material—that relationships are unimportant, or that control is at the heart of the interaction— become relevant. The pedophile, incestuous male, or rapist seeks a sense of control or mastery over his victim. At the same time, the ability to punish the target serves as an outlet for the aggression he feels because of his inability to sustain a relationship.

This orientation indicates that although there is a strong element of rage and anger in these sexual acts, there is also a need to overcome a sense of powerlessness and fear. The sexual material could serve as a means of instruction, demonstrating how to overcome that fear and powerlessness. This is exacerbated by the link to pleasant feelings of sexual arousal that the material generates. The material provides the basis to feel a reward from undertaking the acts described. The above theoretical argument about the function of the material means that mere exposure to the material is not the source of potential harm; rather, it is the use of the material that contributes to any antisocial outcome.

The existence of a large number of investigations serves as the basis for the formal summarization used in the meta-analysis. In the next section we offer a brief justification for the assumptions of meta-analysis and the advantages of using that process.

USE OF META-ANALYSIS

Through meta-analysis, researchers can synthesize the available scientific literature systematically using quantitative procedures. This method provides a means of assessing Type I error as well as various statistical artifacts, such as regression to the mean, restriction in range, and attenuated measurement (Preiss & Allen, 1995). Meta-analysis reduces Type II error by combining sample sizes and therefore reducing confidence intervals, which provides for greater accuracy in the estimation of any statistical parameter (Cooper & Hedges, 1994; Hunter & Schmidt, 1990). When combined with tests for sources of variability (homogeneity or moderator tests), meta-analysis creates the format for formal tests of potential additional theoretical and methodological features that might change or affect the observed relationships.

The advantage of meta-analysis is that it allows the researcher to convert effects to a common metric and assess the variability of effects. This provides the potential for other scientists to replicate the procedures to validate the conclusions of any particular meta-analysis. Unlike traditional narrative reviews, a meta-analysis can be replicated by other observers, who can dispute or agree with the conclusions generated by the summary. There are examples of meta-analyses that have been replicated in which the conclusions generated did not differ substantively from each other (Allen, 1996; Feldman, 1987). More important, the existence of additional studies or studies unknown to the investigator who conducted the original meta-analysis pose no problem; new results or findings can simply be included as part of an updated test.

Empirical investigations often generate different outcomes as measured by the significance test. Unfortunately, Type II error with the significance test often runs in excess of 50%, and therefore inconsistent findings of investigations may reflect nothing more than a high level of Type II error. Comparisons between narrative or box-score reviews and systematic quantitative reviews demonstrate the superiority of meta-analysis as a method of conducting a review of the literature (Allen & Preiss, 1990; Allen et al., 1997; Cook & Leviton, 1980). The conclusions are testable and less subject to wide ranges of variability typical of more traditional literature review methods.

Meta-analysis, by combining samples, reduces the level of Type II error. The average effect is a better estimate of the population parameter because the estimate reduces sampling error. An estimate of an effect derived using meta-analysis provides a higher degree of accuracy than individual investigations that contain larger amounts of sampling error or traditional review methods that have no method to assess random sampling error of individual investigations.

An enormous advantage of meta-analysis is the consideration of potential sources of variation in outcomes associated with additional variables. The examination of moderator variables constitutes much of the process in any meta-analysis. In the next section we detail the procedures used in this meta-analytic investigation.

METHODS

Literature Search

The acquisition of manuscripts for this investigation took place as part of a long-term series of projects testing various aspects of the impact that sexually explicit material generates on consumers. The more than 2,000 manuscripts in our possession were generated using a combination of computer searchers of various databases (ERIC, PsycLIT, COMINDEX, SCA Index, Social Science Citation Index, Sociological Abstracts, Medline) and inspection of the reference sections of manuscripts in our possession and numerous literature reviews specific to this topic (Abel, Becker, Blanchard,

& Djenderedjian, 1978; Abel, Becker, & Cunningham-Rathner, 1984; Abel & Blanchard, 1976; Ashley & Ashley, 1984; Barlow, 1973; Berger, Simon, & Gagnon, 1973; Bjorksten, 1976; Check & Malamuth, 1986; Cline, 1994; Court, 1984; Earls, 1988; Eisler, 1984; Freund, 1976a, 1981; Hui, 1986; Knudsen, 1988; Langevin, 1985; Lonsway & Fitzgerald, 1994; Lyons, Anderson, & Larson, 1994; Malamuth, 1989; Malamuth, Heavey, & Linz, 1993; Marshall & Barbaree, 1978; Murrin & Laws, 1990; Nemes, 1993; Proulx, 1989; Reed, 1989; Weaver, 1994; Yaffe, 1982).[2]

To be included in the meta-analysis, a study had to possess the following characteristics:

1. An identifiable part of the sample had to contain a group of identified criminal sexual offenders (rape, incest, molestation, exhibitionist) who were under arrest, convicted, or in some type of treatment (for their sexual offenses); this group had to be either compared with a control group of persons who had no record of criminal sexual behavior or subjected to a within-group comparison (either longitudinally or to a control stimulus).

2. The study had to use a dependent variable dealing with some measure of the use or exposure to pornography and/or the physiological effects of such material.

3. The study had to use a procedure that could generate quantitative estimates of the effect (thus qualitative or case study methodologies were not included in this meta-analysis).

Table 4.1 provides a list of the studies included along with associated effects for various conditions described in the next section. (More complete information on details for coding decisions and other relevant information is available from the first author.)

Studies were excluded for a variety of reasons. For example, some studies involved the use of clinical case studies for which no quantitative estimates were possible (Abel, Levis, & Clancy, 1970; Barlow, Leitenberg, & Agras, 1969; Beech, Watts, & Poole, 1971; Bergman, 1982; Brown, 1964; Brownell, Hayes, & Barlow, 1977; Davison, 1968; Hammer, 1957; Holmstrom & Burgess, 1980; Kutchinksy, 1976; Laws, 1984; Marquis, 1970; Marshall, 1974; Miller, 1981; Stoller, 1970, 1972; Wyre, 1992); other investigations used female samples (Adams, Haynes, & Brayer, 1983; Cramer & McFarlane, 1994). In some cases, the investigations presented analyses (usually some form of multivariate technique such as multiple regression, MANOVA, discriminant analysis, or canonical correlation) from which effects could not be estimated (Abel, Blanchard, & Barlow, 1981; Castonguay, Proulx, Aubut, McKibben, & Campbell, 1993; Prentky & Knight, 1993); other investigations considered methodological issues and did not meet the above criteria (Blader & Marshall, 1989; Clark, 1972; Csillag, 1976; Davidson & Malcolm, 1985; Earls & Jackson, 1981; Freund, 1971, 1976b; Koss & Gidycz, 1985; Krisak,

Murphy, Stalgaitis, 1981; Laws & Holmen, 1978; McConaghy, 1992; Quinsey & Chaplin, 1988a; Rosen, 1973; Rosen & Kopel, 1978; Rosen, Shapiro, & Schwartz, 1975; Seeley, Abramson, Perry, Rothblatt, & Seeley, 1980). Still other studies used population statistics rather than individual-level analyses to calculate associations (Baron & Straus, 1987, 1989; Baron, Straus, & Jaffee, 1988; Brannigan & Kapardis, 1986; Cochrane, 1978; Court, 1976; Gentry, 1991; Kutchinsky, 1970, 1973a, 1973b, 1985, 1991; Schwalm, 1984), and some studies included sexual offenders but no exposure or measure of exposure to sexually explicit materials (Abel, Becker, Cunningham-Rathner, Mittelman, & Rouleau, 1988; Abel, Becker, & Skinner, 1980; Barbaree & Marshall, 1988; Barbaree, Seto, Serin, Amos, & Preston, 1994; Burt, 1983; Deitz, Blackwell, Dalcy, & Bentley, 1982; Fehrenbach, Smith, Monastersky, & Deisher, 1986; Feild, 1978; Fitch, 1962; Ford & Linney, 1995; Hall & Proctor, 1987; Karacan et al., 1974; Koss & Dinero, 1988; Lanning, 1987; Lipton et al., 1987; Overholser & Beck, 1986; Pacht & Cowden, 1974; Rada, 1976). Finally, some studies did not use sample populations that included identified sexual offenders (for example, studies using males considered "sexually aggressive" do not qualify as criminal sexual offenders) (Athanasiou & Shaver, 1981; Barbaree, Marshall, Yates, & Lightfoot, 1983; Baron & Bell, 1973; Beck, 1984; Berger et al., 1973; Bozman & Beck, 1991; Briere & Runtz, 1989; Dermen, 1990; Donnerstein, 1980; Donnerstein & Berkowitz, 1981; Earls, Quinsey, & Castonguay, 1987; Fisher & Grenier, 1994; Katz, 1970; Malamuth, 1983, 1986; Malamuth, Haber, & Feshbach, 1980; Malamuth, Sockloskie, Koss, & Tanaka, 1991; Meyer, 1969; Miller, 1977; Mosher & Anderson, 1986; Murphy, Haynes, Coleman, & Flanagan, 1985; Rapaport, 1984).

Coding

Use of Sexual Material

The studies included in the meta-analysis examined a variety of functions or conditions under which persons can use sexually materials. We considered three basic types of dependent measures suitable for this analysis: (a) frequency of use, (b) age at first exposure to sexual material, and (c) use of sexual material prior to some form of sexual behavior (masturbation, consensual sex, coercive sex, or criminal sexual behavior). The first measure, frequency, simply concerned how often the person used sexually explicit material. When multiple types of materials were considered, the effect was averaged across material types. The general expectation is that criminal sexual offenders consume pornographic material more often than do individuals in the control group. This finding would support the arguments of those

TABLE 4.1
Effects Associated With Studies

Study Author(s)	Date	Sample Size	Self-Report Data			
			Overall Effect	Amount of Use	Age First Use	Behavior
Becker & Stein	1991	160	.000			
Carter et al.	1987	64	+.276			
Condrun& Nutter	1988	97	.000	+.141	−.141	+.002
Cook & Fosen	1971a, 1971b	129	−.133	−.095	−.303	+.000
Davis & Braucht	1971	365	+.309	+.136	+.193	+.454
Emerick & Dutton	1993	50	+.327			
Goldstein	1973	205	+.084			+.084
Johnson et al.	1971	699	+.039			
Krafka & Prentky	1992	30	.000	.000		
Langevin et al.	1988	279	−.315	−.315		
Linder	1953	153	+.120			+.203
Nutter & Kearns	1993	102	+.050	.000	+.050	+.100
Walker	1971	210	+.232	−.138	.000	+.337

		Sample Size	Physiological Effects			
			Overall	Consensual	Rape	Children
Abel et al.	1977	20	.000	−.213	+.213	
Abel et al.	1977	9	+.302			
Barbaree & Marshall	1989	83	+.350			
Barbaree et al.	1979	20	+.226	+.452		
Baxter et al.	1986	60	−.416			
Earls & Proulx	1986	20	+.061	−.213	+.254	
Fedora et al.	1986	69	+.242			
Fedora et al.	1992	287	+.002			
Frenzel & Lang	1989	191	−.152			

suggesting that such material is more likely to be used by those with criminal intent.

The second measure concerned the age at which the respondent was first exposed to sexually explicit material. The comparison is to the control group on the basis of the mean age of exposure. The expectation is that the criminal sexual offenders will demonstrate a pattern of exposure different from that for the noncriminal controls.

TABLE 4.1
(Continued)

		Sample Size	Physiological Effects			
			Overall	Consensual	Rape	Children
Freund & Langevin	1976	68	+.302			
Freund et al.	1979	214	+.136			
Freund et al.	1986	22	+.043	−.284		
Hall et al.	1988	169	+.005			
Hinton et al.	1980	24	+.254			
Kolarsky & Madlafousek	1972	30	.000			
Kolarsky & Madlafousek	1983	22	+.383			
Lang et al.	1988	60	+.150			+.250
Langevin et al.	1985	40	+.085			
Marques	1981	12	+.049			
Marshall	1988	89	+.320			
Marshall et al.	1982	39	+.656			
Marshall et al.	1986	105	+.233			+.449
Murphy et al.	1986	51	+.416			+.500
Proulx et al.	1994	20	+.167	−.594	+.213	
Quinsey & Chaplin	1984	30	+.694	−.730	+.657	
Quinsey & Chaplin	1988b	39	+.444			
Quinsey et al.	1979	32	+.167			
Quinsey et al.	1981	50	+.385	−.125		
Quinsey et al.	1975	41	+.583			+.583
Seto & Barbaree	1993	36	+.175			
Seto & Walker	1996	97	+.150		+.392	
Wydra et al.	1983	50	+.574	.000		

The final measure concerned the frequency with which the person uses sexual material as part of, or as prelude to, sexual behavior of some kind. One argument is that if sexual material is linked to sexual behavior, then criminal sexual offenders should demonstrate higher levels of association between the use of such material and subsequent sexual behavior. The material has the effect of arousal and creates the need (motivational) or the model (cognitive informational) for the individual to perform some action. If this is true, then criminal sexual offenders should demonstrate a higher level of action after viewing sexual material.

Physiological Effects of Sexual Materials

The dependent measure of the physiological effects of sexual materials concerns the degree of penile arousal created by exposure to such materials. Unlike other physiological measures (blood pressure, galvanic skin response, palmar sweat, muscle tension), penis size is almost exclusively affected by sexual arousal. Penile blood-volume increases that result in erections occur for few reasons other than sexual arousal. This relatively unambiguous response is different from other kinds of physiological responses to particular communication situations, which can be interpreted or psychologically labeled in multiple ways (Allen, 1989). Penile blood volume provides a relatively unambiguous measure of sexual arousal to a stimulus.

This dependent variable ascertains whether the reactions of criminal sexual offenders are different from those of members of noncriminal control groups. Two possible configurations will be considered: (a) general arousal differences and (b) a matching arousal hypothesis. The general arousal difference would indicate that criminal sexual offenders find sexually explicit material more arousing than do noncriminal controls. This would argue for a kind of sensitivity or learning pattern that indicates criminal sexual offenders respond to the material more than do noncriminal controls. This position assumes that sexual material of any kind simply produces stronger reactions in criminal sexual offenders regardless of the content of the material.

The second pattern argues that the content of the material should match the interests of the participants in terms of sexual arousal. Nonsexual offenders should find consensual sexual scenes more arousing physiologically than should rapists. Rapists should be more aroused by rape scenes than by consensual sex scenes. Pedophiles should react more strongly to sexual scenes depicting children than to scenes depicting adults. In this case, it is not the absolute level of arousal (it is possible that rapists would experience some arousal to consensual sex scenes, or nonoffenders to scenes involving nude children) but the relative pattern of arousal that is important. Basically, the argument is that the sexual practices of the individual should match the level of sexual arousal to material depicting those practices. Rapists, for example, compared with noncriminal controls, should be less aroused by depictions of consensual sex but more aroused by rape depictions. This matching hypothesis takes, where possible, the effects of particular types of material and compares the reactions of persons convicted of those particular sexual offenses with the reactions of the control group.

If this explanation is superior to a general arousal model, the average effect from this model should be substantially higher than the average effect for a general model. Consider a study that uses both a rape and a consensual sex scene. The rapists should be more strongly aroused by the rape scene but less aroused than the controls by the consensual sex representation. The first model, general arousal, would average the two effects (one positive, favoring the sexual offender, and one negative, favoring the nonoffender). The net effect might be an average correlation across depictions near zero; the two effects cancel.

The second model, matching the material to the sample, would average the values, but both effects would be coded as positive (because the values are consistent with a matching hypothesis, nonoffenders aroused by consensual scenes and rapists more aroused by coercive sexual scenes). The results would be an average effect much larger than that found using the first model.

Statistical Analysis

Statistical analysis was conducted using a standard variance-centered meta-analysis developed by Hunter and Schmidt (1990). Meta-analysis consists of finding and extracting effects from each study. The common metric used in this analysis was the correlation coefficient because the manipulation of the information is more convenient in that format (the choice of statistic is arbitrary, as conversion can be made to any metric). The effects from each study were then averaged using a weighted averaging procedure. This type of procedure is common to meta-analyses considering the effects of sexual materials (Allen, D'Alessio, & Brezgel, 1995; Allen, Emmers, et al., 1995; Allen et al., 1996; Hall et al., 1993; Lalumiere & Quinsey, 1994).

The final step was the test for homogeneity of the effect. *Homogeneity* simply means that the variability of the effects is due to sampling error rather than to any other factor. *Heterogeneity* indicates that the average effect should be interpreted cautiously. This test was conducted using a chi-square comparison of expected and actual variance in the sample of effects. A nonsignificant chi-square indicates homogeneity; a significant chi-square indicates heterogeneity.

RESULTS

Use of Sexual Materials

Overall, the 13 studies in this analysis demonstrate little difference between sexual criminals and noncriminals in the use of explicit sexual materials (average $r = .062$, $N = 2543$, variance $= .0320$). However, the sample was considered heterogeneous ($\chi^2 = 82.08$, $p < .05$). This average should be interpreted cautiously, but the analysis demonstrates that a conclusion favoring the position that sexual criminals use material more frequently receives only marginal support. Although the direction of the effect is positive, the effect is small and the estimates highly variable.

The frequency of use was examined in 7 studies and demonstrated little distinction ($r = -.054$, $N = 1,212$, variance $= .0313$), but the average effect came from a heterogeneous sample ($\chi^2 = 38.18$, $p < .05$). This finding indicates that criminal sexual offenders use explicit sexual materials slightly less than do members of the nonoffender control groups. However, the large variability in the sample of studies indicates that this conclusion should be viewed with caution. No support exists, however, for a large difference favoring sexual offenders in terms of frequency of use.

The finding was the same for age of first use of pornography (average r = .025, k = 5, N = 903, variance = .0300, χ^2 = 27.08, p < .05). The data, while demonstrating a great deal of variability, demonstrate no support for a conclusion that the sexual criminals were exposed to pornography at earlier ages than were the members of the nonoffender control groups.

The last analysis considered the reports of sexual activity after viewing pornography. The average effect was positive (average r = .234, k = 7, N = 1,261, variance = .0307, χ^2 = 43.39, p < .05). This finding indicates that sexual criminal offenders were more likely to perform some sexual act (masturbation, consensual, or criminal sex) after viewing the material than were control group males. The results support the claim of an association between self-reported use of pornography and subsequent sexual behavior. The sample of effects, however, demonstrates heterogeneity, and any interpretation of the findings should be cautious. However, an examination of the effects for the individual studies (see Table 4.1) reveals no *negative* effects. The reported effects were either zero or positive. That is, any moderator influences or other variables would only differentiate between varying levels of positive associations. That is, under some conditions the effect is larger than under other conditions but positive in both situations. The issue is analogous to the difference between an ordinal and disordinal interaction in ANOVA; the results indicate an ordinal but not a disordinal effect. Although an exact interpretation may not be possible, a general effect in terms of direction is consistent with all the available findings.

The findings, all using self-report methods, do not demonstrate any substantial support for the general conclusion that criminal sexual offenders use pornography more often or at an earlier age than do control group consumers. However, the results do indicate that the outcome from exposure (sexual behavior) is higher for criminal offenders than for controls. It is not the use of pornography that differentiates criminal sexual offenders from controls but the behavioral actions subsequent to exposure.

Physiological Effects of Sexual Materials

The general model of sexual arousal was considered across 32 studies, and the average effect (r = .152, N = 2,099, variance = .0496, χ^2 = 109.19, p < .05) indicates that criminal sexual offenders demonstrated higher levels of sexual arousal than did noncriminal controls. The sample of correlations was heterogeneous, indicating the possible existence of a moderator variable.

The next test was to consider various subclassifications of sexual content in the material. The first was consensual sexual materials, which demonstrated that nonoffender control groups were more greatly sexually aroused to the material than were sexual offenders ($r = -.258$, $k = 7$, $N = 625$, variance $= .0337$, $\chi^2 = 15.22$, $p < .05$). The sample of effects was observed to be heterogeneous. The average effect, however, demonstrates that the controls were generally more aroused than were the sexual offenders. It is important to note that this does not mean that rapists were not aroused, only that they were less aroused when compared with the members of control groups.

The 6 studies involving scenes of rape demonstrated greater arousal for the rapists ($r = .388$, $N = 207$, variance $= .0185$, $\chi^2 = 0.00$, $p > .05$). Unlike other cells, this was homogeneous, indicating that the sample of correlations could be said to vary only as a function of sampling error. The average effect indicates that sexual offenders were much more aroused by sexual materials depicting coercion than were nonoffender controls. Again, this does not mean that the controls were not aroused; rather, the effect compares the relative arousal magnitude for the groups.

The final set of 4 studies examined the effects that materials using children had on the physiological responses of individuals. The average effect is positive ($r = .431$, $N = 214$, variance $= .0148$, $\chi^2 = 0.00$, $p > .05$) and homogeneous. This set of studies found that the criminal sexual offenders were more greatly aroused by materials involving children than were the noncriminal controls.

The matching model could be assessed using 23 estimates; some investigations provided multiple estimates.[3] The average effect is almost three times as large as the general average (average $r = .476$, $N = 1,024$, variance $= .0779$, $\chi^2 = 133.26$, $p < .05$). The sample of correlations was heterogeneous (the variance for this effect was large by comparison), but all the effects were nonnegative (one was zero), indicating that any moderator would compare size of the effect, not the direction of the effect.

There were several instances in which the effect for a rape stimulus indicated more physiological arousal for the rapist sample whereas the consensual stimuli demonstrated more arousal for the control group. This type of outcome supports the idea that sexual practices of the individual correspond to the degree of sexual arousal generated by the material. This matching indicates that there are correspondences among the content of the material, the sexual practices or preferences of the person, and the degree of sexual arousal generated by exposure to that material.

CONCLUSIONS

In this literature summary we have examined how those convicted of sexual offenses are exposed to or react to sexual materials. Understanding this relationship is important for the assessment of whether or not pornography is associated with sexual crime as a possible contributory factor. The first part of the analysis demonstrates that simple frequency of use of sexual material and age at first exposure do not differentiate sexual criminal consumers from noncriminal consumers of sexual material. Analysis of the effects on subsequent behavior (after consumption of sexual material) demonstrates that criminal sexual offenders are more likely than nonoffenders to engage in subsequent sexual behavior. This indicates some association between the material and behavior, although the precise nature of that connection is not evident from this analysis.

The second part of the analysis involved an examination of how sexual criminals react physiologically to materials consistent with the particular crimes for which they were convicted. The findings indicate the possibility that the content of pornography is probably more salient than the explicitness of the material. That is, sexual material or pornography that depicts consensual sex is simply less arousing to rapists and pedophiles than to non-sexual offenders.

The problem is that this meta-analysis does not answer the "chicken and egg" question of media effects. Does the preference for rape, for example, cause the physiological reaction, or do sexual materials teach the consumer to become aroused by such materials? In other words, is the physiological reaction just a manifestation of an existing preference, or do the media help create the preference? Even if the media do not create preferences, one might question the degree to which media representations serve to reinforce preferences or justify behaviors. Whether making such materials unavailable would correspondingly decrease antisocial behavior is unclear. However, it is clear that criminal offenders report using sexual materials prior to sexual acts more frequently than do noncriminal controls. Considering that the preference would exist for material consistent with the particular criminal offense makes the connection more probable than not.

One meta-analysis has demonstrated that educational briefings are sufficient to remove any negative effects of exposure to sexual materials (Allen et al., 1996). The most common method of education is simply to provide a message that reminds study participants (assuming that most are noncriminals) that the media depictions represent fantasy. Participants are told that women do not want to be coerced or raped or treated as sexual objects. This educational briefing contextualizes the mediated experience by reminding the consumer that the experience is fictional and based in fantasy. However, the sexual criminal offender may want the fantasy to become reality and may thus reject the argument contained in the educational material. That is, the process of coercion, rape, or objectification is perhaps the part of the experience necessary for the offender's sexual arousal. Under those assumptions, the impact of such educational material would probably be minimal. Paradoxically, then, those most in need of an educational briefing about sexual material are most likely to remain unaffected. None of the current literature concerning debriefing as it applies to sexual material has considered sexual criminal offenders.

This educational finding contextualizes the previous meta-analyses that have examined the impact of pornography on attitudes (Allen, Emmers, et al., 1995) and behavior (Allen, D'Alessio, & Brezgel, 1995). These meta-analyses did not include convicted sexual offenders and therefore examined the impacts of sexual materials on persons with whom educational efforts would be more effective. These individuals are less likely to draw explicit connections between sexual material and immediate subsequent sexual behavior. The implication is that for non-sexual criminal consumers, the material more likely functions as an aid to sexual fantasy and remains unconnected from experience. The educational materials serve as a reminder of that function and therefore remove the impact of exposure to the materials. However, for the sexual criminal, the material is more likely linked to the reality of sexual behavior, and consuming sexually explicit material serves a different function for this audience. The results of this meta-analysis are consistent with previous efforts but point to the possibility of divergent uses of the same material and possibly different outcomes.

The evidence suggests that sexual material functions differently (something that is used as a prelude to sex) for sexual offenders compared with nonoffenders. The increased arousal for materials consistent with individuals' sexual offenses indicates that the material appeals to the consumer in a particular fashion. Possible additional moderators should involve the level of aggressiveness of the individual. Do more aggressive persons simply view media material differently than do nonaggressive individuals? The nature of the sexual experiences of the viewer should provide some insight into the frame of interpretation for such material. The results of this analysis suggest the need for more research focusing on how mediated images are interpreted by persons in the context of their everyday lives. The nature of the ability of persons to select materials indicates an ability to create a reality by controlling exposure. Why some realities are more appealing than others and the potential self-confirming nature of those realities deserve exploration.

The model described by Malamuth and Billings (1986) merits increased attention. The suggestion of these findings is that for some individuals, sexual materials serve as a contributing factor to sexual aggression. One speculation would be that a comparison of societies with differing levels of sexual information and differing attitudes toward sexuality, or a comparison of individuals within a society, may serve as a basis for estimating "risk" for sexual aggression. This model moves beyond simply examining the frequency or even content of exposure to a view that requires understanding of the audience. The development of models that take a more active view of the audience deserves theoretical and methodological attention. The issue transforms into a consideration of how different types of persons can respond to the same media content differently and increase the probability of sexually aggressive behavior. There is a need to develop a link between mass media effects theories and interpersonal and personal relationship theories. *Media effect* is, in a sense, a misnomer; the real effect is how media contact affects the behavior of an individual engaged in social and personal relationships.

We must make one methodological note about the use of self-report methodology in the consideration of the incidence of use of pornography. Convicted sexual offenders have an incentive to underestimate their frequency of use, either intentionally or unintentionally. Such self-reports may be suspect, given that there is no way to validate their accuracy independently. However, the reverse is true for the physiological measures: Convicted sexual offenders would have every incentive to demonstrate minimal reactions, yet they fail to do so. This indicates that the effects may, in fact, understate the link between sexual practices of criminal offenders and their reactions to sexual material.

The next step is the examination of the link between physiological reaction and psychological classification. Sexuality contains both physiological and psychological elements that work in conjunction. Similarly, sexually explicit materials function with both physiological and psychological reactions. The next step in this project is a meta-analytic examination of the available literature that compares the interplay among these reactions. Mosher (1973) labels much of the reaction to pornography "sexual guilt"; a person becomes physiologically aroused by sexual material but becomes angry, disgusted, or ashamed at the physiological reaction. This incongruity between mental and physiological states may partly explain the issues surrounding the impacts of such material on different audiences.

The simple argument that criminal sexual offenders use pornography more often than others finds no support in this summary. Our meta-analysis did find a difference between sexual criminals and controls—not in the function and frequency of use of sexual material, but in physiological reactions to it. Criminal sexual offenders have been shown to react physiologically more strongly to sexual materials than do nonoffender controls. This difference is heightened when the content of the material matches the sexual offense of the criminal. This correspondence indicates that it is the use of and the reaction to the material that differentiate sexual criminal offenders from nonoffenders. Although the evidence fails to establish a clear causal pattern, the inference of causality is not unwarranted.

NOTES

1. This definition is defective for purposes of policy formulation. The problem is that sexually explicit material varies in effect from person to person. One person might find the Victoria's Secret catalog or a photo in *National Geographic* stimulating. Another person may require scenes

of sadism or other violent sexual behavior to find the material sexually arousing. This definition does not explicate the content or structure of the material; rather, it considers the function that the material serves for the individual. As such, it would be impossible to define in terms of particular content what material would be considered "pornographic," "erotic," or "sexually explicit."

2. The full bibliography of all 2,000 pieces of material consulted for this search is available from the first author as well as a complete set of the calculations and the coding (including the rationales for the decisions) for the various effects from the studies.

3. Several studies have provided multiple comparisons that were included in this section. Such a procedure violates the normal assumptions of independence involved in the estimation of means and variances. A Monte Carlo simulation by Tracz (1985) indicates that the mean and variance estimates of correlations in meta-analyses are not affected by this procedure.

REFERENCES

Note: Asterisks indicate studies included in the meta-analysis.

*Abel, G., Barlow, D., Blanchard, E., & Gould, D. (1977). The components of rapists' sexual arousal. *Archives of General Psychiatry, 34,* 895-903.

Abel, G., Becker, J., Blanchard, E., & Djenderedjian, A. (1978). Differentiating sexual aggressives with penile measures. *Criminal Justice and Behavior, 5,* 315-332.

Abel, G., Becker, J., & Cunningham-Rathner, J. (1984). Complications, consent, and cognitions in sex between children and adults. *International Journal of Law and Psychiatry, 7,* 89-105.

Abel, G., Becker, J., Cunningham-Rathner, J., Mittelman, M., & Rouleau, J. (1988). Multiple paraphilic diagnoses among sex offenders. *Bulletin of the American Academy of Psychiatry and the Law, 16,* 153-168.

Abel, G., Becker, J., & Skinner, J. (1980). Aggressive behavior and sex. *Psychiatric Clinics of North America, 3,* 133-161.

Abel, G., & Blanchard, E. (1976). The measurement and generation of sexual arousal in male sexual deviates. In M. Herson, R. Eisler, & P. Miller (Eds.), *Progress in behavior modification* (Vol. 2, pp. 99-136). New York: Academic Press.

Abel, G., Blanchard, E., & Barlow, D. (1981). Measurement of sexual arousal in several paraphilias: The effects of stimulus modality, instructional set, and stimulus content on the objective. *Behaviour Research and Therapy, 19,* 25-33.

Abel, G., Levis, D., & Clancy, J. (1970). Aversion therapy applied to taped sequences of deviant behavior in exhibitionism and other sexual deviations: A preliminary report. *Journal of Behavioral Therapy and Experimental Psychiatry, 1,* 59-66.

Adams, A., Haynes, S., & Brayer, M. (1983). Cognitive distraction in female sexual arousal. *Psychophysiology, 22,* 689-696.

Allen, M. (1989). A comparison of self-report, observer, and physiological assessments of public speaking anxiety reduction techniques using meta-analysis. *Communication Studies, 40,* 127-139.

Allen, M. (1996). Research productivity and positive teaching evaluations: Examining the relationship using meta-analysis. *Journal of the Association for Communication Administration, 1996,* 77-96.

Allen, M., Bourhis, J., Emmers, T. M., & Sahlstein, E. (1998). Methods of reducing dating anxiety: A meta-analysis. *Communication Reports, 11,* 49-56.

Allen, M., D'Alessio, D., & Brezgel, K. (1995). A meta-analysis summarizing the effects of pornography II: Aggression after exposure. *Human Communication Research, 22,* 258-283.

Allen, M., D'Alessio, D., Emmers, T. M., & Gebhardt, L. (1996). The role of educational briefings in mitigating effects of experimental exposure to violent sexually explicit material: A meta-analysis. *Journal of Sex Research, 33,* 135-141.

Allen, M., Emmers, T. M., Gebhardt, L., & Giery, M. (1995). Pornography and rape myth acceptance. *Journal of Communication, 45*(1), 5-26.

Allen, M., & Preiss, R. (1990). Using meta-analysis to evaluate curriculum: An examination of selected college textbooks. *Communication Education, 39,* 103-116.

Allen, M., Preiss, R., Bielski, N., Cooper, E., Fechner, D., Henry, L., Jacobi, M., Kuhn, J., McClellan, W., & Patterson, K. (1997, April). *Examining textbooks: An analysis examining changes over time.* Paper presented at the annual meeting of the Central States Communication Association, St. Louis, MO.

Ashley, B., & Ashley, D. (1984). Sex as violence: The body against intimacy. *International Journal of Women's Studies, 7,* 352-371.

Athanasiou, R., & Shaver, P. (1981). Correlates of heterosexuals' reactions to pornography. *Journal of Sex Research, 7,* 298-311.

*Avery-Clark, C. (1980). *Differential erection response patterns of sexual child abusers to stimuli describing activities with children.* Unpublished doctoral dissertation, University of Southern California.

*Avery-Clark, C., & Laws, D. (1984). Differential erection response patterns of sexual child abusers to stimuli describing activities with children. *Behavior Therapy, 15,* 71-83.

Bandura, A. (1973). *Aggression: A social learning analysis.* Englewood Cliffs, NJ: Prentice Hall.

Bandura, A. (1977). *Social learning theory.* Englewood Cliffs, NJ: Prentice Hall.

Barbaree, H., & Marshall, W. (1988). Deviant sexual arousal, offense history, and demographic variables as predictors of reoffense among child molesters. *Behavioral Science Law, 6,* 267-280.

*Barbaree, H., & Marshall, W. (1989). Erectile responses among heterosexual child molesters, father-daughter incest offenders, and matched non-offenders: Five distinct age preference profiles. *Canadian Journal of Behavioural Science, 21,* 70-82.

*Barbaree, H., Marshall, W., & Lanthier, R. (1979). Deviant sexual arousal in rapists. *Behaviour Research and Therapy, 17,* 215-222.

Barbaree, H., Marshall, W., Yates, E., & Lightfoot, L. (1983). Alcohol intoxication and deviant sexual arousal in male social drinkers. *Behaviour Research and Therapy, 21,* 365-373.

Barbaree, H., Seto, M., Serin, R., Amos, N., & Preston, D. (1994). Comparisons between sexual and nonsexual rapist subtypes. *Criminal Justice and Behavior, 21,* 95-114.

Barlow, D. (1973). Increasing heterosexual responsiveness in the treatment of sexual deviation: A review of the clinical and experimental evidence. *Behavior Therapy, 4,* 655-671.

Barlow, D., Leitenberg, H., & Agras, W. (1969). Experimental control of sexual deviation through manipulation of the noxious scene in covert sensitization. *Journal of Abnormal Psychology, 74,* 596-601.

Baron, L., & Bell, P. (1973). Sexual arousal and aggression by males: Effects of type of erotic stimuli and prior provocation. *Journal of Personality and Social Psychology, 35,* 79-87.

Baron, L., & Straus, M. A. (1987). Four theories of rape: A macrosociological analysis. *Social Problems, 34,* 467-489.

Baron, L., & Straus, M. A. (1989). *Four theories of rape in American society: A state-level analysis.* New Haven, CT: Yale University Press.

Baron, L., Straus, M. A., & Jaffee, D. (1988). Legitimate violence, violent attitudes, and rape: A test of the cultural spillover theory. *Annals of the New York Academy of Sciences, 528,* 79-110.

*Baxter, D., Barbaree, H., & Marshall, W. (1986). Sexual responses to consenting and forced sex in a large sample of rapists and nonrapists. *Behaviour Research and Therapy, 24,* 513-520.

Beck, J. (1984). *The effect of performance demand and attentional focus on sexual responding in functional and dysfunctional men.* Unpublished doctoral dissertation, State University of New York at Albany.

*Becker, J., & Stein, R. (1991). Is sexual erotica associated with sexual deviance in adolescent males? *International Journal of Law and Psychiatry, 114,* 85-95.

Beech, H., Watts, G., & Poole, A. (1971). Classical conditioning of a sexual deviation: A preliminary note. *Behavior Therapy, 2,* 400-402.

Berger, A., Simon, W., & Gagnon, J. H. (1973). Youth and pornography in social context. *Archives of Sexual Behavior, 2,* 279-308.

Bergman, J. (1982). The influence of pornography on sexual development: Three case histories. *Family Therapy, 9,* 263-269.

Bjorksten, O. (1976). Sexually graphic material in the treatment of sexual disorders. In J. Meyer (Ed.), *Clinical management of sexual disorders* (pp. 161-195). Baltimore: Williams & Wilkins.

Blader, J., & Marshall, W. (1989). Is assessment of sexual arousal in rapists worthwhile? A critique of current methods and the development of a response compatibility approach. *Clinical Psychology Review, 9,* 56-587.

Bozman, A., & Beck, J. (1991). Covariation of sexual desire and sexual arousal: The effects of anger and anxiety. *Archives of Sexual Behavior, 20,* 47-60.

Brannigan, A., & Kapardis, A. (1986). The controversy over pornography and sex crimes: The criminological evidence and beyond. *Australian and New Zealand Journal of Criminology, 19,* 259-284.

Briere, J. N., & Runtz, M. (1989). University males' sexual interest in children: Predicting potential indices of "pedophilia" in a non-forensic sample. *Child Abuse & Neglect, 13,* 65-75.

Brown, P (1964). On the differentiation of homo- or hetero-erotic interest in the male: An operant technique illustrated in a case of a motor-cycle fetishist. *Behaviour Research and Therapy, 2,* 31-35.

Brownell, K., Hayes, S., & Barlow, D. (1977). Patterns of appropriate and deviant sexual arousal: The behavioral treatment of multiple sexual deviations. *Journal of Consulting and Clinical Psychology, 45,* 1144-1155.

Bryant, J., & Brown, D. (1989). Uses of pornography. In D. Zillmann, J. Bryant, & A. Huston (Eds.), *Media, children, and the family: Social scientific, psychodynamic, and clinical perspectives* (pp. 183-195). Hillsdale, NJ: Lawrence Erlbaum.

Burt, M. (1983). Justifying personal violence: A comparison of rapists and the general public. *Victimology, 8,* 131-150.

*Carter, D., Prentky, R., Knight, R., Vanderveer, P., & Boucher, R. (1987). Use of pornography in the criminal and developmental histories of sexual offenders. *Journal of Interpersonal Violence, 2,* 196-211.

Castonguay, L., Proulx, J., Aubut, J., McKibben, A., & Campbell, M. (1993). Sexual preference assessment of sexual aggressors: Predictors of penile response magnitude. *Archives of Sexual Behavior, 22,* 325-334.

Check, J., & Malamuth, N. M. (1986). Pornography and sexual aggression: A social learning theory analysis. In M. L. McLaughlin (Ed.), *Communication yearbook 9* (pp. 181-213). Beverly Hills, CA: Sage.

Christensen, A., Arkowitz, H., & Anderson, J. (1975). Practice dating as treatment for college dating inhibitions. *Behaviour Research and Therapy, 13,* 321-331.

Clark, T. (1972). Penile volume responses, sexual orientation and conditioning performance. *British Journal of Psychiatry, 120,* 126.

Cline, V. (1994). Pornography effects: Empirical and clinical evidence. In D. Zillmann, J. Bryant, & A. Huston (Eds.), *Media, children, and the family: Social scientific, psychodynamic, and clinical perspectives* (pp. 229-247). Hillsdale, NJ: Lawrence Erlbaum.

Cochrane, P. (1978). Sex crimes and pornography revisited. *International Journal of Crime and Penology, 6,* 307-317.

*Condrun, M., & Nutter, D. (1988). A preliminary examination of the pornography experience of sex offenders, paraphiliacs, sexual dysfunction patients, and controls based on Meese Commission recommendations. *Journal of Sex and Marital Therapy, 14,* 285-298.

*Cook, R., & Fosen, R. (1971a). Pornography and the sex offender. In Commission on Obscenity and Pornography, *Technical report of the Commission on Obscenity and Pornography: Vol. 7. Erotica and antisocial behavior* (pp. 149-162). Washington, DC: Government Printing Office.

*Cook, R., & Fosen, R. (1971b). Pornography and the sex offender: Patterns of previous exposure and arousal effects of pornographic stimuli. *Journal of Applied Psychology, 55,* 503-511.

Cook, T., & Leviton, L. (1980). Reviewing the literature: A comparison of traditional methods with meta-analysis. *Journal of Personality, 48,* 449-472.

Cooper, H., & Hedges, L. (1994). (Eds.). *Handbook of research synthesis.* New York: Russell Sage Foundation.

Court, J. (1976). Pornography and sex-crimes: A re-evaluation in the light of recent trends around the world. *International Journal of Criminology and Penology, 5,* 129-157.

Court, J. (1984). The relief of sexual problems through pornography. *Australian Journal of Sex, Marriage, and Family, 5*(2), 97-106.

Cramer, E., & McFarlane, J. (1994). Pornography and the abuse of women. *Public Health Nursing, 11,* 268-272.

Csillag, E. (1976). Modification of penile erectile response. *Journal of Behavioral Therapy and Experimental Psychiatry, 7,* 27-29.

Davidson, P., & Malcolm, P. (1985). The reliability of the rape index: A rapist sample. *Behavioral Assessment, 7,* 283-292.

*Davis, K., & Braucht, G. (1971). Exposure to pornography, character, and sexual deviance. In Commission on Obscenity and Pornography, *Technical report of the Commission on Obscenity and Pornography: Vol. 7. Erotica and antisocial behavior* (pp. 173-243). Washington, DC: Government Printing Office.

Davison, G. (1968). Elimination of a sadistic fantasy by a client-controlled counterconditioning technique. *Journal of Abnormal Psychology, 73,* 84-90.

Deitz, S., Blackwell, K., Daley, P., & Bentley, B. (1982). Measurement of empathy toward rape victims and rapists. *Journal of Personality and Social Psychology, 43,* 372-384.

Dermen, K. (1990). *Alcohol expectancy set, provocation, and predisposition as predictors of male "sexual aggression" toward a female target.* Unpublished doctoral dissertation, State University of New York at Buffalo.

Donnerstein, E. (1980). Aggressive erotica and violence against women. *Journal of Personality and Social Psychology, 39,* 269-277.

Donnerstein, E., & Berkowitz, L. (1981). Victim reactions in aggressive erotic films as a factor in violence against women. *Journal of Personality and Social Psychology, 41,* 710-724.

Downs, D. (1989). *The new politics of pornography.* Chicago: University of Chicago Press.

Duncan, D. (1990). Pornography as a source of information for university students. *Psychological Reports, 66,* 442.

Duncan, D., & Donnelly, J. (1991). Pornography as a source of sex information for students at a private northeastern university. *Psychological Reports, 68,* 782.

Duncan, D., & Nicholson, T. (1991). Pornography as a source of sex information for students at a southeastern university. *Psychological Reports, 68,* 802.

Earls, C. (1988). Aberrant sexual arousal in sexual offenders. *Annals of the New York Academy of Sciences, 528,* 41-48.

Earls, C., & Jackson, D. (1981). The effects of temperature on the mercury-in-rubber strain gauge. *Behavioral Assessment, 3,* 145-149.

*Earls, C., & Proulx, J. (1986). The differentiation of francophone rapists and nonrapists using penile circumferential measures. *Criminal Justice and Behavior, 13,* 419-429.

Earls, C., Quinsey, V., & Castonguay, G. (1987). A comparison of three methods of scoring penile circumference change. *Archives of Sexual Behavior, 16,* 493-500.

Eisler, R. (1984). Violence and male dominance: The ticking time bomb. *Humanities in Society, 7,* 3-17.

*Emerick, R., & Dutton, W. (1993). The effect of polygraphy on the self-report of adolescent sex offenders: Implications for risk assessment. *Annals of Sex Research, 6,* 83-103.

Everywoman. (1983). *Pornography and sexual violence: Evidence of the links.* London: Author.

*Fedora, O., Reddon, J., & Yeudall, L. (1986). Stimuli eliciting sexual arousal in genital exhibitionists: A possible clinical application. *Archives of Sexual Behavior, 15,* 417-427.

*Fedora, O., Reddon, J., Morrison, J., Fedora, S., Pascoe, H., & Yeudall, L. (1992). Sadism and other paraphilias in normal controls and aggressive and nonaggressive sex offenders. *Archives of Sexual Behavior, 21,* 1-25.

Fehrenbach, F., Smith, W., Monastersky, C., & Deisher, R. (1986). Adolescent sexual offenders: Offender and offense characteristics. *American Journal of Orthopsychiatry, 56,* 225-233.

Feild, H. (1978). Attitudes toward rape: A comparative analysis of police, rapists, crisis counselors, and citizens. *Journal of Personality and Social Psychology, 36,* 156-179.

Feldman, K. (1987). Research productivity and scholarly accomplishment of college teachers as related to their instructional effectiveness: A review and exploration. *Research in Higher Education, 26,* 227-298.

Fisher, W., & Grenier, G. (1994). Violent pornography, antiwoman thoughts, and antiwoman acts: In search of reliable effects. *Journal of Sex Research, 31,* 23-38.

Fitch, J. (1962). Men convicted of sexual offenses against children: A descriptive follow-up study. *British Journal of Criminology, 3,* 18-36.

Ford, M., & Linney, J. (1995). Comparative analysis of juvenile sexual offenders, violent nonsexual offenders, and status offenders. *Journal of Interpersonal Violence, 10,* 56-70.

*Frenzel, R., & Lang, R. (1989). Identifying sexual preferences in intrafamilial and extrafamilial child sexual abusers. *Annals of Sex Research, 2,* 255-275.

*Freund, K. (1967a). Diagnosing homo- and heterosexuality and erotic age-preference by means of a psychophysiological test. *Behaviour Research and Therapy, 5,* 209-228.

*Freund, K. (1967b). Erotic preference in pedophilia. *Behaviour Research and Therapy, 5,* 339-348.

Freund, K. (1971). A note on the use of the phallometric method of measuring mild sexual arousal in the male. *Behavior Therapy, 2,* 223-228.

Freund, K. (1976a). Assessment of anomalous erotic preferences in situational impotence. *Journal of Sex and Marital Therapy, 2,* 173-183.

Freund, K. (1976b). Diagnosis and treatment of forensically significant anomalous erotic preferences. *Canadian Journal of Criminology and Corrections, 18,* 181-189.

Freund, K. (1981). Assessment of pedophilia. In M. Cook & K. Howells (Eds.), *Adult sexual interest in children* (pp. 139-179). London: Academic Press.

*Freund, K., Chan, S., & Coulthard, R. (1979). Phallometric diagnosis with "nonadmitters." *Behaviour Research and Therapy, 17,* 451-457.

*Freund, K., & Langevin, R. (1976). Bisexuality in homosexual pedophilia. *Archives of Sexual Behavior, 5,* 415-423.

*Freund, K., Scher, H., Racansky, I., Campbell, K., & Heasman, G. (1986). Males disposed to commit rape. *Archives of Sexual Behavior, 15,* 23-35.

Gentry, C. (1991). Pornography and rape: An empirical analysis. *Deviant Behavior, 17,* 277-288.

*Goldstein, M. (1973). Exposure to erotic stimuli and sexual deviance. *Journal of Social Issues, 29,* 197-219.

*Goldstein, M., Kant, H., Judd, L., Rice, C., & Green, R. (1971). Exposure to pornography and sexual behavior in deviant and normal groups. In Commission on Obscenity and Pornography, *Technical report of the Commission on Obscenity and Pornography: Vol. 7. Erotica and antisocial behavior* (pp. 1-89). Washington, DC: Government Printing Office.

*Hall, G. (1991). Sexual arousal as a function of physiological and cognitive variables in a sexual offender population. *Archives of Sexual Behavior, 20,* 359-369.

Hall, G., & Proctor, W. (1987). Criminological predictors of recidivism in a sexual offender population. *Journal of Consulting and Clinical Psychology, 55,* 111-112.

*Hall, G., Proctor, W., & Nelson, G. (1988). Validity of physiological measures of pedophilic sexual arousal in a sexual offender population. *Journal of Consulting and Clinical Psychology, 56,* 118-122.

Hall, G., Shondrick, D., & Hirschman, R. (1993). The role of sexual arousal in sexually aggressive behavior: A meta-analysis. *Journal of Consulting and Clinical Psychology, 61,* 1091-1095.

Hammer, E. (1957). A psychoanalytic hypothesis concerning sex offenders. *Journal of Clinical and Experimental Psychopathology and Quarterly Review of Psychiatry and Neurology, 18,* 177-184.

*Hinton, J., O'Neill, M., & Webster, S. (1980). Psychophysiological assessment of sex offenders in a security hospital. *Archives of Sexual Behavior, 9,* 205-216.

Holmstrom, L., & Burgess, A. (1980). Sexual behavior of assailants during reported rapes. *Archives of Sexual Behavior, 9,* 427-439.

Hui, C. (1986). Fifteen years of pornography research: Does exposure to pornography have any effects? *Hong Kong Psychological Society Bulletin, 16-17,* 41-62.

Hunter, J. E., & Schmidt, F. L. (1990). *Methods of meta-analysis: Correcting for error and bias in research findings.* Newbury Park, CA: Sage.

*Johnson, W., Kupperstein, L., & Peters, J. (1971). Sex offenders' experience with erotica. In Commission on Obscenity and Pornography, *Technical report of the Commission on Obscenity and Pornography: Vol. 7. Erotica and antisocial behavior* (pp. 163-171). Washington, DC: Government Printing Office.

Karacan, I., Williams, R., Guerrero, M., Salis, P., Thornby, J., & Hursch, C. (1974). Nocturnal penile tumescence and sleep of convicted rapists and other prisoners. *Archives of Sexual Behavior, 3,* 19-26.

Katz, H. (1970). *The effects of previous exposure to pornographic film, sexual instrumentation, and guilt on male verbal aggression against women.* Unpublished doctoral dissertation, University of Connecticut, Storrs.

Knudsen, D. (1988). Child sexual abuse and pornography: Is there a relationship? *Journal of Family Violence, 3,* 253-267.

*Kolarsky, A., & Madlafousek, J. (1972). Female behavior and sexual arousal in heterosexual male deviant offenders. *Journal of Nervous and Mental Disease, 155,* 110-118.

*Kolarsky, A., & Madlafousek, J. (1983). The inverse role of preparatory erotic stimulation in exhibitionists. *Archives of Sexual Behavior, 12,* 123-148.

Koss, M. P., & Dinero, T. E. (1988). Predictors of sexual aggression among a national sample of male college students. *Annals of the New York Academy of Sciences, 528,* 133-147.

Koss, M. P., & Gidycz, C. (1985). Sexual experiences survey: Reliability and validity. *Journal of Consulting and Clinical Psychology, 53,* 422-423.

*Krafka, M., & Prentky, R. (1992). A comparative study of nonparaphilic sexual addictions and paraphilias in men. *Journal of Clinical Psychiatry, 53*, 345-350.

Krisak, J., Murphy, W., & Stalgaitis, S. (1981). Reliability issues in the penile assessment of incarcerates. *Journal of Behavioral Assessment, 3*, 199-207.

Kutchinsky, B. (1970). *Studies on pornography and sex crimes in Denmark.* Washington, DC: New Social Science Monographs.

Kutchinsky, B. (1973a). The effect of easy availability of pornography on the incidence of sex crimes: The Danish experience. *Journal of Social Issues, 29*, 163-183.

Kutchinsky, B. (1973b). Eroticism without censorship: Sociological investigations on the production and consumption of pornographic literature in Denmark. *International Journal of Criminology and Penology, 1*, 217-225.

Kutchinsky, B. (1976). Deviance and criminality: The case of a voyeur in a peeper's paradise. *Diseases of the Nervous System, 37*, 137-151.

Kutchinsky, B. (1985). Pornography and its effect in Denmark and the United States: A rejoinder and beyond. *Comparative Social Research, 8*, 301-330.

Kutchinsky, B. (1991). Pornography and rape: Theory and practice? Evidence from crime data in four countries where pornography is easily available. *International Journal of Law and Psychiatry, 14*, 47-64.

Lalumiere, M., & Quinsey, V. (1994). The discrimination of rapists from non-sex offenders using phallometric measures: A meta-analysis. *Criminal Justice and Behavior, 21*, 150-175.

*Lang, R., Black, E., Frenzel, R., & Checkley, K. (1988). Aggression and erotic attraction toward children in incestuous and pedophilic men. *Annals of Sex Research, 1*, 417-441.

Langevin, R. (1985). An overview of the paraphilias. In M. Ben-Aron, M., Hueker, & C. Webster (Eds.), *Clinical criminology: The assessment and treatment of criminal behavior* (pp. 179-190). Toronto: University of Toronto Press.

*Langevin, R., Ben-Aron, M., Coulthard, R., Heasman, G., Purins, J., Handy, L., Hucker, S., Russon, A., Day, D., Roper, V., Bain, J., Wortzman, G., & Webster, C. (1985). Sexual aggression: Constructing a predictive equation. A controlled pilot study. In R. Langevin (Ed.), *Erotic preference, gender identity and aggression in men* (pp. 39-76). Hillsdale, NJ: Lawrence Erlbaum.

*Langevin, R., Lang, R., Wright, P., Handy, L., Frenzel, R., & Black, E. (1988). Pornography and sexual offenses. *Annals of Sex Research, 1*, 335-362.

Lanning, K. (1987). *Child molesters: A behavioral analysis.* Washington, DC: Department of Justice, Office of Juvenile Justice and Delinquency Prevention. (ERIC Document Reproduction Service No. ED 307 532)

Laws, D. (1984). The assessment of dangerous sexual behavior in males. *Medicine and Law, 3*, 127-140.

Laws, D., & Holmen, M. (1978). Sexual response faking by pedophiles. *Criminal Justice and Behavior, 5*, 343-356.

*Linder, H. (1953). Sexual responsiveness to perceptual tests in a group of sexual offenders. *Journal of Personality, 21*, 364-374.

Lipton, D., McDonel, E., & McFall, R. (1987). Heterosocial perception in rapists. *Journal of Consulting and Clinical Psychology, 55*, 17-21.

Lonsway, K., & Fitzgerald, L. (1994). Rape myths: A review. *Psychology of Women Quarterly, 18*, 133-164.

Lyons, J., Anderson, R., & Larson, D. (1994). A systematic review of the effect of aggressive and nonaggressive pornography. In D. Zillmann, J. Bryant, & A. Huston (Eds.), *Media, children, and the family: Social scientific, psychodynamic, and clinical perspectives* (pp. 271-310). Hillsdale, NJ: Lawrence Erlbaum.

MacKinnon, C. A. (1986). Pornography: Not a moral issue. *Women's Studies International Forum, 9,* 63-78.

MacKinnon, C. A. (1993). *Only words.* Cambridge, MA: Harvard University Press.

Malamuth, N. M. (1983). Factors associated with rape as predictors of laboratory aggression toward women. *Journal of Personality and Social Psychology, 45,* 432-442.

Malamuth, N. M. (1986). Predictors of naturalistic sexual aggression: *Journal of Personality and Social Psychology, 50,* 953-962.

Malamuth, N. M. (1989). Sexually violent media, thought patterns, and antisocial behavior. In G. Comstock (Ed.), *Public communication and behavior* (Vol. 2, pp. 159-204). San Diego, CA: Academic Press.

Malamuth, N. M., & Billings, V. (1986). The functions and effects of pornography: Sexual communications versus feminist models in light of research findings. In J. Bryant & D. Zillmann (Eds.), *Perspectives on media effects* (pp. 83-108). Hillsdale, NJ: Lawrence Erlbaum.

Malamuth, N. M., Haber, S., & Feshbach, S. (1980). Testing hypotheses regarding rape: Exposure to sexual violence, sex differences, and the "normality" of rapists. *Journal of Research in Personality, 14,* 121-137.

Malamuth, N. M., Heavey, C., & Linz, D. (1993). In G. Hall, R. Hirschman, J. Graham, & M. Zaragoza (Eds.), *Sexual aggression: Issues in etiology, assessment, and treatment* (pp. 63-97). Washington, DC: Hemisphere.

Malamuth, N. M., Sockloskie, R. J., Koss, M. P., & Tanaka, J. S. (1991). Characteristics of aggressors against women: Testing a model using a national sample of college students. *Journal of Consulting and Clinical Psychology, 59,* 670-681.

*Marques, J. (1981). Effects of victim resistance strategies on the sexual arousal and attitudes of violent rapists. In R. Stuart (Ed.), *Violent behavior: Social learning approaches to prediction, management, and treatment* (pp. 138-172). New York: Brunner/Mazel.

Marquis, J. (1970). Orgasmic reconditioning: Changing sexual object choice through controlling masturbation fantasies. *Journal of Behavioral Therapy and Experimental Psychiatry, 1,* 263-271.

Marshall, W. (1974). A combined treatment approach to the reduction of multiple fetish-related behavior. *Journal of Consulting and Clinical Psychology, 42,* 613-616.

*Marshall, W. (1988). The use of sexually explicit stimuli by rapists, child molesters, and nonoffenders. *Journal of Sex Research, 25,* 267-288.

Marshall, W., & Barbaree, H. (1978). The reduction of deviant arousal: Satiation treatment for sexual aggressors. *Criminal Justice and Behavior, 5,* 294-303.

*Marshall, W., Barbaree, H., & Butt, J. (1982). Sexual offenders against male children: Sexual preferences. *Behaviour Research and Therapy, 20,* 383-391.

*Marshall, W., Barbaree, H., & Christophe, D. (1986). Sexual offenders against female children: Sexual preference for age of victims and type of behavior. *Canadian Journal of Behavioural Science, 18,* 424-439.

McConaghy, N. (1992). Validity and ethics of penile circumference measures of sexual arousal: A response to McAnulty and Adams. *Archives of Sexual Behavior, 21,* 187-195.

Meyer, T. (1969). *An experimental study of the effect of sexually arousing and verbally violent content on aggressive behavior.* Unpublished master's thesis, Ohio University, Athens.

Miller, C. (1977). *Generalizability of the facilitative effect of anger on sexual arousal.* Unpublished master's thesis, Purdue University.

Miller, F. (1981). Etiological factors in a case of male perversion. *American Journal of Psychoanalysis, 41,* 39-44.

Mosher, D. (1973). Sex differences, sex experience, sex guilt, and explicitly sexual films. *Journal of Social Issues, 29,* 95-112.

Mosher, D., & Anderson, R. (1986). Macho personality, sexual aggression, and reactions to guided imagery of realistic rape. *Journal of Research in Personality, 20,* 77-94.

Murphy, W., Haynes, M., Coleman, E., & Flanagan, B. (1985). Sexual responding of "non-rapists" to aggressive sexual themes: Normative data. *Journal of Psychopathology and Behavioral Assessment, 7,* 37-47.

*Murphy, W., Haynes, M., Stalgaitis, S., & Flanagan, B. (1986). Differential sexual responding among four groups of sexual offenders against children. *Journal of Psychopathology and Behavioral Assessment, 8,* 339-353.

Murrin, M., & Laws, D. (1990). The influence of pornography on sexual crimes. In W. Marshall, D. Laws, & H. Barbaree (Eds.), *Handbook of sexual assault: Issues, theories, and treatment of the offender* (pp. 73-91). New York: Plenum.

Nemes, I. (1993). The relationship between pornography and sex crimes. *Journal of Psychiatry and Law, 20,* 459-481.

*Nutter, D., & Kearns, M. (1993). Patterns of exposure to sexually explicit material among sex offenders, child molesters, and controls. *Journal of Sex and Marital Therapy, 19,* 77-85.

Overholser, J. C., & Beck, S. (1986). Multimethod assessment of rapists, child molesters, and three control groups on behavioral and psychological measures. *Journal of Consulting and Clinical Psychology, 54,* 682-687.

Pacht, A., & Cowden, J. (1974). An exploratory study of five hundred sex offenders. *Criminal Justice and Behavior, 1,* 13-20.

Palczewski, C. (1992, October). *Survivor testimony in the pornography controversy: Assessing credibility in argument from examples in the attorney general's report.* Paper presented at the annual meeting of the Speech Communication Association, Chicago.

Palczewski, C. (1993). Public policy argument and survivor testimony: Pro-ordinance conservatives, confession, mediation and recuperation. In R. McKerrow (Ed.), *Argument and the postmodern challenge: Proceedings of the Eighth SCA/AFA Conference on Argumentation* (pp. 461-467). Annandale, VA: Speech Communication Association.

Preiss, R., & Allen, M. (1995). Understanding and using meta-analysis. *Evaluation & the Health Professions, 18,* 315-335.

Prentky, R., & Knight, R. (1993). Age of onset of sexual assault: Criminal and life history correlates. In G. Hall, R. Hirschman, J. Graham, & M. Zaragoza (Eds.), *Sexual aggression: Issues in etiology, assessment, and treatment* (pp. 43-62). Washington, DC: Taylor & Francis.

Proulx, J. (1989). Sexual preference assessment of sexual aggressors. *International Journal of Law and Psychiatry, 12,* 275-280.

*Proulx, J., Aubut, J., McKibben, A., & Cote, M. (1994). Penile responses of rapists and nonrapists to rape stimuli involving physical violence or humiliation. *Archives of Sexual Behavior, 23,* 295-310.

*Quinsey, V., & Chaplin, T. (1984). Stimulus control of rapists' and non-sex offenders' sexual arousal. *Behavioral Assessment, 6,* 169-176.

*Quinsey, V., & Chaplin, T. (1988a). Penile responses of child molesters and normals to descriptions of encounters with children involving sex and violence. *Journal of Interpersonal Violence, 3,* 259-274.

*Quinsey, V., & Chaplin, T. (1988b). Preventing faking in phallometric assessments of sexual preference. *Annals of the New York Academy of Sciences, 528,* 49-58.

*Quinsey, V., Chaplin, T., & Carrigan, W. (1979). Sexual preference among incestuous and nonincestuous child molesters. *Behavior Therapy, 10,* 562-565.

*Quinsey, V., Chaplin, T., & Upfold, D. (1984). Sexual arousal to nonsexual violence and sadomasochistic themes among rapists and non-sex-offenders. *Journal of Consulting and Clinical Psychology, 52,* 651-657.

*Quinsey, V., Chaplin, T., & Varney, G. (1981). A comparison of rapists' and non-sex offenders' sexual preferences for mutually consenting sex, rape, and physical abuse of women. *Behavioral Assessment, 3,* 127-135.

*Quinsey, V., Steinman, C., Bergersen, S., & Holmes, T. (1975). Penile circumference, skin conductance, and ranking responses of child molesters and "normals" to sexual and nonsexual visual stimuli. *Behavior Therapy, 6,* 213-219.

Rada, R. (1976). Alcoholism and the child molester. *Annals of the New York Academy of Sciences, 273,* 492-496.

Rapaport, R. (1984). *Sexually aggressive males: Characterological features and sexual responsiveness to rape depictions.* Unpublished doctoral dissertation, Auburn University.

Reed, M. (1989). *Research on pornography: The evidence of harm. Pornography's relationship to abnormal sexual behavior/sexual offenders.* Cincinnati, OH: National Coalition Against Pornography.

Rosen, R. (1973). Suppression of penile tumescence by instrumental conditioning. *Psychosomatic Medicine, 35,* 509-513.

Rosen, R., & Kopel, S. (1978). Role of penile tumescence measurement in the behavioral treatment of sexual deviation: Issues of validity. *Journal of Consulting and Clinical Psychology, 46,* 1519-1521.

Rosen, R., Shapiro, D., & Schwartz, G. (1975). Voluntary control of penile tumescence. *Psychosomatic Medicine, 37,* 479-483.

Schwalm, S. (1984). *Violent sexual offenses and the availability, distribution, and consumption of erotic materials.* Unpublished master's thesis, Ohio State University, Columbus.

Seeley, T., Abramson, P., Perry, L., Rothblatt, A., & Seeley, D. (1980). Thermographic measurement of sexual arousal: A methodological note. *Archives of Sexual Behavior, 9,* 77-85.

Segal, Z., & Marshall, W. (1985). Heterosexual social skills in a population of rapists and child molesters. *Journal of Consulting and Clinical Psychology, 53,* 55-63.

*Seto, M., & Barbaree, H. (1993). Victim blame and sexual arousal to rape cues in rapists and nonoffenders. *Annals of Sex Research, 6,* 167-183.

*Seto, M., & Walker, M. (1996). Criterion-related validity of a phallometric test for paraphilic rape and sadism. *Behaviour Research and Therapy, 34,* 175-183.

Stoller, R. (1970). Pornography and perversion. *Archives of General Psychiatry, 22,* 490-499.

Stoller, R. (1972). Pornography and perversion. In D. Holbrook (Ed.), *The case against pornography* (pp. 111-128). London: Willmer Brothers.

Strossen, N. (1995). *Defending pornography: Free speech, sex, and the fight for women's rights.* New York: Scribner.

Tracz, S. (1985). *The effect of the violation of the assumption of independence when combining correlation coefficients in a meta-analysis.* Unpublished doctoral dissertation, Southern Illinois University.

Twentyman, C., & McFall, R. (1975). Behavioral training of social skills in shy males. *Journal of Consulting and Clinical Psychology, 43,* 384-395.

*Walker, C. (1971). Erotic stimuli and the aggressive sexual offender. In Commission on Obscenity and Pornography, *Technical report of the Commission on Obscenity and Pornography: Vol. 7. Erotica and antisocial behavior* (pp. 91-147). Washington, DC: Government Printing Office.

Weaver, J. (1994). Pornography and sexual callousness: The perceptual and behavioral consequences of exposure to pornography. In D. Zillmann, J. Bryant, & A. Huston (Eds.), *Media, children, and the family: Social scientific, psychodynamic, and clinical perspectives* (pp. 215-228). Hillsdale, NJ: Lawrence Erlbaum.

Whitman, W., & Quinsey, V. (1981). Heterosocial skill training for institutionalized rapists and child molesters. *Canadian Journal of Behavioural Science, 13,* 105-115.

*Wydra, A., Marshal, W., Earls, C., & Barbaree, H. (1983). Identification of cues and control of sexual arousal by rapists. *Behaviour Research and Therapy, 21,* 469-476.

Wyre, R. (1992). Pornography and sexual violence: Working with sex offenders. In C. Itzin (Ed.), *Pornography: Women, violence, and civil liberties* (pp. 236-247). New York: Oxford University Press.

Yaffe, M. (1982). Therapeutic uses of sexually explicit material. In M. Yaffe & E. Nelson (Eds.), *The influence of pornography on behaviour* (pp. 119-150). New York: Academic Press.

Zillmann, D., Hoyt, J., & Day, K. (1974). Strength and duration of the effect of aggressive, violent, and erotic communications on subsequent aggressive behavior. *Communication Research, 1,* 286-306.

Zillmann, D., & Sapolsky, B. (1977). What mediates the effect of mild erotica on annoyance and hostile behavior in males? *Journal of Personality and Social Psychology, 35,* 587-596.

CHAPTER CONTENTS

5 The Life Space of Personalized Conflicts

DALE HAMPLE
Western Illinois University

This chapter analyzes interpersonal conflicts by means of Lewin's field theory, which requires a commitment to studying the actor's life space, or perceptions of his or her environment. A particular focus here is on taking conflict personally (TCP), the feeling that interpersonal conflicts are antagonistic, punishing interactions in which an individual believes the other person is trying to hurt him or her on purpose. After two introductory sections on TCP and field theory, the author moves on to a roughly chronological investigation of conflict as seen by people high in TCP. The preconflict, conflict, and postconflict life spaces are all examined. This includes attention to people's affective and cognitive orientations to conflicts, their arguing behaviors (particularly their aggressive actions), and their feelings immediately after an argument is finished. The long-term consequences of personalized conflicts include reduced relational satisfaction and the prospect of violence. Key elements of personalization are thought to begin with the individual's family of origin and to survive into his or her close adult relationships.

A personalized conflict is one that is *taken* personally. That is, the participant feels that opposition is intended to attack self, and not particularly self's position on the substantive topic. Even issue-directed criticisms can be taken personally if the participant is so inclined. This chapter is centrally about what happens when people take on that inclination and why the predisposition may appear.

Scholars have commonly differentiated between conflict actions that are directed at the issues on the table and those that are not. Coser's (1956) classic distinction between realistic and unrealistic conflict is perhaps the best known of these discussions, but related conceptualizations appear in most surveys of conflict management behaviors, with authors usually distinguishing most forcibly between productive and destructive conflicts (e.g., Boardman & Horowitz, 1994; Deutsch, 1994; Lulofs, 1994, pp. 14-16; Wilmot & Hocker,

Correspondence and requests for reprints: Dale Hample, Department of Communication, Western Illinois University, Macomb, IL 61455.

Communication Yearbook 22, pp. 171-207

1998, pp. 40-48) or between substantive and affective conflicts (Collins & Guetzkow, 1964, pp. 111-117). Personalized conflicts, of course, are not seen as being truly substantive. Once a conflict is taken personally, it almost inevitably becomes face oriented (Folger, Poole, & Stutman, 1993, chap. 5), and this invites the interaction to become destructive and potentially to escalate. Personalizing conflict, then, is clearly something to be avoided if possible. Virtually all writers on the topic warn against personalization (or some related idea) and offer instruction on how to steer a conflict, and one's feelings about it, in constructive directions (e.g., Filley, 1975).

In this chapter, the phenomenon of taking conflict personally (TCP) is grounded within a Lewinian framework. This approach has attracted some general attention (e.g., Cupach & Canary, 1997, pp. 59-60; Folger et al., 1993, pp. 18-21; Graziano, Jensen-Campbell, & Hair, 1996), but the literature consists largely of a series of empirical reports. Enough work has been done to justify an effort to sum up, and that is my purpose here.

I begin with two preliminary sections: one that defines the operational construct of taking conflict personally and another that outlines the basic tenets of Lewin's field theory. The three sections that follow explore the effects of TCP prior to conflict engagement, during the conflict itself, and after the conflict has been concluded. The focus of my discussion is TCP, but I report related work as well.

TAKING CONFLICT PERSONALLY

TCP has been defined as "a feeling of being personally engaged in a punishing life event. [The person] feels threatened, anxious, damaged, devalued, insulted" (Hample & Dallinger, 1995, p. 306). Although several studies have been conducted with an early version of the TCP instrument (Dallinger & Hample, 1989), the scale reported in Hample and Dallinger (1995, p. 313) is now preferred. It is a 37-item self-report instrument covering six subscales.

Three of these subscales are the conceptual center of TCP and are sometimes intercorrelated to such an extent that they are simply combined and reported as "core TCP." The first subscale is *direct personalization,* which is a straightforward effort to capture the affect involved in taking conflict personally (e.g., "It really hurts my feelings to be criticized"). *Persecution feelings* is a somewhat more specific construct, reflecting the perception that opposition is directed against self rather than position (e.g., "In conflict discussions I often feel that other people are trying very hard to make sure that I lose"). The third subscale is *stress reactions,* which measures especially intense psychological and physiological negative feelings (e.g., "Sometimes when there are a lot of conflicts in a week, I feel like I'm getting an ulcer").

The other three subscales are *positive relational effects, negative relational effects,* and *like/dislike valence.* The first permits the respondent to report whether he or she really believes that conflicts can strengthen personal or workplace relationships, as virtually all textbooks insist (e.g., "A deep conflict can really bring people together after it's over"). The mirror scale, *negative relational effects,* offers the opportunity for the respondent to give more pessimistic impressions (e.g., "A conflict can really wreck the climate in the workplace"). In the early version of the TCP instrument (Dallinger & Hample, 1989), these two constructs were combined into one subscale, but interpretation was always problematic: If a person got a low score, did it mean that he or she thought conflicts had negative effects on relationships or none at all? These two subscales obviously have a substantial negative correlation, but keeping them separate makes analysis much easier. The negative subscale tends to be directly associated with the core TCP measures, whereas the positive one moves in the opposite direction. The last subscale is *like/dislike valence,* which measures the degree to which a person enjoys conflicts (e.g., "To me, it's fun to argue").

As readers will have inferred from the sample items, these scales reflect the idea that TCP is a stable personality trait. Research to be reviewed in later sections of this chapter confirms, in fact, that TCP scores are validly associated with other traits, permitting, among others, the simple generalization that some people are more predisposed toward personalization than others. However, from the beginning, TCP has been understood as a personality *state* as well. Even people who are not usually inclined to personalize can be made to feel that a particular conflict is aimed at self, and even personalizers can experience productive arguments. TCP has been measured as a state by two methods. One is a self-report instrument that is a simple rewording of the trait measure, administered just after completion of an interpersonal conflict (Hample, Dallinger, & Fofana, 1995). The other state method involved coding participants' postconflict interview comments for expressions of personalization, stress, and so forth (Hample, 1996). Though both enduring and temporary personality features are relevant to Lewinian theory, the state data are particularly on point, as will become clear in the next sections.

FIELD THEORY

Perhaps Lewin's most substantial theoretical work is centered on what he calls field theory (Lewin, 1952). It is a metatheory, an account of the sorts of things that need to be included in a psychological theory of any given kind of behavior (Gold, 1992). Message production, of course, is a behavior, and field theory has recently been applied to that domain (Hample, 1997) and also offered as theoretical grounding for TCP in particular (Hample & Dallinger, 1995).

The most fundamental idea is that psychological behavior (behavior that is in some respect under the actor's control) is affected only by the person and his or her life space (Lewin, 1952, chap. 10). Lewin's frequently cited equation for this is $B = f(P,E)$, meaning that behavior is a joint function of person and environment. The life space is the environment perceived from the actor's point of view (see Graziano et al., 1996, for a recent application of this perspective to interpersonal conflicts). Possibly relevant but unperceived factors are part of the life space's "foreign hull" (Leeper, 1949, pp. 51-52). These factors may affect the state of the life space (e.g., general economic conditions might alter the base probability of succeeding in a job interview), but actors respond only to elements that they themselves perceive. A person may participate more or less simultaneously in several life spaces (Hample, Alajmi, Klein, Ward, & White, 1997; Lewin, 1948, chap. 6), but one will be focal at any given moment.

For many purposes, Lewin (e.g., 1952, p. 196) found it sufficient to represent the life space as two-dimensional, often drawing a circle or oval containing a number of regions. However, when fuller exposition is required, Lewin makes it clear that the life space is more than two-dimensional. One of those additional dimensions is time (Lewin, 1952, chap. 3). Lewin insists that behavior is determined by the state of the life space "in the instant," and therefore there is no need to inquire into participants' childhood experiences, as Freudians do, or into people's past reinforcement schedules, as behaviorists do. However, a person can think about the past and the future, and to the extent that he or she has those in mind, the life space projects backward and forward in time. The development of "time perspective," in fact, is one thing that distinguishes child from adult behavior (Lewin, 1952, pp. 103-104). Certainly, a person's experiences change him or her, and so they can produce predispositions or habits. However, what is important in predicting behavior is not the past experience itself but the behavioral inclination it generates for the present. Future desires are similarly relevant only insofar as they are represented as immediate goals in the instant.

An additional dimension of the life space is reality/irreality. Although this is technically a continuum (Leeper, 1949, pp. 68-71), Lewin (e.g., 1952, p. 246) often simply sketched two planes. Each plane contains a projection of the life space. The plane of reality is where the actor makes his or her most objective perceptions, seeing self, goals, and obstacles more or less as they are. In the plane of irreality, however, the person can imagine, fear, distort, and plan about things that may or may not currently exist. Irreality is not a pathological place; the distinction between reality and irreality is not unlike that between action and intention or that between mundane behavior and daydreaming. Plans and anxieties are mainly sited in the plane of irreality, whereas actions occur in the plane of reality (to the extent that they are accurately perceived).

Lewin (1952, chap. 2) identifies the chief components of a life space, or at least those he thinks to be most likely. Whether these things actually appear depends, of course, only on whether the actor thinks they are present. Within a life space are various *positions,* which are regions that are spatially related to other regions. For instance, the actor may be outside one goal region and simultaneously within another. *Locomotion,* which is Lewin's term for behavior, refers to changes in position from one instant to another. Thus a person might locomote into a goal region. The idea of position is generalized to that of *cognitive structure,* which refers to the constellation of positions within the life space. This takes in the whole perception of the life space, with notice being taken of several regions (thus positions) at once. A *force* is the "tendency to locomotion," is roughly similar to a vector, and may be the resultant vector of several forces perceived simultaneously in the life space. Locomotion from one position to another is determined by forces. A *goal* is not a force, but a *force field.* It is a region of the life space toward which all forces point. Goals have positive valences. A *conflict* appears in the life space when at least two force fields overlap, leading to *frustration* (see Barker, Dembo, & Lewin, 1941) if the individual cannot satisfy all the goals (by moving into their regions or substituting for them).[1] *Equilibrium* appears when the overlap resolves into a resultant force or vector that dictates no movement at all, or when locomotion has satisfied all the forces, leading to satiation and the consequent evaporation of the force fields.

Some other important concepts are scattered throughout the history of field theory's development (see Argyris, 1952; Deutsch, 1954; Hample, 1997). An *obstacle* is a negatively valenced region in the life space. Obstacles are repellent whereas goals are attractive; otherwise there is no difference. Lewin was often content merely to refer to negatively valenced regions, without giving them a distinctive terminology. All regions have *boundaries* that enclose them and distinguish them from their neighboring regions. Some of these boundaries are relatively impenetrable, and these are called *barriers.* Notice that barriers and obstacles are quite different things: One is a force field and the other is a resistant skin around a region, though Deutsch (1954, p. 204) emphasizes that this means that barriers are *restraining forces.* In earlier work, I have suggested that obstacles are understood by the perceiver, whereas barriers are more mysterious (Hample, 1997). Thus not being able to get to a phone to call a person for a date would be an obstacle, but being turned down for a date for no apparent reason would constitute a barrier around the "date" goal region. *Differentiation* refers to the number of parts one perceives in a whole (Lewin, 1952, chap. 5, appendix). A person may be more or less differentiated for his or her life space as a whole or for one element of the life space, such as another person or the individual's goals. *Climate,* an idea Lewin develops mainly in the context of group dynamics (e.g., Lewin, Lippitt, & White, 1939; see Saldern, 1986), is a generalized feature of a life space. Deutsch (1973), one of Lewin's students, concentrated on cooperative versus competitive climates, and other category systems appeared as well. I have suggested that climate may be regarded as a perception that certain sorts of clearly valenced behavior (e.g., personal threats) are expectable and/or that other sorts (e.g., compliments) are not (Hample, 1997;

Hample & Dallinger, 1995). A climate therefore facilitates or impedes certain classes of behaviors. Although the concept of *plan* rarely appears in Lewin's work, the nearly equivalent notion of *distinguished path* does. When a person perceives several possible routes to a goal region and prefers one of them, for whatever reason, the distinguished path is the favored one (see Deutsch, 1954, pp. 195-196; Leeper, 1949).[2]

This brief summary of field theory may be sufficient to provide a skeleton that can be fleshed out in the following sections, which focus much more precisely on interpersonal conflict (for more elaborated discussion of field theory, see Argyris, 1952; Deutsch, 1954; Leeper, 1949). As a kind of summary, note these features of field theory: (a) It takes a subjective orientation, insisting on the priority of the actor's point of view; (b) it is a dynamic theory, in the sense that it regards behavior as a response to various force fields; and (c) it is multidimensional, permitting gradations of time and reality to exercise influence on behavior, provided that the actor brings these variables into the moment of action. These features sound as though they require the actor to be *conscious* of all the factors affecting his or her behavior, but actually they do not (Deutsch, 1954). Field theory can still offer useful descriptions and predictions of behaviors that pursue goals in a habitual way, without consciousness (see Kellermann, 1992).

From this point on, I want to concentrate on interpersonal conflict, and especially on the relevance of personalization and its associated variables. In examining these issues in the preconflict, conflict, and postconflict life spaces, I am aware that some processes and findings have been somewhat arbitrarily placed, but that is to be expected whenever any organization is imposed on a naturally continuous process. It is important to emphasize, however, that my division is an academic one, not necessarily a phenomenological one. That is, I do not suppose that a person taking action during a conflict would necessarily have any immediate orientation to the issues I discuss in the pre- and postconflict life spaces.[3]

THE PRECONFLICT LIFE SPACE

Prior to an interpersonal conflict, let us suppose that the actor can see that a conflict is possible. This supposition, which will often be accurate, permits us to examine the various predispositions and perceptions that people bring to bear on arguments prior to action—what Drake and Donohue (1996) might call a frame for conflict. A person anticipating an argument might, consciously or unconsciously, imagine a life space in the plane of irreality, a life space whose elements and climate foreshadow what the person expects and might therefore cause to happen.

I will not discuss at this point how people come to be predisposed toward taking conflict personally—and, by extension, how others avoid learning this.

A person's TCP levels reflect the whole of his or her past experience with conflict. Personalization is therefore both a precursor and a long-term consequence of conflicts and conflict patterns. I will examine this issue in the final substantive portion of this review. For now, let us just take it as given that people do have predispositions to personalize or not.

In this section, I want to explore several different aspects of the preconflict life space, insofar as we are informed about them by TCP and related constructs. An initial consideration is the climate of this life space. In particular, feelings of anxiety and confidence will be an issue, as will be the desire to avoid engagement. A further matter bearing on the climate is defensiveness, particularly as that construct is understood in the clinical psychology community. The second major part of the section has to do with cognitive organization—the person's perception of likely lines of action in the upcoming conflict. Finally, I will sketch two hypothetical life spaces in order to illustrate some preconflict perceptual and affective differences between those who tend to personalize and those who do not.

Climate

A life space's climate is a pervasive feeling that invites or discourages certain sorts of action. For instance, Deutsch (1973) shows that competitive climates stimulate threats, whereas cooperative climates generate trusting actions. I am unaware of any systematic typology of climates and, on the analogy with efforts to categorize message types (see O'Keefe, 1987), suppose that there will never be one that is completely valid for all investigations. Here, my primary concerns are climates of avoidance, anxiety, confidence, and defensiveness. In each respect, personalization is undesirable.

Considered as a trait, TCP is a predisposition to see conflictive situations as potentially punishing, humiliating, stressful, and hurtful. People high in TCP therefore have avoidant intentions when they anticipate conflict (Dallinger & Hample, 1989; Hample & Dallinger, 1995). The core dimensions of TCP each correlate substantially (from about $r = .40$ to $r = .50$) with Infante and Rancer's (1982) measure of argument avoidance (Hample & Dallinger, 1995). On the other hand, people who do not personalize conflicts welcome them: Based on the valence subscale, people who say they like conflicts score high on Infante and Rancer's measure of argument approach ($r = .58$). Interestingly, these same respondents also say that they are unusually likely to be hostile and nasty during conflicts; the correlation between like/dislike valence and Infante and Wigley's (1986) verbal aggressiveness scale is .34 (Hample & Dallinger, 1995). So personalizers want to avoid conflicts, whereas people low on TCP prefer to dive in and may even seek out chances to do so. In a study of self-reported preferences for different conflict styles, Dallinger and Hample (1995, Study 1) have shown that personalizers have a clear preference for passive, submissive tactics. This evidence points to the conclusion that core TCP predicts the wish to avoid arguments.

Several other studies support this general finding that TCP is associated with avoidant impulses and offer more specific information about people's levels of anxiety and confidence. Personalizers report higher levels of anxiety about communicating: The correlation between the core TCP dimensions and communication apprehension is about .30 (Myers & Bailey, 1991). Given what we know about TCP and argumentativeness, Myers and Bailey's (1991) finding is consistent with the association between communication apprehension and argumentativeness ($r = -.46$; Irizarry, 1997). Women high in generalized anxiety have more negative perceptions about self and relational partner and more negative appraisals of relationships in general (Benton & Allen, 1966). All this implies that people high in TCP are generally more likely to want to avoid interaction of any kind. A roughly opposite climate, a feeling of self-confidence about one's own communicative ability, appears for people who do not generally personalize conflict. Chief executive officers who rate themselves as somewhat lower in TCP than their peers also say that they are more competent in communicating (Barch & Dallinger, 1995). This result is similar to the finding that personalizers see themselves as having worse communicator images (Norton, 1978, 1983) than people with low TCP scores (Dallinger & Adolphson, 1997). Nor are these anxieties and failures of confidence confined merely to the possibility of expressing oneself. Dallinger and Adolphson (1997) also report that personalizers have unusually high levels of apprehension about receiving messages (Wheeless, 1975), with correlations ranging from about .25 to .40 for the core TCP dimensions.

The anticipated climate of the conflictive life space, and its relationship with TCP, has been more directly approached in some further investigations. In his elaborate survey of intact work groups and their supervisors at a large utility company, Lewis (1995) found that when subordinates have high direct personalization scores, they rate their workplace climates as unusually pressured and generally more negative. Those who score high on the positive relational effects subscale, however, perceive more cohesion at work and are more optimistic about their chances for personal recognition. Dallinger and Hample (1995, Study 2) indicate that satisfaction with one's supervisor is lowest for personalizers and highest for those who have low scores on the core TCP dimensions. A related finding in that study is that subordinates who feel most persecuted in conflicts see their supervisors as being more forcing, whereas low personalizers are more likely to perceive compromise as characteristic of the manager. Of course, these may not be perceptual biases: The supervisors' conflict styles may be accurately perceived, and might actually cause the TCP scores. Nonetheless, connections among TCP, climate, and expectations about conflict are again apparent.

To this point, I have reviewed evidence connecting high TCP scores with avoidant wishes, high anxiety and low confidence about communicating, and the perception of generally negative and punishing workplace climates. To finish this discussion of climate, I now want to turn to the idea of defensiveness.

Gibb (1961) introduced the idea of defensiveness to the field of communication. His discussion of the contrast between defensive and supportive climates alerted us to the need for speakers to avoid making others defensive or permitting themselves to be made so. However heuristic Gibb's essay has been, it becomes confusing in detail when one tries to work out whether his climatic features—evaluation, neutrality, and the others—are behaviors, attributions, or feelings (see Eadie, 1982; Hample & Dallinger, 1995). In some respects, Gibb's formulation is closely related to that of personalization, and this has been discussed elsewhere (Hample & Dallinger, 1995). Here, however, I prefer to turn to the earlier (and somewhat more clearly understood and operationalized) construct, ego defense.

Sigmund Freud discussed ego defense at several points in his career, sometimes calling it repression and sometimes referring to it as a superset of mechanisms of which repression was one. The classic formulation of ego defense was finally accomplished by Anna Freud (1966/1934), but confusions about typologies and vocabulary remain within the therapeutic community (see Plutchik, Kellerman, & Conte, 1979, pp. 229-232). Without attempting to settle any of those conceptual problems, we may say that ego-defense mechanisms are those behaviors that people use to protect themselves from stress or punishing life events. These tactics vary from the highly adaptive to the severely incompetent (see Vaillant, 1977, 1993). Over the years, a number of efforts have been made to operationalize typologies of ego-defense mechanisms for the benefit of experimental researchers.

Hample, Benson, Gogliotti, and Jeong (1997) used one of these operationalizations (Andrews, Singh, & Bond, 1993) to evaluate the connection between TCP and ego defense. They believe that the anxieties and avoidant impulses associated with TCP raise the possibility that personalization is, or is related to, immature ego defense. In fact, they report that high personalizers use less mature ego-defense mechanisms than do people lower in TCP. In a related report, Woike, Aronoff, Stollak, and Loraas (1994), using a different operationalization for ego-defense mechanisms (Ihilevich & Gleser, 1993), report that people with less mature defense mechanisms are much more expressive of negative emotions than are people who have more mature defenses. In other sections of this chapter, I show that personalizers tend to be more aggressive and negative during conflict interactions. Therefore, the combination of the Hample, Benson, et al. (1997) and Woike et al. (1994) findings predicts that high personalization, low ego-defense maturity, and expression of extremely negative feelings during arguments are thoroughly associated.

The studies reviewed to this point center mainly on affective expectations about conflict and its climate. Personalizers are apprehensive about conflicts, wish to avoid them, have little confidence in their ability to communicate well, and are motivated to use nonadaptive means of self-defense. This last finding begins to bear more on projected actions during conflict than on feelings about it, and therefore serves as a convenient transition to the other main issue about the preconflict life space, the personalizer's cognitive structure for it.

Cognitive Structure

Following Lewin, I use the term *cognitive structure* to refer to a person's perception of a full life space, all the perceived regions and force fields at once. This is essentially the same idea that is usually called a *plan* in the message production literature (e.g., Berger, 1995, 1997; Waldron, 1997). In the research to be reviewed momentarily, however, the usage is restricted to a particular sort of life space. We will be examining the person's general understanding of how to act during a conflict, and will therefore be looking at projected lines of action prior to an actual conflict (generally, see Louis, 1977). Each expected behavior is a region in the life space, itself located mainly in the plane of irreality. The sequence of adjoining regions connects the person to whatever goal(s) he or she perceives, and is therefore what Lewin calls a distinguished path and what others might label a plan.

The key study discussed in this section regards the idea of a distinguished path as equivalent to a Memory Organization Packet (MOP; Schank, 1982). Using a methodology developed by Bower, Black, and Turner (1979), the researchers asked participants to list, in order, the things that they expect will happen in a typical interpersonal conflict (or restaurant episode, or visit to a doctor's office). The resultant list may be regarded as a description of likely lines of action. In a particular conflict, of course, everything on a given list may not occur, and things not on the list may happen. But the MOP represents the cognitive structure of a conflict prior to its eventuation.

Hample, Dean, Johnson, Kopp, and Ngoitz (1997) therefore asked respondents of known TCP to report the specific acts, in order, of typical face-to-face arguments. People high in TCP were more likely to include acts of physical violence in their descriptions and more likely to mention apologies as an immediate preliminary to the end of the conflict, but less likely to describe a period of calm (or anything else) after the conflict's conclusion. In short, conflict is noticeably more agonistic for personalizers and ends more abruptly. We found some other interesting structural differences between the groups as well: High personalizers, for instance, see disagreement as a preliminary to the start of the conflict, whereas low personalizers report that a lack of agreement appears after the perceived beginning of conflict; escalation also appears sooner for the high personalizers. One interpretation of these findings is that personalizers see conflict as the point and defining feature of the interaction, whereas people low on TCP regard arguments as things that are embedded within nonconflictual episodes.

It may be instructive to examine the scripts provided by two of the respondents in the Hample, Dean, et al. (1997) study. Here is the list of 20 actions (in order) projected by respondent 79, who is unusually high on core TCP (I have edited the grammar and spelling lightly for presentation here):

1. Person isn't thinking correctly.
2. Person's ideas are biased or set in stone.
3. Person tries to take control.
4. Person tries to manipulate other to think the way he or she does.
5. Person forces idea on other.
6. Other person gets mad.
7. Other person takes it personally.
8. Other person tries to stay calm.
9. Other person says they are irrational.
10. Other person changes subject to another.
11. Person gets mad.
12. Both people start to yell.
13. They keep yelling.
14. There is silence.
15. They may not talk for a while.
16. Both people express their ideas.
17. Both people are open to new ideas.
18. Both people can come to a mature agreement.
19. Relationship is settled.
20. Both people are content.

Notice that respondent 79 clearly anticipated an aggressive interaction. Control, manipulation, and force (scripts 3-5) lead immediately to anger and personalization (6-7). Only after another sequence of negative affect and aggressive behaviors (11-14) is the conflict settled. Interestingly, the settlement sequence (16-20) looks almost like a textbook recommendation. However, it is not the initial orientation to conflict for this respondent, for it is expected to occur after a great deal of opposition, attack, and venting. If a conflict were to begin at script 16, as is certainly possible, one supposes that respondent 79 would be very pleasantly surprised.

A contrasting case is respondent 9, whose core TCP scores were unusually low. Here are this person's scripts:

1. Person A makes a comment, remark, or idea to Person B.
2. Person B responds to what Person A said.
3. Person B gives positive feedback (if any).
4. Person B gives negative feedback (if any).

5. Person A responds to the negative response.
6. Person A backs up what they said.
7. Person B says why they are correct in what they said.
8. Person A tries to persuade them as to why they are right.
9. Person B either agrees or disagrees.
10. Persons A and B either agree on it or never do.

Here the projection of regions typical or possible in interpersonal conflict is much less emotionally charged. There may be some negative feedback (scripts 3-4), and the conflict may end in disagreement (9-10), but we see none of the yelling or loss of control that were expected by respondent 79. Respondent 9 obviously does not expect to experience or observe any strong emotional displays in a typical interpersonal argument. Respondent 9 appears to anticipate much more mature and adaptive actions than does respondent 79.

Throughout the study, most respondents, even the nonpersonalizers, were certainly not innocent of conflict's destructive potential, and this is common among many people (see P. J. Benoit & W. L. Benoit, 1990; W. L. Benoit & P. J. Benoit, 1987; Benoit & Hample, 1997). However, the respondents high in TCP were those who featured aggression more prominently and were also those more likely to insist on one or more slots for physical attacks. Although these details are interesting, the conclusion I want to draw here is more general: that trait TCP predicts differing cognitive and affective expectations about the nature of interpersonal conflict.

Conclusions About the Preconflict Life Space

A picture of the anticipated life space for conflicts is beginning to emerge from this narrative review. Figure 5.1 illustrates some of the salient features of the life spaces for high and low personalizers. Both persons (P), I assume, will perceive a goal (G) of some sort (e.g., coming to a resolution of some felt difficulty), and both will see that they cannot enter the goal space without first encountering the region of conflict (C), which comprises the distinguished path. Details of this path are not shown, but the individual's MOPs, such as those just discussed, might be filled in here, each script being a separate region within C.

In spite of these gross similarities, however, some significant differences appear. The high personalizer places a premium on self-defense, signified by the inward-pointing force vectors around P, whereas the low personalizer does not. The attractive valence of the conflict region is also different for the two people: Conflict is attractive for the person low in TCP (bottom figure) but repulsive for the high personalizer. Thus the C region is an obstacle (see Hample, 1997) for high personalizers but not for those more comfortable with arguments. These factors, combined with the anxieties and negative expectations of the person scoring high in core TCP, result in a climate that discour-

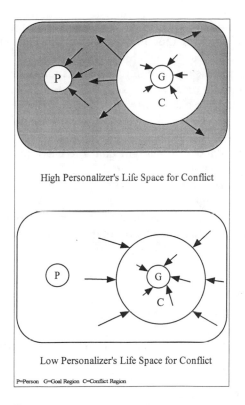

High Personalizer's Life Space for Conflict

Low Personalizer's Life Space for Conflict

P=Person G=Goal Region C=Conflict Region

Figure 5.1. The Preconflict Life Spaces for Personalizers and Nonpersonalizers

ages any movement toward the goal; this impeding climate is represented by the shading in the top figure.

Notice, however, that these are the *anticipated* life spaces, not necessarily those experienced once a conflict begins. As the discussion in the next section indicates, these anticipations do not straightforwardly predict what actually happens in a conflict. The person has not yet, after all, interacted with the environment.

THE CONFLICT LIFE SPACE

The TCP research program is silent regarding why high personalizers would actually engage in conflict. Certainly they want to avoid it. Perhaps situational demands (i.e., the strength of G in Figure 5.1) are irresistible, and/or the repulsive force of C is relatively minor. Perhaps someone else initiates the argument, and escape appears to be impossible or too costly. Or, given our usual research methodology, perhaps the individual is enticed to participate by a friend who recruits him or her for class credit. For whatever reason, a person who wishes to avoid arguments may nonetheless find him- or herself in the middle of one. The analysis in the previous section shows that, given any reasonable choice, high personalizers will escape conflict. But what if they cannot leave the field? The results of the trait TCP research seem to suggest that personalizers might prefer passive or avoidant means of participation; for instance, they might concede early just to be done. That, however, is not at all what we have found.

Based on the existing research, the key phenomena connected with TCP during conflicts are aggression and reciprocity. After treating these separately, I will offer some thoughts about the reasons personalizers are aggressive and conclude by sketching out hypothetical planes of reality and irreality for personalizers.

Aggression

Several investigations have shown that once high personalizers are actually engaged in conflict, they are not passive at all. In Hample and Dallinger (1993) we made the first report of this finding; we were surprised to discover that when people of varying trait TCP actually engaged in interpersonal arguments, the personalizers were more aggressive than the nonpersonalizers. However, using roughly the same methods to code interaction (but with a larger sample), Hample, Dallinger, and Nelson (1994) failed to replicate this finding with much strength. We did discover that people having high scores on positive relational effects are somewhat less likely ($r = -.19$) to be aggressive, but the significant correlations between aggressive codes and core TCP were scattered and negligible. What we did find—and this is quite important here—is that own aggressiveness is very strongly associated with other's aggressiveness. Of the 15 possible correlations between own and other's five aggressive behaviors, 12 were significant and positive, ranging from .26 to .63. This sort of strong pattern did not appear for the other sorts of arguing behaviors coded in the study (i.e., the nonaggressive ones), so the effect seems to be one of reciprocal aggression, not simple reciprocity of all kinds. In other words, the Hample et al. (1994) results suggest that once the conflict begins, behavior responds to real behavior rather than to expectations, regardless of the individual's level of trait TCP. The preconflict life space dissipates and is replaced with the life space containing the actual encounter, on the plane of reality.

The third study in this sequence, conducted by Hample et al. (1995), also failed to find very much connection between trait TCP and the aggressiveness of one's own behaviors and further replicates the Hample et al. (1994) study by reporting that one's own behavioral aggressiveness is predicted by partner's. However, the Hample et al. (1995) study also included one important innovation, a state version of TCP. Immediately after the conflictive conversation, people reported their TCP levels during the conflict. Although technically not a pure measure of state TCP—it is, after all, slightly retrospective—this instrument should give a close assessment of how people feel during the conflict. The state measures do predict arguing behaviors and aggression in particular. The canonical correlation, which predicted arguing behaviors from own state and trait TCP, is significant (R_C = .55), but only because of the high loadings of the state measures. Core TCP (state), in particular, loaded at −.66 on its canonical variate, and was therefore strongly associated with aggression, which loaded at −.96 on the criterion variate. Nonetheless, this effect is still weaker than the association between own and other's arguing behaviors (R_C = .79), with the aggression measures dominating the analysis. In sum, this investigation supports the weak but positive influence of trait TCP on aggression, confirms that other's arguing behaviors are critical in influencing one's own, and suggests that state TCP is predictive of own aggression. Core TCP predicts aggressiveness rather than avoidance or passivity.

Reciprocity

Although the research just reviewed offers some evidence for a link between aggression and personalizing conflicts, the results also indicate a stronger effect for reciprocity of aggressive action. Lewin and his associates found that frustration leads to either aggression or withdrawal (Barker et al., 1941), and it is not hard to connect this result to ours. An attacking move by one's partner in an argumentative discussion creates an obstacle to achievement of one's goals. Given that the experimental situation is a fairly strong barrier to disengagement, aggression is the main available response to the frustration.

Though our research indirectly suggests that high personalizers might be more prone to feeling frustration, the reality is that anyone, regardless of TCP predisposition, might feel impeded by an opponent's attack, and this is why the reciprocity effect is stronger than the TCP result. The phenomenon of symmetrical aggressive exchanges has long been of interest to students of interpersonal communication (Watzlawick, Beavin, & Jackson, 1967, chap. 2), and research focusing on conflict behaviors has also addressed this possibility. Sillars (1980), for instance, reports that avoidant, distributive (i.e., aggressive), and integrative moves in a conflict all tend to call out the same sort of behavior in one's partner. Donohue and Roberto (1993) show that affiliative and antagonistic actions during hostage negotiations tend to be returned in kind. Putnam and Jones (1982) show that impasse dyads, in particular, are very likely to have reciprocal attacking or defending sequences. Putnam and

Poole's (1987, p. 559) substantial literature review offers the conclusion that perceptions, attributions, and behaviors all tend to be reciprocal during conflicts.

"Reciprocity," however, is mainly a summary of empirical observations of behavior, not an explanation of them. The mechanisms by which reciprocity appears are worth examination, and that is no doubt the reason for Putnam and Poole's attention to perceptions and attributions as well as actions. Postulating the other's aggressive behavior—perhaps a confrontation (Bleiberg & Churchill, 1975) or a face-threatening action (Brown & Levinson, 1987)—the person must respond in some way.

The initial response may be affective. Kinney and Segrin (in press) explored some of the emotional consequences of verbal aggression. They found little main effect of other's aggression on recipient's self-esteem, but they did find some interesting interactions. People highly sensitive to negative feedback, and those having some personal guilt about the topic of the attack, had more negative affect, lower self-esteem, and more depression after being attacked. Baron (1989) reports that recipients of destructive criticism have more anger and tension than do those who receive constructive messages. Moffitt, Spence, and Goldney (1986) add that wives are more sensitive to the possibility of rejection than are their husbands. This general idea of sensitivity to negatively toned actions by other has been further explored by Downey and Feldman (1996). They report that people expecting social rejection see it even when it may not be present and are less satisfied with their romantic relationships. Bolger and Zuckerman (1995) rated respondents as to their neuroticism ("Are you a worrier? In general, are your feelings easily hurt?") and asked them to report their conflict experiences daily for 2 weeks. The high neurotics reported having had more conflicts and reacted to them in more stressful ways; analyses show that their greater overall negative affect was due more to their greater reactivity than to their greater exposure. In the previous section, we noticed that people high in TCP are more likely to anticipate aggression in conflicts, so it seems reasonable to suppose that personalizers are probably aggression sensitive, and therefore more prone to suffer the painful results noted by Kinney and Segrin, Baron, Downey and Feldman, and Bolger and Zuckerman.

A number of studies indicate that people faced with barriers to their goals become more aggressive themselves; the relevance of this work here is that other's aggression impedes self's goal achievement in a conflict. Several authors have reported that compliance-gaining efforts become more negative and forceful when the compliance target is stubbornly uncooperative (Bisanz & Rule, 1990; deTurck, 1985; Hample & Dallinger, 1994; Kim, Shin, & Cai, 1998). Mikolic, Parker, and Pruitt (1997) exposed people to repeated annoyances by having confederates withhold supplies necessary to the completion of a joint task. Coding the interactions between participants and confederates,

Mikolic et al. discovered an escalation sequence that satisfies the requirements of a Guttman scale. People proceeded through requests, demands, complaints, angry statements, threats, harassment, and finally abuse as their interactions continued. This study is more on point than those from the compliance-gaining literature because it pretty clearly stimulated genuine interpersonal conflicts. The results of all this work, however, present the same pattern we might anticipate from Barker et al.'s (1941) experiment: Frustration leads to aggression. This is a general phenomenon, not controlled by personalization. However, TCP may well moderate the likelihood of aggression; because personalizers seem to be somewhat more sensitive to hurtful actions in the first place, this might explain the associations we have found between personalization and aggression.

This will not always be the case, however, in a given life space. Cloven and Roloff (1993) designed a study that took into account the individual's impression of partner's capacity for generating discomfort in a romantic relationship and the degree to which the individual feared open conflict with the partner. They found that complaints (i.e., reciprocal aggression) about other's negative behavior were less likely when the other's negative behaviors were seen as more common. This "chilling effect" was more marked for people who were most fearful of having explicit arguments with partner. This study supports Barker et al.'s (1941) finding that frustration can lead to either aggression or withdrawal. The Cloven and Roloff study begins to show what life space elements—perhaps we could summarize them as "the stakes of open conflict"—moderate frustration's effects, and therefore the likelihood that aggression will be reciprocal.

Speculations on the Connection
Between TCP and Aggression

My colleagues and I have given thought to two different explanations for all this. The first account we call "the game face." This suggestion is that personalizers believe that conflicts are inherently antagonistic, and this is why they see arguments as targeting personalities on both sides. In preparing for a conflict, therefore, these people put on a confrontive, hostile game face in much the same way an athlete might. This would produce the aggressiveness we have observed in several studies. The second possibility we call "the cornered rabbit." Personalizers want to be passive and gentle, but they continually find themselves assaulted during conflicts, backed into a small space they cannot escape, and so they desperately respond in kind. This, too, would lead to aggressive messages. Unfortunately, we have no data that directly distinguish these two possible explanations. Even the Hample, Dean, et al. (1997) investigation that explored the cognitive expectations for conflict sequence does not point in one direction in preference to the other.

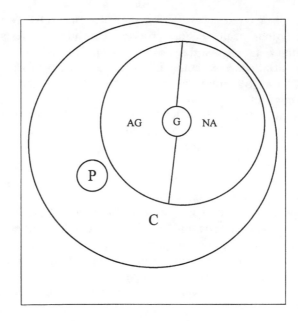

Figure 5.2. Plane of Irreality for Personalizers Engaged in Conflict
NOTE: P = person; G = goal region; C = conflict region; AG = region of aggression; NA = region of nonaggression.

Conclusions About the Conflict Life Space

Still, we can make some pertinent observations about the life space of a personalizer engaged in a conflict. In fact, two life spaces seem to be pertinent: one describing the plane of irreality and the other the plane of reality. The expectations sketched in Figure 5.1 are radically out of place here because the central fact is that P has, for whatever reason, entered the C region, leaving the originally anticipated impeding climate behind. Figure 5.2, illustrating the plane of irreality, indicates what personalizers appear to perceive about the actual conflict life space and shows the two main paths they may take while engaged.

Figure 5.2 proposes that the high personalizer, once engaged in conflict (i.e., occupying the C region), imagines that he or she has two available routes to G: an aggressive one (AG) and another that is not aggressive (NA). Notice that the climate shading of Figure 5.1 is absent. The personalizer's preconflict expectations are now only history, and behavior is controlled by the life space in the instant (Lewin, 1952). This life space, too, has a climate, of course, but the lack of shading in Figure 5.2's C region is intended to suggest that P is either neutral or uncertain about what course the conflict will take.

In Figure 5.3, the plane of reality, the die has been cast. P's partner in the conflict has acted aggressively (in the view of P, who is oversensitive to this

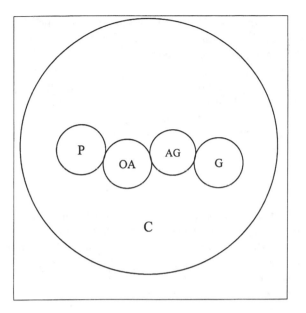

Figure 5.3. Plane of Reality for High Personalizers Faced With Aggression
NOTE: P = person; OA = region of other's aggression; AG = region of aggression; G = goal region; C = conflict region.

possibility), and for P, this may well be decisive in determining a course of locomotion (but recall Cloven & Roloff, 1993). P finds him- or herself, probably unwillingly, drawn into a region of the life space in which the other's aggressiveness (OA) is felt. In fact, it may well be more accurate to say that P believes OA has entered P's region, rather than the other way around. This OA region has negative valence (valence arrows have been omitted from Figures 5.2 and 5.3 to simplify the sketches), but it still serves to instantiate a region of aggressive behaviors (AG) for P to occupy. The AG region has positive valence, partly due to its immediate proximity to the positive G region (Lewin, 1935, chap. 3) and perhaps also partly due to the satisfaction that P might feel in meeting aggression with aggression. In P's view, it is the OA region that gives birth to the AG region and points out the distinguished path of locomotion to G. Thus do personalizers participate in aggressive conflicts.

THE POSTCONFLICT LIFE SPACE

We have conducted relatively little research examining how people differing in TCP feel about conflicts once they are completed. In part, this is because we consider that a person's trait TCP is a sort of affective summary of the person's cumulative feelings about having experienced conflicts during his or her lifetime. In fact, the whole section of this chapter dealing with the preconflict life space might be considered to be a description of how people think and feel about their conflict histories. Still, some approximation of what postconflict life spaces might look like would be interesting. Two studies seem to be on point. Both involved postconflict interviews or instruments. After reviewing them and noting their implications for the life space immediately after a conflict, I will move on to a substantial examination of more long-term postconflict issues.

TCP and the Immediate Aftermath of Conflict

Two TCP studies collected data immediately after participants had engaged in face-to-face conflict. We find evidence that people see themselves as reflecting the conflict partner's affective states (as well as their aggression), and that people's own personalization levels are closely associated with their aggressive reactions to the conflict.

The Hample et al. (1995) investigation has already been mentioned. In addition to the state TCP measures for self, we also asked participants to estimate their partners' state TCP; that is, they estimated the degree to which they thought their partners took the conflict personally, felt stress, and so forth. Although that report does not itself indicate the associations between own and perceived other's state TCP, further examination of the data set yields the following results for the postconflict state measures. Own core TCP is associated with the estimate of other's core TCP ($r = .39$, $p = .01$, two-tailed), and a similar result occurs for negative relational effects ($r = .38$, $p = .01$, two-tailed). The correlations for own and perceived other's positive relational effects and valence scores, however, are not significant (respectively, $r = .21$ and $r = .15$; N is 42 for all these analyses, reflecting the number of dyads in the study). Another set of results of interest here bears on the connections one sees among the other's states. The only significant correlations are between the estimate of other's state core TCP and his or her negative relational effects score ($r = .83$, $p = .000$, two-tailed), other's state core TCP and his or her perceived like/dislike valence ($r = -.42$, $p = .006$, two-tailed), and other's negative relational effects score and his or her valence ($r = -.40$, $p = .009$, two-tailed). These last three correlations parallel, but exceed, the results when the associations among one's own state measures are examined (respectively, $r = .48$, $p = .001$, two-tailed; $r = -.20$, ns; and $r = -.34$, $p = .03$, two-tailed).

These results suggest certain tentative conclusions. People tend to see their conflict partners as having roughly the same core TCP as themselves, and they also perceive coordination in regard to negative relational expectations. These results are consistent with Stamp, Vangelisti, and Daly's (1992) finding that self-reported defensiveness correlates at $r = .60$ with partner's self-reported defensiveness, as well as with some of the data on behavioral reciprocity reviewed in the preceding section. Our results, however, indicate that people do not feel that they and their partners see eye to eye on potential positive outcomes; nor do they particularly sense that they and their partners have the same overall valence for the conflict. When looking at the other participant, people see remarkable overlap between core TCP and expectation of negative relational prospects, and to a lesser degree between the other's state core TCP and his or her overall dislike of the argument. Further, other's dislike for the argument is clearly seen as related to his or her pessimism about relational outcomes. Finally, these overlaps are much more pronounced when the person is looking at other than when looking at self: the other person's TCP manifold is regarded as more homogeneous and less differentiated than one's own.

The other study that examined postconflict feelings is Hample (1996). In that investigation, both partners to a conflict were interviewed separately and immediately afterward, being prompted by exposure to the videotape of the argument, which was divided into 30-second intervals. The interviews were transcribed and coded for mention or evidence of a number of things, including the standard TCP variables. Notice that in contrast to the Hample et al. (1995) study, where state TCP was assessed with a self-report questionnaire, Hample (1996) provides observational measures of state TCP. Still, however, the "state" measure is chronologically postconflict.

Here the data permit us only to see connections between own state TCP and various other of the same person's affective or cognitive elements involved in arguing with another person. One interesting set of results connects people's state TCP with the aggressiveness of their talk during the interviews. Direct personalization, stress reactions, persecution feelings, and like/dislike valence are all positively related to aggressiveness, with correlations ranging from .46 to .70. A notable null finding is that interview TCP is completely uncorrelated with attention to the key instrumental goal for the conflict (considered to be persuasion, winning the argument, coming to a mutual judgment, and so forth). Mentions of obstacles (defined, of course, as negatively valenced regions) are generally connected to the state TCP measures. More obstacles are mentioned by people high in state stress reactions, negative relational effects, and like/dislike valence, and fewer are mentioned by those with low ratings for positive relational effects. The obstacles measure is also predicted by state differentiation for self and other, where differentiation is operationalized as the number of constructs used in talking about a person during the interview (Burleson & Waltman, 1988). The more differentiated a person is during the conflict, the more obstacles he or she perceives. A related finding is that higher state differentiation is associated with more reports of having suppressed or altered some thought prior to utterance (Hample & Dallinger, 1987; Meyer, 1997).

This barrage of results points to several tentative conclusions. State TCP seems to have little differential effect on pursuit of the main goal of the

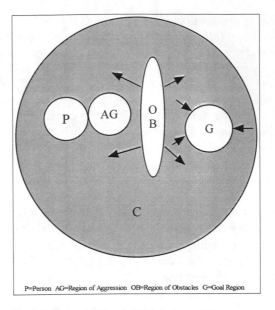

Figure 5.4. Postconflict Life Space for People High in State TCP
NOTE: P = person; AG = region of aggression; OB = region of obstacles; G = goal region; C = conflict region.

interaction, but it does predict awareness of obstacles to that goal and the aggressiveness with which the goal is pursued. The more differentiated a person is—that is, the more details he or she perceives about self and other—the more obstacles he or she notices and the more editing takes place.

Immediately after the conclusion of a conflict, then, we can observe the continuing relevance of personalization to the emotional experience of face-to-face argument. Personalization predicts perception of the other, sensitivity to obstacles, and retrospective aggressive feelings, among other factors. We find some evidence here for the supposition that personalization is part of a complex of potentially self-reinforcing feelings, perceptions, and attributions. The preconflict life space is, after all, a reflection of the individual's conflictual history as well as a continuation of it.

Life Spaces for the Immediate Aftermath of Conflict

In sketching out the postconflict life spaces, it is the second study that offers more guidance in showing the connections among P and the various regions displayed in the earlier figures. The Hample et al. (1995) results mainly indicate perceived overlaps between own and other's feelings. To the degree that a person is focused on the other, these results might be portrayed as a series of intersecting emotional regions, tying own and other's feelings

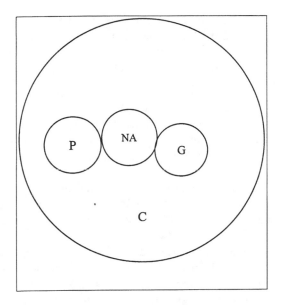

Figure 5.5. Postconflict Life Space for People Low in State TCP
NOTE: P = person; NA = region of nonaggression; G = goal region; C = conflict region.

together. This is not a negligible matter, because conflicts are more likely to be managed productively if the two sides frame the substantive matter in similar ways (e.g., Drake & Donohue, 1996), although two personalizers might still have considerable difficulty even if they have comparable frames (especially if our "game face" speculations are close to being accurate).

However, Figures 5.4 and 5.5 are intended to summarize the results of the Hample (1996) investigation. Figure 5.4 is an effort to show what the life space after a conflict is perceived to be by a typical high personalizer. P spontaneously has aggressive impulses and retrospections and moves into the AG region naturally. However, P is acutely aware of a variety of obstacles (OB) that he or she must endure or avoid while locomoting toward G; the more differentiated P is, the more obstacles he or she perceives and the more editorial effort he or she makes to maneuver around them. For a high personalizing P, the climate of the whole C region is uncomfortable.

Figure 5.5, in contrast, suggests that the postconflict life space for a typical low personalizer is qualitatively different. The hurtful climate is lessened or absent; in fact, the climate of C might even be enjoyable. P is less aggressive in moving toward G.

Looking at Figures 5.4 and 5.5 together, the most striking impression is that the aftermath of a conflict is more detailed and stressful for the high personalizer. This may be expectable, given that negative conflict experiences tend to stand out in an individual's memory (Cloven & Roloff, 1991; Laursen & Koplas, 1995). This structural phenomenon may be both cause and effect of high TCP.

Long-Term Effects of Conflict

Although this chapter is organized chronologically and we appear to be at the end of the sequence, we are really back at the beginning in this substantial subsection. TCP and the related constructs we have been examining grow out of a lifetime's experience. TCP does, after all, have the features of a personality trait, and this involves enduring predispositions. I want to try to explore the place of personalization in individual and relational experience. So in this part of the chapter, my focus is not so much on the immediate aftermath of a particular argument as it is on the consequences of a lifetime of hurtful conflict.

I want to look at several matters, but I must issue one caveat before starting. Most of the literature cited here, in contrast to that cited in the other sections, is focused not on personalization but on a number of related processes. I will periodically indicate my understanding of those variables' connections to taking conflict personally, but the reader should understand that we are moving toward matters that have, for the most part, not been studied in conjunction with the TCP instrument.

The issues that seem of particular importance are these: the persistent connection of negative affect to an individual's interpersonal arguments, the effects of unfavorable conflict experience on marriages and other close relationships, the possibility that violence will emerge from conflicts that are badly managed emotionally, the potential for personalizing cycles, and the considerations that must shape intervention into the problems consequent to personalization. I analyze each issue in turn below.

Persistent Negative Affect

Negative feelings about conflict have deleterious immediate consequences for an individual's ability to manage conflicts productively and reduce his or her ability to learn adaptive arguing behaviors for the future.

TCP reflects a number of negative emotional reactions to the prospect or experience of conflict. My colleagues and I have documented that it is related to anxieties about communicating, stress, punishing workplace climates, and several other feelings. Although we have no evidence to suggest that TCP is anything like the core of the manifold negative affects people may experience about conflicts, it does seem to be part of that collocation. For instance, Hample, Memba, and Seo (1999) have explored the connections among personalization, alexithymia (the inability or unwillingness to express emotions; Johnston, Stinski, & Meyers, 1993), and emotional expressiveness (Balwsick, 1988). The valence subscale of TCP is associated with alexithymia

($r = -.16$), indicating a modest tendency for those who dislike conflicts to swallow their feelings. People who report that they generally like conflict are unusually likely to express hate ($r = .33$) but less likely to show love ($r = -.16$). So those who have negative valence for arguments are reluctant to display their feelings, or at least their negative ones. This pattern of results seems to justify an examination of what other researchers have discovered about negative affect in conflict.

Perhaps the way to begin is by noting that negative experiences in conflict have a tendency to make the conflict seem more important. Laursen and Koplas (1995) interviewed 10th- and 11th-grade students about their daily conflict experiences. The conflicts identified by respondents as "most important" were more likely (than the respondents' other conflict experiences) to be ended by submission or disengagement and less likely to end with negotiation; they were the most emotionally negative of the adolescents' conflicts, both during and after the conflicts; and little constructive learning appeared to be taking place as a result of the arguments. Laursen and Koplas conclude that negative affect is critical in the marking of conflicts as salient. Cloven and Roloff's (1991) results suggest that this is a self-sustaining system: People spend more time thinking about major (than minor) problems, and the more they think about the issue, the worse they feel. So important conflicts are salient, negative, and thought inducing, and each feature reinforces the other two.

The experience and expression of negative feelings appear to have some serious consequences beyond merely making the conflict experientially important. As noted earlier, Kinney and Segrin (in press) have shown that people react very negatively to verbal aggression when they feel guilty about its topic, and Retzinger (1991) shows that shame is implicated in dyadic conflicts that escalate to anger and marital separation. Tangney, Wagner, Fletcher, and Gramzow (1992) make a persuasive case that shame is a more powerful and maladaptive feeling than guilt, having stronger connections to anger, the tendency to blame others, and indirect expressions of hostility. Baron (1989) indicates that people who have received destructive feedback are noticeably more likely to become stubborn or avoidant than are those who have received constructive messages; this, of course, is reminiscent of Barker et al.'s (1941) report that frustration leads to either aggression or withdrawal, both of which are unproductive responses to conflict. Baron also shows that negative feedback calls out anger and tension in its recipients, and these are states that are not only similar to those involved in extreme personalization, but probably also implicated in Baron's respondents' preference for avoidance and nonaccommodation in the future. These results indicate that negatively experienced conflicts lay the foundation for more of the same in the future. The reciprocity effects discussed in previous sections of this chapter are therefore experienced not only momentarily, in the immediate exchange of behaviors, but also in the long term.

Dunn and Brown (1994) visited 3- and 4-year-old children in their homes three times and noted the expression of positive and negative affect at home. The more negative affect was expressed in the home, the poorer the children did on an emotional understanding task. The more negative affect the children displayed, the less other oriented they were in their own conflicts. Exposure to badly managed arguments in early childhood appears to damage children's capacity for handling the emotional elements of conflict. Four-year-old children use markedly less reasoned argumentation when they are upset and are less conciliatory (Tesla & Dunn, 1992), suggesting that the inability to manage conflict productively is both an immediate and a long-term consequence of a negative home environment.

Expression of negative feelings also results in the individual's being seen as less competent and attractive. Watson and Remer (1984) found that when women baldly expressed their negative feelings in a confrontation without also specifying the offending behavior and its consequences, they were rated as less effective, less flexible, less empathic, angrier, and more defensive. Remer (1984) has confirmed most of these results for males as well, although the outcomes for anger and defensiveness were not as pronounced.

One obvious consequence of negative affect is that it shields the person from the benefits of pleasanter emotional states. Berry and Hansen (1996, Study 1) classed people as typically having positive or negative affect on a self-report trait measure, then videotaped them having 6-minute conversations with one another. People with positive affect generally rated themselves as having had higher-quality interactions (enjoyable, natural, pleasant), and this result is supported by observers' ratings of their conversations. In Berry and Hansen's Study 2, participants kept an interaction diary for a week. Positive affect was directly associated with both the frequency of interaction and the enjoyment people felt in their interactions.

We have noticed that personalization is connected to anxiety, and here, too, we find pessimistic results for conflict participants who have negative affect. Baron (1989) reports that the receipt of destructive criticism reduces an individual's self-confidence in the task at hand. In a more relational context, Benton and Allen (1996) identified women who had unusually high levels of anxiety sensitivity, exposed them to either relaxation or hyperventilation instructions, and had their boyfriends act in either an approving or a disapproving manner during an interpersonal conflict. These authors report significant three-way interactions, such that the combination of high anxiety, hyperventilation instructions, and a disapproving boyfriend resulted in unusually negative ratings of self, boyfriend, and their relationship. That this sort of outcome may be common for high-anxiety women is suggested by the preexperimental finding that they already had lower ratings for self, boyfriend, and relationship than did low-anxiety women.

Personalization is a collection of negative feelings. These make conflicts salient but obscure any potentially constructive lessons from them. Negative affect encourages escalation and reduces the individual's ability to orient to the other person. It displays a personal image of inflexibility and self-centeredness. None of these effects, to say the least, encourages any belief that the conflicts to follow later in life will be experienced or handled in a better fashion.

Marriages and Other Close Relationships

As the previous material indicates, the mere possession of negative affect, expressed or not, has serious effects. Some of these bear on a person's most important interpersonal relationships. We know, for example, that personalizers reports less relational satisfaction and less solidarity with relational partners than do nonpersonalizers (Dallinger & Callister, 1997). Furthermore, research marks negative affect as especially important in marriages. Carstensen, Gottman, and Levenson (1995) studied long-term marriages and found that negative affect during conflict declines as the marriages age, and that unhappy marriages have greater exchange of negative emotions than happy ones.

Conflict—or, more particularly, the way an individual orients to it emotionally and behaviorally—has considerable relevance to relational satisfaction and marital happiness (see Roloff, 1987, pp. 491-496, for a review). Gottman (1993b) reports that a predominance of positive over negative behaviors in marital interaction reliably predicts whether the couple is distressed: A negative (or mere lack of positive) predominance predicts that the couple will divorce or consider divorce. The most important negative behaviors include the husband's defensiveness and withdrawal and the wife's criticism and defensiveness. "Flooding," the perception that partner's expression of negative affect was unexpected, intense, and overwhelming, is another variable highly implicated in the eventual dissolution of the marriage. I speculate that flooding might be more common when a nonpersonalizer is suddenly confronted with a personalizer's reaction to an argument. An earlier study indicates that nonverbal affect displays also discriminate between happy and unhappy couples (Gottman, Markman, & Notarius, 1977).

Other studies on hostility and defensiveness confirm the deleterious consequences of negative feelings and behaviors. Koren, Carlton, and Shaw (1980) indicate that distressed couples can be distinguished from nondistressed ones by two factors: The distressed couples make more use of criticism in influence efforts, and the nondistressed couples are more responsive to one another during interactions. These findings are generally supported by Gottman (1993a), who studied 73 married couples for 4 years, coding their conflict interactions. Unstable couples (those for whom divorce was a substantial issue) showed more hostility and anger in their interactions and were more detached in their listening styles. Billings (1979) also reports that distressed couples are more negative than happy couples, but adds the important additional finding that distressed couples also have greater tendencies to reciprocate hostile acts. This latter finding also appears in Walsh, Baucom,

Tyler, and Sayers (1993). Perhaps it is not surprising that unhappy couples have a lower ratio of agreements to disagreements during problem-solving discussions (Gottman et al., 1977), are more aggressive during conflicts, and manage conflict less productively (Yelsma, 1981). The problems that distressed couples have during conflict are exaggerated by the finding that the partners' attributions of one another's intentions are more negative than the actual intentions (Gottman, Notarius, Markman, Bank, & Rubin, 1976).

Worse, negative affect seems to reinforce itself, as is apparent when we examine people's attributions about the causes of conflicts. Collins (1996) asked respondents to give the reasons for the relational partner's having done a negative thing (e.g., declining to cuddle). People high in relational anxiety (i.e., concerned about rejection) were most likely to give negative interpretations and attributions—he or she doesn't love me, isn't dependable, isn't really close to me, and so on. In other words, people who worry about the relationship being in jeopardy perceive that it is in jeopardy in an attributionally ambiguous situation. These relationally anxious respondents also had the most negative emotional reactions to the simulated episodes and were by far the most likely to expect that partner's behavior would start a conflict. As with personalizers, Collins's respondents were highly anxious and negatively predisposed about partner's motives and ended up perceiving just what they were set to see. Moffitt et al. (1986) report that wives are more sensitive to rejection than are husbands.

These negative feelings, which Collins's research suggests are self-fulfilling, are damaging to the most important of our relationships. In the face of negative affect about conflict, relational satisfaction drops, marriages begin to dissolve, interactions become unpleasant, and intimacy erodes. Even relational violence becomes possible, as the following material suggests.

Violence

Negative emotions, including personalization, are indicative, and perhaps causative, of physically aggressive relationships and interactions. As the MOPs study (Hample, Dean, et al., 1997) shows, personalizers are especially likely to believe that the normal progression of an interpersonal conflict includes the possibility of violence. Infante and Rancer (1996, pp. 335-337) summarize research showing a negative association between argumentativeness and relational quality and add that high levels of verbal aggression may be implicated in the pattern of causes for family violence, abused women, corporal punishment of children, and date rape. Given the close associations among argumentativeness, aggression, and personalization, we might expect to find more personalization in violent relationships.

Betancourt and Blair (1992) show that observers' attributions that one person intentionally caused controllable damage to another person's car are highly associated with expected feelings of anger and the likelihood of a violent reaction by the injured party. This connects with Hample and Dallinger's

(1995) finding that personalizers are more likely to rate conflict situations as uncongenial largely because of negative attributions about other's motives. Here, again, is a connection between TCP and negative affect, particularly anger. Expression of anger predicts the appearance of verbal abuse (Yelsma, 1995; generally, see Canary, Spitzberg, & Semic, 1998).

O'Brien, Balto, Erber, and Gee (1995) offer suggestions about the role of violence in an individual's family of origin in shaping that person's perception of conflict as well as his or her reactions to it. They studied college students who self-reported that they did or did not come from homes having physically aggressive parents. Parents' use of physical violence was associated with their higher levels of verbal abuse as well. Students listened to audiotapes of marital conflicts and discussed them at each 30-second interval. Students from physically aggressive homes had fewer constructive comments to offer, had more physiological arousal when listening to the more intense tapes, and experienced more negative feelings about all the tapes. These findings seem to parallel those of Dunn and Brown (1994). The worse a person's experience of conflict, the less he or she seems to learn about managing it constructively.

What these students might have learned about conflict while children is suggested by Kerig (1996), who reports substantial correlations ranging from .38 to .63 among verbal aggression, physical aggression, and child involvement in parents' arguments, based on the parents' self-reports. Worse, all three measures are also associated with frequency and severity of interparent conflict, with correlations ranging from .36 to .58. The children's own reports about parental conflict are closely associated with the parents' perceptions. People in early adulthood show some of these same patterns. Gryl, Stith, and Bird (1991) report that college students in violent relationships, compared with students in nonviolent relationships, have more conflicts and use confrontational and avoidance conflict tactics more often.

Family of origin, and particularly the mother's conflict management ability, also has some predictive involvement in the probability that children will become criminals. Klein, Forehand, Armistead, and Long (1997) show that the likelihood that young adults will commit crimes is predicted by their mothers' problem-solving skills, such that more crimes are committed by the children of mothers who cannot deal deftly with crises. Crisis is known to stimulate stress, a component of TCP, and to make productive conflict management less likely. Holmes and Fletcher-Bergland (1995) point out that organizational crises make preplanning less likely, have a strong tendency to escalate, and may involve greater use of coercive tactics, especially when both parties are equally stressed. Negative affect also endangers negotiations by permitting the possibility of emotional contagion, which can result in conflict escalation (Kumar, 1997). The more disagreement appears within a dyad, the more intense observers rate the conflict as being (Waln, 1982). This suggests that crisis, disagreement, and intensity may form a self-reinforcing cycle. Unexpected crisis, then, may be the most challenging sort of conflict, and mothers' failure to deal with it productively predicts later antisocial behavior in their children.

In sum, physical aggression in conflict seems to be a generator of negative orientations, a barrier to learning how to argue constructively, and a part of a self-replicating system of verbal abuse and violence. Let us turn, then, to an issue periodically mentioned throughout this subsection on the long-term effects of personalized arguments: the possibly cyclical nature of punishing feelings about conflict.

Cycles

The TCP research program has not yet begun serious study of the etiology of personalization. However, the studies reviewed in this subsection seem to suggest that personalization begins in the family of origin and naturally reinforces itself. Parents who lack good conflict resolution skills in the home seem to produce troubled children. These children carry burdens of negative affect and overreaction to conflict throughout their lives, and perhaps into their own marriages.

The issue would seem to be a fairly specific one, focused on the presence of personalization and other psychological traits. More general approaches dealing instead with convenient demographic variables do not appear to hold much promise. Dallinger and Hample's (1993) secondary analysis of the data from several studies shows only the most modest differences between males and females on TCP subscales. Wilson, Cai, Campbell, Donohue, and Drake (1995), after an elaborate review, conclude that the individual/collective cultural values dimension is not very useful in predicting whether representatives from given cultures will actually use different negotiation tactics or get different bargaining outcomes.

So although culture and sex do produce interesting and significant results in some investigations (e.g., Zahn-Waxler, Friedman, Cole, Mizuta, & Hiruma, 1996), we should regard these demographic variables only as stand-ins for the factors of real interest: values, predispositions, and learned emotional experiences. The cycles are sited in the individual and his or her relational networks, not in biology or geography.

A Final Observation on Long-Term Effects

One last thing about TCP, considered as a relatively permanent feature of an individual, needs to be emphasized. Personalization of conflicts is obviously a bad thing and will often impede constructive conflict management. Negative feelings about conflict are often inveighed against by scholars and practitioners, and people are commonly enjoined, more or less, to quit it. "Read my book," the writers seem to say, "and you will see the error of your ways." The problem is that, from the personalizer's point of view, there is no error.

Leaving aside the question of how a person first learned to take conflict personally, the fact that he or she does so leads, as we have seen, to reciprocally bad feelings and behaviors during his or her actual arguments. In other words, for personalizers *conflict really is personal.* As we saw in the examination of research bearing on both the actual conflict life space and the long-term consequences of negatively experienced interpersonal argument, TCP can become a self-fulfilling prophecy. People who expect to be persecuted really are, and those who expect high levels of stress really experience it. They see aggressiveness and defensiveness in the other person, even if it is not objectively present (see Downey & Feldman, 1996, Study 2), and often respond in kind.

Personalization, then, is not necessarily or even primarily a perceptual distortion, and so I suppose that personalizers cannot easily be shown any "error" when they attempt to match their life experiences to whatever textbook recommendations they read. Certainly people can be taught to manage conflict better, even under extremely unpromising conditions (e.g., Bargal & Bar, 1990). But deep and elaborate interventions may be required for people whose *justified* perceptions of conflict are profoundly negative.

Compared with people scoring low on TCP, personalizers have a different conception of conflict. Infante and Rancer (1996, pp. 329-330) make a similar point about people who differ in argumentativeness and verbal aggression: They have markedly different understandings of arguing. People who are highly hostile in arguments do not understand that their aggressive remarks are hurtful, and people who wish to avoid arguments believe that they are essentially agonistic encounters. Although Infante (1995) has outlined several promising approaches to intervening in verbally aggressive habits and situations, the feelings represented by high personalization scores are deep and genuine reflections of the individuals' personal historics, not transient moods that can be eliminated with a little self-discipline.

CONCLUSIONS

My purpose in this chapter has been to review the research bearing on both the predisposition and immediate impulse to take conflict personally. The Lewinian perspective has been convenient for permitting us to see how this essentially emotional experience charges our anticipations and anxieties about conflict, diverts our behaviors into aggressive and punishing paths, and creates painful memories and life histories. Field theory's commitments to a phenomenological perspective and to study of the instant of behavioral production help us to see that taking conflict personally is intense, painful, and self-reproducing. Though I have not yet begun any work on intervention strategies dealing with personalization, my instinct is that successful ones will look more like profound self-analysis than, say, Dewey's process of reflective thinking.

NOTES

1. Though Lewin's dynamic concept of *conflict* will occasionally be useful in this chapter, I more typically use the term to refer to an explicit disagreement between two people.

2. I use the term *plan* whether there is any evidence of an alternative path or not. For communication research, the main issue is simply whether any sequence of behaviors is imagined or projected. The question of choosing between two possible plans adds another layer of complexity to the analysis, and I will not often venture that far.

3. I am worried that readers will confuse this organization with the earlier discussion of how adults are able to bring the past and present to bear while acting "in the instant."

REFERENCES

Andrews, G., Singh, M., & Bond, M. (1993). The defense style questionnaire. *Journal of Nervous and Mental Disease, 181,* 246-256.

Argyris, C. (1952). *An introduction to field theory and interaction theory* (Rev. ed.). New Haven, CT: Yale University, Labor and Management Center.

Balswick, J. O. (1988). *The inexpressive male.* Lexington, MA: Lexington.

Barch, S. L., & Dallinger, J. M. (1995, May). *Assessing HMO CEOs' communication competence and propensity to take conflict personally.* Paper presented at the annual meeting of the International Communication Association, Albuquerque, NM.

Bargal, D., & Bar, H. (1990). Strategies for Arab-Jewish conflict management workshops. In S. A. Wheelan, E. A. Pepitone, & V. Abt (Eds.), *Advances in field theory* (pp. 210-229). Newbury Park, CA: Sage.

Barker, R., Dembo, T., & Lewin, K. (1941). *Frustration and regression: An experiment with young children.* Iowa City: University of Iowa Press.

Baron, R. A. (1989). Negative effects of destructive criticism: Impact on conflict, self-efficacy, and task performance. In M. A. Rahim (Ed.), *Managing conflict: An interdisciplinary approach* (pp. 21-31). New York: Praeger.

Benoit, P. J., & Benoit, W. L. (1990). To argue or not to argue: How real people get in and out of interpersonal arguments. In R. Trapp & J. Schuetz (Eds.), *Perspectives on argumentation: Essays in honor of Wayne Brockriede* (pp. 55-72). Prospect Heights, IL: Waveland.

Benoit, P. J., & Hample, D. (1997, August). *The meaning of two cultural categories: Avoiding interpersonal arguments or cutting them short.* Paper presented at the American Forensic Association/Speech Communication Association Conference on Argumentation, Alta, UT.

Benoit, W. L., & Benoit, P. J. (1987). Everyday argument practices of naive social actors. In J. Wenzel (Ed.), *Argument and critical practices* (pp. 465-474). Annandale, VA: Speech Communication Association.

Benton, F. A., & Allen, G. J. (1996). Relationships between anxiety sensitivity, emotional arousal, and interpersonal distress. *Journal of Anxiety Disorders, 10,* 267-282.

Berger, C. R. (1995). A plan-based approach to strategic communication. In D. E. Hewes (Ed.), *Cognitive bases of interpersonal communication* (pp. 141-180). Hillsdale, NJ: Lawrence Erlbaum.

Berger, C. R. (1997). *Planning strategic interaction: Attaining goals through communicative action.* Mahwah, NJ: Lawrence Erlbaum.

Berry, D. S., & Hansen, J. S. (1996). Positive affect, negative affect, and social interaction. *Journal of Personality and Social Psychology, 71,* 796-809.

Betancourt, H., & Blair, I. (1992). A cognition (attribution)-emotion model of violence in conflict situations. *Personality and Social Psychology Bulletin, 18,* 343-350.

Billings, A. (1979). Conflict resolution in distressed and nondistressed married couples. *Journal of Consulting and Clinical Psychology, 47,* 368-376.

Bisanz, G. L., & Rule, B. G. (1990). Children's and adults' comprehension of narratives about persuasion. In M. J. Cody & M. L. McLaughlin (Eds.), *The psychology of tactical communication* (pp. 48-69). Philadelphia: Multilingual Matters.

Bleiberg, S., & Churchill, L. (1975). Notes on confrontation in conversations. *Journal of Psycholinguistic Research, 4,* 273-278.

Boardman, S. K., & Horowitz, S. V. (1994). Constructive conflict management and social problems: An introduction. *Journal of Social Issues, 50,* 1-12.

Bolger, N., & Zuckerman, A. (1995). A framework for studying personality in the stress process. *Journal of Personality and Social Psychology, 69,* 890-902.

Bower, G. H., Black, J. B., & Turner, T. J. (1979). Scripts in memory for text. *Cognitive Psychology, 11,* 177-200.

Brown, P., & Levinson, S. C. (1987). *Politeness: Some universals in language usage.* Cambridge: Cambridge University Press.

Burleson, B. R., & Waltman, M. S. (1988). Cognitive complexity: Using the role category questionnaire measure. In C. H. Tardy (Ed.), *A handbook for the study of human communication* (pp. 1-35). Norwood, NJ: Ablex.

Canary, D. J., Spitzberg, B. H., & Semic, B. A. (1998). The experience and expression of anger in interpersonal settings. In P. A. Andersen & L. K. Guerrero (Eds.), *Handbook of communication and emotion: Research, theory, applications, and contexts* (pp. 189-213). San Diego, CA: Academic Press.

Carstensen, L. L., Gottman, J. M., & Levenson, R. W. (1995). Emotional behavior in long-term marriage. *Psychology and Aging, 10,* 140-149.

Cloven, D. H., & Roloff, M. E. (1991). Sense-making activities and interpersonal conflict: Communicative cures for the mulling blues. *Western Journal of Speech Communication, 55,* 134-158.

Cloven, D. H., & Roloff, M. E. (1993). The chilling effect of aggressive potential on the expression of complaints in intimate relationships. *Communication Monographs, 60,* 200-219.

Collins, B. E., & Guetzkow, H. (1964). *A social psychology of group processes for decision-making.* New York: John Wiley.

Collins, N. L. (1996). Working models of attachment: Implications for explanation, emotion, and behavior. *Journal of Personality and Social Psychology, 71,* 810-832.

Coser, L. A. (1956). *The functions of social conflict.* New York: Free Press.

Cupach, W. R., & Canary, D. J. (1997). *Competence in interpersonal conflict.* New York: McGraw-Hill.

Dallinger, J. M., & Adolphson, D. L. F. (1997, May). *Taking conflict personally: What roles do communicator style and receiver apprehension play?* Paper presented at the annual meeting of the International Communication Association, Montreal.

Dallinger, J. M., & Callister, M. (1997, August). *Taking conflict personally, solidarity, and relational satisfaction: Interrelationships within arguments.* Paper presented at the American Forensic Association/Speech Communication Association Conference on Argumentation, Alta, UT.

Dallinger, J. M., & Hample, D. (1989, November). *Taking conflict personally: Conceptualization and scale development.* Paper presented at the annual meeting of the Speech Communication Association, San Francisco.

Dallinger, J. M., & Hample, D. (1993). Do women take conflict more personally than men? In C. A. Valentine (Ed.), *Seeking understanding of communication, language and gender* (pp. 176-188). Tempe, AZ: Cyberspace.

Dallinger, J. M., & Hample, D. (1995). Personalizing and managing conflict. *International Journal of Conflict Management, 6,* 287-289.

deTurck, M. A. (1985). A transactional analysis of compliance-gaining behavior: Effects of noncompliance, relational contexts, and actors' gender. *Human Communication Research, 12,* 54-78.

Deutsch, M. (1954). Field theory in social psychology. In G. Lindzey (Ed.), *Handbook of social psychology* (Vol. 2, pp. 181-222). Reading, MA: Addison-Wesley.

Deutsch, M. (1973). *The resolution of conflict: Constructive and destructive processes.* New Haven, CT: Yale University Press.

Deutsch, M. (1994). Constructive conflict resolution: Principles, training, and research. *Journal of Social Issues, 50,* 13-32.

Donohue, W. A., & Roberto, A. J. (1993). Relational development as negotiated order in hostage negotiation. *Human Communication Research, 20,* 175-198.

Downey, G., & Feldman, S. I. (1996). Implications of rejection sensitivity for intimate relationships. *Journal of Personality and Social Psychology, 70,* 1327-1343.

Drake, L. E., & Donohue, W. A. (1996). Communication framing theory in conflict resolution. *Communication Research, 23,* 297-322.

Dunn, J., & Brown, J. (1994). Affect expression in the family, children's understanding of emotions, and their interactions with others. *Merrill-Palmer Quarterly, 40,* 120-137.

Eadie, W. F. (1982). Defensive communication revisited: A critical examination of Gibb's theory. *Southern Speech Communication Journal, 47,* 163-177.

Filley, A. C. (1975). *Interpersonal conflict resolution.* Glenview, IL: Scott, Foresman.

Folger, J. P., Poole, M. S., & Stutman, R. K. (1993). *Working through conflict* (2nd ed.). New York: HarperCollins.

Freud, A. (1966). *The ego and the mechanisms of defense.* New York: International Universities Press. (Original work published 1934)

Gibb, J. R. (1961). Defensive communication. *Journal of Communication, 11*(3), 141-148.

Gold, M. (1992). Metatheory and field theory in social psychology. *Journal of Social Issues, 48,* 67-78.

Gottman, J. M. (1993a). The roles of conflict engagement, escalation, and avoidance in marital interaction: A longitudinal view of five types of couples. *Journal of Consulting and Clinical Psychology, 61,* 6-15.

Gottman, J. M. (1993b). A theory of marital dissolution and stability. *Journal of Family Psychology, 7,* 57-75.

Gottman, J. M., Markman, H., & Notarius, C. (1977). The topography of marital conflict: A sequential analysis of verbal and nonverbal behavior. *Journal of Marriage and the Family, 39,* 461-477.

Gottman, J. M., Notarius, C., Markman, H., Bank, S., & Rubin, M. E. (1976). Behavior exchange theory and marital decision making. *Journal of Personality and Social Psychology, 34,* 14-23.

Graziano, W. G., Jensen-Campbell, L. A., & Hair, E. C. (1996). Perceiving interpersonal conflict and reacting to it: The case for agreeableness. *Journal of Personality and Social Psychology, 70,* 820-835.

Gryl, F. E., Stith, S. M., & Bird, G. W. (1991). Close dating relationships among college students: Differences by use of violence and by gender. *Journal of Social and Personal Relationships, 8,* 243-264.

Hample, D. (1996, May). *A theoretical and empirical effort to describe message production.* Paper presented at the annual meeting of the International Communication Association, Chicago.

Hample, D. (1997). Framing message production research with field theory. In J. O. Greene (Ed.), *Message production: Advances in communication theory* (pp. 171-192). Hillsdale, NJ: Lawrence Erlbaum.

Hample, D., Alajmi, N., Klein, M., Ward, S., & White, J. (1997, May). *Dual think-aloud protocols of message production.* Paper presented at the annual meeting of the International Communication Association, Montreal.

Hample, D., Benson, E., Gogliotti, L., & Jeong, J. (1997, November). *Ego defense and taking conflict personally.* Paper presented at the annual meeting of the National Communication Association, Chicago.

Hample, D., & Dallinger, J. M. (1987). Cognitive editing of argument strategies. *Human Communication Research, 14,* 123-144.

Hample, D., & Dallinger, J. M. (1993). The effects of taking conflict personally on arguing behavior. In R. E. McKerrow (Ed.), *Argument and the postmodern challenge* (pp. 235-238). Annandale, VA: Speech Communication Association.

Hample, D., & Dallinger, J. M. (1994, July). *Why are persuasive messages less polite after rebuffs?* Paper presented at the annual meeting of the International Communication Association, Sydney.

Hample, D., & Dallinger, J. M. (1995). A Lewinian perspective on taking conflict personally. Revision, refinement, and validation of the instrument. *Communication Quarterly, 43,* 297-319.

Hample, D., Dallinger, J. M., & Fofana, J. (1995). Perceiving and predicting the tendency to personalize arguments. In S. Jackson (Ed.), *Argumentation and values* (pp. 434-438). Annandale, VA: Speech Communication Association.

Hample, D., Dallinger, J. M., & Nelson, G. K. (1994). Aggressive and passive arguing behaviors, and their relationship to taking conflict personally. In F. H. van Eemeren, R. Grootendorst, J. A. Blair, & C. A. Willard (Eds.), *Proceedings of the Third ISSA Conference on Argumentation: Vol. 3. Reconstruction and application* (pp. 238-250). Amsterdam: SicSat.

Hample, D., Dean, C., Johnson, A., Kopp, L., & Ngoitz, A. (1997, May). *Conflict as a MOP in conversational behavior.* Paper presented at the annual meeting of the International Communication Association, Montreal.

Hample, D., Memba, B., & Seo, Y. H. (1999). *Taking conflict personally, alexithymia, and expression of emotions.* Paper presented at the annual meeting of the International Communication Association, San Francisco.

Holmes, M. E., & Fletcher-Bergland, T. S. (1995). Negotiations in crisis. In A. M. Nicotera (Ed.), *Conflict and organizations: Communicative processes* (pp. 239-256). Albany: State University of New York Press.

Ihilevich, D., & Gleser, G. C. (1993). *Defense mechanisms.* Odessa, FL: Psychological Assessment Resources.

Infante, D. A. (1995). Teaching students to understand and control verbal aggression. *Communication Education, 44,* 51-63.

Infante, D. A., & Rancer, A. S. (1982). A conceptualization and measure of argumentativeness. *Journal of Personality Assessment, 46,* 72-80.

Infante, D. A., & Rancer, A. S. (1996). Argumentativeness and verbal aggressiveness: A review of recent theory and research. In B. R. Burleson (Ed.), *Communication yearbook 19* (pp. 319-351). Thousand Oaks, CA: Sage.

Infante, D. A., & Wigley, C. J. (1986). Verbal aggressiveness: An interpersonal model and measure. *Communication Monographs, 53,* 61-69.

Irizarry, F. P. (1997, May). *The content validity of the PRCA-24 for measuring communication apprehension and trait argumentativeness.* Paper presented at the annual meeting of the International Communication Association, Montreal.

Johnston, D. D., Stinski, M., & Meyers, D. (1993). Development of an alexithymia instrument to measure the diminished communication of affect. *Communication Research Reports, 10,* 149-160.

Kellermann, K. (1992). Communication: Inherently strategic and primarily automatic. *Communication Monographs, 59,* 288-300.

Kerig, P. K. (1996). Assessing the links between interparental conflict and child adjustment: The conflicts and problem-solving scales. *Journal of Family Psychology, 10,* 454-473.

Kim, M.-S., Shin, H.-C., & Cai, D. (1998). Cultural influences on the preferred forms of requesting and re-requesting. *Communication Monographs, 65,* 47-66.

Kinney, T., & Segrin, C. (in press). Cognitive moderators of negative reactions to verbal aggression. *Communication Studies.*

Klein, K., Forehand, R., Armistead, L., & Long, P. (1997). Delinquency during the transition to early adulthood: Family and parenting predictors from early adolescence. *Adolescence, 32,* 61-80.

Koren, P., Carlton, K., & Shaw, D. (1980). Marital conflict: Relations among behaviors, outcomes, and distress. *Journal of Consulting and Clinical Psychology, 48,* 460-468.

Kumar, R. (1997). The role of affect in negotiations: An integrative overview. *Journal of Applied Behavioral Science, 33,* 84-100.

Laursen, B., & Koplas, A. L. (1995). What's important about important conflicts? Adolescents' perceptions of daily disagreements. *Merrill-Palmer Quarterly, 41,* 536-553.

Leeper, R. W. (1949). *Lewin's topological and vector psychology: A digest and critique.* Eugene: University of Oregon Press.

Lewin, K. (1935). *Dynamic theory of personality.* New York: McGraw-Hill.

Lewin, K. (1948). *Resolving social conflicts.* New York: Harper & Row.

Lewin, K. (1952). *Field theory in social science.* London: Tavistock.

Lewin, K., Lippitt, R., & White, R. K. (1939). Patterns of aggressive behavior in experimentally created "social climates." *Journal of Social Psychology, 10,* 271-299.

Lewis, S. L. (1995). *The relationships between managers' propensity to take conflict personally (TCP), their subordinate workgroups' TCP, and the effects on organizational climate.* Unpublished master's thesis, Western Illinois University.

Louis, M. R. (1977). How individuals conceptualize conflict: Identification of steps in the process and the role of personal/developmental factors. *Human Relations, 30,* 451-467.

Lulofs, R. S. (1994). *Conflict: From theory to action.* Scottsdale, AZ: Gorsuch Scarisbrick.

Meyer, J. R. (1997). Cognitive influences on the ability to address interaction goals. In J. O. Greene (Ed.), *Message production: Advances in communication theory* (pp. 71-90). Mahwah, NJ: Lawrence Erlbaum.

Mikolic, J. M., Parker, J. C., & Pruitt, D. G. (1997). Escalation in response to persistent annoyance: Groups versus individuals and gender effects. *Journal of Personality and Social Psychology, 72,* 151-163.

Moffitt, P. F., Spence, N. D., & Goldney, R. D. (1986). Mental health in marriage: The roles of need for affiliation, sensitivity to rejection, and other factors. *Journal of Clinical Psychology, 42,* 68-76.

Myers, K. A., & Bailey, C. L. (1991). Conflict and communication apprehension in campus ministries: A quantitative analysis. *College Student Journal, 25,* 537-543.

Norton, R. W. (1978). Foundation of a communicator style construct. *Human Communication Research, 4,* 99-112.

Norton, R. W. (1983). *Communicator style: Theory, applications, and measures.* Beverly Hills, CA: Sage.

O'Brien, M., Balto, K., Erber, S., & Gee, C. (1995). College students' cognitive and emotional reactions to simulated marital and family conflict. *Cognitive Therapy and Research, 19,* 707-724.

O'Keefe, D. (1987, November). *Message description.* Paper presented at the annual meeting of the Speech Communication Association, Boston.

Plutchik, R., Kellerman, H., & Conte, H. R. (1979). A structural theory of ego defenses and emotions. In C. E. Izard (Ed.), *Emotions in personality and psychopathology* (pp. 229-257). New York: Plenum.

Putnam, L. L., & Jones, T. S. (1982). Reciprocity in negotiations: An analysis of bargaining interaction. *Communication Monographs, 49,* 171-191.

Putnam, L. L., & Poole, M. A. (1987). Conflict and negotiation. In F. M. Jablin, L. L. Putnam, K. H. Roberts, & L. W. Porter (Eds.), *Handbook of organizational communication: An interdisciplinary perspective* (pp. 549-599). Newbury Park, CA: Sage.

Remer, R. (1984). The effects of interpersonal confrontation on males. *American Mental Health Counselors Association Journal, 6,* 56-70.

Retzinger, S. M. (1991). Shame, anger, and conflict: Case study of emotional violence. *Journal of Family Violence, 6,* 37-59.

Roloff, M. E. (1987). Communication and conflict. In C. R. Berger & S. H. Chaffee (Eds.), *Handbook of communication science* (pp. 484-534). Newbury Park, CA: Sage.

Saldern, M. V. (1986). Kurt Lewin's influence on social emotional climate research in Germany and the United States. In E. Stivers & S. Wheelan (Eds.), *The Lewin legacy: Field theory in current practice* (pp. 30-39). Berlin: Springer-Verlag.

Schank, R. C. (1982). *Dynamic memory: A theory of reminding and learning in computers and people.* New York: Cambridge University Press.

Sillars, A. L. (1980). The sequential and distributional structure of conflict interactions as a function of attributions concerning the locus of responsibility and stability of conflicts. In D. Nimmo (Ed.), *Communication yearbook 4* (pp. 217-235). New Brunswick, NJ: Transaction.

Stamp, G. H., Vangelisti, A. L., & Daly, J. A. (1992). The creation of defensiveness in social interaction. *Communication Quarterly, 40,* 177-190.

Tangney, J. P., Wagner, P., Fletcher, C., & Gramzow, R. (1992). Shamed into anger? The relation of shame and guilt to anger and self-reported aggression. *Journal of Personality and Social Psychology, 62,* 669-675.

Tesla, C., & Dunn, J. (1992). Getting along or getting your own way: The development of younger children's use of argument in conflicts with mother and sibling. *Social Development, 1,* 107-121.

Vaillant, G. E. (1977). *Adaptation to life.* Cambridge, MA: Harvard University Press.

Vaillant, G. E. (1993). *The wisdom of the ego.* Cambridge, MA: Harvard University Press.

Waldron, V. R. (1997). Toward a theory of interactive conversational planning. In J. O. Greene (Ed.), *Message production: Advances in communication theory* (pp. 195-220). Mahwah, NJ: Lawrence Erlbaum.

Waln, V. G. (1982). Interpersonal conflict interaction: An examination of verbal defense of self. *Central States Speech Journal, 33,* 557-566.

Walsh, V. L., Baucom, D. H., Tyler, S., & Sayers, S. L. (1993). Impact of message valence, focus, expressive style, and gender on communication patterns among maritally distressed couples. *Journal of Family Psychology, 7,* 163-175.

Watson, J. J., & Remer, R. (1984). The effects of interpersonal confrontation on females. *Personnel and Guidance Journal, 62,* 607-611.

Watzlawick, P., Beavin, J. H., & Jackson, D. D. (1967). *Pragmatics of human communication: A study of interaction patterns, pathologies, and paradoxes.* New York: W. W. Norton.

Wheeless, L. R. (1975). An investigation of receiver apprehension and social context dimensions of communication apprehension. *Speech Teacher, 24,* 261-268.

Wilmot, W. W., & Hocker, J. L. (1998). *Interpersonal conflict* (5th ed.). Boston: McGraw-Hill.

Wilson, S. R., Cai, D. A., Campbell, D. M., Donohue, W. A., & Drake, L. E. (1995). Cultural and communication processes in international business negotiations. In A. M. Nicotera (Ed.), *Conflict and organizations: Communicative processes* (pp. 201-237). Albany: State University of New York Press.

Woike, B. A., Aronoff, J., Stollak, G. E., & Loraas, J. A. (1994). Links between intrapsychic and interpersonal defenses in dyadic interaction. *Journal of Research in Personality, 28,* 101-113.

Yelsma, P. (1981). Conflict predispositions: Differences between happy and clinical couples. *American Journal of Family Therapy, 9,* 57-63.

Yelsma, P. (1995). Couples' affective orientations and their verbal abusiveness. *Communication Quarterly, 43,* 100-114.

Zahn-Waxler, C., Friedman, R. J., Cole, P. M., Mizuta, I., & Hiruma, N. (1996). Japanese and United States preschool children's responses to conflict and distress. *Child Development, 67,* 2462-2477.

CHAPTER CONTENTS

6 How to Handle Opposing Arguments in Persuasive Messages: A Meta-Analytic Review of the Effects of One-Sided and Two-Sided Messages

DANIEL J. O'KEEFE
University of Illinois, Urbana-Champaign

A random-effects meta-analytic review of the effects of one-sided and two-sided persuasive messages identifies two key moderator variables: whether the two-sided message is refutational or nonrefutational and whether the message is consumer advertising or nonadvertising. Compared with one-sided messages, refutational two-sided messages on nonadvertising topics enjoy significantly greater credibility and persuasiveness, nonrefutational two-sided messages on nonadvertising topics are not significantly different in credibility and are significantly less persuasive, refutational two-sided messages on advertising topics do not differ significantly on either credibility or persuasiveness (though few relevant studies exist), and nonrefutational two-sided messages on advertising topics enjoy significantly greater credibility but do not differ in persuasiveness. Often-mentioned moderators (such as audience initial position and education) appear not to have substantial influence on sidedness effects. Explanations of the observed effects are explored, and foci for future research are identified.

H OW should a persuader handle opposing arguments? In many circumstances, a persuader will at least be aware of some potential arguments supporting the opposing point of view. What should a per-

AUTHOR'S NOTE: My thanks to Sally Jackson for assistance in coding and to Mike Allen for supplying some message texts. A version of this chapter was presented at the 1997 meeting of the National Communication Association.

Correspondence and requests for reprints: Daniel J. O'Keefe, Department of Speech Communication, 244 Lincoln Hall, University of Illinois, 702 S. Wright Street, Urbana, IL 61801-3631; e-mail dokeefe@uiuc.edu

Communication Yearbook 22, pp. 209-249

suader do about these, so far as the persuader's own message is concerned? One possibility, of course, is simply to ignore the opposing arguments, and so not mention or acknowledge them at all; the persuader would offer only constructive (supporting) arguments—that is, arguments supporting the persuader's position. The other possibility is for the persuader not to ignore the opposing arguments, but to deal with them (somehow) while also presenting his or her supporting arguments.

In the research literature on persuasion, this basic contrast—ignoring versus not ignoring opposing arguments—has commonly been captured in the distinction between a "one-sided" message (which ignores opposing arguments) and a "two-sided" message (which, while presenting supportive arguments, also acknowledges opposing arguments). Indeed, there is now a substantial literature on the persuasive effects of variations in message sidedness; this chapter provides a meta-analytic review of this research.

PREVIOUS RESEARCH ON
MESSAGE SIDEDNESS

For quite some time, research evidence has been accumulating on the questions of what persuasive effects are associated with message sidedness variations and how the observed effects might best be explained. As will be seen, primary research provides more than 100 estimates of the size of the effect of sidedness variations on persuasive outcomes.

Despite this accumulated evidence, most secondary discussions of the sidedness literature still mention only a few selected investigations (e.g., Eagly & Chaiken, 1993, pp. 561, 623n2). Even papers aimed at providing integrative treatments of this literature do not consider more than a small proportion of the research evidence. For example, Jackson and Allen (1987) analyze 31 effect sizes, Pechmann (1990) cites 12 primary research studies, Allen's (1991, 1994) meta-analyses are based on 26 and 70 effect sizes, and Crowley and Hoyer's (1994) treatment relies on no more than 20 primary research studies.

Nevertheless, previous discussions of message sidedness effects contain two broad themes that can be useful in guiding a review. First, variations in credibility perceptions may be implicated in sidedness's effects on persuasive outcomes. It is commonly speculated, for example, that acknowledging opposing arguments may, by suggesting the communicator's honesty and lack of bias, boost the communicator's credibility and thereby the message's effectiveness (see, e.g., Hovland, Lumsdaine, & Sheffield, 1949, p. 204; Pechmann, 1990; Settle & Golden, 1974). Allen's (1994) review, having noted Allen et al.'s (1990) finding that sidedness's effects on credibility are consistent with the pattern of effects on persuasive outcomes, suggests the possibility that credibility perceptions might play a causal role in persuasive effects. However, no extant meta-analytic review has systematically considered the effects of sidedness variations on credibility perceptions.[1] Hence the present review examines both persuasion-outcome effects (such as attitude change) and credibility-perception effects.

Second, it is widely anticipated that sidedness effects will be moderated by other factors. Indeed, from the very beginnings of sidedness research, a number of possible moderators have been proposed. Hovland et al. (1949, p. 225), for example, suggested that the audience's educational level is an important determinant of the consequences of sidedness variations. Other proposed moderators have included the audience's initial opinion (Hovland et al., 1949, p. 225), perceived source motivation (Pechmann, 1990), exposure to subsequent opposing communications (Lumsdaine & Janis, 1953), and topic familiarity (Allen, 1991, p. 401n2). Some of these moderators cannot usefully be examined through meta-analytic methods. For example, some factors (such as perceived source motivation) are typically not explicitly measured in primary research and cannot be very satisfactorily assessed post hoc (that is, in the absence of direct measures being made in the primary research).

Two particular moderators, however, recommend themselves to meta-analytic attention. The first is the nature of the two-sided message. Just what sorts of arguments are discussed, and just how they are discussed, may make for different persuasive effects (see Allen, 1991, 1994; Crowley & Hoyer, 1994; Jackson & Allen, 1987; Pechmann, 1990). Two varieties of two-sided messages have been recognized. A *refutational* two-sided message attempts to refute opposing arguments in some fashion; this might involve attacking the plausibility of opposing claims, criticizing the reasoning underlying opposing arguments, offering evidence that is shown to undermine opposing claims, and so forth. A *nonrefutational* two-sided message acknowledges the opposing considerations but does not attempt to refute them directly; it might suggest that the positive supporting arguments outweigh the opposing ones, but it does not directly refute the opposing arguments. Previous discussions have suggested that sidedness effects may vary significantly depending upon whether the opposing arguments are refuted (Allen, 1991, 1994; Crowley & Hoyer, 1994; Jackson & Allen, 1987). Specifically, Allen (1991, 1994) has concluded that there is a persuasive advantage for refutational two-sided messages (over one-sided messages) but no such advantage for nonrefutational two-sided messages; moreover, this effect is reported to be quite general and consistent (that is, unaffected by other moderator variables).

The second moderator of special interest is the topical area of the message, specifically whether the message represents advertising (that is, advertising for a consumer product or service) as opposed to some nonadvertising topic (social or political questions, for example).[2] There has been speculation that nonrefutational two-sided messages may have different effects in consumer advertising contexts than in nonadvertising contexts (O'Keefe, 1990, p. 174).

Although previous discussions of sidedness effects have sometimes been sensitive to the possibility of differences between these persuasion contexts (e.g., Crowley & Hoyer, 1994, p. 562), extant reviews have not systematically examined variations in sidedness effects across these topical areas.

Four other possible moderators were also included in this review, largely because of long-standing (and often-repeated) suggestions that they might influence sidedness effects. One is the audience's initial attitude. Hovland et al. (1949, pp. 212-213) found one-sided messages to be more persuasive than two-sided messages for receivers initially favorable to the advocated view, but found two-sided messages to be more effective with receivers initially opposed to the message's standpoint. Corresponding generalizations about the moderating role of initial audience attitude are common in secondary treatments of the sidedness literature (e.g., Bettinghaus & Cody, 1987, p. 149; Johnston, 1994, p. 142; Pratkanis & Aronson, 1992, p. 155; Reardon, 1991, p. 105; Shimp, 1990, p. 150), but previous meta-analytic reviews have failed to confirm this generalization (Allen, 1991, 1994; Jackson & Allen, 1987).

A second possible moderator is the audience's level of education. Hovland et al. (1949, pp. 213-214) conclude that one-sided messages are more effective than two-sided messages for receivers low in education, whereas two-sided messages have the persuasive advantage with more educated audiences. This, too, often appears in secondary treatments as a generalization about sidedness effects (e.g., Kotler, 1980, p. 482; Shimp, 1990, p. 151), though sometimes phrased in terms of intelligence rather than educational level (e.g., Johnston, 1994, p. 142; Reardon, 1991, p. 105); meta-analytic reviews by Jackson and Allen (1987) and Allen (1994), however, failed to confirm any such general moderating role for audience education.

The third possible moderator is the audience's likely availability of counterarguments. Several commentators have suggested that when receivers have counterarguments available to them, two-sided messages will be more effective than one-sided messages, but when receivers are unlikely to have counterarguments ready to hand, one-sided messages will be more persuasive (e.g., Chu, 1967; Hass & Linder, 1972; Pratkanis & Aronson, 1992, pp. 154-155). Indeed, the availability of counterarguments is sometimes proposed to underlie possible effects (on sidedness outcomes) of other moderator variables. The suggestion is that with receiver opposition to the advocated view, receiver familiarity with the topic, or higher receiver intelligence or education, receivers will likely have counterarguments easily available, thus making two-sided messages more advantageous in such circumstances (McGuire, 1985, p. 272).

The fourth possible moderator is the order of materials in the two-sided message. Jackson and Allen (1987) note that a two-sided message can organize its materials in three ways: by discussing supporting arguments first and then opposing arguments, by discussing opposing arguments first and then supportive arguments, or by interweaving discussion of supportive and opposing arguments. Their review suggests that, at least for refutational two-sided messages, the support-then-refute order might be most persuasive and the refute-then-support order least persuasive. McGuire (1985, p. 272) claims that refutational material can successfully precede supportive materials in two-sided messages, but Crowley and Hoyer's (1994, p. 568) review suggests that two-sided messages should not begin with discussion of opposing considerations.

METHODS

Identification of Relevant Investigations

Literature search. Relevant research reports were located through personal knowledge of the literature, examination of previous reviews and textbooks, and inspection of reference lists in previously located reports. Additionally, searches were made through databases and document-retrieval services using "one-sided," "two-sided," "sidedness," and "refutational" as search bases; these searches covered material at least through August 1997 in PsycINFO, ERIC (Educational Resources Information Center), Current Contents, ABI/Inform, CARL/UnCover (Colorado Association of Research Libraries), Medline, and Dissertation Abstracts Online.

Inclusion criteria. To be included, an investigation had to meet two criteria. First, the study had to compare a one-sided message with a two-sided message without intentionally confounding the sidedness manipulation with other distinct manipulations or with the advocated position. A one-sided message contains only supporting arguments or considerations (that is, arguments or considerations supporting the advocated position). A two-sided message both (a) offers supporting arguments or considerations and (b) at least acknowledges possible opposing arguments or considerations. Generally speaking, an opposing argument or consideration is some argument or consideration that could be raised to support an opposing view (that is, a view opposing that of the advocate) or some argument or consideration that could be raised to undermine the advocated view; thus acknowledging possible opposing arguments or considerations at least means explicitly recognizing the existence of some possible countervailing considerations, some considerations that could (at face value) incline a person against the advocate's viewpoint.

Excluded by this criterion were studies that lacked two-sided messages (e.g., Cronen, 1976; Gaudino & Harris, 1988; Havitz & Crompton, 1990; Kohn & Snook, 1976; McGuire & Papageorgis, 1961; Sheagren, 1997; Thistlethwaite, Kamenetzky, & Schmidt, 1956; Welford, 1972; Weston, 1968) or one-sided messages (e.g., Birkimer et al., 1994; Deuser, 1989; Janis & Feierabend, 1957; Thistlethwaite & Kamenetzky, 1955; Winkel & Huismans, 1986) and designs in which the discussion of opposing arguments and the presentation of supporting arguments appeared in different messages (Kennedy, 1982). Also excluded were quasi-experiments in which sidedness variations were purposefully confounded with other experimental manipulations (e.g., Kasulis & Zaltman, 1977; Koyama, 1982; Reynolds, West, & Aiken, 1990), designs in which receivers were exposed to both one- and two-sided messages in a way that made it impossible to compare the effects of the two message forms (Kosc & Winkel, 1982), and review papers or secondary discussions (e.g., Allen, 1993; Lawson, 1970; O'Keefe, 1993; Ragon, 1996).

As a result of the application of this first criterion, the literature reviewed did not precisely match the literature that might conventionally be labeled as studies of message sidedness. There were two reasons for this. First, some studies—despite not usually being represented as studies of message sidedness effects and despite not themselves mentioning the sidedness literature—involve the same sort of manipulation (of how opposing material is handled) that is common in the message sidedness literature (e.g., Schanck & Goodman, 1939). Second, some studies that have been labeled as studies of message sidedness do not employ manipulations of the sort reviewed here; for example, Wolfinger (1955) and Allen et al. (1990, Replication 1, prochoice [1] messages) varied the elaborateness of the opposing argument or its refutation, but not the presence of opposing arguments (and hence had no one-sided message).

The second inclusion criterion was that the investigation had to contain appropriate quantitative data pertinent to the comparison of persuasive effectiveness or perceived credibility across experimental conditions. Excluded by this criterion were studies of effects on other dependent variables (e.g., Assael & Kamins, 1989; Brenner, Koehler, & Tversky, 1996; Misra & Jain, 1971), including resistance to persuasion (e.g., Insko, 1962; Manis & Blake, 1963; O'Connor & Vann, 1979), and studies not reporting appropriate quantitative information (e.g., Anderson & Golden, 1984; Belch, 1983; Faison, 1961; Gore, 1976; McGinnies, 1966; Sawyer, 1973; Skilbeck, Tulips, & Ley, 1977; Smith, Kopfman, Morrison, & Ford, 1993).

Dependent Variables and Effect Size Measure

Dependent variables. Two dependent variables were of interest. The dependent variable of central interest was persuasiveness (as assessed through measures such as opinion change, postcommunication agreement, behavioral intention, behavior, and the like). When a single study contained multiple indices of persuasion, these were averaged to yield a single summary.

The other dependent variable was credibility (as assessed through measures of communicator or message credibility). Where multiple indices of credibility were available, these were averaged.

Effect size measure. Each comparison between a one-sided message and its two-sided counterpart was summarized using r as the effect size measure.

Differences favoring two-sided versions were given a positive sign; differences favoring one-sided versions were given a negative sign.

When correlations were averaged (e.g., across several dependent measures), the average was computed using the r-to-z-to-r transformation procedure, weighting by n. Wherever possible, multiple-factor designs were analyzed by reconstituting the analysis such that individual-difference factors (but not other experimental manipulations) were put back into the error term (following the suggestion of Johnson, 1989).

Independent Variables

Type of two-sided message. Cases were coded for the type of two-sided message employed. All two-sided messages contain both supportive arguments and acknowledgment of possible opposing arguments. Two main classes of two-sided messages—refutational and nonrefutational—were distinguished on the basis of how the opposing materials were handled.

The contrast between refutational and nonrefutational two-sided messages is a contrast between messages that undertake to attack directly (refute) opposing arguments and messages that acknowledge opposing arguments without attempting refutation; in a sense, the contrast might be expressed by saying that refutational messages attempt to remove the opposing reason, whereas nonrefutational messages do not (but typically might try to overwhelm it with supporting reasons). Refutation involves denying either the truth (e.g., "Some people say this economic policy will increase unemployment, but that's not so, because . . .") or the relevance (e.g., "It's true that my client was convicted of robberies in the past, but past convictions are not evidence of guilt in the current case") of the claim of an opposing argument.

Topic type. The message topics were classified as either advertising or nonadvertising topics. *Advertising* topics were ones in which the advocacy concerned some product or service; the exemplary forms were advertisements for consumer products such as beer, soap, or automobiles (but ads for business products or services were also classified in this category). *Nonadvertising* topics thus included sociopolitical topics (involving public policy questions, broadly understood, such as gun control, creationism, or local educational control) and other topics (such as hypothetical court cases and organ donation).

Audience favorability. Where possible, cases were coded for whether the position advocated by the message was one toward which the audience would generally be favorably or unfavorably disposed. These judgments relied on reported pretest scores or inspection of the population and message. For completely novel topics on which the audience could not possibly have an opinion, as with hypothetical brands of products or hypothetical court cases, the initial opinion was coded as "neutral."

Audience education. Where possible, cases were coded for the audience's level of education. The distinctions drawn were between audiences with no college education, those with some college education, and those having graduated from college.

Counterargument availability. Cases were coded for the degree to which the audience would have access to possible counterarguments. Cases were classified as "high," "low," or "indeterminant" with respect to counterargument availability. This commonly required an estimate of the audience's ability to think up possible objections. In general, if the topic was one on which the audience might well be able to easily bring to mind possible objections, then counterargument availability would be deemed high. So, for instance, if the message topic was a sociopolitical issue that was timely and controversial, then counterargument availability would be presumed to be high (unless some special knowledge/background was likely required). In the case of ads for hypothetical brands of products, when the product class was familiar to the audience (e.g., the audience could be presumed to know something of other brands within that product class), then counterargument availability was coded as high (because the familiarity with the product class would presumably make the audience sensitive to potential shortcomings of the hypothetical brand).

Order of arguments. Two-sided messages can order supportive and opposing materials in at least three ways: first, supportive material followed by opposing material; second, opposing material followed by supporting material; and third, interweaving or alternation of supportive and opposing materials. Where possible, cases were coded for the order of materials in the two-sided message.

Coding reliabilities. Two coders independently classified 15 randomly-selected cases, yielding exact agreements as follows: 100% for type of two-sided message, 87% for topic type, 100% for audience favorability, 93% for audience educational level, 80% for counterargument availability, and 87% for order of arguments. As might be expected from the nature of the judgments involved, counterargument availability was the property most difficult to estimate reliably. All disagreements were resolved through discussion.[3]

Unit of Analysis

In considering how to analyze the present collection of studies, attention to the particular messages employed was important. Every analyzed study contains a comparison of a one-sided message with a two-sided message, and it might be thought that one could simply straightforwardly derive an effect size measure for each study. And indeed this way of proceeding would be appropriate if each study used only one message pair (i.e., compared just one one-sided message to its two-sided counterpart) and if each study used a different message pair (so that messages were never reused).

But these conditions do not hold in this literature. Some investigations have more than one one-sided/two-sided message pair (for instance, when several different topics were used, a different message pair was of course used for each), and some one-sided/two-sided message pairs are used in more than one study. If one is interested in generalizing across message pairs, the common meta-analytic procedure of treating each study as providing one effect size estimate is unsatisfactory.

Thus in the present analysis, the fundamental unit of analysis was the message pair (that is, the pair composed of a one-sided message and its experimental two-sided counterpart). A measure of effect size was recorded for each distinguishable message pair found in the body of studies. Thus, for example, a study reporting separate comparisons between one-sided and two-sided messages on two different topics contributed two observations (because it contained two one-sided/two-sided message pairs, one pair for each topic), whereas a study with a single message pair contributed only one.

Usually, a given message pair was used only in a single investigation, and hence only one effect size estimate was associated with the pair. But some message pairs were used in more than one study, and hence there could be several estimates available of the effect size associated with that message pair. These multiple estimates were averaged to yield a single summary estimate before inclusion in the analysis. Such cumulation occurred in the following cases (see Tables 6.1 and 6.4): Data from Study 1 and Study 2 in Ferrari and Leippe (1992) were combined and reported as "Ferrari and Leippe (1992)"; data from Kamins (1985), Kamins and Assael (1987a), Kamins and Assael (1987b, Experiment 1 and Experiment 2), and Kamins and Marks (1987) were combined and reported as "Kamins refutational"; data from Kamins (1985) and Kamins and Assael (1987b, pretest) were combined and reported as "Kamins nonrefutational"; and data from Ley, Bradshaw, Kincey, Couper-Smartt, and Wilson (1974) and Ley, Whitworth, Woodward, and Yorke (1977) were combined and reported as "Ley messages."

In some cases, the same primary data served as the basis for multiple reports. Sometimes this was made clear by the reports, typically when a given study was reported in a dissertation and in a subsequent journal article (the South African sanctions topic data reported in Allen et al. [1990, Replication 3], in Hale, Mongeau, & Thomas [1991], and in Thomas [1990], recorded here under Thomas [1990]; Belch [1980, 1981]; Earl [1979] and Earl & Pride [1980], recorded here under the former; Paulson [1953, 1954]; Stainback [1983] and Stainback & Rogers [1983], recorded here under the former; Swanson [1983, 1987]) or in both a convention paper and a subsequent publication (Reinard [1984, Experiment 1] and Reinard & Reynolds [1976], recorded here under the former; Smith, Morrison, Kopfman, & Ford [1994] and Smith, Morrison, Molnar, & Ford [1992], recorded here under the former). Sometimes the reports did not make this plain, as when the same primary data were reported (in whole or in part) more than once, without acknowledgment of any relationship (the mass-transit topic data reported in Golden & Alpert [1978] and in Golden & Alpert [1987], recorded here under the former; the deodorant topic data reported in Alpert & Golden [1982] and in Golden & Alpert [1987], recorded here under the latter; Hunt, Domzal, & Kernan [1981] and Hunt & Kernan [1984], recorded here under the former; Hunt & Smith [1987], Hunt, Smith, & Kernan [1985], and Hunt, Smith, & Kernan [1989], recorded here under Hunt & Smith [1987]; Winkel [1984] and Winkel & Kosc [1983], recorded here under the former). Wherever it appeared that a given investigation was reported in more than one outlet, it was treated as a single study and analyzed accordingly.

Random-Effects Analysis

The individual correlations (effect sizes) were initially transformed to Fisher's zs; the zs were analyzed using random-effects procedures described by Shadish and Haddock (1994), with results then transformed back to r. A random-effects analysis was employed in preference to a fixed-effects analysis because of an interest in generalizing across messages (for discussion, see Erez, Bloom, & Wells, 1996; Jackson, 1992, p. 123; Raudenbush, 1994; Shadish & Haddock, 1994). In a random-effects analysis, the confidence interval around an obtained mean effect size reflects not only the usual (human) sampling variation, but also between-studies variance. This has the effect of widening the confidence interval over what it would have been in a fixed-effects analysis (see Shadish & Haddock, 1994, p. 275; for related discussion, see Raudenbush, 1994, p. 306).

RESULTS

Persuasion Effects

Overall effects. A total of 107 distinguishable persuasion effect sizes were available, based on 20,111 respondents. Details for each included case are contained in Table 6.1. The mean effect was −.001; there was no dependable difference in persuasive effectiveness between one-sided and two-sided messages (see Table 6.2).

Individual moderators. Table 6.2 summarizes the observed effects of the various moderator variables. As described there, the form of the two-sided message made a substantial difference to the message's persuasiveness. Refutational two-sided messages enjoyed a dependable persuasive advantage over one-sided messages (mean $r = .077$), whereas nonrefutational two-sided messages were significantly less persuasive than their one-sided counterparts (mean $r = −.049$).

One-sided and two-sided messages did not differ in persuasiveness as a function of whether the messages were advertisements. Neither with advertising messages (mean $r = .002$) nor with nonadvertising messages (mean $r = -.003$) was there a significant difference in persuasiveness between one-sided and two-sided messages.

The audience's initial favorability toward the advocated view appears to have some influence on the relative effectiveness of one- and two-sided messages, though the number of relevant cases was rather small. One-sided messages were significantly more persuasive than two-sided messages when audiences were initially favorable (mean $r = -.138$) or initially unfavorable (mean $r = -.112$). When audiences were initially neutral, there was no significant difference in the effectiveness of one- and two-sided messages (mean $r = -.023$).

Because most investigations used undergraduates as participants, the research evidence concerning the role of audience education is naturally limited. However, this limited research offers little basis for believing that the audience's educational level moderates the general comparison of one- and two-sided messages. No matter whether the audience had no college education, had some college education, was composed of college graduates, or had some mixed or indeterminant level of education, there was no significant difference in effectiveness between one-sided and two-sided messages.

Relatively few investigations employed topics on which the audience could be presumed to have little access to potential counterarguments. But the evidence to date provides no indication that the availability of counterarguments moderates the general comparison of one- and two-sided messages. One-sided and two-sided messages did not differ in effectiveness as a function of the audience's availability of counterarguments.

The order of materials in the two-sided message did not influence the relative effectiveness of one- and two-sided messages. No matter whether the two-sided message discussed supporting arguments and then opposing ones, discussed opposing arguments and then supporting ones, or interwove the discussion of supporting and opposing arguments, one-sided and two-sided messages did not significantly differ in persuasive effectiveness.

Two-sided message type and other moderators. Because of the apparent importance of the contrast between refutational and nonrefutational two-sided messages with respect to persuasive effects, effects involving the joint operation of this moderator variable and other moderator variables are naturally of interest. For example, one might want to know whether the overall difference between refutational and nonrefutational two-sided messages obtains consistently across variations in audience education. Table 6.3 presents results displaying the persuasion effects associated with the joint operation of two-sided message type and each of the other moderator variables.

Unfortunately, as a rule the extant research evidence is insufficient to address such questions, because of the maldistribution of cases across the levels of the moderator. For example, the use of undergraduate respondents is so common in this research domain that the available evidence cannot speak

TABLE 6.1
Persuasion Cases

Study	r	n	Codings
Ahlawat (1991)			
refuted	−.012	261	1/1/2/4/2/1
unrefuted	−.070	261	2/1/2/4/2/1
Alden & Crowley (1995)	.115	281	2/1/4/2/2/4
Allen et al. (1990)			
Replication 1			
refutational, 55 mph	.158	57	1/2/4/2/2/3
refutational, creationism	.330	58	1/2/4/2/2/2
refutational, sex education	.198	54	1/2/4/2/2/4
refutational, prochoice (2)	−.029	53	1/2/4/2/2/2
refutational, adopted kids	−.038	54	1/2/4/2/3/2
refutational, drunk drivers	.296	57	1/2/4/2/2/3
refutational, children's ads	.172	53	1/2/4/2/2/1
nonrefutational, 55 mph	.094	59	2/2/4/2/2/3
nonrefutational, creationism	.082	59	2/2/4/2/2/2
nonrefutational, sex education	−.130	58	2/2/4/2/2/3
nonrefutational, prochoice (2)	−.004	59	2/2/4/2/2/2
nonrefutational, adopted kids	−.090	60	2/2/4/2/3/2
nonrefutational, drunk drivers	−.325	60	2/2/4/2/2/3
nonrefutational, children's ads	−.148	56	2/2/4/2/2/1
Replication 2			
refutational, INF treaty	.210	50	1/2/4/2/1/3
refutational, running	−.051	50	2/2/4/2/2/1
refutational, advertising	.255	64	1/2/4/2/2/4
refutational, SATs	−.122	49	1/2/4/2/2/4
refutational, anarchy	.093	53	1/2/4/2/3/3
refutational, family counseling	.010	52	1/2/4/2/3/3
refutational, political spots	.146	49	1/2/4/2/2/4
nonrefutational, INF treaty	.061	50	2/2/4/2/1/3
nonrefutational, running	−.105	50	2/2/4/2/2/1
nonrefutational, advertising	−.160	70	2/2/4/2/2/4
nonrefutational, SATs	−.209	50	2/2/4/2/2/4
nonrefutational, anarchy	.090	89	2/2/4/2/3/3
nonrefutational, family counseling	.238	52	2/2/4/2/3/4
nonrefutational, political spots	−.194	49	2/2/4/2/2/4
Replication 3			
refutational, elderly	.090	77	1/2/4/2/3/4
nonrefutational, elderly	−.060	77	2/2/4/2/3/4
Belch (1980, 1981)	−.046	230	2/1/2/4/2/3
Bettinghaus & Baseheart (1969)	−.200	120	2/2/3/2/3/3
Chebat et al. (1988)	.048	236	2/2/4/2/2/4
Chebat & Picard (1985)	.083	420	2/1/2/2/2/4
Cho (1996)			
computer	.042	148	1/1/2/4/2/4
coffee	.025	148	1/1/2/4/2/4
Chu (1967)	.012	273	1/2/4/1/3/2

TABLE 6.1
(Continued)

Study	r	n	Codings
Crane (1962)			
juvenile delinquency	.053	92	2/2/4/2/2/3
Red China recognition	.130	75	2/2/4/2/2/3
Crowley (1991)			
Study 1	−.465	175	2/1/2/2/2/3
Study 2	−.523	104	2/1/2/2/2/3
Dipboye (1977)	−.007	80	1/2/2/2/3/2
Dycus (1976)	.293	27	1/2/2/4/2/3
Etgar & Goodwin (1982)	.221	120	2/1/2/2/2/3
Ferguson & Jackson (1982)	−.080	383	1/1/2/2/2/4
Ferrari & Leippe (1992)	.113	79	1/2/4/2/2/4
Ford & Smith (1991)	.146	219	1/2/4/2/2/1
Gardner & Levin (1982)	−.242	40	2/1/2/4/2/4
Golden & Alpert (1987) deodorant	.121	236	2/1/2/4/2/3
Halverson (1975)	−.257	56	1/2/1/2/2/2
Hass & Linder (1972)			
Experiment 2	−.499	27	1/2/4/2/3/2
Experiment 3	.006	150	2/2/2/2/3/4
Hastak & Park (1990)	−.116	124	2/1/2/2/2/2
Hilyard (1966)	−.310	240	2/2/4/2/3/3
Hovland et al. (1949)	.001	402	2/2/4/4/3/4
Hunt & Smith (1987)	−.216	150	1/1/2/2/2/4
Jaksa (1968)	.019	1028	1/2/4/2/3/4
Jarrett & Sherriffs (1953)	−.365	487	2/2/4/2/4/3
Jones (1987)	.004	120	2/2/4/2/2/1
Jones & Brehm (1970)	−.505	84	2/2/2/2/1/4
Kamins refutational	.248	192	1/1/2/2/2/3
Kamins (1989)	.306	77	1/1/2/3/2/1
Kamins et al. (1989)	.290	52	2/1/2/3/2/3
Kamins & Marks (1988)	−.026	170	2/1/4/3/2/3
Kanungo & Johar (1975)	−.050	80	2/1/2/3/2/4
Kaplowitz & Fisher (1985)	.069	1600	2/2/1/4/2/3
Kiesler (1964)	.031	173	1/2/1/2/3/3
Koballa (1984)	.582	58	2/2/4/2/3/3
Koehler (1972)	.063	360	1/2/4/2/3/3
Ley messages	.206	113	1/2/4/4/2/4
Lilienthal (1973)	−.066	120	2/2/4/2/3/3
Lumsdaine & Janis (1953)	.057	88	2/2/4/1/3/3
McCroskey, Young, & Scott (1972)	.249	518	1/2/4/2/3/4
Merenski & Mizerski (1979)	.161	72	2/1/2/3/2/4
Nathan (1981)	−.083	192	1/2/2/2/3/3
Papageorgis (1963)	−.187	310	2/2/3/2/3/4

(continued)

TABLE 6.1
(Continued)

Study	r	n	Codings
Pardini & Katzev (1986)			
control versus 2	.095	40	1/1/4/4/3/4
1 versus 3	.392	40	1/1/4/4/3/4
Paulson (1953, 1954)	−.023	978	2/2/4/2/2/3
Pechmann (1992)			
Study 1	.143	240	2/1/2/4/2/1
Study 2	−.340	80	2/1/2/4/2/1
Rahaim (1984)	.142	110	1/2/4/4/3/3
Reinard (1984)			
Experiment 1	−.027	120	2/2/4/2/3/4
Experiment 2	−.095	360	2/2/4/2/2/4
Roering & Paul (1976)	.022	240	2/1/2/2/2/4
Rosnow (1968)	−.218	197	2/2/4/2/2/4
Sandler (1988)	.183	158	2/1/2/2/2/1
Schanck & Goodman (1939)	−.048	714	2/2/4/3/4/4
Settle & Golden (1974)	.005	120	2/1/2/2/2/4
Sherman, Greene, & Plank (1991)	.082	1173	2/1/4/3/2/4
Sinha & Dhawan (1971)	−.011	100	2/2/4/2/2/4
Smith et al. (1994)	−.050	103	1/2/4/2/2/1
Sorrentino et al. (1988)	−.330	114	2/2/4/2/2/3
Stayman et al. (1987)			
alarm clock	−.149	180	2/1/2/2/2/1
record store	.134	180	2/1/2/2/2/1
Swanson (1983, 1987)			
automobile	.047	311	2/1/4/4/2/2
car wax	−.038	311	2/1/4/4/2/2
Swinyard (1981)	−.049	578	2/1/4/4/2/4
Thomas (1990)			
refutational	.089	130	1/2/4/4/3/3
nonrefutational	−.099	134	2/2/4/4/3/1
Williams et al. (1993)			
Study 1	.141	170	1/2/2/2/1/1
Study 2	.072	97	1/2/2/2/3/4
Williams (1976)	−.061	163	2/1/4/2/2/4
Winkel (1984)	.056	191	1/2/4/2/2/1

NOTE: The coding judgments, in order, are as follows: two-sided message type (1 = refutational, 2 = nonrefutational), topic area (1 = advertising, 2 = nonadvertising), audience initial attitude (1 = favorable, 2 = neutral, 3 = unfavorable, 4 = indeterminant/varied), audience educational level (1 = no college, 2 = some college, 3 = college graduate, 4 = indeterminant/varied), counterargument availability (1 = low, 2 = high, 3 = indeterminant/varied), order of arguments in two-sided message (1 = support then oppose, 2 = oppose then support, 3 = interwoven, 4 = indeterminant).

effectively to the question of whether audience education influences the impact of the refutational-versus-nonrefutational contrast. Of the 88 cases having a distinct level of audience education, 79 involved undergraduates (32 refutational, 47 nonrefutational); only 4 involved respondents without any

TABLE 6.2
Persuasion Effects: Summary of Results

	k	Mean r	95% CI	Q (df)
All cases	107	−.001	−.039, .036	494.1 (106)***
Refutational	42	.077	.026, .128	102.7 (41)***
Nonrefutational	65	−.049	−.098, −.000	352.0 (64)***
Advertising	35	.002	−.068, .071	179.3 (34)***
Nonadvertising	72	−.003	−.048, .042	313.5 (71)***
Favorable initial attitude	10	−.138	−.266, −.009	116.6 (9)***
Unfavorable initial attitude	9	−.112	−.213, −.010	37.7 (8)***
Neutral initial attitude	36	−.023	−.096, .049	195.5 (35)***
Indeterminant/varied attitude	69	.014	−.029, .058	275.8 (68)***
No college education	4	−.021	−.090, .048	2.0 (3)
Some college education	79	−.019	−.065, .028	415.2 (78)***
College graduate	5	.109	−.033, .252	11.0 (4)*
Indeterminant/varied education	24	.034	−.030, .098	54.4 (23)***
High counterargument availability	72	.005	−.040, .051	273.7 (71)***
Low counterargument availability	7	.051	−.240, .342	47.3 (6)***
Indeterminant/varied availability	33	.003	−.069, .075	196.0 (32)***
Support-then-oppose order	22	−.006	−.073, .061	67.5 (21)***
Oppose-then-support order	17	−.055	−.145, .035	34.5 (16)**
Alternation/interwoven	36	.004	−.076, .084	277.3 (35)***
Indeterminant/varied order	41	−.000	−.052, .052	144.8 (40)***

NOTE: Studies that provided a within-study comparison of interest (e.g., a study that included college undergraduates and college graduates, with results reported separately for these conditions) contributed effect sizes to both the relevant specific categories ("some college education" and "college graduate") and the "indeterminant/varied" category. As a result, the number of cases summed across levels of a given moderator sometimes exceeds the total number of cases (107).

$*p < .05; **p < .01; ***p < .001.$

college education (1 refutational, 3 nonrefutational) and only 5 involved college graduates (1 refutational, 4 nonrefutational). In such a circumstance, little can be learned about the joint effects of two-sided message type and audience educational level. For similar reasons, it was not possible to examine usefully the interplay of two-sided message type with variations in initial attitude or counterargument availability.

However, examination of the joint effect of two-sided message type and message topic revealed that the apparent superiority of refutational over nonrefutational forms did not obtain across both advertising and nonadvertising messages. Although for nonadvertising messages there was a dependable advantage for refutational over nonrefutational two-sided messages (refutational mean $r = .081$; nonrefutational mean $r = -.069$), this difference was not apparent for advertising messages. Neither refutational (mean $r = .072$) nor nonrefutational (mean $r = -.022$) two-sided advertising messages were dependably more persuasive than their one-sided counterparts.

TABLE 6.3
Persuasion Effects: Two-Sided Message Type and Other Moderators

	Refutational	*Nonrefutational*
Message topic		
advertising		
mean r	.072	−.022
95% CI	−.057, .200	−.102, .058
k	9	26
Q (df)	35.3 (8)***	143.7 (25)***
nonadvertising		
mean r	.081	−.069
95% CI	.025, .137	−.131, −.007
k	33	39
Q (df)	64.0 (32)***	193.7 (38)***
Audience initial attitude		
favorable		
mean r	−.024	−.201
95% CI	−.156, .108	−.386, −.016
k	4	6
Q (df)	3.9 (3)	111.6 (5)***
unfavorable		
mean r	.027	−.150
95% CI	−.076, .129	−.262, .038
k	2	7
Q (df)	0.0 (1)	30.3 (6)***
neutral		
mean r	.042	−.065
95% CI	−.040, .124	−.166, .035
k	13	23
Q (df)	36.2 (12)***	155.0 (22)***
indeterminant/varied		
mean r	.106	−.042
95% CI	.043, .169	−.095, .011
k	28	41
Q (df)	53.1 (27)**	172.3 (40)***
Audience education		
no college		
mean r	.012	−.038
95% CI		−.122, .047
k	1	3
Q (df)		1.6 (2)
some college		
mean r	.064	−.071
95% CI	.003, .124	−.132, −.009
k	32	47
Q (df)	86.9 (31)***	269.1 (46)***
college graduate		
mean r	.306	.070
95% CI		−.065, .205
k	1	4
Q (df)		7.0 (3)

TABLE 6.3
(Continued)

	Refutational	*Nonrefutational*
indeterminant/varied		
mean *r*	.093	−.003
95% CI	.016, .170	−.083, .076
k	9	15
Q (*df*)	10.2 (8)	40.6 (14)***
Counterargument availability		
high		
mean *r*	.084	−.034
95% CI	.020, .149	−.090, .023
k	24	48
Q (*df*)	59.5 (23)***	205.7 (47)***
low		
mean *r*	.053	.076
95% CI	−.091, .197	−.636, .787
k	4	3
Q (*df*)	5.6 (3)	37.0 (2)***
indeterminant/varied		
mean *r*	.054	−.041
95% CI	−.033, .141	−.157, .075
k	17	16
Q (*df*)	41.2 (16)***	105.3 (15)***
Order of two-sided materials		
support then oppose		
mean *r*	.055	−.050
95% CI	.044, .154	−.134, .034
k	9	13
Q (*df*)	18.8 (8)*	43.7 (12)***
oppose then support		
mean *r*	−.079	−.039
95% CI	−.246, .088	−.096, .018
k	9	8
Q (*df*)	26.4 (8)***	7.9 (7)
alternation/interwoven		
mean *r*	.084	−.055
95% CI	.039, .129	−.169, .059
k	13	23
Q (*df*)	17.3 (12)	232.9 (22)***
indeterminant/varied		
mean *r*	.078	−.046
95% CI	.005, .151	−.107, .015
k	16	25
Q (*df*)	53.1 (15)***	79.1 (24)***

*$p < .05$; **$p < .01$; ***$p < .001$.

The evidence concerning the role of the order of materials in the two-sided message appears to suggest that the general advantage of refutational over nonrefutational two-sided messages is confined to cases in which the opposing and supporting materials are interwoven: In such cases, refutational two-sided messages enjoyed a dependable advantage over one-sided messages (mean $r = .084$), but nonrefutational two-sided messages did not (mean $r = -.055$). When the two-sided message discussed supporting arguments and then opposing arguments, or discussed opposing arguments and then supporting considerations, there was no dependable advantage for either refutational or nonrefutational two-sided messages.

Credibility Effects

Overall effects. A total of 56 distinguishable credibility effect sizes were available, based on 6,937 respondents. Details for each included case are contained in Table 6.4. The mean effect was .091, a significant advantage in perceived credibility for two-sided messages (see Table 6.5).

Individual moderators. The results for the individual moderator variables are summarized in Table 6.5. As indicated there, the general credibility advantage of two-sided messages did not vary as a function of whether the two-sided message was refutational or nonrefutational: Significantly greater credibility resulted from both refutational (mean $r = .113$) and nonrefutational (mean $r = .078$) two-sided messages.

The general credibility advantage of two-sided messages, however, appears restricted to advertising messages (mean $r = .148$). There was no significant difference in perceived credibility between one-sided and two-sided nonadvertising messages (mean $r = .036$). Indeed, the difference between advertising and nonadvertising messages in the size of the two-sided message's credibility advantage was itself marginally significant ($p < .10$).

No studies examined credibility effects with audiences having initially favorable or initially unfavorable attitudes. However, the general advantage of two-sided messages was obtained both in studies in which the audience had an initially neutral attitude (mean $r = .130$) and in studies in which the audience's initial attitude was indeterminant or mixed (mean $r = .066$).

Evidence about the possible effects of the audience's education level on the credibility advantage enjoyed by two-sided messages is limited, by virtue of most studies' having used undergraduate respondents. What very little evidence exists, however, does not hint at any dependable variation in effect across educational level.

Few studies examined credibility effects in circumstances in which counterargument availability was low, undermining any firm conclusions about the role of counterargument availability variations. But one may be confident that the credibility advantage of two-sided messages obtains in circumstances in which the audience has access to potential counterarguments (mean $r = .099$).

The order of materials in the two-sided message appears to influence the relative credibility advantage of one- and two-sided messages (although, again, the research evidence is not extensive). Two-sided messages led to significantly greater credibility than their one-sided counterparts when the two-sided messages either discussed supporting arguments first, followed by opposing arguments (mean $r = .096$), or discussed supporting and opposing considerations in an interwoven fashion (mean $r = .141$). By contrast, there was no significant difference in perceived credibility when the two-sided messages discussed opposing arguments before giving supporting arguments (mean $r = .014$), though few studies of this latter sort exist.

Message topic and other moderators. Because of the apparent importance of message topic variations (specifically, the contrast between advertising and nonadvertising messages) with respect to credibility effects, the joint operation of this moderator with other moderators invites inspection. Table 6.6 displays the credibility effects associated with the joint operation of message topic and each of the other moderator variables.

As will be apparent, the small number of available cases and the uneven distribution of cases across levels of the moderator variable impairs the usefulness of such analysis. For example, there were only four cases in which the audience had a distinguishable level of education other than that of college undergraduate (one case with respondents without any college education, three cases with respondents with college degrees), making impossible any useful examination of the interplay of the advertising-nonadvertising contrast with audience educational level. For similar reasons, it was not useful to consider the joint effects of message topic variations and variations in initial audience attitude or counterargument availability.

However, examination of the joint effect of message topic and two-sided message type indicated that refutational and nonrefutational forms had varying effects on credibility perceptions with advertising and nonadvertising messages. Specifically, for nonadvertising messages, refutational two-sided messages significantly enhanced credibility compared with their one-sided counterparts (mean $r = .117$), but nonrefutational two-sided messages did not (mean $r = -.035$). For advertising messages, nonrefutational two-sided messages produced significantly greater perceived credibility than one-sided messages (mean $r = .160$); refutational advertising messages did not dependably enhance credibility (mean $r = .089$), but there were very few relevant cases ($k = 4$). The enhanced credibility (compared with one-sided messages) of nonrefutational two-sided messages was significantly greater in advertising than in nonadvertising messages ($p < .01$).

With respect to the order of materials in two-sided messages, there were generally too few cases to permit confident conclusions. However, two-sided messages with interwoven supportive and opposing material produced

TABLE 6.4
Credibility Cases

Study	r	n	Codings
Alden & Crowley (1995)	.109	283	2/1/4/2/2/4
Allen et al. (1990)			
Replication 1			
refutational, 55 mph	.162	57	1/2/4/2/2/3
refutational, creationism	.280	58	1/2/4/2/2/2
refutational, sex education	.303	54	1/2/4/2/2/4
refutational, prochoice (2)	−.024	53	1/2/4/2/2/2
refutational, adopted kids	−.001	54	1/2/4/2/3/2
refutational, drunk drivers	.370	57	1/2/4/2/2/3
refutational, children's ads	.250	53	1/2/4/2/2/1
nonrefutational, 55 mph	.101	59	2/2/4/2/2/3
nonrefutational, creationism	.049	59	2/2/4/2/2/2
nonrefutational, sex education	−.142	58	2/2/4/2/2/3
nonrefutational, prochoice (2)	−.015	59	2/2/4/2/2/2
nonrefutational, adopted kids	−.085	60	2/2/4/2/3/2
nonrefutational, drunk drivers	−.193	60	2/2/4/2/2/3
nonrefutational, children's ads	−.095	56	2/2/4/2/2/1
Replication 2			
refutational, INF treaty	.122	50	1/2/4/2/1/3
refutational, running	−.061	50	2/2/4/2/2/1
refutational, advertising	.186	64	1/2/4/2/2/4
refutational, SATs	−.205	49	1/2/4/2/2/4
refutational, anarchy	.071	53	1/2/4/2/3/3
refutational, family counseling	.232	52	1/2/4/2/3/3
refutational, political spots	.191	49	1/2/4/2/2/4
nonrefutational, INF treaty	.051	50	2/2/4/2/1/3
nonrefutational, running	−.087	50	2/2/4/2/2/1
nonrefutational, advertising	−.143	70	2/2/4/2/2/4
nonrefutational, SATs	−.186	50	2/2/4/2/2/4
nonrefutational, anarchy	.020	89	2/2/4/2/3/3
nonrefutational, family counseling	.219	52	2/2/4/2/3/4
nonrefutational, political spots	−.291	49	2/2/4/2/2/4
Chebat & Picard (1988)	.086	434	2/1/2/2/2/4
Cho (1996)	.156	296	1/1/2/4/2/4
Crowley (1991) Study 2	.468	104	2/1/2/2/2/3
Earl (1979)	.003	372	2/1/2/2/2/4
Golden & Alpert (1978)	.168	292	2/1/4/4/2/3
Hastak & Park (1990)	−.043	124	2/1/2/2/2/2
Hunt, Domzal, & Kernan (1981)	.068	114	2/1/2/2/2/4
Hunt & Smith (1987)	−.202	150	1/1/2/2/2/4
Jones & Brehm (1970)	−.020	84	2/2/2/2/1/4
Kamins refutational	.208	410	1/1/2/2/2/3
Kamins nonrefutational	.188	257	2/1/2/2/2/3
Kamins (1989)	.185	76	1/1/2/3/2/1
Kamins et al. (1989)	.420	52	2/1/2/4/2/3

TABLE 6.4
(Continued)

Study	r	n	Codings
Kamins & Marks (1988)	.238	170	2/1/4/3/2/3
Kanungo & Johar (1975)	.060	96	2/1/2/3/2/4
Koehler (1972)	.029	360	1/2/4/2/3/3
Lilienthal (1973)	.091	120	2/2/4/2/3/3
Pechmann (1992)			
Study 1	.151	240	2/1/2/4/2/1
Study 2	.266	80	2/1/2/4/2/1
Sandler (1988)	.174	158	2/1/2/2/2/1
Smith & Hunt (1978)	.197	212	2/1/2/4/2/4
Stainback (1983)	−.038	100	1/2/4/1/2/3
Stayman et al. (1987)			
alarm clock	.072	180	2/1/2/2/2/1
record store	.095	180	2/1/2/2/2/1
Swinyard (1981)	.299	155	2/1/4/4/2/4
Thomas (1990)			
refutational	.110	130	1/2/4/4/3/3
nonrefutational	−.030	134	2/2/4/4/3/1

NOTE: The coding judgments, in order, are as follows: two-sided message type (1 = refutational, 2 = nonrefutational), topic area (1 = advertising, 2 = nonadvertising), audience initial attitude (1 = favorable, 2 = neutral, 3 = unfavorable, 4 = indeterminant/varied), audience educational level (1 = no college, 2 = some college, 3 = college graduate, 4 = indeterminant/varied), counterargument availability (1 = low, 2 = high, 3 = indeterminant/varied), order of arguments in two-sided message (1 = support then oppose, 2 = oppose then support, 3 = interwoven, 4 = indeterminant).

dependably greater credibility enhancement (relative to one-sided messages) in advertising messages (mean $r = .263$) than in nonadvertising messages (mean $r = .064$).

DISCUSSION

Some Key General Findings

Classic moderators. As discussed previously, variables such as initial audience attitude, audience education, counterargument availability, and order of arguments are commonly mentioned as moderators of the persuasive effects of sidedness variations. In the present findings, none of these variables displayed the typically ascribed effects.

There is no support for the conventional view that one-sided messages are to be preferred with audiences initially favorable to the advocated view, but

TABLE 6.5
Credibility Effects: Summary of Results

	k	mean r	95% CI	Q (df)
All cases	56	.091	.048, .134	126.0 (55)***
Refutational	20	.113	.047, .179	41.2 (19)**
Nonrefutational	36	.078	.023, .133	84.5 (35)***
Advertising	22	.148	.085, .211	62.2 (21)***
Nonadvertising	34	.036	−.018, .090	47.3 (33)*
Neutral initial attitude	19	.130	.057, .202	56.6 (18)***
Indeterminant/varied attitude	37	.066	.014, .118	66.2 (36)**
No college education	1	−.038		
Some college education	44	.065	.016, .113	95.2 (43)***
College graduate	3	.178	.070, .285	2.0 (2)
Indeterminant/varied education	9	.181	.096, .266	13.5 (8)
High counterargument availability	43	.099	.044, .153	114.9 (42)***
Low counterargument availability	3	.037	−.111, .185	0.6 (2)
Indeterminant/varied availability	10	.050	−.010, .110	6.1 (9)
Support-then-oppose order	11	.096	.021, .171	12.8 (10)
Oppose-then-support order	7	.014	−.078, .107	5.3 (6)
Alternation/interwoven	20	.141	.066, .216	47.3 (19)***
Indeterminant/varied order	18	.056	−.028, .141	50.1 (17)***

NOTE: Studies that provided a within-study comparison of interest (e.g., a study that included college undergraduates and college graduates, with results reported separately for these conditions) contributed effect sizes to both the relevant specific categories ("some college education" and "college graduate") and the "indeterminant/varied" category. As a result, the number of cases summed across levels of a given moderator sometimes exceeds the total number of cases (56).
*$p < .05$; **$p < .01$; ***$p < .001$.

that two-sided messages are more persuasive with opposed audiences. There have been relatively few studies in which the audience's initial attitude was either favorable or unfavorable, but in both such circumstances one-sided messages appear to enjoy a dependable persuasive advantage.

The typical summary suggests that lower levels of audience education recommend the use of one-sided messages, whereas at higher levels of education two-sided messages are to be preferred. There is only limited evidence available on this question, but the evidence in hand gives no support for such a view.

A common suggestion is that as the audience has more counterarguments ready to hand, the persuasive advantage of two-sided messages will correspondingly increase. There is little empirical evidence bearing on this claim, in good part because few studies have examined the persuasive effects of sidedness variations under conditions in which the audience might be presumed to have relatively little access to counterarguments. What evidence is available, however, gives this suggestion no support.

Finally, contrary to previous suggestions, the present review found no overall dependable differences among the various ways of organizing two-sided messages. For instance, there is no indication here that two-sided messages have a persuasive advantage when opposing materials are discussed after supporting materials but not when opposing materials are discussed before supporting materials.

Refutational and nonrefutational two-sided messages. Previous reviews have pointed to the importance of distinguishing refutational and nonrefutational two-sided forms (Allen, 1991, 1994; Jackson & Allen, 1987), a conclusion underscored by the present findings. Refutational two-sided messages do appear to enjoy a persuasive advantage (over one-sided messages) that nonrefutational two-sided messages do not.

But this advantage may be less general than previously supposed. In particular, although there is a substantial difference between refutational and nonrefutational forms in persuasive effectiveness for nonadvertising messages, that difference appears to be muted for advertising messages. For nonadvertising messages, refutational two-sided messages are significantly more persuasive than one-sided messages, and nonrefutational two-sided messages are significantly less persuasive than one-sided messages; the 95% confidence intervals for these mean effects do not overlap. For advertising messages, neither refutational nor nonrefutational two-sided messages are significantly more persuasive than their one-sided counterparts; the relevant 95% confidence intervals overlap substantially. Taken at face value, these results suggest that the effects of refutational and nonrefutational messages (compared with one-sided messages) are not consistent across advertising and nonadvertising contexts.

However, one should bear in mind the relatively small number of studies of the persuasive effects of refutational advertising ($k = 9$). Given this number of cases, and given the surface similarity in mean persuasive advantages of refutational messages over one-sided messages in nonadvertising (mean $r = .081$) and advertising (mean $r = .072$) contexts, one might entertain a suspicion that in fact there are consistent effects of refutational messages (compared with their one-sided counterparts) in advertising and nonadvertising circumstances.

But it is more difficult to sustain a belief that nonrefutational messages have consistent effects across these contexts. The number of nonrefutational advertising studies is substantial ($k = 26$), and yet the persuasive effects in these studies vary from those observed in nonadvertising studies. In nonadvertising contexts, nonrefutational messages produce significantly less persuasion than do one-sided messages, but no such significant difference obtains in the case of advertising messages. As a result, in nonadvertising

TABLE 6.6
Credibility Effects: Message Topic and Other Moderators

	Advertising	Nonadvertising
Two-sided message type		
refutational		
mean r	.089	.117
95% CI	−.101, .280	.045, .190
k	4	16
Q (df)	19.6 (3)***	21.3 (15)
nonrefutational		
mean r	.160	−.035
95% CI	.095, .225	−.093, .023
k	18	18
Q (df)	42.4 (17)***	14.9 (17)
Audience initial attitude		
neutral		
mean r	.136	−.020
95% CI	.062, .211	
k	18	1
Q (df)	54.9 (17)***	
indeterminant/varied		
mean r	.192	.038
95% CI	.109, .276	−.017, .094
k	4	33
Q (df)	4.5 (3)	47.1 (32)*
Audience education		
no college		
mean r		−.038
k	0	1
some college		
mean r	.102	.039
95% CI	.014, .190	−.020, .099
k	13	31
Q (df)	44.7 (12)***	45.5 (30)*
college graduate		
mean r	.178	
95% CI	.070, .285	
k	3	0
Q (df)	2.0 (2)	
indeterminant/varied		
mean r	.209	.039
95% CI	.136, .282	−.098, .177
k	7	2
Q (df)	6.5 (6)	1.3 (1)

contexts there is a sharp difference between refutational and nonrefutational two-sided forms compared with one-sided messages, but that difference is not so marked in advertising contexts.

TABLE 6.6
(Continued)

	Advertising	Nonadvertising
Counterargument availability		
high		
mean *r*	.148	.022
95% CI	.086, .211	−.062, .105
k	22	21
Q (*df*)	62.2 (21)***	40.1 (20)**
low		
mean *r*		.037
95% CI		−.111, .185
k	0	3
Q (*df*)		0.6 (2)
indeterminant/varied		
mean *r*		.050
95% CI		−.010, .110
k	0	10
Q (*df*)		6.1 (9)
Order of two-sided materials		
support then oppose		
mean *r*	.141	−.007
95% CI	.076, .207	−.131, .115
k	6	5
Q (*df*)	2.9 (5)	4.4 (4)
oppose then support		
mean *r*	−.043	.036
95% CI		−.073, .144
k	1	6
Q (*df*)		4.7 (5)
alternation/interwoven		
mean *r*	.263	.064
95% CI	.151, .375	−.008, .136
k	6	14
Q (*df*)	11.7 (5)*	16.0 (13)
indeterminant/varied		
mean *r*	.089	.007
95% CI	−.002, .181	−.140, .155
k	9	9
Q (*df*)	26.9 (8)***	20.5 (8)**

*$p < .05$; **$p < .01$; ***$p < .001$.

Effects on Credibility. Although credibility has often been mentioned as a possible mediator of sidedness effects (e.g., Allen, 1991, 1994), previous reviews have not systematically considered the effects of sidedness variations on credibility perceptions. One striking general aspect of the present results is the absence of a general parallelism between effects on persuasion and effects on credibility. If credibility perceptions were the key mediating factor influencing the persuasive effects of sidedness variations, then, broadly speaking, the patterns of effects (of sidedness variations) on credibility perceptions should mirror the patterns of effects on persuasive outcomes. But there is no such simple mirroring in these results. For example, even though two-sided messages yield generally greater credibility than their one-sided counterparts, there is no corresponding general difference in persuasiveness between one- and two-sided messages. Such divergences suggest that we cannot explain sidedness's persuasive effects satisfactorily by positing a simple mediating role for credibility.

Previous Explanations

Earlier explanations of sidedness effects sought to account for then-current understandings of the patterns of outcomes associated with sidedness variations. Perhaps it is unsurprising that these explanations prove unsatisfactory in accounting for the present results.

Counterargument Availability. Hovland et al.'s (1949, esp. pp. 270-271) explanation of sidedness effects emphasized one key general moderating factor and two possible mediating factors. A central moderating role was given to the receiver's ability to generate counterarguments (that is, arguments opposed to the advocated view). The suggestion was that for persons capable of generating counterarguments (e.g., persons initially opposed to the advocated view, or persons with greater educational achievement or intellectual capability), two-sided messages will be more persuasive than one-sided messages; for persons not so capable of generating counterarguments, one-sided messages will be more persuasive than two-sided messages.

Two mediating states were mentioned as possibly underlying such effects. One was the receiver's judgment of the communicator's credibility; for persons capable of generating counterarguments, the one-sided message was thought to appear to be biased and so would be less persuasive. The other was the audience's mental rehearsal of counterarguments; the expectation was that for persons capable of generating such counterarguments, the one-sided message would fail to forestall such rehearsal (compared with the two-sided message), thus impairing its persuasive effectiveness.

This account does not fare well given the evidence of the present review. Though the research evidence is limited, there is no indication that the hypothesized key moderating factor—the audience's availability of counter arguments—influences the relative persuasiveness of one-sided and two sided messages. Moreover, the findings concerning more specific factors tha might influence counterargument availability (namely, the audience's initia position and educational level), though also based on small numbers of cases. offer no support to this account: Educational level appears not to influence the persuasiveness of one- and two-sided messages, and one-sided messages are significantly more persuasive than two-sided messages for both initially unfavorable and initially favorable audiences. And, finally, sidedness's effects on credibility do not mirror its effects on persuasive outcomes in the fashion this explanation would suggest.

Reactance. A reactance-based explanation of sidedness effects has been offered by Brehm and Brehm (1981, pp. 12-15; see also Brehm, 1966). These authors suggest that, at least among persons who are aware of the existence of two plausible sides on the issue, two-sided messages will be more persuasive than one-sided messages because a one-sided message represents greater pressure to endorse the advocated view, which will arouse reactance (and thus behavior aimed at restoring threatened freedom). Hence the advantage of two-sided messages would be expected to be especially marked when the audience knows of opposing views—as they would if they held such opposing views, or if they had counterarguments readily available. But such factors do not appear to moderate sidedness effects in the expected ways. As one example, one-sided messages are significantly more persuasive than two-sided messages when audiences are either initially favorable or initially unfavorable.

We might revise this original reactance explanation by attending to the distinction between refutational and nonrefutational two-sided messages. Refutational two-sided messages probably represent greater pressure to endorse than do one-sided messages; refutational two-sided messages have the supporting argumentation characteristic of one-sided messages, plus an explicit attack on counterarguments. By contrast, a nonrefutational two-sided message at least leaves open the possibility that an opposing view would have some merit, and so plausibly might be supposed to represent less pressure to endorse than would a one-sided message. Thus a revised reactance account might suggest that, at least among receivers aware of the existence of two plausible sides, refutational two-sided messages would be the least persuasive (because they represent the greatest pressure to agree), nonrefutational two-sided messages the most persuasive (because they represent the least pressure), and one-sided messages somewhere in between. But even this revised account finds little support in the present findings. For example, among receivers with relatively high availability of counterarguments, refutational two-sided messages are significantly *more* persuasive than one-sided messages—precisely opposite to the expected effect.

Elaboration-Based Message Evaluation. Hale et al. (1991) propose a model in which sidedness variations influence elaboration (the generation of topic-relevant thoughts), which then influences global message evaluations (about bias, fairness, accuracy, and so on), which in turn influence receivers' attitudes. Thus this account suggests that, for instance, a refutational two-sided message might lead receivers to have a greater number of positive thoughts about the position advocated than would a one-sided message, which would lead the two-sided message to be evaluated more positively than the one-sided message, which in turn causes the two-sided message to be more persuasive.

It is difficult to reconcile this model with the research evidence reviewed here. On this account, credibility-related beliefs (evaluations of the degree to which the message is fair, unbiased, informed, and so on) play a key mediating role, and indeed are the proximate cause of sidedness-related attitude change effects. Hence as credibility judgments vary, so (ceteris paribus) should persuasiveness. But, as discussed previously, no such parallelism obtains.

Accounting for Sidedness Effects

The elaboration likelihood model (ELM) describes three possible ways in which a given variable might influence the amount and direction of attitude change (see Petty & Cacioppo, 1986, pp. 16-19): by serving as a persuasive argument, by serving as a peripheral cue, or by influencing the direction or extent of elaboration (issue-relevant thinking). The ELM permits a variable to function in more than one of these ways in different circumstances; for instance, the physical attractiveness of the communicator might commonly serve as a peripheral cue (affecting the receiver's liking for the communicator, and so influencing the operation of a heuristic principle based on liking) but in some circumstances serve as an argument (e.g., in advertisements for beauty products). This might offer a useful framework for explaining sidedness effects.[4]

Nonadvertising Messages. Consider first the case of nonadvertising messages. Sidedness variations might be thought of simply as producing variations in argumentative content (persuasive arguments). Compared with their one-sided counterparts, a nonrefutational two-sided message provides additional arguments opposing the advocated view and a refutational two-sided message provides additional arguments supporting the advocated view. Approached in this way, it is perhaps unsurprising that nonrefutational nonadvertising messages should prove significantly less persuasive, and refutational nonadvertising messages significantly more persuasive, than one-sided messages.

One curiosity concerning the observed effects in nonadvertising contexts is that nonrefutational two-sided messages do not enjoy the same credibility advantage (over one-sided messages) that refutational two-sided messages do. The curiosity arises because, in some sense, the refutational two-sided message does not actually concede anything to opposing views (because it tries to undermine possible counterarguments). The nonrefutational two-sided message might, at least on its face, seem to offer a more candid, less biased, appraisal of the advocated view (because it acknowledges shortcomings without attempting to undermine them). It may simply be that, in nonadvertising contexts, refutation of counterarguments conveys authoritativeness in a way that nonrefutational acknowledgment of counterarguments does not.

Nonrefutational Advertising Messages. Advertising messages present a somewhat more complex picture. Consider first the case of nonrefutational advertising messages. Broadly put, nonrefutational messages do not suffer the same negative consequences in advertising contexts as they do in nonadvertising contexts. In nonadvertising contexts, nonrefutational messages gain no credibility advantage over their one-sided counterparts and are significantly less persuasive; but in advertising contexts, nonrefutational messages are perceived as more credible than their one-sided counterparts and are not significantly different in persuasiveness.

The observed difference in credibility effects between advertising and nonadvertising contexts may reflect the receiver's differing initial expectations about the communicator. Consumer advertising is likely to be met with a good deal of skepticism (about advertising in general or about the specific advertisement encountered). Indeed, by the time they are adolescents, people are "already about as mistrustful of advertising as they can reasonably be" (Boush, Friestad, & Rose, 1994, p. 172). Given this general skepticism, consumers may well anticipate that advertisers will give a one-sided depiction of the advertised product or service, suppressing any undesirable aspects of the advertised object. When instead an advertiser freely acknowledges the opposing considerations, the advertiser's credibility will naturally be enhanced. This effect thus may be related to the well-established finding that communicators advocating unexpected positions (e.g., positions opposed to their apparent self-interests) can enjoy enhanced credibility (Eagly & Chaiken, 1975; Eagly, Wood, & Chaiken, 1978; Walster, Aronson, & Abrahams, 1966; Wood & Eagly, 1981).

Thus nonrefutational acknowledgment of counterarguments boosts the credibility of advertising but not nonadvertising, because the greater initial cynicism regarding advertising permits such acknowledgment to have positive effects on credibility for advertising messages. For nonadvertising messages, the absence of initial skepticism makes any nonrefutational acknowledgment of counterarguments comparatively less surprising (and so relatively ineffective in enhancing credibility).

And, correspondingly, nonrefutational acknowledgment of counterarguments damages the persuasiveness of nonadvertising messages but not that of advertising messages. For nonadvertising messages, whose communicators do not face the entrenched cynicism encountered by advertisers, acknowledgment of counterarguments may not enhance their credibility very much (and so will not enhance acceptance of their supportive reasons), but instead can simply arm the audience with apparently good reasons (persuasive arguments) for rejecting the advocated view, leading to the observed dependably negative effect on persuasion.

For advertising messages, the credibility-enhancement effect of the nonrefutational acknowledgment of counterarguments could have varying effects. It might enhance the believability of both the supportive arguments and the acknowledged counterarguments, with these effects generally canceling each other out. It might boost the counterarguments more than the supportive arguments, thus making the advertisement less persuasive than it would have been. Or the supportive arguments might enjoy the greater benefit of the credibility enhancement, thereby making the advertisement more persuasive. Across a number of nonrefutational advertisements, then, one might well expect to find no dependable overall difference in persuasiveness but a good deal of heterogeneity in effects—which is precisely the pattern observed here.

But these diverse persuasion effects might arise in another way. The enhanced credibility might operate not as a peripheral cue (enhancing the general believability of the message) but as a goad to elaboration. That is, the unexpected candor of a nonrefutational advertising message might evoke closer message scrutiny—which could produce either enhanced or reduced persuasion (depending on, inter alia, the character of the arguments encountered).

Refutational Advertising Messages. As noted earlier, the paucity of relevant studies permits no more than a suspicion that refutational advertising messages are generally more persuasive than their one-sided counterparts. But if refutational advertising messages are eventually shown to be genuinely more persuasive than one-sided messages, it will be worth considering that this effect might come about in various ways. For instance, the effect might be a consequence of the difference in argument content between refutational two-sided messages and one-sided messages (as, ex hypothesi, is the case for nonadvertising messages). Or the appearance of refutation might boost the advertisement's credibility, which in turn leads to enhanced attention to the actual content of the message, which—so long as the argumentative content is of the right sort—leads to enhanced persuasion. The general point is this: Even if refutational messages enjoy a persuasive advantage in both advertising and nonadvertising contexts, that advantage might arise through different processes in the two circumstances (pace William of Ockham). Given the different effects of nonrefutational forms in advertising and nonadvertising contexts, one ought not too easily assume that refutational forms will function identically in the two circumstances.

Nonadvertising Messages Reconsidered. The observed effects suggest that in nonadvertising contexts, persuaders would generally be well-advised to employ refutational two-sided messages in preference to one-sided or nonrefutational two-sided messages. In such contexts, refutational messages enjoy both significantly greater credibility and significantly greater persuasiveness than do one-sided messages, and nonrefutational messages are dependably less persuasive than one-sided messages.

However, this general expectation might be tempered somewhat by a consideration of the effects observed in advertising contexts. As discussed above, the enhanced credibility of nonrefutational two-sided advertising messages (compared with one-sided messages) might reflect the audience's initial anticipation that advertisers will give only a one-sided picture. If so, then it may not be the advertising context per se that gives rise to the phenomenon of credibility enhancement through nonrefutational messages, but rather the background expectations of receivers. That is, whenever receivers have the relevant expectations, such credibility-enhancing effects might be expected. For example, in the domain of risk communication, in circumstances in which a communicator might be expected to discuss only risks or only benefits (e.g., of a given technology or physical/biological hazard), credibility might be enhanced by nonrefutational discussion of both (see Rowan, 1994, p. 405). The general point is that, even given the overall apparent advantage of refutational two-sided messages in nonadvertising contexts, such contexts might nevertheless contain circumstances in which nonrefutational two-sided messages could provide credibility enhancement.

Future Research

Future sidedness research might usefully be directed in four broad ways. First, additional primary research is needed concerning the effects of refutational two-sided advertising messages. The extant research hints that refutational advertising messages are both more credible and more persuasive than one-sided messages, but too few implementations have been studied to permit confident conclusions.

Second, conceptual attention to the particulars of sidedness variations seems warranted. For example, even in nonadvertising contexts, a refutational two-sided message is not guaranteed to be more persuasive than a one-sided message (e.g., Halverson, 1975). Thus a good deal would appear to turn on exactly how the various sidedness treatments are implemented. Surely, for instance, in a refutational two-sided message, it will matter just what counterarguments are refuted; a message refuting implausible minor objections might not have effects identical to those of a message refuting plausible and serious objections. Similarly, in nonrefutational two-sided messages, it might plausibly be supposed that effects could vary depending upon the nature of the opposing considerations that are acknowledged. Systematic conceptualization and study of such variations would plainly be useful (for efforts along such lines, see Crowley & Hoyer, 1994; Pechmann, 1990).

Third (and related to the preceding point), the possibility that the persuasive effects of sidedness variations will sometimes be a consequence of argumentative-content variations (as opposed to, say, the operation of heuristic principles) deserves careful attention. With a sharper conceptualization of argumentative-content variations, researchers might, for instance, examine the numbers and kinds of thoughts generated in different circumstances by different sidedness implementations (for work in this vein, see Hale et al., 1991).

Finally, exploration of the role of initial receiver skepticism seems warranted. Differences in initial mistrust might be responsible for the observed differences in the perceived credibility of nonrefutational messages in advertising and nonadvertising contexts (with nonrefutational two-sided messages perceived to be more credible than one-sided messages in advertising contexts but not in nonadvertising contexts). This possibility might be explored through systematic examination of the relationship between sidedness effects and receivers' background expectations about messages, both in advertising contexts and in nonadvertising circumstances potentially characterized by such mistrust.

NOTES

1. Jackson and Allen (1987) located only three estimates of the effect of sidedness on credibility, and hence did not analyze these closely.

2. The term *advertising* is used here to refer specifically to advertising for consumer products or services. This is potentially misleading, because in fact not all advertising is consumer advertising; for example, advertising can address sociopolitical issues (as when an individual or organization purchases advertising space to present a persuasive message on a public policy issue). But consumer product/service advertising is the most familiar form of advertising, hence the shorthand used here.

3. It would have been desirable to compare the present codings to those in previous reviews, but the only variable for which any previous reviews gave coding information was the nature of the two-sided message (refutational versus nonrefutational). For this variable, the present codings were compared with those of Jackson and Allen's (1987) review, Allen's (1991) review, and the discussion of Allen's (1991) review in O'Keefe (1993). Of the cases included in the present analysis, seven were coded differently here than in one or more previous reviews. Bettinghaus and Baseheart (1969), Etgar and Goodwin (1982), Hovland et al. (1949), Kanungo and Johar (1975), and Kaplowitz and Fisher (1985) were classified as refutational in Allen (1991, Table 2) but as nonrefutational in Jackson and Allen (1987), O'Keefe (1993), and the present review; Koballa (1984) was classified as refutational in Allen (1991) but as nonrefutational in O'Keefe (1993) and in the present review; and Lumsdaine and Janis (1953) was classified as refutational in Allen (1991), Jackson and Allen (1987), and O'Keefe (1993), but nonrefutational in the present review. I discuss all these differences, and rationales for the present codings, in O'Keefe (1993, pp. 88-90, 94n2).

4. Hale et al.'s (1991) model is putatively based on the elaboration likelihood model (but see their note 1, p. 388, for a disclaimer), though it invokes concepts such as "central persuasive cue" (p. 388) that are alien to the ELM (see Petty, Kasmer, Haugtvedt, & Cacioppo, 1987, p. 236).

REFERENCES

Note: Asterisks indicate studies included in the meta-analysis.

*Ahlawat, S. S. (1991). The relative effects of comparative and noncomparative advertising on evaluation processes. *Dissertation Abstracts International, 51,* 2810A. (University Microfilms No. AAG90-35375)

*Alden, D. L., & Crowley, A. E. (1995). Improving the effectiveness of condom advertising: A research note. *Health Marketing Quarterly, 12*(4), 25-38.

Allen, M. (1991). Meta-analysis comparing the persuasiveness of one-sided and two-sided messages. *Western Journal of Speech Communication, 55,* 390-404.

Allen, M. (1993). Determining the persuasiveness of message sidedness: A prudent note about utilizing research summaries. *Western Journal of Communication, 57,* 98-103.

Allen, M. (1994). The persuasive effects of one and two sided messages. In M. Allen & R. W. Preiss (Eds.), *Prospects and precautions in the use of meta-analysis* (pp. 101-125). Dubuque, IA: Brown & Benchmark.

*Allen, M., Hale, J., Mongeau, P., Berkowitz-Stafford, S., Stafford, S., Shanahan, W., Agee, P., Dillon, K., Jackson, R., & Ray, C. (1990). Testing a model of message sidedness: Three replications. *Communication Monographs, 57,* 275-291.

*Alpert, M. I., & Golden, L. L. (1982). The impact of education on the relative effectiveness of one-sided and two-sided communications. In B. J. Walker, W. O. Bearden, W. R. Darden, P. E. Murphy, J. R. Nevin, J. C. Olson, & B. A. Weitz (Eds.), *An assessment of marketing thought and practice* (pp. 30-33). Chicago: American Marketing Association.

Anderson, W. T., Jr., & Golden, L. L. (1984). Bank promotion strategy. *Journal of Advertising Research, 24*(2), 53-65.

Assael, H., & Kamins, M. A. (1989). Effects of appeal type and involvement on product disconfirmation: A cognitive response approach through product trial. *Journal of the Academy of Marketing Science, 17,* 197-207.

*Belch, G. E. (1980). An investigation of the effects of advertising message structure and repetition upon cognitive processes mediating message acceptance. *Dissertation Abstracts International, 41,* 376A. (University Microfilms No. AAG80-15951)

*Belch, G. E. (1981). An examination of comparative and noncomparative television commercials: The effects of claim variation and repetition on cognitive response and message acceptance. *Journal of Marketing Research, 18,* 333-349.

Belch, G. E. (1983). The effects of message modality on one- and two-sided advertising messages. In R. P. Bagozzi & A. M. Tybout (Eds.), *Advances in consumer research* (Vol. 10, pp. 21-26). Ann Arbor, MI: Association for Consumer Research.

*Bettinghaus, E. P., & Baseheart, J. R. (1969). Some specific factors affecting attitude change. *Journal of Communication, 19,* 227-238.

Bettinghaus, E. P., & Cody, M. J. (1987). *Persuasive communication* (4th ed.). New York: Holt, Rinehart & Winston.

Birkimer, J. C., Barbee, A. P., Francis, M. L., Berry, M. M., Deuser, P. S., & Pope, J. R. (1994). Effects of refutational messages, thought provocation, and decision deadlines on signing to donate organs. *Journal of Applied Social Psychology, 24,* 1735-1761.

Boush, D. M., Friestad, M., & Rose, G. M. (1994). Adolescent skepticism toward TV advertising and knowledge of advertiser tactics. *Journal of Consumer Research, 21,* 165-175.

Brehm, J. W. (1966). *A theory of psychological reactance.* New York: Academic Press.

Brehm, S. S., & Brehm, J. W. (1981). *Psychological reactance: A theory of freedom and control.* New York: Academic Press.

Brenner, L. A., Koehler, D. J., & Tversky, A. (1996). On the evaluation of one-sided evidence. *Journal of Behavioral Decision Making, 9,* 59-70.

*Chebat, J. -C., Filiatrault, P., Laroche, M., & Watson, C. (1988). Compensatory effects of cognitive characteristics of the source, the message, and the receiver upon attitude change. *Journal of Psychology, 122,* 609-621.

*Chebat, J. -C., & Picard, J. (1985). The effects of price and message-sidedness on confidence in product and advertisement with personal involvement as a mediator variable. *International Journal of Research in Marketing, 2,* 129-141.

*Chebat, J. -C., & Picard, J. (1988). Receivers' self-acceptance and the effectiveness of two-sided messages. *Journal of Social Psychology, 128,* 353-362.

*Cho, J. -K. (1996). An examination of the attitudinal effects of comparative vs. noncomparative advertising and their causal paths in the context of message sidedness and product involvement. *Dissertation Abstracts International, 56,* 2919A-2920A. (University Microfilms No. AAI95-41589)

*Chu, G. C. (1967). Prior familiarity, perceived bias, and one-sided versus two-sided communications. *Journal of Experimental Social Psychology, 3,* 243-254.

*Crane, E. (1962). Immunization: With and without use of counter-arguments. *Journalism Quarterly, 39,* 445-450.

Cronen, V. E. (1976). The interaction of refutation type, involvement, and authoritativeness. In J. Blankenship & H. G. Stelzner (Eds.), *Rhetoric and communication: Studies in the University of Illinois tradition* (pp. 155-170). Urbana: University of Illinois Press.

*Crowley, A. E. (1991). The golden section: An information theoretic approach to understanding two-sided persuasion. *Dissertation Abstracts International, 51,* 3465A. (University Microfilms No. AAG91-05533)

Crowley, A. E., & Hoyer, W. D. (1994). An integrative framework for understanding two-sided persuasion. *Journal of Consumer Research, 20,* 561-574.

Deuser, P. S. (1989). The application of basic findings within the foot-in-the-door technique, attitude change, and bystander intervention literatures in developing techniques to procure pledges for organ donation. *Dissertation Abstracts International, 50,* 1687B-1688B. (University Microfilms No. AAG89-14137)

*Dipboye, R. L. (1977). The effectiveness of one-sided and two-sided appeals as a function of familiarization and context. *Journal of Social Psychology, 102,* 125-131.

*Dycus, R. D. (1976). Relative efficacy of a one-sided vs. two-sided communication in a simulated government evaluation of proposals. *Psychological Reports, 38,* 787-790.

Eagly, A. H., & Chaiken, S. (1975). An attribution analysis of the effect of communicator characteristics on opinion change: The case of communicator attractiveness. *Journal of Personality and Social Psychology, 32,* 136-144.

Eagly, A. H., & Chaiken, S. (1993). *The psychology of attitudes.* Fort Worth, TX: Harcourt Brace Jovanovich.

Eagly, A. H., Wood, W., & Chaiken, S. (1978). Causal inferences about communicators and their effect on opinion change. *Journal of Personality and Social Psychology, 36,* 424-435.

*Earl, R. L. (1979). An experimental investigation of the effects of advertisement structure, message sidedness, and test results on selected communication variables. *Dissertation Abstracts International, 39,* 4459A. (University Microfilms No. AAG79-00964)

*Earl, R. L., & Pride, W. M. (1980). The effects of advertisement structure, message-sidedness, and performance test results on print advertisement informativeness. *Journal of Advertising, 9*(3), 36-46.

Erez, A., Bloom, M. C., & Wells, M. T. (1996). Using random rather than fixed effects models in meta-analysis: Implications for situational specificity and validity generalization. *Personnel Psychology, 49,* 275-306.

*Etgar, M., & Goodwin, S. A. (1982). One-sided versus two-sided comparative message appeals for new brand introductions. *Journal of Consumer Research, 8,* 460-465.

Faison, E. W. J. (1961). Effectiveness of one-sided and two-sided mass communications in advertising. *Public Opinion Quarterly, 25,* 468-469.

*Ferguson, J. M., & Jackson, D. W., Jr. (1982). Negative information: Asset or liability? In B. J. Walker, W. O. Bearden, W. R. Darden, P. E. Murphy, J. R. Nevin, J. C. Olson, & B. A. Weitz (Eds.), *An assessment of marketing thought and practice* (pp. 34-38). Chicago: American Marketing Association.

*Ferrari, J. R., & Leippe, M. R. (1992). Noncompliance with persuasive appeals for a prosocial, altruistic act: Blood donating. *Journal of Applied Social Psychology, 22,* 83-101.

*Ford, L. A., & Smith, S. W. (1991). Memorability and persuasiveness of organ donation message strategies. *American Behavioral Scientist, 34,* 695-711.

*Gardner, M. P., & Levin, R. S. (1982). Truth and consequences: The effects of disclosing possibly harmful results of product use. In B. J. Walker, W. O. Bearden, W. R. Darden, P. E. Murphy, J. R. Nevin, J. C. Olson, & B. A. Weitz (Eds.), *An assessment of marketing thought and practice* (pp. 39-42). Chicago: American Marketing Association.

Gaudino, J. L., & Harris, A. C. (1988, July). *A strategy for maintaining public opinion support on a controversial issue: An empirical test of resistance theory.* Paper presented at the annual meeting of the Association for Education in Journalism and Mass Communication, Portland, OR. (ERIC Document Reproduction Service No. ED 296 386)

*Golden, L. L., & Alpert, M. I. (1978). The relative effectiveness of one-sided and two-sided communication for mass transit advertising. In H. K. Hunt (Ed.), *Advances in consumer research* (Vol. 5, pp. 12-18). Ann Arbor, MI: Association for Consumer Research.

*Golden, L. L., & Alpert, M. I. (1987). Comparative analysis of the relative effectiveness of one-sided and two-sided communication for contrasting products. *Journal of Advertising, 16*(1), 18-25.

Gore, S. A. (1976). An analysis of responses to one- versus two-sided communications. *Dissertation Abstracts International, 36,* 3671B-3672B. (University Microfilms No. AAG76-00101)

*Hale, J. L., Mongeau, P. A., & Thomas, R. M. (1991). Cognitive processing of one- and two-sided persuasive messages. *Western Journal of Speech Communication, 55,* 380-389.

*Halverson, R. R. (1975). Commitment, cognitive structure, and one- versus two-sided persuasive communications. *Dissertation Abstracts International, 35,* 6164B-6165B. (University Microfilms No. AAG75-13757)

*Hass, R. G., & Linder, D. E. (1972). Counterargument availability and the effects of message structure on persuasion. *Journal of Personality and Social Psychology, 23,* 219-233.

*Hastak, M., & Park, J. -W. (1990). Mediators of message sidedness effects on cognitive structure for involved and uninvolved audiences. In M. E. Goldberg, G. Gorn, & R. W. Pollay (Eds.), *Advances in consumer research* (Vol. 17, pp. 329-336). Provo, UT: Association for Consumer Research.

Havitz, M. E., & Crompton, J. L. (1990). The influence of persuasive messages on propensity to purchase selected recreational services from public or from commercial suppliers. *Journal of Leisure Research, 22,* 71-88.

*Hilyard, D. M. (1966). One-sided vs. two-sided messages: An experiment in counterconditioning. *Dissertation Abstracts, 27,* 1109A-1110A. (University Microfilms No. AAG66-08460)

*Hovland, C. I., Lumsdaine, A. A., & Sheffield, F. D. (1949). *Experiments on mass communication*. Princeton, NJ: Princeton UniversityPress.

*Hunt, J. M., Domzal, T. J., & Kernan, J. B. (1981). Causal attributions and persuasion: The case of disconfirmed expectancies. In A. A. Mitchell (Ed.), *Advances in consumer research* (Vol. 9, pp. 287-292). Ann Arbor, MI: Association for Consumer Research.

*Hunt, J. M., & Kernan, J. B. (1984). The role of disconfirmed expectancies in the processing of advertising messages. *Journal of Social Psychology, 124,* 227-236.

*Hunt, J. M., & Smith, M. F. (1987). The persuasive impact of two-sided selling appeals for an unknown brand name. *Journal of the Academy of Marketing Science, 15*(1), 11-18.

*Hunt, J. M., Smith, M. F., & Kernan, J. B. (1985). The effects of expectancy disconfirmation and argument strength on message processing level: An application to personal selling. In E. C. Hirschman & M. B. Holbrook (Eds.), *Advances in consumer research* (Vol. 12, pp. 450-454). Provo, UT: Association for Consumer Research.

*Hunt, J. M., Smith, M. F., & Kernan, J. B. (1989). Processing effects of expectancy-discrepant persuasive messages. *Psychological Reports, 65,* 1359-1376.

Insko, C. A. (1962). One-sided versus two-sided communications and countercommunications. *Journal of Abnormal and Social Psychology, 65,* 203-206.

Jackson, S. (1992). *Message effects research: Principles of design and analysis.* New York: Guilford.

Jackson, S., & Allen, M. (1987, May). *Meta-analysis of the effectiveness of one-sided and two-sided argumentation.* Paper presented at the annual meeting of the International Communication Association, Montreal.

*Jaksa, J. A. (1968). An experimental study of one-sided and two-sided argument with emphasis on three two-sided speeches. *Dissertation Abstracts, 28,* 4747A. (University Microfilms No. AAG68-06650)

Janis, I. L., & Feierabend, R. L. (1957). Effects of alternative ways of ordering pro and con arguments in persuasive communications. In C. I. Hovland (Ed.), *The order of presentation in persuasion* (pp. 115-128). New Haven, CT: Yale UniversityPress.

*Jarrett, R. F., & Sherriffs, A. C. (1953). Propaganda, debate, and impartial presentation as determiners of attitude change. *Journal of Abnormal and Social Psychology, 48,* 33-41.

Johnson, B. T. (1989). *DSTAT: Software for the meta-analytic review of research literatures.* Hillsdale, NJ: Lawrence Erlbaum.

Johnston, D. D. (1994). *The art and science of persuasion.* Dubuque, IA: Brown & Benchmark.

*Jones, D. B. (1987). Directiveness in promotional communications. *Dissertation Abstracts International, 48,* 1263A. (University Microfilms No. AAG87-19016)

*Jones, R. A., & Brehm, J. W. (1970). Persuasiveness of one- and two-sided communications as a function of awareness there are two sides. *Journal of Experimental Social Psychology, 6,* 47-56.

*Kamins, M. A. (1985). The impact of involvement, advertising type, and expectation level on product evaluation. *Dissertation Abstracts International, 45,* 2185A-2186A. (University Microfilms No. AAG84-15772)

*Kamins, M. A. (1989). Celebrity and noncelebrity advertising in a two-sided context. *Journal of Advertising Research, 29*(3), 34-42.

*Kamins, M. A., & Assael, H. (1987a). Moderating disconfirmation of expectations through the use of two-sided appeals: A longitudinal approach. *Journal of Economic Psychology, 8,* 237-254.

*Kamins, M. A., & Assael, H. (1987b). Two-sided versus one-sided appeals: A cognitive perspective on argumentation, source derogation, and the effect of disconfirming trial on belief change. *Journal of Marketing Research, 24,* 29-39.

*Kamins, M. A., Brand, M. J., Hoeke, S. A., & Moe, J. C. (1989). Two-sided versus one-sided celebrity endorsements: The impact on advertising effectiveness and credibility. *Journal of Advertising, 18*(2), 4-10.

*Kamins, M. A., & Marks, L. J. (1987). Advertising puffery: The impact of using two-sided claims on product attitude and purchase intention. *Journal of Advertising, 16*(4), 6-15.

*Kamins, M. A., & Marks, L. J. (1988). An examination into the effectiveness of two-sided comparative price appeals. *Journal of the Academy of Marketing Science, 16*(2), 64-71.

*Kanungo, R. N., & Johar, J. S. (1975). Effects of slogans and human model characteristics in product advertisements. *Canadian Journal of Behavioral Science, 7*, 127-138.

*Kaplowitz, S. A., & Fisher, B. J. (1985). Revealing the logic of free-riding and contributions to the nuclear freeze movement. *Research in Social Movements, Conflicts, and Change, 8*, 47-64.

Kasulis, J. J., & Zaltman, G. (1977). Message reception and cognitive complexity. In W. D. Perreault, Jr. (Ed.), *Advances in consumer research* (Vol. 4, pp. 93-97). Atlanta, GA: Association for Consumer Research.

Kennedy, B. N. (1982). Contact donors before making solicitations. *Fund Raising Management, 13*(9), 16-17.

*Kiesler, D. J. (1964). Personality factors and attitude and belief change from various types of communications. *Dissertation Abstracts, 25*, 1320. (University Microfilms No. AAG64-08400)

*Koballa, T. R., Jr. (1984). Changing attitudes toward energy conservation: The effect of development advancement on the salience of one-sided and two-sided persuasive communications. *Journal of Research in Science Teaching, 21*, 659-668.

*Koehler, J. W. (1972). Effects on audience opinion of one-sided and two-sided speeches supporting and opposing a proposition. In T. D. Beisecker & D. W. Parson (Eds.), *The process of social influence* (pp. 351-369). Englewood Cliffs, NJ: Prentice Hall.

Kohn, P. M., & Snook, S. (1976). Balanced vs. one-sided communications about drugs. *Journal of Drug Education, 6*, 272-281.

Kose, Z. J., & Winkel, F. W. (1982). Transplantatievoorlichting: De rol van argumentatie pro en contra het donorcodicil. *Gezondheid enSamenleving, 3*, 120-132.

Kotler, P. (1980). *Marketing management: Analysis, planning, and control* (4th ed.). Englewood Cliffs, NJ: Prentice Hall.

Koyama, S. A. (1982). Effects of television camera angle, locus of control, and two-sided/one-sided persuasive messages upon attitudes toward disabled people. *Dissertation Abstracts International, 42*, 5005A. (University Microfilms No. AAG82-12568)

Lawson, R. G. (1970). Relative effectiveness of one-sided and two-sided communications in courtroom persuasion. *Journal of General Psychology, 82*, 3-16.

*Ley, P., Bradshaw, P. W., Kincey, J. A., Couper-Smartt, J., & Wilson, M. (1974). Psychological variables in weight control. In W. L. Burland, P. D. Samuel, & J. Yudkin (Eds.), *Obesity symposium* (pp. 316-337). London: Churchill Livingstone.

*Ley, P., Whitworth, M. A., Woodward, R., & Yorke, R. (1977). The effects of sidedness and fear arousal on willingness to participate in a slimming scheme. *Health Education Journal, 36*, 67-69.

*Lilienthal, R. A. (1973). The effects of one- and two-sided presentation in fear-evoking persuasive communications. *Dissertation Abstracts International, 33*, 5497B. (University Microfilms No. AAG73-12416)

*Lumsdaine, A. A., & Janis, I. L. (1953). Resistance to "counterpropaganda" produced by one-sided and two-sided "propaganda" presentations. *Public Opinion Quarterly, 17*, 311-318.

Manis, M., & Blake, J. B. (1963). Interpretation of persuasive messages as a function of prior immunization. *Journal of Abnormal and Social Psychology, 66*, 225-230.

*McCroskey, J. C., Young, T. J., & Scott, M. D. (1972). The effects of message sidedness and evidence on inoculation against counterpersuasion in small group communication. *Speech Monographs, 39*, 5-212.

McGinnies, E. (1966). Studies in persuasion: III. Reactions of Japanese students to one-sided and two-sided communications. *Journal of Social Psychology, 70*, 87-93.

McGuire, W. J. (1985). Attitudes and attitude change. In G. Lindzey & E. Aronson (Eds.), *Handbook of social psychology* (3rd ed., Vol. 2, pp. 233-346). New York: Random House.

McGuire, W. J., & Papageorgis, D. (1961). The relative efficacy of various types of prior belief-defense in producing immunity against persuasion. *Journal of Abnormal and Social Psychology, 62*, 327-337.

*Merenski, P., & Mizerski, R. (1979). Cognitive effects of advertiser disclaimers. In S. E. Permut (Ed.), *Proceedings of the annual conference of the American Academy of Advertising 1979* (pp. 36-38). New Haven, CT: American Academy of Advertising.

Misra, S., & Jain, S. (1971). Effect of fittingness, type of goods, and type of slogan on brand awareness. *Journal of Applied Psychology, 55*, 580-585.

*Nathan, A. (1981). The effects of source credibility, message style, and group deliberation on mock jury decision-making. *Dissertation Abstracts International, 41*, 3236B. (University Microfilms No. AAG81-04085)

O'Connor, P. J., & Vann, J. W. (1979). Implications of refutational arguments for comparative advertising. In R. S. Franz, R. M. Hopkins, & A. G. Toma (Eds.), *Proceedings of the Southern Marketing Association* (pp. 79-82). Lafayette, LA: Southern Marketing Association.

O'Keefe, D. J. (1990). *Persuasion: Theory and research.* Newbury Park, CA: Sage.

O'Keefe, D. J. (1993). The persuasive effects of message sidedness variations: A cautionary note concerning Allen's (1991) meta-analysis. *Western Journal of Communication, 57*, 87-97.

*Papageorgis, D. (1963). Bartlett effect and the persistence of induced opinion change. *Journal of Abnormal and Social Psychology, 67*, 61-67.

*Pardini, A. U., & Katzev, R. D. (1986). Applying full-cycle social psychology to consumer marketing: The defusing objections technique. *Journal of Economic Psychology, 7*, 87-94.

*Paulson, S. F. (1953). Experimental study of spoken communications: The effects of prestige of the speaker and acknowledgement of opposing arguments on audience retention and shift of opinion. *Dissertation Abstracts, 13*, 270-271. (University Microfilms No. AAG00-04871)

*Paulson, S. F. (1954). The effects of the prestige of the speaker and acknowledgement of opposing arguments on audience retention and shift of opinion. *Speech Monographs, 21*, 267-271.

Pechmann, C. (1990). How do consumer inferences moderate the effectiveness of two-sided messages? In M. E. Goldberg, G. Gorn, & R. W. Pollay (Eds.), *Advances in consumer research* (Vol. 17, pp. 337-341). Provo, UT: Association for Consumer Research.

*Pechmann, C. (1992). Predicting when two-sided ads will be more effective than one-sided ads: The role of correlational and correspondent inferences. *Journal of Marketing Research, 29*, 441-453.

Petty, R. E., & Cacioppo, J. T. (1986). *Communication and persuasion: Central and peripheral routes to attitude change.* New York: Springer-Verlag.

Petty, R. E., Kasmer, J. A., Haugtvedt, C. P., & Cacioppo, J. T. (1987). Source and message factors in persuasion: A reply to Stiff's critique of the elaboration likelihood model. *Communication Monographs, 54*, 233-249.

Pratkanis, A. R., & Aronson, E. (1992). *Age of propaganda: The everyday use and abuse of persuasion.* New York: W. H. Freeman.

Ragon, B. M. (1996). Countering objections to health promotion programming: The objection/rebuttal approach. *Journal of Health Education, 27*, 190-193.

*Rahaim, G. L., Jr. (1984). Eyewitness evidence and the effects of psychological testimony. *Dissertation Abstracts International, 44,* 2599B. (University Microfilms No. AAG83-27134)

Raudenbush, S. W. (1994). Random effects models. In H. Cooper & L. V. Hedges (Eds.), *Handbook of research synthesis* (pp. 301-321). New York: Russell Sage Foundation.

Reardon, K. K. (1991). *Persuasion in practice.* Newbury Park, CA: Sage.

*Reinard, J. C. (1984). The role of Toulmin's categories of message development in persuasive communication: Two experimental studies on attitude change. *Journal of the American Forensic Association, 20,* 206-223.

*Reinard, J. C., & Reynolds, R. A. (1976, November). *An experimental study of the effects of Toulmin's pattern for argument development on attitude change.* Paper presented at the annual meeting of the Western Speech Communication Association, San Francisco. (ERIC Document Reproduction Service No. ED 133 782)

Reynolds, K. D., West, S. G., & Aiken, L. S. (1990). Increasing the use of mammography: A pilot program. *Health Education Quarterly, 17,* 429-441.

*Roering, K. J., & Paul, R. J. (1976). The effect of the consistency of product claims on the credibility of persuasive messages. *Journal of Advertising, 5*(2), 32-36.

*Rosnow, R. L. (1968). One-sided vs. two-sided communication under indirect awareness of persuasive intent. *Public Opinion Quarterly, 32,* 95-101.

Rowan, K. E. (1994). The technical and democratic approaches to risk situations: Their appeal, limitations, and rhetorical alternative. *Argumentation, 8,* 391-409.

*Sandler, D. M. (1988). Consumer involvement as a mediator of advertising "content" vs. "form." *Dissertation Abstracts International, 48,* 1835A-1836A. (University Microfilms No. AAG87-22926)

Sawyer, A. G. (1973). The effects of repetition of refutational and supportive advertising appeals. *Journal of Marketing Research, 10,* 23-33.

*Schanck, R. C., & Goodman, C. (1939). Reactions to propaganda on both sides of a controversial issue. *Public Opinion Quarterly, 3,* 107-112.

*Settle, R. B., & Golden, L. L. (1974). Attribution theory and advertiser credibility. *Journal of Marketing Research, 11,* 181-185.

Shadish, W. R., & Haddock, C. K. (1994). Combining estimates of effect size. In H. Cooper & L. V. Hedges (Eds.), *Handbook of research synthesis* (pp. 261-281). New York: Russell Sage Foundation.

Sheagren, J. R. (1997). Reducing negative social stereotypes: An examination of predictive empathy. *Masters Abstracts International, 35,* 911. (University Microfilms No. AAG13-82758)

*Sherman, E., Greene, J. N., & Plank, R. E. (1991). Exploring business-to-business direct mail campaigns: Comparing one-sided, two-sided, and comparative message structures. *Journal of Direct Marketing, 5*(2), 25-30.

Shimp, T. A. (1990). *Promotion management and marketing communications* (2nd ed.). Chicago: Dryden.

*Sinha, D., & Dhawan, N. (1971). Nature of communication, intelligence, suggestibility, and attitude change. *Journal of the Indian Academy of Applied Psychology, 8*(3), 53-58.

Skilbeck, C., Tulips, J., & Ley, P. (1977). The effects of fear arousal, fear position, fear exposure, and sidedness on compliance with dietary instructions. *European Journal of Social Psychology, 7,* 221-239.

*Smith, R. E., & Hunt, S. D. (1978). Attributional processes and effects in promotional situations. *Journal of Consumer Research, 5,* 149-158.

Smith, S. W., Kopfman, J. M., Morrison, K., & Ford, L. A. (1993, May). *The effects of message sidedness, fear, and prior thought and intent on the memorability and persuasiveness of organ donor card message strategies.* Paper presented at the annual meeting of the International Communication Association, Washington, DC.

*Smith, S. W., Morrison, K., Kopfman, J. E., & Ford, L. A. (1994). The influence of prior thought and intent on the memorability and persuasiveness of organ donation message strategies. *Health Communication, 6,* 1-20.

*Smith, S. W., Morrison, K., Molnar, J. E., & Ford, L. A. (1992, October). *The influence of prior thought and intent on the memorability and persuasiveness of organ donation message strategies.* Paper presented at the annual meeting of the Speech Communication Association, Chicago.

*Sorrentino, R. M., Bobocel, D. R., Gitta, M. Z., Olson, J. M., & Hewitt, E. C. (1988). Uncertainty orientation and persuasion: Individual differences in the effects of personal relevance on social judgments. *Journal of Personality and Social Psychology, 55,* 357-371.

*Stainback, R. D. (1983). The effects of source expertise, message style, and threat appeals on adolescents' intentions to drink alcohol. *Dissertation Abstracts International, 43,* 3777B. (University Microfilms No. AAG83-03355)

*Stainback, R. D., & Rogers, R. W. (1983). Identifying effective components of alcohol abuse prevention programs: Effects of fear appeals, message style, and source expertise. *International Journal of the Addictions, 18,* 393-405.

*Stayman, D., Hoyer, W., & Leon, R. (1987). *Attribute importance in discounting product features in advertising.* Paper presented at the American Marketing Association's Summer Educator's Conference, Toronto.

*Swanson, L. A. (1983). The persuasive effect of volunteering negative information in advertising. *Dissertation Abstracts International, 44,* 562A. (University Microfilms No. AAG83-14750)

*Swanson, L. A. (1987). The persuasive effect of volunteering negative information in advertising. *International Journal of Advertising, 6,* 237-248.

*Swinyard, W. R. (1981). The interaction between comparative advertising and copy claim variation. *Journal of Marketing Research, 18,* 175-186.

Thistlethwaite, D. L., & Kamenetzky, J. (1955). Attitude change through refutation and elaboration of audience counterarguments. *Journal of Abnormal and Social Psychology, 51,* 3-12.

Thistlethwaite, D. L., Kamenetzky, J., & Schmidt, H. (1956). Factors influencing attitude change through refutative communications. *Speech Monographs, 23,* 14-25.

*Thomas, R. M. (1990). The impact of message sidedness on attitudes. *Masters Abstracts International, 28,* 476. (University Microfilms No. AAG13-40460)

Walster, E., Aronson, E., & Abrahams, D. (1966). On increasing the persuasiveness of a low prestige communicator. *Journal of Experimental Social Psychology, 2,* 325-342.

Welford, T. D. (1972). An experimental study of the effectiveness of humor used as a refutational device. *Dissertation Abstracts International, 32,* 7120A. (University Microfilms No. AAG72-17822)

Weston, J. R. (1968). Argumentative message structure and prior familiarity as predictors of source credibility and attitude change. *Dissertation Abstracts, 28,* 3772A. (University Microfilms No. AAG68-04234)

*Williams, K. D., Bourgeois, M. J., & Croyle, R. T. (1993). The effects of stealing thunder in criminal and civil trials. *Law and Human Behavior, 17,* 597-609.

*Williams, T. G. (1976). Effects of an advertising warning message on consumer attitudes and buying intentions. In K. L. Bernhardt (Ed.), *Marketing: 1776-1976 and beyond* (pp. 362-367). Chicago: American Marketing Association.

*Winkel, F. W. (1984). Public communication on donor cards: A comparison of persuasive styles. *Social Science and Medicine, 19,* 957-963.

Winkel, F. W., & Huismans, F. W. (1986). Refutational messages on donor cards: A test of boomerang effects. *Psychological Reports, 59,* 899-910.

*Winkel, F. W., & Kosc, Z. J. (1983). Het donorcodicil: Traditionele versus relativerende voorlichting. *Gezondheid en Samenleving, 4,* 229-237.

Wolfinger, R. E. (1955). *Attitude change toward source and issue resulting from one-sided and two-sided communication.* Unpublished master's thesis, University of Illinois, Urbana-Champaign.

Wood, W., & Eagly, A. H. (1981). Stages in the analysis of persuasive messages: The role of causal attributions and message comprehension. *Journal of Personality and Social Psychology, 40,* 246-259.

CHAPTER CONTENTS

7 Communication Practices of Followers, Members, and Protégés: The Case of Upward Influence Tactics

VINCENT R. WALDRON
Arizona State University West

Changing forms of organization and evolving conceptions of leadership have created the potential for followers to exert increased influence in American organizations. This chapter reviews research from a variety of disciplines on the nature of upward influence messages. Related forms of communication, such as feedback seeking, dissent, and relationship maintenance, are also discussed. Studies of the individual, relational, and organizational antecedents and outcomes of upward influence are presented. The author concludes that this form of communication has important consequences for individual members and leader-follower relationships. He suggests that future research should supplement existing work on influence tactics, with finer-grained analysis of the interactive behavior. The need to rethink traditional (psychological, hierarchical) conceptions of leader-member influence is established and alternate perspectives are explored.

T HE tendencies toward decentralization, team-based organizing, and downsizing in American industry have increased the range and potency of communication options available to followers and members (Gabarro & Kotter, 1993; Graen & Uhl-Bien, 1995). Downsizing and decreasing commitments to job security have elevated the importance of strategic communication as a predictor of employee success, over and above more

AUTHOR'S NOTE: I completed parts of this chapter while serving as visiting professor at the Department of Communication, University of Kentucky, and would like to thank the faculty and students of that institution for their intellectual and material support of this project. My thanks are also extended to the anonymous reviewers for their valuable suggestions.

Correspondence and requests for reprints: Vincent R. Waldron, Department of Communication Studies, Arizona State University West, Phoenix, AZ 85069-7100; e-mail vincrw@asu.edu

Communication Yearbook 22, pp. 251-299

"objective" measures such as seniority and performance level (Keys & Case, 1990; Maslyn, Farmer, & Fedor, 1996; Tepper, Brown, & Hunt, 1993). Changing conceptions of leadership emphasize the essential role of followers in constructing and governing organizations (Graham, 1995). Organizations that facilitate upward influence may be more responsive to internal and external problems, more democratic, and healthier over the long term (Hegstrom, 1995; Krone, 1992; Redding, 1985). Yet, because of the power differential that still characterizes many leader-member relationships, the exertion of influence by followers remains a strategic, complicated, and sometimes threatening activity (Porter, Allen, & Angle, 1981; Tjosvold, 1978). For all of these reasons, the practical and theoretical importance of research on upward influence has grown substantially in recent years.

A review of this research is timely for several reasons. First, studies of upward influence strategies, tactics, and discourse are scattered across the journals of several disciplines, including communication, management, marketing, human resource development, applied psychology, and sociology. Summary and integration of this work will facilitate cross-disciplinary fertilization. Second, research has accumulated to the point where reasonably firm conclusions can be drawn about some aspects of upward influence. Third, although impressive in many regards, the existing research is based largely on individual-psychological models of communication and traditional hierarchical models of leader-member relations. The evolution of communication theory and rapidly changing conceptions of leadership and organization create opportunities for rethinking and enriching upward influence research. Accordingly, in addition to summarizing research conducted within traditional perspectives, this chapter explores new research directions linked to these emerging trends.

SCOPE AND ORGANIZATION OF THE REVIEW

The many studies of the communication behaviors and interactive processes directly associated with *upward* influence are a central concern in this review. Studies of the downward-directed influence tactics used by leaders have received extensive attention elsewhere (Barry & Watson, 1996; Fairhurst, in press; Hellweg, Geist, Jorgenson, & White-Mills, 1990; Krone & Ludlum, 1990). Informal influence processes rather than formal grievance systems or structured negotiation processes are the focus here. Further, the review places communication behaviors and interactions in the foreground and leaves research on the purely psychological or sociopolitical aspects of influence in the background. Finally, because the organizational context and the circumstances experienced by members and followers are assumed to be unique (see below), the vast literature on persuasion and compliance gaining in personal relationships is not reviewed here. However, insights developed from recent reviews of this broader research (see Cody, Canary, & Smith, 1994; Keller-mann & Cole, 1994; O'Keefe, 1994) are applied where appropriate.

The review of the literature begins with a brief discussion of definitions of upward influence and the organizational context in which upward influence occurs. The next and largest section of the chapter reviews the existing empirical research, most of which has been conducted from a traditional (psychological, hierarchical) framework. This section documents the variety of upward influence messages, including tactics and discourse, identified by researchers. This concern with messages and their features is extended to forms of follower communication that appear similar to upward influence. Such behaviors as feedback seeking, impression management, and dissent are reviewed. The essay then proceeds with a consideration of research on factors that account for variation in upward influence behavior, including relational, individual, and situational/contextual characteristics. Research on outcomes of upward influence, such as performance ratings and effects on the leader-member relationship, are then considered. The final part of this chapter is concerned with opportunities for reframing upward influence research by incorporating alternate communication theories, emerging conceptions of leadership/followership, and nonhierarchical organizational forms.

DEFINING UPWARD INFLUENCE

Typical of the definitions of upward influence is that offered by Deluga and Perry (1991), who describe upward influence as an attempt by the subordinate to secure a desired behavior from the superior. Other authors echo early concep-tions of influence as "getting one's way" (Kipnis, Schmidt, & Wilkinson, 1980) or equate it with "political" behavior that occurs outside the formally pre-scribed subordinate role (Porter et al., 1981). Despite slight variations in definitions, nearly all of the empirical work conceptualizes upward influence (if only implicitly) as a deliberate attempt by a subordinate to select tactics that will bring about change in a more powerful target and facilitate achieve-ment of a personal or organizational objective. This definition reflects several debatable but nonetheless prevalent assumptions of most existing studies: Upward influence is an intentional and strategic choice-making process; it is initiated by an individual, not a group; it includes actions that are communi-cative as well as noncommunicative actions; it is oriented up the hierarchical chain; the target is a more powerful *person* (typically the supervisor), as opposed to the larger organizational system; it may result in change of the target's affect, cognition, or behavior, but not the agent's behavior; and it is "directed" by long- or short-term goals.

Perhaps because much of the research has been conducted by applied psychologists and management theorists, prevailing conceptions of upward influence have been more psychological than communicative. Considerable productive research has been conducted from this perspective. But research also might benefit from an expanded definition of influence that emphasizes the social and relational complexities of communication (Fairhurst, in press) and its interactive nature (Barry & Watson, 1996). Followers and members increasingly practice influence as part of teamwork, coaching relationships, mentor-protégé interactions, and other less-hierarchical relationships. Even when influence is practiced in traditional hierarchical settings, as it often is, reconceptualization may be helpful. An expanded view of influence would recognize that follower communication also creates and sustains relational and organizational structures. Through submitting, requesting, questioning, resisting, dissenting, negotiating, agreeing, and numerous other communicative activities, followers to some extent empower (or disempower) leaders, define the quality of their relationships, and affirm or contest organizational values, norms, and procedures. In short, followers not only seek influence within organizational constraints, they participate in and define the larger influence-creating process.

Prevailing views of upward influence are located primarily within a Western cultural frame of reference. Models of the influence process, indeed the very definition of influence and conceptions of how it is "gained," may not translate well across cultures (Krone, Garret, & Chen, 1992). Of course, influence processes have been studied across national cultures, including those of India (Ansari & Kapoor, 1987), Japan (Hirokawa & Miyahara, 1986), and Israel (Erez & Rim, 1982), but studies typically invoke traditional Western conceptual models. Doing so could mask cultural constructs that fundamentally alter how influence is perceived and enacted. In this regard, Graen and Wakabayashi (1994) describe challenges faced by American team leaders in Japanese "transplant" organizations due to differing conceptions of interdependence, harmony, and loyalty—all of which affect the quantity, quality, and outcomes of upward influence efforts. Studies of such concepts as *kuan-hsi* in China (Chang & Holt, 1991) identify relevant cultural differences in relational definitions, social obligations, and the role of the individual.

THE ORGANIZATIONAL CONTEXT
OF UPWARD INFLUENCE

The study of upward influence processes at work is enriched by previous research on compliance gaining in personal relationships and classroom contexts. But organizational life is unique. The existence of overt and covert differences in organizational power make upward influence inherently risky for low-power followers (Porter et al., 1981). More powerful others often control the resources and the rules of engagement that followers must draw upon when framing upward influence messages. The leader-member relationship is often long-lasting, with both a history and a future that must be taken into account. In addition, procedural structure, work roles, job stress, and the nature of the work potentially limit opportunities for persuasive communication and constrain the persuasive options available to followers (Cobb, 1984; Nonis, Sager, & Kumar, 1996). Organizational culture, politics, and socialization can determine the degree to which follower persuasion is considered a "legitimate" activity, its potential social and personal costs, and whether upwardly directed resistance must be overt or covert (Van Maanen & Kunda, 1989). Environmental forces interact with organizational processes to shape influence activity. For example, the degree to which followers are economically secure and employment alternatives are available may contribute to their willingness to engage in upward influence. Workers' connections to larger occupational communities may be more important than intraorganizational factors in determining the rationales used in influence attempts (Van Maanen & Barley, 1984). The support of families and friends as well as the oversight provided by unions and government may partially shape followers' willingness to engage in influence behavior (Bahniuk, Dobos, & Hill, 1991). At work, all of these factors may be more important than individual knowledge and skill in shaping the influence process.

RESEARCH ON UPWARD
INFLUENCE MESSAGES

Early descriptive models of the upward influence process (Cobb, 1984; Porter et al., 1981) drew attention to three questions: (a) What is the nature of upward influence messages? (b) What factors account for variation in influence behavior? and (c) What are the outcomes of upward influence processes? Although these models have been in existence for more than a decade, researchers have yet to test their fit in a holistic manner with causal modeling procedures. Instead, they have tended to isolate parts of the model and to test relationships between key variables.

This section reviews work directly concerned with the nature, form, and quality of upward influence messages—presumably the component of the research most of interest to communication researchers, but one given limited attention in previous analyses of workplace influence (see, e.g., Barry & Watson, 1996). Tactics directly analogous to upward influence tactics (e.g., "power tactics"; Cheng, 1983) are also addressed here. Related forms of communication, such as impression management, are discussed in a later section.

Influence Strategies and Tactics

Strategies are typically identified as general approaches to or blueprints for persuasive action. Tactics are more specific behavioral implementations of a general strategy (for one discussion of this distinction, see Wiemann & Daly, 1994). In addition, researchers sometimes refer to dimensions of persuasion that underlay similar tactics (O'Keefe, 1994). So, for example, any number of tactics involving logic, argument, or explanation might be grouped together based on the underlying dimension of "reasoning" (Kipnis et al., 1980). In the upward influence literature, the terms *tactic* or *tactic type* are frequently used interchangeably with *strategy*—a source of conceptual confusion that has been noted elsewhere (Kellermann & Cole, 1994). In this review, I adopt the naming conventions used by researchers (typically using the term *tactic*), but note differences in the levels of abstraction associated with these terms where applicable.

Studies of persuasion in the workplace have used taxonomy-generating procedures similar to those found in a profusion of earlier work on compliance gaining in interpersonal settings (e.g., Marwell & Schmidt, 1967; for an exhaustive list, see Kellermann & Cole, 1994). But a relatively small number of taxonomic studies have been devoted wholly or in part to describing upward, as opposed to downward, influence tactics (DuBrin, 1989, 1991; Kipnis et al., 1980; Mowday, 1978, 1979; Porter et al., 1981; Schriesheim & Hinkin, 1990; Yukl & Falbe, 1990; Yukl & Tracey, 1992). Several studies have described tactics more indirectly. For example, Schilit and Locke (1982) studied events that put the follower in position to have influence (e.g., discovering valuable information), but only their discussion of tactics is considered in this section. Even within this foundational group of taxonomic studies, few have examined upward influence tactics *exclusively*. Only several have based their taxonomies on thorough, inductively generated data (Kipnis et al., 1980; Schriesheim & Hinkin, 1990; Yukl & Tracey, 1992).

A starting place for much of the research on upward influence messages is the often-referenced study by Kipnis and colleagues (1980) in which the researchers employed an inductive method to identify influence tactics used by working students. They asked respondents to describe their goals and tactics in upward, downward, and horizontal influence situations. Kipnis et al. then developed a list of 370 influence behaviors reportedly used by their sample of 165 employees. They report 14 initial tactics and the percentages of self-reports that referenced them: explanation (17%), direct requests (10%), clandestine acts (8%), exchange (8%), personal negative actions (8%), coalition (7%), persistence (7%), demand (7%), weak ask (6%), gathering evidence (6%), training (6%), self-presentation (5%), administrative sanctions (3%), and reward (2%). In the second stage of their project, more than 700 respondents indicated on 58 Likert-type scales the frequency with which they would use each tactic on first and second attempts.

Based on this study and subsequent work, Kipnis and Schmidt (1982) developed the Profiles of Organizational Influence Scale (POIS; for a review of the whole instrument, see Hellweg et al., 1990). The 27-item Form M subscale measures 6 general tactic categories that subsume the original 14 categories. These categories are described in turn below.

Rationality/reason. This category includes all approaches that use reasoning or logic as the primary basis for persuasion. Rational tactics provide job-related information, explanations, and reasons to the supervisor in an attempt to alter her or his thinking. These tactics work by creating impressions of competence or reasonableness in the mind of the supervisor (Villanova & Bernardin, 1991).

Ingratiation. Defined by Kipnis et al. (1980) as behavior that makes the self appear humble or the leader feel important, ingratiation has been a much-studied form of interpersonal influence (Gordon, 1996; Jones, 1964). In upward influence studies, ingratiation takes at least three forms (Jones & Wortman, 1973; Thacker & Wayne, 1995). The first type, other enhancements, bolsters the identity of the leader through praise, flattery, and approbation (Gordon, 1996; Tjosvold, 1978). Opinion conformity, a second form of ingratiation, involves showing agreement with the target. Statements that gain favor with the target by enhancing the message source's qualities, motives, or achievements are a third form of ingratiation. Upward influence researchers typically consider "friendliness," "liking," and self-presentation tactics to be part of the ingratiation category.

Exchange/bargaining. Tactics in this category involve offering rewards, exchanging resources, or proposing to make sacrifices. Several strategies that appeared in earlier work on interpersonal compliance gaining appear here (see Schenck-Hamlin, Wiseman, & Georgacarakos, 1982). For example, indebtedness tactics, which involve reminding the recipient of obligations based on past exchanges, and promise tactics, which offer future goods, services, or obligations in exchange for compliance, are cited as frequent exchange tactics (e.g., Waldron, Hunt, & Dsilva, 1993).

Assertiveness tactics. Followers using this approach are overt and direct in seeking to influence the leader. These tactics can have a coercive element and may involve raw use of power or will. In the special case of upward influence, such power may stem from technical expertise, information, or social capital, in contrast to the position-based power used by supervisors. Making demands or threats, issuing directives or challenges, and persisting or "wearing down" the supervisor are tactics similar to assertiveness (Mowday, 1978; Waldron et al., 1993). These are also referred to as "pressure" tactics in the literature (Falbe & Yukl, 1992).

Coalition. This tactic involves the development of support among peers, making claims about the degree to which coworkers support one's position, or associating one's position with prevailing or majority opinion. Coalition tactics exploit strength in numbers. Some variation on the coalition tactic (e.g., "group support"; Schilit, 1987a, 1987b) appears in most taxonomic work.

Upward appeal. This tactic involves going "over the head" of the leader in an effort to obtain the desired objective. Upward appeals usually involve the individual's enlisting the support of a more powerful ally to reach persuasive objectives. It is often conceptualized as a secondary tactic when the leader resists initial compliance-gaining efforts (Maslyn et al., 1996; Waldron et al., 1993).

All six of the above-described tactic categories have persisted in the literature, but several new categories have been developed and the behaviors included within each category have been expanded. Two secondary categories cited in the original work by Kipnis et al. (1980) were later dropped, apparently due to a lack of conceptual distinctiveness and insufficient use in upward influence situations. "Sanction" tactics gain compliance by invoking positive or negative organizational sanctions. "Blocking" tactics prevent the recipient from reaching a goal or taking an action by creating interpersonal or organizational barriers and obstructions. Neither of these tactics has received much empirical attention in recent years.

Arguing sensibly that upward influence is distinct from downward influence due to power inequalities that must be considered by the follower, Schriesheim and Hinkin (1990) have studied upward influence exclusively. They suggest that Kipnis et al. (1980) overlooked unique aspects of upward influence because they considered it conceptually similar to horizontal and downward influence. Schriesheim and Hinkin used new and modified survey items in two factor-analytic studies of tactics reported by students and employees. The analyses yielded support for the six original categories of tactics but raised questions about the independence and content validity of the original scale items used by Kipnis et al. (1980). Schriesheim and Hinkin developed a shorter, 18-item instrument for measuring the prominence of the six influence categories in upward influence situations.

Yukl and colleagues (Yukl & Falbe, 1990; Yukl & Tracey, 1992), finding earlier message classification work to be too narrow in its consideration of possible tactic types, have also replicated and extended the work of Kipnis et al. (1980). A contribution of this work is that the authors coded open-ended descriptions of influence episodes rather than relying on a checklist measure such as the POIS. To counter possible social desirability biases, they considered self-reported tactics not just of influence agents, but also of targets. These authors have reported two additional tactic categories that have gained prominence in the literature: inspirational appeals and consultation tactics.

Inspirational appeals. Influenced in part by work on transformational leadership (Bass, 1985), Yukl and Falbe (1990) define inspirational appeals as emotional proposals designed to arouse enthusiasm by appealing to values or ideals or by increasing the recipient's confidence. Other authors have described "allurement" tactics using somewhat similar terms (Lamude, 1993, 1994).

Consultation tactics. Drawing on traditions of participatory management, Yukl and Falbe (1990) define consultation as involving the message recipient in a decision-making process as a way of gaining his or her commitment to the process. Waldron et al. (1993) found that followers used a similar approach when they sought advice from their supervisors as a means of involving them in decisions about adopting new work procedures. Respondents indicated that supervisors invited to offer advice early in the influence process were then more obligated to support the new procedures at a later point.

Alternate Tactics and Classification Schemes

The literature offers some alternatives to Kipnis et al.'s (1980) taxonomy. In some cases, new labels have been applied to tactics that appear very similar. For example, Cheng (1983) uses the term *power strategies* to describe tactics similar to Kipnis et al.'s (1980) influence tactics. But several other taxonomy-building efforts have identified tactics that appear not to fit easily in the Kipnis et al. scheme. Tactics that remove obstacles to compliance represent one alternate type. For example, with "volunteer first" tactics, members persuade leaders to adopt a new procedure or policy by first adopting it themselves (Schriesheim & Tepper, 1989). "Troubleshooting" tactics anticipate problems likely to be experienced by the supervisor due to the persuasive request. For example, a member might explain how she has already arranged for a substitute when requesting an unscheduled day of leave (Waldron et al., 1993).

Followers also gain influence by adhering more closely than normal to organizational rules and roles (Schilit & Locke, 1982). This strategy has been called "formalization" (Waldron et al., 1993); study participants have described such tactics as using the procedures that governed staff meetings as a means of ensuring that reluctant supervisors discussed proposals. In yet another example, the manipulation of emotion has been identified as an understudied influence tactic used by followers (Waldron, 1994). Such tactics as guilt induction, emotion editing, intentional embarrassment, and elicitation of pity have been reported occasionally (Schilit & Locke, 1982; Waldron, 1991). Borrowing from earlier compliance-gaining taxonomies (Marwell & Schmidt, 1967), Lamude (1993) refers to the tactic of "allurement." This approach persuades by implying that the target will ultimately benefit by making others happy or satisfied. As such, it may be a special case of the inspirational appeal tactics identified by Yukl and Falbe (1990).

Finally, some researchers have conceptualized avoidance as a tactic in upward influence situations. Simply choosing to refrain from influence behavior or circumventing the leader are two avoidant approaches reportedly used by followers in face-threatening influence situations (Waldron et al., 1993). Relatedly, "withdrawal," as contrasted with persistence, has been identified as an option in situations where the supervisor offers resistance to the initial influence attempt (Maslyn et al., 1996).

In contrast to these minor additions to the tactic mix, several communication scholars have offered more substantive deviations from the Kipnis et al. (1980) approach. Krone (1992), drawing on Porter et al.'s (1981) model of political behavior, distinguishes among open, strategic, and closed influence attempts. In her analysis of members drawn from five distinct organizations, she classified messages by determining the degree to which the means of influence were overt and the goals of the influence attempt were expressed or hidden. Related to this emphasis on the political nature of influence attempts, other researchers have described deceptive and manipulative tactics (Erez & Rim, 1982; Schilit, 1987a, 1987b; Schilit & Locke, 1982; Schriesheim & Tepper, 1989; Waldron et al., 1993) that expand on the category of "clandestine" tactics originally reported by Kipnis et al. (1980). Despite these additional taxonomic contributions, the most notable feature of the upward influence research may be the consistent use of a relatively small set of tactic categories quite similar to those reported nearly two decades ago.

Tactic Clusters

Researchers have attempted to add parsimony to the taxonomic literature by grouping tactics that appear intuitively to be similar. For example, Kipnis and Schmidt (1983) distinguish among rational (e.g., reason), soft (e.g., ingratiation), and hard (e.g., assertive) dimensions of influence. Soft tactics represent a covert, indirect type of persuasion, in which the follower attempts to manage the identity of the self or the leader. Self-presentation tactics that make the subordinate appear more likable or similar to the leader and ingratiation tactics fit here (Gordon, 1996). Hard tactics communicate persuasive intent more directly and wield power more overtly. These tactics include threats, assertiveness, and direct requests.

Tactic Content

Only recently have upward influence researchers suggested that the "content" of tactics, more than their general form, is likely to influence its effects (but see the discourse-based studies reviewed below). Among the content factors addressed thus far are the importance, feasibility, and desirability of the influence request (Yukl, Kim, & Falbe, 1996). Initial research on the favorability of the request has reported mixed results (Case, Dosier, Murkison, & Keys, 1988). Unfortunately, the factors that make such requests favorable have not been addressed in any detail in this literature. A promising study of 195 MBA students demonstrates that request importance and "enjoyability" (to the recipient) have effects over and above tactic type and power of the agent on target outcomes (Yukl et al., 1996).

Tactic Frequency

Studies reporting on the frequency of tactic use have not been uniform in their results. Rational explanations often appear as one of the most-used tactics (Kipnis et al., 1980; Schilit, 1987a, 1987b), a finding also common in interpersonal communication contexts (Cody et al., 1994). But friendliness/ingratiation, consultation, inspirational appeals, and sometimes coalition tactics have been found to be frequently used in some samples (Chacko, 1988; Tilley, 1988; Yukl & Falbe, 1990). In contrast, it appears that pressure or assertiveness tactics are frequent only with samples of middle- or upper-level managers (Schilit, 1987a). Some researchers report little difference in the relative frequency with which tactics are used (Yukl & Falbe, 1990). The frequency issue is complicated by social desirability biases. The reasoning tactics that appear in many studies to be used most frequently are arguably more socially desirable than ingratiating or pressure tactics.

Tactic Sequencing and Second Attempts

To the credit of upward influence researchers, it has long been recognized in the literature that persuasive episodes often involve more than simple "first-strike" tactics (Barry & Shapiro, 1992; Kipnis et al., 1980; Perreault & Miles, 1978). Theoretical models have specified likely responses to target noncompliance (Cobb, 1984; Kipnis, 1976) and posited that such responses should be calibrated to the reasons for noncompliance (misinformation, inability, organizational barriers). However, empirical work has yet to investigate these theoretical implications fully. Upward influence researchers have generally avoided the study of interactive communication. However, Falbe and Yukl's (1992) analysis of critical influence episodes allowed them to code multiple tactics. It appears from this work and a later study (Yukl, Falbe, & Youn, 1993) that subordinates use softer tactics, such as simple requests, ingratiation, and reasoning, initially and then move to more assertive and exchange-based tactics. This is generally supportive of earlier predictions (Kipnis, 1976). This work also indicates that the mix of tactics increases as the episode progresses, such that second attempts are often of a category distinct from first attempts.

Upward Influence Styles

In a substantive departure from traditional tactic-based views, some communication researchers have conceptualized upward influence behavior in terms of cross-contextual communication styles. For example, Garko (1994) has linked communication style to the upward influence behavior of executive physicians. He found that styles (e.g., animated, contentious, friendly, open) were adjusted to the perceived attractiveness of the target-leader. In another body of work at least indirectly related to upward influence, argumentative and verbally aggressive styles have been contrasted in a series of studies, some in organizational contexts (see Infante & Rancer, 1996, for a comprehensive recent review). Argumentativeness is broadly defined as a willingness to engage in constructive persuasive debate; verbal aggressiveness is associated with a tendency to use personal attacks. Less unique is a study by Kipnis and Schmidt (1988), who revisited their earlier taxonomic work and used cluster analysis to identify upward influence "styles" used by employed students and managers of a health care organization. A "shotgun" style involved extensive use of influence communication, with particularly high levels of bargaining and pressuring tactics. A "bystander" style avoided the use of influence altogether. Employees adopting a "tactician" style used moderate levels of influence and preferred reasoning tactics.

Studies of Discourse

The recent move to study variation in tactic content may signal that researchers are developing an appreciation for finer-grained analysis of the upward influence process. Arguably, it is at the level of conversational behavior that power differences and influence patterns that characterize leader-follower relations are created and sustained. A notable early attempt to frame workplace influence at the discourse level is found in the work of Drake and Moberg (1986). Working from a social exchange paradigm, these theorists note that previous work had focused too extensively on the rewards and resources exchanged during compliance gaining. They argue that the linguistic form of a request can be *intrinsically* rewarding—as when it creates the impression of a special relationship between source and recipient. By creating changed relational definitions (e.g., from coworkers to confidants; from supervisor/subordinate to colleagues), language can have "palliative effects," reducing the degree to which external rewards must be offered as compensation for compliance.

Linguistic forms can also have sedating effects, directing the recipients' attention away from the social exchange calculation. Drake and Moberg (1986) cite as an example the use of indirectness by a supervisor seeking to delegate work: "Working on anything interesting these days?" If the unsuspecting follower indicates that things are routine, a subsequent request to accept an additional work assignment is likely to be answered in the affirmative. According to Drake and Moberg, by highlighting in the mind of the follower the routine nature of the work, the initial request has the effect of labeling the current situation as problematic. In this case, the problem is that the work is unchallenging. The subsequent request to accept a new project is perceived by the follower as a way to resolve the problem rather than as an effort to gain compliance. Drake and Moberg's linguistically oriented work is notable for the careful attention these authors pay to the microdynamics of leader-follower influence and for their acknowledgment of language as the means by which relational and instrumental dimensions of influence are linked.

A series of studies by Fairhurst (1993; Fairhurst & Chandler, 1989) on discourse in leader-member interaction has significantly advanced knowledge in this area. This research reveals that the quality of leader-member exchange can be discerned from patterns of talk. Most relevant here, in Fairhurst's studies leaders and followers in higher-quality exchanges exhibited language patterns indicative of mutual, rather than one-way, influence. Followers exhibited a tendency to question and challenge leader decisions. In a study of the discourse of 16 female leaders and their followers, Fairhurst (1993) found evidence that a mix of aligning (supporting, coaching), polarizing (competitive conflict tactics), and accommodating (polite disagreements) patterns of discourse discriminated between types of leader-member exchange.

Summary and Evaluation of Research on Upward Influence Messages

Two decades of programmatic research on upward influence messages has revealed a remarkable level of agreement among researchers regarding the tactics used in this type of communication. The original categories proposed by Kipnis et al. (1980) remain in use, although the literature has been strengthened by subsequent studies that have validated, modified, and added to their original taxonomy. Although most of the upward influence tactics are familiar to persuasion researchers, the upward adapted and coalition tactics described in these studies appear to be most uniquely adapted to the persuasive situations faced by low-power followers (as opposed to leaders). This literature suggests that rational tactics are preferred in most (but not all) cases and provides at least a preliminary sense of how tactics are sequenced. Research on alternate message schemes is contributed primarily by communication scholars, suggesting the potential value of cross-disciplinary fertilization as researchers describe how abstract tactics are enacted in conversational behavior. This potential "communicative turn" in the upward influence literature should take into account the strengths and weaknesses of the existing compliance-gaining research.

In particular, research on compliance-gaining tactics has received pointed criticism for its excessive reliance on statistical induction (factor analysis), the validity of compliance-gaining scenarios used in surveys, poor conceptualization of tactic examples, failure to consider multiple tactics, and the atheoretical, hodgepodge nature of resulting taxonomies (Hellweg et al., 1990; Kellermann & Cole, 1994; Roloff, 1994). In a particularly comprehensive analysis, Kellermann and Cole (1994) have demonstrated that most taxonomies lack unifying theoretical principles. Within the same taxonomies, they found tactics that were identified by form, goals, content, and other dimensions. This heterogeneity makes generalizable claims difficult and leads to an overabundance of idiosyncratic message coding systems.

The upward influence literature is vulnerable to criticism for failing to derive unifying principles that guide message classification. For example, researchers routinely compare upward appeal tactics, which are defined with reference to the target of the influence attempt, with exchange tactics. This latter type of tactic is defined with reference to the content of the persuasive request. Moreover, some tactics involve face-to-face interaction with the leader (e.g., rational tactics) whereas others (e.g., coalition tactics) sometimes include activities conducted outside the immediate interactive context. The lack of conceptual consistency in the broader compliance-gaining literature has led some commentators to argue for a "feature-based" approach to message classification (e.g., O'Keefe, 1994). Rather than construct comprehensive taxonomies, researchers would classify messages along dimensions posited to be important in a theory of persuasion (prosocialness, degree of imposition, emotionality). Research linking the use of these dimensions to antecedents, situational factors, and outcomes would then contribute to theory development. A theory-driven approach would create improved opportunities for comparing different conceptual accounts of the upward influence process.

The ad hoc nature of message taxonomies creates methodological problems as well. The basis for distinguishing categories becomes problematic for message coders. Isn't it possible to offer an exchange as part of an upward appeal? If so, message coding procedures need to take this conceptual overlap into account. Unfortunately, they typically do not. In fact, it is fair to criticize most upward influence studies for providing very limited information about message coding procedures. Procedures used for category construction, message unitizing, and interrater reliability must be addressed if researchers adopt a more communicative focus.

The great bulk of upward influence studies are based on the written self-reports of MBA students and/or employees, and they suffer from some familiar shortcomings: excessive reliance on hypothetical scenarios, failure to consider dyadic as well as individual processes, biases due to memory limitations and social desirability, and samples that may not be representative of blue-collar and less-educated employees. Retrospective self-report data are complicated by the degree to which respondents can accurately recall their influence behaviors well after the fact. More frequent use of scenarios actually experienced by interactants, as opposed to hypothetical ones, would potentially alleviate this problem. But few researchers have made any attempt to gather data that might increase our confidence that self-reported tactic data correspond closely to real-life patterns of influence.

Regarding the frequency of tactic use, self-report biases in general and social desirability bias in particular remain a major concern. Laudably, some researchers have attempted to control for such bias by including measures of social desirability tendencies in their studies (e.g., Tepper et al., 1993). But a deep-seated preference in the United States for rationale and nonemotive behavior in organizational life may prompt respondents to view themselves as behaving in a rational manner (see Mumby & Putnam, 1992). This frame of reference may make it difficult for employees even to make sense of behavior in nonrational ways. Of course, these same forces might encourage rational tactics, not just in perception but in implementation.

Perhaps even more problematic is the assumption in this research that upward influence is a frequent or salient organizational activity for most employees (Waldron, 1991). The relative importance and frequency of upward influence communication relative to other types of communication (e.g., relationship maintenance) has not been seriously evaluated, but in a "geography" of daily conversation at a large research hospital, Hunt (1994) found that influence episodes were relatively rare compared with the sheer mass of daily task-oriented talk.

Perhaps the most regrettable side effect of the almost exclusive use of survey methods is the limited information they reveal about communication processes. Survey researchers are forced by limited information to conceptualize influence behavior primarily at the abstracted strategy/tactic level. However, tactics such as "rationality" are defined so broadly that they can subsume any number of communicative activities. Obviously the form and nature of evidence presented, the types of arguments used, are significant features of this upward influence approach. Yet these factors have only recently been considered in studies of tactic content. Studies of ingratiation have been more specific about its variations.

The best hope for improvement in this area comes from the relatively few studies conducted at the discourse level. For example, Fairhurst's (1993) work grounds the process of influence in the ordinary communication exchanged between leaders and followers, and provides a richer account of influence behaviors. This line of research may enrich survey-based taxonomic work because it identifies behaviors not typically associated with existing tactic categories (e.g., in-group markers). More important, Fairhurst's studies of leader-member exchange, and her other work on relational control patterns (Courtright, Fairhurst, & Rogers, 1989; Fairhurst, Green, & Snavely, 1984; Fairhurst, Rogers, & Sarr, 1987), are among the few that take seriously the dyadic, interactive nature of influence processes. To make progress, upward influence research will need to capture interactivity more fully.

Perhaps because much upward influence research is relatively recent, some progress has been made in addressing deficiencies found in traditional compliance-gaining research. For example, researchers have long recognized and tried to measure multiple rather than only "first-strike" tactics (Kipnis et al., 1980). Tactic sequencing has been addressed. And compared with research conducted in other contexts, the upward influence research is also somewhat less vulnerable to criticism based on taxonomy proliferation. In fact, there has been remarkable agreement on the basic types of influence tactics used by followers, with most researchers using categories from the original group proposed by Kipnis et al. (1980). It is a strength of this literature that researchers have attempted to improve on the methods of the original work by using both target and agent reports, by using open-ended rather than closed-ended measures, and by broadening the definition of influence behavior. Despite this work, relatively minor modifications have been suggested. The stability and relative brevity of upward influence taxonomies may reflect the limited persuasive options perceived by followers in work contexts. Due to restrictive communication procedures, role requirements, and power differences, followers may in fact find their upward influence options limited. Additional study of higher-power employees might reveal increased variability in behavior (see House & Aditya, 1997). However, researchers may be too willing to accept the limited set of categories reported nearly two decades ago. The tendency for researchers to use very similar methods (checklists completed by MBA students) and to conceptualize influence at the fairly abstracted level of tactics might lead to a false sense of consensus in the research.

Finally, it appears that message classification work could be enriched if more complex views of communication were incorporated. Much of the upward influence literature assumes that communication is essentially unifunctional. Upward influence tactics (almost by definition) are presumed to have a single (persuasive) objective. This perspective can be supplemented by more complex views of interpersonal persuasion in which it is assumed that messages often have identity- and relationship-defining effects (see, e.g., Leichty & Applegate, 1991). Without disputing that many messages are directed toward a primary influence objective, an alternate view would acknowledge that members often find identity and relational concerns of equal or greater salience. For example, members might withdraw from or modify influence attempts if they threaten the members' "good standing," a relational consideration, with a respected leader. Similarly, followers may eschew tactics that are inconsistent with their identities; ingratiation tactics, for example, might be viewed as compromising self-respect.

In these examples, relational and identity goals are conceptualized as constraints on messages designed to achieve the primary influence objective. But identity and relationship management activities can be conceived as primary, if sometimes unintended, routes to influence in and of themselves. Messages that communicate commitment to the leader-member relationship may increase the likelihood that the member will succeed in gaining influence. Messages that demonstrate that a member has internalized organizational expectations may have similar kinds of effects (Waldron, 1991). In short, identity and relational concerns are interdependent with the influence process in a variety of ways.

Messages With Conceptual
Similarities to Upward Influence

It is clear from the preceding review that researchers ostensibly concerned with upward influence include in their taxonomies tactics related to impression management, relationship preservation, and other communication objectives. This tendency is not inherently problematic—much communication theory acknowledges the interdependence of instrumental, relational, and identity management functions of communication. However, the sometimes unacknowledged conceptual overlap in this research can create confusion. In the spirit of developing a more comprehensive picture of the upward influence process, studies of the most relevant and complementary forms of communication are reviewed below. This necessarily brief discussion is intended to encourage cross-fertilization among research programs pertaining to the communication practices of followers, members, and protégés.

Impression Management Tactics

Research on impression management (Ashford & Northcraft, 1992; Deluga, 1991) and the presentation of accounts (Bies, 1987; Bies, Shapiro, & Cummings, 1988; Braaten, Cody, & DeTienne, 1993) is directly relevant to upward influence research. One possibility is that impression management and upward influence are differentiated by their positions in a developmental sequence of relational events. For example, impression management may establish perceptions of competence and trustworthiness early in the leader-member relationship that in time may lead to patterns of reciprocal influence (Liden & Mitchell, 1989; Wayne & Liden, 1985). Members may increase the success rate of upward influence tactics by first accentuating their similarities with the leader (Rao, Schmidt, & Murray, 1995). Wayne, Kacmar, and Ferris (1995) distinguish ingratiation tactics from simple self-promotion, noting that ingratiation involves expressing opinion conformity and support for the other, sharing confidences, or flattery. Both ingratiation and self-promotion have been linked with important outcomes (Gordon, 1996). One study of 96 simulated performance interviews found that use of such impression management behaviors as self- and other-enhancement and expressing opinion conformity was associated with improved performance ratings (Wayne & Kacmar, 1991).

In addition to "proactive" impression management, followers protect their identities by offering accounts for their behavior (Bies et al., 1988; Braaten et al., 1993). Although less obviously related to influence objectives, accounts may indirectly function to alter supervisor behavior. For example, in a disciplinary situation, a supervisor might decide against taking punitive action due to the convincing nature of the account presented by the member (Wood & Mitchell, 1981). In a rapidly developing line of research with implications for leader-member interaction, the nature of the account presented by the member (excuses, apologies, justifications, denials) has been important in determining leader attributions of responsibility and impressions of credibility (Bies & Sitkin, 1992; see also Giacalone & Rosenfeld, 1989). These forms of accounts appear to be directly linked to impressions of intimidation, ingratiation, supplication, dedication, and self-promotion (Braaten et al., 1993).

Upward Maintenance Tactics

Follower behavior in upward influence situations may be dependent on the history and stability of the leader-member relationship. Studies of relationship maintenance tactics bring this relational element to the foreground. One series of studies has identified tactics used by followers to maintain and stabilize relationships with leaders (Waldron, 1991, 1997; Waldron & Hunt, 1992; Waldron et al., 1993). The original study involved factor analysis of responses provided by more than 500 working adults. Four general types of tactics were reported. *Personal-informal* tactics, such as small talk and sharing stories, resembled the patterns of communication exhibited by friends. *Contractual* tactics emphasized follower acceptance of leader expectations and communicated conformity with role prescriptions. Both of these tactics involve behaviors typically classified as ingratiation tactics in the upward influence literature. *Regulative* tactics used avoidance and message distortion, presumably to prevent relationship deterioration. Finally, *direct* tactics overtly defined the nature of the relationship and protested perceived relational injustices in a manner similar to "assertive" influence tactics. These tactics have implications for the upward influence literature because manipulation of the relationship through ingratiation and other tactics is a frequently studied influence route.

Lee and Jablin (1995) have studied maintenance behavior in routine, deteriorating, and escalating situations and have found a generally similar pattern of behaviors. Tactics reported by participants in this study were different from those in the Waldron (1991) study in the escalating situation, which involved a supervisor's wanting to make the relationship more personal then the subordinate desired. Here, procrastination ("I told him/her it was not a good time to help him/her") and conversational refocusing tactics (e.g., redirecting conversational topics) were used to slow relationship development. Tepper (1995) has replicated and extended the Waldron (1991) study in the management literature. He located an additional "extracontractual" form of maintenance that involved behavior that exceeded role expectations (e.g., being more accessible than necessary).

Feedback-Seeking Tactics

It is almost axiomatic in the literature that supervisor feedback changes behavior, but the strategic upward feedback behavior of subordinates has received heightened attention in recent years. In an impressive example, Atwater, Roush, and Fischthal (1995) studied 978 leaders and their 1,232 followers. They found significant postfeedback changes in supervisor behavior (as reported by subordinates) as a function of upward negative feedback. Even more relevant is recent work in the area of "feedback seeking," which conceptualizes followers as active participants rather than passive receivers in the feedback process. Larson's (1989) model of feedback and work by Ashford and colleagues (e.g., Ashford & Cummings, 1983; Ashford & Northcraft, 1992; Northcraft & Ashford, 1990) and Morrison and Bies (1991) link feedback with impression management processes (see the previous discussion). They view monitoring and proactive inquiry as communication behaviors that followers use to manipulate the feedback behavior of supervisors. For example, by seeking feedback with carefully worded inquiries, followers can discourage supervisors from delivering negative feedback—an action that supervisors are hesitant to take anyway (Larson, 1989).

The tactic of proactive inquiry has conceptual links to the "consultation" tactics studied in the upward influence literature (Yukl & Falbe, 1990). Moreover, the decision to seek feedback is affected by many of the same variables thought to affect upward feedback tactic use, including perceived costs to self, performance level, prevailing norms, and goal characteristics (Ashford & Northcraft, 1992). Feedback researchers have determined that feedback valence (positive or negative) and sensitivity to situational cues are relevant dimensions of feedback behavior (Geddes, 1993; Larson, Glynn, Fleenor, & Scontrino, 1987). Upward influence scholars might consider the potential of these alternate dimensions for coding upward influence tactics.

Messages of Dissent

Research on messages of dissent and processes of employee resistance is related to upward influence, as are studies of "voice" (Hirschman, 1970) and moral outrage (e.g., Bies, 1987). Arguably, the practice of responsible dissent in day-to-day interactions is a defining characteristic of democratic organizing (Cheney, 1995) and employee empowerment (Chiles & Zorn, 1995). In addition, theorists have argued on the basis of morality and organizational effectiveness that leaders should encourage the expression of "principled dissent" by employees (Gorden, Infante, & Graham, 1988; Graham, 1986, 1988). Yet even aggressively democratic forms of organizing have been found to discourage followers from confronting directly those work practices with which they disagree (Gorden, Holmberg, & Heisey, 1994). This urge to suppress dissent, even in participative organizational structures, makes dissent a potentially rich area for study (Hegstrom, 1995) and one conceptually similar to the area of upward influence.

Voice is the label associated by Hirschman (1970) with employee efforts to protest and alter unsatisfactory work conditions. Persuasive efforts to alter work roles or work routines, change job descriptions, or protest unethical practices have also been examined under this label (Jones, 1986). Voice can take a variety of strategic forms, ranging from quiet murmurings to threats and/or collective action (Graham & Keeley, 1992). These latter two behaviors resemble assertive- and coalition-type upward influence tactics. Perhaps a key difference between these two forms of communication is the target. In most studies, upward influence is assumed to be directed at an individual; resistance is typically defined as a response to a system or cultural practice. For example, in their study of the culture of Disneyland, Van Maanen and Kunda (1989) found that employee resistance strategies in that culture are often covert rather than "voiced." Prevailing cultural norms and supervisory controls enforce an ethic of extreme cheerfulness, even in the face of customer abuse. Employees resist these norms covertly, most notably with the "seat belt squeeze"—a tactic that, under the guise of concern about visitor safety on amusement rides, involves a strong yank on the seat belts of obnoxious customers to ensure a painful degree of snugness.

Despite the existence of good work in the area of dissent (see Farrell & Rusbult, 1992), only limited attention has been paid to the dynamics of dissent messages. Yet evidence for their importance is abundant. For example, a study of 253 employees from a variety of organizational types found support for a link between the ability to express critical voice and organizational commitment of employees (Gorden & Infante, 1991). A major factor influencing downward influence behavior of leaders is their anticipation of dissent and resistance by followers (Sullivan, Albrecht, & Taylor, 1990). These studies suggest the need for cross-fertilization in the upward influence and organizational dissent literatures.

Power-Gaining Tactics

In contrast to research on "power tactics," which bears close resemblance to traditional compliance-gaining research (Cheng, 1983; Richmond, McCroskey, & Davis, 1986), a recent line of inquiry resides more comfortably within research on career development, mentoring, and social support. This research establishes the importance of relational communication that connects followers with mentors, peers, coaches, family members, and others (Bahniuk et al., 1991; Bahniuk, Hill, Kogler, & Darus, 1996). This work takes the notion of coalition-building tactics in the upward influence literature to a new level of specificity and expands it in ways that recognize the web of connections that facilitates or impedes upward influence efforts. Moreover, this research recognizes that influence is a process with elements that expand beyond traditionally defined organizational boundaries and has outcomes (e.g., life satisfaction, career development) that extend beyond short-term measures of effectiveness (see also Steil & Weltman, 1992).

Summary and Critique: Studies
of Related Message Types

The above discussion reveals that a rich body of research not typically associated with upward influence is nonetheless quite relevant. It seems clear that researchers need to do a better job of distinguishing these related forms of communication. For example, relationship maintenance tactics, messages of dissent, and upward influence behavior have all been conceptualized around the concept of assertiveness/directness. Relationship maintenance, impression management, and upward influence researchers have all described tactics related to ingratiation. Research on feedback seeking, relationship maintenance, and impression management has described attempts by subordinates to protect their identities through proactive inquiry and aggressive facework.

One explanation for this phenomenon is simply that research on these topics is too compartmentalized. Researchers operating in different spheres have failed to integrate their findings. If this is the case, an increasingly interdisciplinary approach to research on the communication activities of followers is called for. But it now appears obvious that the similarities in this research are due to the existence of broad theoretical principles that underlay communication in all of these related contexts (see O'Keefe, 1994). Future research should specify these underlying principles. The supposed objective (influence, relationship maintenance) of communication may be less important than the degree to which (for example) it disguises the follower's motives (Krone, 1992) or threatens the supervisor's face (Tjosvold, 1974; Waldron et al., 1993).

Another alternative is for researchers to specify the conceptual relations among tactics (for an example, see Deluga, 1991). It may be that impression management tactics create initial impressions, relationship maintenance tactics sustain them, and upward influence tactics are adjusted to them (for speculations about possible temporal relations, see Rao et al., 1995; Waldron, 1991). These temporal relations may span the course of a developing leader-member relationship, a series of interactions, or a single conversation. In this regard, work by Fairhurst and her colleagues on control sequences, although oriented to downward influence by managers, has established that tactic choice changes substantially after the first attempt (see, e.g., Fairhurst et al., 1984). Yet another possibility is that *most* messages are multifunctional in nature. If that is the case, researchers should develop coding schemes that simultaneously code messages in terms of their responsiveness to identity, relational, and instrumental concerns (among others).

Finally, in the interpersonal persuasion literature researchers have been able to locate numerous types of persuasive subgoals, some of which relate directly to relationship maintenance, identity protection, and resistance (Cody et al., 1994). This work associates goals with relevant types of tactics and specifies the degree to which tactics overlap across goals. Similar research directed exclusively at the broad range of communicative activities related to upward influence would be useful in imposing order on this far-flung literature.

SITUATIONAL FACTORS AFFECTING
UPWARD INFLUENCE BEHAVIOR

Theorists have identified relational, individual, and situational/contextual factors that ought to account for variation in upward influence tactic use (Cobb, 1984; Porter et al., 1981). Empirical studies of these factors are reviewed below.

Relationship Factors

This subsection reviews the research that has focused on qualities of the leader-follower relationship and their role in upward influence messages.

Leader-Member Exchange Quality

The much-researched leader-member exchange (LMX) perspective essentially describes leadership as a relational phenomenon involving the exchange of resources between leader and member (for recent discussions see Graen & Uhl-Bien, 1991, 1995; Graen & Wakabayashi, 1994). The theory posits that, rather than adopt an average leadership style to be used with all followers, leaders instead develop differentiated leadership approaches calibrated to the quality of their relationships with members. According to the theory, limitations on resources and time make it possible for leaders to develop high-quality leadership exchanges with some, but typically not all, followers. In leadership exchanges, supervisors invest social resources (e.g., communication, support, mentoring) to create high levels of trust, loyalty, and mutual understanding and reduced social distance (Dienesch & Liden, 1986). A characteristic of "mature" leadership exchanges is the exercise of reciprocal influence (Graen & Uhl-Bien, 1991). Lower-quality relationships (supervisory exchanges) are characterized by the exchange of monetary resources and are managed more contractually and formally. LMX quality and upward influence behavior have been linked in the literature, in part because LMX theory is one of the few that acknowledges follower influence on the leadership process.

Research cast at the level of tactics confirms the link between upward influence and LMX. Krone (1992), who conceptualizes upward influence as "political behavior" (Porter et al., 1981), found that members of leadership exchanges were less political (i.e., covert, deception based) and more open (i.e., overt, logic based) in their influence attempts. One dimension of LMX that might explain infrequent use of deception might be trust, which has been positively associated with the use of prosocial influence tactics in previous studies (Latib, 1989). However, the amount of variance accounted for by LMX in the Krone study was only 2% of the total. Using scenario-based rather than summary measures, Waldron et al. (1993) found effects of larger magnitude (up to 18% of variance), particularly in situations where the influence objective was organizational rather personal. We reasoned that members of leadership exchanges found such situations less threatening to the relationship and their individual identities. These members were also more likely to use the strategic tactic of soliciting the manager's advice and less likely to use the manipulative tactic of deception.

In an earlier study, Dockery and Steiner (1990) established a link between exchange quality and the use of ingratiation, exchange, and assertiveness tactics. Similarly, Deluga and Perry (1991) found that higher-quality exchanges are characterized by limited use of "hard" influence tactics, such as assertiveness or coercion. Consistent with this pattern, Maslyn et al. (1996) found that LMX quality was negatively associated with the use of persistence and positively associated with withdrawal in situations where the leader resisted initial attempts to obtain resources. In contrast, Waldron et al. (1993) studied an organizational scenario in which a supervisor resisted a proposed innovation and found exchange quality to be *negatively* associated with avoidance tactics and positively associated with what the researchers called direct tactics (e.g., asking for an explanation). Studies with discourse-level implications also confirm that members in leadership exchanges have more opportunities to exert control and influence (Fairhurst et al., 1987) and do so through such conversational devices as topic control and extension, framing positions, and sustaining challenges to leader positions (Fairhurst, 1993; Fairhurst & Chandler, 1989). These contrasting results indicate that the relationship between LMX and assertive-direct behavior varies. Organizational constraints (Green, Anderson, & Shivers, 1996), the level of analysis (tactics versus discourse), and, perhaps, the maturity of the relationship (Graen & Uhl-Bien, 1991, 1995) may account for this variation.

LMX quality has also been linked to related kinds of follower communication. Several studies of impression management processes indicate that followers' use of ingratiating behavior may be instrumental in developing leadership exchanges (Liden & Mitchell, 1989). Relatedly, member communication that is focused on the supervisor rather than the self has been associated with positive affect and increased liking (Wayne & Ferris, 1990). Liking may be one of several factors that constitute leadership exchanges (Dienesch & Liden, 1986; Dockery & Steiner, 1990). Studies of relationship maintenance tactics confirm that members of leadership exchanges report using more informal, open, and personal relational talk, similar to that used by friends (Waldron, 1991). But it has also been found that followers in leadership exchanges report high levels of "contractual" behavior, including seeking information about leader expectations and demonstrating conformity to rules (Waldron, 1991). Lee and Jablin (1995) found similar behavior patterns when relationships were stable. Members of low-quality exchanges engaged in more protective, deceptive, and avoidant communication, except in deteriorating situations, where they apparently threw caution to the wind and chose more direct tactics.

In general, this research indicates that the quality of the leader-member relationship is a substantial factor in accounting for the upward influence behavior of followers. The pattern of results suggests that members of low-quality exchanges might adopt more assertive tactics when the supervisory relationship is deteriorating and perhaps unsalvageable. In contrast, members of high-quality exchanges are more routinely open and direct in their interactions with leaders but less assertive in situations that threaten the relationship, as when influence behavior has previously failed. Perhaps these individuals experience enough influence in their routine interactions with leaders that highly assertive behavior is rarely necessary and may even threaten the relationship.

In a sense, this pattern of results confirms in the organization context a finding that has been reported frequently in the interpersonal literature: The degree of social distance separating agent and recipient appears to be a primary situational factor that shapes persuasive behavior (Cody et al., 1994). This research also suggests that members not only react to LMX quality in predictable ways, they also *create* it (through tactics designed to demonstrate liking and conformity) and sustain it through conversational devices and tactics that signal acceptance of influence opportunities, negotiate controls, and manage threats to the identities of self, supervisor, and the relationship.

Power and Power Differences

Results pertaining to LMX quality imply that upward influence changes as a function of power and social distance (Fairhurst, 1993). Supporting evidence for the effects of power is found in studies indicating that tactic use varies with the direction of the influence attempt. Upwardly-directed influence is more likely to be based on logic and reason than on assertiveness or resource exchange—presumably because the message sender lacks the legitimate power and resources needed to make these tactics credible (Chacko, 1990; Erez, Rim, & Keider, 1986; Schilit & Locke, 1982). But differences due to direction tend to be mixed, small, and, in some cases, nonexistent (Kipnis et al., 1980; Yukl & Tracey, 1992).

The magnitude of the power difference between leader and follower should be a more important determinant of tactic use (Tjosvold, Andrews, & Struthers, 1992). One possibility is that power differential has a "chilling effect" that encourages low-power individuals to avoid the exercise of influence for fear of the consequences (Cloven & Roloff, 1993). In fact, some studies have found that lower-power followers use influence tactics less frequently and with less variety than do upper-level followers (Ferris & Judge, 1991; Thacker

& Wayne, 1995). In a survey of 500 employees, Waldron and Hunt (1992) found that followers located higher in the organizational hierarchy were more likely to use direct tactics to maintain their relationships with leaders. These included explicit discussion of relational expectations and injustices. Mainiero (1986) reports similar findings, indicating that high levels of relational dependency are associated with passivity and acquiescence in influence situations.

In general, it appears that as followers become more powerful through position, expertise, information access, or other power bases, their tactical options increase and their tactics become more assertive, particularly when the influence attempt appears to be "legitimate" from the organization's point of view.

Relationship Maturity

Socialization perspectives indicate that the maturity, longevity, and developmental stage of relationships constitute another dimension that may potentially affect influence behavior (Jablin & Krone, 1994). Schilit (1986, 1987a, 1987b) studied the influence activities of midlevel managers and concludes that the length (in years) of the leader-member relationship is a strong predictor of the degree and type of influence activity. In longer-term relationships, members appear to view themselves as less vulnerable, or at least more willing to take risks in influence situations. This view is consistent with theoretical depictions of the development of "mature" leader-member exchanges (Bauer & Green, 1996; Graen & Uhl-Bien, 1991, 1995). But this theoretical perspective suggests that such mature relationships develop from mutual investments of social resources rather than the mere passage of time. In this regard, a study of maintenance tactics used in supervisory relationships ranging in length from 3 months to more than 10 years found no substantive changes in upwardly directed maintenance behavior over time (Waldron & Hunt, 1992).

Individual Difference Factors

Individual characteristics of leaders and members have been proposed as factors that may shape influence behavior (Porter et al., 1981).

Sex Differences

Researchers have frequently analyzed the effects of sex differences on upward influence tactic choice (Ansari, 1989; DuBrin, 1989; Kipnis et al., 1980; Yukl & Falbe, 1990) and have generally found small or no effects due to the sex of agent and target. In an exception, Lamude (1993) found gender differences in a study of successful upward influence tactics described by 162 male and female managers. The results suggest that the females in this study preferred inspirational and "allurement" tactics with both male and female managers. In contrast, the males appeared more likely to adjust their tactics depending on the sex of the recipient. Contrary to expectations, Lamude found males more likely to use inspiration, ingratiation, and liking tactics with male leaders and pressure tactics with female leaders.

More promising is research suggesting that upward influence tactics may have differential effects for males and females on outcomes such as promotability assessments and salary attainment (Kipnis & Schmidt, 1988). Dreher, Dougherty, and Whitely (1989) attempted to account for disparities in the salaries of 212 male and 82 female business graduates. They found no substantive differences in the upward influence tactics of the men and women, but they discovered that exchange tactics were linked to salary size for men and reasoning tactics acted similarly for women. In a study linking upward influence tactics with performance ratings and the receipt of mentoring from supervisors, Tepper, Brown, and Hunt (1993) found an interaction between sex and tactic use. Males who used "stronger" tactics received higher performance ratings and more career-related mentoring. Women who used "weaker" tactics received more psychosocial mentoring. Tepper and his colleagues conclude that male and female followers are expected to use influence in different ways, and that violation of these expectations may yield negative outcomes. More recently, Thacker and Wayne (1995) found that gender and influence tactic use failed to interact to affect promotability ratings. But this result may be due to their use of only three tactics as a basis for comparison.

Subordinate Personality/Disposition

Porter et al. (1981) have posited that individual differences in personality characteristics ought to affect the political behavior of followers. One candidate characteristic is Machiavellianism (Grams & Rogers, 1990), which has been predicted to affect the decision to persist or withdraw from upward influence episodes. But this factor was not found to be an important predictor of influence tactics used by 285 employees of a large nonprofit organization (Maslyn et al., 1996), and it was correlated with the use of only one tactic (blocking) in another study (Vecchio & Sussmann, 1991). In contrast, middle-level followers with a high need for achievement and internal locus of control were found to be more influential in decision making in one study (Schilit, 1986), and they may be more likely to use reason and coalition tactics (Chacko, 1990). A summary of the literature on argumentativeness (Infante & Rancer, 1996) indicates that subordinates differ in their willingness and ability to engage in constructive debate about controversial issues. Subordinates characterized by high levels of argumentativeness apparently receive positive ratings from supervisors. In sum, only a few dispositional factors have been studied thus far. In most cases the amount of variance accounted for by these factors is relatively small.

Age and Experience

Deluga and Perry (1991) found that age was negatively related to the frequency of use of all influence tactics. In contrast, Maslyn et al. (1996) found that work experience made employees less likely to withdraw from influence situations in which they met resistance. This difference might be attributed to the association of work experience with political savvy, a factor previously predicted to encourage influence behavior (Porter et al., 1981).

Leadership Style

In early theoretical work, the style enacted by leaders was posited to affect influence tactics (Cobb, 1986). Since that time, followers have been shown to prefer reasoning tactics when leaders use a participative style (Ansari & Kapoor, 1987) and hard tactics when leaders are low in initiation and consideration (Chacko, 1990; Cheng, 1983). A series of surveys of employees indicates that those with supervisors who encouraged argumentativeness were more likely to express voice, be committed, and report satisfaction with their work situation (for representative work, see Gorden & Infante, 1991; Gorden et al., 1988; Infante, Anderson, Martin, Herington, & Kim, 1993; Infante & Gorden, 1989; Infante & Rancer, 1996). In contrast, verbally aggressive supervisors may have a dampening effect on employee voice.

Subordinate Performance Level

LMX researchers suggest that high-performing employees might "earn" the right to engage in extracontractual influence and thus shape organizational decisions (Graen & Uhl-Bien, 1995). Followers who routinely communicate information about their conformity to performance expectations have been found to be more likely to have achieved high-quality exchanges with their leaders (Waldron, 1991; Waldron et al., 1993). Wayne et al. (1995) found no direct effect for subordinate performance level on the use or effects of ingratiation. Perhaps performance level directly contributes to relational perceptions, which in turn may affect influence tactic use. Of course, influence tactic choice may then alter perceptions of performance and relational quality, as suggested in the impression management and feedback literatures (e.g., Larson, 1989; Wayne & Liden, 1985).

Situational/Contextual Factors

Researchers have noted that the unique characteristics of organizations, roles, and work situations may be more important than individual or relational differences in predicting how followers behave in influence situations.

Goal of the Influence Attempt

In the interpersonal literature, it has become almost a truism that persuasive strategies vary with influence objectives (Cody et al., 1994)—a point apparently taken to heart by upward influence researchers. Researchers have consistently contrasted the tactics used to achieve two types of goals (Schmidt & Kipnis, 1984): personal (e.g., getting time off) and organizational (e.g., acquiring support for a project). Adding to research using this personal/organizational distinction, Yukl and associates (Yukl & Falbe, 1990; Yukl, Guinan, & Sottolano, 1995) have found that the most common purposes of upward influence are requesting approval, acquiring resources, and building managerial support for projects or ideas.

Research suggests that personal goals are more likely to be approached with exchange, ingratiation, and other soft tactics, whereas organizational objectives are (somewhat) more likely to be approached with rationality or hard tactics (Ansari & Kapoor, 1987; Erez et al., 1986; Kipnis et al., 1980; Waldera, 1988; Waldron et al., 1993). Prevailing organizational norms may serve to legitimate the exercise of influence by subordinates when the goal is perceived as consistent with organizational objectives (Porter et al., 1981). Power differences and threat to self may be mitigated in such situations. Confirming this, in a recent study 283 employees rated personal goal situations as more threatening to their identity and supervisory relationship, a factor attributed to the lower level of legitimacy associated with personal requests in organizational environments (Waldron, 1997). Measures of perceived threat were more directly associated with tactic use than was the goal itself.

Several studies indicate that coalition building is a tactic used frequently when followers promote change and new ideas to leaders (Howell & Higgins, 1990). In addition, the importance of the goals to the follower is apparently a significant predictor of influence behavior (Mowday, 1978). At least one upward influence study demonstrates that persistence with the supervisor (or another supervisor outside the chain of command) is positively associated with goal importance (Maslyn et al., 1996). In addition, when the likelihood of achieving the influence goal is high, rational tactics might be used, but when it is low, followers may resort to harder tactics (Kipnis, Schmidt, Swaffin-Smith, & Wilkinson, 1984).

Job Level

Lower-level employees have less discretion and autonomy when choosing influence tactics and tend to use influence less frequently than do upper-level employees (Ferris & Judge, 1991; Thacker & Wayne, 1995). Persons in supervisory positions are generally found to use a wider range of upward influence tactics than do those in lower power positions (Ansari, 1989) and may be more likely to use persistence or upward appeal influence methods (Case et al., 1988; Vecchio & Sussmann, 1991).

Structural Features

Structural features of organizations have not been addressed extensively in the upward influence literature. Size of organization and centralization of authority were found to have small effects in a study reported by Krone (1992). Erez and Rim (1982) found in their study of 125 Israeli managers that rational tactics were more likely to be used in large organizations. The degree of latitude, structure, and certainty associated with organizational roles and relationships appears to constrain influence behavior (Green et al., 1996). Role uncertainty was the strongest predictor of influence activity in a study by Cobb (1986), who also found that the power of the larger work unit affected employees' decisions to seek influence.

Political and Cultural Factors

Models of upward influence have often conceptualized it as a political process unique to organizations, in which organizational members operate from power bases of various types, attempt to accrue power through influence behavior, adapt their behavior to prevailing cultural norms, and seek to advance the interests of themselves or their work groups (Mayes & Allen, 1977; Porter et al., 1981; Schein, 1977). Cultural values and assumptions determine which types of influence objectives and tactics are viewed as legitimate (Porter et al., 1981) and can function to value or devalue the influence messages of a particular gender, ethnic group, or subculture. It has been argued that follower and leader argumentativeness is instrumental in promoting perceptions of democracy in American organizations (Infante & Rancer, 1996). Yet the *empirical* research on upward influence rarely acknowledges the larger political forces in organizations that shape follower behavior, apparently leaving such questions to critical theorists and ethicists (e.g., Graham, 1995).

There is some evidence supporting the importance of these macro factors in the upward influence process. Krone (1992) found that company identity was more important than a host of structural and relational factors in accounting for subordinates' use of influence attempts. In a study of five companies, she reasoned that socialization processes made interactants aware of the degree to which political behavior could be open, strategic, or manipulative. Although typically not concerned with upward influence per se, existing ethnographic research has done a better job of documenting the relationship between cultural practices and influence activities of members. For example, in their study of the culture of Disneyland, Van Maanen and Kunda (1989) found that prevailing cultural norms and supervisory controls enforced on employees an ethic of extreme cheerfulness that was often affirmed but sometimes resisted overtly by employees. It is clear from this work that employees do not simply react to organizational culture, they create it, in part through their decisions to resist or contest cultural values. Another indirect connection to issues of power and culture can be made through the leadership literature. The extent to which leaders create political and cultural conditions that facilitate follower autonomy and influence is a criterion useful in distinguishing among emerging perspectives of leadership (Graham, 1995; see also below).

Summary and Critique: Studies of Relational, Individual, and Contextual Factors

The research indicates that relationship factors have broad effects on influence tactic use. Contextual factors are clearly important, but cultural and political factors are somewhat understudied by upward influence researchers. Individual differences appear to have small or nonexistent effects on upward influence behavior.

With regard to relationship factors, the accumulating body of empirical research on leader-member exchange quality affirms theoretical claims about the importance of follower influence in the leadership-making process. The importance of position power and power disparity is also well supported. However, additional research is needed on the potentially complex connection between relationship development and upward influence (Bauer & Green, 1996). The quantity and nature of influence activity should change as relationships mature. For example, early in a relationship, influence behavior may be oriented more toward altering relational definitions in a manner that builds trust and liking. These activities may have the long-term effects of increasing opportunities for reciprocal (rather than one-way) influence, reducing the risk associated with influence attempts, and emboldening followers to resist leader influence behavior. As researchers design studies to examine relationship maturity, they must consider more than the mere passage of time. Memories of past encounters, the accumulated track record of expressed relational commitments, trust, and the development of unique rather than merely conventional ways of relating all mark changes in relationship quality that should shape influence behavior in later relationship stages. The rate or quality of relationship development may be accelerated or delayed due to the nature of the work performed, the degree to which leader-member interaction is possible, and other constraints (Green et al., 1996).

Upward influence research has been limited by its tendency to consider only traditional, hierarchical supervisory relations as the context for influence. With changing organizational forms (see below) comes a whole new set of important relationships. Relationships with coaches, formal mentors, informal mentors, team leaders, senior team members, project champions, and peers potentially involve different kinds of power relations, obligations, influence objectives, and influence tactics. At the time of this writing, increasing numbers of work relationships involve telecommuting and temporary workers, but little research has documented the means of influence exercised in these relationships.

The value of studying alternate relational forms is illustrated in a study by Tepper (1995), who found different patterns of upward maintenance behavior in formal and informal mentoring relationships. Recent conceptual extensions of leader-member exchange theory to team relationships provide theoretical guidance for researchers studying influence in teams (see Graen & Uhl-Bien, 1991, 1995; Seers, 1989). Ethnographic research indicates that team members control status-equal peers with tactics ranging from value-based appeals to traditional bureaucratic coercion (e.g., Barker, 1993). But the effects of social networks on upward influence behavior, in particular the contributions of peer advice and peer modeling, have yet to be fully investigated. Nor have the effects of friendship and family network support been fully considered (but see Bahniuk et al., 1996).

The research on individual differences is less promising. An exception is the evidence suggesting that sex differences and tactic choices interact with social expectations to affect outcomes (Tepper et al., 1993). Additional work in this area may explain sex differences in salaries and other critical individual outcomes. Leadership style is an individual-level factor that has received surprisingly limited research attention, given the many models of leadership that have emerged in recent decades (see the discussion below). The degrees to which autonomy is respected and follower influence is encouraged are features that discriminate among leadership approaches (Graham, 1991, 1995). Researchers should explore how different leadership styles are associated with the upward influence activities of followers. Another promising direction is found in research on the behaviors of "difficult" subordinates (Monroe, DiSalvo, Lewis, & Borzi, 1990). In fact, the abusive communicative tendencies of both subordinates and supervisors require additional study, as they are likely sources of work stress.

Finally, research on contextual factors affecting influence behavior is suggestive but, as yet, underdeveloped. The importance of influence goals is clearly established, but the full range of influence objectives and situational factors shown to affect influence behavior has yet to be investigated. These objectives and factors include (among others) request legitimacy, homophily, apprehension, and perceived consequences (Cody et al., 1994). Underlying features of goals that account for their effects on message design need to be identified. The type and nature of face threat inherent in goals might constitute one such feature (Lim & Bowers, 1991; Tjosvold, 1974), but face-threatening communication is complex and nuanced enough to require discourse-level, rather than tactic-level, data. In pursuing further study of influence situations and goals, researchers should be careful to validate their measures of situational features (Roloff, 1994).

Structural factors appear to have small effects in most studies. One potentially important but understudied (in this literature) structural feature is role characteristics. Roles have received theoretical attention (Cobb, 1984) but limited empirical research (Cobb, 1986). It appears that employees use more upward influence behavior when they experience high levels of role conflict (Deluga, 1989). A recent study of salespersons' influence tactics demonstrated that role conflict was positively associated with the use of assertive upward influence, whereas role ambiguity was positively associated with exchange and coalition-building tactics (Nonis et al., 1996). Upward influence tactics appeared in this study to mediate the effects of role stressors on important outcomes, such as intent to leave the organization. In other words, these tactics may be a means by which employees cope with the effects of structural factors beyond their control.

Finally, the relative lack of attention paid by researchers to macro-level forces must be remedied. The strong tendency in this literature to conceptualize upward influence at individual and dyadic levels probably accounts for the current dearth of research. Researchers oversimplify influence processes when they fail to analyze and critique political, cultural, occupational, and economic factors that shape the perceived legitimacy of influence behavior. The rationales offered in influence attempts, the goals of influence, and whether upward influence is even considered an option by followers are all shaped by these forces. Understanding the role of social and cultural expectations is prerequisite to unraveling the findings regarding sex differences reported above.

OUTCOMES OF UPWARD INFLUENCE

Research on the outcomes of upward influence is relatively recent and sparse. Outcomes can be personal (e.g., obtaining a salary increase), relational (e.g., improved trust), or collective (e.g., improved organizational decision making). As only the former two have been studied extensively, they are considered in this section. I take up the neglect of collective outcomes in the summary and critique subsection below.

Individual Outcomes

Generally, upward influence behavior has been shown to have facilitating effects on measures of individual success. Over and above more "objective" factors, such as years of experience, employee use of upward influence behavior accounts for variation in supervisor judgments of promotability (Ferris, Judge, Rowland, & Fitzgibbons, 1994; Thacker & Wayne, 1995) and performance ratings (Tepper et al., 1993). In this regard, Dreher et al. (1989) found no significant effect for assertiveness on salary attainment, but did find positive effects for exchange tactics (in a male sample) and reasoning tactics (in a female sample). In contrast, Waldera (1988) found that employees grouped by supervisors based on effectiveness showed no differences in influence tactic preference.

Several additional studies have examined the effects of specific types of influence tactics on performance evaluation (Ferris et al., 1994; Judge & Bretz, 1994). From this work it appears that "soft" influence tactics affect performance evaluation indirectly. For example, self-promotion and ingratiation tactics have been shown to produce affective responses in supervisors, which in turn negatively or positively affect performance ratings. The effects of ingratiation tactics have been mixed in this regard, with studies claiming both positive (Judge & Bretz, 1994) and negative effects (Thacker & Wayne, 1995) on performance outcomes.

The complexity of the link between tactics and outcomes is illustrated in Thacker and Wayne's (1995) study of 157 university employees. These researchers linked the use of reasoning and ingratiation to promotability assessments. When only supervisory employees were considered, reasoning tactics were positively associated with promotability (beta = .25) and assertiveness tactics were negatively associated with promotability (beta = −.18). Thacker and Wayne found ingratiation also to be negatively correlated (beta = −.26) with supervisor rankings of promotability. But for lower-level employees neither of these tactics was associated with promotability assessments. These results suggest that the relationships between tactic use and outcomes are mediated by employee latitude and role expectations (Porter et al., 1981).

In an interesting twist on other studies, Falbe and Yukl (1992) defined three possible outcomes of influence attempts as cognitive commitment, behavioral compliance, or resistance. As previous authors have found in interviews with practicing managers (Case et al., 1988; Schilit, 1987a, 1987b), they report evidence that multiple tactics were perceived by followers to be more successful in gaining supervisor commitment than the use of just one tactic. Success in achieving the three outcomes varied with the mix of tactics, but not in systematic ways. Although suggestive, the study's results are qualified by apparently imprecise coding procedures (no chance-correcting reliability statistic is reported) and by the self-report nature of outcome measures. In another study with implications for the use of multiple tactics, Kipnis and Schmidt (1988) found that their "tactician" style, characterized by the repeated use of reason, was associated with higher salaries than were the "shotgun" and "bystander" approaches.

Relationship Outcomes

In some studies, assertiveness and repetition tactics have appeared to create negative effects on leader-member relations (Barry & Bateman, 1992; Rao et al., 1995). One interpretation of the accumulated research on leader-member exchange theory is that the influence activities of the follower are instrumental in moving the relationship to a "mature stage" characterized by high degrees of trust, support, and mutual benefit (Graen & Uhl-Bien, 1991).

In one of the few studies that has examined the effects of upward influence tactics on coworker relations, Wayne et al. (1995) used an artificial work situation that required groups of undergraduates to cooperate with a confederate who used (or did not use) ingratiation tactics with the group's supervisor. Workers with an ingratiating peer rated their mutual supervisor higher on measures of satisfaction and fairness, an indication that ingratiation has effects not only on the target but on the perceptions of third parties. Interestingly, ingratiating confederates were themselves viewed no differently than confederates who refrained from ingratiation. Others have suggested that repeated use of ingratiating behavior may result in negative relational perceptions (Liden & Mitchell, 1989).

Summary and Critique of Outcomes Research

The empirical research on outcomes is not yet extensive. Generally speaking, this literature suggests that the influence behaviors of followers can have substantive personal and organizational effects (Schilit, 1987a). It supports the notion that "effective subordinancy" involves followers who are active in the decision-making process and willing to confront the leader under some conditions (Downs & Conrad, 1982). But the results of outcome studies have not been uniformly supportive of this notion, partially due to methodological inconsistencies and the tendency to measure outcomes in diverse ways (Falbe & Yukl, 1992). Outcomes can be immediate, as when the influence attempt leads directly to changed behavior in the leader. In contrast, long-term or cumulative effects may be observed in periodic performance evaluations or measures of upward mobility. It may be useful to distinguish global judgments of effectiveness (overall performance) from more specific ones (e.g., evaluations of persuasiveness). These finer distinctions have yet to be made in the literature.

Particularly problematic is the lack of research linking upward influence to collective outcomes. This is partially due to the exclusion of research on formal bargaining processes and participation systems from this review. But the likelihood that voice, upward influence, and resistance processes are essential to the collective success of the organization remains underinvestigated in the upward influence literature (cif., Redding, 1985). Most notable is the lack of "hard" measures of variables such as reduced turnover, increased innovation, redistributed resources, and improved safety, which might be expected to change as a function of the persuasive efforts of followers. In an exception, Nonis et al. (1996), building on work by Deluga (1989), provide preliminary evidence that upward influence activity is linked to intent to leave the organization, but they do not report actual measures of turnover. Their study does suggest, however, that influence tactics may help employees cope with role stress, which is a potentially important individual outcome with implications for the collective health of workers. In addition, some evidence indicates that employees who experience opportunities to voice their concerns are more committed to their organizations (Gorden & Infante, 1991). But on the whole, considerably more work is needed on the outcomes associated with organizational health, responsiveness, employee morale, and work satisfaction. In addition, the exercise of upward influence is obviously linked to organizational democracy, citizenship, and the ethical obligations of followers and leaders. Traditional upward influence research has not engaged these issues.

REFRAMING UPWARD
INFLUENCE RESEARCH

It is clear from the preceding review that traditional upward influence research has produced a steady and programmatic stream of contributions regarding influence tactics, their outcomes, and the factors that affect their use. As I have indicated throughout this chapter, communication research and theory will be useful in articulating more specifically the interactive processes that constitute the influence process, nominating theories and coding procedures that improve message categorization, and conceptualizing the connections between upward influence and related forms of communication. But in addition to making incremental improvements in traditional models, upward influence research might benefit from a fundamental rethinking of its assumptions. Two emerging trends—changing conceptions of leader-follower relations and new organizational forms—make this reassessment timely. I review both briefly below before concluding the chapter with a discussion of selected communication concepts that might reframe the upward influence research.

Evolving Conceptions of
Leadership and Followership

The existing upward influence literature has been somewhat unresponsive to changing conceptions of leadership and followership (see, e.g., Fairhurst, in press; Graham, 1995; Hollander & Offerman, 1990). Traditional perspectives on leadership view the leader as a power broker whose primary purposes are to direct and control followers using a system of concrete resources, rules, and orders. In this view, follower roles are relatively passive and characterized by limited autonomy. Followers seek guidance and sometimes inspiration from the leader and concern themselves with implementing leader plans. Upward influence is rare, necessarily strategic, likely to be resisted, and risky when viewed from this perspective.

In recent years, theorists have described or advocated numerous alternative or updated models of leadership, including charismatic leadership (House & Howell, 1992), transformational leadership (Bass, 1985), transactional leadership (e.g., Graen & Uhl-Bien, 1995), servant leadership (for a review see Graham, 1991), stewardship (Block, 1993), learning leadership (Senge, 1990), and "super leadership" (Manz & Sims, 1991). Although very different, these views all direct attention away from the traditional hierarchical view of leadership as a process of allocating resources and directing people and toward views that emphasize consensus-forming, value-defining, and rhetorical dimensions. Leadership is often viewed as a relational rather than an individual phenomenon (Graen & Uhl-Bien, 1995; Hollander, 1995; Hollander & Julian, 1990). Moreover, "leadership" is increasingly distinguished from "management" (for an early discussion, see Hickman, 1990). Leaders are more likely than managers to consider the "big picture," to construct persuasive visions, to initiate change, and to thrive in environments characterized by disorder and ambiguity. Researchers should investigate whether upward influence is more frequent and/or different in the presence of "true" leadership. Perhaps influential followers are a defining characteristic of leadership, when it is defined in this way.

Most striking in this literature is the growing sense that leadership is primarily a process of empowering followers. In a narrow sense, empowerment means sharing power and emboldening followers to take action in support of a vision created by a charismatic leader (see Bass, 1985). However, conceptions of servant or transformational leadership extend this notion (Graham, 1991, 1995). The leader's role is to create conditions that encourage followers to exert influence as active participants in organizational governance. Rather than charismatic exhortations, leaders encourage autonomy and create the expectation that followers think for themselves, responsibly question the status quo, and create for themselves a system of organization that meets the needs of all members and conforms to shared ethical principles. This view of the process differs radically from the traditional models and necessitates rethinking of the follower role.

Followers and their activities have received considerable attention over the years from leadership researchers (Lantis, 1987). However, changing conceptions of leadership have spawned renewed speculation in the practitioner (Bennis, 1991; Buhler, 1993) and academic literatures about the important and diverse contributions of followers (Graham, 1995; Hollander, 1992). The most important implication of this work is that followers should experience expanded opportunities for influence (in all directions) in many organizations. For example, upward influence might be not just an exercise in "getting one's way" but also a process of exploring new ideas and questioning assumptions in dialogue with leaders and peers (Senge, 1990). In some cases, such as with charismatic leaders, follower influence might involve "reigning in" unrealistic visions or unethical persuasive practices of orator-leaders. In research cast from these alternate leadership perspectives, traditional factors like power difference might be less important in shaping influence tactic use than such considerations as follower/leader perceptions of shared responsibility, organizational values, and perceived opportunities for learning. Future research must better account for these leader-follower dynamics and their implications for the frequency, quality, context, and motives of follower influence. One fruitful place to begin this process might be in the upper echelons of organizations, where both followers and leaders have relative autonomy and many opportunities for joint influence (see House & Aditya, 1997).

Upward Influence in a
Changing Work Environment

In the past decade, team-based, decentralized decision making has continued to be embraced in American organizations. To increase flexibility, employee commitment, and responsiveness, organizations have flattened organizational structures and shared power with teams of employees who are closer than they formerly were to work processes and customers. The tendency toward team-based organizing can alter radically the context within which employees exercise influence. Even the term *upward influence* must be rethought as traditional hierarchical and bureaucratic controls are replaced with systems of concertive control. In team-based models, control is rooted in the efforts of peers to promote conformity with values accepted by the team. Leaders become coaches, resource providers, or facilitators. Employees who seek to expand their influence do so within a web of interpersonal relationships with status-equal peers. Traditional studies of upward influence do not apply well in this context.

Relationship-based views of the influence process may translate most readily to team environments. Graen and Wakabayashi (1994) view mutual influence and the transformation from self-concern to concern for the collective good as products of mature leader-member relationships. By facilitating the development of such relationships, organizations lay the groundwork for effective teamwork (Graen & Uhl-Bien, 1991; Seers, 1989), which requires the investment of social resources, the exercise of influence, and extracontractual commitment by members. Through development of mature exchanges in relationships with team members, coaches, and key persons in the extended organizational network, members develop more widespread influence and gain access to resources that facilitate team success (Graen & Wakabayashi, 1994).

On the other hand, employees in team-based organizations still find themselves attempting to influence more powerful others. The advantaged party may be a coach, an emergent team leader, or a senior member of the team. The functions of team leaders in Japanese transplant organizations (e.g., directing the work process, selecting workers) sound similar to traditional definitions of supervision (see Graen & Wakabayashi, 1994). In such organizations, power disadvantages might develop less from traditional position power than from differences in technical expertise, seniority, team loyalty, network centrality, cultural knowledge, or information access. But the fact remains that members must cope with status inequality.

Moreover, it appears that in at least some team-based organizations, the value-based system of control designed and enforced by peers can become more restrictive and powerful than the bureaucratic systems they replace. Barker (1993) followed the development of teams in a manufacturing plant and found that member behavior was initially controlled by a shared sense of values and norms. With time, however, teams developed a fairly complex set of behavioral rules to regulate such things as tardiness, and the rules were enforced in a fairly ruthless manner by team members themselves. What this means is that team-based organizing has the potential to restrict member autonomy and influence in a manner less observable but potentially more potent than in traditional authority systems. Rather than create influence messages for a single supervisor within the constraints imposed by a system of overt, "legitimate" controls, members must consider multiple peer-managers as the "audience" for influence attempts (see Wayne et al., 1995). They must operate within a system of less overt, potentially more ambiguous, value-based constraints (see Tompkins & Cheney, 1985). As a team member, the initiator of the influence message has to some extent contributed to the real or imagined consensus on which team rules are based, a fact that complicates the influence process and no doubt discourages members from arguing with the status quo. In short, the locus of power has moved much closer to home.

Numerous social and organizational forces ensure that teams will remain influential in the American workplace (Fairhurst, in press). Given this reality, upward influence researchers should expand their models in the following ways. First, they should document the prevalence of concertive control and its effects on the form and content of influence behavior. Persuasive messages might increasingly be constructed on appeals to idiosyncratic team values rather than organizational goals. Second, the notion of multiple audiences needs to be accounted for. Messages are created and shared with multiple team members rather than single supervisors. The influence process might helpfully be reframed as a web of relationships, in contrast to a process occurring within the leader-follower dyad. Influence is created, resisted, and redefined as team members interact across this web. A kind of "spreading activation" model of influence might better account for the way that influence is communicated across the organization. This view of influence directs attention to the way ideas, arguments, and emotions "flow" through the web, altering decisions in a mostly unconscious manner. It can be contrasted with a more individualistic, strategic view of persuasion.

Third, in team-based organizations, coalition-forming tactics might be more widely used. Because member status differences are less accentuated than in more hierarchical organizations, influence may be more a process of recruiting a critical mass of peer support and building *horizontal* influence than a process of constructing arguments for more powerful decision makers. Even more than in traditional organizations, influence and power may be a process of constructing a more tightly woven web of social connections and supports. Members might obtain disproportional influence in team and organizational decision processes when they activate this web, shape the meanings of messages flowing across it, "pump" emotion into it, or otherwise "agitate" the team into rethinking its otherwise taken-for-granted decision premises.

Alternate Perspectives Derived From Communication Research and Theory

Some existing communication research can make obvious, if incremental, contributions to the prevailing (mostly psychological) stream of upward influence studies. For example, research on argumentation and persuasion could be helpful as researchers grapple with "tactic content"—the features of messages that make them persuasive to leaders. Planning theory (Berger, 1997) might help researchers to frame questions about how subordinates construct influence strategies based on previous work experiences, about the qualities of such strategies, and, most intriguing, about how subordinates are likely to modify these strategies in response to thwarting by the supervisor. Research on social networks and network roles provides an obvious starting place for the spreading activation model of influence described above. Most important is the need for communication theorists to help identify the theoretical features that underlie existing tactic taxonomies (Kellermann & Cole, 1994). Additional development of ad hoc taxonomies will not help this literature, and research extending existing taxonomies is unlikely to foster innovative conceptions of the influence process.

More interesting is the possibility that communication researchers might participate in a fundamental reframing of the upward influence literature. Considerable recent theorizing in communication calls attention to the cultural, temporal, and nondeterminate qualities of communication (see Werner & Baxter, 1994). The assumptions common in upward influence research— that communication is a linear process, that individual tactic choices "cause" certain outcomes, that situational variables can be separated from the communication processes—are all contested by this approach. At a minimum, a reading of this literature would encourage upward influence researchers to incorporate time in their models, consider dyads and other social units rather than individuals as the appropriate level of analysis, and focus on the role of influence processes in the construction of meaning rather than as a cause of outcomes. One concrete application to this literature would be the research on relational dialectics (Baxter, 1990). From this perspective relationships do not merely develop on an orderly course from socially distant to intimate. Instead, they involve oppositional tensions between bipolar relational features such as autonomy and interdependence or stability and change (Baxter, 1990). Communication is the process through which relational partners manage the tensions between the poles, by (for example) agreeing to share decisions (or not) or engaging in more or fewer joint activities. Conceived in this way, upward influence might be a process of altering the definition of the leader-member relationship along dimensions of autonomy/interdependence. The type (unilateral, reciprocal) and intensity of influence activities might increase, decrease, or remain stable at various times in the relationship, depending on the relational and individual needs of the participants.

One additional communication metaphor that might be useful in reframing the literature is that of a "campaign." Mass communication research establishes that persuasion involves multiple channels, multiple sources of support, and messages created to meet interim objectives as well as final goals. Researchers approaching upward influence in this way might produce research that documents how followers cooperate in the influence process and how messages are evaluated and adapted during different stages of the persuasive process. Finally, interpersonal communication researchers have increasingly concerned themselves with the routine communication activities that define and sustain interpersonal relationships. This is applied most obviously to the workplace in research on relationship maintenance tactics (Lee & Jablin, 1995; Tepper, 1995; Waldron, 1991). But existing research can be faulted for focusing too much on relatively "dramatic" persuasion events that in reality may be experienced relatively infrequently by most followers. The actual day-to-day communication activities of followers are not well documented, but it seems certain that most of this communication is more mundane and less strategic than the typical upward influence study presumes (Hunt, 1994). These less exciting but more prevalent interactions may ultimately determine the quality of leader-member relationships and predispose followers to use certain influence tactics when the need arises (Tepper, 1995; Waldron, 1991). Researchers may need to entertain the possibility that followers communicate in a more mindless and less purposeful manner than is often assumed.

In conclusion, this review reveals that upward influence researchers have made extensive progress in understanding a very important aspect of organizational life. The potential for interdisciplinary cross-fertilization, the impact of new forms of organizing, and the importance of this type of communication to followers and leaders make it likely that new and creative research will be produced in the near future. Perhaps the most compelling need at this point is for additional theoretical work to supplement what is a body of largely intuitive and variable-analytic studies. Researchers typically continue to adopt an implicit or explicit social exchange perspective. The most provocative theoretical work arguably was completed more than a decade ago (Cobb, 1984; Porter et al., 1981). It is puzzling that researchers have not tested these early models more systematically and holistically with causal modeling techniques. However, it seems certain that communication theory and research will be helpful in constructing reinvigorated models of the upward influence process.

REFERENCES

Ansari, M. A. (1989). Effects of leader sex, subordinate sex, and subordinate performance on the use of influence strategies. *Sex Roles, 20,* 283-293.

Ansari, M. A., & Kapoor, A. (1987). Organizational context and upward influence tactics. *Organizational Behavior and Human Decision Processes, 40,* 39-49.

Ashford, S. J., & Cummings, L. L. (1983). Feedback as an individual resource: Personal strategies of creating information. *Organizational Behavior and Human Performance, 32,* 370-398.

Ashford, S. J., & Northcraft, G. B. (1992). Conveying more (or less) than we realize: The role of impression-management in feedback seeking. *Organizational Behavior and Human Decision Processes, 53,* 310-334.

Atwater, L., Roush, P., & Fischthal, A. (1995). The influence of upward feedback on self and the follower ratings of leadership. *Personnel Psychology, 48,* 35-59.

Bahniuk, M. H., Dobos, J., & Hill, S. E. K. (1991). The impact of mentoring, collegial support, and information adequacy on career success: A replication. In J. W. Neuliep (Ed.), *Replication research in the social sciences* (pp. 419-444). Newbury Park, CA: Sage.

Bahniuk, M. H., Hill, S. E., Kogler, D., & Darus, H. J. (1996). The relationship of power-gaining communication strategies to career success. *Western Journal of Communication, 60,* 358-378.

Barker, J. B. (1993). Tightening the iron cage: Concertive control in self-managing teams. *Administrative Science Quarterly, 38,* 408-437.

Barry, B., & Bateman T. S. (1992). Perceptions of influence in managerial dyads: The role of hierarchy, media, and tactics. *Human Relations, 65,* 555-574.

Barry, B., & Shapiro, D. L. (1992). Influence tactics in combinations: The interactive effects of soft versus hard tactics and rational exchange. *Journal of Applied Social Psychology, 22,* 1429-1441.

Barry, B., & Watson, M. R. (1996). Communication aspects of dyadic social influence: A review and integration of conceptual and empirical developments. In B. R. Burleson (Ed.), *Communication yearbook 19* (pp. 269-317). Thousand Oaks, CA: Sage.

Bass, B. M. (1985). *Leadership and performance beyond expectations.* New York: Free Press.

Bauer, T., & Green, S. (1996). Development of leader-member exchange: A longitudinal test. *Academy of Management Journal, 39,* 1538-1536.

Baxter, L. A. (1990). Dialectical contradictions in relationship development. *Journal of Social and Personal Relationships, 7,* 69-88.

Bennis, W. (1991). Leading followers, following leaders. *Executive Excellence, 8,* 5-7.

Berger, C. B. (1997). *Planning strategic interaction.* Mahwah, NJ: Lawrence Erlbaum.

Bies, R. J. (1987). The predicament of injustice: The management of moral outrage. In L. L. Cummings & B. M. Staw (Eds.), *Research in organizational behavior* (Vol. 9, pp. 289-319). Greenwich, CT: JAI.

Bies, R. J., Shapiro, D. L., & Cummings, L. L. (1988). Causal accounts and managing organizational conflict: Is it enough to say it's not my fault? *Communication Research, 15,* 381-399.

Bies, R. J., & Sitkin, S. B. (1992). Explanation as legitimation: Excuse-making in organizations. In M. L. McLaughlin & M. J. Cody (Eds.), *Explaining one's self to others: Reason-giving in a social context* (pp. 183-198). Hillsdale, NJ: Lawrence Erlbaum.

Block, P. (1993). *Stewardship: Choosing service over self-interest.* San Francisco: Berret-Koehler.

Braaten, D. O., Cody, M. J., & DeTienne, K. B. (1993). Account episodes in organizations: Remedial work and impression management. *Management Communication Quarterly, 6,* 219-250.

Buhler, P. (1993, March). The flip side of leadership: Cultivating followers. *Supervision, 54,* 17-19.

Case, T., Dosier, L., Murkison, G., & Keys, B. (1988). How managers influence superiors: A study of upward influence tactics. *Leadership and Organizational Development Journal, 9,* 25-31.

Chacko, H. E. (1988). Upward influence: How administrators get their way. *Cornell Hotel & Restaurant Administration Quarterly, 29,* 48-50.

Chacko, H. E. (1990). Methods of upward influence, motivational needs, and administrators' perceptions of their supervisors' leadership styles. *Group and Organization Studies, 15,* 253-265.

Chang, H. C., & Holt, R. G. (1991). More than a relationship: Chinese interaction and the principle of kuan-hsi. *Communication Quarterly, 39,* 251-271.

Cheney, G. (1995). Democracy in the workplace: Theory and practice from the perspective of communication. *Journal of Applied Communication Research, 23,* 1-25.

Cheng, J. L. C. (1983). Organizational context and upward influence: An experimental study of the use of power tactics. *Group and Organization Studies, 8,* 337-355.

Chiles, A. M., & Zorn, T. E. (1995). Empowerment in organizations: Employees' perceptions of the influences of empowerment. *Journal of Applied Communication Research, 23,* 167-200.

Cloven, D., & Roloff, M. E. (1993). The chilling effect of aggressive potential on the expression of complaints in intimate relationships. *Communication Monographs, 60,* 199-209.

Cobb, A. T. (1984). An episodic model of power: Toward an integration of theory and research. *Academy of Management Review, 9,* 382-393.

Cobb, A. T. (1986). Informal influence in the formal organization: Psychological and situational correlates. *Group and Organization Studies, 11,* 229-253.

Cody, M. J., Canary, D. J., & Smith, S. W. (1994). Compliance-gaining goals: An inductive analysis of actors' goal types, strategies, and successes. In J. A. Daly & J. M. Wiemann (Eds.), *Strategic interpersonal communication* (pp. 33-90). Hillsdale, NJ: Lawrence Erlbaum.

Courtright, J. A., Fairhurst, G. T., & Rogers, L. E. (1989). Interaction patterns in organic and mechanistic systems. *Academy of Management Journal, 32,* 773-802.

Deluga, R. J. (1989). Employee influence strategies as possible stress-coping mechanisms for role conflict and role ambiguity. *Basic and Applied Social Psychology, 10,* 329-335.

Deluga, R. J. (1991). The relationship of upward-influencing behavior with subordinate-impression management characteristics. *Journal of Applied Social Psychology, 21,* 1145-1160.

Deluga, R. J., & Perry, J. T. (1991). The relationship of subordinate upward influencing behavior, satisfaction, and perceived superior effectiveness with leader-member exchanges. *Journal of Occupational Psychology, 64,* 239-252.

Dienesch, R., & Liden, R. C. (1986). Leader-member exchange model of leadership: A critique and further development. *Academy of Management Review, 11,* 618-634.

Dockery, T. M., & Steiner, D. D. (1990). The role of the initial interaction in leader-member exchange. *Group and Organization Studies, 15,* 395-413.

Downs, C. W., & Conrad C. (1982). Effective subordinancy. *Journal of Business Communication, 19,* 28-36.

Drake, B. H., & Moberg, D. J. (1986). Communicating influence attempts in dyads: Linguistic sedatives and palliatives. *Academy of Management Review, 11,* 567-584.

Dreher, G., Dougherty, T., & Whitely, W. (1989). Influence tactics and salary attainment: A gender-specific analysis. *Sex Roles, 20,* 535-550.

DuBrin, A. J. (1989). Sex differences in endorsement of influence tactics and political behavior tendencies. *Journal of Business and Psychology, 4,* 3-14.

DuBrin, A. J. (1991). Sex and gender differences in tactics of influence. *Psychology Reports, 68,* 635-646.

Erez, M., & Rim, Y. (1982). The relationships between goals, influence tactics, and personal and organizational variables. *Human Relations, 35,* 871-878.

Erez, M., Rim, Y., & Keider, I. (1986). The two sides of the tactics of influence: Agent vs. target. *Journal of Occupational Psychology, 59,* 25-39.

Fairhurst, G. (1993). The leader-member exchange patterns of women leaders in industry: A discourse analysis. *Communication Monographs, 60,* 321-351.

Fairhurst, G. (in press). Dualisms in leadership communication research. In F. M. Jablin & L. L. Putnam (Eds.), *Handbook of organizational communication* (2nd ed.). Thousand Oaks, CA: Sage.

Fairhurst, G., & Chandler, T. (1989). Social structure in leader-member interaction. *Communication Monographs, 56,* 215-239.

Fairhurst, G., Green, S. G., & Snavely, B. K. (1984). Face support in controlling poor performance. *Human Communication Research, 11,* 272-295.

Fairhurst, G., Rogers, L., & Sarr, R. (1987). Manager-subordinate control patterns and judgments about the relationship. In M. L. McLaughlin (Ed.), *Communication yearbook 10* (pp. 395-415). Newbury Park, CA: Sage.

Falbe, C. M., & Yukl, G. (1992). Consequences for managers of using single influence tactics and combinations of tactics. *Academy of Management Journal, 35,* 638-652.

Farrell, D., & Rusbult, C. E. (1992). Exploring the exit, voice, loyalty, and neglect typology: The influence of job satisfaction, quality of alternatives, and investment size. *Employee Rights and Responsibilities Journal, 5,* 201-218.

Ferris, G. R., & Judge T. A. (1991). Personnel/human resources management: A political influence perspective. *Journal of Management, 17,* 447-488.

Ferris, G. R., Judge, T. A., Rowland, K. M., & Fitzgibbons, D. E. (1994). Subordinate influence and the performance evaluation process: A test of a model. *Organizational Behavior and Human Decision Processes, 58,* 101-135.

Gabarro, J. J., & Kotter, J. P. (1993, May-June). Managing your boss. *Harvard Business Review, 71,* 150-157.

Garko, M. G. (1994). Communicator styles of powerful physician executives in upward-influence situations. *Health Communication, 6,* 159-172.

Geddes, D. (1993). Examining the dimensionality of performance feedback messages: Source and recipient perceptions of influence attempts. *Communication Studies, 44,* 200-215.

Giacalone, R. A., & Rosenfeld, P. E. (Eds.). (1989). *Impression management in the organization.* Hillsdale, NJ: Lawrence Erlbaum.

Gorden, W. I., Holmberg, K., & Heisey, D. R. (1994). Equality and the Swedish work environment. *Employee Rights and Responsibilities Journal, 7,* 141-160.

Gorden, W. I., & Infante, D. A. (1991). Test of a model of organizational commitment. *Communication Quarterly, 39,* 144-145.

Gorden, W. I., Infante, D. A., & Graham, E. E. (1988). Corporate conditions conducive to employee voice. *Employee Rights and Responsibilities Journal, 1,* 101-111.

Gordon, R. A. (1996). Impact of ingratiation on judgments and evaluations: A meta-analytic investigation. *Journal of Personality and Social Psychology, 71,* 54-70.

Graen, G., & Uhl-Bien, M. (1991). The transformation of professionals into self-managing and partially self-designing contributors: Towards a theory of leadership making. *Journal of Management Systems, 3,* 33-48.

Graen, G., & Uhl-Bien, M. (1995). Relationship-based approach to leadership: Development of leader-member exchange (LMX) theory over 25 years: Applying a multi-level, multi-domain perspective. *Leadership Quarterly, 6,* 219-247.

Graen, G., & Wakabayashi, M. (1994). Cross-cultural leadership-making: Bridging American and Japanese diversity for team advantage. In H. C. Triandis, M. D. Dunnette, & L. M. Hough (Eds.), *Handbook of industrial and organizational psychology* (Vol. 4, pp. 415-446). New York: Consulting Psychologists Press.

Graham, J. W. (1986). Principled organizational dissent: A theoretical essay. In B. M. Staw & L. L. Cummings (Eds.), *Research in organizational behavior* (Vol. 8, pp. 1-52). Greenwich, CT: JAI.

Graham, J. W. (1988). Transformational leadership: Fostering follower autonomy, not automatic followership. In J. G. Hunt, B. R. Baglia, H. P. Dachler, & C. Schriesheim (Eds.), *Emerging leadership vistas* (pp. 73-79). Lexington, MA: Lexington.

Graham, J. W. (1991). Servant-leadership in organizations: Inspirational and moral. *Leadership Quarterly, 2,* 105-119.

Graham, J. W. (1995). Leadership, moral development, and citizenship behavior. *Business Ethics Quarterly, 5,* 43-54.

Graham, J. W., & Keeley, M. (1992). Hirschman's loyalty construct. *Employee Rights and Responsibilities Journal, 5,* 191-200.

Grams, W. C., & Rogers, R. W. (1990). Effects of power on use of influence tactics. *Journal of General Psychology, 117,* 71-82.

Green, S. G., Anderson, S. E., & Shivers, S. L. (1996). An examination of the effects of organizational constraints on leader-member exchange. *Organizational Behavior and Human Decision Processes, 66,* 203-214.

Hegstrom, T. G. (1995). Focus on organizational dissent: A functionalist response to criticism. In J. Lehtonen (Ed.), *Critical perspectives on communication research and pedagogy* (pp. 83-94). St. Ingbert, Germany: Rohrig University Press.

Hellweg, S. A., Geist, P., Jorgenson, P. F., & White-Mills, K. (1990). An analysis of compliance-gaining instrumentation in the organizational communication literature. *Management Communication Quarterly, 4,* 244-271.

Hickman, C. R. (1990). *Mind of a manager, soul of a leader.* New York: John Wiley.

Hirokawa, R. Y., & Miyahara, A. (1986). A comparison of influence strategies utilized by managers in American and Japanese organizations. *Communication Quarterly, 34,* 250-264.

Hirschman, A. O. (1970). *Exit, voice, and loyalty.* Cambridge, MA: Harvard University Press.

Hollander, E. P. (1992). The essential interdependence of leadership and followership. *Current Directions in Psychological Science, 1*(2), 71-75.

Hollander, E. P. (1995). Ethical challenges in the leader-follower relationship. *Business Ethics Quarterly, 5,* 55-65.

Hollander, E. P., & Julian, L. R. (1990). Relational features of organizational leadership and followership. In K. E. Clark & M. B. Clark (Eds.), *Measures of leadership* (pp. 83-97). West Orange, NJ: Leadership Library of America.

Hollander, E. P, & Offerman, L. R. (1990). Power and leadership in organizations. *American Psychologist, 45,* 179-189.

House, R. J., & Aditya, R. N. (1997). The social scientific study of leadership: Quo vadis? *Journal of Management, 23,* 409-473.

House, R. J., & Howell, J. M. (1992). Personality and charismatic leadership. *Leadership Quarterly, 3,* 81-108.

Howell, J., & Higgins, C. A. (1990). Leadership behaviors, influence tactics, and career experiences of champions of technological innovation. *Leadership Quarterly, 1,* 249-264.

Hunt, M. D. (1994). The subordinate's view: A communication inventory of talk between subordinates and their supervisors (Doctoral dissertation, University of Kentucky, 1994). *Dissertation Abstracts International, 55*(04), 534B.

Infante, D. A., Anderson, C. M., Martin, M. M., Herington, A. D., & Kim, J. (1993). Subordinates' satisfaction and perceptions of supervisors' compliance-gaining tactics, argumentativeness, verbal aggressiveness, and style. *Management Communication Quarterly, 6,* 307-325.

Infante, D. A., & Gorden, W. I. (1989). Argumentativeness and affirming communicator style as predictors of satisfaction/dissatisfaction with subordinates. *Communication Quarterly, 37,* 81-90.

Infante, D. A., & Rancer, A. S. (1996). Argumentativeness and verbal aggressiveness: A review of recent theory and research. In B. R. Burleson (Ed.), *Communication yearbook 19* (pp. 319-351). Thousand Oaks, CA: Sage.

Jablin, F. M., & Krone, K. J. (1994). Task/work relationships: A life-span perspective. In M. L. Knapp & G. R. Miller (Eds.), *Handbook of interpersonal communication* (2nd ed., pp. 621-675). Thousand Oaks, CA: Sage.

Jones, E. E. (1964). *Ingratiation: A social psychological analysis.* New York: Appleton-Century-Crofts.

Jones, E. E., & Wortman, C. (1973). *Ingratiation: An attributional approach.* Morristown, NJ: General Learning.

Jones, G. R. (1986). Socialization tactics, self-efficacy, and newcomers' adjustment to organizations. *Academy of Management Journal, 29,* 262-279.

Judge, T. A., & Bretz, R. D. (1994). Political influence behavior and career success. *Journal of Management, 20,* 43-65.

Kellermann, K., & Cole, T. (1994). Classifying compliance-gaining messages: Taxonomic disorder and strategic confusion. *Communication Theory, 4,* 3-60.

Keys, B., & Case, T. (1990). How to become an influential manager. *Academy of Management Executive, 4,* 38-51.

Kipnis, D. (1976). *The powerholders.* Chicago: University of Chicago Press.

Kipnis, D., & Schmidt, S. (1982). *Profiles of organizational influence strategies.* Toronto: University Associates.

Kipnis, D., & Schmidt, S. (1983). An influence perspective on bargaining within organizations. In M. H. Bazerman & R. J. Lewicki (Eds.), *Negotiating in organizations* (pp. 303-319). Beverly Hills, CA: Sage.

Kipnis, D., & Schmidt, S. (1988). Upward-influence styles: Relationship with performance evaluations, salary, and stress. *Administrative Science Quarterly, 33,* 528-542.

Kipnis, D., Schmidt, S., Swaffin-Smith, C., & Wilkinson, L. (1984). Patterns of managerial influence strategies: Shotgun managers, tacticians, and bystanders. *Organizational Dynamics, 12,* 58-67.

Kipnis, D., Schmidt, S., & Wilkinson, I. (1980). Intraorganizational influence tactics: Explorations in getting one's way. *Journal of Applied Psychology, 65,* 440-452.

Krone, K. J. (1992). A comparison of organizational, structural, and relationship effects on subordinates' upward influence choices. *Communication Quarterly, 40,* 1-15.

Krone, K. J., Garret, M., & Chen, L. (1992). Managerial communication practices in Chinese factories: A preliminary investigation. *Journal of Business Communication, 29,* 229-252.

Krone, K. J., & Ludlum, J. T. (1990). An organizational perspective on interpersonal influence. In J. P. Dillard (Ed.), *Seeking compliance: The production of interpersonal influence messages* (pp. 123-142). Scottsdale, AZ: Gorsuch Scarisbrick.

Lamude, K. G. (1993). Supervisors' upward influence tactics in same-sex and cross-sex dyads. *Perceptual and Motor Skills, 77,* 1067-1070.

Lamude, K. G. (1994). Supervisors' influence tactics for handling managers' resistance. *Psychological Reports, 75,* 371-374.

Lantis, M. (1987). Two important roles in organizations and communities. *Human Organization,* *46,* 189-199.

Larson, J. R., (1989). The dynamic interplay between employees' feedback-seeking strategies and supervisors' delivery of performance feedback. *Academy of Management Review, 14,* 409-422.

Larson, J. R., Glynn, M. A., Fleenor, C. P., & Scontrino, M. P. (1987). Exploring the dimensionality of managers' performance feedback to subordinates. *Human Relations, 39,* 1083-1102.

Latib, M. A. S. (1989). The relative importance of personal, relational and perceived target attributes in determining upward influence strategies in subordinate-superior interaction [CD-ROM]. Abstract from: SilverPlatter File: Dissertation Abstracts Item: AA18912446.

Lee, J., & Jablin, F. M. (1995). Maintenance communication in superior-subordinate work relationships. *Human Communication Research, 22,* 220-257.

Leichty, G., & Applegate, J. (1991). Social-cognitive and situational influences on the use of face-saving persuasive strategies. *Human Communication research, 17,* 451-484.

Liden, R. C., & Mitchell, T. R. (1989). Ingratiation in the development of leader-member exchanges. In R. A. Giacalone & P. Rosenfeld (Eds.), *Impression management in the organization* (pp. 343-361). Hillsdale, NJ: Lawrence Erlbaum.

Lim, T., & Bowers, J. H. (1991). Facework: Solidarity, approbation, and tact. *Human Communication Research, 17,* 415-450.

Mainiero, L. A. (1986). Coping with powerlessness: The relationship of gender and job dependency to empowerment strategy usage. *Administrative Science Quarterly, 31,* 633-653.

Manz, C., & Sims, H. P. (1991). Super leadership: Beyond the myth of heroic leadership. *Organizational Dynamics, 19,* 18-35.

Marwell, G., & Schmidt, D. R. (1967). Dimensions of compliance-gaining behaviors. *Sociometry, 30,* 350-364.

Maslyn, J. M., Farmer, S. M., & Fedor, D. D. (1996). Failed upward influence attempts: Predicting the nature of subordinate persistence in pursuit of organizational goals. *Group and Organization Management, 21,* 461-480.

Mayes, B. T., & Allen, R. W. (1977). Toward a definition of organizational politics. *Academy of Management Review, 2,* 672-678.

Monroe, C., DiSalvo, V. S., Lewis, J. J., & Borzi, M. G. (1990). Conflict behaviors of difficult subordinates: Interactive effects of gender. *Southern Communication Journal, 56,* 12-23.

Morrison, E. W., & Bies, R. J. (1991). Impression management in the feedback-seeking process: A literature review and research agenda. *Academy of Management Review, 16,* 522-541.

Mowday, R. T. (1978). The exercise of upward influence in organizations. *Administrative Science Quarterly, 23,* 137-156.

Mowday, R. T. (1979). Leader characteristics, self-confidence, and methods of upward influence in organizational decision situations. *Academy of Management Journal, 22,* 709-725.

Mumby, D. K., & Putnam, L. L. (1992). The politics of emotion: A feminist reading of bounded rationality. *Academy of Management Review, 17,* 465-486.

Nonis, S., Sager, J., & Kumar, K. (1996). Salespeople's use of upward influence tactics in coping with role stress. *Journal of the Academy of Marketing, 24,* 44-56.

Northcraft, G. B., & Ashford, S. J. (1990). The preservation of self in everyday life: The effects of performance expectations and feedback context on feedback inquiry. *Organizational Behavior and Human Decision Processes, 47,* 42-64.

O'Keefe, D. J. (1994). From strategy-based to feature-based analyses of compliance gaining message classification and production. *Communication Theory, 4,* 61-68.

Perreault, W. D., & Miles, R. H. (1978). Influence strategy mixes in complex organizations. *Behavioral Science, 23,* 86-98.

Porter, L. W., Allen, R. W., & Angle, H. L. (1981). The politics of upward influence in organizations. In L. L. Cummings & B. M. Staw (Eds.), *Research in organizational behavior* (pp. 109-149). Greenwich, CT: JAI.

Rao, A., Schmidt, S. M., & Murray, L. H. (1995). Upward impression management: Goals, influence strategies, and consequences. *Human Relations, 48,* 147-167.

Redding, W. C. (1985). Rocking boats, blowing whistles, and teaching speech communication. *Communication Education, 34,* 245-258.

Richmond, V. P., McCroskey, J. C., & Davis, L. M. (1986). The relationship of supervisor use of power and affinity-seeking strategies with subordinate satisfaction. *Communication Quarterly, 34,* 178-193.

Roloff, M. E. (1994). Validity assessment of compliance gaining exemplars. *Communication Theory, 4,* 69-80.

Schein, V. (1977). Individual power and political behaviors in organizations: An inadequately explored reality. *Academy of Management Review, 2,* 64-72.

Schenck-Hamlin, W. J., Wiseman, R. L., & Georgacarakos, G. N. (1982). A model of properties of compliance-gaining strategies. *Communication Quarterly, 30,* 92-100.

Schilit, W. K. (1986). An examination of individual differences as moderators of upward influence activity in strategic decisions. *Human Relations, 39,* 933-953.

Schilit, W. K. (1987a). An examination of the influence of middle-level managers in formulating and implementing strategic decisions. *Journal of Management Studies, 24,* 271-293.

Schilit, W. K. (1987b). Upward influence activity in strategic decision making. *Group and Organization Studies, 12,* 343-368.

Schilit, W. K., & Locke, E. (1982). A study of upward influence in organizations. *Administrative Science Quarterly, 27,* 304-316.

Schmidt, S., & Kipnis, D. (1984). Managers' pursuit of individual and organizational goals. *Human Relations, 37,* 781-794.

Schriesheim, C., & Hinkin, T. (1990). Influence tactics used by subordinates: A theoretical and empirical analysis and refinement of the Kipnis, Schmidt, and Wilkinson subscales. *Journal of Applied Psychology, 75,* 246-257.

Schriesheim, C., & Tepper, B. (1989). *Interpersonal influence tactics in organizations: Content-analytic and experimental investigations.* Unpublished manuscript, University of Miami, School of Business Administration.

Seers, A. (1989). Team-member exchange quality: A new construct for role-making research. *Organizational Behavior and Human Decision Processes, 43,* 118-135.

Senge, P. (1990). *The fifth discipline.* Garden City, NY: Doubleday.

Steil, J. M., & Weltman, K. (1992). Influence strategies at home and work: A study of sixty dual career couples. *Journal of Social and Personal Relationships, 9,* 65-88.

Sullivan, J., Albrecht, T., & Taylor, S. (1990). Process, organizational, relational, and personal determinants of managerial compliance-gaining communication strategies. *Journal of Business Communication, 4,* 331-355.

Tepper, B. (1995). Upward maintenance tactics in supervisory mentoring and nonmentoring relationships. *Academy of Management Journal, 38,* 1191-1205.

Tepper, B., Brown, S. J., & Hunt, M. D. (1993). Strength of subordinates' upward influence tactics and gender congruency effects. *Journal of Applied Social Psychology, 23,* 1903-1919.

Thacker, R. A., & Wayne, S. J. (1995). An examination of the relationship between upward influence tactics and assessments of promotability. *Journal of Management, 21,* 739-756.

Tilley, G. C. (1988). A study of intraorganizational influence processes: The relationship between a superordinate's perception of influence strategies and effectiveness [CD-ROM]. Abstract from: SilverPlatter File: Dissertation Abstracts Item: AA1882244.

Tjosvold, D. (1974). Threat as a low-power person's strategy in bargaining: Social face and tangible outcomes. *International Journal of Group Tensions, 4,* 494-510.

Tjosvold, D. (1978). Affirmation of the high-power person and his position: Ingratiation in conflict. *Journal of Applied Social Psychology, 104,* 57-68.

Tjosvold, D., Andrews, I. R., & Struthers, J. T. (1992). Leadership influence: Goal interdependence and power. *Journal of Social Psychology, 132,* 39-50.

Tompkins, P. K., & Cheney, G. C. (1985). Communication and unobtrusive control in contemporary organizations. In R. D. McPhee & P. K. Tompkins (Eds.), *Organizational communication: Traditional themes and new directions* (pp. 179-210). Beverly Hills, CA: Sage.

Van Maanen, J., & Barley, S. R., (1984). Occupational communities. In L. L. Cummings & B. M. Staw (Eds.), *Research in organizational behavior* (Vol. 6, pp. 287-365). Greenwich, CT: JAI.

Van Maanen, J., & Kunda, G. (1989). Real feelings: Emotional expression and organizational culture. In L. L. Cummings & B. M. Staw (Eds.), *Research in organizational behavior* (Vol. 11, pp. 43-104). Greenwich, CT: JAI.

Vecchio, R., & Sussmann, M. (1991). Choice of influence tactics: Individual and organizational determinants. *Journal of Organizational Behavior, 12,* 73-80.

Villanova, P., & Bernardin, H. J. (1991). Performance appraisal: The means, motive, and opportunity to manage impressions. In R. A. Giacolone & P. E. Rosenfeld (Eds.), *Applied impression management* (pp. 81-96). Newbury Park, CA: Sage.

Waldera, L. M. (1988). A study of key variables related to the directness of upward influence strategies and to self perceptions of upward influence. *Dissertation Abstracts International, 50,* 02B.

Waldron, V. R. (1991). Achieving communication goals in superior-subordinate relationships: The multi-functionality of upward maintenance tactics. *Communication Monographs, 58,* 289-306.

Waldron, V. R. (1994). Once more, with feeling: Reconsidering the role of emotion in work. In S. A. Deetz (Ed.), *Communication yearbook 17* (pp. 388-416). Thousand Oaks, CA: Sage.

Waldron, V. R. (1997, November). *Managing threats and maintaining relationships: Toward a model of followership.* Paper presented at the annual meeting of the National Communication Association, Chicago.

Waldron, V. R., & Hunt, M. D. (1992). Hierarchical level, length, and quality of supervisory relationship as predictors of subordinates' use of maintenance tactics. *Communication Reports, 5,* 82-89.

Waldron, V. R., Hunt, M. D., & Dsilva, M. (1993). Towards a threat management model of upward communication: A study of influence and maintenance tactics in the leader-member dyad. *Communication Studies, 44,* 254-272.

Wayne, S. J., & Ferris, G. R. (1990). Influence tactics, affect, and exchange quality in supervisor-subordinate interactions: A laboratory experiment and field study. *Journal of Applied Psychology, 75,* 487-499.

Wayne, S. J., & Kacmar, K. M. (1991). The effects of impression management on the performance appraisal process. *Organizational Behavior and Human Decision Processes, 48,* 70-88.

Wayne, S. J., Kacmar, K. M., & Ferris, G. R. (1995). Coworker responses to others' ingratiation attempts. *Journal of Managerial Issues, 8,* 277-289.

Wayne, S. J., & Liden, R. C. (1985). Effects of impression management on performance ratings: A longitudinal study. *Journal of Management, 38,* 232-260.

Werner, C. M., & Baxter, L. A. (1994). Temporal qualities of relationships: Organismic, transactional, and dialectical views. In M. L. Knapp & G. R. Miller (Eds.), *Handbook of interpersonal communication* (2nd ed., pp. 322-379). Thousand Oaks, CA: Sage.

Wiemann, J. M., & Daly, J. A. (1994). Introduction: Getting your own way. In J. A. Daly & J. M. Wiemann (Eds.), *Strategic interpersonal communication* (pp. vii-xiv). Hillsdale, NJ: Lawrence Erlbaum.

Wood, R., & Mitchell, T. (1981). Manager behavior in a social context: The impact of impression management on attributions and disciplinary actions. *Organizational Behavior and Human Performance, 28,* 356-378.

Yukl, G., & Falbe, C. M. (1990). Influence tactics and objectives in upward, downward, and lateral influence attempts. *Journal of Applied Psychology, 75,* 132-140.

Yukl, G., & Tracey, B. (1992). Consequences of influence tactics used with subordinates, peers, and the boss. *Journal of Applied Psychology, 77,* 525-535.

Yukl, G., Falbe, C. M., & Youn, J. Y. (1993). Patterns of influence behavior for managers. *Group and Organization Studies, 18,* 5-28.

Yukl, G., Guinan, P., & Sottolano, D. (1995). Influence tactics used for different objectives with subordinates, peers, and supervisors. *Group and Organization Management, 20,* 272-296.

Yukl, G., Kim, H., & Falbe, C. M. (1996). Antecedents of influence outcomes. *Journal of Applied Psychology, 81,* 309-317.

CHAPTER CONTENTS

8 The Crisis of Political Communication: Normative Critiques of News and Democratic Processes

ERIK P. BUCY
Indiana University

PAUL D'ANGELO
Villanova University

Over the past 25 years, political communication researchers have presented mounting evidence of how the press fails its public mission by not adequately informing the electorate, presenting an accurate picture of civic affairs, or fostering a sense of connectedness to governing institutions. Perceived shortcomings of the political communication system and sustained controversy in the field over the nature and extent of media deficiencies have led scholars to articulate a crisis of communication for citizenship and a crisis of political communication research. Focusing on the literature of the press's expanding role in the "modern campaign," this chapter describes the schisms and disciplinary divides among scholars and identifies two valuative propositions emerging from normative critiques of news and democratic processes. The review also addresses the field's historical ambivalence toward normative theory and discusses contemporary democratic expectations of the press. Finally, three developments within political communication theory and research—public journalism, constructionism, and electronic democracy—are reviewed to illustrate how the field might resituate communication in public life.

IN the two and a half decades since the field of political communication cast doubt and closed ranks on the limited effects model of media influence (Chaffee, 1975; Gitlin, 1978; McCombs & Shaw, 1972), a substan-

AUTHORS' NOTE: We wish to thank Jay Blumler and Michael Gurevitch for their encouragement and helpful comments on an earlier version of the manuscript.

Correspondence and requests for reprints: Erik P. Bucy, 327 Radio-TV Building, Indiana University, Bloomington, IN 47405-6901; e-mail ebucy@indiana.edu

Communication Yearbook 22, pp. 301-339

tial body of literature critical of media performance in the public sphere has emerged in response to the press's recognized impact on civic affairs (see Blumler & Gurevitch, 1995; Graber, 1984; Iyengar & Reeves, 1997).[1]

The growth of "media politics" (Arterton, 1984), for example, has prompted researchers to examine more closely the press's increased structural role. Political scientists, looking for an explanation for the decline in voter turnout, institutional trust, and the influence of the political parties that began in the 1960s, have set the tone for the resulting interdisciplinary critique of news and democratic processes (McLeod, Kosicki, & Rucinski, 1988), advancing arguments that implicate the media in the erosion of confidence in government (Lipset & Schneider, 1983; Robinson, 1975, 1976, 1977), citizen capacities to know and understand politics (Graber, 1988; Neuman, 1986), and participation in civic and associational life (Putnam, 1995a, 1995b). Rising levels of political apathy, cynicism, and mistrust have also been attributed to the news media (Cappella & Jamieson, 1996, 1997), especially television, which in Rothman's (1979) view has directly "contributed to the decay of traditional political and social institutions" (p. 346). Putnam (1995b) cites survey evidence suggesting that television viewing displaces "nearly every social activity outside the home, especially social gatherings and informal conversations" (p. 679).[2]

Though argued from a variety of perspectives, these diverse criticisms converge on the inability of the mass media to meet the demands of an idealized democratic system, a vision of which has driven much political communication research since the early voting studies (Chaffee & Hochheimer, 1985). According to the assumptions of this system, Chaffee and Hochheimer (1985) observe, citizens "should be concerned, cognizant, rational and accepting of the political system," and "the institutions of communication should be comprehensive, accurate, and scrupulously fair and politically balanced" (p. 268). To the degree that news organizations and individual journalists are perceived to fall short of such normative criteria, they are accused of trivializing political discourse and weakening the accountability of public officials (Iyengar, 1996; Postman, 1986), of being overly intrusive, interpretive, and evaluative (Patterson, 1993), liberally biased (Efron, 1971; Lichter & Rothman, 1986), partisan actors (Page, 1996; Patterson & Donsbach, 1996) who are elitist, self-serving, and arrogant (Fallows, 1996), ill suited for the role of coalition builder (Patterson, 1993), fixated on conflict and mired in a tabloid culture that specializes in prediction rather than assessment (Fallows, 1996; Kurtz, 1993, 1996), carnivorous (Patterson, 1994), and producers and purveyors of just "bad news" (Lichter & Noyes, 1996; Patterson, 1996a, 1996b).[3]

In the opinion of a growing number of political communication scholars, American democracy has reached a crisis because the necessary conditions for civic participation—namely, adequate information, an accurate picture of public life, and a sense of connectedness to governmental institutions (Blumler, 1983; Hacker, 1996)—have been endangered substantially by the press (see, e.g., Bennett, 1996a; Blumler & Gurevitch, 1995; Hacker, 1996; Kellner, 1990; Zarefsky, 1992). In particular, Blumler and Gurevitch (1995) argue that the increased "professionalization of political advocacy" of recent decades and organization of civic life around media imperatives serves to marginalize the role of citizens in contemporary democracies. Instead of the active participation envisioned in political science models of "strong democracy" (Barber, 1984; Fishkin, 1991), civic engagement now largely consists of exposure to the "white noise" (Bennett, 1992) of distorted news coverage (Bennett, 1996b; Fallows, 1996) and manipulative advertising (Diamond & Bates, 1992; Jamieson, 1992; Kern, 1989), staged events that are transient and ephemeral (Boorstin, 1964; Dayan & Katz, 1992), discussion and presentation of issues and ideas in sound-bite form (Jamieson, 1988; Kurtz, 1996), and citizen feedback that occurs mainly via scripted talk shows and terse public opinion surveys (Dahlgren, 1995).

Citizens thus have few substantive opportunities to participate in and to influence public policy making and are likely to withdraw from the political process altogether. The public sphere has consequently become more the domain of political professionals and advocacy specialists who dictate agendas and less the province of ordinary citizens, who constitute an increasingly passive public (Blumler, 1990; Blumler & Gurevitch, 1995). Because this diminished role for citizenship so egregiously contradicts the image of a deliberative, informed citizenry called for by democratic theory, civic life has entered a crisis, precipitated, according to this view, not by media coverage per se but by conceiving the political system in the image of the media, (Zarefsky, 1992) and by conducting politics according to the imperatives and values of news (Patterson, 1993).

TWO DIMENSIONS OF THE CRISIS

Following Blumler's (1983) explanation of the crisis of communication and democracy, in this review we develop and elaborate an internal and an external dimension to the crisis of political communication. "The *external dimension,*" Blumler writes, "stems from the crisis of legitimacy that is currently being experienced by the institution long considered central to the aims of Western democracies—the news media" (p. 166). Blumler points to three reasons for journalism's legitimacy crisis: (a) the inability of many groups with a stake in civic affairs to recognize themselves in stereotypical media portrayals, (b) the undermining of conventional assumptions about the nature of news by academic studies depicting journalists as "active creators of political reality" (Graber, 1982), and (c) the growing trend of blaming the messenger for the message (p. 167). In this chapter, the external dimension of the crisis addresses the veritable litany of problems ascribed to the performance of the press in the "real world" of democratic processes, focusing to a large extent on the press's expanding role in what has come to be known as the "modern campaign" (Chaffee, 1981; Davis, 1990; Patterson, 1980; Rose, 1994). Journalism's legitimacy crisis parallels the erosion of confidence in political institutions and has accelerated in recent years, according to numerous public opinion polls (Cappella & Jamieson, 1996; Valente, 1997). We refer to the external dimension of the crisis, involving the news media's problematic political performance, as the "crisis of communication for citizenship" (Blumler & Gurevitch, 1995; Entman, 1989).

"The *internal dimension,*" Blumler (1983) continues, "is well reflected in Stuart Hall's description of the recent history of mass media research as a 'movement from essentially a behavioral to an ideological perspective' " (pp. 167-168). Hall's (1982) characterization of the field implies the undesirable (if not false) choice for Blumler between a group of "hard-nosed, value-free behavioral positivists" in one camp and "critical researchers, determined to unmask the ideological functions of mass communications" in another. Whereas Nimmo and Sanders (1981a) felt that these different perspectives could coexist and generate desirable diversification, Nimmo and Swanson (1990) later viewed the resulting schisms as propelling an inevitable fragmentation of knowledge across the internal boundaries of the field. Other students of the political communication process have characterized the internal dimension of the crisis not just as a matter of competing perspectives, social science versus critical, but in terms of disciplinary divides—a problem of "shocking mutual ignorance or disregard" (Graber, 1987, p. 10) among political scientists, mass communication scholars, and rhetoricians (Jamieson & Cappella, 1996; McLeod et al., 1988). As when practitioners or lay critics overlook the existing research literature and present their observations about media and politics as new, this can result in a situation of redundancy, where "researchers continue to rediscover the wheel" (Meadow, 1985, p. 172). Perhaps worse, as Entman (1993) observes, "because of the lack of interchange among the disciplines, hypotheses thoroughly discredited in one field may receive wide acceptance in another" (p. 51).

For many political communication researchers, the tension between achieving social scientific rigor and articulating normative standards for the press in a complex democracy presents a dilemma. Perhaps more than any other area of communication inquiry, political research "cannot evade normative assumptions of how social institutions 'ought to' work" (McLeod, Kosicki, & McLeod, 1994, p. 123). Yet, although much media and politics research provides a provocative assessment of the role of news in democratic processes, documenting for instance the negative tenor and "horse-race" angle of campaign coverage (Patterson, 1980, 1993) or the shrinking sound bite (Adatto, 1990; Hallin, 1992) and its effect on political discourse (Jamieson, 1988), historically the field has stopped "far short of telling us the role that news can or should play" (Davis, 1990, p. 177). Some scholars have attributed this normative reticence to an overemphasis on the empirical quest for what *is* at the expense of articulating a preferred democratic role for the media (Nimmo & Sanders, 1981a).

From the above discussion, three defining characteristics of the internal dimension of the crisis emerge: (a) a paucity of horizontal dialogue and integration in the field, (b) a reluctance to utilize empirical findings as a springboard for the development of a cogent normative theory of the press and democracy, and (c) the growing trend of media reductionism, or tendency to blame seemingly intractable social-political problems on the press. We refer to the internal dimension of the crisis as the "crisis of political communication research." We use the term *crisis* here not to indicate impending failure but to signal less alarmingly a situation that has perhaps reached a critical phase. The role of normative theory in research presents a guiding theme for a literature review that builds upon and develops Blumler's bifurcation of the crisis of political communication. A careful reading of the literature reveals that mainstream political communication research levels an impressive indictment against the press for failing democracy (the external dimension) while the field itself is suffering from a crisis of purpose in its inability to advance a coherent theory of political journalism and effectuate reforms of the media-political system (the internal dimension).

ORGANIZATION AND APPROACH

To illustrate how these two dimensions of the crisis operate in the literature, we have organized this chapter into four major sections. First, we present existing normative theories of press and democracy to place the growing number of media critiques in context. Second, we examine the internal dimension—the crisis of political communication research. While saturated with empirical assessments of communication processes, many of them harshly critical of the news media, the field, with a few notable exceptions (e.g., Gurevitch & Blumler, 1990; Peterson, 1956; Rosen, 1996; Schudson, 1995), has struggled with the theoretical development of new normative models for the American media-political system, typically offering pragmatic solutions aimed at resolving the external crisis instead (e.g., Graber, 1993b; Lichter & Noyes, 1996; Patterson, 1993; Robinson, 1975; Sabato, 1991).[4]

Third, we organize our discussion of the external dimension—the crisis of communication for citizenship—in terms of two propositions that emerge from crisis critiques: News media distort political reality and fail their information role, and press roles intrude into democratic processes. Finally, we review three developments within political communication theory and research—public journalism, constructionism, and electronic democracy—to illustrate how the field might resituate communication in public life.

Because the universe of political communication scholarship is so large (see Johnston, 1990; Kaid & Wadsworth, 1985), we review here only works that are in some way critical of press performance in politics. Studies included in this review focus on, but are not limited to, literature of presidential press coverage in the context of the modern campaign. In our discussion of the internal crisis, the works cited mainly include overviews, intellectual histories, and synoptic articles. The section on the external crisis references a broad range of research articles, books, essays, and, to a lesser degree, more popular commentaries authored by journalists and articles in journalism trade magazines.

To some extent we seek to address (or redress) in this chapter a central problematic raised by Nimmo and Swanson (1990) in their comprehensive review of the field. Political communication, these authors state, "would do well to move away from context-based conceptions of itself, particularly the uni-centric campaign touchstone, toward an organizing framework grounded in basic questions about how communication and politics intersect" (p. 11). The two propositions we present later in the chapter attempt such an organizing framework, with an eye toward clarifying the disparate and sometimes contradictory claims about media and politics. Addressing what is conceptually common in empirical findings and normative critiques may allow for a more coherent and meaningful literature about press performance to emerge, improving our understanding of the field.

Although Nimmo and Swanson (1990) caution against our becoming "preoccupied" with philosophical and theoretical questions about the "center" of the field, we consider a certain amount of disciplinary reflexivity to be important, and perhaps necessary, given the fragmentation within political communication, the extent to which mass media are now integrated into political life, and the enthusiasm with which researchers continue to investigate the problems instigated by this condition. We cannot hope to address in this review all of the deep, metatheoretical issues involved in these debates, though such issues surely need to be addressed further. Moreover, such issues plumb deep into the intellectual history of the field, an endeavor that we can only sketch here.

NORMATIVE THEORIES OF
THE PRESS AND DEMOCRACY

The Social Responsibility Theory of the Press

Normative theories of democracy run deep in the Western canon, beginning with the republican ideas of Aristotle and Plato. Less developed are normative theories of the *press and democracy* that philosophically examine "how media *ought* to operate if certain social values are to be observed or attained"

(McQuail, 1994, p. 4). In the modern era, the relationship of the mass media to government has been seriously addressed at least since Lippmann's (1922/ 1965) seminal analysis. But it was not until after World War II that explicit normative standards for press performance appeared in prescriptive form (McQuail, 1992). Perhaps the most cogent single body of criticism of press performance and recommendations for improvement was formulated in 1947 by the Commission on the Freedom of the Press (known as the Hutchins Commission), which Peterson (1956) elaborated as the social responsibility theory of the press.

In its report, the commission attempted to reconcile the commercial imperatives of the media industry to the informational needs of democratic society and essentially threatened the press, including print as well as broadcast journalism, with regulation unless it better fulfilled its social responsibilities. The report enumerated five public services that society requires of its communication system. In exchange for constitutional protection and freedom from prior restraint by the government, it is the duty of the press to provide "a truthful, comprehensive, and intelligent account of the day's events in a context which gives them meaning." The press should also serve as "a forum for the exchange of comment and criticism," give a "representative picture of the constituent groups in society," help in the "presentation and clarification of the goals and values of the society," and "provide full access to the day's intelligence" (Hutchins, 1947). Together, these normative standards provided an early benchmark, albeit one that was vague and readily satisfied by existing practices, against which to assess press performance.

The emphasis on a public service mission for the press grew out of a concern, among other things, over the increasing difficulty for citizens to speak and be heard in a mass society. Freedom of the press, social responsibility theory argues, "is a somewhat empty right for the person who lacks access to the mass media" (Peterson, 1956, p. 94) and whose voice is not adequately represented in the range of published opinion. Some safeguards should be developed, then, to ensure effective access to or opinion representation by the mass media. Another reason for the emergence of social responsibility theory was an increase in media criticism. As the press grew in size and importance and began to consolidate in the early part of the twentieth century, media critiques increased in force and intensity and took on an antitrust, antimonopoly tone (Peterson, 1956). Partially to address these criticisms, Peterson (1956) recommended that an independent agency should be established to appraise press performance and to report on it each year.

The National News Council

A quarter century after the Commission on the Freedom of the Press issued its recommendations, the Markle Foundation and the Twentieth Century Fund underwrote the creation of the National News Council in 1973, amid the tumult of the Watergate scandal. Modeled after the British Press Council, the National News Council was created in an effort "to discipline and defend the American news media" (Brogan, 1985, p. 3). But, as with the Hutchins Commission, the National News Council faced vigorous opposition from the print and broadcast media, especially from the *New York Times,* which led the refusal to cooperate. Defending freedom of the press, *Times* publisher Arthur Ochs Sulzberger wrote in 1973, "does not begin with an unjustified confession that our own shortcomings are such that we need monitoring by a press council" (quoted in Brogan, 1985, p. 27). Not surprisingly, the National News Council "died of poverty and neglect" after a decade of obscure existence (Brogan, 1985, p. 3). Even so, a state-level Minnesota News Council has thrived since 1971, and broadcast journalist Mike Wallace of CBS has recently advocated reintroducing the news council concept nationally (Shepard, 1997). In the absence of government regulation or formal monitoring of the press, normative media criticisms from academics, watchdog groups, and media critics within journalism serve to apply the pressure necessary to maintain a certain consensual standard of press performance.

Contemporary Democratic
Expectations of the Press

Contemporary democratic expectations of the mass media have been summarized by Schudson (1995) as well as by Gurevitch and Blumler (1990) as a set of seven or eight normative goals. McLeod et al. (1994) have connected the democratic standards identified by Gurevitch and Blumler to specific constraints and conventions, performance problems, and presumed individual and societal effects of the mass media found in criticism. But they admit there are problems associated with using such a framework as a base for theory building, in part because many media criticisms are inconsistently supported by reliable evidence. "Discussions of news media faults too often fail to distinguish criticisms based on unsystematic observation from those based on more solid evidence" (McLeod et al., 1994, p. 127). Table 8.1 illustrates the normative goals identified by Schudson (1995) for a media system dedicated to democracy.

Despite the existence of normative standards for journalism, as well as long-standing codes of ethics by professional associations, Schudson (1995) notes, "we are a long way from a coherent normative theory of journalism," adding that "there is little to push news institutions to change this" (p. 29). Democracy in the contemporary world is scarcely conceivable without the mass media, Schudson observes, but whether the press serves the social-political system as well as it might is an open question. Unlike other industries, American journalism is not significantly challenged from abroad. And unlike higher education, the mainstream media are not encouraged to innovate through a diversity of models from within. "Journalism, even at its research

TABLE 8.1
Normative Goals for a Media System Dedicated to Democracy

---

1. News media should provide citizens fair and full information so that they can make sound decisions as citizens.

2. News media should provide coherent frameworks to help citizens comprehend the complex political universe. They should analyze and interpret politics in ways that enable citizens to understand and to act.

3. News media should serve as common carriers of the perspectives of the varied groups in society; they should be, in the words of Gans (1979), "multiperspectival."

4. News media should provide the quantity and quality of news that people want; that is, the market should be the criterion for the production of news.

5. News media should represent the public and speak for and to the public interest in order to hold government accountable.

6. News media should evoke empathy and provide deep understanding so that citizens at large can appreciate the situation of other human beings in the world and so elites can come to know and understand the situation of other human beings, notably non-elites, and learn compassion for them.

7. News media should provide a forum for dialogue among citizens that not only informs democratic decision making but is, as a process, an element in it.

NOTE: Reprinted by permission of the publisher from *The Power of News,* by Michael Schudson, Cambridge, MA: Harvard University Press, Copyright (c) 1995 by the President and Fellows of Harvard College.

centers and with its foundation supporters, seems overcome with the charms of celebrity, commercial success, and national reach" (Schudson, 1995, p. 30).

Gurevitch and Blumler (1990) have identified several structural obstacles that hinder the press in its fulfillment of its democratic expectations, chief of which are conflicts among certain values that may necessitate trade-offs and compromises. "There are tensions, for example, between the principle of editorial autonomy and the ideal of offering individuals and groups wide-ranging access to the media" (p. 271). Second, knowledge and status differentials separating ordinary citizens from political elites impose limits on the "participatory energy" the system can generate. Third, although democratic theory presupposes an engaged citizenry, in a free society people may choose to be decidedly apolitical. Fourth, press performance depends in large measure on the broader social, political, and economic environment in which the media operate. Moreover, the internal constraints media institutions place on themselves limit their ability to serve a purely democratic purpose. "Through their acceptance of the imperatives of competition, and in their adherence to a self-generated and self-imposed set of professional standards, they shape their contributions to the political process in ways that may well fall short of the democratic ideals they claim to serve" (Gurevitch & Blumler, 1990, p. 283).

The contradictions inherent in many democratic expectations of the mass media, stemming from institutional constraints and conflicts among competing values, arguably prevent the media from fulfilling their social responsibilities. Yet the press, as a democratic institution, remains responsive to prevailing sentiments (Gurevitch & Blumler, 1990) even if it is resistant to reform. So long as popular media criticism relies on unsystematic observations and empirical scholars fail to link knowledge derived from scientific methods with the development of normative theory, research itself may be implicated in the crisis of the public sphere. In the next section we consider the implications of scholarly reticence to enter into the fray and correct the flaws of media and democracy uncovered by research.

THE INTERNAL DIMENSION: THE CRISIS OF POLITICAL COMMUNICATION RESEARCH

Periodically in the social sciences, controversies brought on by intensive critical attention to an issue or perspective cause a discipline or field to enter a period of intense self-examination. Frequently, these debates are the result of ongoing paradigm shifts in theory or method, as occurs in the physical sciences (Kuhn, 1970). Whatever their eventual outcome, such crises are rarely short-lived, readily resolved, or easily forgotten. Three social scientific eruptions—the cognitive revolution that psychology underwent in the 1950s and 1960s (Baars, 1986), the ongoing challenge to rational choice models of voting and legislative behavior in political science (Green & Shapiro, 1994), and the now-celebrated "ferment in the field" era of communication research (Gerbner, 1983)—speak to the contestable nature of these intellectual debates. Scholarly fields are subject to their critical moments. In this section we assert that political communication may be nearing such a critical moment as it matures into a bona fide interdisciplinary subfield. The causes for this concern stem from (a) the field's initial suppression of normative theory, (b) the tendency among researchers to embrace uncritically the assumptions of elite pluralism to maintain research consensus, and (c) the lack of media openness to reform. We address each of these concerns in turn.

Suppressing Normative Theory

As normative theories of press and democracy crystallized in the middle of the twentieth century, mainstream political communication began to move in another direction, developing along empirical, positivist, behavioral lines of inquiry that characterized its social scientific origins in sociology, psychology, and political science. The seminal voting studies conducted by Lazarsfeld and his associates at Columbia University in the 1940s and 1950s (Berelson, Lazarsfeld, & McPhee, 1954; Katz & Lazarsfeld, 1955; Lazarsfeld, Berelson, & Gaudet, 1944) were particularly influential in cultivating a "radically empirical perspective" in the field of communication generally (Davis, 1990, p. 150) and moving political communication down a decisively nonnormative path. In this environment of Cold War consensus and high public confidence in political institutions, Hallin (1994) observes, "it was possible for social scientists to proclaim the 'end of ideology' and to put forward a vision of social science as a source of neutral expertise, closely tied to governing institutions, and at the same time serving society as a whole" (p. 172; see also Bell, 1960). Indeed, Davis (1990) notes that "the very idea of normative theory was called into question" (p. 150) in the field's nascent stages.

A researcher's conception of the way the world should be functions as a guiding influence on how research projects proceed (Nimmo & Sanders, 1981a). In deploying scientific methods, early election researchers did not altogether abandon the philosophical tenets of normative theory to interpret their findings but embraced them implicitly rather than explicitly (Chaffee & Hochheimer, 1985). The empirical perspective of political communication research was guided at midcentury by the theory of elite pluralism, which "envisions a complex social order consisting of myriad groups, social organizations, and bureaucracies, each with countervailing interests and values" (Davis, 1990, p. 153) and discourages broad citizen participation in government and even interest group activities. Given the assumptions of a marginalized electorate in elite pluralist thinking, it is easy to see how a minimal effects model of media influence and, later, a two-step flow theory emphasizing the importance of opinion leaders or elites in the political persuasion process (Katz & Lazarsfeld, 1955) could flourish.

Over the years, Chaffee (1975) observes, there has been a "latent anguish in the social sciences in attempting to reconcile normative beliefs in democracy and press freedom with persistent evidence of less-than-ideal levels of competence and performance on the part of either the electorate or the mass media" (p. 14). Concerned about advancing the field through good science, Davis (1990) notes:

> American academics have been reluctant to develop normative theories of media because such theories are inherently "value laden" and speculative. Only in the past decade have we come to the full realization that elite pluralism was itself a normative theory with rather clear implications for the role of media in politics. As long as media research showed that news was effective in serving the functions considered important by elite pluralism, there was little need for changes in the news production process. But now that we have identified so many problems with news, we also need to provide a constructive perspective on what news could do to serve and improve politics. (pp. 177-178)

Some recent political communication scholarship has stressed the importance of including an explicit normative component beyond the obligatory passing remark or concluding comment about a research finding's importance to "democratic theory." Entman (1989) and Patterson (1993), for example, combine normative criteria with quantitative methods to address substantively what a theory of political communication might look like. Several synoptic overviews written by communication scholars addressing normative concerns have built upon the social responsibility theory of the press (e.g., Altschull, 1984; Gurevitch & Blumler, 1990; McLeod et al., 1994; Schudson, 1995). Still other works critique traditional normative theory from a sociological perspective and suggest new roles and public interest models for the mass media that are not necessarily political (e.g., Curran, 1996; Gans, 1979, 1983; McQuail, 1996).

Maintaining Research Consensus

Although removed to a certain extent from the outside world, social science is nevertheless embedded in the real world of politics and ideological struggle (Lanigan & Strobl, 1981). In this way, communication research as a branch of the social sciences has been actively political since its beginning (Simpson, 1994). Upon divorcing themselves from intentional normative pursuits in the 1950s, political communication researchers became "ideologically wedded" to the prevailing assumptions of elite pluralism, much in the same way that the "high modernism" of the Cold War consensus "made it possible for journalists to feel that they could be part of the political 'Establishment,' and yet remain neutral and independent" (Hallin, 1994, p. 172). On firm political ground through the mid-1960s, media researchers worked in the comfort of general ideological agreement (McLeod et al., 1994; Simpson, 1994). In this milieu, research questions narrowed and political communication research from the 1940s to the 1960s "was confined within a fairly narrow set of topics, focusing on media content and individual voting behavior within relatively stable political systems" (McLeod et al., 1994, p. 123).

As we have noted, Blumler's (1983) assessment of "the ferment within" is predicated on differing research and ideological perspectives that separate scholars. Ferment within in the field of political communication is thus partially manifested in the paradigm cleavage between social scientific/elite-pluralist approaches on the one hand and critical research on the other. Although initially viewed as a source of welcome intellectual diversity (Nimmo & Sanders, 1981a), this paradigm cleavage has more recently been regarded as a problem due to its promotion of methodological and theoretical fragmentation (Nimmo & Swanson, 1990). There is an ideological component to this argument, too: In the critical view, political communication research itself is an expression of normative assumptions, even when it professes merely to describe or explain objective reality (Lanigan & Strobl, 1981). Political communication appears to be in a position where it must address the disciplinary divides and lack of horizontal integration *within* in order to more adequately, and with firm theoretical basis, address the crisis *beyond*—the crisis of communication for citizenship.

Media Openness to Reform

Openness refers to the news media's willingness or ability to respond to reforms suggested by normative critiques. Several scholars have commented on the relative imperviousness of the media to outside criticism and suggestion (e.g., Avery & Eadie, 1993; Robinson, 1975). Jamieson (1996c), in an effort to influence media performance in real time, discovered the recalcitrance of the press firsthand during the 1996 presidential campaign. After making a near-heroic effort to monitor and analyze media and candidate discourse during the general election, faxing some 18 campaign briefings to 275 reporters over a 9-week period and posting them on the Internet home page of the Annenberg School, she candidly reflected that the influence of political communication scholars on the conduct of presidential campaigns "may never be more than modest."

One aspect of the crisis of political communication research derives from the lack of agreement within the field on the best solutions or approaches to remedy media practices that are seen as deficient from the standpoint of democracy. Here, a schism opens between pragmatists and ritualists. Sabato (1991), for example, pragmatically offers recommendations to correct the press's propensity to intrude into the private lives of political candidates. To restore public faith in politics, Sabato suggests raising campaign journalism standards by, among other things, resisting the reporting of rumors, preserving areas of legitimate privacy for public officials, and treating all candidates equally. Similarly, Patterson (1993) suggests that journalists should move away from interpretive forms of reporting centered on their own views of political reality, first, by resisting the temptation to lace political coverage with judgments about the motives of presidential candidates and, second, by allowing the candidates to speak at length rather than reducing their stump speeches to sound bites.

Political science pragmatists, valuing political institutions over media institutions, quite naturally want to impose reforms to remedy perceived press deficiencies in politics. Some communication scholars, however, define the situation as one of mutual culpability. "If real reform is wanted," Swanson (1992) writes, "it must begin with the institutions that create political communication—ineffectual political parties, officeholders obsessed with media coverage and campaign fundraising . . . a *system* that punishes rather than rewards seriousness in political discourse and courage in political action" (pp. 399-400, emphasis added). Swanson singles out news as only one of several players, most of whom are political, implicated in the crisis. The burgeoning public journalism movement argues that a realistic approach to reform might be to adapt some perceived strengths of the press, such as the editorial page and community coverage, to existing modes of professional practice in a way that might reinvigorate democratic dialogue (Rosen, 1996). Common to these and other recommendations for improving press performance (see Graber, 1993b; Kurtz, 1993; Lichter & Noyes, 1996; Robinson, 1975) is their prescriptive and practical orientation.

Within political communication, however, models and accounts of news and democratic processes have been developed that would seem to short-circuit the efficacy of such reforms. Scholars who regard the routines of media-politics as symbolic spectacles of a largely unchanging social order, for instance, advance a ritualistic view to explain the processes by which campaigns are conducted, policies are made, and public opinion is formed (Bennett, 1980, 1992; Edelman, 1964, 1988; Gurevitch & Kavoori, 1992; Nimmo, 1987). Writing on "myth, ritual, and political control," Bennett (1980) observes that, "despite its good intentions, the standard criticism that elections are not living up to their potential as broad-based policy forums misses the crucial point: in their existing institutional framework elections have no such potential" (p. 163).

Ritual perspectives see substantial fundamental agreement among mainstream political actors; their relatively superficial differences are merely portrayed melodramatically by the media to engender excitement and imbue political events with a sense of importance. Edelman (1964) observes that the ritual of campaign speeches and political discussion mostly consists of "the exchange of clichés among people who agree with each other. The talk, therefore, serves to dull the critical faculties rather than to arouse them" (pp. 17-18). Historical accounts of American journalism's development, which view the evolution of the press as an organic, centuries-long social process (e.g., Emery & Emery, 1996; Leonard, 1986; Schudson, 1978, 1995), would also seem to preclude the forced implementation of pragmatic press reforms. Dahlgren (1992) brands as "uncritical" scholars who assume that journalism can be remedied through the types of pragmatic recommendations implicit in liberal or elite-pluralist models of democracy. Accepting the general incorrigibility of the press, Bennett (1996b) asserts that viewers should become better critics of journalism to see through the "illusions" promulgated by the structural (nonideological) biases of reporting.

Political communication is scarcely at a loss to advance pragmatic solutions for resolving the problems of the press and democracy. But the cumulative weight of research findings has not significantly altered media performance, as the press exhibits a comfortable imperviousness to outside criticism. Despite disagreement, scholarly dissonance over the media's *openness* to reform should not prevent political communication researchers from assuming that the press *can* be reformed. The lack of disciplinary interchange in the field (see Entman, 1993) arguably inhibits the development of new normative models that might be used for more effective reform efforts, however. In Gans's (1983) view, such models are a necessary precondition for media criticism, for "only if we give serious and systematic thought to news norms and news media purposes do we have a right to tell journalists and others whether and how to improve the news" (pp. 183-184). In the next section we outline the consolidation of the field and elaborate the problems of the press and democracy as the crisis of communication for citizenship.

THE EXTERNAL DIMENSION:
THE CRISIS OF COMMUNICATION FOR CITIZENSHIP

Consolidation of the Field
and the Turn to Strong Effects

Communication research emerged as a distinct domain of investigation in the decade from 1945 to 1955 with the publication of classic works by Berelson, Hovland, Lasswell, Lazarsfeld, Merton, and Schramm, among others (see Delia, 1987). But it would take another two decades for the "subfield" of political communication to develop its own unity and sense of identity. One of the reasons for political communication's belated consolidation was its cross-disciplinary origins. Then, as now, the study of media and politics spanned a wide variety of research topics and traditions, including rhetorical analysis, propaganda analysis, persuasion and attitude change studies, public opinion research, voting behavior studies, and systems analysis (Delia, 1987; Nimmo & Sanders, 1981a). Political communication was not identified as a discrete area of social scientific research until the mid-1950s (Eulau, Eldersveld, & Janowitz, 1956; Nimmo & Sanders, 1981a).[5] As if to make up for its late arrival, political communication has produced a voluminous literature in the span of a few short decades. The boundaries of the field have widened considerably, moving beyond the "voter persuasion paradigm" with the development of cognitive, institutional, cultural, cross-national, critical, feminist, postmodern, and constructionist perspectives (see Johnston, 1990; Kaid & Wadsworth, 1985; McLeod et al., 1994; Nimmo & Sanders, 1981b; Swanson & Nimmo, 1990). The field has become so diffuse that bridging disciplinary divides and finding common themes among these disparate approaches is now a concern (Graber, 1987; Jacobs & Shapiro, 1996; Jamieson & Capella, 1996).

Another reason for the field's belated development involves limited effects conceptions of media influence that dampened interest in research. "Partly because Berelson (1959) prematurely declared the death of communication research in 1959," McLeod et al. (1988) observe, "a virtual moratorium on political media research prevailed until the 1972 campaign" (p. 9). The field's rebirth coincided with the rise of a stronger, more cognitively oriented effects paradigm, memorialized by Chaffee (1975) in an important edited volume (Jamieson & Cappella, 1996). Numerous edited volumes, readers, and core texts addressed exclusively to political communication have subsequently appeared, solidifying political communication's interdisciplinary status, including books written or edited by Kraus and Davis (1976); Graber (1980, 1984); Nimmo and Sanders (1981b); Jamieson and Campbell (1982); Sanders, Kaid, and Nimmo (1984); Denton and Woodward (1985); Paletz (1987); Alger (1989); Swanson and Nimmo (1990): Semetko, Blumler, Gurevitch, and Weaver (1991); Davis (1994); Blumler and Gurevitch (1995); Swanson and Mancini (1996); and Iyengar and Reeves (1997). Several of these works are now in their second or later editions (e.g., Graber, 1996a).

Energized by a renewed conviction that media may indeed have profound, if not "massive," cognitive and electoral effects (Ansolabehere & Iyengar, 1995; Iyengar, 1991; Iyengar & Kinder, 1987; Mutz, Sniderman, & Brody, 1996), and provoked by an interest in "media politics" following the image-oriented election campaigns of the Reagan-Bush era (Arterton, 1984; Bennett, 1996b; Jamieson, 1996b; Kellner, 1990; Kerbel, 1995; Parenti, 1986), researchers in the field are well on their way to making the 1990s an important decade for political communication scholarship.[6]

Established journals in both communication and political science, including *American Politics Quarterly* (Welch, 1991), the *Journal of Communication* (Siefert, 1991), *Communication Monographs* (Burgoon, 1992), *American Behavioral Scientist* (Payne, 1993, 1997), *Communication Research* (Chaffee & Jamieson, 1994), *Journalism and Mass Communication Quarterly* (Folkerts, 1995), *Research in Political Sociology* (Wasburn, 1995), the *Annals of the American Academy of Political and Social Science* (Jamieson, 1996a), *Media, Culture & Society* (Sparks, 1996), and *PS: Political Science & Politics* (Hauck, 1996), have featured special symposia on media and politics, focusing particularly on election research and the impact of new communication technologies on politics. To gauge the health of the public sphere in the 1990s means to analyze the media's role in political life.

Origins of the External Crisis in Media Politics

The origins of the external crisis of communication for citizenship can be traced to two developments within the media/politics nexus: the rise of the modern campaign and the evolution of what Blumler (1990) calls the modern publicity process. The modern process of presidential selection materialized in the late 1960s. "The turning point appears to be the Democratic National Convention of 1968, a fractious and, according to some, illegitimate nominating convention" (Rose, 1994, p. xii). Following the nomination by party regulars of Hubert Humphrey, who did not enter a single primary, progressive Democrats demanded a more open nominating system. The ensuing McGovern-Fraser reforms of 1970 favoring direct-vote primaries over caucuses opened a vacuum in the political system between candidates and voters, giving the press a more prominent role in the candidate selection process (Arterton,

1984; Barber, 1978; Patterson, 1980, 1993). Institutional changes to the political system, including open and fluid nominating procedures, candidate-centered electioneering, the rise of political consulting, and public financing of presidential campaigns, diminished the influence of the political parties, giving rise to what Patterson (1980) calls the "mass media election." As the ability of parties to deliver votes has declined, Swanson (1992) notes, "campaigning and governing have become steadily more intertwined with the priorities and interests of political journalism" (p. 398).

Leading political actors must accordingly adopt the twin roles of policy maker and publicist and remain ever mindful of how decisions are liable to be influenced by how they will play in the press. Thus, Blumler (1990) notes, "the modern publicity process puts a high premium on getting the *appearance* of things right" (p. 106). In the contest for influence over popular perceptions, candidates and political advocates see themselves engaged in competitive struggle not just with their political opponents but increasingly with the press itself. Not wanting to leave opinion formation to chance, they employ strategies to shape the news consistent with their message. In such a milieu, certain features of political coverage, including journalists' fixation on process over substance and "disdaining the news" (Levy, 1981), or coloring reports of events with judgmental words or phrases to demonstrate the reporter's distance from the event's public relations purpose, can thus be regarded as attempts by journalists to reestablish editorial control over the news (Blumler & Gurevitch, 1996). "Such a publicity process," Blumler and Gurevitch (1996) note, "is not exactly rich in vitamins for citizenship" and tends to "narrow the debate; make negative campaigning more central; foster cynicism; and, over-represent newsmaking as a field of power struggle rather than a source of issue clarification" (p. 129).

Perspectives on the External Crisis

The crisis of communication for citizenship surfaces in at least three different "real-world" contexts: (a) the discourse of individual rhetors, (b) the relationships between political and media institutions, and (c) the political-economic structures of society that critical scholars argue limit the range of free expression. Although these research emphases frequently overlap and are often addressed within the same studies, some general patterns can be discerned.

From a rhetorical standpoint, Zarefsky (1992, p. 413) has identified a "crisis in American political communication" owing in part to a debasement of political debate, which has been formatted for television. In the presidential debates, visual emphasis on confrontation and restrictions on response times quicken the pace and add an element of drama, but, Zarefsky notes, these same conventions "thwart sustained discussion of serious issues; they encourage one-liners and canned mini-speeches" (p. 412). Communication technology is also indicted for placing discursive restrictions on the form and content of political discourse (Jamieson, 1988; Postman, 1986) and for "charming the modern voter" (Hart, 1994) by making distant political figures seem closer, more accessible, and more responsive than they really are (see also Meyrowitz, 1985). Jamieson (1992) suggests that traditional genres of political dialogue, including reasoned argument, engagement in ideas, and accountability, have been corrupted by the transmogrification of campaigning into a series of visually evocative ads and sound-bite stump speeches, which in turn are given adlike news coverage. "Candidates are learning to act, speak, and think in television's terms" (Jamieson, 1992, p. 206), and the news, largely due to the shrinking sound bite in both broadcast and print journalism (Adatto, 1990; Hallin, 1992; Jamieson, 1988; Mickelson, 1989), has substituted rhetorical assertion for factual evidence.

Institutional approaches, particularly those elaborated by Blumler and Gurevitch (1995, 1996), propose that the roots of perceived media deficiencies are systemic, that is, "they inhere in the very structures and functioning of present-day political communications systems" (Blumler & Gurevitch, 1995, p. 4). In this view, the failures of political communication practices to serve democracy stem from the interplay of political and media institutions, as well as audiences. The role relationships between journalists and politicians have been described in terms of mutual dependency and reciprocal influence (Blumler & Gurevitch, 1995). With the rise of attack journalism by the press (Sabato, 1991) and media management strategies by political consultants (Sabato, 1981), however, these relationships have become increasingly vitriolic. "The resulting combination of denigrated politicians and frustrated journalists has been a recipe for the emergence of an adversarial climate that seems unprecedentedly fierce and abiding—a chronic state of partial war" (Blumler & Gurevitch, 1996, p. 129). Writing about the "political-media complex," which, like President Dwight Eisenhower's fabled military-industrial complex, "wields influence at every level of society," Swanson (1992, 1997) suggests that particularized interests often cause government and media organizations to conflict with each other despite their mutual dependency in the battle over public opinion. In this competitive struggle, the public interest per se is not represented; rather, voter attention and approval are treated as "commodities to be produced by the most efficient means possible and bartered for advantage" (Swanson, 1992, p. 399).

From a political-economic perspective, Kellner (1990) argues that the news media "not only have failed in recent years to carry out the democratic functions of providing the information necessary to produce an informed citizenry but also have promoted the growth of excessive corporate and state power" (p. xiii). Corporate control of media institutions, the decline in the newspaper industry of economic and editorial competition, and the growing concentration of media institutions into fewer and fewer hands (Bagdikian, 1992) have constricted the range of expressed opinion while benefiting conservative, moneyed interests at the expense of a vibrant public sphere. At the same time, the trend toward deregulation in broadcasting has resulted in television's becoming "increasingly embedded in the corporate structure of big business" (Curran, 1996, p. 86). Argued from within a political-economic or neo-Marxist framework, critical authors see the performance of political journalism as less of a problem than the limitations that corporate capitalism and organizational imperatives place on the professional freedoms of individual reporters (Gitlin, 1980; Hallin, 1994; Kellner, 1990). Herman and Chomsky (1988) apply a propaganda model to the political performance of the media, depicting how an underlying elite consensus largely structures the news and marginalizes dissent while allowing dominant special interests to get their message across to the public.

Although rhetorical, institutional, and political-economic arguments provide insight into the crisis of the public sphere, no single emphasis is inclusive enough to unify the disparate crisis literature. In the following section we propose two valuative propositions to address what is conceptually common in empirical findings and/or normative critiques of the media and politics. In addition to organizing the literature, these propositions represent a device for encouraging communication across disciplinary divides and furthering consensus, or at least coherence, rather than fragmentation in the field.

PROPOSITIONS EMERGING
FROM NORMATIVE CRITIQUES

News Media Distort Political Reality
and Fail Their Information Role

The first proposition emerging from normative critiques, that news media distort political reality and fail their information role, involves one of the most important criteria by which political communication scholars criticize political news coverage: distortion. In the literature, distortionist arguments surface in at least three research contexts: (a) in studies of ideological bias and the work routines of journalists, (b) in the criticism that print and broadcast media traffic primarily in images, and (c) in the experimental literature on framing and priming.

Ideological distortion relates to how media messages are thought to be infused with partisan bias, mainly liberal. Only a few empirical studies have purported to show that such liberal biases are systematically evident in political coverage (e.g., Efron, 1971; Lichter & Rothman, 1986), and several investigators have not found much evidence to support the claim that either political reporting or journalists themselves are in fact very liberal (Patterson & Donsbach, 1996; Robinson & Sheehan, 1983; Stevenson, Eisinger, Feinberg, & Kotok, 1973; Weaver & Wilhoit, 1986; see also Dennis, 1997). In a recent cross-national survey of newspaper and broadcast journalists from

Germany, Great Britain, Italy, Sweden, and the United States, Patterson and Donsbach (1996) found that news workers' beliefs are "accurately characterized as slightly left of center rather than as unambiguously liberal," consistent with "Gans' (1979) conclusion that most journalists hold 'progressive' but 'safe' views" (p. 465). Yet the charge of liberal bias in the media continues to have currency among citizens and conservative politicians, especially during presidential elections, where the charge has become a part of campaign lore (Hunter, 1996).

Bias in the news has also come under broad scholarly scrutiny. Ideological bias has been discredited by research that characterizes the news media/candidate organization interface as a site of mutual interaction and influence (Arterton, 1984; Blumler & Gurevitch, 1995). As Nimmo (1978) observes, political news is the joint creation of journalists who assemble and report events and political communicators who promote them. The classic newsroom ethnographies (e.g., Breed, 1955; Epstein, 1973; Gans, 1979; Tuchman, 1978) as well as more politically oriented scholarship (e.g., Entman & Paletz, 1980; Parenti, 1986) have also contested the notion that news messages purvey any systematic political slants. Indeed, these studies argue that news has a profoundly *conservatizing* influence on public opinion and discourse because the boundaries for what news professionals consider newsworthy are more or less tightly drawn around official views and sources. Kellner (1990) attributes the "crisis of democracy" to such a conservatizing influence.

In exonerating the press of overt ideological bias, scholars have demonstrated more insidious forms of distortion in political news. Narrative emphases on "stock political plots" centered on conflict and competition (Bennett & Edelman, 1985) and emotionally charged "condensation symbols" (Edelman, 1988), for example, are held to depreciate the democratic value that elections should be based on sound and wide-ranging policy debates. Bennett (1996b) labels as "information biases" the tendency for political news to be personalized, dramatized, fragmented, and normalized. Entman (1989) also identifies evaluation and production biases, or slants, in various types of political news, including information about campaigns. In another context, Hart, Jerome, and McComb (1984) have analyzed presidential speech making for the presence of certain formulaic "rhetorical biases."

Given the lack of overt ideological bias in political reporting, some researchers have emphasized the *nonideological* biases that infuse campaign news. Patterson (1980) has noted that, whereas candidates prefer "diffuse" issues with broad appeal, journalists tend to mold these generalities into "clear-cut" issues that neatly divide the candidates. This "issue bias" is a form of distortion that stresses differences and conflict over broad policy commitments (Patterson, 1980, 1993). Another distortion observed in the literature is the press's increased emphasis on campaign or strategy-based news (Jamieson, 1993; Kerbel, 1994). Campaign issues—issues arising from campaign incidents, tactical decisions, or errors in judgment (Patterson, 1980)—often displace the coverage of policy issues in this analysis. Nonideological distortion, then, evacuates the kinds of substantive issue debate and information on which voters can purposively act as a reasoning citizenry and results in less of the balance of issues that candidates themselves stress. The press is thus held to fail its informational role.

Fortified by Lippmann's (1922/1965) views that news is but a beacon shining on the political world and people are necessarily kept mostly in the dark by the information they do receive, Patterson (1980) also shows that in a comparison of news coverage to the candidates' own discourse on the campaign trail, literal distortion is evident. The medium around which candidates most organize their campaigns, he notes, has the least use for diffuse policy appeals: "Television's preference for action film, brief statements, and interpretive reporting produces an issue agenda that is the severest distortion of the one that the candidate is trying to establish" (p. 42). Nimmo and Combs (1990) take the distortion line a step further by arguing that media coverage transforms political reality into fantasy, divorcing political action from its real-world basis: "Reality is created, or constructed, through communication—not expressed by it [and] for any situation there is no single reality, no one objective truth, but multiple, subjectively derived realities" (p. 4).

Central to the critique that media coverage invariably distorts the political process is the observation that the press has grown more visual and less verbal in recent decades and that television, a medium that literally traffics in images, dominates campaign communication, altering the way candidates communicate with the public and approach elective office (e.g., Bennett, 1996a; Donovan & Scherer, 1992; Graber, 1996a). In the process, the role of journalists, the packagers of images, is enhanced. In a study of televised "image bites" drawn from the network news tapes of Hallin's (1992) sound-bite study, Barnhurst and Steele (1997) found that presidential election reports became faster paced and more visual from 1968 to 1992; images and video clips multiplied and journalists began to appear more frequently and dramatically on screen. Out of the same data, Steele and Barnhurst (1996) also found that, compared with news sources, on-air correspondents talk longer and have increased their share of airtime even as the total time allotted for campaign discussion on television has shrunk. Such an emphasis on image over substance and focus on journalists as political actors will, in Bennett's (1996b) view, inevitably have the effect of distorting viewers' sense of political consequences.

From a postmodern perspective, Schram (1991) argues that the "grammar of electronic electioneering" has altered campaigns in such a way that journalists are now "obsessed with finding the 'true' self of each candidate, with demystifying the image to get at the soul and thereby designate the one true leader" (p. 211). Candidates in the (post)modern campaign must therefore devise the proper image to convey symbolically who they are and what issues they stand for. In Arterton's (1984) analysis, the images projected by candidates intersect with the images of candidates already shared by the press. Journalists develop these "press images," or consensual beliefs about candidates, in response to campaign themes and the reaction of activists and voters to those themes (p. 119). The electorate then receives these images as information about the campaign. The increased propagation of images in the modern campaign is considered by distortionist authors to render the electorate more or less incapable of rational self-governance.

Another way the news is held to distort political reality is through the related processes of framing, the emphasis in a communication text on some aspects of a perceived reality over others in such a way as to promote a particular interpretation or evaluation (Entman, 1993), and priming, the ability of news programs to affect the criteria by which individuals judge political leaders (Iyengar, 1991; Iyengar & Kinder, 1987). Situated within the political information-processing literature, much recent research on framing and priming makes some reference to normative criteria in assessing specific findings (see Ansolabehere & Iyengar, 1995; Iyengar, 1991, 1996; Iyengar & Kinder, 1987; Mutz et al., 1996). Undergirding experimental findings of strong cognitive effects of media exposure is a concern that the news, by portraying recurring issues as unrelated episodic events and assigning responsibility to individual perpetrators at the expense of more general, thematic information, "contributes to the trivialization of public discourse and the erosion of electoral accountability" (Iyengar, 1991, p. 143).

At bottom, distortionist authors argue that images in the modern campaign place a heavy burden on the capacities of citizens to make sense out of politics and hold officials accountable, even those who take a more or less attenuated view of the level of rationality required for voters to become effectively informed (Popkin, 1991). And yet, although media distortion research tends to disparage the quality of political information available in the press, reserving the harshest criticism for television, a number of political knowledge studies conducted by empiricists have found the information environment, print as well as broadcast, to be more than adequate (see Alvarez, 1996; Graber, 1988, 1996d) and attention to television news to be a fairly consistent predictor of issue knowledge (Chaffee & Frank, 1996; Weaver, 1996; Zhao & Chaffee, 1995). The contrasting approaches and findings of the distortion and knowledge studies—an emphasis on message production in an anemic media landscape on the one hand, compared to a cognitive focus on the abilities of voters to navigate a robust information environment on the other—serve to illustrate the disciplinary divides that partially characterize the internal dimension of the crisis.

Press Roles Intrude Into Democratic Processes

A second proposition arising from crisis critiques concerns how press roles intrude into democratic processes (Davis, 1992; Matthews, 1978; Sabato,

1991). Theories of democracy have traditionally held that the news media's primary purpose is to disseminate political information and educate the electorate, in essence performing a conduit role. But stipulated in libertarian and social responsibility theories of the press is the notion that the news should safeguard the rights of individuals by serving as a watchdog against government. Consequently, journalists frequently adopt an adversarial posture toward current or potential power holders, serving as an independent check on political aspiration (Martin, 1981; Rivers, 1970). These conflicting roles place the press in a dilemma, as it must scrutinize political actors and rely on political institutions for information at the same time. The relationship between the news media and government ranges, then, from open conflict to open cooperation. Although political communication research has demonstrated the powerful slants and biases that can stem from adversarial reporting (Entman, 1989), including the erosion of political legitimacy and weakening of political authority (Robinson, 1975, 1976), the conduit role has been viewed as serving existing social relations (Parenti, 1986) and, in the context of the modern campaign and modern publicity process, the designs of candidates and policy advocates (Arterton, 1984; Blumler, 1990). Parenti (1986) observes that the media's overarching role of reality definer interferes with the attainment of a true pluralistic society: "The press does many things and serves many functions, but its major role, its irreducible responsibility, is to continually recreate a view of reality supportive of existing social and economic class power" (p. 10).

Since the sweeping campaign reforms of the early 1970s, election researchers have documented a proliferating number of press roles in politics. Journalists, according to the roles literature, act as agenda setters, winnowers, surrogate electorates, power brokers, and kingmakers (Arterton, 1984; Joslyn, 1984; Matthews, 1978). To these roles Davis (1992) adds mentioner, categorizer, expectation setter, and chief critic. Indeed, the news media are so intertwined with politics that they no longer merely "depict the political environment; they *are* the political environment" (Graber, 1996a, p. 274). Increasingly, journalists are viewed as partisan actors themselves (Page, 1996; Patterson & Donsbach, 1996). Nevertheless, the adversarial model of a feisty, autonomous press endures, Blumler and Gurevitch (1995) have noted, partly because it prescribes *how* journalists should regard leading politicians and government figures—suspiciously. The adversarial ethos assumes that wielders of power "should be carefully watched lest they abuse their powers, exceed their mandates, commit blunders they would prefer to conceal, and elevate themselves to positions of nonaccountable authority" (Blumler & Gurevitch, 1995, pp. 27-28).

Working with an adversarial model of press-candidate relations, Sabato (1991) describes the major media's proclivity to attack candidates in terms of a progression of roles. Since the New Deal, Sabato argues, journalists have gone from being lapdogs (submissive conduits) to watchdogs (aggressive adversaries) to junkyard dogs (sleazemongers) intent on destroying political reputations. Donohue, Tichenor, and Olien (1995) argue for a less autonomous "guard dog" perspective on the role of the press, which regards the news media as a sentry not for society as a whole but for groups with power and influence: "What may seem to be a tug-of-war is, from the guard dog perspective, primarily a result of reporting and reflecting the conflicting views among divided political or economic bodies" (p. 122).

Augmenting these models are the policing duties the press has assumed in evaluating candidate fitness for office, most notably the "character cop" role in evidence since at least the 1972 presidential campaign and especially prominent since Gary Hart's forced withdrawal from the 1988 Democratic primaries (Davis, 1992; Graber, 1996a; Strentz, 1989). By displacing more substantive information about a candidate's policy positions or public record, character issue news is held to have a corrosive effect on attitudes toward political figures (Strentz, 1989). Sabato (1991) comments that a focus on character becomes "a strained effort to find a sometimes real, sometimes manufactured 'pattern' of errors or shortcomings that will automatically disqualify a candidate" (p. 67).

Defenders of interpretive journalism argue that the news is well within its ethical mandate to scrutinize the private lives of public officials. Belsey (1992) claims that objective reporting styles have of necessity become more interpretive because journalism otherwise would be too vulnerable to campaign manipulation. Journalistic studies have commented on the difficulty reporters experience in getting out from under the manipulative grasp of professional political operatives in order to maintain their autonomy (see Hertsgaard, 1988; Spear, 1984). Arterton's (1978) notion of a press crisis, or "period in which the candidate and campaign operatives undergo persistent questioning from journalists relating to a single topic" (pp. 48-49), can be extrapolated to journalists' use of character issues to resist orchestration. Moreover, rhetorical scholars argue that character, as revealed through candidate mistakes and gaffes, can serve as a dependable basis upon which voters may make candidate judgments (Bitzer, 1981; Johannesen, 1991).

Complicating the conduit and adversarial roles is the news media's relationship to the electorate. Beyond transmitting information and holding public officials accountable, political journalism has assumed an intermediary role between candidates and officeholders, who require coverage to communicate with the electorate, and voters, whose civic actions depend to some degree on the information they receive from news. The power of the press in the modern campaign derives in part, then, from the media's role in "democratizing" politics (Davis, 1992). Media provide critical linkages between citizens and officials, facilitating horizontal communication between two socially and politically disparate groups (Blumler & Gurevitch, 1996). But increased dependency on the mass media as an electoral intermediary is not regarded as a boon to democracy (Kerbel, 1995; Patterson, 1993). With its own economic and storytelling imperatives, the news is unqualified or unable to assume such a role (Hallin, 1992; Schudson, 1995). Patterson (1993) regards the press as a miscast institution, one that is neither democratically accountable nor very well suited for coalition building—a major task of elections. As with other political scientists, he would like to see this intermediary role retrenched and the parties revitalized. Rather than asking more of the press, he suggests relieving the press of responsibilities it has assumed but cannot or ought not perform and reforming the electoral process—namely, by shortening it, "so that communication during the campaign is more instructive" (p. 210).

As the numbers and kinds of press roles in politics have proliferated, press power has come under increased scrutiny. Among other ways, press power is viewed as the ability to set the public agenda, influence public opinion, marginalize dissent, decide candidate viability or electability through favorable or unfavorable coverage, determine criteria for political judgments, and frame political news in ways that significantly affect attributions of responsibility (Gitlin, 1980; Iyengar, 1991; Matthews, 1978; McCombs & Shaw, 1972; McLeod et al., 1994). Through the press's structural position in the modern campaign, "the media's actions, and sometimes mere presence," Lichter and Noyes (1996) argue, "cause significant changes in the electoral process, as well as in candidate and voter behavior" (p. 23). Institutionally, Blumler and Gurevitch (1995) stress that media influence is relative, either enhanced or diminished by the political strength or weakness of other players in the political arena. Consistent with this theme, Robinson (1977) argues that television has a parasitic relationship with weak institutions, diminishing the significance of the political parties for instance, and a symbiotic relationship with strong institutions, making the presidency even more powerful and imperious.

Normative critics take a suspicious view of press power because, unlike the different branches of government, each of which acts as a check upon the others, there is no formal check on the "fourth estate." Because press power is not subject to countervailing institutional pressure, journalists are held to lack real accountability. Therefore, their watchdog status comes into question and their political motives are questioned. Bagdikian (1992), a former journalist, asserts that media power *is* political power: "The mass media become the authority at any given moment for what is true and what is false, what is reality and what is fantasy, what is important and what is trivial. There is no greater force shaping the public mind" (p. xxvi).

RESITUATING COMMUNICATION IN PUBLIC LIFE

Three developments within political communication suggest ways that the media may actually nurture citizenship and illustrate how the field might resituate communication in public life: public journalism, constructionism, and electronic democracy. All of these perspectives produce cogent critiques of the press and democracy, thus contributing to the external crisis literature, yet by positioning the press as a vital element of civic participation and public opinion formation, they open new avenues for theorizing media and democracy—and ultimately reforming the press.

Public Journalism:
A New Normative Theory of the Press

Since the work of Alexis de Tocqueville (1840/1969), newspapers have been regarded as a positive influence on citizenship. Public, or civic, journalism argues that this prosocial feature of the press should be carried a step further: Rather than remaining detached, the press should adopt an activist agenda beyond telling the news and become a fair-minded, engaged participant in public life (Merritt, 1995). Public journalism—a new and developing normative theory of the press—acknowledges that public support for journalism has eroded and that newspapers in particular have a substantial role to play in reviving civic life, cultivating citizenship, and improving public dialogue, particularly at the local level (Glasser, 1991; Merritt, 1995; Rosen, 1996; Stepp, 1996). Rosen (1996) hopes the public journalism movement "might develop into a kind of public philosophy for a re-energized press" (p. 50).

Less altruistically, public journalism is also seen as a way to restore journalism's sagging reputation. Revitalizing civic life is important to the news business because a "public that does not attend to public affairs, that retreats deeply into private life and concerns, has no need of journalists and journalism" (Merritt, 1995, p. 10). Consistent with the earlier social responsibility theorists, advocates of public journalism accede that the press is implicated in the problems of civil society and has a responsibility to maintain the kind of civic climate that gives democratic politics a chance to do its work (Rosen, 1996, p. 4). Without sacrificing its objectivity, balance, and professionalism, journalism should promote democracy without advocating particular solutions, thereby becoming a civic catalyst. Public journalism views the press, then, as an important actor in the political arena, but not in a partisan sense. In a *Washington Post* column that helped launch the movement, Broder (1990) declared that "it is time for those of us in the world's freest press to become activists, not on behalf of a particular party or politician, but on behalf of the process of self-government" (p. A-15).

Although there has been a constituency for Broder's call within journalism, it has not been his colleagues in the national media, Rosen (1996) notes. Instead, Broder's appeal for a more activist press "helped inspire some of the early experiments in public journalism at the local level" (p. 72), particularly at small to medium-size newspapers such as the *Charlotte Observer, Minnea-*

polis Star Tribune, and *Norfolk Virginian-Pilot.* Public journalism, which by 1995 had been tried in one form or another at more than 150 news organizations (Rosen, 1996), adheres to a theory of praxis in the public sphere and encourages media organizations to (a) forge alliances with community groups and listen to citizens on a regular basis as part of an ongoing civic dialogue, (b) sponsor deliberative forums where agendas can be shaped, and (c) prod citizens and government officials to act on the public's judgment (Stepp, 1996).

In the tradition of Dewey (1927) and later writers who have advocated an enhanced social-political role for critics and public intellectuals (e.g., Avery & Eadie, 1993; Jacoby, 1987; Klumpp & Hollihan, 1989; Lentricchia, 1983), Rosen (1994), the leading academic proponent of public journalism, argues that communication scholars, or "media intellectuals," also have a *political* responsibility to restore vitality to the public sphere. Rather than remaining critically detached, critics of media and public life should become moral actors (Klumpp & Hollihan, 1989) and effectuate their theoretical ideals by bringing citizens and media organizations together to make civic life more open and participatory so that citizens can be recast as actors in, rather than passive spectators of, the public drama (Clark, 1997; Rosen, 1994).

Inasmuch as public journalism represents an attempt to involve citizens in the news process and transform a one-way implement of mass communication, the newspaper, into a public forum for two-way interactive discussion, it also implies that the press should relinquish some of its power to decide what is important and how information is portrayed. Perhaps understandably, then, the major media have generally not been supportive of public journalism's suggestion to redefine journalism as a "discussion." As with the failed National News Council, the *New York Times* has set the tone, with former executive editor Max Frankel (1995) asserting that "American journalism sorely needs improvement . . . [but] reporters, editors and publishers have their hands full learning to tell it right. They should leave reforms to the reformers" (p. 30).

Constructionism

Constructionist approaches to civic involvement and public opinion formation also see forums for democratic action as essential to staving off cynicism and apathetic responses to the pseudoenvironment of mediated politics.[7] Constructionist studies foreground social interaction and, in the research setting, group and depth interviews. The talk in such interactional research settings becomes an opportunity for socially meaningful opinion production rather than the impersonal, positivist extraction of information assumed to be preexisting inside people's heads (Dahlgren, 1995). Recent research programs taking a constructionist approach, for instance, have found that political beliefs and shared knowledge of the world are determined largely by how people, in social contexts, actively interpret the images and messages carried by mass media (Gamson, 1992; Just et al., 1996; Neuman, Just, & Crigler, 1992).

"Constructionism focuses on 'common knowledge' as opposed to 'public opinion' [and] emphasizes that the structuring and framing of information is not unique to each individual but aggregates into the cultural phenomenon of shared perspectives and issue frames" (Neuman et al., 1992, p. 18). Consistent with this position, Dahlgren (1995) asserts that "without discussion among citizens, the label 'public' becomes meaningless" (p. 151). Constructionism thus posits that, as active meaning makers, citizens are not as ill informed, apathetic, and cynical as conventional opinion surveys imply. Even if they can recall from memory only a limited number of political facts, ordinary citizens possess the ability to "uncover the connections between private circumstances and public affairs, and critically to analyze current issues within the context of group interaction" (Dahlgren, 1995, p. 153). The democratic promise of such an active citizenry may be mitigated, however, by the disjuncture "between what the mass media emphasize and what the media audience tells us is important and relevant to their lives" (Neuman et al., 1992, p. 111).

Electronic Democracy

A recently revitalized area of political communication research focuses on the role that use of electronic media plays in civic and associational life. In this literature, the mass media are seen as central to the process of community building and have the power to influence substantially the bonds of social connectedness and trust that weave together the societal fabric (Arterton, 1987; Pool, 1990; Putnam, 1995a, 1995b). As in previous research (e.g., Robinson, 1975), television receives special attention. More current scholarship in this tradition has been directed at the relationship between mass media and the fate of various traditional associations that Tocqueville (1840/1969) admired as the building blocks of American democracy. The Tocquevillean ideal is captured by the influential 19th-century French writer's observation that "Americans of all ages, all stations in life, and all types of disposition, are forever forming associations" (p. 513) and working together in common cause. Putnam (1995a, 1995b), a "neo-Tocquevillean" critic of the media, asserts that the introduction of television into American society in the 1950s was a major factor in the subsequent decline of social trust, community networks, and participation in civic organizations. Partly due to the corrosive influence of television on civic life, Putnam argues, the country's supply of social capital, or citizen engagement in public affairs, has eroded (see also Mancini, 1997). This privatization of public life through technological means, according to Pool (1990), will "promote individualism and will make it harder, not easier, to govern and organize a coherent society" (p. 262). Newspaper reading, which shows a positive association with social trust and group membership in Putnam's study, is usually spared such criticism.

Another approach to analyzing the relationship between news media and citizenship is offered by the participatory potential of the "new media," which a growing body of literature on electronic democracy views as a possible answer to the exclusionary nature of traditional one-way mass media systems (Arterton, 1987; Friedland, 1996; Glass, 1996; Graber, 1996b; Grossman, 1995; Hacker, 1996; Rash, 1997). A basic tenet of this literature is that interactive media, especially talk radio, call-in television, and the Internet and World Wide Web, have the capacity to engage ordinary citizens directly in democratic processes. Though flanked by utopians and pessimists at the extreme ends, some new media researchers argue that interactive media involvement, especially involvement in talk radio, call-in television, and Internet use, might be conceptualized as a substantive mode of civic participation and opinion activity rather than a distraction or detriment to democracy (e.g., Bucy, D'Angelo, & Newhagen, 1997; Hofstetter et al., 1994; O'Sullivan, 1995; Page & Tannenbaum, 1996; Pan & Kosicki, 1997). From this perspective, questions about democratic legitimacy and civic involvement in the face of low voter turnout, decreased traditional participation, and an apparently ill-informed mass electorate (Neuman, 1986) may be explained by an important criterion variable that is not being measured: civic engagement *through* media. Graber (1996b) contends that the chief change brought about by the new media is the empowerment of media users: "Thanks to the new electronic networks, individuals can now inform people worldwide and mobilize them for political action" (p. 34).

CONCLUSION

The preceding review of normative critiques of news and democratic processes leads us to three concluding remarks about political communication scholarship. First, in order to address effectively the external crisis—the crisis of communication for citizenship—political communication scholars perhaps need to accept the historical fact that the press as an institution has only evolved organically, in response to broad cultural changes, over a period of decades, if not centuries (Emery & Emery, 1996; Leonard, 1986; Schudson, 1978, 1995), and typically not in direct response to calls for press reform. Since the rise of the modern campaign and modern publicity process (Blumler, 1990), however, the political press has changed dramatically, guided by professional values and the economic imperatives of the market rather than by a coherent normative theory of journalism (Schudson, 1995). The consequences of this institutionally driven arrangement are well reflected in the crisis of communication for citizenship, which the field has resoundingly substantiated. Second, political communication researchers are ideally situated to fill this theoretical vacuum and have begun to do so, as the burgeoning public journalism, constructionist, and electronic democracy literatures indicate, but must be willing to exchange their normative reticence and prescriptive exuberance for a renewed commitment to systematic evaluation of news norms and news media purposes (Gans, 1983). In this way, the field may resolve some of the internal tensions between producing scientific knowledge and building normative theory. Third, even so, political communication scholars should proceed with realistic expectations. To the degree that researcher assessments of political coverage are contrasted with idealized conceptions (Chaffee & Hochheimer, 1985) rather than desired but attainable practices, the gulf between normative preferences of press conduct and actual media performance is only apt to widen. Because of the impervious quality of the press to most criticism (Avery & Eadie, 1993; Brogan, 1985; Jamieson, 1996c; Rosen, 1996), scholars should not pin their hopes of solving social or political problems on press reforms. As Lippmann (1922/1965) noted of the shortcomings of American democracy 75 years ago, "The trouble lies deeper than the press, and so does the remedy" (p. 229).

NOTES

1. Contemporaries of researchers who conducted the early voting studies introducing the concept of limited media effects challenged this notion from the outset (see Lang & Lang, 1959).

2. Although this literature review is not limited to a U.S. context, we focus here on the trends and patterns of American political communication research. Many of the arguments are undoubtedly applicable to other industrial democracies.

3. This criticism has not gone unnoticed by the press. *Washington Post* columnist Richard Harwood (1996) recently observed: "The academic community, once smitten with the media [during the Vietnam and Watergate eras], has gone revisionist, producing books and tracts in great numbers denouncing the press for cynicism, ignorance, and mindless arrogance that endanger democracy and the political process. We are also capitalist tools, as Noam Chomsky and Ralph Nader frequently remind us" (p. A-23).

4. Curran (1996) and Keane (1991) have proposed and elaborated public interest models of communication, and McQuail (1992, 1996) has written extensively about a framework of norms for media performance, but these proposals seem more suited to a European or Canadian communication context, which is more accepting of government intervention than the American commercial media system.

5. Whereas empirical studies of political communication processes were somewhat slow to develop, rhetorical essays on the history or criticism of political discourse have appeared in the *Quarterly Journal of Speech* since its founding in 1915 (Nimmo & Sanders, 1981a).

6. In recognition of the growing importance of communication research to politics, the journal *Political Communication* came under the joint sponsorship of the political communication divisions of the American Political Science Association and the International Communication Association in 1993 (Graber, 1993a). In 1996, the journal grew by 25%, increasing its annual number of pages to 500 (Graber, 1996c). Also in 1996 a second major scholarly journal devoted to media and politics, the *Harvard International Journal of Press/Politics,* was founded with the interdisciplinary intent to "stimulate dialogue among different branches of scholarship and

leapfrog the sadly parochial borders that now separate scholars from journalists" (Kalb & Norris, 1996, p. 1).

7. This research tradition has also been called *constructivism,* a term that has been applied in a more general sense to the study of human communication (see Delia, 1977; Swanson, 1981). The basic focus of both constructionism and constructivism is on interpretive processes.

REFERENCES

Adatto, K. (1990). *Sound bite democracy: Network evening news presidential campaign coverage, 1968 and 1988* (Research Paper R-2). Cambridge, MA: Harvard University, Joan Shorenstein Barone Center.

Alger, D. E. (1989). *The media and politics.* Englewood Cliffs, NJ: Prentice Hall.

Altschull, J. H. (1984). *Agents of power: The role of the news media in human affairs.* New York: Longman.

Alvarez, R. M. (1996). *Information and elections.* Ann Arbor: University of Michigan Press.

Ansolabehere, S., & Iyengar, S. (1995). *Going negative: How attack ads shrink and polarize the electorate.* New York: Free Press.

Arterton, F. C. (1978). The media politics of presidential campaigns: A study of the Carter nomination drive. In J. D. Barber (Ed.), *Race for the presidency: The media and the nominating process* (pp. 26-54). Englewood Cliffs, NJ: Prentice Hall.

Arterton, F. C. (1984). *Media politics: The news strategies of presidential campaigns.* Lexington, MA: Lexington.

Arterton, F. C. (1987). *Teledemocracy: Can technology protect democracy?* Newbury Park, CA: Sage.

Avery, R. K., & Eadie, W. F. (1993). Making a difference in the real world. *Journal of Communication, 43*(3), 174-179.

Baars, B. J. (1986). *The cognitive revolution in psychology.* New York: Guilford.

Bagdikian, B. H. (1992). *The media monopoly* (4th ed.). Boston: Beacon.

Barber, B. R. (1984). *Strong democracy: Participatory politics for a new age.* Berkeley: University of California Press.

Barber, J. D. (Ed.). (1978). *Race for the presidency: The media and the nominating process.* Englewood Cliffs, NJ: Prentice Hall.

Barnhurst, K. G., & Steele, C. A. (1997). Image-bite news: The visual coverage of elections on U.S. television, 1968-1992. *Press/Politics, 2*(1), 40-58.

Bell, D. (1960). *The end of ideology: On the exhaustion of political ideas in the fifties.* New York: Free Press.

Belsey, A. (1992). Privacy, publicity, and politics. In A. Belsey & R. Chadwick (Eds.), *Ethical issues in journalism and the media* (pp. 77-92). London: Routledge.

Bennett, W. L. (1980). Myth, ritual, and political control. *Journal of Communication, 30*(4), 154-167.

Bennett, W. L. (1992). White noise: The perils of mass mediated democracy. *Communication Monographs, 59,* 401-406.

Bennett, W. L. (1996a). *The governing crisis: Media, money, and marketing in American elections* (2nd ed.). New York: St. Martin's.

Bennett, W. L. (1996b). *News: The politics of illusion* (3rd ed.). New York: Longman.

Bennett, W. L., & Edelman, M. (1985). Toward a new political narrative. *Journal of Communication, 35*(4), 156-171.

Berelson, B. R. (1959). The state of communication research. *Public Opinion Quarterly, 23,* 1-6.

Berelson, B. R., Lazarsfeld, P., & McPhee, W. (1954). *Voting.* Chicago: University of Chicago Press.

Bitzer, L. F. (1981). Political rhetoric. In D. Nimmo & K. R. Sanders (Eds.), *Handbook of political communication* (pp. 225-248). Beverly Hills, CA: Sage.

Blumler, J. G. (1983). Communication and democracy: The crisis beyond and the ferment within. *Journal of Communication, 33*(3), 166-173.

Blumler, J. G. (1990). Elections, the media, and the modern publicity process. In M. Ferguson (Ed.), *Public communication: The new imperatives* (pp. 101-113). London: Sage.

Blumler, J. G., & Gurevitch, M. (1995). *The crisis of public communication.* London: Routledge.

Blumler, J. G., & Gurevitch, M. (1996). Media change and social change: Linkages and junctures. In J. Curran & M. Gurevitch (Eds.), *Mass media and society* (2nd ed., pp. 120-137). London: Edward Arnold.

Boorstin, D. J. (1964). *The image: A guide to pseudo-events in America.* New York: Harper & Row.

Breed, W. (1955). Social control in the newsroom: A functional analysis. *Social Forces, 33,* 326-335.

Broder, D. S. (1990, January 3). Democracy and the press. *Washington Post,* p. A-15.

Brogan, P. (1985). *Spiked: The short life and death of the National News Council.* New York: Twentieth Century Fund Press.

Bucy, E. P., D'Angelo, P., & Newhagen, J. E. (1998). New media use as political participation. In L. L. Kaid & D. Bystrom (Eds.), *The electronic election: Perspectives on 1996 campaign communication* (pp. 335-347). Mahwah, NJ: Lawrence Erlbaum.

Burgoon, J. K. (Ed.). (1992). Are media news spectacles perverting our political processes? [Chautauqua] *Communication Monographs, 59,* 397-420.

Cappella, J. N., & Jamieson, K. H. (1996). News frames, political cynicism, and media cynicism. *Annals of the American Academy of Political and Social Science, 546,* 71-84.

Cappella, J. N., & Jamieson, K. H. (1997). *Spiral of cynicism: The press and the public good.* New York: Oxford University Press.

Chaffee, S. H. (Ed.). (1975). *Political communication: Issues and strategies for research.* Beverly Hills, CA: Sage.

Chaffee, S. H. (1981). Mass media in political campaigns: An expanding role. In R. E. Rice & W. J. Paisley (Eds.), *Public communication campaigns* (pp. 181-198). Beverly Hills, CA: Sage.

Chaffee, S. H., & Frank, S. (1996). How Americans get political information: Print versus broadcast news. *Annals of the American Academy of Political and Social Science, 546,* 48-58.

Chaffee, S. H., & Hochheimer, J. L. (1985). The beginnings of political communication research in the United States: Origins of the "limited effects" model. In E. M. Rogers & F. Balle (Eds.), *The media revolution in America and Western Europe* (pp. 267-296). Norwood, NJ: Ablex.

Chaffee, S. H., & Jamieson, K. H. (Eds.). (1994). Campaign '92: Communication and the political process [Special issue]. *Communication Research, 21*(3).

Clark, C. (1997). In favor of civic journalism. *Press/Politics, 2*(3), 118-124.

Curran, J. (1996). Mass media and democracy revisited. In J. Curran & M. Gurevitch (Eds.), *Mass media and society* (2nd ed., pp. 81-119). London: Edward Arnold.

Dahlgren, P. (1992). Introduction. In P. Dahlgren & C. Sparks (Eds.), *Journalism and popular culture* (pp. 1-23). London: Sage.

Dahlgren, P. (1995). *Television and the public sphere.* London: Sage.

Davis, D. K. (1990). News and politics. In D. L. Swanson & D. Nimmo (Eds.), *New directions in political communication* (pp. 147-184). Newbury Park, CA: Sage.

Davis, R. (1992). *The press and American politics: The new mediator.* New York: Longman.

Davis, R. (Ed.). (1994). *Politics and the media.* Englewood Cliffs, NJ: Prentice Hall.

Dayan, D., & Katz, E. (1992). *Media events: The live broadcasting of history.* Cambridge, MA: Harvard University Press.

Delia, J. G. (1977). Constructivism and the study of human communication. *Quarterly Journal of Speech, 63,* 66-83.

Delia, J. G. (1987). Communication research: A history. In C. R. Berger & S. H. Chaffee (Eds.), *Handbook of communication science* (pp. 20-98). Newbury Park, CA: Sage.

Dennis, E. E. (1997). How "liberal" are the media, anyway? The continuing conflict of professionalism and partisanship. *Press/Politics, 2*(4), 115-119.

Denton, R. E., & Woodward, G. (1985). *Political communication in America.* New York: Praeger.

Dewey, J. (1927). *The public and its problems.* New York: Henry Holt.

Diamond, E., & Bates, S. (1992). *The spot: The rise of political advertising on television* (3rd ed.). Cambridge: MIT Press.

Donohue, G. A., Tichenor, P. J., & Olien, C. N. (1995). A guard dog perspective on the role of the media. *Journal of Communication, 45*(2), 115-132.

Donovan, R. J., & Scherer, R. (1992). *Unsilent revolution: Television news and American public life.* New York: Cambridge University Press.

Edelman, M. (1964). *The symbolic uses of politics.* Urbana: University of Illinois Press.

Edelman, M. (1988). *Constructing the political spectacle.* Chicago: University of Chicago Press.

Efron, E. (1971). *The news twisters.* Los Angeles: Nash.

Emery, M., & Emery, E. (1996). *The press and America: An interpretive history of the mass media* (8th ed.). Boston: Allyn & Bacon.

Entman, R. M. (1989). *Democracy without citizens: Media and the decay of American politics.* New York: Oxford University Press.

Entman, R. M. (1993). Framing: Toward clarification of a fractured paradigm. *Journal of Communication, 43*(4), 51-58.

Entman, R. M., & Paletz, D. L. (1980). Media and the conservative myth. *Journal of Communication, 30*(4), 180-191.

Epstein, E. J. (1973). *News from nowhere: Television and the news.* New York: Random House.

Eulau, H., Eldersveld, S. J., & Janowitz, M. (Eds.). (1956). *Political behavior.* New York: Free Press.

Fallows, J. (1996). *Breaking the news: How the media undermine American democracy.* New York: Pantheon.

Fishkin, J. (1991). *Democracy and deliberation: New directions for democratic reform.* New Haven, CT: Yale University Press.

Folkerts, J. (Ed.). (1995). Election research [Symposium]. *Journalism & Mass Communication Quarterly, 72,* 7-105.

Frankel, M. (1995, May 20). Fix-it journalism. *New York Times Magazine,* p. 30.

Friedland, L. A. (1996). Electronic democracy and the new citizenship. *Media, Culture & Society, 18,* 185-212.

Gamson, W. A. (1992). *Talking politics.* New York: Cambridge University Press.

Gans, H. J. (1979). *Deciding what's news: A study of* CBS Evening News, NBC Nightly News, Newsweek, *and* Time. New York: Pantheon.

Gans, H. J. (1983). News media, news policy, and democracy: Research for the future. *Journal of Communication, 33*(3), 174-184.

Gerbner, G. (Ed.). (1983). Ferment in the field [Special issue]. *Journal of Communication, 33*(3).

Gitlin, T. (1978). Media sociology: The dominant paradigm. *Theory and Society, 6,* 205-253.

Gitlin, T. (1980). *The whole world is watching: Mass media in the making and unmaking of the New Left.* Berkeley: University of California Press.

Glass, A. J. (1996). On-line elections: The Internet's impact on the political process. *Press/Politics, 1*(4), 140-146.

Glasser, T. L. (1991). Communication and the cultivation of citizenship. *Communication, 12*(4), 235-248.

Graber, D. A. (1980). *Mass media and American politics.* Washington, DC: Congressional Quarterly Press.

Graber, D. A. (1982). The impact of media research on public opinion studies. In D. C. Whitney & E. Wartella (Eds.), *Mass communication review yearbook* (Vol. 3, pp. 555-564). Beverly Hills, CA: Sage.

Graber, D. A. (1984). *Media power in politics.* Washington, DC: Congressional Quarterly Press.

Graber, D. A. (1987). Researching the mass media-elections interface: A political science perspective. *Mass Comm Review, 14*(1), 3-19.

Graber, D. A. (1988). *Processing the news: How people tame the information tide* (2nd ed). New York: Longman.

Graber, D. A. (1993a). Editor's prospectus. *Political Communication, 10*(1), vii.

Graber, D. A. (1993b). Making campaign news user friendly: The lessons of 1992 and beyond. *American Behavioral Scientist, 37,* 328-336.

Graber, D. A. (1996a). *Mass media and American politics* (5th ed.). Washington, DC: Congressional Quarterly Press.

Graber, D. A. (1996b). The "new" media and politics: What does the future hold? *PS: Political Science & Politics, 29,* 33-36.

Graber, D. A. (1996c). *Political Communication*: A progress report. *Political Communication Report, 8,* 1, 6.

Graber, D. A. (1996d). Say it with pictures. *Annals of the American Academy of Political and Social Science, 546,* 85-96.

Green, D. P., & Shapiro, I. (1994). *Pathologies of rational choice theory: A critique of applications in political science.* New Haven, CT: Yale University Press.

Grossman, L. K. (1995). *The electronic republic: Reshaping democracy in the information age.* New York: Viking.

Gurevitch, M., & Blumler, J. G. (1990). Political communication systems and democratic values. In J. Lichtenberg (Ed.), *Democracy and the mass media* (pp. 269-289). Cambridge: Cambridge University Press.

Gurevitch, M., & Kavoori, A. P. (1992). Television spectacles as politics. *Communication Monographs, 59,* 415-419.

Hacker, K. L. (1996). Missing links in the evolution of electronic democratization. *Media, Culture & Society, 18,* 213-232.

Hall, S. (1982). The re-discovery of "ideology": Return of the repressed in media studies. In M. Gurevitch, T. Bennett, J. Curran, & J. Woollacott (Eds.), *Culture, society and the media* (pp. 56-90). London: Methuen.

Hallin, D. C. (1992). Sound bite news: Television coverage of elections, 1968-1988. *Journal of Communication, 42*(2), 5-24.

Hallin, D. C. (1994). *We keep America on top of the world: Television journalism and the public sphere.* London: Routledge.

Hart, R. P. (1994). *Seducing America: How television charms the modern voter.* New York: Oxford University Press.

Hart, R. P., Jerome, P., & McComb, K. (1984). Rhetorical features of newscasts about the president. *Critical Studies in Mass Communication, 1,* 260-286.

Harwood, R. (1996, September 6). Deconstructing Bob Woodward. *Washington Post,* p. A-23.

Hauck, R. J. P. (Ed.). (1996). Media and politics [Symposium]. *PS: Political Science & Politics, 29,* 10-36.

Herman, E. S., & Chomsky, N. (1988). *Manufacturing consent: The political economy of the mass media.* New York: Pantheon.

Hertsgaard, M. (1988). *On bended knee: The press and the Reagan presidency.* New York: Farrar, Straus & Giroux.

Hofstetter, C. R., Donovan, M. C., Klauber, M. R., Cole, A., Huie, C. J., & Yuasa, T. (1994). Political talk radio: A stereotype reconsidered. *Political Research Quarterly, 47,* 467-479.

Hunter, A. (1996, January/February). Why the right hates the media: Conservatives and the "new class." *Extra!* 9(1), 19-21.

Hutchins, R. (1947). *A free and responsible press.* Chicago: University of Chicago Press.

Iyengar, S. (1991). *Is anyone responsible? How television frames political issues.* Chicago: University of Chicago Press.

Iyengar, S. (1996). Framing responsibility for political issues. *Annals of the American Academy of Political and Social Science, 546,* 59-70.

Iyengar, S., & Kinder, D. (1987). *News that matters: Television and American opinion.* Chicago: University of Chicago Press.

Iyengar, S., & Reeves, R. (Eds.). (1997). *Does the media govern? Politicians, voters, and reporters in America.* Thousand Oaks, CA: Sage.

Jacobs, L. R., & Shapiro, R. Y. (1996). Toward the integrated study of political communications, public opinion, and the policy-making process. *PS: Political Science & Politics, 29,* 10-13.

Jacoby, R. (1987). *The last intellectuals: American culture in the age of academe.* New York: Basic Books.

Jamieson, K. H. (1988). *Eloquence in an electronic age: The transformation of political speechmaking.* New York: Oxford University Press.

Jamieson, K. H. (1992). *Dirty politics: Deception, distraction, and democracy.* New York: Oxford University Press.

Jamieson, K. H. (1993). The subversive effects of a focus on strategy in news coverage of presidential campaigns. In Twentieth Century Fund (Ed.), *1-800-president: The report of the Twentieth Century Fund Task Force on Television and the Campaign of 1992* (pp. 35-61). New York: Twentieth Century Fund Press.

Jamieson, K. H. (Ed.). (1996a). The media and politics. *Annals of the American Academy of Political and Social Science, 546.*

Jamieson, K. H. (1996b). *Packaging the presidency: A history and criticism of presidential campaign advertising* (3rd ed.). New York: Oxford University Press.

Jamieson, K. H. (1996c, November 22). Scholarship and the discourse of election campaigns. *Chronicle of Higher Education,* pp. B4-B5.

Jamieson, K. H., & Campbell, K. K. (1982). *The interplay of influence: Mass media and their publics in news, advertising, politics.* Belmont, CA: Wadsworth.

Jamieson, K. H., & Cappella, J. N. (1996). Bridging the disciplinary divide. *PS: Political Science & Politics, 29,* 13-17.

Johannesen, R. L. (1991). Virtue ethics, character, and political communication. In R. E. Denton (Ed.), *Ethical dimensions of political communication* (pp. 69-90). New York: Praeger.

Johnston, A. (1990). Selective bibliography of political communication research, 1982-1988. In D. L. Swanson & D. Nimmo (Eds.), *New directions in political communication* (pp. 363-389). Newbury Park, CA: Sage.

Joslyn, R. (1984). *Mass media and elections.* New York: Random House.

Just, M. R., Crigler, A. N., Alger, D. E., Cook, T., Kern, M., & West, D. M. (1996). *Crosstalk: Citizens, candidates, and the media in a presidential campaign.* Chicago: University of Chicago Press.

Kaid, L. L., & Wadsworth, A. J. (1985). *Political campaign communication: A bibliography and guide to the literature, 1973-1982.* Metuchen, NJ: Scarecrow.

Kalb, M., & Norris, P. (1996). Editorial. *Press/Politics, 1*(1), 1-2.

Katz, E., & Lazarsfeld, P. F. (1955). *Personal influence.* New York: Free Press.

Keane, J. (1991). *The media and democracy.* Oxford: Polity.

Kellner, D. (1990). *Television and the crisis of democracy.* Boulder, CO: Westview.

Kerbel, M. R. (1994). *Edited for television: CNN, ABC, and the 1992 presidential campaign.* Boulder, CO: Westview.

Kerbel, M. R. (1995). *Remote and controlled: Media politics in a cynical age.* Boulder, CO: Westview.

Kern, M. (1989). *Thirty-second politics: Political advertising in the eighties.* New York: Praeger.

Klumpp, J. F., & Hollihan, T. A. (1989). Rhetorical criticism as moral action. *Quarterly Journal of Speech, 75,* 84-97.

Kraus, S., & Davis, D. (1976). *The effects of mass communication on political behavior.* University Park: Pennsylvania State University Press.

Kuhn, T. (1970). *The structure of scientific revolutions* (2nd ed.). Chicago: University of Chicago Press.

Kurtz, H. (1993). *Media circus: The trouble with America's newspapers.* New York: Times Books.

Kurtz, H. (1996). *Hot air: All talk, all the time.* New York: Times Books.

Lang, K., & Lang, G. E. (1959). The mass media and voting. In E. Burdick & A. J. Brodbeck (Eds.), *American voting behavior* (pp. 217-235). Glencoe, IL: Free Press.

Lanigan, R. L., & Strobl, R. L. (1981). A critical theory approach. In D. Nimmo & K. R. Sanders (Eds.), *Handbook of political communication* (pp. 142-167). Beverly Hills, CA: Sage.

Lazarsfeld, P. F., Berelson, B., & Gaudet, H. (1944). *The people's choice.* New York: Duell, Sloan & Pearce.

Lentricchia, F. (1983). *Criticism and social change.* Chicago: University of Chicago Press.

Leonard, T. C. (1986). *The power of the press: The birth of American political reporting.* New York: Oxford University Press.

Levy, M. R. (1981). Disdaining the news. *Journal of Communication, 31*(3), 24-31.

Lichter, S. R., & Noyes, R. (1996). *Good intentions make bad news: Why Americans hate campaign journalism* (2nd ed.). Lanham, MD: Rowman & Littlefield.

Lichter, S. R., & Rothman, S., with Lichter, L. S. (1986). *The media elite: America's new power brokers.* Bethesda, MD: Adler & Adler.

Lippmann, W. (1965). *Public opinion.* New York: Free Press. (Original work published 1922)

Lipset, S. M., & Schneider, W. (1983). *The confidence gap: Business, labor, and government in the public mind.* New York: Free Press.

Mancini, P. (1997). The gap between citizens and government. *Press/Politics, 2*(3), 131-135.

Martin, L. J. (1981). Government and the news media. In D. Nimmo & K. R. Sanders (Eds.), *Handbook of political communication* (pp. 445-465). Beverly Hills, CA: Sage.

Matthews, D. R. (1978). "Winnowing": The news media and the 1976 presidential nominations. In J. D. Barber (Ed.), *Race for the presidency: The media and the nominating process* (pp. 55-78). Englewood Cliffs, NJ: Prentice Hall.

McCombs, M. E., & Shaw, D. L. (1972). The agenda-setting function of the press. *Public Opinion Quarterly, 36,* 176-187.

McLeod, J. M., Kosicki, G. M., & McLeod, D. M. (1994). The expanding boundaries of political communication effects. In J. Bryant & D. Zillmann (Eds.), *Media effects: Advances in theory and research* (pp. 123-162). Hillsdale, NJ: Lawrence Erlbaum.

McLeod, J. M., Kosicki, G. M., & Rucinski, D. M. (1988). Political communication research: An assessment of the field. *Mass Comm Review, 15*(1), 8-15, 30.

McQuail, D. (1992). *Media performance: Mass communication and the public interest.* London: Sage.

McQuail, D. (1994). *Mass communication theory: An introduction* (3rd ed.). London: Sage.

McQuail, D. (1996). Mass media in the public interest: Towards a framework of norms for media performance. In J. Curran & M. Gurevitch (Eds.), *Mass media and society* (2nd ed., pp. 66-80). London: Edward Arnold.

Meadow, R. G. (1985). Political communication research in the 1980s. *Journal of Communication, 35*(1), 157-173.

Merritt, D. (1995). *Public journalism and public life: Why telling news is not enough.* Hillsdale, NJ: Lawrence Erlbaum.

Meyrowitz, J. (1985). *No sense of place: The impact of electronic media on social behavior.* New York: Oxford University Press.

Mickelson, S. (1989). *From whistle stop to sound bite.* New York: Praeger.

Mutz, D., C., Sniderman, P. M., & Brody, R. A. (Eds.). (1996). *Political persuasion and attitude change.* Ann Arbor: University of Michigan Press.

Neuman, W. R. (1986). *The paradox of mass politics: Knowledge and opinion in the American electorate.* Cambridge, MA: Harvard University Press.

Neuman, W. R., Just, M. R., & Crigler, A. N. (1992). *Common knowledge: News and the construction of political meaning.* Chicago: University of Chicago Press.

Nimmo, D. (1978). *Political communication and public opinion in America.* Santa Monica, CA: Goodyear.

Nimmo, D. (1987). Elections as ritual drama. In L. P. Develin (Ed.), *Political persuasion in presidential campaigns* (pp. 159-173). New Brunswick, NJ: Transaction.

Nimmo, D., & Combs, J. E. (1990). *Mediated political realities* (2nd ed.). New York: Longman.

Nimmo, D., & Sanders, K. R. (1981a). The emergence of political communication as a field. In D. Nimmo & K. R. Sanders (Eds.), *Handbook of political communication* (pp. 11-36). Beverly Hills, CA: Sage.

Nimmo, D., & Sanders, K. R. (Eds.). (1981b). *Handbook of political communication.* Beverly Hills, CA: Sage.

Nimmo, D., & Swanson, D. L. (1990). The field of political communication: Beyond the voter persuasion paradigm. In D. L. Swanson & D. Nimmo (Eds.), *New directions in political communication* (pp. 7-47). Newbury Park, CA: Sage.

O'Sullivan, P. B. (1995). Computer networks and political participation: Santa Monica's teledemocracy project. *Journal of Applied Communication Research, 23,* 93-107.

Page, B. I. (1996). The mass media as political actors. *PS: Political Science & Politics, 29,* 20-24.

Page, B. I., & Tannenbaum, J. (1996). Populistic deliberation and talk radio. *Journal of Communication, 46*(2), 33-54.

Paletz, D. (Ed.). (1987). *Political communication research: Approaches, studies, assessments.* Norwood, NJ: Ablex.

Pan, S., & Kosicki, G. M. (1997). Talk show exposure as an opinion activity. *Political Communication, 14,* 371-388.

Parenti, M. (1986). *Inventing reality: The politics of the mass media.* New York: St. Martin's.

Patterson, T. E. (1980). *The mass media election: How Americans choose their president.* New York: Praeger.

Patterson, T. E. (1993). *Out of order.* New York: Knopf.

Patterson, T. E. (1994). Legitimate beef: The presidency and a carnivorous press. *Media Studies Journal, 8*(2), 21-26.

Patterson, T. E. (1996a). Bad news, bad governance. *Annals of the American Academy of Political and Social Science, 546,* 97-108.

Patterson, T. E. (1996b). Bad news, period. *PS: Political Science & Politics, 29,* 17-20.

Patterson, T. E., & Donsbach, W. (1996). News decisions: Journalists as partisan actors. *Political Communication, 13,* 455-468.

Payne, J. G. (Ed.). (1993). Campaign '92: New frontiers in political communication [Special issue]. *American Behavioral Scientist, 37*(2).

Payne, J. G. (Ed.). (1997). Campaign '96: Messages for the new millennium [Special issue]. *American Behavioral Scientist, 40*(8).

Peterson, T. (1956). The social responsibility theory of the press. In F. S. Siebert, T. Peterson, & W. Schramm (Eds.), *Four theories of the press* (pp. 73-103). Urbana: University of Illinois Press.

Pool, I. de S. (1990). *Technologies without boundaries: On telecommunications in a global age.* Cambridge, MA: Harvard University Press.

Popkin, S. (1991). *The reasoning voter: Communication and persuasion in presidential campaigns.* Chicago: University of Chicago Press.

Postman, N. (1986). *Amusing ourselves to death: Public discourse in the age of show business.* New York: Penguin.

Putnam, R. D. (1995a). Bowling alone: America's declining social capital. *Journal of Democracy, 6,* 65-78.

Putnam, R. D. (1995b). Tuning in, tuning out: The strange disappearance of social capital in America. *PS: Political Science & Politics, 28,* 664-683.

Rash, W., Jr. (1997). *Politics on the nets: Wiring the political process.* New York: W. H. Freeman.

Rivers, W. (1970). *The adversaries: Politics and the press.* Boston: Beacon.

Robinson, M. J. (1975). American political legitimacy in an era of electronic journalism: Reflections on the evening news. In D. Carter & R. Adler (Eds.), *Television as a social force: New approaches to TV criticism* (pp. 97-139). New York: Praeger.

Robinson, M. J. (1976). Public affairs television and the growth of political malaise: The case of "The selling of the Pentagon." *American Political Science Review, 70,* 409-432.

Robinson, M. J. (1977). Television and American politics: 1956-1976. *Public Interest, 48,* 3-39.

Robinson, M. J., & Sheehan, M. A. (1983). *Over the wire and on TV: CBS and UPI in campaign '80.* New York: Russell Sage Foundation.

Rose, G. (1994). *Controversial issues in presidential selection* (2nd ed.). Albany: State University of New York Press.

Rosen, J. (1994). Making things more public: On the political responsibility of the media intellectual. *Critical Studies in Mass Communication, 11,* 363-388.

Rosen, J. (1996). *Getting the connections right: Public journalism and the troubles in the press.* New York: Twentieth Century Fund Press.

Rothman, S. (1979). The news media in post-industrial America. In S. M. Lipset (Ed.), *The third century America as a post-industrial society* (pp. 346-388). Chicago: University of Chicago Press.

Sabato, L. J. (1981). *The rise of political consultants: New ways of winning elections.* New York: Basic Books.

Sabato, L. J. (1991). *Feeding frenzy: How attack journalism has transformed American politics.* New York: Free Press.

Sanders, K. R., Kaid, L. L., & Nimmo, D. (Eds.). (1984). *Political communication yearbook 1984.* Carbondale: Southern Illinois University Press.

Schram, S. F. (1991). The post-modern presidency and the grammar of electronic electioneering. *Critical Studies in Mass Communication, 8,* 210-216.

Schudson, M. (1978). *Discovering the news.* New York: Basic Books.

Schudson, M. (1995). *The power of news.* Cambridge, MA: Harvard University Press.

Semetko, H. A., Blumler, J. G., Gurevitch, M., & Weaver, D. H., with Barkin, S., & Wilhoit, G. C. (Eds.). (1991). *The formation of campaign agendas: A comparative analysis of party and media roles in recent American and British elections.* Hillsdale, NJ: Lawrence Erlbaum.

Shepard, A. C. (1997, April). Going public. *American Journalism Review,* pp. 24-29.

Siefert, M. (Ed.). (1991). Texts of destruction and insurrection: International politics and the press [Special issue]. *Journal of Communication, 41*(4).

Simpson, C. (1994). *Science of coercion: Communication research and psychological warfare, 1945-1960.* New York: Oxford University Press.

Sparks, C. (Ed.). (1996). Electronic democracy [Special issue]. *Media, Culture & Society, 18*(2).

Spear, J. C. (1984). *Presidents and the press: The Nixon legacy.* Cambridge: MIT Press.

Steele, C. A., & Barnhurst, K. G. (1996). The journalism of opinion: Network news coverage of U.S. presidential campaigns, 1968-1988. *Critical Studies in Mass Communication, 13,* 187-209.

Stepp, C. S. (1996, May). Public journalism: Balancing the scales. *American Journalism Review,* pp. 38-40.

Stevenson, R. L., Eisinger, R. A., Feinberg, B. M., & Kotok, A. B. (1973). Untwisting the news twisters: A replication of Efron's study. *Journalism Quarterly, 50,* 211-219.

Strentz, H. (1989). *News reporters and news sources: Accomplices in shaping and misshaping the news.* Ames: Iowa State University Press.

Swanson, D. L. (1981). A constructivist approach. In D. Nimmo & K. R. Sanders (Eds.), *Handbook of political communication* (pp. 169-191). Beverly Hills, CA: Sage.

Swanson, D. L. (1992). The political-media complex. *Communication Monographs, 59,* 397-400.

Swanson, D. L. (1997). The political-media complex at 50: Putting the 1996 presidential campaign in context. *American Behavioral Scientist, 40,* 1264-1282.

Swanson, D. L., & Mancini, P. (Eds.). (1996). *Politics, media, and modern democracy: An international study of innovations in electoral campaigning and their consequences.* Westport, CT: Praeger.

Swanson, D. L., & Nimmo, D. (Eds.). (1990). *New directions in political communication.* Newbury Park, CA: Sage.

Tocqueville, A. de. (1969). *Democracy in America.* Garden City, NY: Doubleday. (Original work published 1840)

Tuchman, G. (1978). *Making news: A study in the construction of reality.* New York: Free Press.

Valente, J. (1997, March 2). Do you believe what newspeople tell you? *Parade,* pp. 4-6.

Wasburn, P. C. (Ed.). (1995). *Research in political sociology* (Vol. 7). Greenwich, CT: JAI.

Weaver, D. H. (1996). What voters learn from media. *Annals of the American Academy of Political and Social Science, 546,* 34-47.

Weaver, D. H., & Wilhoit, G. C. (1986). *The American journalist: A portrait of U.S. news people and their work.* Bloomington: Indiana University Press.

Welch, S. (Ed.). (1991). Media, campaigns, and elections [Symposium]. *American Politics Quarterly, 19*(1).

Zarefsky, D. (1992). Spectator politics and the revival of public argument. *Communication Monographs, 59,* 411-414.

Zhao, X., & Chaffee, S. H. (1995). Campaign advertisements versus television news as sources of political issue information. *Public Opinion Quarterly, 59,* 41-65.

CHAPTER CONTENTS

9 Communication and Customer Service

WENDY S. ZABAVA FORD
Western Michigan University

Service providers play a central role in organizations. This chapter integrates research on communication behaviors engaged in by providers in customer service interactions. Providers' customer service styles may reflect a combination of courteous, personalized, and manipulative communication behaviors. The exact behaviors demonstrated in any given service interaction are greatly influenced by the provider's status, the customer's status, and time pressure. Providers may engage in courteous service behaviors, including phatic speech, nonverbal immediacy, and verbal immediacy. They may also offer personalized service by demonstrating a customer orientation, interaction involvement, information sharing, and social support. In addition, they may engage in manipulative service through such behaviors as bureaucratization, interaction control, compliance gaining, and emotion management. Whereas courteous and personalized service practices appear to contribute to customer satisfaction and compliance as well as provider job satisfaction, manipulative service practices have been more strongly linked to sales and tips as well as provider burnout. Future research is necessary to heighten our awareness of the role and impact of communication in customer service interactions.

C USTOMER service is a communication process in which an organizational representative presents products or professional assistance in exchange for another individual's money or cooperation. The organizational representative, commonly labeled a *service provider,* may perform any of a variety of roles, such as cashier, food server, bank teller, receptionist, physician, nurse, lawyer, counselor, hairdresser, flight attendant, bartender, salesperson, teacher, or consultant. The other service participant, commonly labeled a *customer,* may be any consumer, patient, student, client, shopper, caller, diner, or passenger to whom the provider offers products or assistance. The customer may even be a member of the same organization—an "internal customer"—such as an employee served by a payroll clerk, a manager served

Correspondence and requests for reprints: Wendy S. Zabava Ford, Department of Communication, Western Michigan University, Kalamazoo, MI 49008.

Communication Yearbook 22, pp. 341-375

by an administrative assistant, or a telecommuter served by a technical support provider.

Customer service is widely heralded as one of the major keys to success for any organization. Retail enterprises, government agencies, schools, and hospitals are equally concerned about attracting and retaining customers, promoting "service excellence," "getting close to the customer," and securing "consumer involvement" in their programs. Given the central role of customer service in organizations, a number of studies have been conducted to examine service practices and provide direction for service improvement. Most of these studies have focused specifically on provider communication behaviors.

Customer service providers have a unique role as organizational representatives. Often labeled *front-end personnel* or *boundary spanners,* providers represent the organization in the minds of customers. What providers say and do in their brief moments with customers leaves deep impressions regarding the values and orientation of the organization. Service providers' behaviors also have an immediate influence on organizational outcomes, such as sales and customer satisfaction. Therefore, these behaviors should be given serious attention.

My purpose in this chapter is to explore the communication behaviors engaged in by customer service providers. I first describe communication behaviors that are reflected in customer service styles and examine the key predictors of variation in these behaviors. I then present a general taxonomy of behaviors that illustrate three categories of customer service; this is followed by a discussion of the potential impact of service communication behaviors on organizational outcomes. I close the chapter with conclusions and recommendations for further research examining communication and customer service.

CUSTOMER SERVICE STYLES

Providers may develop customer service styles that incorporate a variety of communication behaviors. These behaviors may range from the bureaucratic norms of postal clerks (Goodsell, 1976) to the language choices of physicians (Thompson & Pledger, 1993), emotional displays of supermarket cashiers (Rafaeli & Sutton, 1990), information sharing by computer consultants (Guinan & Scudder, 1989), and informal counseling by hairdressers, lawyers, and bartenders (Cowen, 1982). Unfortunately, the specific service behaviors addressed by researchers have varied dramatically, making it difficult to generalize toward common theories regarding customer service practices.

In 1994, Ford and Etienne identified three broad categories of customer service behaviors that capture the wide range of communication behaviors addressed in prior studies. I further elaborated on these categories (Ford, 1998), providing the basis for portions of this chapter. These categories are: courteous service, personalized service, and manipulative service.

Courteous service is friendly service. It is service used to forge an immediate "bond" between the provider and customer. Common examples of courteous service behaviors are greetings, smiles, eye contact, small talk, humor, and the use of names.

Personalized service is tailored service, or service that attempts to address the unique needs of individual customers. Examples of personalized service include asking questions to identify customers' concerns, offering options and helpful advice, listening attentively and responding sensitively to customers' problems, explaining complex issues in simple language, and providing informal counseling and support.

Manipulative service is strategic service, or service that involves attempts to deceive or control customers. Some examples of manipulative service behaviors are fake smiles, sales pitches, threats and rewards, bureaucratic routines, emotional detachment from customers, mindless reliance on standardized "scripts," and attempts to dominate the course of the service interaction.

Service providers are likely to develop customer service styles that include some combination of courteous, personalized, and manipulative communication behaviors. For example, a postal service employee may extend courteous service by smiling at customers and greeting them warmly as they approach the service desk. The employee may also personalize service interactions by listening attentively to customers' questions and providing appropriate responses and support. In addition, the employee may engage in manipulative service by adhering to standard scripts and procedures that facilitate efforts to process customers quickly and accurately.

Service providers may alter their communication behaviors to correspond to different stages of their interactions with customers. For instance, Olshavsky (1973) found that salespersons complete three distinct, consecutive phases during the sales process: orientation, evaluation, and consummation. His observations of 40 complete sales interactions revealed that the salespersons used different combinations of questions, information sharing, and selling behaviors in each phase of the sales process.

Although service providers are likely to employ some combination of behaviors representing the three service categories during the course of their interactions with customers, they may rely more heavily on one particular category of behaviors over others. For instance, food servers may develop a style of "fast and friendly" service that is dominated by manipulative behaviors for processing customers quickly and influencing tip size but also includes some courteous gestures such as sincere smiles and a little small talk. As another example, many physicians may have an overall "patient-centered" style comprising primarily personalized service behaviors to ensure that they sufficiently address patients' unique concerns, but their style may also include some manipulation to influence the patients' ultimate compliance with treatment recommendations.

The exact customer service styles applied by providers will likely depend on various service predictors. Spiro and Perreault (1979), in their examination of salespersons' communication behaviors, determined that the salespersons tended to employ different mixes of communication strategies in their interactions with customers depending on situational variables. For instance, they found that salespersons were more likely to engage in a mix of closed, deceptive strategies with customers they perceived as very "important" and were less likely to apply such strategies when their products were not much different from their competitors' products. The next section presents a discussion of additional customer service predictors that are likely to influence service styles.

CUSTOMER SERVICE PREDICTORS

A significant body of research examining the conditions under which providers are likely to use particular service behaviors has accumulated over a short period of time. Ford and Etienne (1994) identify three broad categories of service predictors: provider variables, customer variables, and context variables. Examples of the personal characteristics of providers that have been related to their service communication practices are gender (Ford, 1995), personality (Etienne, 1994), and identification with the organization (Rafaeli, 1989b). Examples of personal characteristics of customers that have also been related to service practices are gender (Rafaeli, 1989b), dress (Krapfel, 1988), and race (McCormick & Kinloch, 1986), as well as customer behaviors such as aggressiveness (Krapfel, 1988) and sociability (Hester, Koger, & McCauley, 1985). Contextual variables related to customer service include busyness (Sutton & Rafaeli, 1988) and the availability of organization-sponsored interventions for improving customer service (Elizur, 1987).

Although the specific characteristics of service interactions may vary, three overarching factors appear to be consistently related to service provider behaviors: provider status, customer status, and time pressure. These factors may be the best predictors of providers' choices to engage in courteous, personalized, or manipulative service behaviors.

Provider Status

Providers vary in their level of training and experience in preparation for a service role. As the expertise and professional status of providers increase, so does the likelihood that the providers will be expected to engage in personalized service behaviors tailored to meet customers' unique needs. The influence of provider status on customer service styles is apparent in discussions of service norms within various occupations. For instance, whereas research regarding physicians' communication behaviors has focused primarily on personalized service practices, such as sharing information and offering social support, research on frontline employees' behaviors in fast-food restaurants has tended to focus on manipulative tactics, such as prompting customers to order fries and displaying scripted smiles.

Gutek (1995) argues that in routine service encounters, such as those observed in fast-food restaurants, providers are considered functionally equivalent. That is, customers should be able to expect the same level of service from any provider in a particular position. Service routines are not performed with great expertise attained through professional training, but with a tendency to follow a narrow script required of all providers in that position. As a result, providers in routine service interactions are highly interchangeable and easily replaced, whereas providers in nonroutine service interactions are more likely to be well-trained professionals selected for their unique qualifications.

Providers of expert or professional status will not always deliver highly personalized service. We can all recall instances in which physicians rushed through appointments, hairdressers were unfriendly, and professors never learned their students' names. Although the status of these providers may have dictated a customer service style emphasizing personalized service behaviors, additional variables could account for their greater reliance on manipulation or simple courtesy. These variables include customer status and time pressure.

Customer Status

Customers are commonly treated differently based on their perceived social status. Research has found that low-status customers are likely to receive less courteous and personalized service than are high-status customers. Rafaeli (1989b) observed checkout interactions in grocery stores and found that clerks generally displayed more courteous gestures toward male customers, including more greetings, smiles, eye contact, and thank-yous. She suggests that these results may reflect a tendency to attribute higher status to men.

Zinkhan and Stoiadin (1984) observed checkout interactions in department stores in which clerks were approached by female and male customers (research confederates) simultaneously and found that male customers were generally served first. This finding held true regardless of the gender of the clerk, the gender of the department (male products, female products, neutral products), or the type of store (high price, moderate price, low price). In a follow-up study, Stead and Zinkhan (1986) determined that male customers were particularly likely to receive service priority when in business dress (coat and tie) rather than in casual dress (jeans and shirt), further reinforcing the idea that service is influenced by customer status.

Krapfel (1988) also examined customer status as a predictor of service treatment. He conducted an experiment in which clerks from department stores observed a videotape of a female customer attempting to obtain reimbursement for a damaged product. He found the clerks' responses to the customer varied depending on whether the customer in the videotape was dressed professionally or casually. The well-dressed customer was significantly more likely to receive a full refund or exchange.

Customer status is even an issue in professional services of a very personal and critical nature, such as health care. In a large-scale assessment of physician-patient interactions, Waitzkin (1985) found that physicians tended to share less information with patients of lower social status and education levels. The physicians gave fewer explanations to these patients and were less willing to offer multilevel explanations, or explanations in which technical information is followed with translations in simple language. To some extent, the physicians' behaviors may have been in response to the patients' behaviors. Waitzkin explains that lower-class and less-educated patients are more hesitant to ask questions and are likely to express their interests only nonverbally, whereas physicians tend to expect patients to express their needs verbally and may erroneously perceive patients' hesitancy in asking direct questions as disinterest in information. In Waitzkin's study, a survey of patients revealed that lower- and upper-class patients did not differ in the amount of information they desired from their physicians, although observations of interactions showed that they did differ in the amount of information they *received* from their physicians.

Waitzkin's (1985) findings are consistent with those of other researchers, suggesting that low-status customers are less likely to receive courteous and personalized service than are high-status customers. However, his discussion reveals that low-status customers may engage in behaviors that elicit less individualized service from their providers.

Time Pressure

A third strong predictor of customer service behaviors is time pressure. Sutton and Rafaeli (1988) conducted an investigation intended to link convenience store sales with employee courtesy, but what they found surprised them. In busier stores with higher sales, employees were actually less likely to display positive emotions toward customers. Sutton and Rafaeli determined that stores where there was great time pressure placed on employees to handle larger numbers of customers tended to foster norms of processing customers without personal shows of friendliness. This idea was reaffirmed in follow-up studies (Rafaeli, 1989b; Rafaeli & Sutton, 1990).

My own analysis of the service behaviors of grocery store cashiers complements Sutton and Rafaeli's (1988) findings (Ford, 1993). I observed and timed cashier-customer checkout interactions and found that cashiers displayed a greater number of courteous nonverbal behaviors, such as head nods and eye contact, as the interactions grew longer.

Even in instances in which providers and customers are both of high status, time pressure may interfere with the provider's ability to provide individualized service. As Beck and Ragan (1995) note, "To many health care providers, who remain pressed for time to accurately attend to strictly medical elements of the health care encounter, communication may be a nicety that remains temporally impossible" (p. 74). Mental health clinicians interviewed in a study by Scheid (1996) reinforced how time pressures interfere with their ability to provide the personalized service demanded by customers. Said one clinician, "We need more space, more hours in the day, more energy to respond to the demands" (p. 33). Cordes and Dougherty (1993), in a review of the literature on burnout among service providers, found that individuals who attempt to maintain high performance standards despite insufficient time and resources are very likely to experience increased emotional exhaustion.

A recently conducted study further demonstrates that time pressure is a clear predictor of differences in service behaviors (McNitt & Ford, 1997). In a survey of a small sample of teleservice providers, the providers rated their use of 50 different communication behaviors during "typical" interactions and during interactions occurring at a "busy" time. They reported using the courteous service behaviors an average of 50.3% of the time in typical interactions, but only 35.7% of the time in busy interactions. The providers reported using the personalized service behaviors 61.2% of the time in typical interactions, but only 53.3% of the time in busy interactions. Regarding personalized service behaviors, providers were particularly less likely to "try to obtain as much information as possible from the consumer," reporting they used this behavior 92% of the time in typical interactions and 72.7% of the time in busy interactions, or to "listen patiently to the consumer," reporting this behavior in 93.6% of typical interactions and 73.6% of busy interactions.

Whereas the providers in the McNitt and Ford (1997) study were likely to *decrease* their use of courteous and personalized service behaviors under time pressure, they were likely to *increase* their use of manipulative behaviors under pressure. They reported using manipulative service behaviors only 21.6% of the time during typical interactions, but 26.7% of the time during busy interactions. At busy times, they were especially likely to "purposefully avoid discussing certain topics with the consumer," reporting this behavior in only 33.3% of typical interactions but in 53.2% of busy interactions, and to "cut off nonessential conversation," a behavior they reported in 25.5% of typical interactions but in 47.7% of busy interactions. These findings do suggest that customer service styles tend to be less courteous and personalized and more manipulative when providers experience time pressure.

TABLE 9.1
Taxonomy of Customer Service Behaviors

Courteous Service	Personalized Service	Manipulative Service
Phatic speech	Customer orientation	Bureaucratization
Nonverbal immediacy	Interaction involvement	Interaction control
Verbal immediacy	Information sharing	Compliance gaining
	Social support	Emotion management

TAXONOMY OF
CUSTOMER SERVICE BEHAVIORS

A growing body of research reveals that a variety of categories of courteous, personalized, and manipulative communication behaviors may be engaged in customer service interactions. These categories, summarized in Table 9.1, are presented in detail in the following pages. The categories are not intended be exhaustive, but they do illustrate a wide range of behaviors that may support providers' overall customer service styles.

Courteous Service

Typically when we speak of customer service, we are thinking of courteous service. Courteous service is friendly service. It is service that creates an immediate bond between the provider and customer that allows for a positive interaction. That bond is often labeled *rapport,* or a sense of comfort or ease developed between persons. Service providers are more likely to engage in courteous service when they are under little time pressure. Three categories of courteous service derived from the research literature are phatic speech, nonverbal immediacy, and verbal immediacy.

Phatic Speech

Phatic speech involves the exchange of pleasantries to build goodwill between people. It functions to keep lines of communication open (DeVito, 1970, p. 15). Greeting and thanking behaviors are two forms of phatic speech that may leave strong lasting impressions on customers. Research by Asch (1946) and Higgins, Rholes, and Jones (1977) demonstrates that individuals' memories and attitudes are influenced most by information they receive first (primacy effect) or last (recency effect). The research suggests that greeting a customer early in an interaction and thanking a customer late in an interaction may be two of the most important behaviors engaged in by service providers. Perhaps this is why Elizur (1987), in a feedback intervention designed to improve bank employee friendliness, guided the employees to use courteous behaviors at least twice during each customer service interaction:

first, when a new customer approached, and second, at the completion of service.

Additional forms of phatic speech may be used throughout customer service interactions. Hester et al. (1985), Komaki, Blood, and Holder (1980), and McCormick and Kinloch (1986) identify small talk or "chitchat" as a form of expression consistent with courteous or friendly service in their research in malls, fast-food restaurants, supermarkets, and discount stores. Their idea is that simply talking with customers helps to establish the rapport necessary for a positive service interaction. However, based on their research on bank tellers, Crowell, Anderson, Abel, and Sergio (1988) and Ketrow (1991) argue that providers need to keep small talk to a minimum to avoid prolonging the service interaction unduly. This suggests that there is such a thing as being "too courteous" in communicating with customers, particularly if the customers place great importance on speed of service.

Nonverbal Immediacy

Phatic speech may be complemented by nonverbal immediacy in courteous service interactions. Mehrabian (1967) defines immediacy as "the degree of directness and intensity of interaction between two entities" (p. 325). Following immediacy theory, as service providers become more nonverbally direct or "immediate" with customers, they are able to reduce psychological distance and thereby promote friendlier relations with the customers.

One of the most commonly researched nonverbal immediacy behaviors in customer service interactions is eye contact. Eye contact is widely regarded as a critical behavior for displaying involvement and attentiveness toward another person; however, the frequency with which providers make eye contact during service interactions varies dramatically. Elizur (1987) found that Israeli bank employees typically used an average of 7.2 eye contacts per service interaction, but increased to an average of 12.2 eye contacts immediately after feedback interventions. Ketrow (1991) found that tellers in a U.S. bank, on average, spent 6.6 seconds in direct eye contact per service encounter. My own assessment of eye contact exhibited by cashiers in U.S. grocery stores found that cashiers used anywhere from zero to 44 eye contacts per interaction, depending, to a large degree, on interaction length (Ford, 1995). The ratio of eye contacts per minute of interaction length averaged 2.3.

Smiling, as another form of nonverbal immediacy, is the clearest visible display of a person's emotional state and is therefore considered critical in setting a positive tone in customer service interactions. Elizur (1987) found that Israeli bank employees used an average of 0.6 smiles per interaction, then increased to 2.8 smiles per interaction immediately following feedback interventions. Ketrow (1991) observed an average of 1.8 smiles per interaction among U.S. bank tellers, with an average of only 0.1 frowns per interaction. My own measurement of grocery store cashiers' overall facial expressions while customers were paying, using a 5-point scale ranging from a deep frown (1) to a broad smile (5), found an average expression of 3.5 (between a neutral expression and a slight smile; Ford, 1995).

Although eye contact and smiling are the most commonly researched displays of nonverbal immediacy in customer service interactions, several other courteous nonverbal behaviors have been studied. Head nods and physical distance in cashier-customer interactions have been observed, for instance. Head nods, commonly used to demonstrate following or agreeing with what customers are saying, were displayed between zero and 8 times per minute of interaction length, but the average was only 0.4 times per minute (Ford, 1995). Physical distance, estimated from shoulder to shoulder between the cashier and customer while the customer was paying, ranged from one-half foot to three feet, with an average distance of two feet. Smaller distances indicate greater nonverbal immediacy.

Ketrow (1991) observed a broad range of nonverbal immediacy behaviors among bank tellers. In addition to assessments of eye contact and smiling, Ketrow found the tellers used an average of 1.1 head nods and 0.2 touches per interaction. The tellers also leaned forward toward customers an average of 1.7 times. They leaned backward, distancing themselves from customers, an average of 0.2 times. Most tellers rotated their bodies toward customers at angles of within 45 degrees, thereby facing customers more directly, an average of 6.4 times per interaction, and rotated away from customers, beyond 45 degrees, an average of only 0.1 times. Ketrow's findings illustrate that nonverbal immediacy cues vary considerably.

Verbal Immediacy

Service providers may also use verbal communication to create a sense of "immediacy" with customers. Subtle stylistic differences in speech, such as reliance on present tense instead of past tense or the choice of the word *we* over the word *you,* can create feelings of psychological closeness during an interaction. These speech forms represent what Mehrabian (1971) describes as "a language within language" (p. 89), that is, a form of speech communication that conveys meaning beyond the mere content of the words. Service providers may select from a wide range of strategies to foster a level of immediacy that is most comfortable for them and for their customers.

A first strategy for increasing verbal immediacy is to become more temporally and spatially responsive to the customer. *Temporal responsiveness* refers to the immediacy of time in an interaction. For instance, a service provider may begin talking with the customer quickly, rather than make the customer wait. Crowell et al. (1988) have suggested that a bank teller should verbally acknowledge a customer within 5 seconds from the moment the customer is within one yard of the teller's window. Immediacy of time is also enhanced by speaking in present tense rather than past tense, such as in the statement

"I am working on your computer problem" as opposed to "I have been working on your computer problem."

Spatial responsiveness refers to physical closeness, which may be expressed verbally. Mehrabian (1971, pp. 90-91) explains how adjectives and demonstrative pronouns may be used to increase spatial responsiveness. For instance, a service provider may convey immediacy by simply saying, "Here is the part you wanted," instead of "There is the part you wanted." Immediacy may also be increased by saying, "These people need help" or "This woman needs help," as opposed to "Those people need help" or "That woman needs help." *Here, this,* and *these* are more spatially immediate language forms than *there, those,* and *that.*

In addition to increasing temporal and spatial responsiveness, a second strategy for conveying immediacy is to make direct references to topics. Mehrabian (1971, pp. 92-97) explains that a person may reveal negative feelings toward something by avoiding references to certain topics or by referring to the topics in ambiguous ways. For instance, if a customer asks a sales representative, "How do you like this hat on me?" the representative might say, "I'm not the right person to ask" (avoidance), "I like the whole outfit on you" (an overinclusive statement), "I like the color of the hat on you" (an overspecific statement), or even "That hat just doesn't seem 'right' for you" (a euphemism). These responses are nonimmediate because they make no reference or only an ambiguous reference to impressions of the hat on the customer.

A third strategy for enhancing verbal immediacy is to use language that shows acceptance of responsibility for one's own feelings or actions (Mehrabian, 1971, pp. 97-101). Service providers often avoid responsibility for their statements by using conditional language such as "This seems to be a problem" instead of "This is a problem." Or they may preface statements with tentative phrases such as "I think," "It seems to me," or "It is possible that." Refusing to make direct references to themselves also enables persons to avoid responsibility, as in the statement "It is evident that your books are overdue." An alternative, more immediate statement would be "I see that your books are overdue."

Verbal immediacy is also enhanced by the individual's showing a willingness to share responsibility. For instance, a service provider may suggest to the customer that "we need to work on this problem," rather than indicate that only one party should be responsible for resolving the problem. Language for sharing responsibility has been used in measuring the verbal immediacy of teachers, who may refer to "our" class or work that "we" are doing, instead of "my" class or work that "you" are doing (Gorham, 1988).

A fourth strategy for creating verbal immediacy is not recognized in Mehrabian's defining work on immediacy, but has since been reflected in a body of research assessing teacher immediacy in interactions with students (e.g., Christophel, 1990; Gorham, 1988; Sanders & Wiseman, 1990). The strategy is to use language generally reserved for personal relationships. Examples include self-disclosure about personal experiences, individual feedback or praise, inquiries about persons' opinions, humor, and conversation about topics unrelated to the immediate service context. Personal language also includes addressing oneself or the customer by name or, even more immediate, by first name. Gorham's (1988) research in teaching contexts and work by Crowell et al. (1988) in banking contexts have encouraged the use of names in these respective service environments. However, the use of names and other forms of language suggesting personal relationships may be resented by customers who do not desire high levels of immediacy with their service providers.

Personalized Service

Surprenant and Solomon (1987) define personalized service as "any behaviors occurring in the interaction intended to contribute to the individuation of the customer. That is, the 'customer' role is embellished in the encounter through specific recognition of the customer's uniqueness as an individual over and above his/her status as an anonymous service recipient" (p. 87). Personalized service is tailored service, which by nature consumes more time than other service behaviors. It is generally expected of high-status providers, such as physicians, lawyers, and management consultants. Four identifiable communication strategies that represent personalized service are a customer orientation, interaction involvement, information sharing, and social support.

Customer Orientation

Perhaps the most basic form of personalization is a customer orientation. Service providers who focus on customers' needs, interests, or behaviors and who give appropriately tailored service are customer oriented. This form of service is generally desired in upscale contexts, such as expensive department stores or restaurants, as well as in contexts where customers make decisions requiring major personal or financial commitment, such as health care and legal services.

Surprenant and Solomon (1987) describe two forms of service that may demonstrate a customer orientation. First is "option personalization." Following this approach, service providers offer several options to their customers. Examples include a bank employee describing alternative checking plans and a doctor suggesting several treatment alternatives. The customer is ultimately in control of determining the best option. However, given a narrow number of available options, this form of customer-oriented service is limited in its ability to address fully the customer's unique needs.

A second form of customer-oriented service proposed by Surprenant and Solomon, "customized personalization," is perhaps a stronger example of personalized service. Service providers who attend to the unique needs of the customer and provide helpful advice toward meeting those needs are giving truly customized service. Customized personalization may be combined with option personalization so that the customer is offered several service options and given appropriate advice as to which option to select, thereby increasing the customer's confidence that he or she has selected the best option.

Sales strategies may also be chosen for their ability to demonstrate a customer orientation. Saxe and Weitz (1982) researched and developed an instrument for assessing customer-oriented selling. Items in the scale reveal fundamental differences between customer-oriented salespersons and selling-oriented salespersons. Saxe and Weitz suggest that customer-oriented salespersons are more concerned with the customer's goals and interests than their own. They are also less likely to use high-pressure tactics or deception to influence customers. They may instead provide information and clarification to help customers make decisions.

Interaction Involvement

A customer orientation requires interaction involvement. Cegala (1981) defines interaction involvement as the extent to which one is fully engaged, both cognitively and behaviorally, in a conversation. Such engagement on the part of the service provider is necessary to ensure complete understanding of the customer's perspective and needs and to demonstrate a wholehearted effort toward meeting those needs. A provider who is fully involved with the customer is an active listener, both mentally attuned and physically responsive to the customer.

Interaction involvement as a form of personalized service is similar to nonverbal immediacy as a form of courteous service. Both categories of behavior rely heavily on nonverbal cues displayed toward customers. However, interaction involvement differs from nonverbal immediacy in one major respect: Interaction involvement is more than getting "close" to customers; it represents an interactive listening process in which the provider demonstrates both attentiveness and responsiveness to the customer's problems or needs. Unfortunately, interaction involvement has hardly been researched in customer service contexts. We must rely on a few studies in broader interpersonal contexts to appreciate the potential applications of interaction involvement in customer service contexts.

Cegala (1981) has identified three dimensions of interaction involvement. The first of these is attentiveness. The truly involved service provider focuses complete attention on the customer with a pure desire to obtain as much information as possible. The provider does not tune out parts of the conversation. Even when explaining things to a customer, an attentive provider is observing the customer's reactions to the explanation.

Attentiveness is displayed in many ways. Badzinski and Pettus (1994) illustrate how persons may demonstrate nonverbally that they are involved or uninvolved with others. They found that judges may be perceived differently by juries based on their nonverbal behaviors toward trial participants. In their study, Badzinski and Pettus manipulated the level of involvement of judges in simulated courtroom trials. The contrasting elements of judges' nonverbal behaviors included the following (p. 313):

- *High involvement:* forward lean, body and head oriented toward the defendant, open arms, looking "intently" at the defendant, and nodding frequently in response to the defendant's remarks
- *Low involvement:* backward lean with rocking motion, arms crossed or close to body, avoiding visual contact with the defendant, and engaging in frequent object adaptors such as pen tapping and paper shuffling

Such high-involvement and low-involvement behaviors are not restricted to the courtroom context. One may observe similar attentive or inattentive behaviors during any service interaction.

The second dimension of interaction involvement is perceptiveness (Cegala, 1981). In the service context, *perceptiveness* refers to the provider's ability to interpret correctly what the customer is trying to communicate. For instance, a highly perceptive provider can identify a customer's specific needs so that he or she can offer the appropriate products or services to meet those needs. Highly perceptive providers can also identify how their customers feel about them and adjust their communication behaviors accordingly. Illustrative of the value of perceptiveness in customer service interactions, Weitz (1978) found that the most effective salespersons were able to develop accurate impressions of customers' beliefs about product performance and use these impressions in selecting specific influence strategies.

The third dimension of interaction involvement is responsiveness (Cegala, 1981). The involved service provider, after attending completely to the customer and perceiving the customer's needs accurately, will respond in a timely and appropriate manner. Different messages from customers require different types of responses from providers. Northouse and Northouse (1992, pp. 174-180) discuss several verbal responses used in health care interviews. First is *restatement,* which is paraphrasing or repeating the customer's message to acknowledge that it was heard and understood. Second is *reflection,* or mirroring the emotions or attitudes of the customer to acknowledge that the customer's feelings were also recognized and understood. Third is *clarification,* which involves the use of questions that invite the customer to describe or give an example of a concern so that the provider might more easily pinpoint the concern. Fourth is *interpretation,* which differs from the other three verbal responses in that it temporarily shifts the focus of the conversation back to the provider. Providers use interpretation when expressing what they believe to be their customers' concerns, providing their own perspectives on the customers' situations.

Information Sharing

Central to the role of providers of professional services is the responsibility of conveying information that may be technical in nature and thereby unfamiliar to the customer. Toward that end, service providers often exhibit additional personalized behaviors that serve to facilitate the process of information exchange between themselves and their customers.

Professionals may be successful at sharing information with customers if they use simple language when discussing technical topics. In one study, Thompson and Pledger (1993) tested physicians' ability to select words appropriate for conveying information to their patients. The study was based on a list of 50 medical terms that a panel of 10 physicians indicated they normally use with patients, including such terms as *chronic, sutures,* and *acute.* Interviews with 224 subjects (71% with college degrees) revealed that many of these terms were not as familiar to patients as the physicians believed. None of the terms was identified correctly by all subjects. The average proportion of subjects who possessed vague or incorrect knowledge of a given term was 28%. Several terms were misunderstood by as many as 60-80% of subjects. Thompson and Pledger's study suggests that professional service providers may have difficulty selecting words that match their customers' levels of understanding.

To facilitate the process of information sharing, service providers may be encouraged to use "framing" behaviors. Framing involves recasting information or questions into forms that others can easily understand. Guinan and Scudder (1989, pp. 447-449) describe several framing behaviors employed by computer software development staff with internal organizational customers. Examples include outcome frames, or defining the goals or desired outcomes of an interaction (e.g., "What I want to get an idea of today is what you do and what you want the computer to do for you"); backtrack frames, or clarifying or repeating information to indicate the quality of understanding and to review progress (e.g., "I would like to review what we have said to this point"); and metaframes, or asking the customer to look beyond the current perspective (e.g., "Let's not assume the worst; let's look at the positive contributions that you have made in the past 2 years").

Service providers can make several other changes in how they communicate information to customers. Waitzkin's (1985) analyses of 336 physician-patient interactions reveal a few variables worth examining. One is time spent communicating information to customers. Waitzkin found that physicians spent an average of only 1.3 minutes giving information to patients, though they perceived they spent 8.9 minutes giving information. Spontaneity of explanations is also an important variable—that is, whether the service provider volunteers explanations spontaneously or gives explanations only in response to customers' questions. Waitzkin found that 71.4% of physicians' explanations were spontaneous. Another variable is whether explanations are "multilevel," or involve technical explanations followed by explanations translated into simpler language. Only 12% of explanations coded in Waitzkin's study were multilevel in nature. One more variable in communicating information is the discrepancy in technical level between providers' explanations and customers' questions. Waitzkin found that 72% of physicians' responses to patients' questions were nondiscrepant. In most instances, the physicians responded to patients at the patients' technical level.

Social Support

Tolsdorf (1976) describes social support as "any action or behavior that functions to assist the focal person in meeting his personal goals or in dealing with the demands of any particular situation" (p. 410). Social support is generally expected of any service provider who regularly hears customers' problems. These include providers in recognized "helping" professions, such as nurses and social service agents; those who maintain long-term relationships with customers, such as hairdressers and investment brokers; and others perceived to be in potentially helpful roles, such as bartenders and police officers. Socially supportive behaviors may take many forms that are not often recognized in the formal job descriptions of service providers. These may be as diverse as providing helpful suggestions, showing sensitivity to a customer's feelings, telling jokes, or even entertaining a customer's baby.

Barrera and Ainlay (1983) researched and developed a general taxonomy of socially supportive behavior. The taxonomy reveals four categories of supportiveness: directive guidance, nondirective support, positive social interaction, and tangible assistance. Each of these categories may be applied to customer service contexts.

According to Barrera and Ainlay (1983), directive guidance involves "actions on the part of helpers to provide support of a practical nature, aimed at aiding the recipient in improving his or her performance through increased understanding and skill" (p. 140). Directive guidance may include giving advice or instructions on how to do something, clarifying expectations of persons, or giving feedback to a customer. Service providers may also give directive guidance by following up on customers to determine whether they need additional assistance or by providing the names of persons customers may see for further assistance.

Service providers may also give nondirective support, which Barrera and Ainlay (1983) describe as behaviors typically associated with counseling. Nondirective support may be exhibited through listening and providing encouraging feedback to customers as they talk through personal problems; expressing interest, concern, affection, or respect for the customer; and making oneself clearly available to the customer. Cowen (1982) found that some service providers, including hairdressers, lawyers, and bartenders, are regularly called upon to listen to customers' personal problems, though few have professional counseling training. These providers, Cowen found, do often engage in response strategies similar to those used by mental health professionals, including offering support and sympathy, presenting alternatives, and just listening. However, some do not. Lawyers reported offering support and sympathy, but were also prone to be more directive, such as by asking questions, giving advice, and pointing out consequences of bad ideas. Some service providers in all three categories admitted to offering disconfirming responses that might free them from the responsibilities of nondirective support, such as telling customers to "count their blessings," trying to change the topic, or trying to get customers to talk with someone else.

Barrera and Ainlay's (1983) third category of social support is positive social interaction, which they conceptualize as "engaging in social interactions for fun and relaxation" (p. 136). Service providers may exhibit this form of social support by joking or kidding with customers, talking about the customers' interests, or performing diversionary activities with customers. These activities typically extend beyond expectations for rapport building and offer an opportunity for providers to establish more personal relationships with customers.

As a final form of social support, service providers may give tangible assistance to customers, which may include material aid, such as money or physical objects, and behavioral assistance, or "sharing of tasks through physical labor" (Barrera & Ainlay, 1983, p. 136). Barrera and Ainlay's examples of tangible assistance included giving or loaning money or possessions and providing transportation or a place to stay. These examples are not typical of customer service interactions, but other forms of tangible assistance have been documented in research in retail settings. For instance, tangible support has been observed in grocery stores, such as a clerk's chasing after a customer who left a bag of groceries at the checkout stand and another's entertaining a customer's baby while the customer wrote out a check to pay for the groceries (Ford, 1992). Other forms of tangible support may be provided routinely to customers, such as assistance with heavy packages, house calls or deliveries, looking after personal belongings, and providing cab fare or free meals.

Manipulative Service

Any time a service provider makes an attempt to deceive or control the customer, that provider is engaging in manipulative service. Manipulative service is "strategic" service. It involves the use of a clear strategy for achieving the provider's objectives. The objectives may vary from increasing sales or tips to managing a challenging situation, such as a long line of waiting customers or an "uncooperative" customer. Four representative manipulative strategies are bureaucratization, interaction control, compliance gaining, and emotion management.

Bureaucratization

Service providers often exercise control over customers through strict adherence to bureaucratic rules and procedures during service interactions. These providers are "all business" and are therefore not inclined to engage in small talk or other behaviors that are not essential for "processing" customers quickly. The providers effectively distance themselves from customers by maintaining a formal, impersonal posture and following bureaucratic routines.

One study that focused on the use of bureaucratization as an approach to customer service was conducted by Goodsell (1976), who researched the extent to which postal clerks in Costa Rica and the United States adhered to bureaucratic communication norms with customers. His observations of service providers were based on three norms that govern interpersonal encounters in bureaucracies, as discussed by Katz and Danet (1973, pp. 4-5): affective neutrality, specificity, and universalism. *Affective neutrality* refers to emotional detachment from customers—maintaining a neutral tone, rather than displaying positive or negative emotions; *specificity* refers to strictly limiting communication in service to essential business; and *universalism* refers to the practice of treating all customers equally.

Goodsell (1976) found that postal clerks in both Costa Rica and the United States tended to conduct service interactions in a bureaucratic mode. The clerks did not typically greet customers or respond warmly when customers greeted them. Approximately 53% of Costa Rican clerks and 44% of U.S. clerks continued to display an unemotional, officious, or discourteous demeanor when giving instructions to customers on how to send packages. The clerks also tended to stick to "official business." Only 16% of Costa Rican clerks engaged in nonessential talk, compared with 48% of U.S. clerks. Further, in managing customer disagreements concerning postage rates, only 22% of Costa Rican clerks took time to explain their reasons for denying customers' requests, whereas 75% of U.S. clerks elaborated on reasons for denying requests.

As a test of adherence to the bureaucratic norm of universalism in customer service encounters, Goodsell (1976) manipulated the status of customers and observed whether postal clerks treated customers of high status differently than customers of low status. Four male observers, who posed as customers in the service encounters, each played either a high-status or low-status role in their respective countries. Goodsell found clear evidence of status differentiation in the clerks' treatment of the customers. For instance, postal clerks in both Costa Rica and the United States were significantly more likely to display a positive demeanor in responses to customers who disagreed with postage rates if the customers were of high status. The clerks were also more likely to elaborate on reasons for denying postage rate adjustments when the customers were of high status. Universalism, as a norm of bureaucratic treatment, was not upheld among most postal service clerks. Many engaged in discriminatory service practices.

Overall, Goodsell's (1976) research demonstrated that bureaucratic norms are not adhered to unconditionally among postal clerks in Costa Rica and the United States. This should not be surprising. Katz and Eisenstadt (1960) found that it is common for service providers to break bureaucratic norms, a practice they label "debureaucratization," when faced with pressures from customers who seek more personalized service.

Interaction Control

Beyond bureaucratization of service, service providers may use a variety of strategies to direct the course of an interaction with a customer. They may exercise control over the timing of the service interaction as well as the content and sequence of topics addressed in the interaction. They may also employ strategies to ensure that their control is not relinquished to the customer as the interaction progresses.

Interaction control often begins with the provider's ability to determine when to initiate service with a customer. Stead and Zinkhan (1986) found that service clerks in department stores were likely to initiate interactions more readily with some customers than with others. When two customers approached service clerks simultaneously, the clerks appeared to rely on stereotypes associated with customer gender and dress to determine which to wait on first. Pauley (1988) also found discrimination in service providers' decisions concerning when to offer assistance to customers. Observations at shoe stores revealed that salespersons waited longer before approaching customers who may be perceived as "fat." These studies show distinct patterns of provider control over the initiation of interactions with customers. Waiting lines are also used as a form of control over when to initiate encounters with customers, as are the telephone service equivalent, putting callers on "hold." (For an enlightening discussion of the experience of waiting in line, see Maister, 1985.)

Once a service interaction has been initiated, the service provider may exercise strategies for directing the flow of conversation during the interaction. One of the most common tools for interaction control at this stage is the service "script." Scripts are mental schemata that specify sequences of behavior or routines to be performed in given situations. Ashforth and Fried (1988) describe how individuals may learn scripts gradually as they gain experience in performing their roles, until eventually they perform the scripts automatically or mindlessly. Once a service provider is able to follow a script automatically, that provider is no longer inclined to provide more personalized or courteous service.

Scripts are commonly used to exercise control in teleservice interactions. Whalen and Zimmerman (1987) conducted research on the opening sequences of phone scripts used by emergency service dispatchers for police, fire, and paramedic services. They found that the service dispatchers tended to skip the "greeting" sequence and "howareyou" sequence common in casual calls, starting instead with an exchange of identifying information, followed by the reason for the call. The opening script enables the provider to control the course of an interaction by constraining the caller's topics to information the provider deems most appropriate for directing an efficient service interaction.

Iacobucci (1990) has also investigated scripts used in teleservice interactions. Her research on customer calls for billing services in a telephone company has produced findings that complement and extend Whalen and Zimmerman's (1987) findings. Iacobucci found that service providers in the telephone company used similar opening sequence scripts as the emergency dispatchers. Providers constrained opening topics to an identification sequence followed by a reason-for-calling sequence. The teleservice providers continued to follow institutionalized scripts while handling customers' billing concerns. As customers gave "accounts" (excuses or justifications for their billing problems), the providers consistently responded with "formulations" (company-mandated lines) to recast customer queries into business terms.

Another communication strategy that service providers often employ to control the flow of interactions with customers is directive questioning. Service providers may ask one question or a series of questions that lead the conversation in a particular direction. Perhaps the most popular form of directive questioning is prompting. Martinko, White, and Hassell (1989) describe the prompt as "a stimulus condition that sets the occasion for behavior to occur" (p. 94). One example of prompting is asking a burger purchaser at a fast-food restaurant, "Would you like fries with that?" The service provider, who may have included the prompt as part of a standard service script, effectively controls the course of the interaction by ensuring the customer considers purchasing fries as the next stage of the interaction.

Compliance Gaining

In many service interactions, providers have the goal of influencing their customers' behaviors. Sometimes the goal is in the best interests of the customer, such as when a doctor tries to persuade a patient to take a prescribed medication or when a teacher attempts to influence a student to complete homework assignments. Other times, the goal is more clearly in the best interests of the service provider, such as when a salesperson tries to talk a customer into purchasing an expensive luxury item or when a professor works to recruit students to volunteer for an experiment. In situations in which service providers hope to secure customer compliance with their behavioral expectations, compliance-gaining strategies are likely to be used.

There is a vast body of research on communication techniques for compliance gaining. Kellermann and Cole (1994) recently reviewed the literature and found 74 different compliance-gaining taxonomies with more than 820 defined strategies. The earliest and most widely used taxonomy was developed by Marwell and Schmitt (1967) and includes 16 alternative strategies. Examples include promising a reward for compliance (e.g., "If you buy this car, I'll throw in a free stereo"), threatening to punish for noncompliance (e.g., "If you don't buy the car today, I cannot guarantee the $2,000 rebate"), and rewarding the customer before requesting compliance (e.g., "I will give you $50 just for test-driving this new car today").

Many of the compliance-gaining strategies described in the literature are reflected in stimulus-response approaches to sales, which follow the assumption that a salesperson may control the outcomes of a sales interaction by applying a specific sales tactic to stimulate a desired customer response. Numerous investigations have evaluated the impact of different types of persuasive messages (stimuli) on the probability of a sale (response). Early studies by Brock (1965), Farley and Swinth (1967), Jolson (1975), Capon (1975), and others have compared the relative effectiveness of two or more alternative sales pitches. However, Weitz (1981), in a review of this literature, found that the preponderance of these studies have shown no consistent differences in sales effectiveness across message strategies.

Tybout, Sternthal, and Calder (1983) describe two sequential request strategies that are also commonly used in compliance-gaining attempts. The "foot-in-the-door" technique "involves asking people to comply with a critical large request after they have complied with a small request" (p. 280). An example would be a jewelry salesperson asking a customer to purchase an expensive watch after the salesperson has already gotten "a foot in the door" by soliciting the customer's commitment to purchase a relatively inexpensive watch. The other request strategy, which Tybout et al. call the "door-in-the-face" technique, involves "asking people to comply with a critical small request after they have rejected a large request" (p. 280). An example would be a jewelry salesperson asking a customer to purchase an inexpensive watch after the salesperson has already gotten "a door in the face" when the customer rejected a request to purchase a relatively expensive watch.

Compliance-gaining strategies may include discriminative listening behaviors. Discriminative listening involves focusing intently on particular cues with meaning. For instance, salespersons are commonly taught to recognize "closing cues," or "comments and body language that suggest buyers may be ready to purchase products" (Kurtz, Dodge, & Klompmaker, 1988, p. 216). Once they discriminate closing cues, the salespersons know to try their next trick to move the customer toward a purchase commitment.

Emotion Management

Bureaucratization, interaction control, and compliance gaining are often complemented by emotion management, or any effort to convey an emotional image considered most appropriate for meeting the goals of an interaction. Emotion management involves deceptive behavior. Hochschild (1979) describes it as the "act of trying to change in degree or quality an emotion or feeling" (p. 561). Hochschild emphasizes the word *trying,* arguing that emotion management is not always successful. A service provider is engaging in emotion management when there is inconsistency between the emotions the provider feels and the emotions he or she attempts to display toward customers.

Hochschild (1979) identifies two broad types of emotion management: (a) evocation, or attempts to produce emotions that are initially absent; and (b) suppression, or attempts to quell emotions that are initially present. Following Hochschild's typology, examples of emotion management in service interactions can range from conjuring up smiles and warm greetings for customers the providers are not really happy to see to avoiding yelling or glaring at customers who harass the providers.

Emotion management may begin with the management of facial expressions. Tidd and Lockard (1978), for instance, have demonstrated significant effects of smile manipulations in service interactions. In their experiment, a cocktail server approached 96 customers with either a "maximal smile" (mouth corners turned up enough to expose teeth in a broad smile) or a "minimal smile" (mouth corners turned up noticeably, but with no teeth showing). The 48 customers she approached with a maximal smile left a total of $23.20 in tips, whereas the 48 customers she approached with a minimal smile left only $9.40 in tips. These results indicate that displaying false smiles may be advantageous to service providers.

Service providers may manage additional nonverbal and verbal cues to secure desired responses from customers. Crusco and Wetzel (1984) found that food servers might increase a tip by simply touching the customer's palm or shoulder while returning change. Lynn and Mynier (1993) have also shown that food servers might increase tips by squatting down next to customers' tables, rather than standing. In addition, Garrity and Degelman (1990) found that increased tips resulted from food servers' giving their first names to customers in initial introductions. Each of these studies suggests that service providers may be rewarded for their attempts to display feelings of closeness toward their customers.

CUSTOMER SERVICE IMPACT

Despite widespread recognition of the importance of customer service and a large body of literature describing customer service behaviors, relatively few scholarly studies have assessed the impact of these behaviors. When studies have been conducted, they have often confirmed managers' personal beliefs and anecdotal evidence regarding the effects of particular service practices on customers. In some instances, scholarly studies have challenged conventional wisdom regarding the impact of popular service practices on customers. In very rare instances have studies attempted to address the impact of service practices on the providers expected to use them. In the next few pages, I review several studies that examine customer service impact on customers and providers.

Impact on Customers

The foremost goal of customer service in most organizations is simple: to boost sales. Most of the research attempting to link service and sales has focused on manipulative tactics engaged in by salespersons. These studies have traditionally examined canned sales pitches, but, as Weitz (1981) observes, sales pitches do not produce consistent results. Multiple request strategies have also been found to be only minimally effective (Beaman, Cole, Preston, Klentz, & Steblay, 1983; Fern, Monroe, & Avila, 1986). However, prompting practices have been consistently linked to sales. For instance, Martinko et al. (1989) found that fast-food servers were able to increase french fry purchases by prompting customers to order fries with their sandwiches. Similarly, Ralis and O'Brien (1986) and Mirman (1982) found that prompting could be used by food servers in formal dining restaurants to increase wine and dessert sales, and Dickinson and O'Brien (1982) found that it could be used in beauty salons to increase hair-care product sales. Prompting is also the thrust of cross-selling practices common in banks and other retail enterprises. Johnson and Seymour (1985) found that one bank's cross-selling system was successful in increasing the average number of sales per service interaction as well as the average percentage of available services that each customer used.

As salespersons shift away from manipulative strategies and adopt a customer-oriented approach, significant effects on sales have been observed. Saxe and Weitz (1982) found that salespersons who perceived themselves as more customer oriented tended to receive higher sales ratings from their supervisors. Additional personalized or courteous service practices have not been linked to sales.

Organizational researchers have recently refocused their attention away from sales and toward satisfaction as a desirable outcome of service. The current prevailing view is that customer satisfaction has a greater impact on organizational performance in the long run than do immediate sales. Recent theories that have been subjected to rigorous empirical evaluations propose that customers' perceptions of service quality will predict their satisfaction and, ultimately, their intentions to return to an organization for products or services in the future (e.g., Anderson & Sullivan, 1993; Gotlieb, Grewal, & Brown, 1994). The research has further shown that customers are most likely to experience dissatisfaction when their expectations for service are not fulfilled, such as when employees are less courteous, efficient, and caring than expected.

Customer satisfaction has been of particular interest in retail banking. However, research by Crowell et al. (1988), Ketrow (1991), and Brown and Sulzer-Azaroff (1994) has not successfully linked banks' courteous service practices with customer satisfaction. Health care organizations have also been interested in customer satisfaction and have generally found relationships between physicians' use of courteous and personalized behaviors and their patients' satisfaction (Buller & Buller, 1989; Burgoon et al., 1987). Among educational enterprises, studies have linked teachers' clarity, as well as their verbal and nonverbal immediacy inside and outside the classroom, to student satisfaction (Fusani, 1994; Gorham, 1988; Powell & Harville, 1990; Sanders & Wiseman, 1990).

In many service contexts, the central concern of providers is not sales or satisfaction, but compliance. Health care providers are acutely concerned about patients' lack of compliance with their advice. Patients' failure to adhere to treatment regimens is a pervasive problem and, as Stone (1979) notes, "one category of factors that is consistently found to be related to adherence is that of the quality of the *interaction between physician and patient*" (p. 37). Substantial research has been conducted to examine communication and compliance in health care contexts. Based on a review of research conducted primarily in the 1960s and 1970s, Stone (1979) notes that health care providers should have two key concerns when communicating with patients:

> Two aspects of the interaction are important: (1) the effectiveness with which the necessary information is given to the patient to enable him or her to carry out recommended actions, and (2) the emotional impact of the interaction. This latter aspect refers specifically to the interpersonal message sent by the physician to the patient, which may elicit satisfaction, unhappiness, or anger. (pp. 37-38)

Research regarding information sharing related to patient compliance has produced the most convincing results. For instance, Boyd, Covington, Stanaszek, and Coussons (1974) demonstrated that providers' failure to give sufficient information was a major contributor to drug defaulting. Additional studies have also linked providers' use of an affiliative communication style with patient compliance. In a review of literature regarding provider empathy and patient compliance, Squier (1990) reports on a substantial body of research that illustrates relationships among provider interpersonal style, patient satisfaction and motivation, and patient adherence to the provider's advice. However, the studies have produced some inconsistent results and have been inconclusive in determining exactly which affiliative behaviors are most important in securing compliance.

Impact on Providers

Naturally, every organization hopes to reinforce service practices that will have a positive impact on customers. However, little consideration is given to the potential impact of service practices on the providers expected to apply them. In some instances, providers may find their service practices personally rewarding, as when these practices lead to increased income and job satisfaction. In other instances, providers may experience heightened levels of stress and burnout associated with their service practices.

Money remains one of the key motivators for behavior change, and nowhere is this more clear than among service providers who work for tips or sales commissions. Research demonstrates that even small behavior changes may have significant financial consequences for providers. Providers may increase their tips and sales commissions by delivering rehearsed prompts or pitches, smiling at customers, touching customers, squatting down to converse at their customers' level, or even simply sharing their names with customers (e.g., Brock, 1965; Crusco & Wetzel, 1984; Garrity & Degelman, 1990; Lynn & Mynier, 1993; Ralis & O'Brien, 1986; Tidd & Lockard, 1978). Each of these strategies represents a form of manipulative service grounded in deception or control.

Although manipulative service practices may be financially rewarding for some service providers, they may ultimately lead to provider burnout. Parkinson's (1991) study of hairdressers provides one example of the relationship between manipulative service and burnout. Parkinson found that hairdressers who engaged in deceptive impression management tactics, such as exhibiting friendliness toward persons they really disliked, were more likely to experience psychological distress and dissatisfaction with their jobs.

Scheid (1996) also examined the relationship between service practices and burnout. She conducted a qualitative study of the emotional labor performed by clinicians in mental health centers, hypothesizing that emotional labor—akin to emotion management, entailing managing one's feelings and expressing appropriate emotions as part of one's job (Hochschild, 1983)—is professionally dictated and may uniquely contribute to the burnout experienced by these providers. Burnout was very high among the clinicians, with the most commonly reported symptoms including anger or resentment, discouragement or indifference, and feeling tired or exhausted all day.

The relationship between communication and burnout among service providers has been further illustrated by a review of the burnout literature conducted by Cordes and Dougherty (1993). These authors cite several studies whose findings suggest that the directness, frequency, intensity, and duration of interpersonal interactions may influence the level of burnout experienced. For instance, studies have indicated that burnout increases as the number of customers increases, as the intensity of customers' needs or problems increases, as the amount of time spent with customers increases, and as the amount of time on break, away from customers, decreases.

Personalized service practices may be more intrinsically rewarding overall than manipulative service practices. Abramis and Thomas (1990) conducted one study that demonstrates a clear relationship between personalized service practices and job satisfaction. The researchers surveyed 100 working adults regarding their job satisfaction and their views of their employer's service practices. Responses indicated that employees were most satisfied with their jobs when they were satisfied with their employer's service practices, specifically personalized service practices. When organizations make services accessible to customers, take customer complaints seriously, follow up on sales and complaints, and ensure that technical and management employees spend time with customers, employees are more satisfied with their work. In addition, an organization with established procedures and norms supportive of employees' efforts to serve customers is also likely to have satisfied employees. High service standards, consideration of customer service practices in performance reviews and bonuses, and norms for communicating customer information up to higher levels of the organization are strongly related to job satisfaction.

Adams and Parrott (1994) also found a connection between personalized service practices and employee job satisfaction. Their study involving nurses and parents of hospitalized children indicates that nurses who had formal rules to present to parents about their roles in caring for their children tended to experience higher levels of job satisfaction than did nurses who assessed their satisfaction prior to adopting the formal rules. This study provides further evidence that personalized service policies and practices may be intrinsically rewarding for service providers.

CONCLUSIONS AND RESEARCH DIRECTIONS

Customer service providers have been the focus of significant research attention. Their service styles may incorporate courteous, personalized, and manipulative communication behaviors. Their typical behaviors may vary depending on their status, their customers' status, and whether they are experiencing time pressure. Providers may display courteous or friendly service through phatic speech, nonverbal immediacy, and verbal immediacy behaviors. They may also demonstrate personalized or tailored service through a customer orientation, interaction involvement, information sharing, and social support. Providers may rely on manipulative service strategies as well, including bureaucratization, interaction control, compliance gaining, and emotion management.

Customer service behaviors should be appreciated for the impact they have on both customers and providers. Manipulative service practices have been commonly linked to sales and tips, but also to provider burnout. Courteous service practices and, to an even greater degree, personalized service practices have been linked to customer satisfaction and compliance as well as provider job satisfaction.

Additional research is needed to continue exploring the role of provider communication behaviors in customer service interactions. Particularly critical are studies that will further our understanding of service predictors, service technology, customer participation, and service impact. Future research regarding the changing nature of service is also needed.

Service Predictors

In this chapter I have posited three key predictors of customer service approaches: provider status, customer status, and time pressure. Empirical evidence derived from research in customer service contexts reveals that providers will opt for more personalized service behaviors when they are of high status, their customers are of high status, and there is little time pressure for service completion. However, there is no empirical evidence that clearly determines the relative weight of these three service predictors. Which predictor accounts for the most variation in providers' service behaviors? There is also no empirical evidence clearly demonstrating whether control over the three key predictors would influence providers' behaviors. For instance, can organizations increase personalized service practices by hiring better-trained service providers, by socializing providers to believe that all customers are important, or by allowing providers to spend more time with individual customers? Can organizations, likewise, increase their overall use of more efficient manipulative service practices by hiring unskilled service providers, socializing them to treat customers anonymously, and enforcing strict time limitations for service interactions?

Service Technologies

Our most salient images of customer service tend to focus on face-to-face interactions with boundary-spanning employees, such as store clerks, bank tellers, food servers, sales associates, and government bureaucrats. However, an increasing range of services is offered over the telephone. Charland (1993) found that the teleservice industry represents one of the fastest-growing markets in the United States, with more than 600,000 service providers responding to 700,000 toll-free numbers nationwide. The number of telephone service operations has grown so fast that the toll-free "800" prefix can no longer accommodate all teleservice needs.

As the teleservice industry continues to grow, so does the need for research that examines communication processes engaged in teleservice contexts. Surprisingly few studies have explored teleservice communication practices. Although these investigations have increased our awareness of the development and maintenance of telephone scripts (e.g., Iacobucci, 1990; Whalen & Zimmerman, 1987), they have provided little information regarding the specific communication behaviors exhibited by teleservice providers.

Service interactions are also increasingly making use of computer technologies. These technologies are often accessed through the telephone. For instance, Brooks (1992) describes how banks are using switch/computer integrating systems that identify callers then automatically route the calls and caller data to customer service representatives. Draper, Arend, and Diamond (1989) discuss the use of voice-response systems that automatically update and present recorded information to callers through computer-generated voices programmed to sound like human voices. Additional technologies also allow for some services to be fully computerized (e.g., the automated teller machine).

It seems that reliance on new technologies will result in more routinized forms of service because the machines must be programmed to handle a wide range of customers. This indicates that we should see an overall increase in manipulative service practices. However, the use of technologies may also enable more individualized service in instances in which providers with training and experience that can match the sophistication of computer programming are available to identify and address customers' unique situations. This indicates a possible increase in personalized service practices as well. Further research is necessary if we are to understand fully the implications of service technologies for communication practices.

Customer Participation

Additional research must also recognize the role of the customer in the context of service interactions. Most of the research attention has been given to service providers, but our understanding of communication as a transactional process would suggest that providers are likely to adjust their communication behaviors in response to messages received from customers. A few studies have supported this idea. Hester et al. (1985), for instance, followed customers through shopping malls and found that those who tended to display more courteous behaviors toward service providers also tended to receive more courteous service in return. In addition, Rafaeli (1989a), in her research among grocery store cashiers, found that customers and providers commonly engaged in a "struggle for control" over the course of the service interaction.

Soldow and Thomas (1984) observed similar struggles for control in sales interactions as customers and salespersons negotiated the nature of their relationship. Krapfel (1988) also found that customers who engaged in more aggressive communication behaviors were less likely to have their requests treated seriously by salespersons than were customers who engaged in less assertive behaviors.

There is also growing recognition of the integral role of customers as "partial employees" or "coproducers" contributing to the service process. Customers are often required to contribute resources, including information and effort, to obtain services (Mills & Moberg, 1982). Partial employee behaviors include stating hairstyle preferences to a beautician, providing records of one's credit history to a loan officer, and serving oneself at a salad bar or buffet (Kelley, Donnelly, & Skinner, 1990).

Research regarding the role and contributions of customers in service interactions is seriously lacking. Our knowledge of the influence of customers on the overall service received is particularly limited, as is our knowledge of the influence of the customer on the overall effectiveness of customer service interactions toward achieving the customer's and provider's objectives.

Service Impact

There has been surprisingly little research in the area of service impact as well. Most investigations have looked only at traditional impact variables associated with particular service approaches, such as the impact of manipulative service on sales and the impact of courteous and personalized service on customer satisfaction. As a result, we know little about the broader effects of service choices. For instance, do manipulative service practices, while increasing sales, also result in lower customer satisfaction? Likewise, do personalized service practices, while influencing customer satisfaction, have overall positive or negative effects on sales? In addition, do courteous service practices have a sufficient impact on sales or customer satisfaction or other variables that they should be deemed worthwhile as a service alternative?

The narrow focus on traditional variables regarding service impact also prevents us from realizing the full long-term impact of service choices. In my own work, I have identified customer discretionary behavior (CDB) as a long-term service outcome worth investigating (Ford, 1995). CDB represents "any behavior a customer voluntarily performs, beyond purchasing products or services, which may be helpful or harmful to an organization" (p. 67). In my investigation of the effects of courteous service behaviors in grocery stores, I found that as cashiers displayed more courtesy, customers responded with more positive evaluations of service and a greater likelihood of engaging in two forms of CDB: recommending the store to friends and shopping at the store when other stores are closer. Future investigations into the links between service communication behaviors and long-term service outcomes would be worthwhile.

Additional research should also pay more attention to the often-neglected service provider. Ashforth and Humphrey (1993) assert that service providers who do not identify with the communication behaviors they perform in their service roles may experience deleterious effects such as low self-esteem or depression. This idea has received some attention conceptually, particularly in the writing of Hochschild (1983), but has received little attention empirically. Pressure to conform to particular customer service approaches may have harmful effects, and these have not been sufficiently documented. Potential positive effects of service communication behaviors, such as impact on employee job satisfaction, have also not been sufficiently examined.

Service Revolution

A final significant area for future research is an exploration of the impact of the changing nature of service on society. Gutek (1995) has observed that we are experiencing a service revolution. This revolution is characterized by a decreasing reliance on personal "service relationships" and an increasing reliance on anonymous "service encounters." Service relationships, Gutek explains, "occur when a customer has repeated contact with a particular provider. When a customer and provider have a relationship, they get to know each other, both as individuals and as role occupants" (p. 7). Service encounters, on the other hand, "typically consist of a single interaction between a customer and provider, and they are typically fleeting rather than lengthy. Over time, the customer's successive contacts involve different providers rather than the same provider so that in encounters, provider and customer are strangers to each other" (p. 8).

As organizations restructure their service operations into large enterprises intended to respond efficiently to masses of customers, they find they are unable to foster the personal relationships they may have previously desired with customers. As a result, they rely increasingly on service encounters, rather than service relationships, to meet their customers' needs. Unfortunately, relatively little is known about the unique dynamics of customer service encounters. What are the forms of communication engaged in by service providers within the constraints of brief service encounters? How might these communication forms influence service outcomes? What can be done to further our understanding of the role of communication in changing service interactions?

Service environments are changing rapidly. As organizations continue to embrace brief encounters, the telephone, and new technologies as their means of communicating with customers, there will be a growing need to increase our awareness of the dynamics of these evolving service interactions. To date, we have not achieved a full appreciation of the predictors and impact of courteous, personalized, and manipulative service practices, or of the influence of customers on service transactions. Research that explores these issues will lead to a better understanding of the nature and influence of customer service interactions in our society.

REFERENCES

Abramis, D. J., & Thomas, C. (1990). Effects of customer service communication on employees' satisfaction. *Psychological Reports, 67,* 1175-1183.

Adams, R. J., & Parrott, R. (1994). Pediatric nurses' communication of role expectations to parents of hospitalized children. *Journal of Applied Communication Research, 22,* 36-47.

Anderson, E. W., & Sullivan, M. W. (1993). The antecedents and consequences of customer satisfaction for firms. *Marketing Science, 12,* 125-143.

Asch, S. (1946). Forming impressions of personality. *Journal of Abnormal and Social Psychology, 41,* 258-290.

Ashforth, B. E., & Fried, Y. (1988). The mindlessness of organizational behaviors. *Human Relations, 41,* 305-329.

Ashforth, B. E., & Humphrey, R. H. (1993). Emotional labor in service roles: The influence of identity. *Academy of Management Review, 18,* 88-115.

Badzinski, D. M., & Pettus, A. B. (1994). Nonverbal involvement and sex: Effects on jury decision making. *Journal of Applied Communication Research, 22,* 309-321.

Barrera, M., & Ainlay, S. L. (1983). The structure of social support: A conceptual and empirical analysis. *Journal of Community Psychology, 11,* 133-143.

Beaman, A. L., Cole, C. M., Preston, M., Klentz, B., & Steblay, N. M. (1983). Fifteen years of foot-in-the-door research: A meta-analysis. *Personality and Social Psychology Bulletin, 9,* 181-196.

Beck, C. S., & Ragan, S. L. (1995). The impact of relational activities on the accomplishment of practitioner and patient goals in the gynecologic examination. In G. L. Kreps & D. O'Hair (Eds.), *Communication and health outcomes* (pp. 73-85). Cresskill, NJ: Hampton.

Boyd, J. R., Covington, T. R., Stanaszek, W. F., & Coussons, R. T. (1974). Drug-defaulting, II: Analysis of noncompliance patterns. *American Journal of Hospital Pharmacy, 31,* 485-491.

Brock, T. C. (1965). Communicator-recipient similarity and decision change. *Journal of Personality and Social Psychology, 1,* 650-654.

Brooks, C. M. (1992, April). Improve service quality by phone. *Bank Marketing,* pp. 36-38.

Brown, C. S., & Sulzer-Azaroff, B. (1994). An assessment of the relationship between customer satisfaction and service friendliness. *Journal of Organizational Behavior Management, 14,* 55-75.

Buller, M. K., & Buller, D. B. (1989). Physicians' communication style and patient satisfaction. *Journal of Health and Social Behavior, 28,* 375-388.

Burgoon, J. K., Pfau, M., Parrott, R., Birk, T., Coker, R., & Burgoon, M. (1987). Relational communication, satisfaction, compliance-gaining strategies, and compliance in communication between physicians and patients. *Communication Monographs, 54,* 307-324.

Capon, N. (1975). Persuasive effects of sales messages developed from interaction process analysis. *Journal of Business Administration, 60,* 238-244.

Cegala, D. J. (1981). Interaction involvement: A cognitive dimension of communicative competence. *Communication Education, 30,* 109-121.

Charland, W. (1993, October 18). Economy: Teleservice call centers emerge as new source of middle class jobs. *Christian Science Monitor,* p. 6.

Christophel, D. (1990). The relationships among teacher immediacy behaviors, student motivation, and learning. *Communication Education, 39,* 323-340.

Cordes, C. L., & Dougherty, T. W. (1993). A review and an integration of the research on job burnout. *Academy of Management Review, 18,* 621-656.

Cowen, E. L. (1982). Help is where you find it: Four informal helping groups. *American Psychologist, 37,* 385-395.

Crowell, C. R., Anderson, D. C., Abel, D. M., & Sergio, J. P. (1988). Task clarification, performance feedback, and social praise: Procedures for improving the customer service of bank tellers. *Journal of Applied Behavior Analysis, 21,* 65-71.

Crusco, A. H., & Wetzel, C. G. (1984). The Midas touch: The effects of interpersonal touch on restaurant tipping. *Personality and Social Psychology Bulletin, 10,* 512-517.

DeVito, J. A. (1970). *The psychology of speech and language: An introduction to psycholinguistics.* New York: Random House.

Dickinson, A. M., & O'Brien, R. M. (1982). Performance measurement and evaluation. In R. M. O'Brien, A. M. Dickinson, & M. P. Rosow (Eds.), *Industrial behavior modification: A management handbook* (pp. 51-64). Elmsford, NY: Pergamon.

Draper, J., Arend, M., & Diamond, S. (1989, July). Voice technology abets new services. *Wall Street Computer Review,* pp. 59-69.

Elizur, D. (1987). Effect of feedback on verbal and non-verbal courtesy in a bank setting. *Applied Psychology: An International Review, 36,* 147-156.

Etienne, C. N. (1994). *Personality type as a predictor of employee courtesy in customer service encounters.* Unpublished master's thesis, University of Arkansas at Little Rock.

Farley, J. U., & Swinth, R. L. (1967). Effects of choice and sales message on customer-salesman interaction. *Journal of Applied Psychology, 51,* 107-110.

Fern, E. F., Monroe, K. B., & Avila, R. A. (1986). Effectiveness of multiple request strategies: A synthesis of research results. *Journal of Marketing Research, 23,* 144-152.

Ford, W. S. Z. (1992). *Analysis of the cashier-customer interaction, predictors and outcomes: Evaluation of alternative structural equation models.* Unpublished doctoral Dissertation, University of Maryland at College Park.

Ford, W. S. Z. (1993, May). *Employee behaviors, predictors, and outcomes in customer service encounters: Argument for a structural equation modeling approach to full model analysis.* Paper presented at the annual meeting of the International Communication Association, Washington, DC.

Ford, W. S. Z. (1995). Evaluation of the indirect influence of courteous service on customer discretionary behavior. *Human Communication Research, 22,* 65-89.

Ford, W. S. Z. (1998). *Communicating with customers: Service approaches, ethics, and impact.* Creskill, NJ: Hampton.

Ford, W. S. Z., & Etienne, C. N. (1994). Can I help you? A framework for the interdisciplinary literature on customer service encounters. *Management Communication Quarterly, 7,* 413-441.

Fusani, D. S. (1994). "Extra-class" communication: Frequency, immediacy, self-disclosure, and satisfaction in student-faculty interaction outside the classroom. *Journal of Applied Communication Research, 22,* 232-255.

Garrity, K., & Degelman, D. (1990). Effect of server introduction on restaurant tipping. *Journal of Applied Social Psychology, 20,* 168-172.

Goodsell, C. T. (1976). Cross-cultural comparison of behavior of postal clerks towards clients. *Administrative Science Quarterly, 21,* 140-150.

Gorham, J. (1988). The relationship between verbal teacher immediacy behaviors and student learning. *Communication Education, 37,* 40-53.

Gotlieb, J. B., Grewal, D., & Brown, S. W. (1994). Consumer satisfaction and perceived quality: Complementary or divergent constructs? *Journal of Applied Psychology, 79,* 875-885.

Guinan, P. J., & Scudder, J. N. (1989). Client-oriented interactional behaviors for professional-client settings. *Human Communication Research, 15,* 444-462.

Gutek, B. A. (1995). *The dynamics of service: Reflections on the changing nature of customer/provider interactions.* San Francisco: Jossey-Bass.

Hester, L., Koger, P., & McCauley, C. (1985). Individual differences in customer sociability. *European Journal of Social Psychology, 15,* 453-456.

Higgins, E., Rholes, W., & Jones, C. (1977). Category accessibility and impression formation. *Journal of Experimental Social Psychology, 13,* 141-154.

Hochschild, A. R. (1979). Emotion work, feeling rules, and social structure. *American Journal of Sociology, 85,* 551-575.

Hochschild, A. R. (1983). *The managed heart: Commercialization of human feeling.* Berkeley: University of California Press.

Iacobucci, C. (1990). Accounts, formulations and goal attainment strategies in service encounters. *Journal of Language and Social Psychology, 9,* 85-99.

Johnson, E. M., & Seymour, D. T. (1985). The impact of cross selling on the service encounter in retail banking. In J. A. Czepiel, M. R. Solomon, & C. F. Surprenant (Eds.), *The service encounter: Managing employee/customer interaction in service business* (pp. 225-239). Lexington, MA: Lexington.

Jolson, M. A. (1975). The underestimated potential of the canned sales presentation. *Journal of Marketing, 39,* 75-78.

Katz, E., & Danet, B. (Eds.). (1973). *Bureaucracy and the public: A reader in official-client relations.* New York: Basic Books.

Katz, E., & Eisenstadt, S. N. (1960). Some sociological observations on the response of Israeli organizations to new immigrants. *Administrative Science Quarterly, 5,* 113-133.

Kellermann, K., & Cole, T. (1994). Classifying compliance-gaining messages: Taxonomic disorder and strategic confusion. *Communication Theory, 4,* 3-60.

Kelley, S. W., Donnelly, J. H., & Skinner, S. J. (1990). Customer participation in service production and delivery. *Journal of Retailing, 66,* 315-335.

Ketrow, S. M. (1991). Nonverbal communication and client satisfaction in computer-assisted transactions. *Management Communication Quarterly, 5,* 192-219.

Komaki, J., Blood, M. R., & Holder, D. (1980). Fostering friendliness in a fast food franchise. *Journal of Organizational Behavior Management, 2,* 151-164.

Kraptel, R. E. (1988). Customer complaint and salesperson response: The effect of the communication source. *Journal of Retailing, 64,* 181-198.

Kurtz, D. L., Dodge, H. R., & Klompmaker, J. E. (1988). *Professional selling* (5th ed.). Homewood, IL: Business Publications.

Lynn, M., & Mynier, K. (1993). Effect of server posture on restaurant tipping. *Journal of Applied Social Psychology, 23,* 678-685.

Maister, D. H. (1985). The psychology of waiting lines. In J. A. Czepiel, M. R. Solomon, & C. F. Surprenant (Eds.), *The service encounter: Managing employee/customer interaction in service business.* Lexington, MA: Lexington.

Martinko, M. J., White, J. D., & Hassell, B. (1989). Operant analysis of prompting in a sales environment. *Journal of Organizational Behavior Management, 10,* 93-107.

Marwell, G., & Schmitt, D. R. (1967). Dimensions of compliance-gaining behavior: An empirical analysis. *Sociometry, 30,* 350-364.

McCormick, A. E., & Kinloch, G. C. (1986). Interracial contact in the customer-clerk situation. *Journal of Social Psychology, 126,* 551-553.

McNitt, J. L., & Ford, W. S. Z. (1997, April). *Development of an instrument for assessing communication approaches in teleservice contexts.* Paper presented at the annual meeting of the Eastern Communication Association, Baltimore.

Mehrabian, A. (1967). Orientation behaviors and nonverbal attitude communication. *Journal of Communication, 17,* 324-332.

Mehrabian, A. (1971). *Silent messages.* Belmont, CA: Wadsworth.

Mills, P. K., & Moberg, D. J. (1982). Perspectives on the technology of service organizations. *Academy of Management Review, 7,* 80-88.

Mirman, R. (1982). Performance management in sales organizations. In L. Frederiksen (Ed.), *Handbook of organizational behavior management* (pp. 427-475). New York: John Wiley.

Northouse, P. G., & Northouse, L. L. (1992). *Health communication: Strategies for health professionals* (2nd ed.). Norwalk, CT: Appleton & Lange.

Olshavsky, R. W. (1973). Customer-salesman interaction in appliance retailing. *Journal of Marketing Research, 10,* 208-212.

Parkinson, B. (1991). Emotional stylists: Strategies of expressive management among trainee hairdressers. *Cognition and Emotion, 5,* 419-434.

Pauley, L. L. (1988). Customer weight as a variable in salespersons' response time. *Journal of Social Psychology, 129,* 713-714.

Powell, R. G., & Harville, B. (1990). The effects of teacher immediacy and clarity on instructional outcomes: An intercultural assessment. *Communication Education, 39,* 369-379.

Rafaeli, A. (1989a). When cashiers meet customers: An analysis of the role of supermarket cashiers. *Academy of Management Journal, 32,* 245-273.

Rafaeli, A. (1989b). When clerks meet customers: A test of variables related to emotional expressions on the job. *Journal of Applied Psychology, 74,* 385-393.

Rafaeli, A., & Sutton, R. I. (1990). Busy stores and demanding customers: How do they affect the display of positive emotion? *Academy of Management Journal, 33,* 623-637.

Ralis, M. T., & O'Brien, R. M. (1986). Prompts, goal setting and feedback to increase suggestive selling. *Journal of Organizational Behavior Management, 8,* 5-18.

Sanders, J. A., & Wiseman, R. L. (1990). The effects of verbal and nonverbal teacher immediacy on perceived cognitive, affective, and behavioral learning in the multicultural classroom. *Communication Education, 39,* 341-353.

Saxe, R., & Weitz, B. A. (1982). The SOCO Scale: A measure of the customer orientation of salespeople. *Journal of Marketing Research, 19,* 343-351.

Scheid, T. L. (1996, August). *Burned-out emotional laborers: An analysis of emotional labor, work identity, and burnout.* Paper presented at the annual conference of the American Sociological Association, New York.

Soldow, G. F., & Thomas, G. P. (1984). Relational communication: Form versus content in the sales interaction. *Journal of Marketing, 48,* 84-93.

Spiro, R. L., & Perreault, W. D. (1979). Influence use by industrial salesmen: Influence-strategy mixes and situational determinants. *Journal of Business, 52,* 435-455.

Squier, R. W. (1990). A model of empathic understanding and adherence to treatment regimens in practitioner-patient relationships. *Social Science & Medicine, 30,* 325-339.

Stead, B. A., & Zinkhan, G. M. (1986). Service priority in department stores: The effects of customer gender and dress. *Sex Roles, 15,* 601-611.

Stone, G. C. (1979). Patient compliance and the role of the expert. *Journal of Social Issues, 35,* 34-59.

Surprenant, C. F., & Solomon, M. R. (1987). Predictability and personalization in the service encounter. *Journal of Marketing, 51,* 86-96.

Sutton, R. I., & Rafaeli, A. (1988). Untangling the relationship between displayed emotions and organizational sales: The case of convenience stores. *Academy of Management Journal, 31,* 461-487.

Thompson, C. L., & Pledger, L. M. (1993). Doctor-patient communication: Is patient knowledge of medical terminology improving? *Health Communication, 5,* 89-97.

Tidd, K. L., & Lockard, J. S. (1978). Monetary significance of the affiliative smile: A case for reciprocal altruism. *Bulletin of the Psychonomic Society, 11,* 344-346.

Tolsdorf, C. C. (1976). Social networks, support, and coping: Exploratory study. *Family Process, 15,* 407-417.

Tybout, A. M., Sternthal, B., & Calder, B. J. (1983). Information availability as a determinant of multiple request effectiveness. *Journal of Marketing Research, 20,* 280-290.

Waitzkin, H. (1985). Information giving in medical care. *Journal of Health and Social Behavior, 26,* 81-101.

Weitz, B. A. (1978). The relationship between salesperson performance and understanding of customer decision making. *Journal of Marketing Research, 15,* 501-516.

Weitz, B. A. (1981). Effectiveness in sales interactions: A contingency framework. *Journal of Marketing, 45,* 85-103.

Whalen, M. R., & Zimmerman, D. H. (1987). Sequential and institutional contexts in calls for help. *Social Psychology Quarterly, 50,* 172-185.

Zinkhan, G. M., & Stoiadin, L. F. (1984). Impact of sex role stereotypes on service priority in department stores. *Journal of Applied Psychology, 69,* 691-693.

CHAPTER CONTENTS

10 Communication in Families With an Aging Parent: A Review of the Literature and Agenda for Future Research

SUSAN ANNE FOX
Western Michigan University

This chapter reviews the research findings in the area of intergenerational relations within families that have an aging adult, including theoretical approaches to aging. The author advances a new perspective on communication between family members over the life span that uses social identity theory and communication accommodation theory, arguing that the roles that family members play over time create a unique situation over the life span that may be intergroup in nature. Within this intergroup situation the family must systematically adapt to the changing physiological, mental, emotional, and intellectual differences that occur from birth to death. These roles can create stereotypical expectations based on group differences—where once the context was almost exclusively interpersonal, the changing ages create a situation more intergroup in nature. The chapter concludes with a discussion of some future research directions this interdisciplinary perspective may follow.

> Oh let me do that, Mom. You shouldn't be doing that at *your* age.
> *Overheard comment made by a daughter to an elderly mother*

COMPARED with previous eras, today families are bearing fewer children, elderly parents are living longer, and more women are in the workforce. All factors mediate the dynamics occurring in intergenerational families. Moreover, rises in divorce rates, teenage pregnancies, and single parenting are contributing to the increasing role of grandparents in raising grandchildren (Burton, 1992). Although social service programs exist to help families adapt to the changing needs of their members, the primary

Correspondence and requests for reprints: Susan Fox, Department of Communication, Western Michigan University, Kalamazoo, MI 49008; e-mail fox@wmich.edu

Communication Yearbook 22, pp. 377-429

source of assistance is still other family members. These social changes have also increased the amount of support and caregiving families are having to give. Lang (1995) has found that the poverty rate among older adults would increase up to 42% if they did not live with their relatives. As Lee and Sheehan (1989) note, "Instances of older persons who are truly isolated from their families are very rare, and few older Americans who require aid or assistance are forced to rely solely on formal agencies" (p. 117). Only 5% of elderly adults are living in institutions at any given time (Palmore, 1980), and families provide 80-90% of medical and personal care as well as help with household tasks, transportation, and shopping needs for the elderly (Mares, 1995). Children who provide assistance, however, experience strain from giving care to older adults, and the psychological well-being of both adult children and older parents may change as the result of giving and receiving assistance (Sheehan & Nuttall, 1988). This may contribute to the increasingly noted problem of elder abuse (see, e.g., Gold & Gwyther, 1989; Noelker & Townsend, 1987; Steinmetz, 1988). Therefore, the importance of the family in providing social support and caregiving for older adults has been well documented by researchers (Cantor, 1975; Cicirelli, 1989; Lee & Ishii-Kuntz, 1987; Marks, 1996). Given the changing nature of intergenerational issues, researchers need to investigate how these changes are affecting the behavior and communication of people within family settings (Cicirelli, 1989; Thompson, 1989).

These issues highlight the need for research concerning communication in families that include older adult members. With the importance of these changing issues in American life, researchers need to determine if and how changes in communication occur in families with an aging parent. Given the lack of research that has focused specifically on communication in intergenerational settings, my purposes in this chapter are fourfold. First, I present a review of the research findings related to the psychological and communicative issues involved in families. I then review the area of intergenerational communication that is centered primarily on stranger and institutional contexts and apply it to family contexts. Following that discussion, I address the theoretical perspectives related to aging and incorporate a new theoretical backdrop to the study of communication within families using an intergroup perspective. Finally, I present a number of possible future research directions for the study of communication in intergenerational families, involving psychological, methodological, and theoretical considerations.

ISSUES SURROUNDING THE FAMILY

Many different definitions of family exist, and researchers have relied on definitions that limit who can be considered a "family." For this chapter, I extend Fitzpatrick's (1990) definition of a family as a group to "whom an individual is related by blood or marriage" to include also adoptions and postdivorce relationships, such as former stepchildren and mothers-in-law. Most researchers contend that, unlike friendships, relationships within families, such as those between siblings, grandparents, and grandchildren, are not voluntary, and that although people can neglect family obligations, their family memberships cannot be broken (Lee & Sheehan, 1989; Matthews & Sprey, 1989; Wood, 1982). Fitzpatrick (1990) lists certain assumptions of families and their interactions, including (a) there are multiple types of well-functioning families; (b) families differ from one another in basic organization and worldview; (c) families are guided by different paradigms and organized by different regimes; (d) family paradigms vary, but within this variability distinct primary forms can be identified; (e) families guided by different paradigms will have different interactional styles, both within the family and between the family and the external environment; and (f) families guided by different paradigms will have different strengths and weaknesses. I apply these assumptions later to the discussion of future research on family communication.

The next subsection looks at psychological issues related to families in general, parent-child (primarily adult-adult), sibling, and grandchild-grandparent relationships as they relate to families with at least one aging member. It is important to note that the majority of the studies described below have their roots in psychology, gerontology, and sociology, and thereby look at variables tangentially related but not specifically investigating communication. In these areas there is a dearth of literature on actual or perceived *communication* within families, and "the role of communication in the relationship development process" (Holladay et al., 1996, p. 4). Research that has been done in these areas views communication very broadly. Rossi and Rossi (1990) measured communication only in relation to helping behavior and included it as a nominal "yes/no" variable. Even in Mancini's (1989) edited volume *Aging Parents and Adult Children* there is virtually no mention of communication in families. When communication is mentioned, it is in relation to communication difficulties between adult-child caregivers and their parents with Alzheimer's disease outside naturally occurring situations (Blieszner & Shifflett, 1989). Therefore, these studies are good springboards for future studies that will examine communication variables, but fall short of examining communication within intergenerational settings.

In the past 15 years, the field of family studies (primarily comprising sociologists) has done much to increase the knowledge of intergenerational family research. However, even in this area there have been few studies that have specifically addressed either perceived or observed communication in families. Moreover, there has been little cross-fertilization of this research in the psychological and communication literatures. This chapter incorporates literature in all of these areas, thereby serving as an interdisciplinary review of intergenerational family research.

Psychological Issues

Researchers have studied the psychological roles within families and how these roles change over the life span. There are inherent role structures within families, and relationships are organized by cognitive processes, role expectations, and scripts that the family ascribes (Quinn, 1989; Sillars, 1995). Scripts for interaction are set at an early age, and parent-child interactions become habituated around issues such as amount of conformity required by the family and openness of interactions (Fitzpatrick, 1990). Even though an adult child can be successful and powerful in other contexts, within the family he or she may revert to a childhood role in certain family interactions. Furthermore, the roles within families are constantly changing and being renegotiated over the life span. A person starts in a role as a child, then usually moves to being a spouse, then a parent, and then possibly a grandparent or even a great-grandparent (Cicirelli & Nussbaum, 1989).

These life-span changes affect the whole family unit. When the adult child finds that his or her parents are not immortal as once thought, this may cause distress and a change in the communication occurring in the family. The roles within the family may reverse as the parents age, and children may begin parenting their parents (Osterkamp, 1996). Prusank (1993) notes these role differences with adult children and older parents:

> It must be noted that as the lifespan of parents and children reaches the point where the parents are elderly and the children are actually adult children, the participants find themselves in a reversal of roles regarding who is disciplining whom. That is, adult children find themselves in the position of "disciplining" their parents. (pp. 151-152)

These changing roles can cause transformations in independence. Blieszner and Mancini (1987) found that, for older adults, one of the most desired aspects of relationships with adult children was avoidance of direct interference in each other's lives. Losing independence and having to rely on children for different forms of support is a great fear of the elderly (Clark & Anderson, 1967; Downs, 1989). If the older person does become dependent, that dependency can be of a financial, physical, and/or socioemotional nature (Brubaker & Brubaker, 1989). These changing family roles may greatly alter the power structure of the family, and older adults may become dependent on their children and grandchildren. The loss of independence also affects decision making for the older adult, which can go from his or her being autonomous to having to share autonomy with a younger person, to paternalistic decision making, such that the younger person is making decisions for the parent (Cicirelli, 1993). Although not yet studied, these different types of dependencies may have different effects on the psychological well-being and communication of younger and older family members.

Decisions made by the adult child can cause feelings of resentment in the older person (Cicirelli, 1993; Sheehan & Dwyer, 1989). Consequently, actions taken by family members toward an elderly person may lead to more stable functioning at the cost of psychological distress, thus both having positive and negative effects (Hughes & Gove, 1981). Disagreements between perceptions of who is making decisions can also influence the overall quality of the parent-child relationship (Cicirelli, 1993). Horowitz, Silverstone, and Reinhardt (1991) found that elderly family members were more likely to report that they had the final say and had, in fact, made a decision, whereas family caregivers reported that the elderly family member "gave in" when there was a disagreement about a decision.

There are also instances wherein older parents may interfere with their children's parenting styles, thereby attempting to influence the children's decision making. There is, however, evidence that suggests that methods of parenting may be changing from when older adults were new parents. Hunter (1997) recently found that grandmothers are relied upon for help in child care and parental guidance. Olsen (1993), in a study of parenting differences between mothers and grandmothers, found that mothers reported being more nurturing toward their children than grandmothers were to their children. If grandmothers feel that less nurturance is appropriate in caregiving, they may react negatively if their daughters begin to take care of them in a nurturing way when they are older. Therefore, it is important that both sides of the decision-making process be explored.

Another factor related to the psychological issues within families is the amount of responsibility family members feel toward each other. Thompson (1989) notes that both parents and adult children feel responsibility to the other and that both would rather give than receive assistance (Brody, Johnsen, Fulcomer, & Lang, 1983). Adult children have to balance feelings of responsibility toward their aging parents and their desire to allow them to live an autonomous life. Some adult children, however, may find that they provide assistance to aging parents more because of feelings of obligation than because of feelings of liking and love. Jarrett (1985) discovered that many children do not like or love their parents. Other more recent research has found that college students have positive affection and respect for grandparents (Kennedy, 1990), but that attitudes toward parents are not as favorable (Manolis, Levin, & Dahlstrom, 1997). Manolis et al. (1997) found that Generation Xers (those born between 1964 and 1990) reported more negative affect toward parents than did baby boomers (those born between 1942 and 1962), so feelings of obligation could be decreasing as society changes. There is evidence that contradicts these studies, however. Aldous's (1987) data indicate that older adults are keeping intergenerational connections voluntarily as opposed to obligatorily.

Feelings of liking, however, do not preclude feelings of responsibility and obligation that children have toward the parents who helped them. In this regard, people usually endorse filial responsibility, at least in the abstract (Schorr, 1980; Thompson, 1989). Walker, Pratt, Shin, and Jones (1989) and Flax (1981) found that caregiving daughters felt as though they were "paying back" their mothers for earlier care their mothers had given them. But if daughters provided care and attributed it to obligatory motives, they reported less intimacy in their relationships than did daughters who perceived their caregiving as a discretionary task (Walker et al., 1989). This idea that there are discretionary and obligatory motives for behavior also affects the care receiver. The mothers in Walker et al.'s study, not surprisingly, believed that the caregiving daughters' motives were more of a discretionary than an obligatory nature, even when the daughters reported the contrary.

There is evidence that obligatory filial responsibility is changing. Yankelovich (1981) found that 67% of his respondents believed that "children do not have any obligation to their parents regardless of what their parents did for them" (p. 104). For many of these children, the fact that they did not ask to be born releases them of any obligation to care for their parents. Thompson (1989) quotes Vivian Gornick's memoirs of her relationship with her mother as indicative of the changing feelings of responsibility: "I'm saying that nowadays love has to be earned. Even by mothers and sons" (p. 261). Kornhaber and Woodward (1981) found effects of what they term a "new social contract" on the relationships between grandparents and grandchildren: "Under the terms of the new social contract, no one is obliged to anyone else" (p. 97; see, however, Cherlin & Furstenberg, 1986). Relatedly, parents' filial responsibility expectations are negatively related to their morale, perhaps because of the gap between high expectations and low fulfillment of those expectations (Lee, Netzer, & Coward, 1994). Hamon and Blieszner (1990) found, however, that there were moderate levels of agreement between adult children and older parents on the types of family responsibilities they expected to either perform or receive. Even with these possible changing feelings of interfamilial obligation, many children do feel responsibility toward their parents, and families continue to be the main source of assistance for older adults.

Many of the issues surrounding families in which there is an aging adult are intricately related to power and control. Decision making is related to power and control, and having decisions made for you is related to loss of that power and control. Umberson (1987) asserts that social control is largely an indirect process that can develop subtly over many years of interaction. Harwood, Giles, and Ryan (1995) note that in intergroup relationships, power relationships are important when two group members are interacting. It follows that this would be especially true of families in which ascribed power may change over the life span. These issues of power and control, and how the communicative process is involved in social control attempts in personal relationships, constitute a relatively new area of research (Patterson, 1985) that needs to be expanded in future research endeavors to include family relationships.

The position of the sandwich generation, those middle-aged persons living with both adolescent or adult children and elderly parents, can complicate relational dynamics, especially given the large numbers of women in the workplace. Zal (1992) has examined the conflicts in identities of the different members of the sandwich layers. Halpern (1994) highlights the issues of dependency, demands of work outside and inside the home, and the reoccupied empty nest. Raphael and Schlesinger (1993) have found that socioeconomic status and health of the elderly parents are related to family interaction factors. Schlesinger (1989) found that although the sandwich does create stress on the middle generation, the general patterns of interaction are not necessarily negative. Loomis and Booth (1995) have noted that the changes in responsibilities that result for the caregiver in a sandwich family have little to no effect on the caregiver's well-being, even taking into consideration outside work and gender. They suggest that this may be related to the fact that people with strong marriages are the ones most likely to accept further responsibilities.

Giving and receiving assistance as well as decision making from family members can change and strain the relationships taking place within the family (for a review, see Query & Flint, 1996; for an annotated bibliography of family caregiving, see Schultz, 1994). In one study, more than one in five women aged 35-64 reported caring for relatives or friends during the previous year (Marks, 1996). Cicirelli (1983) found that 52% of adult children experienced strain, and 34% felt substantial strain when acting in a caregiving role, showing the stressful nature of the caregiving process. Montgomery, Gonyea, and Hooyman (1985) differentiated between subjective and objective burden in caregiving and found unique factors predicting each type of burden; they conclude that there may be different ways to reduce each type of burden. The difficulties of this strain may be caused by a lack of recognition and appreciation given to the caregiver (Foulke, Alford-Cooper, & Butler, 1993), and Wearing and Wearing (1996) point out the need for recognition of the caregiving activities grandparents take part in for their grandchildren.

Dunkle (1985) also points out that caregiving arrangements can have adverse effects on the health of an elderly family member, especially if reciprocal exchanges of assistance do not exist; such adverse effects may mediated by reciprocal exchanges of assistance. In a study of depression, Dunham (1995) found that older adults who received support from an adult child were more depressed than those who did not. Dwyer, Lee, and Jankowski (1994) found, however, that reciprocity does not directly or indirectly affect the satisfaction of older women. Therefore, caregiving, although by its nature designed to be helpful, may have negative effects on both participants as well as the family as a whole.

Perceptions of aid in caregiving situations can also influence family situations. Although some research has shown that mothers underestimate the amount of care they receive, Walker and Allen (1991) did not find that mothers underestimated the aid they received from adult daughters. They found that when there was incongruence in perceptions, it was because mothers overestimated the amount of aid they received. Zweibel and Lydens (1990) found an association between incongruence and the extent to which the care receivers reported worrying that their caregivers do too much for them. It seems, then, that for older adults, being the recipients of care is stress producing. This highlights the need to research helping expectations and perceptions of caregiving and care receiving in intergenerational family situations.

The need of older people to remain self-sufficient and independent is well-known, but ways in which adult children can help their parents achieve this have not been given sufficient attention (Cicirelli, 1989). It has been suggested that adult children may contain their involvement and interference in order to preserve parental independence (Brody, Johnsen, & Fulcomer, 1984). There are also those who believe that not taking action, not making decisions, and not providing services to elderly parents may be the most caring, responsible course adult children can take (Gubrium, 1988; Matthews & Rosner, 1988; Noddings, 1984). In one study, adult daughters indicated that they respected their mothers' rights to make their own decisions, but noted that many times allowing them to make those decisions required an extra effort (Cicirelli, 1993). Qualls (1995) emphasizes that "the very purpose of families to support individual development makes evident a significant dialectic between individual autonomy and familial independence" (p. 484).

Osterkamp (1996) has focused on attributions of ability and motivation as ways in which people make judgments about the performance of family members. This contributes to familial relations by highlighting the role of the perceived responsibility people attribute to another's behavior. Subsequently, these perceptions may contribute to adult children's prematurely taking over the decision-making processes of aging parents. Osterkamp had 48 women (ages 35-55) read vignettes about troublesome behavior by either a 71-year-old mother, a 44-year-old sister, or a 23-year-old daughter. This person perception study found that the 71-year-old mother was rated as less responsible (due to age and illness) for her behavior than the younger vignette characters. Although Osterkamp did not investigate actual communication toward older and younger family members, lowered perceptions of responsibility in real-life situations could translate into domineering behavior of an adult child toward an aging adult. This dominance could, in turn, lessen the ability of the aging parent to make decisions or have autonomous control of his or her life. If an adult child attributes negative behaviors of the parent (such as forgetting to pay bills) to the detrimental effects of the aging process, the adult child may begin to take over decision making for the parent unnecessarily, bypassing avenues that could have been beneficial to both parent and child (Rodin & Langer, 1980).

It is also useful to stress the importance of culture in this discussion of responsibility, perceptions, and caregiving in intergenerational family situations. Research on intergenerational families has focused primarily on Caucasian families, but there is abundant research that shows that other cultures view intergenerational family relations differently than do North American Caucasian families. Black American families may have higher levels of interaction and stronger emotional bonds than do White American families (Taylor & Chatters, 1991; see also Burton & Dilworth-Anderson, 1991, for a review of Black elderly as aged parents, grandparents, and kin keepers). Black and Anglo grandparents' perceived strengths and needs are also different (Strom, Collinsworth, Strom, & Griswold, 1993). Kivett (1993), however, found that "high levels of family affect are not unique to the Black elderly" (p. 170). Taylor (1987) found that adult children are important in the informal social support networks of elderly Blacks, and, as in Caucasian families, kin keeping among Blacks is done primarily by women. Miner and Uhlenberg (1997) found no racial differences in exchange of instrumental support, but did find that Blacks were more likely to report that they provided expressive support, operationalized as "advice, encouragement, moral or emotional support" (p. 147). Dietz (1995) found that older Mexican Americans report that they did not receive as much instrumental support from family members, such as financial support or help with heavy household chores, as they expected. Ishii-Kuntz (1997) found differences in intergenerational relationships among Korean, Chinese, and Japanese families in North America—a finding that highlights the need to differentiate not only between seemingly larger cultures, such as Asian and American, but also between the subcultures within those larger cultures (see also Rindfull, Liao, & Tsuya, 1992). Sangree's (1992) investigation of the changing status of the elderly in Africa also highlights the need to expand what has been a primarily ethnocentric focus on intergenerational communication to include other cultures.

Overall, the nonvoluntary and arguably obligatory nature of family relations, along with cultural factors, compounds the issues related to these complex relationships. These issues, combined with the changes occurring within aging individuals, may lead to difficult transitory experiences for families. Although some of this research mentions communication as a component of family interactions, none of the research cited thus far has discussed how these issues are verbally or nonverbally manifested through family discourse. It would be useful to investigate in future studies how family roles, feelings of responsibility and obligation, and issues related to power and control are managed discursively. Given the issues of responsibility, power, and role structures, let us now turn to the different types of family relationships, including parent-child, sibling, and grandparent-grandchild relationships.

Intergenerational Familial Interactions

A number of studies have focused on intergenerational contact between family members with an aging adult. The focus of this research, however, has been primarily psychological and rarely communicative, so the studies mentioned here are descriptive of contexts in which intergenerational contact occurs. For example, researchers have found that, in general, later-life adults tend to maintain strong and close relationships with parents, brothers, and sisters through physical and phone contact (Argyle & Henderson, 1985; Cicirelli, 1982). Larson, Mannell, and Zuzanek (1986) found that older family members spend a large portion of time with family members engaged in day-to-day maintenance tasks (such as cooking and helping with housework) and in passive activities as opposed to active ones (watching television versus going on vacations together).

In an interview study of parent-child interactions, close to 50% of elderly adults who had children had seen one of them the day before or on the day of the interview (Cicirelli, 1983). Shanas (1979) found that most older parents live within an hour's drive of at least one child. As will be discussed below, frequency of interaction has, for the most part, been found to be unrelated or negatively related to the morale of the aging parent (Dowd & La Rossa, 1982; Mancini, 1979), so mere contact does not ensure positive interactions.

Parent-child relations can influence medical care in certain contexts (Beisecker & Thomspon, 1995). For example, triadic health care encounters (when the patient is elderly and the third party is a younger family member) can change the nature of the care that the patient receives. In a study that looked at the influence of companions on medical encounters of older patients, Beisecker (1989) found that companions may initiate comments toward a doctor for the elderly patient when the doctor is not addressing them. She describes three roles that a companion (most commonly a spouse or adult child) can play in the health encounter: the watchdog, who verifies information of both the patient and doctor; significant other, who provides feedback; and surrogate patient, who answers questions directed at the patient. (The latter of these could be considered highly patronizing behavior—see below.) Coe (1987) has also found that companions act as interpreters and negotiators for the dyadic health encounter. Given the important role that a family caregiver can play in an older patient's treatment compliance (Morgan & Zhao, 1993), it is essential that this context be explored further.

Related to medical care are long-term care issues. The amount of personal care older adults need has been found to influence whether or not caregivers discuss institutionalization (Gonyea, 1987, cited in Bromley & Blieszner, 1997). Bromley and Blieszner (1997) studied adult children with healthy parents to determine whether adult children had considered, discussed, planned, or decided on long-term care issues with their independent parents. They found that adult children with more family stressors were more likely to give *consideration* to future dependency concerns, but those with fewer stressful life events occurring in their families were more likely to enter into *discussions* with their parents. Furthermore, adult children who felt as though they had an egalitarian relationship with their parents were more likely to discuss long-term care issues with them. Therefore, it may be that nonegalitarian families with life stressors such as failing health—the families in which discussion of long-term care is most important—are the least likely to discuss care in a collaborative manner.

Parent-child relations have also been studied in terms of intergenerational conflict (Keith, 1995; Suitor & Pillemer, 1988). Fingerman (1996) uncovered many sources of tension (e.g., intrusiveness, inappropriate care of self or other, or exclusion) in the aging mother-adult daughter relationship. Suitor and Pillemer (1988) found that only 46% of elderly parents living with adult children reported that they had had disagreements with their resident children in the previous year. These results were based on such issues as how money is spent, division of household chores, drug use, relationships with friends, and jobs. Likewise, Sheehan and Nuttall (1988) found that adult children caregivers who reported more intense interpersonal conflict in their relationships with their elderly parent recipients were significantly more likely to report greater strain and negative emotion. In their study, however, interpersonal conflict in the relationship between the elder and the caregiver was determined by a single item assessing the quality of the relationship on a scale from 1 (conflict-ridden) to 5 (harmonious). Therefore, the nature of these disagreements, the conflict strategies used, and how or whether the situations were resolved were not measured in any of these studies.

Sibling relationships also play a major role throughout people's lives. Cicirelli and Nussbaum (1989) point out the difference between sibling relationships and other relationships: Siblings have an ascribed relationship (via a common biological heritage and intimate family experiences) that is, in most cases, the longest relationship individuals have in their lifetimes. McKay and Caverly (1995) characterize the sibling relationship as egalitarian, unlike (usually) the parent-child relationship. A review of the studies concerning sibling contact have found that roughly one-half of all people over age 65 see a sibling at least once a week, although the proportions of older people reporting weekly contact with siblings has ranged from 17% to 69% in various studies (Cicirelli & Nussbaum, 1989; supported more recently by Atchley, 1991; see also Connidis's work of the past 15 years—1983, 1989, 1992, 1994; Connidis & Campbell, 1995).

The functions of sibling relationships are unlike those of either parent-child relationships or friendships and seem to be gender differentiated. Most sibling aid comes from unmarried sisters (Foulke et al., 1993; O'Bryant, 1988), and siblings in general give more psychological support than actual instrumental help. Unlike parent-child relationships, sibling relationships in old age are based on companionship, reminiscence, and perceptual validation (Cicirelli, 1980) and are less binding than either marriage or parent-child relationships (Connidis & Campbell, 1995). Anderson (1984) found that study participants who were widowed reported increasing their reliance on extended kin in times of personal crisis more than did married subjects. O'Bryant (1988) found that sibling interaction is a factor in widows' well-being. Connidis and Campbell (1995) found that emotional closeness is an important factor determining how much contact and confiding siblings have with each other. Brody, Hoffman, Kleban, and Schoonover (1989) found negative intersibling interactions to be related to lowered levels of closeness. For families with a chronically ill older adult, sibling relationships are a major determinant of the amount and kind of care the ill member receives (Feinauer, Lund, & Miller, 1987). As in studies of parent-child contact, however, sibling relationships do not seem to have a strong effect on the psychological well-being of older adults (Argyle & Furnham, 1983; Larson, 1978).

Women are more likely to be the "kin keepers" in families (Leach & Braithwaite, 1996), although type of aid to family members can depend on the marital status of the woman (Gallagher & Gerstel, 1993). Older siblings reminisce with each other about the past more than do older people with their adult children (Cicirelli, 1980), and this may be due to siblings' jointly constructed and shared experiences. Parker and Lew (1996) note that "studies have indicated that reminiscence leads to a number of positive outcomes for older adults, such as improved emotional well-being and cognitive functioning" (p. 9; note that these researchers found that young adults reminisce more often than do older people, especially in times of transition, so viewing reminiscence as a life-span behavior is warranted).

Also within the family is the grandparent-grandchild relationship, which has received substantial attention in the literature. Even though the age of grandparents can range from 30 to 120, and grandparenthood often occurs in middle age (Downs, 1989), it is often assumed that grandparents, in general, belong to the group considered elderly. Mares (1995) notes that age, frequency of interaction, geographic proximity, the parent-grandparent relationship, and gender all affect the relationship between grandparents and grandchildren. Other researchers have developed typologies of "grandparenting" to describe the different roles that grandparents play. Cherlin and Furstenberg's (1985) typology includes detached, passive, supportive, authoritative, and influential grandparents. Mares's (1995) review of Neugarten and Weinstein's (1964) typology includes the funseeker, surrogate parent, reservoir of family wisdom, and distant figure. The most common kinds of grandparents are funseekers and distant figures; the former most often joke with grandchildren, give them money, and watch television with them. In another context, Webb (1985) found that the topics university students most often discuss with their grandparents are family, school, education, and health. According to Sanders and Trystad (1989), "Grandchildren and stepgrandchildren go to grandparents for advice, receive information about family heritage, and to turn for personal advice" (p. 73). Cherlin and Furstenberg (1986) list some of the behaviors grandparents had engaged in with their grandchildren during the previous year: 91% reported that they joked with grandchildren, 77% had talked about growing up, 68% had given advice, 39% had disciplined their grandchildren, and 14% had helped settle disagreements between the grand-children and the children's parents. Feinauer et al. (1987) found that both children and grandchildren of a chronically ill grandparent who lived with them perceived a lack of communication as the primary problem faced by the family. When questioned as to what more positive communication would include, the family members' solutions were limited.

One of the most frequently reported forms of communication in grandparent-grandchild interactions comes in the form of shared experiences, events, or family history through stories (Kornhaber & Woodward, 1981; for a review of reminiscence behavior, see Parker & Law, 1996). McKay (1993) asserts that narratives are one way people come to know themselves and that such narratives may satisfy higher-order needs such as self-realization and self-esteem. Moreover, she suggests that it is through storytelling that grandparents achieve a sense of continuity in their own lives and a way to communicate insight to younger generations. Storytelling and reminiscence, many times more broadly categorized as "narratives," have important social functions such as justification, criticism, and social solidification (Gergen & Gergen, 1983).

Holladay et al. (1996) found that a granddaughter's feelings of closeness with a maternal grandmother were predicted by the opportunity to visit alone, the absence of parental criticism of the grandmother, and the importance parents place on the grandmother. Using the same data set, these researchers also investigated turning points and dialectics in grandmother-granddaughter interactions. They found, as others have, that parents are important relational mediators in the grandparent-grandchild interaction. Holladay et al.'s research helps to increase our knowledge about the psychological aspects related to closeness between grandparents and grandchildren.

Grandparenting has also changed in American society as grandparents have taken on a more active role in the raising of grandchildren. Increases in joblessness, rates of teenage pregnancy, single parenting, and in some areas drug addiction have contributed to the increase in interactions between grandparents and grandchildren (Burton, 1992). Droddy (1993) sampled 59 grandmothers between the ages of 46 and 65 who were raising their grand-children and found that these grandparent-grandchild(ren) families were primarily the result of the inability of the biological parents to care for the child(ren) owing to drug abuse, child abuse, and lack of financial support. Divorce also increases grandchildren's interactions with maternal grandpar-ents if custody of the children resides with the mother (McKay & Caverly, 1995). Additionally, custodial grandparents take on more financial and emo-tional responsibility than do noncustodial grandparents (Mares, 1995). Not surprisingly, given the correlation between health and age, McKay and Caverly (1995) found that younger grandparents help with grandchildren more than do older grandparents.

Outcomes of Intergenerational Interactions

The above discussion highlights issues surrounding the dynamics within families. One starting point for future communication research involves the outcomes of intergenerational contact between family members. Voluntary social relationships have been shown to influence competent performance, stress, and crises and to influence both susceptibility and recovery from disease (Kasl & Cooper, 1995). Because it is not clear that intergenerational familial contact has the same result as voluntary relationships, it is important to look at the communication occurring in families. Let us now turn to possible outcomes that could be mediated by intergenerational communication.

In research conducted more than 20 years ago, Arling (1976) found that contact with friends and neighbors contributed to a higher quality of life (operationalized as less loneliness and worry and greater feelings of usefulness) than did contact with family members. Recent studies also support this finding. Mares (1995), in a review of intergenerational familial contact, found little evidence that contact with children has a positive effect on the morale of elderly adults. Many times the frequency of older adults' interaction with their adult children is either unrelated (Blau, 1981; Mancini, 1979) or negatively related to the morale of the older persons (Dowd & La Rossa, 1982). Wood and Robertson (1978) found that for older adults, friends contribute more positively to morale than do grandchildren. Lee and Sheehan (1989), however, note that in some cases morale is related to whether parents value independence and autonomy or expect and feel entitled to assistance from children in later life. Similarly, Lawton, Silverstein, and Bengtson's (1994) findings support the hypothesis that "contact and affection between adult children and their parents are casually related, creating the possibility that adult intergenerational relationships may be improved by promoting social contact" (p. 67). These outcomes may be gender specific, however. Lee and Sheehan (1989) found that men who see and receive assistance from their adult children less often have higher morale than do those who have more contact; no such relationship existed for women. Exchange patterns within families, and particularly in intergenerational relationships, may be different from those involving unrelated persons (Lee & Sheehan, 1989). Therefore, even though family relationships may be strong, interactive, and meaningful, the role that family members play in contributing to an individual's morale in old age may be limited (Mares, 1995).

Research on intergenerational programs with strangers has found that context and type of contact are very important (see Fox & Giles, 1993). In the field of intergenerational family studies, contact is often used as a blanket variable not accounting for the subtexts that may be occurring in the contact situation. For example, frequency of association has been operationalized as letters and/or telephone calls, informal home visits, joint celebration of holidays and birthdays, going together for entertainment and vacations, and joint community and church activities (Aldous, 1987). Zweibel and Lydens (1990) as well as Mancini and Blieszner (1989) point out the importance of determining the type of contact (e.g., voluntary versus obligatory) that is occurring in intergenerational settings. If contact with family members is of a caregiving or obligatory nature, this can decrease morale and well-being. Future research on the effects that different contexts and types of communication have on intergenerational morale could aid in increasing positive and decreasing negative communication situations.

Blieszner and Mancini (1987), in a study of parental roles and responsibilities, used vignettes of family interactions to elicit reactions and suggestions. One vignette described occasional family arguments and visits based on obligation. Participants responded that to improve the quality of the relationships of interactants in the vignette, the older mother should "talk over her feelings with the children, try having less frequent visits, plan more interesting and enjoyable activities during the visits, and let the children know that she wants them to visit her when their hearts are really in it" (p. 179). Participants reacting to another vignette involving a grandmother who wanted to help more with her grandchildren suggested the grandmother emphasize open discussion with the daughter, follow the daughter's rules for the children's behavior, and abstain from criticizing either the children or the daughter's parenting style.

Other researchers have used communication as a variable, but have done so using perceptions and not actual measures of communication. For example, Travis (1995) discusses the idea of affective assistance as "enhancing feelings of self-esteem, contentment, life satisfaction, hope of recovery, dignity, and general well-being" (p. 460), but does not discuss how it is accomplished communicatively. Although Rossi and Rossi (1990) addressed social interaction and affective closeness, such as frequency and type of contact, they did not investigate the communication that is occurring in these interactions. Embedded in their measure of "extent of help" were three nominal (yes/no) measures involved with communication (advice on a decision, telling about job prospects, and comforting in personal crisis). These measures did not look at the communication involved in these helping situations. Likewise, their measure of affective closeness was based on an interval-level "very tense and strained" to "very close and intimate" (p. 30) question. Silverstein, Parrott, and Bengtson (1995) differentiated between affectual solidarity and normative solidarity. Affectual solidarity involves the degree of emotional intimacy, whereas normative solidarity deals with service and responsibility for others. Interestingly, they asked, "How good is communication with your parent?" as an affectual solidarity question, whereas "listening to problems and giving advice" was seen as part of serving older parents' needs. Daughters felt that they had good communication and often listened to and gave advice to their older parents. This research, although important to inspire future research, lacks specificity in its investigation of the intricacies of communication occurring in family situations.

Few researchers have looked at actual intergenerational communication in family contexts. Webb (1985) found that grandparent-grandchild dyads most commonly discussed family, school, education, and health topics. Montepare, Steinberg, and Rosenberg (1992) examined the speech of young adult women to their parents and grandparents during telephone conversations. They found that speakers used more baby talk and congeniality when talking to grandparents than to parents, which was then interpreted by outside observers as being attributable to familial obligation more than to the perceived cognitive abilities of the grandparents. Hummert and Mazloff (1993, cited in Hummert, 1994) determined that one situation in which patronizing speech occurs is when disputes arise with family members. Therefore, there is some indication that patronizing speech may occur in the context of family situations, but more research needs to pinpoint the details of such communication.

In sum, few studies have looked at the actual communication taking place within families. Even the field of family studies, which has contributed abundantly to intergenerational family research (especially the field of caregiving), has focused not on actual behaviors but mainly on psychological issues such as social mobility, perceptions of care, feelings of responsibility, and caregiving. On this point, Cicirelli and Nussbaum (1989) note that although researchers have determined that siblings continue to interact throughout life (and have uncovered several functions of this interaction), the process of the interaction and actual communication itself have yet to be studied. Connidis and Campbell (1995) measured "amount of confiding" using one question on a "never" to "about everything" continuum, which, although a step toward incorporating communication, does little to resolve the nature of intergenerational communication. Blieszner and Shifflett (1989) found a relationship between affection and communication, but this was restricted to adult children's frustration with the ability of a parent with Alzheimer's disease to communicate. They conclude their discussion with a call for more research in the area of communication. Couper and Sheehan (1987), who list 19 considerations regarding caring for a dependent older persons, include improved communication and problem solving-skills as a way to reverse old patterns of behavior. They do not, however, describe how these communication behaviors are achieved. As discussed below, researchers studying nonfamilial intergenerational interactions have done much to determine various issues in problematic communication, such as beliefs about talk, patronizing speech, and painful self-disclosures, but little to determine what constitute positive and satisfying interactions (although see Williams & Giles, 1996), especially as they relate to the family context.

NONFAMILIAL INTERGENERATIONAL CONTEXTS:
CHANGES OVER THE LIFE SPAN,
STEREOTYPES, AND COMMUNICATION

Because of the scarcity of research on intergenerational communication within families, we must rely on communication in stranger intergenerational communication situations to glean information about what may be occurring within a family context. I begin this section by examining the changes in communication that occur due to aging and how the research on stereotypes of the elderly informs the research on intergenerational communication (see also Nussbaum, Hummert, Williams, & Harwood, 1996). By reviewing this research, we can begin to see how people, especially younger people, may be interacting and communicating with older people based on expected decreases in mental and communicative abilities. Much of the research conducted on communication between younger and older people has been done in the context of institutions (i.e., hospitals and nursing homes), so we must be careful not to generalize the findings in these situations to other contexts. Although the family context is vastly different from nonfamilial intergenerational interaction, the following discussion can help to illuminate what may be occurring in family situations.

In reviewing the changes in communication over the life span, Coupland, Nussbaum, and Coupland (1991) concluded that the findings are inconsistent. There does seem to be evidence demonstrating that changes in speech production, linguistic knowledge, and processing occur among all elderly. Moreover, they suggest that these changes include older adults' use of "less complex syntactic structure, more syntactic errors, and poorer linguistic processing" (p. 92) when communicating. They also argue that there may be a tendency for more extroverted, socially active, low-self-monitoring older adults to exhibit more off-target verbosity. Emery (1986) suggests that lowered linguistic ability appears to be a by-product of aging. However, there is reason to believe that older people in some contexts may have abilities above those of younger interlocutors. Smith, Reinheimer, and Gabbard-Alley (1981) found that older women adapted more efficiently in crowded and closed environments than did younger women. Given that most research uses younger adults as a ruler for determining what is "normal" and "ideal," it is not surprising that older adults have fallen short in this comparison.

Perhaps more important to intergenerational communication than the actual deficits that may affect older adults are the stereotypes younger people hold about older people. Palmore (1980), whose work has discovered great inaccuracies in the facts and beliefs people hold about aging, has shown that "many, if not most, of the 'problems of aging' stem from or are exacerbated by prejudice and discrimination against the aged" (p. 333). In general, research on stereotypes of and attitudes toward the elderly has found that younger people hold predominantly negative attitudes toward and stereotypes of the elderly (Fox & Giles, 1993; Kite & Johnson, 1988), although some research has determined that multiple stereotypes do exist (Hummert, 1990). In work on multiple stereotypes of older adults, Hummert, Shaner, and Garstka (1995) have found some stereotypes that are positive. These researchers have replicated and extended the work of Brewer, Dull, and Lui (1981) and have found positive stereotypes such as the sage, John Wayne conservative, perfect grandparent, and liberal matriarch/patriarch (for a more extensive review see Hummert et al., 1995). There are also negative stereotypes of older adults, such as the severely impaired, mildly impaired, despondent, recluse, vulnerable, shrew/curmudgeon, bag lady/vagrant, and nosy neighbor. These stereotypes can set up expectations regarding older people's communication (Hummert, 1994). For example, beliefs exist that the John Wayne conservative would have less trouble communicating (e.g., less trouble talking when pressed for time, fewer hearing difficulties, better storytelling abilities, and better word recognition) than people included in the more negative stereotypes such as the despondent older adult. All in all, the research shows that older adults judged as fitting negative stereotypes are seen as having more communicative difficulties than those who fit positive stereotypes (Hummert, 1994).

Harwood et al. (1995, p. 142) summarize a number of studies in which comparisons are made between younger and older communicators. Their findings related to attitudes toward elderly speech include the following:

- Younger people "evaluate older speakers as more vulnerable and less competent" (Giles, Coupland, Henwood, Harriman, & Coupland, 1990; Ryan & Laurie, 1990; Steward & Ryan, 1982).
- Younger people "have negative expectations regarding their elders' receptive and expressive skills in conversation" (Ryan, See, Meneer, & Trovato, 1992).
- Younger people "process and interpret messages from older speakers in an ageist manner" (Giles, Henwood, et al., 1992).
- Younger people "recall older speakers' messages less efficiently" (Giles, Henwood, et al., 1992).
- Younger people "blame older speakers more for external adverse conditions, such as noise" (Ryan & Laurie, 1990).
- Younger people "seek information from older people that involves views of incompetence" (Ng, Moody, & Giles, 1991).
- Younger people "believe older people are less effective compliance-gainers" (Dillard, Henwood, Giles, Coupland, & Coupland, 1990).
- Younger people "believe older people relish small talk more" (Giles, Coupland, & Wiemann, 1992).
- Younger people "believe older people are underaccommodative to their conversational needs" (Coupland, Coupland, et al., 1988; Giles & Williams, 1994).

Researchers acknowledge stereotypes as a contributing factor affecting speech toward older adults (Hummert et al., 1995), and the elderly themselves believe stereotypes are one reason for certain types of speech directed toward them (Giles, Fox, & Smith, 1993). This has been highlighted by Giles, Williams, and Coupland (1990): "Since being elderly is associated with declining health . . . older people may be treated communicatively in a stigmatized and unhealthy fashion, irrespective of the older person's actual subjective healthy identity" (p. 17). Let us now turn to how these stereotypes may be manifesting themselves communicatively in intergenerational contexts between younger and older individuals in nonfamily contexts.

Most studies examining intergenerational communication have been done either in the context of institutional settings in which younger and older people interact in health care situations (e.g., caregivers and elderly) or in more contrived older and younger stranger interactions. Given the more intimate nature of family situations, it is important not to apply these findings zealously to speculations about what could be occurring in family settings where the relationships are quite different. These studies only give us a launching point from which to understand the types of communications—such as age disclosures, painful self-disclosures (PSDs), and patronizing speech—that do occur in intergenerational communication settings and may be related to family contexts.

One characteristic of intergenerational communication has been labeled "painful self-disclosure" (Coupland, Coupland, Giles, & Wiemann, 1988), or the disclosure, usually by older people, of information about medical problems, family losses, or accidents they have experienced. Younger interactants do not generally reciprocate with PSDs of their own; rather, they predominantly manage the PSDs of elders with bland responses. This is a developing line of research in which taxonomies of types of PSDs as well as types of responses are being investigated (Coupland, Coupland, & Giles, 1991). Coupland, Coupland, Giles, and Henwood (1991), in a follow-up to the original PSD study, found that younger people attributed older people's PSDs to egocentric floor hogging and insensitivity. PSDs may function for older people as testaments to younger people of the resilience of older people and the experiences they have endured (Coupland, Coupland, & Giles, 1991; see also Harwood et al., 1995). Younger people have been found to use deflections in their conversations with older people, one form of which includes a discounting response to older people's troubles-talk (see Grainger, Atkinson, & Coupland, 1990). In this way, younger people may cast off and minimize older people's communication through comments such as "You're no different from anybody else" or "Things aren't that bad."

Another form of communication that occurs in younger-older dyads is that of the age disclosure (Coupland, Coupland, & Giles, 1989). This occurs as older people divulge their age (in years or via other linguistic strategies) in a seemingly spontaneous manner. Younger people usually respond to such disclosures in routinized ways, such as "Why, 87, good heavens, you don't look 87!" (Giles, Fox, Harwood, & Williams, 1994). Age disclosure, therefore, may be an impression management strategy used by older people.

Patronizing Communication

The area on which much of the recent intergenerational communication has focused is that of speech from younger to older adults. This often takes the form of more syntactically simplistic, redundant, nonverbally high-pitched, and tonally exaggerated communication termed "baby talk," "elderspeak," and "patronizing talk." Recently this area has been broadened to encompass all "patronizing communication" (see Ryan, Hummert, & Boich, 1995, for a review of this area). Caporael (1981) and Ashburn and Gordon (1981) originally studied speech within a nursing home context and found that speech addressed to the older residents was similar to that of baby talk to children. Culbertson and Caporael (1983) found that about 24% of speech addressed to incapacitated residents included baby talk. Baby talk is more specifically defined as speech that includes slower speech rates, higher pitch, shorter sentences, terms of endearment, simple vocabulary and grammar, and increased repetitions (Caporael & Culbertson, 1986; Culbertson & Caporael, 1983). Caporael, Lukaszewski, and Culbertson (1983) found that health professionals viewed the use of baby talk as communicating nurturing support. Judgments of baby talk seem to depend on the listener, however, with lower-functioning elderly having a greater liking for baby talk (Caporael et al., 1983; O'Connor & Rigby, 1996; Ryan & Cole, 1990).

Ryan, Bourhis, and Knops (1991) conducted the initial study examining the evaluations of patronizing talk in institutional settings. Using a vignette format of a younger nurse talking to an older patient in either neutral or patronizing speech, they discovered that people rated the nurse negatively if she used patronizing talk versus speech of a more neutral style. Giles et al. (1993) explored potential differences in the evaluations of patronizing speech between young and elderly respondents and found similar results. More recently, studies have shown that in terms of evaluations of interlocutors there is a pattern of blaming and denigrating the individual, who is spoken to in a patronizing way (Ryan, Boich, & Klemenchuk-Politcski, 1994; Ryan, Meredith, & Shantz, 1994, cited in Harwood et al., 1995). Therefore, this type of communication can have effects on other people's beliefs (and possibly communication) about older people in these contexts, regardless of the health or communicative ability of the older people involved.

Grainger (1995) has highlighted the controlling nature of discourse usually found in institutional settings. She defines *nurturing discourse* as being related most to relational, caring goals, and *routine management discourse* as being related to more task-oriented, controlling goals. Both of these types of speech are found to be patronizing, however (Hummert & Mazloff, 1993, cited in Hummert & Ryan, in press). Caporael et al. (1983) further discovered that caregivers expected that "adult speech" or non-baby talk would not be as effective as baby talk for interacting with older care receivers. Caregivers in a health care setting therefore face a predicament of accommodating to the needs of older people while at the same time conveying respect and nurturance in accomplishing job-related tasks (Nussbaum, Thompson, & Robinson, 1988).

Hummert and Ryan (in press) have created a model for patronizing talk that juxtaposes care and control as ways to convey either respect or disrespect for older individuals. They assert that it is a linguistic challenge to construct acceptable messages that are simultaneously high in control and low in care but that are still respectful. Their model includes four types of patronizing talk that vary according to the level of control or care: (a) directive talk, which is low in care and high in control; (b) baby talk, which is high in care and control; (c) overly personal talk, which is high in care and low in control; and (d) superficial talk, which is low in control and care.

Although many older people find baby talk and patronizing speech to be irritating and offensive (Giles et al., 1993), recent research has attempted to determine if this type of speech is effective toward accomplishing certain instrumental goals. Kemper, Vandeputte, Rice, Cheung, and Gubarchuk (1995) explored the use of elderspeak and determined that older listeners benefited from speech adjustments found in elderspeak with regard to the task of reproducing a map described by a younger subject. Comprehension and recall of spoken language also increases if focal stress is placed in ways similar to elderspeak (Cohen & Faulkner, 1986). Therefore, as the caregivers in Caporael et al.'s (1983) study believed, it may prove to be more efficient for caregivers to use baby talk to institutionalized elderly to accomplish nonrelational goals, even though it may diminish the well-being of these older adults.

There is also evidence that patronizing speech is sometimes directed at younger people. Giles and Williams (1994) indicated that younger adults found speech from older people to be patronizing. They discovered three categories of patronizing speech: elder overprotectiveness, not listening, and disapproval of individual actions (the last category based on negative stereotypes of youth). This type of patronizing speech may be especially relevant to grandparent-grandchild relationships.

It is important to note that it is through perception that speech is deemed patronizing (Fox & Giles, 1993; Harwood et al., 1995; Hummert & Ryan, in press). This may be exceedingly important in a family context, in which there may be an expectation that communication be more nurturing and therefore patronizing speech is seen as more acceptable.

The effects of intergenerational communication need to be examined in future research, especially in terms of the outcomes of patronizing speech styles on recipients. Ryan, Giles, Bartolucci, and Henwood (1986) have proposed the communicative predicament of aging model (see below) to address this issue, and although recent research has investigated these effects (see Ryan et al., 1995), the model has not been applied to family communication. These researchers' view includes the idea that an older person may find patronizing speech demeaning and irritating but may tolerate it. This, however, may behaviorally confirm younger people's stereotypes and beliefs and reinforce their patronizing behavior. Patronizing communication from younger to older people may then become routinized, and the elderly can develop mindless or passive patterns to respond to it (Kreps, 1990; Rook, 1995). Relatedly, deflections by younger people toward older people's troubles-talk may undermine older people's self-worth and psychological well-being and actually increase their dependent behaviors. The outcome of long-term repeated instances of this talk in encounters could then lead to negative outcomes, including lessened psychological activity, personal control, and self-esteem. Harwood and Giles (1996) assert, however, that there may be both positive and negative outcomes from patronizing encounters given the role of cognition as a mediator of evaluations related to patronizing communication.

Relating Past Intergenerational
Research to the Family Context

The research reviewed above indicates that there are negative stereotypes of the elderly that may contribute to less satisfying communication between younger and older people. Much of the intergenerational literature seems to be based on younger people's perception that older people have communication deficiencies and therefore younger people feel that older people are not sensitive to their communicative needs. Although it is difficult to generalize the intergenerational research reviewed above to the specialized context of the family, I will attempt in this subsection to address issues relating past intergenerational research to this context.

One issue that future research needs to flesh out is whether younger family members hold stereotypes of older family members and, if so, the features of these stereotypes. Because research on intergenerational communication is based on the stereotypes that younger people hold of older people in general, it is premature to assume that those stereotypes hold true under family situations. Support for this hesitation comes from the research on known versus general elderly, which has found that younger people stereotype "general" older people using negative characteristics (e.g., generally ill, tired, not sexually interested, mentally slower, forgetful, and unproductive) whereas they rate "known" older people more positively on these and other such dimensions (Kocarnik & Ponzetti, 1986; Weinberger & Millham, 1975). Moreover, the more information that is known about a target individual, the less negative are the attitudes held toward them. (Levin, 1988; Sanders & Pittman, 1987). In support of this, Downs (1989) cites research indicating that "children with grandparents and great-grandparents demonstrate less prejudice toward old age than children with no living grandparents" (p. 269). Because family members who interact together are known to each other, there may be fewer negative stereotypes present in family interactions. For example, "grandfathers have been characterized as either imposing authoritarians who frightened and challenged grandchildren or as helpless and feeble older men" (Kivett, 1985, p. 569). This may become a stereotype that both grandfathers and grandchildren act upon. As I will argue below, however, there may be situations in which younger family members behave toward older members as being typical "elderly," and therefore stereotype them according to broad stereotypical categories.

The findings regarding PSDs, age disclosures, and patronizing speech may be problematic in their application to family settings. Age disclosures may be less likely given the fact that within the family context members may be well aware of the ages of the other members. On the other hand, age disclosures may be more likely if older family members seek to assert authority by using them. Likewise, PSDs related to bereavement or other circumstances may already be known to family members. Such disclosures may be redundant with known information, and they may be more common in families because of the history that the family shares. Furthermore, attributions made about an older person who uses PSDs might be very different in family situations than in stranger interactions, and the circumstances may be more closely linked to future behavior within the family. Finally, given that patronizing speech is "in the ear of the beholder," what might be considered condescending in an institutional setting might be considered nurturing in a family setting. Even though patronizing speech in family contexts may be perceived as nurturing, however, this may not prevent negative long-term effects of such communication.

Other issues surrounding the context of intergenerational family communication exist, but it is important to provide a theoretical framework in which to couch these issues. I will now review the theories related to the aging process and intergenerational communication, returning thereafter to the family communication context as it applies to these theories.

THEORETICAL FRAMEWORKS FOR
INTERGENERATIONAL FAMILY COMMUNICATION

Theories Related to Aging

There are many different theories used to explain the aging process and family relations within families with older adults. Although none of these approaches specifically describes, predicts, and explains communication within a family context, each can be used as a starting point for understanding some of the psychological underpinnings that are important in intergenerational family situations. Some theories have been used to describe the aging individual in relation to social bonds (activity, disengagement, and continuity theory); others have been used to explain the helping behavior of adult children toward their aging parents (exchange theory, obligation theory, and attachment theory).

Three theories are most often cited as being related to the aging process: disengagement theory, activity theory, and, more recently, continuity theory. Rook (1995) has reviewed two of these theories, disengagement and activity, based on explaining how and if older people's levels of social activity (and therefore well-being) change in later life. Disengagement theory views the later stages of aging as a time when older people retire from their social roles and activities, allowing them to prepare for their impending death. This withdrawal benefits society because it allows scarce resources, such as jobs, to be opened up to younger people. On the other hand, activity theorists believe that to adjust to later life most effectively, people must maintain social networks for as long as possible. These theorists believe that it is society that abandons the elderly instead of vice versa. The more recently developed continuity theory posits that older adults attempt to retain a sense of continuity and order in their lives by retaining past experiences of themselves and their social worlds (see Atchley, 1993, for a review). According to Atchley (1989), individuals transition through different stages and call on past experiences in order to interpret these changes. From the perspective of continuity theory, it is through this stability in action and connection to the past that older people adapt to aging.

There are, however, communicative predictions that can be made based on the disengagement, activity, and continuity theories. Disengagement theory would suggest that persons disengaging from society would likely communicate less to younger people and more to those who could help them prepare for their death. Activity theory would suggest that in order to maintain social networks, persons would increase their communication within these networks. Continuity theory has been linked to reminiscence as a way to understand one's life through the telling of life stories (Parker & Lew, 1996). Although all of these theories focus mostly on the intrapersonal rather than interpersonal ramifications of aging, there are connections that can be drawn from them to the area of communication.

Cicirelli (1989) believes that attachment theory can best account for the motivation that adult children have to help elderly parents. *Attachment* "refers to an emotional or affectional bond between two people" (Cicirelli, 1989, p. 169), and the theory explains that as parents grow old, children seek to guard and protect the attachment the younger persons have to the older. This may be maintained symbolically, through writing and telephoning, if visits are not possible. Attachment, however, is not necessarily positive and may be negative (labeled "insecure" by Ainsworth, Blehar, Waters, & Wall, 1978). Positive and negative attachments may have the same behavioral outcomes in terms of helping behavior toward older parents. For example, whether an adult child has a positive or negative attachment to an aging parent, the child may decide that an institution is the place the parent should live. In the case of a positive attachment, the placement could be attributed to protecting the aging parent. On the other hand, a person who has a negative attachment to an aging parent may use institutionalization of the parent to decrease feelings of responsibility toward him or her, or to avoid or resist feelings of attachment (see Ainsworth et al., 1978). Although attachment theory covers psychological motivation of behavior and has yet to be applied to communication, its application to communicative behavior could be fruitful.

Obligation theory is a gratitude-based approach to intergenerational caring in later life that is in theoretical opposition to attachment theory. Jarrett (1985) asserts that obligation, not attachment, is the basic motivation of caregiving for the elderly. He argues that closeness in family relations will most likely fade over the life span and rejects attachment theory as a viable explanation for caregiving. Furthermore, the caregiving situation itself may be accompanied by strain felt by the caregiver, which can lead to lowered feelings of closeness and therefore more psychological distancing (Johnson & Catalano, 1983). Kivett's (1988) finding that obligation characterized adult sons' relationships with rural elderly fathers suggests that obligation may be a more important motivation for sons than for daughters. Therefore, for obligation theorists, care for parents in old age comes from a sense of duty or responsibility and not necessarily a sense of caring (Cicirelli, 1989). This theory informs us of possible motivations for behavior of family members but has not yet been applied to communication in family situations.

Other theories related to the field of communication that are not specifically related to aging have also been used to explain changes in behavior over the life span. Exchange theory is based on the idea that if benefits received are not equal to benefits given, a relationship becomes psychologically taxing and damaging to an individual's self-esteem (Lee, 1985). This may be true not only for people who feel as though they are exerting more assistance (e.g., caregiving) than they are receiving, but also for people who feel they are receiving an inordinate amount of assistance. This relates to the research described earlier showing that older persons who receive assistance from children have lower morale and higher depression than do those who provide assistance (Stoller, 1985). Ingersoll-Dayton and Antonucci (1988) found, however, that elderly persons in their study did not feel as much distress at receiving unreciprocated instrumental care from adult children as they did at receiving such care from other caregivers. Therefore, "intergenerational exchanges may be unbalanced at both ends of the family life cycle, but balanced and equitable over the entire course of the life cycle" (Lee & Sheehan, 1989, p. 128), making the measurement and substantiation of this theory very complex in predicting different types of behavior. Applying this theory to the perceived and experienced costs and rewards of intergenerational communication (e.g., listening to an older family member's PSDs) may help our understanding of families.

Although there are other theories related to aging (e.g., commitment theory; see Blieszner & Shifflett, 1989), the theories mentioned above are the most commonly cited in the intergenerational literature. Bear in mind that these theories have been applied primarily to Western or American intergenerational situations, and many cultural differences may exist that could contradict these theories' assumptions. Nevertheless, these theories are useful in viewing aging and social networks, and may serve to expand our knowledge of intergenerational family communication. Furthermore, all of these theories may explain intergenerational behavior given certain contexts and participants. As yet, these theories have not specifically incorporated communicative issues. The following approach, which synthesizes two theories, social identity theory and communication accommodation theory, is an attempt to create an explanation of communicative behavior that is occurring in intergenerational situations in general and family interactions specifically.

Social Identity Theory

Social identity theory (SIT) has been applied to intergenerational interactions in other bodies of work (Fox & Giles, 1993; Giles, Coupland, & Wiemann, 1990; Harwood et al., 1995; Williams & Giles, 1996). Historically, however, SIT has not been applied to the context of family communication. Therefore, I briefly review the theory below, concentrating on its application to family situations.

Social identity theory is based upon the concepts of personal and social identity, the latter of which is an important part of our social and communicative lives. An individual's social identity stems from his or her membership in social groups and the status and social standing of those groups in relation to others. Tajfel and Turner (1979) believe that it is through categorizing others and comparing group memberships that we understand and cope with the uncertainty that contributes negatively to our lives (Harwood et al., 1995). Social identity theory posits that individuals compare their social groups with other groups in order to seek positive social identity (Tajfel & Turner, 1986). Hogg and Abrams (1993) argue that we "actively construct a social categorization that minimizes intracategory differences and maximizes intercategory differences around relevant contrasting ingroup and outgroup prototypes" (p. 186). Positive social identity, it is argued, can be attained through psychological and communicative distinctiveness in relation to other groups (Giles & Coupland, 1991).

At any one time, an individual belongs to a large number of social groups, so the idea of multiple memberships is also important (Hamilton, Gibbons, Stroessner, & Sherman, 1992). The salience of the situation determines which social group's identity is most important in a given interaction. Likewise, if social categories are salient, self-stereotyping or other-stereotyping may take place (Hewstone & Brown, 1986). For example, during election campaigns, political party membership may be more important to people than at nonelection times. When political party membership is salient, a "Republican" would most likely stereotype a "Democrat" in ways that accentuate the differences and minimize the similarities of these groups.

Behavior (and thus communication) toward members of other groups can therefore be based on stereotypes and not individual differences. Harwood et al. (1995) assert that in intergenerational situations people use age as a determinant of a social group membership and that people categorize others on the basis of age-related stereotypes and attitudes. A younger group member may seek to differentiate from an older person who, although attempting to seek a positive identity, may assume the identity that has been placed on him or her by others (Louw-Potgeiter & Giles, 1987). It is therefore important that we seek to understand the ways people claim and disclaim memberships (Harwood et al., 1995).

Communication Accommodation Theory

Communication accommodation theory (CAT) explains the process by which social identity theory is manifest behaviorally. CAT posits that people attempt to attain a positive social identity psychologically and behaviorally through the linguistic strategies of accommodation, which include convergence, divergence, or maintenance. *Convergence* has been defined as "a strategy whereby individuals adapt to each other's communicative behaviors in terms of a wide range of linguistic/prosodic/nonvocal features including speech rate, pausal phenomena and utterance length, phonological variants, smiling, gaze, and so on" (Giles & Coupland, 1991, p. 63). *Divergence* refers to the accentuation of these communicative differences between individuals. Communication accommodation theory explains that the motivation to adjust speech styles results from individuals' need to express values, attitudes, and intentions toward each other (Giles & Coupland, 1991).

Applying CAT to SIT explains why communicative divergence can occur when a person desires to communicate disapproval or maintain differentiation from another person due to group membership. Divergence, like convergence, can be found in such features as self-disclosure, gestures, head nodding, facial effects, posture, and eye gaze, as well as shifting or switching the topic (for discussion of divergent responses to elderly painful self-disclosures, see Giles & Coupland, 1991).

Important to this discussion of CAT and intergenerational communication are the ideas of over- and underaccommodating. Patronizing speech, mentioned above, is one way in which younger people can overaccommodate to the perceived psychological and communicative needs of older persons. Underaccommodation can occur when a younger interactant pays little regard to the needs of an older interactant and when communication is based on stereotypes that are irrelevant to the latter's personalized attributes and style. Ryan et al. (1986) describe four communication strategies based on the principles of CAT that younger people use when interacting with older people. First is the notion of sensory overaccommodation, which is speech based on age-stereotyped physical or sensory disabilities. These could include paralinguistics such as speaking loudly or slowly to an older person. Second is dependency-related overaccommodation, which has been defined as "excessive and directive disciplinary talk to older people that can linguistically control and contribute to older people's loss of independence" (Fox & Giles, 1993, p. 445). The third strategy, age-related divergence, is related to the concept of group membership and occurs when younger people diverge from older people in order to differentiate. Finally, intergroup overaccommodation, found to be most common, takes place when younger people accommodate to the expectation of the older group's speech without consideration of the individual (i.e., intergroup rather than interpersonal).

Relatedly, the communication predicament of aging model (see Ryan et al., 1995) proposes that in situations where negative stereotypes toward the elderly are present, younger interlocutors may constrain the communication situation in such a way that negative and dissatisfying communications occur for both interactants. The consequences for older persons of long-term exposure to such negative and dissatisfying communication include lowered self-esteem and decreased psychological well-being. For younger interactants reinforcement of negative stereotypes can result, along with fear of their own aging in the future.

Application of SIT and CAT
to Intergenerational Family Contexts

It is important that SIT and CAT be applied to the family context. For example, given that feelings of obligation seem to be present in family contexts, these feelings may contribute to speech styles that do not occur in stranger settings. Moreover, if obligation increases care but decreases feelings of closeness over the life span (Jarrett, 1985), interpersonal feelings may be reduced to more group-related distinctions (in this case "young versus old") and thus may justify the use of patronizing talk. Similarly, if an older family member is dependent on younger members, overaccommodation, possibly in the form of patronizing speech, could become more extreme. Supportive communication (as well as positive health outcomes) may be better achieved through a younger person's dismissal of false worries (Giles, Williams, & Coupland, 1990) and deflection of an older person's painful self-disclosures.

SIT may be relevant in family contexts in ways that have not yet been examined. Because many different social identities can operate at once, a single individual can have such identities as "woman," "mother," "daughter," "grandmother," and "wife" within the same family situation. It may be that the role that contributes to the most positive identity (e.g., grandmother) is the one that the individual asserts. For adult children with older parents, the younger person's need to differentiate and attain a positive identity may constrain the ability of the older parent to maintain a positive identity. For example, a younger family member may attempt to assume a more dominant family role by acting in a way that conveys to the older family member, "You are too old for that sort of thing," resulting in the older person's lowered positive social identity.

Thompson (1989) suggests that some intergenerational interactions, such as those occuring in nursing homes, are based on younger persons' treatment of older persons as "generalized others." Similarly, as adult children grow older and closer to "old age," they may seek to differentiate from their elderly parents in an attempt to maintain an identity based upon being young and productive. An adult child may begin to make decisions for the older parent not based on the capability of the particular older person, but based on the stereotype the younger has of old age bringing a decrease in ability.

"Family identity" may also be invoked in situations involving intergenerational interactions. In regard to social comparison and group identity, there may be intergroup issues going on not only within the family, but also between families. The whole notion of "keeping up with the Joneses" assumes that families are comparing themselves to one another. The attributions family members make about their behavior (whether psychologically or discursively) compared to that of other families (e.g., "I still take care of my mother, but Betty placed her aging mother in a nursing facility") may mediate communication within and between families.

These are just a few of the ways in which SIT and CAT may be applicable to families. This application of theory to family intergenerational communication may lead to important directions for future work and needs further theoretical development and refinement. Given the scant research in the field of family intergenerational communication, I turn now to a discussion of some future research directions that are important to the theoretical development of SIT and CAT, as well as to the field of family communication in general.

FUTURE RESEARCH DIRECTIONS

Any future research involving family communication would be strengthened by a theoretical framework. Such research also needs to be conducted with specific background assumptions, psychological variables, contextual variables, and methodologies that can contribute to the quality, validity, generalizability, and utility of the research.

Theoretical Assumptions

Communication is transactional, and this is especially true of family communication. Maynard (1988-1989) discusses this in terms of an "interaction order" wherein interactants jointly facilitate and constrain the roles, identities, and communication of each other within conversations and relationships. From this perspective, both parents and children must be viewed as reciprocally influencing each other (Glass & Dunham, 1989). For example, in decision making by an adult child for an older family member (assuming a level of good health in the latter), the older parent must at some level give up control to that child. It would be naive, however, to think that a negotiation of this sort is conducted as a formal dialogue (Quinn, 1989). The subtleties of the power relations in these transactional interactions can be virtually unrecognizable within one specific interaction, but over time they can take the form of habituated behaviors.

Family communication must also incorporate a life-span identity framework. Coupland and Nussbaum, in their edited volume *Discourse and Lifespan Identity* (1993), focus on the idea that the self is a constantly changing and developing identity that evolves processually through communication. This conceptualization is different from a view that focuses on age identities and life stages. As Coupland, Nussbaum, and Grossman (1993) note: "Lifespan change does not merely 'happen.' It is both experienced by and enacted by people" (p. xiii). In this way, although there may be age-related capstones (e.g., the ability to vote at age 18), the communicative and psychological aspects of identity are cocreated within communication and relationships. "A life-span perspective alerts us to the changes that may ensue across adult development" (Tinsley & Parke, 1984, p. 165; see also Blieszner, 1986), and it is crucial that communication scholars be aware of and include this perspective in future theoretical and research endeavors.

The transactional and life-span approaches to communication lend themselves to viewing family relationships as interacting systems. Some of the research conducted on intergenerational communication has moved away from the fact that family relations are systemic (Matthews & Sprey, 1989). A systems perspective, however, asserts that what occurs within any subsystem of a family affects and is also affected by the events within other subsystems (Cicirelli & Nussbaum, 1989). Divorce is one example of how families are interconnected structural systems, given that many times divorced mothers must rely on their own parents for assistance in child care.

Aldous (1990) also asserts that a family life-course perspective is important to the investigation of intergenerational families. She argues that research should take into account the consideration of "how societal events affect the families experiencing them as well as changes in the family institution over broad sweeps of time" (p. 579). For example, the proportion of young adults still living with their parents has changed considerably over the past 20 years in the United States. Aldous cautions researchers about applying a developmental stages approach to families when life stressors unrelated to normal stage development may be causing changes in those families.

The field of intergenerational family communication is still in its early stages of development, so incorporating a transactional, life-span, and systems approach is not counternormative to the field. The field of intergenerational communication—in particular, the subarea of that field focused within families—is ripe for future research. Many different issues need to be addressed, and many different methodologies can be utilized to determine the intricacies that are occurring within family communication contexts. A number of researchers have put forth calls for more research in this area:

> Clearly affection and communication are significant dimensions of any close relationship, but little research on affection and communication between adult children and their aged parents exists. More research should investigate these variables in both normal and problematic late life parent-child relationships. (Blieszner & Shifflett, 1989, p. 240)

> Both the work on family subsystems and the work on family paradigms would be enriched by exploring how differential information processing is converted into family communication practices. (Fitzpatrick, 1990, p. 217)

> We do not have a clear understanding of the messages shared by siblings in later life or how these messages have changed over the lifetime, which may reflect the changing functions of the relationship. We do not know how individuals couched within a family context have maintained their relationship through communication as many as nine decades. Finally, we do not know the pragmatic role that sibling communication plays in serving the functions of companionship, reminiscence and helping behavior. (Cicirelli & Nussbaum, 1989, p. 296)

> The role of communication in dyadic family caregiving decision making needs to be recognized as an important area for future study if an increasing number of frail elders in American society are to retain some degree of autonomy in caregiving decision making. (Cicirelli, 1993, p. 232)

A life-span, transactional, and systems approach will enhance future research in intergenerational communication. Having stated these basic underlying assumptions, I turn now to essential psychological and communicative variables as well as contexts and methodologies that researchers need to keep in mind when examining communication in intergenerational family situations.

Psychological Variables

Factors such as proximity, age (although see discussions of contextual and psychological measures of age; e.g., Mares & Cantor, 1992), family roles, number of siblings, health, perceptions of responsibility, economic consid-erations, emotional closeness, and parents' marital status can enhance or inhibit the development of functional families. Kulis (1987) found that social mobility can also affect relationships between elderly parents and their adult children. Political and religious orientations may also contribute to differ-ences in communication within families. These variables may also influence the social identities that family members hold. For example, the age of the grandparent is related to the amount of help parents receive (McKay & Caverly, 1995). It may be that a younger grandparent, possibly in an attempt to demonstrate a positive social identity as a fun and young person, will help with child rearing more than might an older grandparent, who may not feel the need to assert a young identity.

The changing power structures in families, especially among the growing numbers of American sandwich families in which three generations live together, are fertile ground for future studies. Given the increase in sandwich living arrangements (children, adult children, and elderly parents), it is important to determine how the family members maintain their power and identity through communicative discourse. The changing roles and identities of the intergenerational family members and the interdependencies of these relationships need to be explored via the communication occurring in them.

Life changes such as widowhood can change how people, especially elderly women, interact with others. Anderson (1984) has found that after the death of a spouse, widows increase their reliance on children and siblings while allowing more voluntary relationships to disintegrate. Life changes such as divorce and death have a great impact on families, and more research is needed to examine the communication that occurs as an outcome of these situations.

As I have mentioned above, future research should also determine whether family members hold different stereotypes of each other and how these stereotypes contribute to communication within families. Ascertaining when age is a salient group dimension may be an even more important area for future research because it could reveal when different convergent or divergent communication strategies are used. Finally, the roles of contact, morale, and well-being within families would be made clearer through examination of the communication occurring in the family context.

More and more research indicates that gender is an important variable in psychological, sociological, and communicative issues related to intergenera-tional family ties and interactions. Snyder and Miene (1994) found that younger women seem to be more aware of and concerned with aging than are men. Women are also more likely to maintain family ties than are men (Leach & Braithwaite, 1996), and grandmothers tend to be involved with grand-daughters whereas grandfathers spend more time with grandsons (Hagestad, 1985). In terms of gender identity shifts in later life, men and women both report that men's identities change more than do women's (Sillars & Zietlow, 1993). This may be due to a softening of gender stereotypes after fatherhood and into retirement, when males display more reflective, dependent, and affiliative behaviors.

Daughters are more often caregivers to older adults than are sons (Mares, 1995), so gender differences also exist in relation to care. These differences may be the result of socialization (i.e., caregiving is seen as nurturing and therefore "woman's work") or they may exist because women have greater affection or feelings of obligation toward their parents. In fact, Noelker and Townsend (1987) found that 92% of daughters in their study, but only 62% of sons, considered themselves caregivers. Such identities may be mediated, however, by the type of care being given. Montgomery and Kamo (1989) and Sarantakos (1990) point out that sons, more than daughters, take on more of a managerial role than a direct caregiver role. They are more likely to purchase services and support elder parents financially, whereas women spend more time in direct helping behavior. This may be attributed, in part, to higher employment rates among sons. Even with this difference in time in actual caregiving, sons and daughters feel equal levels of burden (Montgomery & Kamo, 1989). Silverstein et al. (1995) notes that "intergenerational affection is the factor that most motivates daughters to provide support, while filial obligation, legitimization of inheritance, and frequency of contact most motivate sons" (p. 465). Dwyer and Seccombe (1991) found contradictory evidence suggesting that husbands believed they spent more time than wives in caregiving tasks. Matthews's (1995) study of brother-sister dyads highlights the need for research into the gender composition of the sibling group as a potentially important context within which parent care is negotiated. Relating this issue to communication within families, perhaps patronizing talk is used more often by female caregivers than by male caregivers, but because of the types of nurturing care females provide, older family members' psychological well-being is not affected. Research in this area could shed light on the types of burdens and stress both caregivers and receivers experience, how this stress is managed communicatively, and how differing communication behaviors contribute to that stress.

The psychological variables discussed above could serve as basic building blocks for future research, but they must be kept in mind and either examined or controlled for in the study of intergenerational family interactions.

Contextual Variables

Also important to future research are contextual variables that affect family interactions. As mentioned above, future research needs to account for the cultures within which families are interacting. Culture, in this sense, is any overriding paradigm by which a family interacts, be it based on political, religious, or ethnic ideals. The culture can significantly affect not only the values and attitudes of a family, but also the communicative behaviors of family members interacting among themselves or with other people. Family members in religiously based cultures, such as the Amish, assist each other without governmental aid of any kind (Brubaker & Brubaker, 1989), and they therefore have a set of beliefs about using social services available for older adults that is different from that found in other cultures. Compared with mainstream U.S. culture, Middle Eastern cultures view aging as a more positive experience, increasing elders' status and prestige (Coupland, Nussbaum, & Coupland, 1991). In industrialized societies such as those in Western Europe and North America, production is viewed as crucial to the success of a society, and thus retirement from work and older adults who are no longer productive are often seen as draining important resources. Sillars (1995) describes American families "as a constellation of separate personalities kept in dynamic equilibrium through continual (verbal) negotiation of relationships" (p. 390). More collectivist cultures view the family unit as more important than the identities of its separate members. Recent research, however, has found that Asian cultures do not necessarily have positive stereotypes and evaluations of the elderly or aging, as was once believed (Ota et al., 1996). Barber (1984) found that within Australian families, power positions play a part in family members' abilities to predict attitudes and behaviors. Researchers need to account for families' diverse backgrounds and belief systems in future studies aimed at explaining communication within families.

There are also differences among American subcultures that future research needs to address. McKay and Caverly (1995) found womanhood and matriarchy to be dominant in African American cultures. Kivett's (1993) research reveals cultural distinctions between Blacks and Whites in regard to the grandmother role. Dwyer and Miller (1990) found differences in caregiving between rural elders and those living in large cities. Relatedly, Pyke and Bengtson (1996) found that differentiating between individualist and collectivist American families revealed that the former found caregiving to be troublesome and burdensome whereas for the latter caregiving was a labor of love. These findings highlight the need for researchers to pay special attention to subcultural influences.

With the high rates of divorce and the changing nature of families today, it is also important for research to determine the effects that stepfamily connections have on intergenerational relations and communication. Henry, Ceglian, and Matthews (1992) found that mothers perceived that stepgrandmothers were less expressive to their stepgrandchildren than to their grandchildren. This differential treatment of grandchildren and stepgrandchildren may influence children's emotional well-being. "Grandchildren report having and desiring more contact, rate the relationships as more important, and report more involvement in social and personal roles, expected behaviors, and higher relationship strength than stepgrandchildren" (Sanders & Trystad, 1989, p. 71). How these feelings arise from communicative interactions between (step)grandchildren and (step)grandparents needs to be explored further.

Rising rates of divorce and teenage pregnancy, as well as financial difficulties, have increased the numbers of grandparents who have a larger role in the upbringing of grandchildren; thus future studies need to address grandparent-grandchild interactions. Cherlin and Furstenberg (1986) have observed that "strong, functional intergenerational ties are linked to family crises, low incomes, and instability rather than to health, prosperity, and stability" (p. 197). Therefore, although people do not wish to have strife, it may build intergenerational cohesion. Research examining whether and how communication differs for families with and without crises is lacking and should be undertaken by researchers in the future.

Given the difficulty in studying intergenerational family communication in home settings, researchers could begin studying family interactions within institutional contexts. Petronio and Kovach's (1996) research on issues among nursing staff, residents, and family members of institutionalized aged in Scotland is an example of research that has begun to look at such interactions. These researchers found that control of information, manifestations of guilt, decision-making rights, problematic behaviors of the family, and changing family structures were five main issues relevant to the institutional context. Although the interactions are constrained by the fact that the elderly in these institutions are usually limited by their surroundings and their health, it is a context that could be designed to be less intrusive than studies taking place within a home environment. This could also be a place to study reminiscence and storytelling within a family context to determine whether such communicative exchanges serve to differentiate or affirm family relationships (Buchanan & Middleton, 1993; McKay, 1993).

Educational contexts could also be utilized to study intergenerational communication. Strom and Strom (1993a, 1993b) suggest that educational programs developed for grandparents can increase family cohesion, and perhaps such classes can be used as a forum for studying communication in families. Strom and Strom (1992) found attitudinal improvement in grandparents who had taken weekly classes designed to help them adjust to their changing role and build satisfying relationships. Training workshops also are available to help family and friends communicate with institutionalized elderly (Shulman & Mandel, 1988). Within these contexts research could be designed to explore the effects of such education on family communication.

Future research also needs to examine the communication processes in family caregiving situations. Schmall and Pratt (1989) point out the need for a focus on the family caregiver and note that strategies such as family conferences, support groups, and educational programs can give attention to this undernoted group. Other factors that have been shown to affect caregiving outcomes are the duration of caregiving responsibility and whether the care members reside together (Hoyert & Seltzer, 1992). Seccombe, Ryan, and Austin (1987) found that size of responsibility, caregiver's capacity, long-range welfare, age, and motivation are all important caregiving factors.

Newhouse and McAuley (1987) highlight the use of informal structures as opposed to formal structures in the caregiving experience. Informal structures, however, may allow people to tap into their caregiving role, triggering negative stereotypes of older people as frail, dependent, and needy. Pyke and Bengtson's (1996) exploratory finding that collectivist families provide care more out of love than out of obligation may then have a negative side. Because there is a higher incidence of overcare, this could affect elderly members' levels of dependency, health, and well-being. Dwyer and Miller (1990) differentiate between stress and burden, the former being a subjective reaction to the demands of caregiving and the latter characterized by caregiving's emotional costs. Although stress and burden may be positively related, it could be an important distinction to make so that future research can investigate whether there are differences in communication between them. Likewise, it would be useful to explore whether the communication occurring in these contexts is of a type that increases caregiving efficiency at the expense of elderly people's feelings of independence.

Future caregiving studies also need to elaborate on how interpersonal conflict and caregivers' attitudes and expectations operate within the caregiving situation. Hunter (1997) has suggested that future research should include "an examination of the negotiations and conflicts within multigeneration family systems about who receives support, when, and under what conditions" (p. 265). Among the issues that need to be explored are the source of conflict between the caregiver and the elder, the influence of other family members in increasing or alleviating conflict, and the influence of increasing levels of functional or mental dependence on the quality of the relationship between the elder and caregiver (Sheehan & Nuttall, 1988). Keith (1995) asserts that "given the propensity for stress and the possibilities for intrafamilial conflict engendered by the work of caregiving, it can be important to assist family members in maximizing opportunities to share the burden and to engage in cooperative, rather than atomistic or competitive, caregiving" (p. 188).

Another area that needs to be developed is that of health care and decision-making contexts. Beisecker and Thompson (1995) indicate that the presence of a caregiver influences patient-physician interaction as well as compliance with a treatment regime. This may be especially true for family caregivers. Bromley and Blieszner (1997) emphasize the need to determine when and how intergenerational discussions of long-term care occur. Participants in Blieszner and Mancini's (1987) study expressed communicative uncertainty because although they "recognized the value of discussing their wishes for care in a future medical emergency and for the disposal of their property in the event of their death, [they] raised questions about precisely how to carry out such conversations" (p. 179).

More important than studying institutional and health-related contexts is the study of intergenerational family communication in natural settings. As

Thompson (1989) notes, "If we want to understand the immediate context of intergenerational responsibility, we should study ordinary life day by day, not just dramatic circumstances in which the elderly parent is decrepit, destitute, thoroughly dependent, or dying" (p. 263; see also Gubrium, 1988, 1992). Suitor, Pillemer, Keeton, and Robison (1995) stress the significance of looking at families with older parents who are in good health instead of families in which illness, dependency, and role reversal are present. Researchers need to remember that only 5% of the elderly are institutionalized (Palmore, 1980) and that many elderly will remain relatively healthy until death. It may be that day-by-day routinized interactions have a greater effect on the well-being and self-esteem of family members than do anomalous contexts involving strangers.

Communication Variables

With psychological and contextual variables accounted for, it is crucial that future research focus on the actual communication that is occurring in families. Giles and Coupland (1991), in their discussion of intergenerational communication and the principles of CAT, state that not only do the dynamics of young-elderly conversations appear to involve a mutually disturbing imbalance of power (identified by the concepts of over- and underaccommodation) but there may be sufficient evidence to show that younger people actually elicit problematic communication from the elderly, even though they report that they do not like this type of communication. Future research should examine the role of PSDs, age disclosures, and deflections, especially as they relate to caregiving situations within families. It may be that "younger people can create and promote negative intergenerational communication as much as or more than older people thrust it upon them" (Fox & Giles, 1993, p. 443).

In reference to studying patronizing communication in naturalistic contexts, Hummert and Ryan (in press) suggest that future research include interview studies involving younger and older participants "regarding their awareness of their own patronizing talk and the dilemmas of balancing care and control." This research needs to address not only stranger or caregiver interactions, but also family interactions. Given Mares's (1995) conclusion that there is little evidence that contact with children influences the morale of older people, it may be that nonfamilial caregivers and strangers have even less effect. It will be useful for research to determine whether certain types of communication considered patronizing among strangers are perceived similarly within families. More than this, research needs to determine the effects of such talk on older adults in family contexts.

Barbato and Perse (1992, 1996) have looked at communication motives throughout the life span. Their results suggest that, in general, parents' motives for communicating with children (e.g., affection, pleasure, relaxation) are relationally oriented and quite stable over time. Although Barbato and Perse did not look specifically at communication, the communication motives in families constitute another area for future research; such motives may mediate the communication occurring in intergenerational family situations.

There is also a need to explore if and how communication contributes to the incidence of elder abuse. Douglass (1983) has found that elder abuse is a substantial although underreported problem (see Pedrick-Cornell & Gelles, 1982, for an early review of the literature), and "elder abuse occurs primarily within the intimate, caregiving context" (Qualls, 1995, p. 476). Perhaps, as with Infante, Chandler, and Rudd's (1989) counterintuitive finding that violent spouses are less argumentative than spouses in nonviolent marriages, families in which elder abuse takes place may be less argumentative and the elder adult more passive than in nonabuse situations. Moreover, it may be in situations with passive adults who are patronized by adult children that abuse is most prevalent. Given the importance of this social problem, future research needs to focus on communication in elder abuse situations.

The communicative relationship between siblings is also an important area for future research. Given possible gender differences in feelings of obligation toward older parents and the differences in caregiving that occur (Montgomery & Kamo, 1989), research could determine how caregiving roles (and social identities) affect changes in communication between older and younger siblings. Moreover, how sibling members communicatively negotiate the sharing of caregiving roles is an area ripe for future study.

Fitzpatrick's (1990) assumptions about families and their interactions can also be used to frame future communication research. For example, the assumption that there are multiple family types makes it necessary for researchers to hesitate before hypothesizing that certain intergenerational communication strategies will always have positive or negative effects on family members. Referring back to Ryan and Cole's (1990) finding that some institutionalized elderly enjoy patronizing speech, it may be that some families thrive whereas others deteriorate when their communication includes such talk. The four typologies of parent-child communication that Fitzpatrick (1990) uses as a framework (pluralistic, protective, laissez-faire, consensual) can be used to predict satisfaction and communication strategies within families. For example, if the parent-child communication within a family was pluralistic (i.e., valuing open communication and the discussion of differing opinions) when the children were young, we may be able to predict how the adult children will interact with the aging parent when discussing the option of nursing home care. Similarly, a protective environment might lead to a unilateral decision by an adult child who sees an aging parent as needing care. Sillars (1995) discusses the idea of a comfort zone that families have in relation to disclosures, negativity, criticism, punishment, relationship talk, "mind reading," and other variables that should be of concern to researchers.

These communication variables can be used to help explain the dynamics occurring in intergenerational family settings.

Methodologies for Future Research

With the inclusion of relevant psychological and communicative variables, it is also important that future research utilize appropriate methodologies to optimize these studies. One aspect of research that has been criticized is the use of single variables such as "frequency of interaction" or "exchange of aid" to assess the quality of intergenerational family relationships (Mangen, Bengtson, & Landry, 1988). Future research needs to address many dimensions of family interactions, such as degree of intimacy desired, degree of conformity, and degree of openness (Fitzpatrick, 1990). Doolittle and Wiggins (1993) point out the importance of family cohesion, adaptability, and communication as factors in promoting positive health. Aldous (1995) highlights the need for research to focus not only on the interactional dynamics but also on the consequences of family interactions. Quinn (1983) proposes a model of intergenerational family relationships based more on qualitative measures, such as quality of the relationship and filial responsibility, than on quantitative measures, such as frequency of interaction or residential proximity.

Future research also needs to triangulate methodologies and variables, and many researchers have called for the use of multiple methods in investigating intergenerational family communication. Kin-keeping research has utilized the "diary: diary-interview" method of data collection, which involves keeping a detailed diary of interactions over a period of time, followed up by interviews (Leach & Braithwaite, 1996). Rook (1995) suggests studying single communicative episodes within a particular dyad, multiple communication episodes that occur in a particular dyad, or multiple episodes across a set of relationships. Cicirelli and Nussbaum (1989) have suggested utilizing multiple methods that include various conversation-analytic techniques.

It is imperative that researchers look at intergenerational communication longitudinally and not just cross-sectionally. Roan and Raley (1996) conclude from their longitudinal study that most cross-sectional research fails to find changes that occur over time between mother's widowhood and subsequent intergenerational social support. Silverstein et al. (1995) also note the need for longitudinal data in studies of family relationships.

Thompson (1989) points out that researchers rarely consider both generations or the nature of their relations. Discourse analysis is one method that incorporates this perspective. For example, Thompson notes that elder identities are often manufactured for older people through the linguistic choices of younger conversational partners (such as eliciting painful self-disclosures; Coupland, Coupland, & Giles, 1991). As mentioned above, however, an older person may be asserting a positive "look at what I have survived" identity by engaging in such talk. In this way, interactants are acting and acted upon in a mutually transactional way. Discourse analysis is one way to show changes in identity and relationships.

Much of the research that has taken place in family studies and gerontology has focused on the parent-child dyad rather than the whole family. Mancini and Blieszner (1989) suggest that future research should investigate the family as the unit of analysis instead of the dyad. This is exemplified by Matthews and Rosner's (1988) work, which shows that caregiving is many times a team effort of siblings. These researchers discovered that although most studies have focused on one primary caregiver, if there are two sibling caregivers (usually sisters), they both contribute in unique but regular ways to caregiving for older parents. Future research should attempt to determine how the whole family mobilizes to provide care to older adults—how family members negotiate fulfillment of needs and establish norms and expectations.

Relatedly, it is important to differentiate among various measures of family relations, such as relationship quality, closeness, and contact. Many studies focus on the family member closest to a given other member but attempt to generalize findings to all family members. Other studies look at a mean for the family relations, which is confounded by the number of family members. Connidis and Campbell (1995) analyzed data using both the closest siblings and the entire sibling network as an independent variable and found differences in predictors of closeness and confiding between these two vantage points. Suitor et al. (1995), who assert that relationship quality is an intervening variable in family relationships, do not specifically include a communication component in their definition. They discuss "positive family involvement," "less conflict," "feelings of closeness," and "positive relations" as indicative of relationship quality, all of which could be measured via communication. It is important that future research not only use qualitative and quantitative measures but also clearly define and operationalize measurements.

Nonfamilial Variables

Given that many families are spread out over vast distances, it is also important to continue the study of friendship within older adults' lives. Friendships with age peers have been found to have a positive relationship with emotional well-being among older adults (Mares, 1995; see also Adams & Blieszner, 1995; Matthews, 1995). Frequency of interaction with friends has been shown to be positively related to well-being and morale in older persons, and interaction often serves a companion function as opposed to a social support function (Lee & Ishii-Kuntz, 1987). For older adults, friends have been found to contribute more positively to morale than grandchildren (Wood & Robertson, 1978), and contact with friends and neighbors has been found to contribute more to improved quality of life (operationalized as less loneliness and worry and greater feelings of usefulness) than contact with family members (Arling, 1976). Adelman, Parks, and Albrecht (1987) note that although friendships may not differ significantly across the life span, the voluntary nature of the relationship may contribute to the enhanced self-esteem and perceived control that older people feel. Larson et al. (1986) assert that "it is kin whom you confide in and count on; it is friends whom you enjoy" (p. 122). Rawlins (1995) maintains that "friendship appears to be a protected and privileged relationship during old age, reflecting its vulnerable, voluntary basis, and specialized functions" (p. 252). Rook (1995) suggests that the companionship that brings elderly persons' well-being above a baseline level is most often found in friendships, not in the family. Therefore, it may be that the most positive contribution family members can possibly make to one another is the time to spend with friends.

CONCLUSION

Clearly, all of the variables and issues discussed above cannot be accounted for in one research study. A programmatic research agenda, however, should systematically investigate these variables and their contributions to communication and the effects that this communication has on family relationships. Future theoretical work could begin by developing a model of intergenerational communication within families that amalgamates important psychological and communicative variables with the concepts of social identity theory and communication accommodation theory to explain communication between family members. This communication may be based not on interpersonal but on intergroup variables, such as when children begin to see their parents more as "old people" than as parents. When age is salient in these family contexts, interactions may be based on the stereotypes associated with old age, such as decreased ability to communicate. Harwood et al. (1995) succinctly acknowledge the need for this link between intergroup theory and gerontology: "The development of an intercourse between intergroup theory and social gerontology seems essential in the face of increasing recognition to the importance of age groups as collectives with political power, specific communicative needs and practices, and identities that are distinct from one another" (p. 133). This could lead to explanations and, more important, predictions about the types of communication strategies that are occurring in family communication contexts.

My main goal in writing this chapter has been to emphasize the need for future research in the area of intergenerational family communication. I would stress that this research must be concerned with three major objectives. First, research needs to determine whether and how communication changes within families over the life span. Second, it is important to increase our understanding of the communicative ways in which younger and older members may be colluding in the aging process of the entire family through their social identities. Finally, research needs to inform us as to the positive and negative effects of these changes on all family members' psychological well-being and feelings of worth. Mindful investigation of the communication occurring within families and the effects this communication has on family members can serve to increase the possibility of creating environments that allow for more satisfying intergenerational communication, increased psychological well-being, and better physical health.

REFERENCES

Adams, R., & Blieszner, R. (1995). Aging well with friends and family. *American Behavioral Scientist, 39,* 209-224.

Adelman, M. B., Parks, M. R., & Albrecht, T. L. (1987). Supporting friends in need. In T. L. Albrecht & M. B. Adelman (Eds.), *Communication and social support* (pp. 105-125). Newbury Park, CA: Sage.

Ainsworth, M. S., Blehar, M. C., Waters, E., & Wall, S. (1978). *Patterns of attachment: A psychological study of the strange situation.* Hillsdale, NJ: Lawrence Erlbaum.

Aldous, J. (1987). New views on the family life of the elderly and the near-elderly. *Journal of Marriage and the Family, 49,* 227-234.

Aldous, J. (1990). Family development and the life course: Two perspectives on family change. *Journal of Marriage and the Family, 52,* 571-583.

Aldous, J. (1995). New views of grandparents in intergenerational context. *Journal of Family Issues, 16,* 104-122.

Anderson, T. B. (1984). Widowhood as a life transition: Its impact on kinship ties. *Journal of Marriage and the Family, 46,* 105-114.

Argyle, M., & Furnham, A. (1983). Sources of satisfaction and conflict in long-term relationships. *Journal of Marriage and the Family, 45,* 481-493.

Argyle, M., & Henderson, M. (1985). *The anatomy of relationship.* Harmondsworth, Middlesex: Penguin.

Arling, G. (1976). The elderly widow and her family, neighbors and friends. *Journal of Marriage and the Family, 38,* 757-768.

Ashburn, G., & Gordon, A. (1981). Features of a simplified register in speech to elderly conversationalists. *International Journal of Psycholinguistics, 8*(3), 7-31.

Atchley, R. C. (1989). A continuity theory of normal aging. *Gerontologist, 29,* 137-144.

Atchley, R. C. (1991). Family, friends, and social support. In R. C. Atchley (Ed.), *Social forces and aging* (pp. 150-152). Belmont, CA: Wadsworth.

Atchley, R. C. (1993). Continuity theory and the evolution of activity in later adulthood. In J. R. Kelly (Ed.), *Activity and aging: Staying involved in later life* (pp. 5-16). Newbury Park, CA: Sage.

Barbato, C. A., & Perse, E. M. (1992). Interpersonal communication motives and the life position of elders. *Communication Research, 19,* 516-531.

Barbato, C. A., & Perse, E. M. (1996, November). *"I don't care if you are 65. You are still my baby!" Examining parents' communication motives throughout the lifespan.* Paper presented at the annual meeting of the Speech Communication Association, San Diego, CA.

Barber, C. E. (1984). The influence of power and dependency on role-taking accuracy in three-generational families. *Australian Journal of Sex, Marriage and Family, 5,* 77-87.

Beisecker, A. E. (1989). The influence of a companion on the doctor-elderly patient interaction. *Health Communication, 1,* 75-95.

Beisecker, A. E., & Thompson, T. (1995). The elderly patient-physician interaction. In J. F. Nussbaum & J. Coupland (Eds.), *Handbook of communication and aging research* (pp. 397-416). Mahwah, NJ: Lawrence Erlbaum.

Blau, Z. S. (1981). *Aging in a changing society.* New York: Watts.

Blieszner, R. (1986). Trends in family gerontology research. *Family Relations, 35,* 555-562.

Blieszner, R., & Mancini, J. A. (1987). Enduring ties: Older adults' parental role and responsibilities. *Family Relations, 36,* 176-180.

Blieszner, R., & Shifflett, P. A. (1989). Affection, communication, and commitment in adult-child caregiving for parents with Alzheimer's disease. In J. A. Mancini (Ed.), *Aging parents and adult children* (pp. 231-243). Lexington, MA: Lexington.

Brewer, M. B., Dull, V., & Lui, I. (1981). Perceptions of the elderly: Stereotypes as prototypes. *Journal of Personality and Social Psychology, 41,* 656-670.

Brody, E. M., Hoffman, C., Kleban, M. H., & Schoonover, C. B. (1989). Caregiving daughters and their local siblings: Perceptions, strains, and interactions. *Gerontologist, 29,* 529-538.

Brody, E. M., Johnsen, P. T., & Fulcomer, M. C. (1984). What should adult children do for elderly parents? Opinions and preferences of three generations of women. *Journal of Gerontology, 39,* 736-746.

Brody, E. M., Johnsen, P. T., Fulcomer, M. C., & Lang, A. M. (1983). Women's changing roles and help to elderly parents: Attitudes of three generations of women. *Journal of Gerontology, 38,* 597-607.

Bromley, M. C., & Blieszner, R. (1997). Planning for long-term care: Filial behavior and relationship quality of adult children with independent parents. *Family Relations, 46,* 155-162.

Brubaker, T. H., & Brubaker, E. (1989). Toward a theory of family caregiving: Dependencies, responsibility, and use of services. In J. A. Mancini (Ed.), *Aging parents and adult children* (pp. 245-257). Lexington, MA: Lexington.

Buchanan, K., & Middleton, D. J. (1993). Discursively formulating the significance of reminiscence in later life. In N. Coupland & J. F. Nussbaum (Eds.), *Discourse and lifespan identity* (pp. 55-80). Newbury Park, CA: Sage.

Burton, L. M. (1992). Black grandparents rearing children of drug-addicted parents: Stressors, outcomes, and social service needs. *Gerontologist, 32,* 744-751.

Burton, L. M., & Dilworth-Anderson, P. (1991). The intergenerational family roles of aged black Americans. *Marriage and Family Review, 16,* 311-330.

Cantor, M. (1975). Life space and the social support system of the inner city elderly of New York. *Gerontologist, 15,* 23-27.

Caporael, L. R. (1981). The paralanguage of caregiving: Baby talk to the institutionalized aged. *Journal of Personality and Social Psychology, 40,* 876-884.

Caporael, L. R., & Culbertson, G. H. (1986). Verbal response modes of baby talk and other speech at institutions for the aged. *Language and Communication, 6,* 99-112.

Caporael, L. R., Lukaszewski, M. P., & Culbertson, G. H. (1983). Secondary baby talk: Judgments by institutionalized elderly and their caregivers. *Journal of Personality and Social Psychology, 44,* 746-754.

Cherlin, A., & Furstenberg, R. R. (1985). Styles and strategies of grandparenting. In V. L. Bengtson & J. F. Robertson (Eds.), *Grandparenthood* (pp. 97-116). Beverly Hills, CA: Sage.

Cherlin, A., & Furstenberg, R. R. (1986). *The new American grandparent: A place in the family, a life apart.* New York: Basic Books.

Cicirelli, V. G. (1980). Sibling influence in adulthood: A life span perspective. In L. W. Poon (Ed.), *Social support networks and the care of the elderly: Theory, research, practice, and policy* (pp. 93-107). New York: Springer.

Cicirelli, V. G. (1982). Sibling influence throughout the lifespan. In M. E. Lamb & B. Sutton-Smith (Eds.), *Sibling relationships: Their nature and significance across the lifespan* (pp. 267-284). Hillsdale, NJ: Lawrence Erlbaum.

Cicirelli, V. G. (1983). Adult children and their elderly parents. In T. H. Brubaker (Ed.), *Family relationships in later life* (pp. 31-46). Beverly Hills, CA: Sage.

Cicirelli, V. G. (1989). Helping relationships in later life: A reexamination. In J. A. Mancini (Ed.), *Aging parents and adult children* (pp. 167-179). Lexington, MA: Lexington.

Cicirelli, V. G. (1993). Intergenerational communication in the mother-daughter dyad regarding caregiving decisions. In N. Coupland & J. F. Nussbaum (Eds.), *Discourse and lifespan identity* (pp. 215-236). Newbury Park, CA: Sage.

Cicirelli, V. G., & Nussbaum, J. F. (1989). Relationships with siblings in later life. In J. F. Nussbaum (Ed.), *Life-span communication: Normative processes* (pp. 283-299). Hillsdale, NJ: Lawrence Erlbaum.

Clark, M., & Anderson, B. G. (1967). *Culture and aging: An anthropological study of older Americans.* Springfield, IL: Charles C Thomas.

Coe, R. M. (1987). Communication and medical care outcomes: Analysis of conversations between doctors and elderly patients. In R. A. Ward & S. S. Tobin (Eds.), *Health in aging* (pp. 180-193). New York: Springer.

Cohen, G., & Faulkner, D. (1986). Does "elderspeak" work? The effect of intonation and stress on comprehension and recall of spoken discourse in old age. *Language and Communication, 6,* 91-98.

Connidis, I. A. (1983). Integrating qualitative and quantitative methods in survey research on aging: An assessment. *Qualitative Sociology, 6,* 334-352.

Connidis, I. A. (1989). Siblings as friends in later life. *American Behavioral Scientist, 33,* 81-93.

Connidis, I. A. (1992). Life transitions and the adult sibling tie: A qualitative study. *Journal of Marriage and the Family, 54,* 972-982.

Connidis, I. A. (1994). Sibling support in older age. *Journal of Gerontology: Social Sciences, 49,* 309-317.

Connidis, I. A., & Campbell, L. D. (1995). Closeness, confiding, and contact among siblings in middle and late adulthood. *Journal of Family Issues, 16,* 722-745.

Couper, D. P., & Sheehan, N. W. (1987). Family dynamics for caregivers: An educational model. *Family Relations, 36,* 181-186.

Coupland, J., Coupland, N., Giles, H., & Wiemann, J. M. (1988). My life in your hands: Processes of self-disclosure in intergenerational talk. In N. Coupland (Ed.), *Styles of discourse* (pp. 201-253). London: Croom Helm.

Coupland, J., Nussbaum, J. F., & Coupland, N. (1991). The reproduction of aging and agism in intergenerational talk. In N. Coupland, H. Giles, & J. M. Wiemann (Eds.), *"Miscommunication" and problematic talk* (pp. 85-102). Newbury Park, CA: Sage.

Coupland, N., Coupland, J., & Giles, H. (1989). Telling age in later life: Identity and face implications. *Text, 9,* 129-151.

Coupland, N., Coupland, J., & Giles, H. (1991). *Language, society and the elderly: Discourse, identity and ageing.* Oxford: Basil Blackwell.

Coupland, N., Coupland, J., Giles, H., & Henwood, K. (1988). Accommodating the elderly: Invoking and extending a theory. *Language in Society, 17,* 1-41.

Coupland, N., Coupland, J., Giles, H., & Henwood, K. (1991). Intergenerational talk: Goal consonance and intergroup dissonance. In K. Tracy (Ed.), *Understanding face-to-face interaction: Issues linking goals and discourse* (pp. 79-100). Hillsdale, NJ: Lawrence Erlbaum.

Coupland, N., & Nussbaum, J. F. (Eds.). (1993). *Discourse and lifespan identity.* Newbury Park, CA: Sage.

Coupland, N., Nussbaum, J. F., & Grossman, A. (1993). Introduction: Discourse, selfhood, and the lifespan. In N. Coupland & J. F. Nussbaum (Eds.), *Discourse and lifespan identity.* Newbury Park, CA: Sage.

Culbertson, G. H., & Caporael, D. R. (1983). Baby talk speech to the elderly: Complexity and content of messages. *Personality and Social Psychology Bulletin, 9,* 305-312.

Dietz, T. L. (1995). Patterns of intergenerational assistance within the Mexican American family: Is the family taking care of the older generation's needs? *Journal of Family Issues, 16,* 344-356.

Dillard, J. P., Henwood, K., Giles, H., Coupland, N., & Coupland J. (1990). Compliance-gaining young and old: Beliefs about influence in different age groups. *Communication Reports, 3,* 84-91.

Doolittle, N. O., & Wiggins, S. D. (1993). Present and future health care for an aging society: A proactive self-health approach. *Marriage and Family Review, 18,* 57-71.

Douglass, R. L. (1983). Domestic neglect and abuse of the elderly: Implications for research and service. *Family Relations, 32,* 395-402.

Dowd, J. J., & La Rossa, R. (1982). Primary group contact and elderly morale: An exchange/power analysis. *Sociology and Social Research, 66,* 184-197.

Downs, V. C. (1989). The grandparent-grandchild relationship. In J. F. Nussbaum (Ed.), *Life-span communication: Normative processes* (pp. 257-281). Hillsdale, NJ: Lawrence Erlbaum.

Droddy, F. M. (1993). Grandparents raising grandchildren: The unrecognized family structure. *Dissertation Abstracts International, 54*(1-A), 332.

Dunham, C. C. (1995). A link between generations: Intergenerational relations and depression in aging parents. *Journal of Family Issues, 16,* 450-465.

Dunkle, R. E. (1985). Comparing the depression of elders in two types of caregiving arrangements. *Family Relations, 34,* 235-240.

Dwyer, J. W., Lee, G. R., & Jankowski, T. B. (1994). Reciprocity, elder satisfaction, and caregiver stress and burden: The exchange of aid in the family caregiving relationship. *Journal of Marriage and the Family, 56,* 35-43.

Dwyer, J. W., & Miller, M. K. (1990). Differences in characteristics of the caregiving network by area of residence: Implications for primary caregiver stress and burden. *Family Relations, 39,* 27-37.

Dwyer, J. W., & Seccombe, K. (1991). Elder care as family labor: The influence of gender and family position. *Journal of Family Issues, 12,* 229-247.

Emery, O. B. (1986). Linguistic cues in the differential diagnosis of Alzheimer's disease. *Clinical Gerontologist, 6,* 59-61.

Feinauer, L. L., Lund, D. A., & Miller, J. R. (1987). Family issues in multigenerational households. *American Journal of Family Therapy, 15,* 52-61.

Fingerman, K. L. (1996). Sources of tension in the aging mother and adult daughter relationship. *Psychology and Aging, 11,* 591-606.

Fitzpatrick, M. A. (1990). Aging, health and family communication: A theoretical perspective. In H. Giles, N. Coupland, & J. M. Wiemann (Eds.), *Communication, health and the elderly* (pp. 213-228). Manchester: Manchester University Press.

Flax, J. (1981). The conflict between nurturance and autonomy in mother-daughter relationships and within feminism. In E. Howell & M. Bayes (Eds.), *Women and mental health* (pp. 51-69). New York: Basic Books.

Foulke, S. R., Alford-Cooper, F., & Butler, S. (1993). Intergenerational issues in long term planning. *Marriage and Family Review, 18,* 73-95.

Fox, S. A., & Giles, H. (1993). Accommodating intergenerational contact: A critique and theoretical model. *Journal of Aging Studies, 7,* 423-451.

Gallagher, S. K., & Gerstel, N. (1993). Kinkeeping and friend keeping among older women: The effect of marriage. *Gerontologist, 33,* 675-681.

Gergen, K. J., & Gergen, M. M. (1983). Narratives of the self. In T. R. Sarabin & K. E. Scheibe (Eds.), *Studies in social identity* (pp. 254-273). New York: Praeger.

Giles, H., & Coupland, N. (1991). *Language: Contexts and consequences.* Pacific Grove, CA: Brooks/Cole.

Giles, H., Coupland, N., Henwood, K., Harriman, J., & Coupland, J. (1990). The social meaning of R.P.: An intergenerational perspective. In S. Ramsaran (Ed.), *Studies in the pronunciation of English: A commemorative volume in honor of A. C. Gimson* (pp. 191-221). London: Routledge.

Giles, H., Coupland, N., & Wiemann, J. M. (Eds.). (1990). *Communication, health and the elderly.* Manchester: Manchester University Press.

Giles, H., Coupland, N., & Wiemann, J. M. (1992). "Talk is cheap" . . . but "my word is my bond": Beliefs about talk. In K. Bolton & H. Kwok (Eds.), *Sociolinguistics today: Eastern and Western perspectives* (pp. 218-243). London: Routledge.

Giles, H., Fox, S. A., Harwood, J., & Williams, A. (1994). Talking age and aging talk: Sociolinguistic parameters of intergenerational communication. In M. L. Hummert, J. M. Wiemann, & J. F. Nussbaum (Eds.), *Interpersonal communication in older adulthood: Interdisciplinary theory and research* (pp. 130-160). Thousand Oaks, CA: Sage.

Giles, H., Fox, S. A., & Smith, E. (1993). Patronizing the elderly: Intergenerational evaluations. *Research in Language and Social Interaction, 26,* 129-150.

Giles, H., Henwood, K., Coupland, N., Harriman, J., et al. (1992). Language attitudes and cognitive mediation. *Human Communication Research, 18,* 500-527.

Giles, H., & Williams, A. (1994). Patronizing the young: Forms and evaluations. *International Journal of Aging and Human Development, 39,* 33-55.

Giles, H., Williams, A., & Coupland, N. (1990). Communication, health and the elderly: Frameworks, agenda and a model. In H. Giles, N. Coupland, & J. M. Wiemann (Eds.), *Communication, health and the elderly* (pp. 1-28). Manchester: Manchester University Press.

Glass, J. L., & Dunham, C. (1989). Factors influencing intergenerational consensus in adulthood. In J. A. Mancini (Ed.), *Aging parents and adult children* (pp. 135-150). Lexington, MA: Lexington.

Gold, D. T., & Gwyther, L. P. (1989). The prevention of elder abuse: An educational model. *Family Relations, 38,* 8-14.

Gonyea, J. G. (1987). The family and dependency: Factors associated with institutional decision-making. *Journal of Gerontological Social Work, 10,* 61-77.

Grainger, K. (1995). Communication and the institutionalized elderly. In J. F. Nussbaum & J. Coupland (Eds.), *Handbook of communication and aging research* (pp. 417-436). Mahwah, NJ: Lawrence Erlbaum.

Grainger, K., Atkinson, K., & Coupland, N. (1990). Responding to the elderly: Troubles-talk in the caring context. In H. Giles, N. Coupland, & J. M. Wiemann (Eds.), *Communication, health and the elderly* (pp. 192-212). Manchester: Manchester University Press.

Gubrium, J. F. (1988). Family responsibility and caregiving in the qualitative analysis of the Alzheimer's disease experience. *Journal of Marriage and the Family, 50,* 197-207.

Gubrium, J. F. (1992). Qualitative research comes of age in gerontology. *Gerontologist, 32,* 581-582.

Hagestad, G. O. (1985). Continuity and connectedness. In V. L. Bengtson & J. F. Robertson (Eds.), *Grandparenthood* (pp. 31-48). Beverly Hills, CA: Sage.

Halpern, J. (1994). The sandwich generation: Conflicts between adult children and their aging parents. In D. D. Cahn (Ed.), *Conflict in personal relationships* (pp. 143-160). Hillsdale, NJ: Lawrence Erlbaum.

Hamilton, D. L., Gibbons, P. A., Stroessner, S. J., & Sherman, J. W. (1992). Stereotypes and language use. In G. Semin & K. Fiedler (Eds.), *Language, interaction and social cognition* (pp. 102-128). London: Sage.

Hamon, R. R., & Blieszner, R. (1990). Filial responsibility expectations among adult child-older parent pairs. *Journal of Gerontology, 45,* 110-112.

Harwood, J., & Giles, H. (1996). Reactions to older people being patronized: The roles of response strategies and attributed thoughts. *Journal of Language and Social Psychology, 15,* 395-421.

Harwood, J., Giles, H., & Ryan, E. B. (1995). Aging, communication, and intergroup theory: Social identity and intergenerational communication. In J. F. Nussbaum & J. Coupland (Ed.), *Handbook of communication and aging research* (p. 133-159). Mahwah, NJ: Lawrence Erlbaum.

Henry, C. S., Ceglian, C. P., & Matthews, D. W. (1992). The role behaviors, role meanings, and grandmothering styles of grandmothers and stepgrandmothers: Perceptions of the middle generation. *Journal of Divorce and Remarriage, 17,* 1-22.

Hewstone, M., & Brown, R. H. (1986). Contact is not enough: An intergroup perspective on the contact hypothesis. In M. Hewstone & R. H. Brown (Eds.), *Contact and conflict in intergroup encounters: Social psychology and society* (pp. 1-44). Oxford: Basil Blackwell.

Hogg, M. A., & Abrams, D. (1993). Towards a single-process uncertainty-reduction model of social motivation in groups. In M. A. Hogg & D. Abrams (Eds.), *Group motivation: Social psychological perspectives* (pp. 173-190). New York: Harvester Wheatsheaf.

Holladay, S., Hardin, D., Lee, M., Denton, D., Lacovich, R., & Coleman, M. (1996, November). *Examining communication in grandparent-grandchild relationships.* Paper presented at the annual meeting of the Speech Communication Association, San Diego, CA.

Horowitz, A., Silverstone, B. M., & Reinhardt, J. P. (1991). A conceptual and empirical exploration of personal autonomy issues within family caregiving relationships. *Gerontologist, 31,* 23-33.

Hoyert, D. L., & Seltzer, M. M. (1992). Factors related to the well-being and life activities of family caregivers. *Family Relations, 41,* 74-81.

Hughes, M., & Gove, W. R. (1981). Living alone, social integration, and mental health. *American Journal of Sociology, 87,* 48-74.

Hummert, M. L. (1990). Multiple stereotypes of elderly and young adults: A comparison of structure and evaluations. *Psychology and Aging, 5,* 182-193.

Hummert, M. L. (1994). Stereotypes of the elderly and patronizing speech. In M. L. Hummert, J. M. Wiemann, & J. F. Nussbaum (Eds.), *Interpersonal communication in older adulthood: Interdisciplinary theory and research* (pp. 162-184). Thousand Oaks, CA: Sage.

Hummert, M. L., & Mazloff, D. (1998). *Elderly adults' perceptions of patronizing speech: Situations and responses.* Unpublished manuscript, University of Kansas.

Hummert, M. L., & Ryan, E. B. (in press). Toward understanding variations in patronizing talk addressed to older adults: Psycholinguistic features of care and control. *International Journal of Psycholinguistics.*

Hummert, M. L., Shaner, J. L., & Garstka, T. A. (1995). Cognitive processes affecting communication with older adults: The case for stereotypes, attitudes, and beliefs about communication. In J. F. Nussbaum & J. Coupland (Eds.), *Handbook of communication and aging research* (pp. 105-131). Mahwah, NJ: Lawrence Erlbaum.

Hunter, A. G. (1997). Counting on grandmothers: Black mothers' and fathers' reliance on grandmothers for parenting support. *Journal of Family Issues, 18,* 251-269.

Infante, D. A., Chandler, T. A., & Rudd, J. E. (1989). Test of an argumentative skill deficiency model of interspousal violence. *Communication Monographs, 56,* 163-177.

Ingersoll-Dayton, B., & Antonucci, T. C. (1988). Reciprocal and nonreciprocal social support: Contrasting sides of intimate relationships. *Journal of Gerontology, 43,* 65-73.

Ishii-Kuntz, M. (1997). Intergenerational relationships among Chinese, Japanese, and Korean Americans. *Family Relations, 46,* 23-32.

Jarrett, W. H. (1985). Caregiving within kinship systems: Is affection really necessary? *Gerontologist, 25,* 5-10.

Johnson, C. L., & Catalano, D. J. (1983). A longitudinal study of family supports to impaired elderly. *Gerontologist, 23,* 612-618.

Kasl, S. V., & Cooper, C. L. (Eds.). (1995). *Stress and health: Issues in research methodology.* New York: John Wiley.

Keith, C. (1995). Family caregiving systems: Models, resources, and values. *Journal of Marriage and the Family, 57,* 179-189.

Kemper, S., Vandeputte, D. D., Rice, K., Cheung, H., & Gubarchuk, J. (1995). Speech adjustments to aging during a referential communication task. *Journal of Language and Social Psychology, 14,* 40-59.

Kennedy, G. E. (1990). College students' expectations of grandparent and grandchild role behaviors. *Gerontologist, 30,* 43-48.

Kite, M. E., & Johnson, B. T. (1988). Attitudes toward older and younger adults: A meta-analysis." *Psychology and Aging, 3,* 233-244.

Kivett, V. R. (1985). Grandfathers and grandchildren: Patterns of association, helping, and psychological closeness. *Family Relations, 34,* 554-571.

Kivett, V. R. (1988). Older rural fathers and sons: Patterns of association and helping. *Family Relations, 37,* 62-67.

Kivett, V. R. (1993). Racial comparisons of the grandmother role: Implications for strengthening the family support system of older black women. *Family Relations, 42,* 165-172.

Kocarnik, R. A., & Ponzetti, J. J. (1986). The influence of Intergenerational contact on child care participants' attitudes toward the elderly. *Child Care Quarterly, 15,* 244-250.

Kornhaber, A., & Woodward, K. L. (1981). *Grandparents/grandchildren: The vital connection.* Garden City, NY: Anchor.

Kreps, G. L. (1990). A systematic analysis of health communication with the aged. In H. Giles, N. Coupland, & J. M. Wiemann (Eds.), *Communication, health and the elderly* (pp. 135-154). Manchester: Manchester University Press.

Kulis, S. (1987). Socially mobile daughters and sons of the elderly: Mobility effects within the family revisited. *Journal of Marriage and the Family, 49,* 421-433.

Lang, S. (1995). Living with family keeps many elderly persons out of poverty. *Human Ecology Forum, 23,* 25.

Larson, R. (1978). Thirty years of research on the subjective well-being of older Americans. *Journal of Gerontology, 33,* 109-125.

Larson, R., Mannell, R., & Zuzanek, J. (1986). Daily well-being of older adults with friends and family. *Psychology and Aging, 1,* 117-126.

Lawton, L., Silverstein, M., & Bengtson, V. L. (1994). Affections, social contact, and geographic distance between adult children and their parents. *Journal of Marriage and the Family, 56,* 57-68.

Leach, M. S., & Braithwaite, D. O. (1996). A binding tie: Supportive communication of family kinkeepers. *Journal of Applied Communication Research, 24,* 200-216.

Lee, G. R. (1985). Theoretical perspectives on social networks. In W. J. Sauer & R. T. Coward (Eds.), *Social support networks and the care of the elderly* (pp. 21-37). New York: Springer.

Lee, G. R., & Ishii-Kuntz, M. (1987). Social interaction, loneliness, and emotional well-being among the elderly. *Research on Aging, 9,* 459-482.

Lee, G. R., Netzer, J. K., & Coward, R. T. (1994). Filial responsibility expectations and patterns of intergenerational assistance. *Journal of Marriage and the Family, 56,* 559-565.

Lee, G. R., & Sheehan, C. L. (1989). Elderly parents and their children: Normative influences. In J. A. Mancini (Ed.), *Aging parents and adult children* (pp. 117-133). Lexington, MA: Lexington.

Levin, W. C. (1988). Age stereotyping: College student evaluations. *Research on Aging, 10,* 134-148.

Loomis, L. S., & Booth, A. (1995). Multigenerational caregiving and well-being: The myth of the beleaguered sandwich generation. *Journal of Family Issues, 16,* 131-148.

Louw-Potgieter, J., & Giles, H. (1987). Imposed identity and linguistic strategies. *Journal of Language and Social Psychology, 6,* 261-286.

Mancini, J. A. (1979). Family relationships and morale among people 65 years of age and older. *American Journal of Orthopsychiatry, 49,* 292-300.

Mancini, J. A. (Ed.). (1989). *Aging parents and adult children.* Lexington, MA: Lexington.

Mancini, J. A., & Benson, M. J. (1989). Aging parents and adult children: New views on old relationships. In J. A. Mancini (Ed.), *Aging parents and adult children* (pp. 285-295). Lexington, MA: Lexington.

Mancini, J. A., & Blieszner, R. (1989). Aging parents and adult children: Research themes in intergenerational relations. *Journal of Marriage and the Family, 51,* 275-290.

Mangen, D. J., Bengtson, V. L., & Landry, P. H., Jr. (Eds.). (1988). *Measurement of intergenerational relations.* Newbury Park, CA: Sage.

Manolis, C., Levin, A., & Dahlstrom, R. (1997). A Generation X scale: Creation and validation. *Educational and Psychological Measurement, 57,* 666-684.

Mares, M. L. (1995). The aging family. In M. A. Fitzpatrick & A. L. Vangelisti (Eds.), *Explaining family interactions* (pp. 344-374). Thousand Oaks, CA: Sage.

Mares, M. L., & Cantor, J. (1992). Elderly viewers' responses to televised portrayals of old age: Empathy and mood management versus social comparison. *Communication Research, 19,* 459-478.

Marks, N. F. (1996). Caregiving across the lifespan: National prevalence and predictors. *Family Relations, 45,* 27-36.

Matthews, S. H. (1995). Gender and the division of filial responsibility between lone sisters and their brothers. *Journals of Gerontology, 50,* 312-320.

Matthews, S. H., & Rosner, T. T. (1988). Shared filial responsibility: The family as the primary caregiver. *Journal of Marriage and the Family, 50,* 185-195.

Matthews, S. H., & Sprey, J. (1989). Older family systems: Intra- and intergenerational relations. In J. A. Mancini (Ed.), *Aging parents and adult children* (pp. 63-77). Lexington, MA: Lexington.

Maynard, M. (1988-1989). Health maintenance through stress management: A wellness approach for elderly clients. *Activities, Adaptation and Aging, 13,* 117-127.

McKay, V. C. (1993). Making connections: Narrative as the expression of continuity between generations of grandparents and grandchildren. In N. Coupland & J. F. Nussbaum (Eds.), *Discourse and lifespan identity* (pp. 173-184). Newbury Park, CA: Sage.

McKay, V. C., & Caverly, R. S. (1995). Relationships in later life: The nature of inter- and intragenerational ties among grandparents, grandchildren, and adult siblings. In J. F. Nussbaum & J. Coupland (Eds.), *Handbook of communication and aging research* (pp. 207-225). Mahwah, NJ: Lawrence Erlbaum.

Miner, S., & Uhlenberg, P. (1997). Intragenerational proximity and the social role of sibling neighbors after midlife. *Family Relations, 46,* 145-153.

Montepare, J. M., Steinberg, J., & Rosenberg, B. (1992). Characteristics of vocal communication between young adults and their parents and grandparents. *Communication Research, 19,* 479-492.

Montgomery, R. J., Gonyea, J. G., & Hooyman, N. R. (1985). Caregiving and the experience of subjective and objective burden. *Family Relations, 34,* 19-26.

Montgomery, R. J., & Kamo, Y. (1989). Parent care by sons and daughters. In J. A. Mancini (Ed.), *Aging parents and adult children* (pp. 213-230). Lexington, MA: Lexington.

Morgan, D. L., & Zhao, P. Z. (1993). The doctor-caregiver relationship: Managing the care of family members with Alzheimer's disease. *Qualitative Health Research, 2,* 133-164.

Neugarten, B. L., & Weinstein, K. K. (1964). The changing American grandparent. *Journal of Marriage and the Family, 26,* 199-206.

Newhouse, J. K., & McAuley, W. J. (1987). Use of informal in-home care by rural elders. *Family Relations, 36,* 456-460.

Ng S. H., Giles, H., & Moody, J. (1991). Information-seeking triggered by age. *International Journal of Aging and Human Development, 33,* 269-277.

Noddings, N. (1984). *Caring: A feminine approach to ethics and moral education.* Berkeley: University of California Press.

Noelker, L. S., & Townsend, A. L. (1987). Perceived caregiving effectiveness: The impact of parental impairment, community resources, and caregiver characteristics. In T. H. Brubaker (Ed.), *Aging, health, and family: Long-term care* (pp. 58-79). Newbury Park, CA: Sage.

Nussbaum, J. F., Hummert, M. L., Williams, A., & Harwood, J. (1996). Communication and older adults. In B. R. Burleson (Ed.), *Communication yearbook 19* (pp. 1-47). Thousand Oaks, CA: Sage.

Nussbaum, J. F., Thompson, T., & Robinson, J. D. (1988). *Communication and aging.* New York: Harper & Row.

O'Bryant, S. L. (1988). Sibling support and older widows' well-being. *Journal of Marriage and the Family, 50,* 173-183.

O'Connor, B. P., & Rigby, H. (1996). Perceptions of baby talk, frequency of receiving baby talk and self-esteem among community and nursing home residents. *Psychology and Aging, 11,* 147-154.

Olsen, S. F. (1993). Intergenerational transmission, generational differences, and parenting. *Dissertation Abstracts International, 54*(2-A), 696-697.

Osterkamp, L. (1996, May). *The effects of age and family relationship on judgments about troublesome behavior of a family member.* Paper presented at the Third International Conference on Communication, Aging, and Health, Kansas City, MO.

Ota, H., Giles, H., Harwood, J., Pierson, H. D., Gallois, C., Ng, S. H., Lim, T. S., Ryan, E. B., Maher, J., & Somera, L. (1996, November). *A neglected dimension of communication and aging: Filial piety across eight nations.* Paper presented at the annual meeting of the Speech Communication Association, San Diego, CA.

Palmore, E. (1980). The Facts on Aging Quiz: A review of the findings. *Gerontologist 20,* 669-672.

Parker, R., & Lew, R. (1996, November). *An exploration of reminiscence behavior in young and older adults.* Paper presented at the annual meeting of the Speech Communication Association, San Diego, CA.

Patterson, M. L. (1985). The evolution of a functional model of nonverbal exchange: A personal perspective. In R. L. Street, Jr., & J. N. Cappella (Eds.), *Sequence and pattern in communicative behavior* (pp. 190-205). Baltimore: Edward Arnold.

Pedrick-Cornell, C., & Gelles, R. J. (1982). Elder abuse: The status of current knowledge. *Family Relations, 31,* 457-469.

Petronio, S., & Kovach, S. S. (1996, November). *Tensions and issues between nursing staff, residents, and family members of institutionalized aged in Scotland.* Paper presented at the annual meeting of the Speech Communication Association, San Diego, CA.

Prusank, D. T. (1993). Contextualizing social control: An ethnomethodological analysis of parental accounts of discipline interactions. In N. Coupland & J. F. Nussbaum (Eds.), *Discourse and lifespan identity* (pp. 132-153). Newbury Park, CA: Sage.

Pyke, K. D., & Bengtson, V. L. (1996). Caring more or less: Individualistic and collectivist systems of family eldercare. *Journal of Marriage and the Family, 58,* 379-392.

Qualls, S. H. (1995). Clinical interventions with later-life families. In R. Blieszner & V. H. Bedford (Eds.), *Handbook of aging and the family* (pp. 474-487). Westport, CT: Greenwood.

Query, J. L., Jr., & Flint, L. J. (1996). The caregiving relationship. In N. Vanzetti & S. Duck (Eds.), *A lifetime of relationships* (pp. 455-483). Pacific Grove, CA: Brooks/Cole.

Quinn, W. H. (1983). Personal and family adjustment in later life. *Journal of Marriage and the Family, 45,* 57-73.

Quinn, W. H. (1989). Scripts, transaction, and transition in family relations over the life course. In J. A. Mancini (Ed.), *Aging parents and adult children* (pp. 45-62). Lexington, MA: Lexington.

Raphael, D., & Schlesinger, B. (1993). Caring for elderly parents and adult children living at home: Interactions of the sandwich generation family. *Social Work Research and Abstracts, 29,* 3-8.

Rawlins, W. K. (1995). Friendships in later life. In J. F. Nussbaum & J. Coupland (Eds.), *Handbook of communication and aging research* (pp. 227-257). Mahwah, NJ: Lawrence Erlbaum.

Rindfull, R. R., Liao, R. F., & Tsuya, N. O. (1992). Contact with parents in Japan: Effects on opinions toward gender and intergenerational roles. *Journal of Marriage and the Family, 54,* 812-822.

Roan, C. L., & Raley, R. K. (1996). Intergenerational coresidence and contact: A longitudinal analysis of adult children's response to their mother's widowhood. *Journal of Marriage and the Family, 58,* 708-717.

Rodin, J., & Langer, E. J. (1980). Aging labels: The decline of control and the fall of self-esteem. *Journal of Social Issues, 36,* 12-29.

Rook, K. S. (1995). Support, companionship, and control in older adults' social networks: Implications for well-being. In J. F. Nussbaum & J. Coupland (Eds.), *Handbook of communication and aging research* (pp. 437-463). Mahwah, NJ: Lawrence Erlbaum.

Rossi, A. S., & Rossi, P. H. (1990). *Of human bonding: Parent-child relations across the life course.* New York: Aldine de Gruyter.

Ryan, E. B., Boich, L. H., & Klemenchuk-Politeski, L. (1994, May). *Patronizing behavior in health care: Is ignoring the older, accented speaker excusable?* Paper presented at the International Conference on Communication, Aging and Health, Hamilton, ON.

Ryan, E. B., Bourhis, R. Y., & Knops, U. (1991). Evaluative perceptions of patronizing speech addressed to elders. *Psychology and Aging, 6,* 442-450.

Ryan, E. B., & Cole, R. L. (1990). Evaluative perceptions of interpersonal communication with elders. In H. Giles, N. Coupland, & J. M. Wiemann (Eds.), *Communication, health and the elderly* (pp. 172-190). Manchester: Manchester University Press.

Ryan, E. B., Giles, H., Bartolucci, G., & Henwood, K. (1986). Psycholinguistic and social psychological components of communication by and with the elderly. *Language and Communication, 6,* 1-24.

Ryan, E. B., Hummert, M. L., & Boich, L. H. (1995). Communication predicaments of aging: Patronizing behavior toward older adults. *Journal of Language and Social Psychology, 14,* 144-166.

Ryan, E. B., & Laurie, S. (1990). Evaluations of older and younger adult speakers: Influence of communication effectiveness and noise. *Psychology and Aging, 5,* 514-519.

Ryan, E. B., Meredith, S. D., & Shantz, G. B. (1994). Evaluative perceptions of patronizing speech addressed to institutionalized elders in contrasting conversational contexts. *Canadian Journal on Aging, 13,* 236-248.

Ryan, E. B., See, S. K., Meneer, W. B., & Trovato, D. (1992). Age-based perceptions of language performance among younger and older adults. *Communication Research, 19,* 423-443.

Sanders, G. F., & Pittman, J. F. (1987). Attitudes of youth toward known and general target elderly. *Journal of Applied Gerontology, 6,* 464-475.

Sanders, G. F., & Trystad, D. W. (1989). Stepgrandparents and grandparents: The view from young adults. *Family Relations, 38,* 7-75.

Sangree, W. H. (1992). Grandparenthood and modernization: The changing status of male and female elders in Tiriki, Kenya, and Irigwe, Nigeria. *Journal of Cross-Cultural Gerontology, 7,* 331-361.

Sarantakos, S. (1990). Anatomy of family care. *Australian Journal of Marriage and Family, 11,* 73-83.

Schlesinger, B. (1989). The "sandwich generation": Middle-aged families under stress. *Canada's Mental Health, 37*(3), 11-14.

Schmall, V. L., & Pratt, C. C. (1989). Family caregiving and aging: Strategies for support. *Journal of Psychotherapy and the Family, 5,* 71-87.

Schorr, A. (1980). *" . . . thy father and thy mother . . .": A look at filial responsibility and family policy* (DHHS Publication No. 13-11953). Washington, DC: Government Printing Office.

Schultz, C. L. (1994). Annotated bibliography. *Australian Journal of Marriage and Family, 15,* 106-120.

Seccombe, K., Ryan, R., & Austin, C. D. (1987). Care planning: Case manager's assessment of elders' welfare and caregivers capacity. *Family Relations, 36,* 171-175.

Shanas, E. (1979). Social myth as hypothesis: The case of the family relations of old people. *Gerontologist, 19,* 3-9.

Sheehan, C. L., & Dwyer, J. W. (1989). Parent-child exchanges in the middle years: Attachment and autonomy in the transition to adulthood. In J. A. Mancini (Ed.), *Aging parents and adult children* (pp. 99-116). Lexington, MA: Lexington.

Sheehan, N. W., & Nuttall, P. (1988). Conflict, emotion, and personal strain among family caregivers. *Family Relations, 37,* 92-98.

Shulman, M. D., & Mandel, E. (1988). Communication training of relatives and friends of institutionalized elderly persons. *Gerontologist, 28,* 797-799.

Sillars, A. L. (1995). Communication and family culture. In M. A. Fitzpatrick & A. L. Vangelisti (Eds.), *Explaining family interactions* (pp. 375-399). Thousand Oaks, CA: Sage.

Sillars, A. L., & Zietlow, P. H. (1993). Investigations of marital communication and lifespan development. In N. Coupland & J. F. Nussbaum (Eds.), *Discourse and lifespan identity* (pp. 237-261). Newbury Park, CA: Sage.

Silverstein, M., Parrott, T. M., & Bengtson, V. L. (1995). Factors that predispose middle-aged sons and daughters to provide social support to older parents. *Journal of Marriage and the Family, 57,* 465-475.

Smith, M. J., Reinheimer, R. E., & Gabbard-Alley, A. (1981). Crowding, task performance, and communicative interaction in youth and old age. *Human Communication Research, 7,* 259-272.

Snyder, M., & Miene, P. K. (1994). Stereotyping of the elderly: A functional approach. *British Journal of Social Psychology, 33,* 63-68.

Steinmetz, S. K. (1988). *Duty bound: Elder abuse and family care.* Newbury Park, CA: Sage.

Steward, M. A., & Ryan, E. B. (1982). Attitudes toward young and older adult speakers: Effects of varying speech rate. *Journal of Language and Social Psychology, 1,* 91-110.

Stoller, E. P. (1985). Exchange patterns in the informal support networks of the elderly: The impact of reciprocity on morale. *Journal of Marriage and the Family, 47,* 335-342.

Strom, R., Collinsworth, P., Strom, S., & Griswold, D. (1993). Strengths and needs of black grandparents. *International Journal of Aging and Human Development, 36,* 255-268.

Strom, R., & Strom, S. (1992). Grandparents and intergenerational relationships. *Educational Gerontology, 18,* 607-624.

Strom, R., & Strom, S. (1993a). Grandparent development and influence. *Journal of Gerontological Social Work, 20,* 3-16.

Strom, R., & Strom, S. (1993b). Grandparents raising grandchildren: Goals and support groups. *Educational Gerontology, 19,* 705-715.

Suitor, J. J., & Pillemer, K. (1988). Explaining intergenerational conflict when adult children and elderly parents live together. *Journal of Marriage and the Family, 50,* 1037-1047.

Suitor, J. J., Pillemer, K., Keeton, S., & Robison, J. (1995). Aged parents and aging children: Determinants of relationship quality. In R. Blieszner & V. H. Bedford (Eds.), *Handbook of aging and the family* (pp. 223-242). Westport, CT: Greenwood.

Tajfel, H., & Turner, J. C. (1979). An integrative theory of intergroup conflict. In W. G. Austin & S. Worchel (Eds.), *The social psychology of intergroup relations* (pp. 33-53). Monterey, CA: Brooks/Cole.

Tajfel, H., & Turner, J. C. (1986). The social identity theory of intergroup relations. In S. Worchel & W. G. Austin (Eds.), *Psychology of intergroup relations* (pp. 7-24). Chicago: Nelson-Hall.

Taylor, R. J. (1987). Receipt of support from family among black Americans: Demographic and familial differences. *Journal of Marriage and the Family, 48,* 67-77.

Taylor, R. J., & Chatters, L. M. (1991). Extended family networks of older black adults. *Journal of Gerontology, 46,* 210-217.

Thompson, L. (1989). Contextual and relational morality: Intergenerational responsibility in later life. In J. A. Mancini (Ed.), *Aging parents and adult children* (pp. 259-282). Lexington, MA: Lexington.

Tinsley, B. R., & Parke, R. D. (1984). Grandparents as support and socializing agents. In M. Lewis (Ed.), *Beyond the dyad* (pp. 161-194). New York: Plenum.

Travis, S. S. (1995). Families and formal networks. In R. Blieszner & V. H. Bedford (Eds.), *Handbook of aging and the family* (pp. 459-473). Westport, CT: Greenwood.

Umberson, D. (1987). Family status and health behaviors: Social control as a dimension of social integration. *Journal of Health and Social Behavior, 28,* 306-319.

Walker, A. J., & Allen, K. R. (1991). Relationships between caregiving daughters and their elderly mothers. *Gerontologist, 31,* 389-396.

Walker, A. J., Pratt, C. C., Shin, H. Y., & Jones, L. L. (1989). Why daughters care: Perspectives of mothers and daughters in a caregiving situation. In J. A. Mancini (Ed.), *Aging parents and adult children* (pp. 199-212). Lexington, MA: Lexington.

Wearing, B. M., & Wearing, C. G. (1996). Women breaking out: Changing discourses on grandmotherhood? *Journal of Family Studies, 2,* 165-177.

Webb, L. (1985). Common topics of conversation between young adults and their grandparents. *Communication Research Reports, 2,* 156-163.

Weinberger, L. E., & Millham, J. (1975). A multi-dimensional, multiple method analysis of attitudes toward the elderly. *Journal of Gerontology, 30,* 343-348.

Williams, A., & Giles, H. (1996). Intergenerational conversations: Young adults' retrospective accounts. *Human Communication Research, 23,* 220-250.

Wood, V. (1982). Grandparenthood: An ambiguous role. *Generations, 22,* 67-71.

Wood, V., & Robertson, J. F. (1978). Friendship and kinship interaction: Differential effect on the morale of the elderly. *Journal of Marriage and the Family, 40,* 367-375.

Yankelovich, D. (1981). *New rules: Searching for self-fulfillment in a world turned upside down.* New York: Random House.

Zal, H. M. (1992). *The sandwich generation: Caught between growing children and aging parents.* New York: Insight/Plenum.

Zweibel, N., & Lydens, L. A. (1990). Incongruent perceptions of older adult/caregiver dyads. *Family Relations, 39,* 63-67.

CHAPTER CONTENTS

11 Adult Friendship: Examples of Intercultural Patterns

ELISABETH GAREIS
Baruch College, City University of New York

Intercultural friendship provides one of the main avenues for meaningful interpersonal contact and is considered a catalyst for successful sojourn experiences and positive attitudes toward the host culture. Yet one of the most common complaints of foreign sojourners in the United States is the lack of friendship with Americans. This chapter examines the unique challenges of intercultural friendship formation by discussing definitional issues, highlighting prominent theoretical frameworks for research in intercultural relationship development, and exploring the factors instrumental in intercultural friendship formation, including culture, personality, self-esteem, friendship elements, expectations, adjustment stage, communicative competence, demographic variables, proximity, host-culture elements, and chemistry. The focus is on foreign students on U.S. campuses. Examples from their experiences are supplied, culture-specific patterns are described, and international perceptions of U.S. friendship patterns are discussed.

B E it in the course of travel, studies, business, or immigration, prolonged contact between people from different cultures is becoming increasingly common. Many kinds of relationships ensue, ranging from superficial contact to the formation of close friendships. Although there are plenty of examples of more or less peaceful coexistence and loose-knit associations across cultures, making close friends across cultures poses more of a challenge, owing to the many dimensions of intercultural friendship not existent in intracultural friendship.

In this literature review, I explore these dimensions by providing definitional information, highlighting theoretical approaches to intercultural relationship research, examining the factors influencing intercultural friendship formation, and suggesting directions for future research. The focus is on the experiences of foreign students in the United States, who constitute one of

Correspondence and requests for reprints: Elisabeth Gareis, Department of Speech, Baruch College, City University of New York, New York, NY 10010; e-mail address: egareis@baruch.cuny.edu

Communication Yearbook 22, pp. 431-468

the most researched sojourner groups in the field of intercultural communication and represent a large number of cultures.

DEFINITION OF FRIENDSHIP

Friendship studies usually attempt to define the term *friend*. Definitions often contain three tiers: a reference to the degree of formalization of kinship and friendship ties, a delineation of relationship descriptors, and a listing of the functions and values of friendship.

Formalization

Most studies make mention of the fact that friendship in the United States is not formalized. In many other societies, friendship carries with it social rituals, public ceremonies, behavioral norms, and well-developed sets of rights and obligations. The Bangwa of the Cameroon, for example, have a custom analogous to arranged marriage in which parents give their child a best friend, and the friends assume lifelong commitments and obligations to each other (Rubin, 1985).

Even if friendship is not institutionalized, as in the above example, many cultures feature elements of formalization that are absent from American friendship. In Germany, for instance, a ceremony called *Brüderschafttrinken* demarcates the threshold between acquaintanceship and close friendship. This ceremony requires that two people, each holding a class of beer, wine, or liquor, entwine arms and then drink from their glasses, and possibly kiss each other on the cheeks or mouth (Rubin, 1985). The ceremony precedes the change from the formal form of address, *Sie,* to the familiar *Du* and thus helps the interactants change their relationship from a public to a private one.

In the United States, only kinship has an institutional form. Friendship is voluntaristic; there are no friendship rituals or ceremonies, and existing behavioral norms, rights, and obligations are ambiguous and merely implied (Bell, 1981).

Relationship Descriptors

A factor very much connected to the ambiguity accompanying the lack of formalization is the absence of linguistic forms to delineate clearly different kinds of relationships. Thus in the United States the term *friend* is used to describe a variety of relationships, ranging from short-term, superficial ones to ones that are long-standing and deeply committed (Matthews, 1986). For the exacting language user, terms such as *acquaintance, casual friend, close friend,* and *best friend* offer the promise of a differentiation; however, even they have no clear demarcation, as is illustrated by Merriam-Webster's (1997) equivocal definition of an acquaintance as "a person whom one knows but who is not a particularly close friend," with the highly subjective term *close friend* not defined in the dictionary. This lack of definitive criteria and the above-mentioned absence of formalization make it very difficult to differentiate among the possible terms and determine the existence of friendship (Matthews, 1986). It is under this premise that Rubin (1985) states:

> Without institutional form, without a clearly defined set of norms for behavior or an agreed-upon set of reciprocal rights and obligation, without even a language that makes distinctions between the different kinds of relationships to which we apply the word, there can be no widely shared agreement about what is a friend. Thus it is that one person will claim as a friend someone who doesn't reciprocate; that another who has been called a good friend says, when I ask him about his relationship, "Oh, yeah, John, we worked together a year or so ago. Haven't seen him since." (p. 8)

Despite the lack of established definitions, most studies focus on the description of what seems to correlate with best and close friendships, disregarding more casual relationships. One criterion for differentiation lies in numbers. Thus, when asked how many friends—meaning casual friends—they have, people respond with numbers as high as 30 to 50 (Matthews, 1986). Close friendships, on the other hand, are fairly consistently limited to numbers between 3 and 7 (Pogrebin, 1987), and best friendship should by definition include only a single person. To draw more descriptive lines separating these three dimensions, we might utilize Du Bois's (1974) interpretation of exclusive, close, and casual friendships. Thus exclusive friendships are marked by a dyadic character, inclusive intimacy (i.e., confidences and responsibilities), and assumed permanence; close friendships occur in multiple dyads with selective intimacy and hoped-for durability; and casual friendships are polyadic, with incidental intimacy and an unstressed attitude toward durability.

Although average numbers of close friendships may be similar across cultures (limits are probably set by the time and effort it takes to maintain close relationships), definitional differences often cause misunderstandings detrimental to friendship formation. One of the most basic observations concerning American and German friendship patterns, for example, is the linguistic relationship between the English word *friend* and the German equivalent *Freund*. The words look alike, but the German term has a narrower connotation, referring to close friends exclusively. This difference presents a stumbling block that causes much confusion and limitless debate. Thus many German sojourners—oblivious to the fact that the correct translation of *Freund* would be *close friend* and not simply *friend*—assert that being an

American's friend does not necessarily mean much and that the concept of American friendship, in general, is inflated (Gareis, 1995).

Although the resemblance of the words *friend* and *Freund* makes mistranslations between English and German more likely, similar differences in semantic width exist in other languages. To mention only a couple of examples, Swedish uses the term *van* for close friends and *bekant* for casual friends and acquaintances, and Japanese differentiates among *shin-yuu* (close friends), *tomo* (friends, in general), and *shiriai* (acquaintances). Foreign students whose native languages feature separate terms for close friends as opposed to casual friends or acquaintances are susceptible to incorrect translations. It therefore comes as no surprise that they often evaluate American friendships as shallow and devoid of intimacy. Although this judgment may be based on more than linguistic generalizations, definitional differences play an unfortunate role in prompting misunderstandings and subsequent stereotyping.

Functions and Values

Despite the definition problems, research findings widely agree on the functions and values of friendship. Intracultural studies list proximity, homophily, reciprocal liking, and self-disclosure as necessary elements for friendship formation (Fehr, 1996; Pogrebin, 1987; Rawlins, 1992; Reohr, 1991). Of these elements, homophily appears to be the single most important. It encompasses similarities among persons with regard to age, appearance, gender, race, marital status, education, intelligence, residence, social class, economic situation, social status, personality traits, interests, opinions, attitudes, and values (Bell, 1981; Dodd, 1998; Hammer, 1989; H. J. Kim, 1991; Lee & Boster, 1991; Matthews, 1986; Paige, 1983; Strom, 1988).

Respondents in U.S. friendship studies are also fairly unanimous concerning the traits to be valued in a friend. The qualities most frequently mentioned are trust, honesty, and loyalty, followed by mutuality, generosity, warmth, supportiveness, and acceptance (Bell, 1981; Matthews, 1986; Parlee, 1979; Pogrebin, 1987; Rubin, 1985).

Intercultural studies on friendship functions and values are rare, but those that have been conducted point to similarities across cultures. Thus Argyle and Henderson (1984), in a study involving participants from Great Britain, Italy, Hong Kong, and Japan, found a set of friendship rules that were endorsed in all four locales. These rules include sharing news of success, showing emotional support, volunteering help in time of need, striving to make the other person happy while in each other's company, trusting and confiding in each other, and standing up for the other person in his or her absence. Less universal, but still significant, are repaying debts and favors, being tolerant of other friends, not nagging, not criticizing in public, avoiding jealousy or criticism of other relationships, and respecting privacy. German,

Indian, and Taiwanese students have shown similar agreement; study participants tended to focus on common interests or values and trustworthiness in sharing confidences when describing their ideal friend (Gareis, 1995).

Even when compared to antiquity, friendship functions and values remain fairly constant. Thus Aristotle (1953) differentiates between perfect friendships in which friends "desire the good of one another" (p. 233) and pleasant or useful friendships in which "the friend is not loved for being what he is in himself but as the source, perhaps of some pleasure, perhaps of some advantage" (p. 232). Thus if the purpose of the friendship is to gain status and power or even just pleasure, the friendship cannot be considered good. Good friendship automatically brings with it both pleasant and useful values, but it is not based on them (Paine, 1974). Pogrebin (1987) mirrors this distinction in what she calls communal theory and exchange theory. Communal theory says that the friend him- or herself is the reward and that real friends give to make each other happy, not to get something back. Exchange theory, on the other hand, stipulates that friendships require an exchange of resources and exist only as long as equal benefits can be derived; these benefits may include love but also comprise status, goods, money, and information. In a parallel notion, Du Bois (1974) uses the terms *expressive* and *instrumental* to differentiate between friends of virtue and friends of pleasure or utility. Both Du Bois (1974) and Cohen (1961) then employ these concepts to claim that with increasing materialism, intimacy decreases and friendships slide on the continuum from exclusive to close to casual and purely expedient, thus deviating further and further from Aristotle's prototype of the perfect friendship.

The general agreement on the basic functions and values of friendship can be deceiving and can lead to minimization of differences. A closer look at each element reveals that although cultures may agree on main characteristics of close friendship, the importance and manifestations of each trait may differ greatly. When comparing friendship in Australia and Brazil, for example, Morse (1983) found that Brazilians had greater expectations with respect to liking and sharing confidences than did Australians. Likewise, Höllinger and Haller (1990) report that Australians fall behind Americans when it comes to frequency of contact. In addition to the degree of importance, the specific incarnation of traits may vary across cultures. Male friends in India, for example, are allowed to show affection through more touching behavior (e.g., holding hands) than are male friends in the United States (Berman, Murphy-Berman, & Pachauri, 1988; Brown, 1986; Gareis, 1995; Roland, 1986). And although self-disclosure is a characteristic of friendship around the globe, in some cultures (such as Japan) the amount of self-disclosure as well as its rate is more modest than in the United States (Barnlund, 1989). General commonalities in friendship functions and values should therefore be regarded with caution and examined with respect to their culture-specific characteristics.

THEORETICAL APPROACHES
TO INTERCULTURAL
RELATIONSHIP RESEARCH

To study the process of intra- and intercultural communication, several theoretical frameworks have been developed. Approaches that apply to relationship research in general and friendship research in specific include uncertainty and anxiety reduction theory, social penetration theory, communication competence theory, and the self-other construal perspective.

Uncertainty and
Anxiety Reduction Theory

Uncertainty reduction theory stresses that initial interactions are marked by ambiguity (Berger, 1979; Berger & Calabrese, 1975; Gudykunst, 1995). This ambiguity is influenced by such factors as the amount of communication taking place, nonverbal affiliative expressiveness, information seeking, intimacy of communication content, reciprocity, similarity, and liking (Berger & Calabrese, 1975). Although uncertainty exists in both intra- and intercultural relationship formation, interactants in intercultural situations are usually more dissimilar with respect to cultural elements and therefore less able to predict and explain the words and actions of their counterparts. In addition, second-language competence and linguistic differences in uncertainty reduction strategies may represent obstacles to effective intercultural communication (Gudykunst, 1985; Gudykunst, Sodetani, & Sonoda, 1987).

A similar theory focuses on anxiety reduction (Gao & Gudykunst, 1990; Gudykunst, 1995; Witte, 1993). In addition to reducing uncertainty, interactants need to control anxiety to form satisfactory relationships across cultures. The goal is to achieve optimal levels of anxiety. Whereas too little anxiety may convey a noncaring and uninterested attitude, too much anxiety prevents interactants from focusing on the other person.

Both the uncertainty and the anxiety reduction approaches promote the gathering of information (Gudykunst & Hammer, 1988). The type of information sought may differ from culture to culture, however. Whereas members of individualist cultures, for example, tend to seek person-based information, members of collectivist cultures focus on group-based information (Gudykunst & Nishida, 1986). Encounters between interactants unaware of this distinction may therefore be somewhat confusing or frustrating.

Uncertainty and anxiety reduction theory indicates that intercultural interactants are more likely to encounter difficulties than are intracultural interactants, especially in the beginning stages of friendship formation. To reduce uncertainty and anxiety during intercultural friendship initiation, more openness and sustained interest may be required than in intracultural friendship formation.

Social Penetration Theory

Social penetration theory posits that interpersonal relationships gradually progress from outer to central areas of the interactants' personalities (Altman & Taylor, 1973). Through self-disclosure, the amount as well as the depth of exchange is increased until intimate personality layers are reached. Four stages of relationship development can be observed: an orientation stage at the very beginning of the relationship, the exploratory affective exchange at the acquaintanceship level, the affective exchange at the initial stage of friendship, and the stable exchange characteristic of established friendships.

Social penetration theory emphasizes reciprocity in self-disclosure. This mutual increase in self-disclosure can occur in a linear fashion or cyclically, with alternating periods of openness and restraint (Altman, Vinsel, & Brown, 1981; VanLear, 1987). Because self-disclosure strategies differ across cultures and reciprocity in conversation is influenced by linguistic competence, social penetration is considered more difficult interculturally than intraculturally (VanLear, 1987). If intercultural interactants have differing expectations concerning the timing and content of self-disclosure, for example, or are unable to interpret important nuances correctly due to linguistic difficulties, reciprocity may not occur at sensitive junctions, and the development of friendship may be jeopardized.

Communication Competence Theory

Communication competence can be defined as a combination of cognitive, affective, and behavioral components (Collier, 1988; Gudykunst & Kim, 1992; Kim, 1988; Spitzberg & Cupach, 1984). In intercultural interactions, cognitive competence involves the knowledge of language, nonverbal behaviors, and communication rules of the host culture. The affective dimension includes attitudes, motivation, empathy, and acknowledgment of cultural differences. Finally, behavioral competence pertains to the application of cognitive and affective qualities in social interaction with host nationals.

Although sojourners are expected to familiarize themselves with the host culture's communication norms and accommodate to its members (Gallois, Franklyn-Stokes, Giles, & Coupland, 1988), literature in second-language acquisition stresses that the effectiveness of intercultural interactions is also influenced by the host nationals' ability to adapt their speech behavior to nonnative speakers (de Heredia, 1986; Gass & Varonis, 1985; Long, 1983).

Another element affecting at least the perception of communication of sojourners as well as host nationals is the predisposition toward talking, or willingness to communicate (McCroskey & Richmond, 1990). This predisposition differs among individuals and across cultures and can thus lead to frustration and stereotyping in intercultural encounters with mismatched partners.

Communication competence theory applies to friendship formation in all of the above-mentioned areas: Many sojourners are nonnative speakers and are still developing communication competence in the target language and culture; host nationals are frequently unskilled in adapting their speech behavior to nonnative speakers; and differences in the amount and importance of talking often cause misperceptions concerning interest and intent of interactants. Potential friends have to overcome these obstacles to move from the initiation phase of friendship to the more stable maintenance stage.

Self-Other Construal Perspective

Self-other construal theory concerns self-perceptions and their relationship to perceptions of self by others (Adams-Webber, 1985; Kelly, 1955). It has been found, for example, that a person's self-ratings are not always congruent with others' ratings of him or her (Schrauger & Schoeneman, 1979). This dichotomy results from the self's attribution of behavior causality to external situations as opposed to the other's focus on internal traits of the self (Funder, 1980; Furnham, Jaspars, & Fincham, 1983; Jones & Nisbett, 1971).

Intercultural contexts complicate the self-other construal perspective. For one, concepts of self and other differ across cultures. Whereas the independence of self and self-actualization are important goals in individualist cultures, the self is interdependent and defined in relation to others in collectivist cultures (Gao, 1996; Gudykunst & Kim, 1992; Markus & Kitayama, 1991; Page & Berkow, 1991). As a consequence, self-concept plays a less significant role in the collectivist relationship formation process (Klopf, 1987).

Independent of individualist or collectivist backgrounds, self-perception issues also arise during sojourn experiences. Zaharna (1980), for example, describes as self-shock the process in which sojourners are confronted by inconsistent, conflicting self-images in the host country. This clash is caused by unexpected negative responses of hosts to behaviors and traits considered desirable in the sojourner's home culture. The challenge for the sojourner is to maintain consistency and sameness of self in the face of the radical behavior changes accompanying adjustment.

Individuals experiencing confusion due to cultural differences in self-perception or self-shock are in a state of instability that may impede friendship formation. With ratings of self and others more complicated in inter- than in intracultural settings, sojourners may find it difficult to attract appropriate friends among host nationals and determine their compatibility.

INTERCULTURAL FRIENDSHIP:
THE CASE OF FOREIGN STUDENTS
ON U.S. CAMPUSES

The area of intercultural contact with possibly the most significant impact on the future of international relations is that of the interaction of foreign and native students on the world's university campuses. Because many of these individuals may be destined to fill influential positions and make decisions of far-reaching import later in their lives, campus relationships may prove to be extremely important for international relations.

Unfortunately, close intercultural relationships in general and the intercultural friendship experiences of foreign students in particular have not been given due attention until recently. Hull (1978) states that when he asked the foreign student respondents in a study in the United States for suggestions on how to increase meaningful contacts with Americans, they could not come up with any that had not been "discussed in the literature and tried again and again in U.S. higher education" (p. 185). The measures to which Hull refers (integrated housing, international clubs, international nights, and the like) provide commendable opportunities for contact but ultimately leave the interacting individuals on their own and helpless as to how to make the contact meaningful and intimate. In many institutions, these measures continue to be the sole attempts at improving intercultural relations, and very little has been done to examine their effectiveness and learn about the actual friendship networks and preferences of foreign students (Furnham & Alibhai, 1985).

Yet foreign student satisfaction and well-being in the United States are integrally tied to host-country interaction in general and the development of close friendships with Americans in specific (Locke, 1988; Rohrlich & Martin, 1991; Searle & Ward, 1990). Contacts with host nationals are also of immense importance for facilitating overall adjustment and are said to be the most influential factor in changing international images (Dziegielewska, 1988; Furnham & Alibhai, 1985; Yum, 1988). As Hull (1978) notes, however, contact per se does not result in positive attitudes. Research findings agree that one of the conditions for positive attitudinal change following intergroup contact is intimate rather than casual contact (Gudykunst, 1979; Yum, 1988). Incidentally, the phenomenon of friendship satisfies not only this but also most other conditions posited for the reduction of stereotypes and ethnocentric attitudes in intergroup contact; that is, cooperation, equal status and competence, value similarity, positive outcomes, future interaction, individuation of interactants, voluntariness, variety of contexts, equal number of interactants, and favorable climate (Stephan & Stephan, 1985).

Even though intercultural friendship has immense potential for the improvement of international relations, the reality on U.S. campuses is fraught with problems. Thus the common thread running through the respective research literature is foreign student disappointment with the lack of American friends (Furnham & Alibhai, 1985; Hull, 1978; Trice & Elliott, 1993). Likewise, most manuals for foreign student advisers, handbooks for foreign students, and general-interest books for business personnel, immigrants, and tourists warn sojourners about American friendship patterns (Althen, 1988; Lanier, 1996; Stewart & Bennett, 1991; University of Iowa, 1991). These sources describe Americans as friendly and warm during initial contact, but note that close friendships between sojourners and Americans are extremely rare; if they do happen, they are usually short-lived, less intense, and center on activities and academic or professional, rather than intimate, concerns (Klein, Alexander, Miller, Haack, & Bushnell, 1986).

In attempting to explain American friendship patterns, some publications elaborate on their cautionary descriptions with details or examples. Thus it is frequently mentioned that Americans have difficulty forming close friendships in general, not just across cultures (Althen, 1988; Du Bois, 1956; Stewart & Bennett, 1991). In addition, it is asserted that Americans tend to keep personal feelings and thoughts to themselves; that when socializing, they prefer doing activities together rather than just sitting and talking (Althen, 1988); and that they frequently compartmentalize their friends into friends at work, friends at school, tennis friends, and so on (University of Iowa, 1991). Another characteristic noted is that Americans avoid commitment and obligation (Stewart & Bennett, 1991). Thus foreigners often feel they cannot call on Americans freely or ask them for help. Americans may also be very hospitable and easily invite foreigners into their homes, but no strings are attached to this gesture, which is a fact that baffles visitors who either think they have to reciprocate or see such an invitation as the sign of a budding close friendship (Lanier, 1996).

To what extent this mosaic represents the status quo of American friendship patterns is open to question. Many of the details remind one of idiosyncratic, nongeneralizable aspects of American friendship. Thus low self-disclosure, a preference for activities over talking, and compartmentalization of friends have been ascribed more to male than to female friendship styles (Bell, 1981; Jones, Bloys, & Wood, 1990; Mitchell, 1986; Pogrebin, 1987; Rubin, 1985).

Likewise, lack of commitment and permanence are characteristic of some friendship styles but not others. Thus Matthews (1986), in a study using oral biographies of senior citizens and focusing on friendship patterns emerging over the life course, has distinguished three personality types: independent, discerning, and acquisitive. Matthews's respondents who were grouped in the independent category did not acknowledge ever having had close friends. Their contacts are friendly relations rather than friendships. Because independents focus on the present, they do not feel the necessity of a commitment for maintaining those relations after separation or life turnings. Yet independents are not isolated or unhappy; they usually know many people, but these others appear more like an undifferentiated mass than like individuals with whom close ties are to be established. Respondents classified as discerning, on the other hand, made clear distinctions between friends and friendly relations. For people in this category, close friendships are very important and are usually maintained throughout life. Discerning individuals do not have many of these close friends, and with a focus on the past, they are likely to stand alone in old age because as these few friends die away, they are not replenished. By contrast, acquisitive individuals collect a variety of friendships throughout life. Some of these friendships are long-term, some short-term, but they all are close and committed, at least for the duration of geographic proximity. In addition to having past and current friends, acquisitive people look to the future as well and make a conscious effort to add new friends, usually at turning points in life. Levels of commitment and duration may thus be determined more through personal friendship style than through culture-specific patterns. It may be the case that independent and acquisitive personalities are more prevalent in the United States than elsewhere, resulting in the above-mentioned negative evaluations made by sojourners; however, respective research does not exist at the moment to throw light on this possibility.

Of all the issues listed in the intercultural literature for foreign students, the biggest problem seems to be that initial displays of friendliness or gestures such as invitations to an American's home are often misinterpreted as signaling the desire for a close friendship, and many foreigners feel betrayed when this perceived promise is not fulfilled (Paige, 1983). A similar situation of disappointment arises when friendships are actually formed but then quickly fade as the American party moves or undergoes other life changes. It comes as no surprise that frustrated foreigners often conclude that American relationships are superficial in nature (Althen, 1988).

In an attempt to aid foreign visitors' understanding of American friendship patterns, intercultural publications often supply rationales for points of contention. Du Bois (1956), for instance, observes that at least some constituents of friendship are culturally determined and mentions by way of example that U.S. friendships are marked by high spread, low obligation, low duration, and high trust; in other words, American friendships tend to be widespread and trusting, but lacking in a sense of obligation and permanence. She cautions Americans about entering relationships with persons from high-obligation and high-duration cultures because it is in such relationships that American openness and friendliness are often interpreted as promises of closer involvement, and a sense of disappointment and failure ensues on the part of the foreigners when this promise is not realized. To exemplify the issue, Kalberg (1987) points out that German sojourners often miss the bond of inner obligation within groups common in their home culture. Germans are further confused by weak in-group/out-group boundaries in the United States, which allow fast and relatively uncomplicated transitions from one to the other. As a result, American personal relationships tend to appear superficial and devoid of substance to Germans sojourners who are unfamiliar with these cultural differences.

From another angle, Du Bois (1956) warns that the proverbial American friendliness might "appear to foreigners as a tactless intrusion into cherished areas reserved for close relationships" (p. 62) and is, therefore, doubly problematic. Du Bois also notes that the role of interpersonal relations in a culture in general needs to be analyzed. In the United States, for example, there is more emphasis on material well-being than on relationships, and Americans place a lower value on interpersonal relations in general than do people in some other cultures. On a narrower scale, we must also give attention to the degree of importance assigned to friendships within the hierarchy of these interpersonal relations and take into account cultural or individual discrepancies to avoid frustrating experiences.

Besides these general pointers, publications also supply specific reasons based on U.S. history and national traits in an attempt to analyze American idiosyncrasies. Thus the high spread and compartmentalization of friendships is explained by Stewart and Bennett (1991) as a function of the wish to be popular; they purport that popularity and friendship are "matters of social success and not the conditions for establishing deep relationships" (p. 108). Stewart and Bennett also supply a reason for the perceived unavailability or inconvenienced reaction of Americans when it comes to assisting others. They state that Americans in need of help, support, or solace frequently search for professional help rather than make demands on friends. The most prominent explanation for the fear of close involvement and the lack of sense of commitment and obligation given in the literature, however, is the American ideal of independence and self-reliance. Research has shown that, when asked about values, Americans rank freedom first, well ahead of friendship (Connecticut Mutual Life Report on American Values in the '80s, cited in Pogrebin, 1987), an attitude leading to understandable caution with people who do want to get closely involved (Althen, 1988). Another reason for the fear of involvement and simultaneously for the perceived short duration of American friendships can be found in American mobility patterns. Having grown up in families that might have changed their residence every few years, many Americans either have not had sufficient practice in forming close friendships or have developed self-protective habits of keeping relationships casual in order not to get hurt upon the repeated separations (Bell, 1981). When turnings in adult life are also accompanied by frequent moving, chances for the survival of friendships become slim. American historic mobility patterns do not match ideals of commitment, responsibility, obligation, and permanence; the result is that people have learned to develop instant intimacy but also to let go quickly and with ease (Rubin, 1985).

Whatever the explanations, the fact remains that especially during the first year of a sojourn, contacts of foreign students with Americans are limited beyond modest expectations, and these students often feel insecure, self-conscious, lonely, and powerless (Owie, 1982; Klein et al., 1986). This social alienation from the host country can have different effects: It can lead to physical isolation and a retreat into a private world; it can cause an immersion into work and studies; or it can foster a banding together with fellow nationals or students from other countries (Owie, 1982; Klein et al., 1986; Strom, 1988; Winter, 1986). Thus Bochner, McLeod, and Lin (1977) found that of the three social networks of foreign students, the primary one is monocultural and functions as an outlet for ethnic and cultural values among conationals. It is followed by a secondary network with host nationals that serves mainly instrumental purposes, such as academic and professional assistance. The tertiary, much less salient, network consists of other internationals and fulfills recreational needs. Whereas interaction with fellow nationals can alleviate some adjustment stress and consequently be of vital importance to sojourners (Bochner et al., 1977), a prolonged and exclusive reliance on home-country support can have distinct disadvantages. Thus it has been shown that sojourner satisfaction increases the more close friends are from the host country and the fewer close friends are from the home country (Locke, 1988). Some foreign students point out that fellow nationals are arbitrarily thrown together and that the pool of truly suitable friends is therefore limited; they also remark that conational friendships result in too many obligations (parties, help, and so on) and often focus on gossip about other people's sojourn experiences and degrees of undesirable assimilation (Tjioe, 1972). In addition, foreign student isolation from host-country interactions can create a vicious circle of impeded English improvement and perpetual contact difficulties (Bochner, Hutnik, & Furnham, 1985).

FACTORS INFLUENCING INTERCULTURAL
FRIENDSHIP FORMATION

Presupposing this mostly undesirable status quo and the absence of formal rules for establishing and maintaining intercultural friendships (Argyle & Henderson, 1984), the question arises of what exactly influences intercultural friendship formation. Concerning the specific case of foreign students in the United States, 11 key factors can be identified: culture, personality, self-esteem, friendship elements, expectations, adjustment stage, communicative competence, demographic variables, proximity, U.S. elements, and what we may call chemistry.

The first five variables (culture, personality, self-esteem, friendship elements, and expectations) focus on the predisposition of the individual sojourner. Adjustment stage and communicative competence constitute the major factors present in the testing ground of the actual sojourn. Demographic variables and proximity might be labeled auxiliary and add minor influences.

Whereas the factors just listed are all to some extent influenceable and changeable by the sojourners, the last two (U.S. elements and chemistry) are givens and are largely out of their control.

Culture

The first of the key factors is culture. Culture, of course, is a vast concept. Even if one can delineate cultural versus political boundaries and focus on deep as opposed to formal components of culture, myriad aspects can be considered. These include basic assumptions and value systems; the relationship between humans and nature; social structure; sex roles; sources of support; the importance of status; the locus of control; conflict resolution; mobility; the concepts of achievement, work, and play; uncertainty avoidance; past, present, and future orientation; thought patterns; and verbal communication styles and nonverbal communication aspects (kinesics, proxemics, and haptics). Aspects of deep culture also include dichotomies such as individualism versus collectivism, doing versus being, the importance of material possessions versus interpersonal relationships, monochronic time versus polychronic time, and many more. Cultures can differ along all of these criteria and influence intercultural friendship formation, even though some may play more prominent roles than others.

Individualism Versus Collectivism

Invariably, the distinction between individualist and collectivist outlooks is mentioned as a major variable in intercultural interaction. In general, individualism stresses "individual initiative, action, and interests" (Merriam-Webster, 1997). Collectivism, on the other hand, is marked by an emphasis on social relationships and can be defined as a concept in which values, rights, and duties originate in the group, not the individual (Hofstede, 1980; Triandis, 1988; Verma, 1985; Yum, 1997). In addition to this basic characterization, the terms serve as an umbrella for a whole host of differences, including conflicting levels of obligation, self- versus other-orientation, verbal versus nonverbal communication prevalence, and low versus high context (i.e., meaning explicit in messages versus internalized meaning or meaning embedded in settings).

If two potential interactants are fairly typical representatives of individualist and collectivist cultures, these differences have to be dealt with and can pose significant obstacles in the development of the friendship. To list just a few examples, most people's goals and attitudes in individualist cultures overlap only slightly with the goals and attitudes of their various in-groups. By contrast, in-groups in collectivist societies not only are fewer in number and less formed by free choice but also provide a much greater match in outlook and dominate all aspects of people's lives (Triandis, 1988; Verma, 1985). Perhaps as a consequence, persons from individualist cultures are attracted to out-group members with desirable personal attributes, whereas persons from collectivist cultures look for desirable cultural or social role attributes (Ting-Toomey, 1989)—a fact that can lead to some misunderstanding and alienation if interactants are not aware of it.

Another side effect of this in-group orientation is that the individualist trappings of contact initiation (such as small talk and smiling) are less important in collectivist cultures. There, friendships are often predetermined by the social networks into which persons are born and do not require as much initiative as in individualist cultures (Barnlund, 1989; Hofstede, 1980). Collectivist sojourners in an individualist culture who are not aware of this distinction and are unfamiliar with individualist friendship formation strategies may therefore be at a disadvantage in making friends.

Yet another example of the potential problems in interactions between individualists and collectivists is the difference in conflict management. Conflicts in individualist cultures are mostly caused through violations of space, power, and individual fairness. By contrast, conflict in collectivist societies tends to be related to group loyalty, commitment, obligation, and trust. In addition, individualist conflict management employs a direct approach focused on substance, whereas collectivist conflict resolution is more indirect and concerned with face maintenance and relational processes (Ting-Toomey, 1997). Because of the cultural focus on harmony, conflicts appear to be less frequent in collectivist societies. In Japanese culture, for example, intuition and respect are cultivated from an early age, and ambiguity, circumlocution, euphemism, and silence are used to avoid antagonizing others (Barnlund, 1989). Japanese thus often disguise or conceal their inner convictions to prevent friction and maintain harmony. Americans, on the other hand, show less inhibition about sharing negative kinds of information. If conflicts arise between potential or established friends from individualist and collectivist cultures, these differences are frustrating and often exacerbate the friction.

Researchers have found that dissimilarity of cultures, in general, is a powerful predictor of difficulties in sociocultural adjustment (Du Bois, 1974; Rohrlich & Martin, 1991; Schaffer & Dowling, 1966; Searle & Ward, 1990). Cultural similarity, on the other hand, gives attributional confidence—that is, makes behavior explanations and predictions easier, and therefore increases interpersonal attraction during initial encounters, paving the way for deeper involvement (Lee & Boster, 1991). Because one of the functions of close relationships is to affirm self and identity, it is understandable that foreign students from cultures dissimilar to the host culture often band together with conationals or fellow students from similar or neighboring countries (Furnham & Alibhai, 1985; Rubin, 1985). In the case of a foreign student from a collectivist culture in the individualist United States, this bonding is further aided by automatic, preexisting group memberships and the frequent absence of peer support for venturing out and establishing relationships beyond the conational network (Paige, 1983; Tjioe, 1972). The fate of social isolation is sealed when unfavorable attitudes, prejudice, and discrimination against foreign-looking individuals on the part of host-country nationals create additional barriers and solidify intergroup relations (Schaffer & Dowling, 1966; Ting-Toomey, 1989). Thus, on the extreme ends of the social distance continuum, culture dissimilarity contributes to social isolation, whereas culture similarity facilitates intercultural interaction.

As with all generalizations, we have to keep in mind, however, that there is variety among individuals and not everybody fits the typical mold. People from all cultures have the potential for unique interpersonal styles and in their individual identities might be closer to a given contact culture than others (Dziegielewska, 1988; Roland, 1986). Just as these personal perceptions of similarity ultimately determine social distance, we must take care to see each person as an individual and not label individuals with national generalizations that do not apply.

Public Versus Private Realm

Differences do not have to be as extensive as that between individualism and collectivism to pose obstacles. Even two fairly closely related cultures can exhibit patterns that make interaction difficult for the uninitiated. Germany and the United States, for example, feature an unequal distribution of public and private personality layers, leading to much intercultural confusion and consternation. The phenomenon, which can be seen as an example of the potential intercultural complications of social penetration, was first described by Lewin (1948). Despite its distant publication date, the findings of Lewin's treatise continue to reverberate in more recent literature and therefore serve well as a basis for analysis. At the core of Lewin's comparison is a juxtaposition of American and German personality types. Although persons from both cultures have the same number of personality layers, ranging centripetally from public layers on the outside to an innermost private center, in the United States all but the central innermost layer are public domain, whereas in Germany only the outermost first layer is considered such.

This dichotomy results in several phenomena. The most obvious one concerns perceived social distance. The larger number of public layers in the United States by necessity contain a greater variety of contact features in a graded but fluid mixture of formal and informal functions. Americans therefore appear open and friendly, easily start conversations with strangers, and invite people for lunch or into their homes quite readily. Social distance in Germany is much larger than in the United States, and the one peripheral public layer is characterized by formality and reserved solely for all external interactions, such as business relations and other impersonal events. For this reason Germans seem unfriendly (Tjioe, 1972) or arrogant and formal (Kalberg, 1987) to Americans, who expect much greater congeniality in public situations and no obstacles to more amicable exchanges at such a peripheral point. One has to penetrate the German boundary between the thin public layer and the underlying private layer to gain access to the friendliness and openness so unobstructed in the American pattern. Once one has achieved this, however, one has reached the private core of the German personality and a vast area of friendship potential with a gradual and now unrestricted transition from friendliness to warmth, compassion, and finally to the most intimate regions. The public and private layer situation for Americans is reversed. Whereas Americans are easily accessible in the outer layers (which is the fact often falsely interpreted as a promise of friendship by Germans and other foreigners), the innermost private core is very difficult to enter and is considered even less permeable than in Germans. Thus Americans have relatively more close relations without a deep level of involvement and often less permanence.

Interestingly, the German configuration of public and private layers is found not only in Germany but in other European and Asian cultures as well. The situation is exacerbated by a linguistic peculiarity of English, which has only one form of the second-person pronoun (*you*) and is characterized by general informality (e.g., the widespread use of first names). In many other languages, the threshold between public and private is marked by changes in forms of address and the second-person pronoun (e.g., from *Sie* to *Du* in German, from *vous* to *tu* in French, and from *usted* to *tu* in Spanish). Lewin's analysis thus provides an explanation why not only Germans but also other foreigners often judge American friendships as shallow or superficial. Assuming that many sojourners in the United States are mainly exposed to the public layers of Americans and never "crack the nut" of the intimate inner layer, it is indeed understandable that they would perceive an absence of depth. On the other hand, one can also comprehend why some Americans abroad value the relatively more easily attainable deeper emotional bonds inherent in German and other European or Asian friendship patterns, and why some feel that this closer involvement brings out hidden aspects of their personalities (Winter, 1986).

Another effect of the public and private layer dichotomy is the degree of compartmentalization. With Americans having available many public layers and thus a broad field of action for a variety of relationships, different areas of life are clearly separated, and relationships are often based on interests (Kalberg, 1987). A case in point for this compartmentalization is the structure of American social events. When socializing in groups, Americans tend to have more or less brief contacts with many people, inquiring about occupations and interests at the beginning of conversations and preferring more issue- than person-oriented formats for these brief interactions (Kalberg, 1987). This is often said to be a sign of pragmatism and the search for mutual profitability (Winter, 1986). By contrast, Germans, for example, approach relationships more holistically, trying to base friendships more on character than on interests and preferring a slower pace and a longer observation period in the development of these friendships. Likewise, they frequently are frustrated by the hurried pace of American social gatherings and by being so quickly labeled according to their occupations or interests (Kalberg, 1987).

The more holistic orientation of Germans is deeply connected with another phenomenon. Whereas the outer personality layers are the seat of action and appearance, as is emphasized in the active, achievement-oriented American, the inner layers are the realm of morals and ideas (Lewin, 1948). It is this inner focus combined with the more holistic perception that results in the great importance of ideology and related status in Germany and the fact that Germans tend to apply the whole person when confronted with a task. Therefore, whereas Americans are able to stay uninvolved and are also less in danger of personal friction because the sensitive inner layer of intimacy is small and closed, Germans seem more intense or even impatient, egotistical, and aggressive (Tjioe, 1972). If, for example, two politicians fight in the United States, they might emerge on cordial terms afterward because the fight takes place in the safe, outer layers and can be compartmentalized there. In Germany, on the other hand, disagreement concerning politics—or, in fact, any subject that matters—involves the whole person and is therefore inseparable from moral disapproval; within friendships, this is often regarded as a tragedy (Mead, 1966).

The reasons for the unique constellation of private and public layers in the United States are not fully determined. One could speculate that the phenomenon is related to the settlement history of the United States and the diversity of the U.S. population. Another theory is that Calvinism laid the foundation for the pattern, due to its premium on worldly success and the subsequent importance and positive role of the public sphere (Kalberg, 1987). Irrespective of its origins, the constellation of public and private layers represents one of the most powerful differences between the United States and other cultures and is the cause of much misunderstanding.

Cultural Knowledge

Cultural differences do not have to be detrimental to friendship formation. Any difference can be ameliorated by cultural awareness of one or both interactants. Cultural knowledge comprises familiarity with the elements of deep culture, including hidden assumptions underlying surface signals, and an ease in using them in daily life (Y. Y. Kim, 1991). Together with language skills, a grasp of the host culture is an essential factor in decreasing misunderstandings and making interpersonal interaction attractive (Gao & Gudykunst, 1990; Gudykunst, 1991). Unfortunately, few studies concerning the United States and even fewer in many other cultures have delved into enough culture-specific details to answer all but the most common questions (Althen, 1995). Research is needed to eliminate this deficiency.

Personality

Personality is the second key factor influencing friendship formation. Effects can take place on a global level, with respect to a person's identity, or on a narrower level, with respect to specific personality traits. On a global level, individuals can define their identities along personal or cultural dimensions, leading to the identification of five different personality types (Ting-Toomey, 1986): Balanced identifiers have clear personal and cultural identities; personal identifiers have a clear view of themselves but no strong cultural identity; cultural identifiers are less sure of their personal selves but have a great understanding of themselves as cultural beings; marginal identifiers are low on both the personal and cultural scales; and ambivalent identifiers experience perpetual tension between personal and cultural identities.

Strom (1988) found that sojourners with strong cultural identification—possibly out of a fear of losing their identities—spend their energies in the home-country milieu, do not interact as much with host nationals, and consequently have the fewest American friends. Being at least somewhat culture-less, personal and marginal identifiers have more friends and are better adjusted to the host society. One possible reason for this dichotomy is that cultural identification may promote intergroup instead of interpersonal behavior. Intergroup behavior occurs when communication is based on others' group membership, whereas interpersonal communication focuses on the other person as an individual (Tajfel, 1978), which in turn encourages relationship formation. Related to this phenomenon, it might be pointed out that individuals who do not define themselves along the lines of their mainstream home culture often find support in marginal groups of fellow outsiders (Rubin, 1985). These groups may have an ethnic or sexual-orientation focus and, in being semi-imposed by discriminatory practices in the mainstream culture, may exhibit an ambivalence between choice and self-doubt hidden behind defensiveness (Rubin, 1985). However, they may also serve to provide a haven for people of certain political persuasions (e.g., environmentalists, socialists, neofascists), people with a certain common lifestyle (e.g., hippies, the ultrarich of the international jet set), intellectuals, artists, and similar groups marginal in their specific societies. These "global in-groups" cross borders and create a common ground for intercultural encounters, eclipsing other comparatively minor cultural dissimilarities.

Besides the nature of identification, other personality factors have been found to influence successful adjustment and intercultural interaction. Among these are empathy, patience, flexibility, broad categorization, resilience, resourcefulness, tolerance for ambiguity, world-mindedness, preparedness for change, extroversion, honesty, and sense of humor (Althen, 1988; Gudykunst, 1991; Kim, 1989, 1991; Paige, 1983; Rohrlich & Martin, 1991; Searle & Ward, 1990). In general, then, open and creative individuals with stable self-images and a high degree of sensitivity toward others possess a favorable starting position considering intercultural contact, whereas closed, rigid, and habitual personalities marked by a strong cultural definition and intergroup anxiety are at a disadvantage (Y. Y. Kim, 1991; Strom, 1988; Winter, 1986).

Self-Esteem

The third key factor concerning intercultural friendship formation, self-esteem, goes hand in hand with personality to the extent that one of its aspects, self-awareness, might be grouped in either category. Self-awareness and self-knowledge are the prerequisites of self-acceptance and therewith self-esteem. Taking it a step further, self-awareness, self-knowledge, and self-acceptance lead to other-awareness, other-knowledge, and other-acceptance and are, therefore, important ingredients in effective communication and successful intercultural contact (Saral, 1979; Ting-Toomey, 1989). If individuals know themselves, they are better able to disclose their identities and reduce uncertainty in interactions, which is an essential element in the development of close relationships (Ting-Toomey, 1986). Research has found that individuals with high self-esteem are less alienated from others and more open and direct in their need for affiliation and friendship (Strom, 1988). People with self-confidence and joy and pride in their ability to function in the new environment are also more likely to reach out, initiate contact, and persevere in their pursuit of friendship—skills that are of immeasurable importance considering that host-country nationals, having established support groups and being dominant in their surroundings, often do not take the first step in interactions with foreign sojourners (Klein et al., 1986; Paige, 1983; Strom, 1988; Winter, 1986).

Self-esteem shows its positive influence even preceding actual intercultural contact. Thus sojourners with a high level of confidence about getting along with Americans and optimism about their ability to adapt have been found to befriend Americans more easily than have others (Klein et al., 1986). It has to be mentioned, however, that if the levels of self-esteem reach exaggerated proportions and preclude a realistic and sensitive perception of others, conditions will in all likelihood turn sour—as with any extreme offshoot of something originally positive. Thus individuals with overwhelming egos at times react to intercultural challenges in a defensive manner and with an inflated self-image not conducive to friendship formation (Winter, 1986). Likewise, weak self-esteem has negative consequences in intercultural interactions. Because it usually carries with it anxiety and fears of, for example, negative evaluations by strangers, being subjected to domination, not being able to use English correctly, or receiving blows to one's self-concept (Gudykunst, 1991; Strom, 1988), a lack of self-esteem often leads to avoidance of contact with strangers and overall withdrawal, or in some cases to an obsessional perseverance with similar negative results (Du Bois, 1956; Gudykunst, 1991).

Researchers have found that cultural identifiers tend to have less self-esteem than do people who are not enmeshed in their home cultures, leaving the question open as to which is the cause and which the effect (Strom, 1988). This phenomenon is exacerbated if the home country has a low national status in the host society, which often results in defensive or chauvinistic attitudes (Bochner et al., 1977). In general, conditions are most favorable with a combination of high self-esteem, high accorded national status, and low identification with the home culture; the reverse scenario of low self-esteem, low accorded national status, and high identification with the home culture usually leads to little involvement in the new environment and the absence of close host-culture relationships (Du Bois, 1956).

Friendship Elements

The research literature agrees that the main function of friendship is homophily, or similarity between friends. Homophily is considered important universally because people in every culture develop self- and role identities through interaction with similar others (Strom, 1988). Considering findings on dissimilarities between cultures, one could be tempted to presume that homophily stipulations are difficult to fulfill in intercultural contact, thus making uncertainty reduction a daunting task. However, recent research suggests that attitudinal similarity in friendship formation is a much stronger variable than cultural similarity and even language competence (H. J. Kim, 1991).

This finding supports the above-mentioned observations concerning the bonding within what were earlier referred to as global in-groups (e.g., people with strong political value systems, unconventional lifestyles). It also suggests the hypothesis that pronounced and developed persuasions (opinions, attitudes, and values) and strong interests—among others, providing the shared and superordinate goals and task-orientation conducive to relationship development (Hammer, 1989; Lee & Boster, 1991; Paige, 1983)—override other, less controllable considerations and open the door for meaningful and relatively uncomplicated interaction. Finally, a strong international orientation and interest in intercultural contacts on the side of the host national may eclipse other homophily stipulations.

Related to the discovered importance of attitudinal similarity is another finding by Gudykunst, Nishida, and Chua (1987). Following Altman and Taylor's (1973) social penetration theory, these researchers tested the four stages of social penetration (orientation, exploratory affective exchange, affective exchange, and stable exchange) in intercultural relationship formation. They found that close friendship occurs during the affective and stable exchange stages. Whereas cultural and sociological data play a role during initial contact and often introduce problematic intercultural complexities, cultural dissimilarities have little impact once people move to the friendship stage. In this stage, intra- as well as intercultural interactions have a person-alistic focus; that is, each person is treated uniquely, predictions are based on psychological data, and cultural stereotypes are broken down. Thus intercul-tural friendships may be more difficult to initiate but should be fairly similar to intracultural friendship in the maintenance stage.

Expectations

Expectations concerning the sojourn make up the fifth factor influencing intercultural friendship formation. These include expectations related to the developmental stages of the sojourners, motivations, and expected outcomes. Corresponding to the intracultural equivalent, the developmental stage of the individual bears significantly on the formation of intercultural friendship. Aspects of homophily such as age, maturity, sophistication, and related lifestyle elements (e.g., marital status and the existence of children) strongly influence the nature and quantity of host-country friendships (National Asso-ciation for Foreign Student Affairs, 1967). Thus a foreign student in the company of a spouse or family can usually expect to spend a significantly smaller amount of time with host nationals (Fahrlander, 1980), which in turn reduces the chances of friendship formation.

Closely related are motivation and expected outcomes. Concerning moti-vation, we can differentiate between task-oriented and adaptive motivation. Often the main reason for graduate students to go abroad is to obtain a degree or professional training (Bochner et al., 1977). Individuals with such a task orientation usually remain anchored in the home culture and are not im-mensely concerned about forming friendships with host nationals (Klein et al., 1986). Their opposites are cross-cultural seekers, "who are interested in self-development through interpersonal contact with the host" (Klein et al., 1986, p. 116). Cross-cultural seekers, on one hand, have more potential for interaction and development of friendships with host nationals (Hull, 1978; Paige, 1983; Klein et al., 1986). On the other hand, they also are exposed to more stress and frustration when their high hopes of contacts are not imme-diately fulfilled (Klein et al., 1986). Whereas it has been reported that numbers of friends increase during the second sojourn year, first-year levels are usually lower than expected (Fahrlander, 1980; Klein et al., 1986).

On a related note, intercultural adjustment and friendship formation are also related to realistic expectations of difficulties (Searle & Ward, 1990) and the expected length of sojourn (Hull, 1978). Research has reported that married graduate students from East Asia or Africa are most limited in their host-country interactions (Locke, 1988) and Western Europeans are compara-tively satisfied with this facet of their stay (Hull, 1978). Given that, in contrast to Asian and African students, Western Europeans often come to the United States primarily to gather cultural experience (Hull, 1978), these examples illustrate the extent to which expectations and motivation influence intercultural interaction.

Adjustment Stage

Closely related to developmental stages, motivation, and expected outcomes but rooted more firmly in the actual sojourn than the individual's predisposition is the sixth factor affecting intercultural friendship formation, adjustment stage. The term *adjustment stage* here serves as an umbrella term for two dimensions of adjustment: stages of intercultural sensitivity and culture shock.

Stages of Intercultural Sensitivity

Superimposed on specific sojourn experiences is the overall development of the individual as an interculturally sensitive being. Bennett (1986) lists six stages in this process: denial (no recognition of difference due to absence of contact), defense (recognition of difference, but resulting in negative evaluations and feelings of superiority), minimization (focus on commonalities with a recognition of only superficial differences, such as food or dress), acceptance (recognition of other culture's beliefs, behaviors, values, and patterns of daily life as viable alternatives), adaptation (empathy and bicultural repertoire), and integration (internalization of different frames of reference, cultural marginality of individual). It must be noted that the last three stages are defined as ethnorelative, with equal footing for diverse cultures; the first three are ethnocentric (i.e., the individual's home culture is central to a reality from which other cultures stray).

Although minimization, with its focus on commonalities, is still considered an ethnocentric stage, it represents a mild side of the phenomenon. Ethnocentrism at its worst is marked by a perception of in-group superiority, lack of concern and sensitivity for out-groups, avoidance or limitation of interaction with out-groups, and ridicule and outright hostility (Gudykunst, 1991). Needless to say, ethnocentric attitudes are not conducive to intercultural friendship formation. To develop close relationships with host nationals, sojourners must accept them on their own terms (Hanvey, 1979). Unfortunately, mere contact, even if sustained, will not automatically move individuals toward more understanding and the ethnorelative end of the spectrum—as is illustrated by many immigrants and long-term sojourners who, after years, are still separated or isolated from the host culture (Berry, 1980; Dziegielewska, 1988; Hanvey, 1979). This is true even if the ethnocentric individual encounters a person deviating from the preconceived stereotypes, because such a person is frequently seen as a mere exception to a still-existing rule (Dziegielewska, 1988). To move to the ethnorelative stages of intercultural sensitivity, individuals must participate with members of the other culture and must have a readiness to respect and accept (Hanvey, 1979; Roland, 1986); then, time and perhaps special training techniques can bring about a true change.

A possible example of this double standard is the frequently heard assertion of sojourners that their relationships are atypical or nonaverage and deviate from the less compatible norm (Gareis, 1995). In their delineations of this norm, familiar descriptors surface, and Americans in general are depicted mirroring the cautionary notes in the literature geared to foreign sojourners. Thus the average American is characterized as merely fun-loving and activity oriented, initially friendly but then closed, not interested in serious talks or sharing of personal matters, self-centered, volatile, and unreliable. It remains to be resolved whether this discrepancy between actual positive experience and general negative definition reflects a tendency to reiterate commonly held stereotypes automatically and to consider deviants exceptions to the rule or whether foreign students indeed seek out atypical and nonaverage Americans to be their close friends.

The existence of this double standard brings up another interesting issue: Foreign sojourners may be more content with their friendship experiences than reported. It is feasible that at least some of the negative image of American friendship in foreign student literature is based on stereotypical notions (including the definitional differences mentioned earlier) and does not reflect actual friendship experiences. Double standards and definitional subtleties may not always be detected in research studies (especially if they employ only survey instruments and do not have qualitative elements). Thus the bleak portrayal of American friendship in the intercultural literature may not be entirely correct. If a faulty assumption exists, however, it would also explain the dichotomy between the generally positive portrayal of American friendship in intracultural publications contrary to the dismal picture provided concerning the intercultural friendship experiences of foreign students.

Culture Shock

In addition to stages of intercultural sensitivity, culture shock has to be considered as an adjustment factor. Upon entering a different culture, individuals usually go through several fairly predictable stages of adjustment: the honeymoon stage, during which the sojourner is positively excited and fascinated by the new; a crisis stage, marked by complaints, hostility, and refuge with fellow nationals, brought on by the stress and frustration associated with having to live in an unfamiliar environment and interact according to strange rules; a recovery stage, with feelings of superiority toward the host country during which composure and a sense of humor are regained; and finally an adjustment stage, which is marked by an ease of communication and the acceptance of host culture ways as just an alternative way of living (Oberg, 1979). Evidently the last stage of culture shock corresponds with the acceptance stage of intercultural sensitivity described above. It must be noted, however, that mere contact does not bring on this acceptance. Thus if a sojourner cannot manage adjustment stress and frustration, is not ready to accept host-culture ways, and does not participate, he or she might not be able to fight through the crisis stage of culture shock and may instead opt for flight and withdrawal, leading to prolonged or indefinite isolation from host-country nationals (Y. Y. Kim, 1991).

Communicative Competence

The next key factor, communicative competence, is by nature integrally tied to the interaction process and therefore is one of the most often mentioned forces influencing sociocultural adjustment and friendship formation. Assuming that most sojourners are nonnative speakers of the host country's language, the focus here is on second-language competence. Traditionally, communicative competence in the second-language context has been defined as mere linguistic proficiency. In line with general communication competence theory, this narrow definition, however, has long been discarded in favor of a more comprehensive picture featuring a wide range of elements.

Thus Chen (1988) differentiates between two dimensions specifically addressing intercultural communicative competence, communication skills and personal attributes, each of which consists of a number of separate components. Only the first component of communication skills, message skills, partially resembles the traditional image of foreign-language competence. Thus it comprises verbal language skills, descriptiveness, and comprehension. In addition, however, it extends the original definition to include supportive verbal and nonverbal behavior (e.g., reinforcements, eye contact, head nods, facial expressions, proximics) and other speech communication skills (e.g., effective organization and expression of messages, listening skills, negotiating meaning and clarifications, giving feedback). The other components of communication skills are social skills (e.g., empathy, identity maintenance), flexibility in choosing appropriate behaviors, and interaction management (e.g., turn taking, being attentive, perceptive, and responsive). The second dimension of intercultural communicative competence, personal attributes, includes self-awareness, self-disclosure, a friendly and sincere self-concept, and social relaxation (i.e., low levels of anxiety both verbally and nonverbally). Spitzberg and Hecht (1984) add to this list of personal attributes the degree of involvement or expressiveness and other-orientation.

Relatedly, but from a slightly different angle, Hammer (1989) divides intercultural communicative competence into culture-general competence, which applies to intercultural interactions regardless of the specific culture, and culture-specific elements, those unique to the communication practices of individual cultures. Culture-general skills include the ability to interact with strangers, deal with misunderstandings, adjust to different communication styles (Y. Y. Kim, 1991), and reduce uncertainty (Gudykunst, 1991).

Culture-specific elements include all the verbal and nonverbal manifestations of a culture but also the rules and rituals connected with communication. Thus thinking styles, levels of verbal ability, the structure and meaning of language functions (such as greetings, small talk, and invitations), the amount of self-disclosure, the selection of topics, the thoroughness with which topics are discussed, and the choice of conversation partners for specific topics can all vary among cultures and contribute to the success or failure of friendship initiation and maintenance (Barnlund, 1979; Gareis, in press; Kartalova, 1996). To exemplify two of these elements, Russian students in the United States (Kartalova, 1996) as well as German sojourners (Gareis, 1995) at times complain about shallowness in American interactions and assert that conversations with friends in their home countries explore topics more in depth. Likewise, differences in thinking style often stand in the way of effective communication (Bennett, 1996; Kaplan, 1988). Bennett (1996) reports on a Nigerian student, for instance, whose nonlinear and holistic thinking style caused impatience in his American counterparts, who were more accustomed to the linear and dichotomous cognitive style common in the United States. In turn, the student felt patronized and treated like a child, because in his culture linear ways of thinking and speaking are employed only with children who are not old enough to understand the more high-context and nonlinear communication patterns used by adults.

Of all cultural contrasts in communication patterns, differences between individualist and collectivist cultures are especially pronounced, with language competence, expressiveness, and self-disclosure being more important in individualist than collectivist societies (Y. Y. Kim, 1991; Sanders, Wiseman, & Matz, 1991; Saral, 1979; Ting-Toomey, 1989). With respect to Japanese culture, for example, Kindaichi (as cited in Nishida, 1996) asserts that talking too much (especially among men and with out-group members) is considered inappropriate and projects a negative image. Concerning expressiveness, differences are also reflected in nonverbal communication. In a study on Japanese, English, and Italian culture, for example, Shimoda, Argyle, and Bitti (1978) found that the facial expressions used by Japanese for emotions were less clear than those used by the English and Italians. Results were similar no matter whether English, Italian, or Japanese subjects themselves judged the facial expressions. Communication patterns differ significantly during friendship initiation, but research does indicate that contrasts are diminished once in-groups and friendships are formed. Self-disclosure patterns, for example, differ very much during the acquaintance stages of contact but tend to be comparable in the more personalized communication of close relationships (Gudykunst, Nishida, & Chua, 1987; Wheeler, Reis, & Bond, 1989). In addition, the somewhat greater tendency for women than men to self-disclose among friends seems to be comparable across East and West (Goodwin & Lee, 1994; Morse, 1983).

For effective intercultural communication and the formation of friendships, it is also important to avoid intergroup posturing, which is especially pronounced when cultures have a history of dominance and subjugation and which intensifies and perpetuates in-group/out-group problems (Y. Y. Kim, 1991). During intergroup posturing, interactions are based on cultural identities and stereotypes, leading to the deindividuation of out-group members (Lee & Boster, 1991). Gudykunst (1991) posits that the development of close intercultural relationships is possible only through the exchange of psychological, intimate data and that only this exchange should be considered interpersonal communication. All other communication, such as intergroup communication, is noninterpersonal by definition. On a more phenomenological note, Saral (1979) reasons that each culture selects and develops only aspects of human potential, leading to different states of consciousness comparable perhaps to the states of normal waking versus dream. The challenge in intercultural communication therefore is to gain the awareness and ability to communicate among these various states of consciousness.

No matter which level of perception is taken as a base of operations, the research literature agrees that communicative competence plays a crucial role in the establishment of intercultural relationships and that proficiency in the respective skills is one of the major predictors in interpersonal attraction and successful interaction (H. J. Kim, 1991; Lee & Boster, 1991; Strom, 1988). On a concrete level, in addition to providing the actual link between two interactants, communication competence is indispensable for gathering information about the host culture and thereby facilitating the acquisition of cultural knowledge (Chen, 1988). The real or perceived lack of language skills, in contrast, exacerbates fears of making mistakes and often leads nonnative speakers to avoid seeking out, initiating, or prolonging contact (Lee & Boster, 1991; University of Iowa, 1991).

Demographic Variables

Adjustment stages and communicative competence represent the main factors influencing friendship formation at the actual sojourn level. The research literature, however, frequently points to a number of minor variables that serve as auxiliaries for sociocultural adjustment. Thus it is often mentioned that previous transition experiences facilitate adjustment and the establishment of host-country relationships (Kim, 1989; Paige, 1983; Rohrlich & Martin, 1991; Yum, 1988). Research findings also suggest that socioeconomic status and level of education positively influence interpersonal contact (Li & Yu, 1974). Some correlation may also exist among the degree of interactions, fields of study, and source of support. Thus one study found that foreign students in the humanities and students without scholarships report more contact than others (Hull, 1978). Likewise, foreign students with an urban home-culture background may adjust and interact with more ease than so-journers from rural areas (Du Bois, 1956; Rohrlich & Martin, 1991). A study by Strom (1988), however, did not confirm these tendencies and revealed no effect of student's major and size of hometown on the formation of intercultural friendship.

The external variable most often mentioned in the research literature is gender. Findings are also dispersed, however, and therefore inconclusive. Thus one study reports that females have more intercultural friendships than do males (Heydari, 1988); another merely mentions a higher degree of concern for making friends among females (Rohrlich & Martin, 1991); and a third, investigating social alienation, finds no difference between men and women (Owie, 1982). Other researchers note that women in some cultures are not meant to have friends but get their support from kin and neighbors instead (Du Bois, 1974). Asian women are educated not to open conversations or initiate contact (Tjioe, 1972). This type of cultural background can pose immense obstacles to the establishment of host-country friendships in the United States.

Proximity

The ninth and last of the factors controllable by the foreign sojourner is proximity. The research literature agrees that proximity to host nationals and contact frequency improve the likelihood of positive intercultural relationships (Klein et al., 1986; Paige, 1983; Strom, 1988). To create favorable conditions in this respect, living situations in proximity with host nationals or, even better, shared lodging and frequent participation in community and other activities are advisable (Hull, 1978). Unfortunately, institutions at times unwittingly counteract the positive effects of proximity by encouraging or at least not discouraging "international house"-type associations, in which foreign students live and form friendships with other internationals but not with Americans (Bochner et al., 1977). Often, sojourners also find it difficult to find the time for frequent contact with Americans, given the time they must devote to study in order to do well in a foreign-language and educational situation (National Association for Foreign Student Affairs, 1967). As to the most favorable type of contact, if time allows, research findings differ. Whereas the National Association for Foreign Student Affairs in 1967 suggested that informal, unstructured, and natural meetings best promote intercultural friendship formation, the trend nowadays seems to be toward formalized and directed contact experiences. Thus structured projects like the International Community Workshop, during which foreign students function as learning resources in elementary and secondary schools, have been found to have positive influence on the formation of close relationships (Gudykunst, 1979; Paige, 1983).

U.S. Elements

Whereas the preceding factors influencing intercultural friendship formation are to some extent controllable or changeable by the foreign student, the last two are givens that cannot be directly manipulated by the sojourner. U.S. elements are factors rooted in the idiosyncrasies of Americans or the status quo of American life that the foreign student must confront and manage to the best of his or her ability. Ideal surroundings would, of course, be receptive and favorable toward out-groups and offer plenty of institutional support, providing a fertile ground for intercultural interaction and friendship formation (Fahrlander, 1980; Paige, 1983; Rohrlich & Martin, 1991). The reality in the United States, as well as in other countries, however, falls short of this ideal, producing a residue of complaints and discontent on the part of many sojourners.

As noted earlier, the problems encountered in the pursuit of friendship are one of the main sources of foreign student dissatisfaction. Americans are seen as friendly but not easy to befriend, too busy and self-absorbed to focus on others, more business oriented than human oriented, superficial in their relationships, and indifferent about the existence of foreign students (Dziegielewska, 1988; Elenwo, 1988; Roland, 1986).

Although some of these complaints might reflect the characteristics of highly individualist societies and the particularities of American friendship patterns, it needs to be pointed out that members of dominant cultures, already having established circles of friends and kin, in general do not seek out intercultural relationships or find that establishing contact is easy (Paige, 1983). This is especially true when out-group members are seen banding together in conational cohorts or when sojourners appear extremely shy, introverted, and reserved (Tjioe, 1972; University of Iowa, 1991). Thus it is often only during international crises or other international events that attention temporarily turns to sojourners from specific cultures. Too frequently, however, this attention results only in the affirmation of intergroup differences and the presence of stereotypes—resulting, no doubt, from the spirit of competition for resources or superiority that is often the focus of the publicity (Heydari, 1988; Paige, 1983; Tjioe, 1972). Even if conditions are not conflict-laden and ordinary interaction takes place, Americans frequently relate to foreign students only in their student roles or approach them as cultural representatives in ethnic terms (Bochner et al., 1977; Strom, 1988). As a Nepalese student in a study by Hull (1978) succinctly put it: "The foreign student shouldn't be treated like a museum piece" (p. 187). From a foreign student's perspective, Americans then often appear ethnocentric, generally ignorant of other cultures, and disinterested in overcoming their lack of awareness (Klein et al., 1986).

A handbook for foreign students notes in defense of American students that many American undergraduates, especially those from rural areas, have virtually no experience with people who are significantly different from themselves, and therefore tend to be afraid or at least reserved concerning foreign students (University of Iowa, 1991). Graduate students may be more cosmopolitan, but unfortunately they often lack the time for social contacts. Other population groups that have been found to be more open-minded and interested in interacting with foreign students are people with low church attendance (Heydari, 1988) and students with majors in history, languages, and literature (Shearer, 1965/1966). In addition to culture- or personality-focused complaints, sojourners also frequently point to specific communication problems and comment that Americans should show more sensitivity by adjusting their rate of speech and vocabulary selection, increasing their listening skills, and avoiding paternalisms (such as baby talk or higher volume during communication difficulties) (Strom, 1988).

The list of complaints is long, and areas of contentment or admiration are often not mentioned or at least not put into print. A closer look at the grievances reveals, however, that whereas some of the complaints are unique to the United States, others seem to be applicable to the intercultural experiences of foreign students in general, regardless of the specific host culture. This observation is not meant to serve as an excuse, however. Thus, with a focus on the future and the improvement of conditions worldwide, Americans should promote more cross-cultural education and learn to see sojourners as individuals with varied identities (Spodek, 1983; Strom, 1988). It also must be noted that foreign students should not, as they often are, be subject to a double standard (i.e., foreign students are supposed to do well academically, master English, have enough money, behave well, be honest, be quiet politically, be chaste, have no personal problems, live in a particular place after graduation, and do certain kinds of work) (Althen, 1995). Double standards and other intergroup attitudes on the part of host nationals set sojourners apart and thus inhibit intercultural interaction.

Unfortunately, host-culture elements influencing friendship formation are the most difficult to alter, especially because there is often no perceived need for change in the host society. It can be assumed or at least hoped, however, that the increasing internationalization of the world and interdependence among cultures will remedy this situation and open the doors for change even in dominant host cultures.

Chemistry

The last key factor influencing friendship formation is possibly the most important, but also the least tangible. For lack of a better word, we can call it chemistry. *Chemistry* is defined by Merriam-Webster (1997) as a "strong mutual attraction, attachment, or sympathy." Probably due to its vague and nonphysical nature, the concept has received only minimal attention in the research literature. Thus I found only two references with a more or less cursory mention of the subject. Dziegielewska (1988), in a phenomenological paper, sketches chemistry as an "invisible bond" (p. 67) and notes that "what draws us into the relationship that deserves the name friendship . . . [is] an interest in the essential person of the other" (p. 59). A more explicit analysis of the concept of chemistry in its broadest psychical sense is provided by Chang and Holt (1991) in their description of the Buddhist concept *yuan,* or secondary causation. In Buddhist philosophy, "any relationship has its roots in uncounted numbers of lifetimes and is situated in a complex web of interdependent causative factors that are outside the control, or even the comprehension of the human mind" (p. 34). Thus when two individuals meet, their karmic selves, built up through these lifetimes, meet; and it is *yuan* that will determine who will be involved with whom, to what degree, in what kind of relationship, and for how long. Having *yuan* with another person means that the conditions are right for the meeting. Out of many contacts, only a few have *yuan.* When there is a lot of *yuan,* the relationship will last for a long time; but even the smallest such encounters are important, and their occurrence might have been prepared for thousands of years. *Yuan,* of course, cannot be forced; one must wait until conditions are right. By the same token, however, two individuals will meet if they are destined to, even if they live thousands of miles apart.

The concept of predestined or invisible bonds exists in a variety of cultures; if this view is correct, destiny is ultimately responsible for whether a relationship will come to fruition or not. It may therefore not matter whether two individuals are from the same culture; if they have chemistry or are connected through *yuan,* their relationship may blossom regardless. Consequently, even if all other factors are favorable, the final decisive force behind friendship formation lies with the presence or absence of this last factor.

As the intangibility of chemistry shows, it is necessary to remember that a logical and comprehensive compilation of knowledge does not suffice to explain friendship or any other complex concept involving whole beings and their intricate connections and interdependencies (Dziegielewska, 1988). As Saral (1979) writes, we need to "free ourselves from our deep rooted addiction to sensing and coding reality in rigid and narrow patterns" (p. 83) and cease occupying ourselves with surface structures and the segmentation of human nature into variables (p. 82). Only if we can focus on cultural experience holistically and the existential linkage between all human beings can we begin to understand the nature of authentic connection and the true meaning of friendship (Dziegielewska, 1988; Saral, 1979).

CONCLUSION

Making friends across cultures is complex. Sojourners are confronted with new and unfamiliar patterns and the realization that the behavioral repertoires that worked in their home countries have become inefficient (Fahrlander, 1980; Mead, 1966; National Association for Foreign Student Affairs, 1967). Due to the complexity of intercultural friendship formation, many possible areas for future research present themselves, including the following:

- Researchers need to seek more culture-specific information about friendship patterns.
- Further investigation is warranted into the existence of various personality types concerning friendship formation. Thus researchers need to determine whether friendship types such as the independent, discerning, and acquisitive types described by Matthews (1986) also exist in cultures other than the United States and how prevalent each is across cultures.
- Investigations are needed concerning the role of homophily as a multifaceted factor versus the single commonality of an international perspective.
- Research needs to address issues of communicative competence specifically related to friendship formation and development, and researchers need to design strategies for the integration of these issues into foreign student orientation and language classes.
- The role of gender in intercultural friendship formation requires clarification.
- More knowledge is needed with respect to such intangible concepts as chemistry and *yuan*.
- Training techniques should be developed for involved third parties (e.g., foreign student personnel, immigration workers, intercultural trainers, foreign language educators) so that they may support sojourners in their quest for close friends.
- Research needs to investigate the reasons for the dichotomy between the positive descriptions of actual friendship experiences in the intracultural literature and the generally negative portrayals in intercultural publications.
- If some foreign students are quite able to form intercultural friendships and are satisfied with the experience, help needs to be directed toward sojourners who are not as successful. For this purpose data on the following issues need to be collected: the characteristics of discontented students, their desire for close involvement, their willingness to put forth an effort to change their situation, and specific problem areas and the skills necessary for their eradication.
- Research is needed on the duration of intercultural friendships, specifically after foreign students return to their home countries.
- It has been purported that social networks and communities are dissolving worldwide (Maybury-Lewis, 1992). Although this trend may allow for greater creativity and individual expression, it also is said to be responsible for an increase in social stress, isolation, and alienation. The effects of this trend on intercultural friendship formation should be studied. Special consideration should be given to collectivist cultures, where traditionally close-knit bonds may be endangered by the complexity and mobility of modern life (Barnlund, 1989).

These and no doubt countless other issues await examination in the future. Considering the relevance of global understanding and a peaceful coexistence of the world's cultures on one hand and the perfect suitability of friendship to foster the necessary awareness and promote precious bonds on the other, the issues listed seem pressing and should be researched without delay.

Although gaps in knowledge are vast and the task of filling them might appear overwhelming, we must keep in mind that intercultural friendships are being formed and do prosper worldwide. Uncovering the secrets of their success should be a rewarding experience and enriching for both sojourners and researchers in our increasingly intercultural world.

REFERENCES

Adams-Webber, J. (1985). Self-other contrast and the development of personal constructs. *Canadian Journal of Behavioural Science, 17,* 303-314.

Althen, G. (1988). *American ways: A guide for foreigners in the United States.* Yarmouth, ME: Intercultural Press.

Althen, G. (1995). *The handbook of foreign student advising.* Yarmouth, ME: Intercultural Press.

Altman, I., & Taylor, D. (1973). *Social penetration.* New York: Holt, Rinehart & Winston.

Altman, I., Vinsel, A., & Brown, B. (1981). Dialectic conceptions in social psychology: An application to social penetration and privacy regulation. In L. Berkowitz (Ed.), *Advances in experimental social psychology* (Vol. 14, pp. 76-100). New York: Academic Press.

Argyle, M., & Henderson, M. (1984). The rules of friendship. *Journal of Social and Personal Relationships, 1,* 211-237.

Aristotle. (1953). *The ethics of Aristotle* (J. A. K. Thomson, Trans.). Baltimore: Penguin.

Barnlund, D. C. (1979). Verbal self-disclosure: Topics, targets, depths. In E. C. Smith & L. F. Luce (Eds.), *Toward internationalism: Readings in cross-cultural communication* (pp. 83-101). Rowley, MA: Newbury House.

Barnlund, D. C. (1989). *Communicative styles of Japanese and Americans: Images and realities.* Belmont, CA: Wadsworth.

Bell, R. R. (1981). *Worlds of friendship.* Beverly Hills, CA: Sage.

Bennett, M. J. (1986). A developmental approach to training for intercultural sensitivity. *International Journal of Intercultural Relations, 10,* 179-196.

Bennett, M. J. (1996). Beyond tolerance: Intercultural communication in a multicultural society. *TESOL Matters, 6*(3), 6.

Berger, C. R. (1979). Beyond initial interactions. In H. Giles & R. St. Clair (Eds.), *Language and social psychology* (pp. 122-144). Oxford: Basil Blackwell.

Berger, C. R., & Calabrese, R. J. (1975). Some explorations in initial interaction and beyond: Toward a developmental theory of interpersonal communication. *Human Communication Research, 1,* 99-112.

Berman, J. J., Murphy-Berman, V., & Pachauri, A. (1988). Sex differences in friendship patterns in India and in the United States. *Basic and Applied Social Psychology, 9,* 61-71.

Berry, J. W. (1980). Acculturation as varieties of adaptation. In A. M. Padilla (Ed.), *Acculturation: Theory, models and some new findings* (pp. 9-25). Boulder, CO: Westview.

Bochner, S., Hutnik, N., & Furnham, A. (1985). The friendship patterns of overseas and host students in an Oxford student residence. *Journal of Social Psychology, 125,* 689-694.

Bochner, S., McLeod, B. M., & Lin, A. (1977). Friendship patterns of overseas students: A functional model. *International Journal of Psychology, 12,* 277-294.

Brown, R. H. (1986). Self and polity in India and the United States. In R. H. Brown & G. V. Coelho (Eds.), *Tradition and transformation: Asian Indians in America* (pp. 1-25). Williamsburg, VA: College of William and Mary, Department of Anthropology.

Chang, H. C., & Holt, G. R. (1991). The concept of yuan and Chinese interpersonal relationships. In S. Ting-Toomey & F. Korzenny (Eds.), *Cross-cultural interpersonal communication* (pp. 28-57). Newbury Park, CA: Sage.

Chen, G. M. (1988, April). *Relationships of the dimensions of intercultural communication competence.* Paper presented at the annual meeting of the Eastern Communication Association. (ERIC Document Reproduction Service No. ED 297 381)

Cohen, Y. A. (1961). Patterns of friendship. In Y. A. Cohen (Ed.), *Social structure and personality: A casebook* (pp. 351-386). New York: Holt, Rinehart & Winston.

Collier, M. J. (1988). A comparison of conversations among and between domestic culture groups: How intra- and intercultural competencies vary. *Communication Quarterly, 36,* 122-144.

de Heredia, C. (1986). Asymmetric communication in bilingual exchanges. *Studies in Second Language Acquisition, 8,* 369-389.

Dodd, C. H. (1998). *Dynamics of intercultural communication* (5th ed.). New York: McGraw-Hill.

Du Bois, C. (1956). *Foreign students and higher education in the United States.* Washington, DC: American Council on Education.

Du Bois, C. (1974). The gratuitous act: An introduction to the comparative study of friendship patterns. In E. Leyton (Ed.), *The compact: Selected dimensions of friendship* (pp. 15-32). Toronto: University of Toronto Press.

Dziegielewska, J. (1988). The intercultural dimension of friendship: A study in the phenomenology of communication. *Dissertation Abstracts International, 50,* 301A. (University Microfilm No. 89-09316)

Elenwo, E. (1988). International students' self-perceived expectations and the reality-shock in cross-cultural encounters (Doctoral dissertation, United States International University, 1988). *Dissertation Abstracts International, 49,* 2404A.

Fahrlander, R. S. (1980). Social participation and adjustment of foreign students at the University of Nebraska-Lincoln (Doctoral dissertation, University of Nebraska, Lincoln, 1980). *Dissertation Abstracts International, 41,* 810A.

Fehr, B. (1996). *Friendship processes.* Thousand Oaks, CA: Sage.

Funder, D. C. (1980). On seeing ourselves as others see us: Self-other agreement and discrepancy in personality ratings. *Journal of Personality, 48,* 473-493.

Furnham, A., & Alibhai, N. (1985). The friendship networks of foreign students: A replication and extension of the functional model. *International Journal of Psychology, 20,* 709-722.

Furnham, A., Jaspars, J., & Fincham, F. D. (1983). Professional and naive psychology: Two approaches to the explanation of social behaviour. In J. Jaspars, F. D. Fincham, & M. Hewstone (Eds.), *Attribution theory and research: Conceptual, developmental and social dimensions.* London: Academic Press.

Gallois, C., Franklyn-Stokes, A., Giles, H., & Coupland, N. (1988). Communication accommodation in intercultural encounters. In Y. Y. Kim & W. B. Gudykunst (Eds.), *Theories in intercultural communication* (pp. 157-185). Newbury Park, CA: Sage.

Gao, G. (1996). Self and other: A Chinese perspective on interpersonal relationships. In W. B. Gudykunst, S. Ting-Toomey, & T. Nishida (Eds.), *Communication in personal relationships across cultures* (pp. 81-101). Thousand Oaks, CA: Sage.

Gao, G., & Gudykunst, W. B. (1990). Uncertainty, anxiety, and adaptation. *International Journal of Intercultural Relations, 14,* 301-317.

Gareis, E. (1995). *Intercultural friendship: A qualitative study.* Lanham, MD: University Press of America.

Gareis, E. (in press). Rhetoric and intercultural friendship formation. *International and Intercultural Communication Annual: Rhetoric in Intercultural Contexts, 22.*

Gass, S. M., & Varonis, E. M. (1985). Variation in native speaker speech modification to non-native speakers. *Studies in Second Language Acquisition, 7,* 37-57.

Goodwin, R., & Lee, I. (1994). Taboo topics among Chinese and English friends: A cross-cultural comparison. *Journal of Cross-Cultural Psychology, 25,* 325-338.

Gudykunst, W. B. (1979). The effects of an intercultural communication workshop on cross-cultural attitudes and interaction. *Communication Education, 28,* 179-187.

Gudykunst, W. B. (1985). A model of uncertainty reduction in intercultural encounters. *Journal of Language and Social Psychology, 4,* 79-98.

Gudykunst, W. B. (1991). *Bridging differences: Effective intergroup communication.* Newbury Park, CA: Sage.

Gudykunst, W. B. (1995). Anxiety/uncertainty management (AUM) theory: Current status. In R. L. Wiseman (Ed.), *Intercultural communication theory* (pp. 8-58). Thousand Oaks, CA: Sage.

Gudykunst, W. B., & Hammer, M. R. (1988). Strangers and hosts: An uncertainty reduction based theory of intercultural adaptation. In Y. Y. Kim & W. B. Gudykunst (Eds.), *Cross-cultural adaptation: Current approaches* (pp. 106-139). Newbury Park, CA: Sage.

Gudykunst, W. B., & Kim, Y. Y. (1992). *Communicating with strangers: An approach to intercultural communication.* New York: McGraw-Hill.

Gudykunst, W. B., & Nishida, T. (1986). Attributional confidence in low- and high-context cultures. *Human Communication Research, 12,* 525-549.

Gudykunst, W. B., Nishida, T., & Chua, E. (1987). Perceptions of social penetration in Japanese-North American dyads. *International Journal of Intercultural Relations, 11,* 171-189.

Gudykunst, W. B., Sodetani, L. L., & Sonoda, K. T. (1987). Uncertainty reduction in Japanese-American/Caucasian relationships in Hawaii. *Western Journal of Speech Communication, 51,* 256-278.

Hammer, M. R. (1989). Intercultural communication competence. In M. K. Asante & W. B. Gudykunst (Eds.), *Handbook of international and intercultural communication* (pp. 247-260). Newbury Park, CA: Sage.

Hanvey, R. G. (1979). Cross-cultural awareness. In E. C. Smith & L. F. Luce (Eds.), *Toward internationalism: Readings in cross-cultural communication* (pp. 46-56). Rowley, MA: Newbury House.

Heydari, A. (1988). An empirical test of two conceptual models concerning American students' social distance from international students (Doctoral dissertation, South Dakota State University, 1988). *Dissertation Abstracts International, 49,* 2419A.

Hofstede, G. (1980). *Culture's consequences: International differences in work-related values.* Beverly Hills, CA: Sage.

Höllinger, F., & Haller, M. (1990). Kinship and social networks in modern societies: A cross-cultural comparison among seven nations. *European Sociological Review, 6,* 103-124.

Hull, W. F., IV. (1978). *Foreign students in the United States of America: Coping behavior within the educational setting.* New York: Praeger.

Jones, D. C., Bloys, N., & Wood, M. (1990). Sex roles and friendship patterns. *Sex Roles, 23,* 133-145.

Jones, E. E., & Nisbett, R. E. (1971). *The actor and the observer: Divergent perceptions of the causes of behavior.* Morristown, NJ: General Learning Press.

Kalberg, S. (1987). West German and American interaction forms: One level of structured misunderstanding. *Theory, Culture & Society, 4,* 603-618.

Kaplan, R. B. (1988). Cultural thought patterns in intercultural education. In J. S. Wurzel (Ed.), *Toward multiculturalism* (pp. 207-221). Yarmouth, ME: Intercultural Press.

Kartalova, Y. B. (1996). Cross-cultural differences in American and Russian general conventions of communication. *Pragmatics and Language Learning Monograph Series, 7* 71-96. (ERIC Document Reproduction Service No. ED 400 705)

Kelly, G. A. (1955). *The psychology of personal constructs.* New York: W. W. Norton.

Kim, H. J. (1991). Influence of language and similarity on initial intercultural attraction. In S. Ting-Toomey & F. Korzenny (Eds.), *Cross-cultural interpersonal communication* (pp. 213-229). Newbury Park, CA: Sage.

Kim, Y. Y. (1988). *Communication and cross-cultural adaptation: An integrative theory.* Clevedon, England: Multilingual Matters.

Kim, Y. Y. (1989). Intercultural adaptation. In M. K. Asante & W. B. Gudykunst (Eds.), *Handbook of international and intercultural communication* (pp. 275-294). Newbury Park, CA: Sage.

Kim, Y. Y. (1991). Intercultural communication competence: A systems-theoretic view. In S. Ting-Toomey & F. Korzenny (Eds.), *Cross-cultural interpersonal communication* (pp. 259-275). Newbury Park, CA: Sage.

Klein, M. H., Alexander, A. A., Miller, M. H., Haack, L. J., & Bushnell, N. J. (1986). Indian students in the United States: Personal and professional issues in cross-cultural education. In R. H. Brown & G. V. Coelho (Eds.), *Tradition and transformation: Asian Indians in America* (pp. 115-132). Williamsburg, VA: College of William and Mary, Department of Anthropology.

Klopf, W. D. (1987). *Intercultural encounters: The fundamentals of intercultural communication.* Inglewood, CA: Morton.

Lanier, A. R. (1996). *Living in the U.S.A.* (5th ed.). Yarmouth, ME: Intercultural Press.

Lee, H. O., & Boster, F. J. (1991). Social information for uncertainty reduction during initial interactions. In S. Ting-Toomey & F. Korzenny (Eds.), *Cross-cultural interpersonal communication* (pp. 189-212). Newbury Park, CA: Sage.

Lewin, K. (1948). Some social-psychological differences between the United States and Germany. In K. Lewin, *Resolving social conflict* (pp. 3-33). New York: Harper & Brothers.

Li, W. L., & Yu, L. (1974). Interpersonal contact and racial prejudice: A comparative study of American and Chinese students. *Sociological Quarterly, 15,* 559-566.

Locke, R. J. (1988). The interpersonal environments of students from other countries enrolled at Cornell University (New York) (Doctoral dissertation, George Washington University, 1988). *Dissertation Abstracts International, 50,* 373A.

Long, M. H. (1983). Linguistic and conversational adjustments to non-native speakers. *Studies in Second Language Acquisition, 5,* 177-193.

Markus, H. R., & Kitayama, S. (1991). Culture and the self: Implications for cognition, emotion, and motivation. *Psychological Review, 98,* 224-253.

Matthews, S. H. (1986). *Friendships through the life course: Oral biographies in old age.* Beverly Hills, CA: Sage.

Maybury-Lewis, D. (1992). *Millennium: Tribal wisdom and the modern world.* New York: Viking.

McCroskey, J. C., & Richmond, V. P. (1990). Willingness to communicate: Differing cultural perspectives. *Southern Communication Journal, 56,* 72-77.

Mead, M. (1966, August). Different lands, different friendships. *Redbook,* pp. 38, 40.

Merriam-Webster. (1997). *WWWebster dictionary* [On-line]. Available: http://www.m-w.com/dictionary.htm

Mitchell, C. (1986). Adult friendship patterns: The implications of autonomy, connection and gender. *Dissertation Abstracts International, 47,* 382B. (University Microfilms No. 86-06859)

Morse, S. J. (1983). Requirements for love and friendship in Australia and Brazil. *Australian Journal of Psychology, 35,* 469-476.

National Association for Foreign Student Affairs. (1967). *American-foreign student relationships: Guidelines.* Washington, DC: Author. (ERIC Document Reproduction Service No. ED 018 832)

Nishida, T. (1996). Communication in personal relationships in Japan. In W. B. Gudykunst, S. Ting-Toomey, & T. Nishida (Eds.), *Communication in personal relationships across cultures* (pp. 102-121). Thousand Oaks, CA: Sage.

Oberg, K. (1979). Culture shock and the problem of adjustment in new cultural environments. In E. C. Smith & L. F. Luce (Eds.), *Toward internationalism: Readings in cross-cultural communication* (pp. 43-45). Rowley, MA: Newbury House.

Owie, I. (1982). Social alienation among foreign students. *College Student Journal, 16,* 163-165.

Page, R. C., & Berkow, D. N. (1991). Concepts of the self: Western and Eastern perspectives. *Journal of Multicultural Counseling and Development, 19,* 83-93.

Paige, R. M. (1983). Cultures in contact: On intercultural relations among American and foreign students in the United States university context. In D. Landis & R. W. Brislin (Eds.), *Handbook of intercultural training* (Vol. 3, pp. 102-129). New York: Pergamon.

Paine, R. (1974). Anthropological approaches to friendship. In E. Leyton (Ed.), *The compact: Selected dimensions of friendship* (pp. 1-14). Toronto: University of Toronto Press.

Parlee, M. B. (1979). The friendship bond. *Psychology Today, 13*(4), 43-54, 113.

Pogrebin, L. C. (1987). *Among friends.* New York: McGraw-Hill.

Rawlins, W. K. (1992). *Friendship matters: Communication, dialectics, and the life course.* New York: Aldine de Gruyter.

Reohr, J. R. (1991). *Friendship: An exploration of structure and process.* New York: Garland.

Rohrlich, B. F., & Martin, J. N. (1991). Host country and reentry adjustment of student sojourners. *International Journal of Intercultural Relations, 15,* 163-182.

Roland, A. (1986). The Indian self: Reflections in the mirror of American life. In R. H. Brown & G. V. Coelho (Eds.), *Tradition and transformation: Asian Indians in America* (pp. 43-52). Williamsburg, VA: College of William and Mary, Department of Anthropology.

Rubin, L. B. (1985). *Just friends: The role of friendship in our lives.* New York: Harper & Row.

Sanders, J. A., Wiseman, R. L., & Matz, S. I. (1991). Uncertainty reduction in acquaintance relationships in Ghana and the United States. In S. Ting-Toomey & F. Korzenny (Eds.), *Cross-cultural interpersonal communication* (pp. 79-98). Newbury Park, CA: Sage.

Saral, T. B. (1979). The consciousness theory of intercultural communication. In M. K. Asante, E. Newmark, & C. A. Blake (Eds.), *Handbook of intercultural communication* (pp. 77-84). Beverly Hills, CA: Sage.

Schaffer, R. H., & Dowling, L. R. (1966). *Foreign student friends* (Cooperative Research Project No. 5-0806). Bloomington: Indiana University. (ERIC Document Reproduction Service No. ED 010 008)

Schrauger, J. S., & Schoeneman, T. J. (1979). Symbolic interactionist view of self-concept: Through the looking glass darkly. *Psychological Bulletin, 86,* 549-573.

Searle, W., & Ward, C. (1990). The prediction of psychological and sociocultural adjustment during cross-cultural transitions. *International Journal of Intercultural Relations, 14,* 449-464.

Shearer, R. (1966). A comparative study of American graduate student friends of foreign students (Doctoral dissertation, Indiana University, 1965). *Dissertation Abstracts International, 26,* 5250.

Shimoda, K., Argyle, M., & Bitti, P. R. (1978). The intercultural recognition of emotional expressions by three national racial groups: English, Italian and Japanese. *European Journal of Social Psychology, 8,* 169-179.

Spitzberg, B. H., & Cupach, W. R. (1984). *Interpersonal communication competence.* Beverly Hills, CA: Sage.

Spitzberg, B. H., & Hecht, M. L. (1984). A component model of relational competence. *Human Communication Research, 10,* 575-599.

Spodek, H. (1983). Integrating cross-cultural education in the postsecondary curriculum. In D. Landis & R. W. Brislin (Eds.), *Handbook of intercultural training* (Vol. 3, pp. 81-101). New York: Pergamon.

Stephan, W. G., & Stephan, C. W. (1985). Intergroup anxiety. *Journal of Social Issues, 41,* 157-175.

Stewart, E. C., & Bennett, M. J. (1991). *American cultural patterns: A cross-cultural perspective.* Yarmouth, ME: Intercultural Press.

Strom, W. O. (1988). Cross-cultural friendships on the university campus: Testing the functional and identity validation models (Doctoral dissertation, University of Iowa, 1988). *Dissertation Abstracts International, 49,* 3204A.

Tajfel, H. (1978). Interindividual and intergroup behaviour. In H. Tajfel (Ed.), *Differentiation between social groups* (pp. 27-60). London: Academic Press.

Ting-Toomey, S. (1986). Interpersonal ties in intergroup communication. In W. B. Gudykunst (Ed.), *Intergroup communication* (pp. 114-126). Baltimore: Edward Arnold.

Ting-Toomey, S. (1989). Identity and interpersonal bonding. In M. K. Asante & W. B. Gudykunst (Eds.), *Handbook of international and intercultural communication* (pp. 351-373). Newbury Park, CA: Sage.

Ting-Toomey, S. (1997). Managing intercultural conflicts effectively. In L. A. Samovar & R. E. Porter (Eds.), *Intercultural communication: A reader* (8th ed., pp. 392-404). New York: Wadsworth.

Tjioe, L. E. (1972). *Asiaten über Deutsche: Kulturkonflikte ostasiatischer Studentinnen in der Bundesrepublik* [Asians about Germans: Cultural conflicts of female East Asian students in the Federal Republic of Germany]. Frankfurt: Thesen Verlag.

Triandis, H. C. (1988). Collectivism vs. individualism: A reconceptualization of a basic concept in cross-cultural social psychology. In C. Bagley & G. K. Verma (Eds.), *Cross-cultural studies of personality, attitudes, and cognition* (pp. 60-95). London: Macmillan.

Trice, A. D., & Elliott, J. (1993). Japanese students in America: College friendship patterns. *Journal of Instructional Psychology, 20,* 262-264.

University of Iowa, Office of International Education and Services. (1991). *Handbook for foreign students and scholars 1991-1992.* (Available from the Office of International Education and Services, University of Iowa, Iowa City, IA 52242)

VanLear, C. A., Jr. (1987). The formation of social relationships: A longitudinal study of social penetration. *Human Communication Research, 13,* 299-322.

Verma, J. (1985). The ingroup and its relevance to individual behaviour: A study of collectivism and individualism. *Psychologia, 28,* 173-181.

Wheeler, L., Reis, H., & Bond, M. (1989). Collectivism and individualism in everyday social life: The middle kingdom and the melting pot. *Journal of Personality and Social Psychology, 57,* 79-86.

Winter, G. (1986). German-American student exchange: Adaptation problems and opportunities for personal growth. In R. M. Paige (Ed.), *Cross-cultural orientation: New conceptualizations and applications* (pp. 311-339). Lanham, MD: University Press of America.

Witte, K. (1993). A theory of cognitive and negative affect: Extending Gudykunst and Hammer's theory of uncertainty and anxiety reduction. *International Journal of Intercultural Relations, 17,* 197-216.

Yum, J. O. (1988). Multidimensional analysis of international images among college students in Japan, Hong Kong, and the United States. *Journal of Social Psychology, 128,* 765-777.

Yum, J. O. (1997). The impact of Confucianism on interpersonal relationships and communication patterns in East Asia. In L. A. Samovar & R. E. Porter (Eds.), *Intercultural communication: A reader* (8th ed., pp. 78-88). New York: Wadsworth.

Zaharna, R. S. (1980). Self-shock: The double-binding challenge of identity. *International Journal of Intercultural Relations, 13,* 501-525.

AUTHOR INDEX

SUBJECT INDEX

ABOUT THE EDITOR

MICHAEL E. ROLOFF is Professor in the Department of Communication Studies at Northwestern University. He received his PhD in communication from Michigan State University in 1975. His research and teaching interests are in the general area of interpersonal influence. He has published articles and offers courses focused on persuasion, interpersonal compliance gaining, conflict management, and bargaining and negotiation. He has coedited four research volumes for Sage Publications: *Persuasion: New Directions in Theory and Research, Social Cognition and Communication, Interpersonal Processes,* and *Communication and Negotiation.* He is the author of *Interpersonal Communication: The Social Exchange Approach.* His articles have appeared in such journals as *Communication Monographs, Communication Research, Human Communication Research, International Journal of Conflict Management,* and *Personal Relationships.* In addition to editing the *Communication Yearbook,* he currently serves on the editorial boards of seven academic journals.

ABOUT THE CONTRIBUTORS

MIKE ALLEN (PhD, Michigan State University, 1987) is Professor in the Department of Communication at the University of Wisconsin–Milwaukee. His research interests include the various methods of social influence that exist within organizations, persons, society, and the culture. His more than 100 published works include two edited books and articles in the fields of communication, psychology, medicine, law, interpersonal relationships, and women's studies. His current focus is an examination of the various methods used in HIV/AIDS educational efforts.

ERIK P. BUCY (PhD, University of Maryland, 1998) is Assistant Professor in the Department of Telecommunications at Indiana University, Bloomington. His research interests focus on user experiences of interactive media, psychological responses to emotion-laden images, and the impact of new communication technologies. A former staff writer for the *Los Angeles Herald Examiner* and contributor to the *Los Angeles Times,* he served as deputy press secretary and national scheduler for Jerry Brown's 1992 presidential campaign. The author of two trade books, he has published in the *Journal of Broadcasting and Electronic Media* and is coauthor (with Paul D'Angelo and John E. Newhagen) of a chapter titled "New Media Use as Political Participation" in *The Electronic Election: Perspectives on 1996 Campaign Communication,* edited by L. L. Kaid and D. Bystrom (1998). During the 1996 election campaign, he was part of a national team of political communication scholars researching the campaign, directed by Dr. Lynda Lee Kaid at the University of Oklahoma.

DAVID D'ALESSIO (PhD, Michigan State University, 1997) is Assistant Professor of Communication at the University of Connecticut, Stamford. He is a former polymer chemist, former computer graphic artist, former TV engineer, and former animator. His research interests include the various reasons people choose to consume mass media and the effects such activities generate. He has published in *Human Communication Research, Journal of Sex Research,* and the *Journal of Broadcasting & Electronic Media.*

PAUL D'ANGELO (MA, Temple University, 1992) is an Instructor at Villanova University and a doctoral candidate in the Mass Media and Communication Program at Temple University. His research interests center on rhetorical aspects of election news, in particular "character issue" news, and the effects of reflexive news coverage on public cynicism. His work entails discourse analysis of news frames and strategies by which mainstream journalists assert their cultural authority when covering political campaigns. He has published on information, ideological dilemmas, and Persian Gulf War news in the *Electronic Journal of Communication* and is coauthor (with Erik P. Bucy and John E. Newhagen) of a chapter titled "New Media Use as Political Participation" in *The Electronic Election: Perspectives on 1996 Campaign Communication,* edited by L. L. Kaid and D. Bystrom (1998). A former staff writer for the Temple University News Bureau, he has written extensively for marketing research firms and has taught as an adjunct faculty member in communication at several universities in the Philadelphia area. During the 1996 election campaign, he was part of a national team of political communication scholars researching the campaign, directed by Dr. Lynda Lee Kaid at the University of Oklahoma.

TARA M. EMMERS-SOMMER (PhD, Ohio University) is Assistant Professor in the Department of Communication at the University of Oklahoma. Her research interests include problematic communication and conflict in interpersonal relationships and the impact of media on attitudes toward women. Her research has appeared in the *Journal of Communication, Communication Quarterly, Communication Reports, Communication Research Reports, Personal Relationships,* and the *Journal of Sex Research.* She is coauthor, with Daniel J. Canary, of a new book titled *Sex and Gender Differences in Personal Relationships: Toward an Activity-Based Perspective.*

WENDY S. ZABAVA FORD (PhD, University of Maryland) is Associate Professor of Organizational Communication at Western Michigan University. Her research has appeared in such publications as *Human Communication Research, Management Communication Quarterly, Communication Education,* and the *Electronic Journal of Communication.* She recently published a book titled *Communicating With Customers: Service Approaches, Ethics, and Impact.* Her primary research interests are in the areas of communication and customer service and organizational assessment and development.

SUSAN ANNE FOX (PhD, University of California, Santa Barbara, 1994) is Assistant Professor of Communication at Western Michigan University. Her area of expertise is interpersonal communication, with an emphasis on intergroup communication. Her research focuses on problematic communication between groups, with a concentration on intergenerational, interability, illness, and weight-related contexts. She incorporates both qualitative and quantitative methodologies in her research. Her work on intergenerational communication has appeared in the *Journal of Language and Social Psychology, Journal of Aging Studies, Journal of Applied Communication Research,* and *Interpersonal Communication and Older Adults.*

PATRICIA A. FULFS (MA, University of Illinois, Urbana-Champaign, 1997) is a PhD student at the University of Texas at Austin, studying cultural studies, film, and media. Her research interests include the political and cultural articulations of the body in contemporary horror films.

ELISABETH GAREIS (EdD, University of Georgia, 1992) is Assistant Professor in the Department of Speech at Baruch College/City University of New York. Her major research interests are in intercultural communication and second-language acquisition, with specific emphasis on intercultural friendship formation, oral communication competence in English as a second language, and the use of video in intercultural training and language instruction. Her recent publications include *Intercultural Friendship: A Qualitative Study* and the textbook series *A Novel Approach* (coauthored with M. Allard, S. Gill, and J. Saindon), which focuses on the use of literature and film in language education.

HOWARD GILES (PhD, University of Bristol, England, 1971; D.Sc., University of Bristol, England, 1997) is Chair of Communication at the University of California, Santa Barbara, and Affiliate Professor of Linguistics and Psychology there, as well as Honorary Professor of Psychology and Communication at the University of Wales, Cardiff. Previously, he served as Head of the Department of Psychology at the University of Bristol. He is founding coeditor of both the *Journal of Language and Social Psychology* and the *Journal of Asian Pacific Communication,* general editor of the book series Language and Language Bchaviors, and coeditor of the book series Social Psychology and Society. He has published widely in the areas of language attitudes, intercultural communication and relations, and intergenerational communication, and is a Fellow of the British Psychological Society, the International Communication Association, and the Gerontological Association of America. He is President-Elect of the International Communication Association.

DAENA J. GOLDSMITH (PhD, University of Washington, 1990) is Assistant Professor of Speech Communication at the University of Illinois, Urbana-Champaign. Her research focuses on developing explanations for better and worse ways of seeking and providing social support in close relationships. She has also examined sociocultural variability in these supportive communication processes. Her recent work has appeared in *Human Communication Research, Journal of Social and Personal Relationships,* and *Communication Yearbook 18.*

DALE HAMPLE (PhD, University of Illinois, 1975) is Professor of Communication at Western Illinois University. His research interests include the cognitive and personality issues in message production, argumentation, conflict, and persuasion. His recent publications include a chapter in John Greene's *Message Production: Advances in Communication Theory* as well as articles in *Communication Quarterly, International Journal of Conflict Management, Communication Reports, Communication Monographs,* and the proceedings of the Alta and Amsterdam argumentation conferences.

MIN-SUN KIM (PhD, Michigan State University, 1992) is Associate Professor in the Department of Speech at the University of Hawaii at Manoa. Her research interests focus on the role of cognition in conversational styles among people of different cultural orientations. She has applied her models (based on conversational constraints) in the areas of requesting, re-requesting, and conflict styles. Her publications have appeared in a variety of journals. She is the recipient of numerous top awards in major international communication conferences, most recently at the 1999 International Communication Association. Currently, she serves as a reviewer for various communication journals, and as Associate Editor for *Communication Reports.* She is also working on a book about non-Western perspectives on human communication.

LAURA LEETS (PhD, University of California, Santa Barbara, 1995) is Assistant Professor of Communication and an affiliate faculty member of the Comparative Studies in Race and Ethnicity Program at Stanford University. Her primary area of research interest is intergroup communication, with an emphasis on harmful speech, ethnic identity, and language. Her recent research has appeared in *Human Communication Research, Journal of Language and Social Psychology, Journal of Multilingual and Multicultural Development,* and *Multilingua: Journal of Cross-Cultural and Interlanguage Communication.*

DANIEL J. O'KEEFE (PhD, University of Illinois, Urbana-Champaign) is Associate Professor in the Department of Speech Communication at the University of Illinois, Urbana-Champaign. His work focuses on research synthesis in persuasion and argument. He is the author of *Persuasion: Theory and Research,* and his research has appeared in *Communication Monographs, Human Communication Research, Communication Theory, Argumentation and Advocacy,* and other journals. He has received the National Communication Association's Charles H. Woolbert Research Award as well as the association's Golden Anniversary Monograph Award.

VINCENT R. WALDRON (PhD, Ohio State University, 1989) is Associate Professor of Communication Studies at Arizona State University West. There, in addition to teaching courses in organizational communication and interpersonal communication, he has served in such roles as founding director of the community-university research partnership, and Director of the Social Interaction Research Laboratory. His research concerns the tactical and cognitive aspects of face-to-face communication. His work has appeared recently in *Health Communication, Communication Education,* and the *Communication Yearbook.*